International Directory of

COMPANY

HISTORIES

VOLUME 76

Editor

Tina Grant

ST. JAMES PRESS
An imprint of Thomson Gale, a part of The Thomson Corporation

THOMSON
™
GALE

Detroit • New York • San Francisco • San Diego • New Haven, Conn. • Waterville, Maine • London • Munich

International Directory of Company Histories, Volume 76

Tina Grant, Editor

Project Editor
Miranda H. Ferrara

Editorial
Virgil Burton, Donna Craft, Louise Gagné,
Peggy Geeseman, Julie Gough, Linda Hall,
Sonya Hill, Keith Jones, Lynn Pearce,
Maureen Puhl, Holly Selden,
Justine Ventimiglia

Imaging and Multimedia
Lezlie Light, Michael Logusz

Manufacturing
Rhonda Dover

Product Manager
Gerald L. Sawchuk

LIBRARY OF CONGRESS CATALOG NUMBER 89-190943

ISBN: 1-55862-580-1

BRITISH LIBRARY CATALOGUING IN PUBLICATION DATA
International directory of company histories. Vol. 76
I. Tina Grant
33.87409

This title is also available as an e-book
ISBN 1-55862-624-7
Contact your Thomson Gale sales representative for ordering information

Printed in the United States of America
10 9 8 7 6 5 4 3 2 1

CONTENTS

Company Histories

The St. James Press series *The International Directory of Company Histories (IDCH)* is intended for reference use by students, business people, librarians, historians, economists, investors, job candidates, and others who seek to learn more about the historical development of the world's most important companies. To date, *IDCH* has covered over 7,700 companies in 76 volumes.

Inclusion Criteria

Most companies chosen for inclusion in *IDCH* have achieved a minimum of US$25 million in annual sales and are leading influences in their industries or geographical locations. Companies may be publicly held, private, or nonprofit. State-owned companies that are important in their industries and that may operate much like public or private companies also are included. Wholly owned subsidiaries and divisions are profiled if they meet the requirements for inclusion. Entries on companies that have had major changes since they were last profiled may be selected for updating.

The *IDCH* series highlights 10% private and nonprofit companies, and features updated entries on approximately 50 companies per volume.

Entry Format

Each entry begins with the company's legal name, the address of its headquarters, its telephone, toll-free, and fax numbers, and its web site. A statement of public, private, state, or parent ownership follows. A company with a legal name in both English and the language of its headquarters country is listed by the English name, with the native-language name in parentheses.

The company's founding or earliest incorporation date, the number of employees, and the most recent available sales figures follow. Sales figures are given in local currencies with equivalents in U.S. dollars. For some private companies, sales figures are estimates and indicated by the abbreviation *est.* The entry lists the exchanges on which a company's stock is traded and its ticker symbol, as well as the company's NAIC codes.

Entries generally contain a *Company Perspectives* box which provides a short summary of the company's mission, goals, and ideals, a *Key Dates* box highlighting milestones in the company's history, lists of *Principal Subsidiaries, Principal Divisions, Principal Operating Units, Principal Competitors,* and articles for *Further Reading.*

American spelling is used throughout *IDCH*, and the word "billion" is used in its U.S. sense of one thousand million.

Sources

Entries have been compiled from publicly accessible sources both in print and on the Internet such as general and academic periodicals, books, annual reports, and material supplied by the companies themselves.

Cumulative Indexes

IDCH contains three indexes: the **Index to Companies**, which provides an alphabetical index to companies discussed in the text as well as to companies profiled, the **Index to Industries**, which allows researchers to locate companies by their principal industry, and the **Geographic Index**, which lists companies alphabetically by the country of their headquarters. The indexes are cumulative and specific instructions for using them are found immediately preceding each index.

Suggestions Welcome

Comments and suggestions from users of *IDCH* on any aspect of the product as well as suggestions for companies to be included or updated are cordially invited. Please write:

The Editor
International Directory of Company Histories
St. James Press
27500 Drake Rd.
Farmington Hills, Michigan 48331-3535

AB	Aktiebolag (Finland, Sweden)
AB Oy	Aktiebolag Osakeyhtiot (Finland)
A.E.	Anonimos Eteria (Greece)
AG	Aktiengesellschaft (Austria, Germany, Switzerland, Liechtenstein)
A.O.	Anonim Ortaklari/Ortakligi (Turkey)
ApS	Amparteselskab (Denmark)
A.Š.	Anonim Širketi (Turkey)
A/S	Aksjeselskap (Norway); Aktieselskab (Denmark, Sweden)
Ay	Avoinyhtio (Finland)
B.A.	Buttengewone Aansprakeiijkheid (The Netherlands)
Bhd.	Berhad (Malaysia, Brunei)
B.V.	Besloten Vennootschap (Belgium, The Netherlands)
C.A.	Compania Anonima (Ecuador, Venezuela)
C. de R.L.	Compania de Responsabilidad Limitada (Spain)
Co.	Company
Corp.	Corporation
CRL	Companhia a Responsabilidao Limitida (Portugal, Spain)
C.V.	Commanditaire Vennootschap (The Netherlands, Belgium)
G.I.E.	Groupement d'Interet Economique (France)
GmbH	Gesellschaft mit beschraenkter Haftung (Austria, Germany, Switzerland)
Inc.	Incorporated (United States, Canada)
I/S	Interessentselskab (Denmark); Interesentselskap (Norway)
KG/KGaA	Kommanditgesellschaft/Kommanditgesellschaft auf Aktien (Austria, Germany, Switzerland)
KK	Kabushiki Kaisha (Japan)
K/S	Kommanditselskab (Denmark); Kommandittselskap (Norway)
Lda.	Limitada (Spain)
L.L.C.	Limited Liability Company (United States)
Ltd.	Limited (Various)
Ltda.	Limitada (Brazil, Portugal)
Ltee.	Limitee (Canada, France)
mbH	mit beschraenkter Haftung (Austria, Germany)
N.V.	Naamloze Vennootschap (Belgium, The Netherlands)
OAO	Otkrytoe Aktsionernoe Obshchestve (Russia)
OOO	Obschestvo s Ogranichennoi Otvetstvennostiu (Russia)
Oy	Osakeyhtiö (Finland)
PLC	Public Limited Co. (United Kingdom, Ireland)
Pty.	Proprietary (Australia, South Africa, United Kingdom)
S.A.	Société Anonyme (Belgium, France, Greece, Luxembourg, Switzerland, Arab speaking countries); Sociedad Anónima (Latin America [except Brazil], Spain, Mexico); Sociedades Anônimas (Brazil, Portugal)
SAA	Societe Anonyme Arabienne
S.A.R.L.	Sociedade Anonima de Responsabilidade Limitada (Brazil, Portugal); Société à Responsabilité Limitée (France, Belgium, Luxembourg)
S.A.S.	Societá in Accomandita Semplice (Italy); Societe Anonyme Syrienne (Arab speaking countries)
Sdn. Bhd.	Sendirian Berhad (Malaysia)
S.p.A.	Società per Azioni (Italy)
Sp. z.o.o.	Spólka z ograniczona odpowiedzialnoscia (Poland)
S.R.L.	Società a Responsabilità Limitata (Italy); Sociedad de Responsabilidad Limitada (Spain, Mexico, Latin America [except Brazil])
S.R.O.	Spolecnost s Rucenim Omezenym (Czechoslovakia)
Ste.	Societe (France, Belgium, Luxembourg, Switzerland)
VAG	Verein der Arbeitgeber (Austria, Germany)
YK	Yugen Kaisha (Japan)
ZAO	Zakrytoe Aktsionernoe Obshchestve (Russia)

$	United States dollar	ISK	Icelandic krona
£	United Kingdom pound	ITL	Italian lira
¥	Japanese yen	JMD	Jamaican dollar
AED	Emirati dirham	KPW	North Korean won
ARS	Argentine peso	KRW	South Korean won
ATS	Austrian shilling	KWD	Kuwaiti dinar
AUD	Australian dollar	LUF	Luxembourg franc
BEF	Belgian franc	MUR	Mauritian rupee
BHD	Bahraini dinar	MXN	Mexican peso
BRL	Brazilian real	MYR	Malaysian ringgit
CAD	Canadian dollar	NGN	Nigerian naira
CHF	Swiss franc	NLG	Netherlands guilder
CLP	Chilean peso	NOK	Norwegian krone
CNY	Chinese yuan	NZD	New Zealand dollar
COP	Colombian peso	OMR	Omani rial
CZK	Czech koruna	PHP	Philippine peso
DEM	German deutsche mark	PKR	Pakistani rupee
DKK	Danish krone	PLN	Polish zloty
DZD	Algerian dinar	PTE	Portuguese escudo
EEK	Estonian Kroon	RMB	Chinese renminbi
EGP	Egyptian pound	RUB	Russian ruble
ESP	Spanish peseta	SAR	Saudi riyal
EUR	euro	SEK	Swedish krona
FIM	Finnish markka	SGD	Singapore dollar
FRF	French franc	THB	Thai baht
GRD	Greek drachma	TND	Tunisian dinar
HKD	Hong Kong dollar	TRL	Turkish lira
HUF	Hungarian forint	TWD	new Taiwan dollar
IDR	Indonesian rupiah	VEB	Venezuelan bolivar
IEP	Irish pound	VND	Vietnamese dong
ILS	new Israeli shekel	ZAR	South African rand
INR	Indian rupee	ZMK	Zambian kwacha

International Directory of

COMPANY
HISTORIES

The Advertising Council, Inc.

261 Madison Avenue, 11th Floor
New York, New York 10016
U.S.A.
Telephone: (212) 922-1500
Fax: (212) 922-1676
Web site: http://www.adcouncil.org

Not-for-Profit Company
Founded: 1942
Sales: $12 million
NAIC: 541800 Advertising and Related Services

The Advertising Council, Inc., is a New York City-based not-for-profit corporation that coordinates public service advertising campaigns, enlisting the volunteer services of advertising and communications companies and media facilities, and distributes the public service announcements (PSAs) to media outlets that run them free of charge. All told, the Ad Council receives about $1.3 billion in donated radio and television airtime and print space each year. The organization serves both government agencies and other non-profit groups. Ad Council campaigns have included some of the best known advertising of the past half-century, including such well-known slogans as "A mind is a terrible thing to waste," and "Friends don't let friends drive drunk." Advertising Council campaigns have also introduced several iconic characters, including Rosie the Riveter, Smokey the Bear, and McGruff the Crime Dog.

Wartime Roots of PSAs in the Civil War

Public service advertising in America was usually related to war efforts before the advent of the Ad Council. During the Civil War of the 1860s, for example, newspapers ran ads urged men to volunteer for the Army and made fundraising appeals to fund the war. During World War I, the U.S. government commissioned full-color posters to boost enlistment, recruit workers for war industries, and sell Liberty bonds. Much of the advertising work was done at cost and a lot of the media was donated, a harbinger of the Ad Council model a generation later. In the meantime, the concept of corporate advertising had emerged in the early 1900s, as corporations and trade associations sought to sway public opinion on important issues of the day that affected commerce. During the difficult days of the 1930s, when America suffered through the Great Depression, business was held in a poor light by many. The advertising industry had its share of critics as well, and by the start of the 1940s advertisers felt pressure to justify its place in the business world. The Association of National Advertisers and the American Association of Advertising Agencies commissioned studies, and the Advertising Research Foundation conducted polls to gain an understanding of how advertising was viewed and what was its perceived purpose. Not surprisingly, many in the industry wanted to develop an ad campaign to sell the idea of ad campaigns, to pitch the importance of advertising in creating jobs, lowering prices, and building wealth. When the two advertising associations decided to hold a joint meeting to discuss the plight of the industry in November 1941, one of the speakers took a different approach. His name was James Webb Young.

Young, whose formal education never went beyond eighth grade, worked his way up from office boy at the J. Walter Thompson agency to writer and eventually vice-president. In his 30 minute address at the joint meeting, Young maintained that the promotion of advertising lost sight of a more important goal, reviving confidence in business, of which advertising was a mere tool. But he went further, arguing that advertising should be used to promote the greater good: "It ought to be used to wipe out such diseases of ignorance as childbed fever. It ought to do the nutritional job this country needs to have done. It ought to be the servant of music, of art, of literature and of all the forces of righteousness." At the heart of Young's vision was an organization, a council, that would marshal the resources of the advertising community to promote worthy social causes, funded by business but with freedom and autonomy. The nobility of the effort would redound favorably on the reputation of advertising and business in general in the eyes of the public.

Young's call was taken up with enthusiasm by the attendees and committees were established to organize what the meeting minutes referred to as "the new Advertising Council, or whatever it is to be called." But war was raging around the world and within a matter of weeks, the United States would be drawn into the conflict following the Japanese attacks on Pearl Harbor in December 1941. The war effort took precedence, as virtually every industry rallied to the call to service, including advertising. In 1942 the organization became known as the War Advertising Council. It operated out of both New York and Washington, D.C., under the auspices of the Office of War Information, funded by $100,000 raised from ad agencies and media associations.

Ad Council's World War II Effort

The War Council's first assignment was to convince Americans not to hoard vital materials needed in the war effort that were now to be rationed, including rubber, sugar, and wool. The first full-fledge Ad Council campaign, also launched in 1942, was the sale of war bonds that would help finance the war. The campaign would run in some form until 1980, war bonds later becoming known as Savings Bonds. Also in 1942 the Ad Council created a campaign to urge Americans to be careful about discussing information that might be of interest to the enemy. One slogan, "Loose Lips Sink Ships," would be remembered long after the war ended. Generally forgotten was "Keep it Under Your Stetson," a slogan that revealed a practice at the time of tying brand names to war ads. Not only did the companies involved pay for the ads, the government believed it was important that trademarks be kept alive in the marketplace during a war of uncertain duration. Some companies went too far, however, placing what were called brag ads. Legendary adman Raymond Rubicam commented at the time, "A ball bearing manufacturer informed us that the subject of ball bearings is on everyone's lips nowadays, and sugar was an Axis-killer and castor beans had left the medicine cabinet for the battlefield." He also said that according to Madison Avenue air conditioners were responsible for sinking enemy ships and water conditioners for destroying Panzer tanks. The War Advertising Council stepped in to curb this practice, which dissipated within a year.

The War Advertising Council also produced a campaign to recruit women workers for war industries, which had to deal with a shortage of workers because of the millions of men serving in the military. The effort was personified by the invention of Rose the Riveter, who proclaimed to women, "We can do it!" Approximately two million women answered the call and went to work. Not only did their involvement help sustain the war economy, it began to change society's view of women's role outside of the home. It was also during the war, in 1944, that the Ad Council launched its longest running campaign, Forest Fire Prevention and its famous slogan, "Only You Can Prevent Forest Fires." At the time, the vast majority of forest fires were the result of accident, and the lack of available manpower hindered the government's ability to respond. Many conscientious objectors to the war, in fact, were recruited to

fight the fires. Disney allowed Bambi to be used in the first poster, but the dear was soon replaced by an Ad Council creation that became an American icon: Smokey Bear, who would become Smokey the Bear in the 1950s. It was also during World War II that the Ad Council established a 50-year relationship with the American Red Cross, helping the organization in blood drives, the recruitment of volunteers, and fund raising.

As the end of the war neared in 1945, President Roosevelt, before his death, urged the War Advertising Council to remain active after the peace. By now, the image of American business was much improved and James Young's vision for the Ad Council had been affirmed, as it became apparent that public service provided business with the kind of positive public relations no amount of money could buy. Theodore Repplier, who served as the War Advertising Council's executive director, commented, "The war never stopped. Only the enemy has changed." The organization reverted back to The Advertising Council name and in 1947 Repplier was named its first president.

After the war, the Ad Council continued to urge forest fire prevention, sell savings bonds, and work with the Red Cross. It also launched campaigns that dealt with veteran's rights and housing, tolerance for religious and ethnic groups, the danger of nuclear weapons, and the value of world trade. In 1947 the Ad Council began working with the National Safety Council in an effort to cut down the staggering number of highway fatalities. With the onset of the Cold War between Communist countries and the West, the Ad Council supported Radio Free Europe and promoted freedom and free enterprise. During the 1950s the organization moved beyond radio, print ads, and billboards to use comic books and television. Perhaps the most important, and successful Ad Council campaign of the 1950s was the drive to get parents to have their children immunized against Polio, a childhood scourge for many years. Also during the 1950s the Ad Council formed the Campaigns Review Committee to examine each campaign at every stage of its development and execution in an effort to make it as effective as possible.

New Projects in the 1960s

The Ad Council tackled a number of new subjects in the 1960s. It was also during this period that advertisers ceased to sponsor their own television shows and the networks took control of programming. As a result, the influence of advertisers on Ad Council spots was diminished. The organization also refined its operating procedure, as agencies donated their efforts to create the advertising and media companies ran the campaigns free of charge. In 1961 the Ad Council began promoting the Peace Corps, the volunteer organization envisioned by President Kennedy. The recruitment effort would last three decades.

Pollution was becoming a concern in America and in 1961 the Ad Council launched the Keep American Beautiful campaign, which ran until 1983. It originally focused on "litter bugs," but also dramatized the effects of other forms of pollution. The best known television spot in the campaign was aired on Earth Day in 1971 and featured a tearful Native American actor, Iron Eyes Cody, and the slogan, "People start pollution. People can stop it." Called "The Crying Indian," the PSA won a pair of Clios and was ranked 50th among the top 100 advertising campaigns of the 20th Century by *Ad Age* magazine. "It also

Key Dates:

1941: Advertising associations meet to plan Advertising Council.
1942: Ad Council formed and becomes The War Advertising Council for duration of World War II.
1943: Rosie the Riveter is created.
1944: Smokey Bear character is created.
1958: A polio vaccine campaign is launched.
1962: The Peace Corps campaign is launched.
1972: "A mind is a terrible thing to waste" tagline is coined for the United Negro College Fund campaign.
1988: An AIDS prevention campaign is launched.
2002: Campaign For Freedom, a joint venture with three other agencies, is launched.

represent what some critics believed was wrong with the Ad Council," according to John McDonough writing for *Advertising Age.* "The Keep American Beautiful campaign rested on the premise that 'people start pollution, people can stop it.' But what people and how? 'The damage done by litter is . . . inconsequential.' writer Kennen Peck noted in *The Progressive* in 1983, 'compared to the damage done by industrial pollution . . .' While different versions of the '70s campaign spots showed smokestacks as well as garbage, critics argued that by placing responsibility for pollution on individuals rather than institutions, the campaign was a powerful political decoy devised by corporate interests to divert public attention from the real issues of industrial waste."

Criticism was not new to the Ad Council, however. In the beginning, Republicans accused the organization of being an arm of the Roosevelt reelection effort, and others claimed the Ad Council was only trying to prevent the taxation of advertising. In 1950 one headline-seeking politician claimed that the Ad Council, along with the Ford Foundation, was little more than a Communist Front. The Ad Council was also criticized in the 1960s for being slow to recognize the plight of minorities and the conditions in America's urban centers. In response, the organization began addressing more sensitive topics. During the 1970s the Ad Council began its work on behalf of the United Negro College Fund, best known for the slogan, "A mind as a terrible thing to waste." During the 1970s the Ad Council also tackled once-taboo subjects like venereal disease and child abuse. Also of note in the 1970s, the Ad Council began working with the National Crime Prevention Council, urging Americans to "Take a bite out of crime," as espoused by one of the Ad Council's most popular characters, the trench coat-wearing McGruff the Crime Dog, who would issue a wealth of safety tips to children and adults alike.

In the 1980s, Ad Council campaigns took on drug abuse. At the behest of First Lady Nancy Regan, it created the "Just Say No" campaign, and later in the decade began to work with the Partnership for a Drug-Free America. Also in the 1980s the Ad Council launched a Drunk Driving Prevention campaign, which coined the slogan, "Friends Don't Let Friends Drive Drunk," as well as a Safety Belt Education campaign that featured Vince & Larry, the Crash Test Dummies and the tagline, "You Could Learn A Lot From a Dummy." While the anti-drug campaigns had little impact, the auto safety efforts proved highly effective. In 1988 the Ad Council tackled the controversial issue of AIDS, urging prevention through the use of condoms.

International Influence in 1990s and Beyond

The 1990s saw the Ad Council extend its influence beyond North America. With the fall of Communism in Eastern Europe, the Ad Council helped in the organization of volunteer Ad Councils in emerging democracies such as Russia and the Ukraine. It also aided similar efforts in other countries, including Belgium and Thailand. In 1994 the Ad Council launched a campaign to prevent domestic violence. It was at this point that the organization decided that instead of targeting a wide variety of messages it would focus much of its resources on a single topic: children. In 1995 the Ad Council announced the initiative, "Commitment 2000: Raising a Better Tomorrow," a 10-year effort that would pursue a range of issues relating to children, from violence to education and healthcare. Some of the current campaigns, such as drunk driving, would be recast to include children.

While the Ad Council might have focused its mission, it still remained ready to respond to new challenges. In the aftermath of the September 11, 2001, terrorist attacks, the organization was quick to become involved. Employees of Texas ad agency GSDM&M were in Maryland in a client meeting when the attacks unfolded. As they drove home to Texas (because air flights were suspended) they decided to create a PSA that celebrated America's diversity. The agency's president contacted the Ad Council about being a partner in the endeavor, and for the first time in its history the Ad Council became the sole signatory of a PSA. The result was the "I am an American" spot, featuring a wide range of men and women, young and old, of different races declaring "I am an American." The spot was on the air within ten days of the attacks.

Also during this time, three advertising industry associations met to plan an advertising campaign to celebrate freedom. The Ad Council was enlisted to manage the Campaign for Freedom. Unlike traditional Ad Council campaigns that were developed by a single agency, this would be the joint work of four agencies, and instead of relying on the backing of a sponsoring organization, the Ad Council itself raised the necessary funds to cover costs. After several months of development, the Campaign for Freedom was ready to launch in time for the Fourth of July holiday in 2002. A second phase was timed to coincide with the second anniversary of the September 11 attacks. The campaign evolved into a long-term effort called "Explore Freedom."

While the essential mission of the Ad Council remained unchanged, the organization was finding new ways to disseminate its messages. Just as it was quick to embrace television in the 1950s, it seized on the possibilities of the Internet as early as 1998, not only advertising on the Web but serving as a host. As Nat Ives wrote in the *New York Times* in 2005, "These days, Ad Council campaigns receive exposure in forms like Internet video, e-cards from American Greetings, taxi-top signs and video kiosks in stores. Google supports the campaigns through a grant program that allows nonprofit groups to secure keyword search terms; when Web surfers enter searches for those terms, links to public service ads appear next to the regular search results.'' The Ad Council was also taking steps to improve the television time slots for its PSAs, typically relegated to the early morning hours. The organization created what it called an ''up-front'' model that allowed media companies to determine what issues they wanted to support and time commitments could be secured ahead of time. As a result of these changes, the Ad Council, more than 60 years old, remained a vital force in American culture.

Principal Divisions

Campaign Review; Industries Advisory; Media; Public Issues Advisory.

Further Reading

''Ad Council Focuses on Children In Campaigns for Next 10 Years,'' *Wall Street Journal,* May 16, 1995, p. B8.

Albiniak, Paige, ''The Ad Council,'' *Broadcasting & Cable,* June 27, 2005, p. 24.

Elliott, Stuart, ''The Question Is: What is the Role of the Ad Council?'' *New York Times,* June 10, 1997, p. D9.

Fass, Allison, ''Public Service Ads Had a Record Year in 200, and the Ad Council Has High Hopes About 2001,'' *New York Times,* August 3, 2001,p. C4.

Ives, Nat, ''In the Struggle for Times and Space, Public Service Spots Are Finding New Way to Hold Their Own,'' *New York Times,* May 13, 2005,p. C6.

''Matters of Choices,'' New York, New York, The Advertising Council, 2002.

McDonough, John, ''Ad Council at 60—Facing a Crossroads,'' April 29, 2002, p. C4.

O'Connell, Vanessa, ''U.S. Plans a Campaign to Boost Morale,'' *Wall Street Journal,* September 21, 2001, p. B8.

—Ed Dinger

Agilysys...

Agilysys Inc.

6065 Parkland Boulevard
Mayfield Heights, Ohio 44124
U.S.A.
Telephone: (216) 587-3600
Web site: http://www.agilysys.com

Public Company
Incorporated: 1963
Employees: 1,386
Sales: $1.6 billion (2005)
Stock Exchanges: NASDAQ
Ticker Symbol: AGYS
NAIC: 421690 Other Electronic Parts and Equipment
    Wholesalers

Agilysys Inc., formerly known as Pioneer-Standard Electronics, Inc., operates as a leading distributor and reseller of enterprise technology solutions. The company markets its products and solutions through its Enterprise Solutions Group and its KeyLink Systems Group. The latter serves Agilysys's reseller partners and distributes computer systems that include server and storage hardware and software. Agilysys's Enterprise Solutions Group caters to large corporations that need help streamlining information technology systems. The company also provides software applications to the retail and hospitality industries. Agilysys sold off its Industrial Electronics Division in 2003 and adopted its current moniker shortly thereafter.

"Vacuum Tubes by the Pound": 1921–63

The U.S. electronic components distribution business was born in the 1920s in Courtland Street in lower Manhattan, a location that came to be known as Radio Row because of its profusion of radio parts stores. Before the commercial battery-operated radio was developed, ham radios ruled the industry, and in 1921 Charles Avnet, the founder of the firm that would lead the industry 70 years later, opened one of the first electronics distributorships for ham radio replacement parts, passive components, and connectors on Radio Row—only to see it fall victim to the Depression in 1931. In the 1930s Avnet tested the

waters again with a car radio kit and antenna manufacturing business, which succumbed to competition and went bankrupt as well. Small radio and electrical goods stores were springing up across the country, however, in major U.S. port cities like Boston, Philadelphia, and Chicago. In 1922, for example, industry pioneer Charles Kierulff (later part of the Arrow Electronics empire) opened his own radio parts store in Los Angeles, and in 1928 Allied Radio, a mail-order radio parts store, opened in Chicago.

By 1932 the radio parts distribution industry had reached Ohio, where a small distributorship named Standard Radio Supply—Pioneer-Standard's first incarnation—opened for business in Dayton. Around the same time an entrepreneur named Murray Goldberg founded Arrow Radio on New York's Radio Row to sell used radio equipment, marking the birth of the firm, Arrow Electronics, which together with Avnet would dominate the industry in the 1990s. For all of this entrepreneurial fervor, however, it was only with the explosion in manufacturing brought on by World War II that the U.S. electronics industry really came into its own. Simple ham radio parts suddenly became high-priority defense products, and for security reasons the federal government banned the manufacturing of radio sets for home or hobbyist use. With their traditional customers now off limits, radio part resellers and distributors like Standard Radio turned to the U.S. military and the war industry for sustenance. Charles Avnet, for example, made his third and finally successful attempt at business success at the height of the war by buying surplus electrical and electronic parts and selling them to the government. After the war, the private radio and electronic parts market was flooded by government war surplus parts, and the electronics distribution industry flourished. Among the many distributors who began in the postwar electronics boom were two new Cleveland firms, Premier Industrial Corporation and Pioneer-Standard's other forerunner, Pioneer Electronics Supply, both of which opened in 1946.

In 1947 the invention of the solid-state transistor rendered the vacuum tube obsolete, and during the 1950s the emergence of the television provided a new outlet for industry sales. In 1953, Wyle Electronics was formed in California, and a year

Company Perspectives:

Agilysys strives to be the preferred strategic link between its suppliers and customers by providing differentiated value that is rewarded. The company's role is to provide customers with solutions to integrate their systems, improve the efficiency of their business, and solve information technology challenges.

later Marshall Industries began business in the same state. Charles Avnet's distributorship incorporated as Avnet Electronics Supply Co. in 1955 and saw its sales climb above the $1 million mark for the first time. By the mid-1950s, some electronic parts distributors were selling parts for televisions, car radios, and sound systems, primarily to the consumer market, and in the late 1950s the growing U.S. space industry provided another lucrative new market. A growing number of Original Equipment Manufacturers (OEMs) began to join the consumer market as buyers of industry products, and industry firms began selling power electronics products and high-current devices for heavy equipment in addition to TV and radio components. To lessen its dependence on the military market, the electronic components industry increasingly began to sell its products directly to distributors like Avnet, Pioneer, and Standard, who for their part began to develop new methods to protect their prices and inventories from the competition and demand swings of the electronics market.

Pioneer-Standard Electronics: 1963–71

As the semiconductor industry began to grow in importance in the 1960s, electronics distributor Hamilton Electro (later acquired by Avnet) popularized the "broad-line" approach to distributing by carrying a range of electronics products from a variety of manufacturers rather than a limited line of select goods. It thus created the industry niche that Pioneer-Standard would later exploit on its path to industry leadership. By 1963 the electronic parts distribution business had grown into a roughly $500 million industry, and Cleveland's Pioneer Electronics Supply merged with Dayton's Standard Radio Supply to form Pioneer-Standard Electronics, incorporated in Ohio. Three years later in 1966, Pioneer-Standard purchased 50 percent of Frontier Electronics (itself founded in 1964) of Gaithersburg, Maryland, and rechristened it Pioneer-Washington and then later Pioneer/Technologies Group. By the mid-1960s, Pioneer's sales of electronic components and audio equipment stood at $5 to $9 million. In 1966 Preston (Pete) Heller, Jr., the CEO who would preside over Pioneer-Standard's growth into an industry giant, joined the firm as an executive vice-president of the Pioneer Division after a career with Crane Packing Company, Inland Steel, and Arthur Young & Company. Throughout the 1960s the leading firms in the electronics distribution industry grew by acquisition. In addition to Pioneer-Standard's purchase of Frontier, Avnet acquired Time Electronics, for example, and an investment group bought up Arrow Electronics. In its 1969 annual report Arrow's management sketched the future of the electronics distribution industry: It would soon be dominated by "those few substantial distribution companies with the financial resources, the professional management, and the modern con-

trol systems necessary to participate in the industry's current consolidation phase."

Pioneer Going Public: 1971–82

In 1969 Pete Heller was named Pioneer's president and director, and James L. Bayman (later Heller's successor as CEO) joined the firm as the general manager of its Dayton branch after several years in management positions in the electronics industry. Despite the national recession of 1970–71, several electronics distribution firms broke the $100 million sales level in the early 1970s, and by 1971 total industry sales were closing in on $1 billion. The industry solidified its place in the electronics industry food chain by developing product return privileges and further price protection guarantees. With sales at roughly $13 million, in June 1970 Pioneer-Standard registered an initial public offering (IPO) of company stock with the Securities and Exchange Commission. The $2.47 million in common stock sold quickly in January 1971, and Pioneer-Standard joined 14 other electronics distributors in the publicly owned arena (by the mid-1990s, only nine—Pioneer-Standard, Arrow, Avnet, Bell Industries, Jaco Electronics, Marshall Industries, Milgray Electronics, Sterling Electronics, and Wyle Electronics—remained).

Although Wall Street ignored the electronics distribution industry in the early 1970s, under Heller's command Pioneer-Standard raised its net income from $949,000 in 1973 to $2.33 million in 1975 and investors were soon watching its stock price with anticipation. Between 1975 and 1980 the electronics distribution industry as a whole grew at an annual pace of 17 percent as distributors grabbed a larger share of the electronics parts market and the largest firms grew even larger. As the growth of the computer industry began to spark investors' interest in electronics distributors in the late 1970s, industry earnings began to climb, carrying stock prices with them. Pioneer-Standard topped the $36 million mark in sales in 1976, and in 1977 sales broke past the $46 million mark. By 1980, the stocks of many distributors were selling at four to five times their 1971 prices, and Pioneer-Standard's net income had reached $3.95 million.

The onset of the recession of the early 1980s interrupted Pioneer's ascent, however, and in mid-1980 Heller was forced to admit to securities analysts that "if business remains flat and expenses remain frozen, profits will be under great pressure. . . . We're no different from any other concern in the industry." Unless the industry could cut costs or raise prices, he warned, its sales would have to grow at a 20 percent clip to match 1979 profit levels. As Wall Street saw stocks fall 24 percent between 1981 and 1982, distributors' stocks performed even worse. Many industry firms reported losses, and stock price declines of 50 percent were not unusual.

The Computer Revolution: 1982–89

In 1982 IBM introduced personal computers with greater computing power than any that had previously been marketed to American business. Almost immediately, sales of computer electronics were accounting for nearly 20 percent of the distribution industry's sales. With businesses and consumers buying PCs to power spreadsheet, word processing, and video game applications, the computer segment of the electronic distribu-

Key Dates:

1932:	Standard Radio Supply opens for business in Dayton, Ohio.
1946:	Premier Industrial Corporation and Pioneer Electronics Supply are established.
1963:	Pioneer Electronics Supply merges with Standard Radio Supply to form Pioneer-Standard Electronics.
1966:	The company buys 50 percent of Frontier Electronics (later known as Pioneer/Technologies).
1970:	Pioneer-Standard goes public.
1982:	The electronics distribution division of the Harvey Group of New York is acquired.
1994:	Canada-based Zentronics is purchased.
1995:	Pioneer-Standard acquires the remaining 50 percent of Pioneer/Technologies, which is renamed Pioneer-Standard of Maryland.
2003:	The company sells off its Industrial Electronics Division and changes its name to Agilysys Inc.; Kyrus Corporation is acquired.
2004:	Inter-American Data Inc. is purchased.

tion market was enjoying an annual growth rate of almost 100 percent, and price/performance ratios for industrial electronics began to improve by leaps and bounds every year. To capitalize on the trend, in late 1982 Heller engineered a $50 million credit agreement with four Ohio banks that enabled Pioneer-Standard to purchase the electronics distribution division of the Harvey Group of New York, pay down its existing debts, and cover its existing capital requirements. By early 1983, the electronics distribution industry had recovered from its recession and enjoyed an 18-month expansion in which sales grew at a 30 percent annual clip. Heller was named Pioneer-Standard's chairman and CEO in 1983, and by March 1984 the company's net income had recovered from its prerecession level, and then some, to $4.1 million.

The early 1980s was a period of heavy capital spending in the U.S. semiconductor industry, and Pioneer-Standard stock began to be touted as a way for investors to "play" the semiconductor industry without investing directly in the major semiconductor makers like AMD, Intel, and National Semiconductor. By 1984 Pioneer had established a distributor relationship with computer product maker Symbios Logic Inc. of Colorado; Peter Heller's future successor, James Bayman, had been promoted to president and chief operating officer; and the company's net income was climbing toward $3.67 million. The company established its System Integration Value-Added Center (SIVAC), a customer support/cost-control consulting service, in 1985 and in 1986 founded its End-User sales group to provide greater focus to its sales efforts. In 1989 Pioneer-Standard acquired California-based distributor Compumech Technologies and its net income broke past the $6.7 million mark on sales of more than $250 million.

The Keys to the Kingdom: 1990–97

For all Pioneer-Standard's steady expansion, however, by the late 1980s it had become apparent to many companies in the distribution industry that growth alone was no longer enough. Despite increasing industry sales, electronic components were becoming cheaper and cheaper to make, and distribution industry profit margins were declining. Firms like Pioneer-Standard were forced to scratch for improved cost savings and offer value-added services to maintain their profits and market share. In a crowded industry of 1,000 or more players, companies had to find new ways to distinguish themselves from their competitors.

For Pioneer-Standard's James Bayman, offering value-added services in addition to distribution became "the keys to the kingdom" of bigger profits and stronger market share. In fact, when it had begun offering systems integration services to customers in the mid-1970s, Pioneer-Standard had already started transforming itself from a plain-vanilla parts distributor to a value-added firm. By the late 1980s, however, there was no turning back. Electronics industry suppliers were reducing the number of distributors with which they worked and expecting more from the ones they kept. (Intel, for example—one of Pioneer's two largest suppliers—was among the first electronics manufacturers to insist that its distributors understand and technically support the products they sold.)

By 1990, Pioneer-Standard was not only supplying bowling automation system components for supplier AMF, for example, it was participating in their manufacture as well. "They [AMF] get the order," Bayman told *Barron's* magazine. "We configure it. We load the software, and ship it directly to the bowling alley, where it's installed by AMF service people." Similarly, in 1990 Pioneer-Standard opened "demonstration centers" in five U.S. cities, where its sales staff showed small- and medium-sized software companies how to adapt their products for use with DEC's computers. By 1997, Pioneer-Standard would be offering everything from product evaluation, demand generation services, warehousing, and package labeling to technology "migration" consulting and upgrading services and Internet and firewall design and connection services. Moreover, in addition to its army of increasingly technically trained sales people Pioneer-Standard added 150 "field application engineers" (FAEs) to support its sales force. The image of the electronics distributor as a mere "parts" supplier with only a big warehouse and a team of salesmen was giving way to automated warehouses, bar-coding of product shipments, overnight product delivery, and stock-tracking software and electronic data interchange systems for accurate, real-time sales and inventory information. By 1996, Pioneer-Standard could claim the highest FAE-to-salesperson ratios in the industry.

Pioneer-Standard opened its Central Distribution Center in Cleveland in 1990 and acquired the LCS computer systems division of the U.K. firm Lex Service plc the same year. By 1991 Pioneer's vow to become "a solutions company" seemed to be coming true, and its share of the North American electronics distribution market rose from 5.5 percent in 1990 to 5.8 percent. Following further expansion to the West Coast, Pioneer's sales surged to $552 million in 1992, representing 6.6 percent of the total North American electronics distribution market. In 1993 Pioneer acquired Siemens Components Inc.'s Hamilton/Hall-Mark distribution franchise and won a crucial vote of confidence for its campaign (called "FutureStart") to become a quality-driven distributor when the International

Standards Organization certified Pioneer as compliant with its ISO-9002 international quality standards program.

In 1994 Pioneer entered the international distribution market for the first time by acquiring Zentronics, one of Canada's largest industrial electronics and computer products distributors, from United Westburne Inc. for $10 to $12 million. While its share of Pioneer/Technologies was enabling it to make further inroads into the California distribution market, Pioneer signed a distribution agreement with California-based integrated circuit maker Atmel and won service awards from 15 of its suppliers and customers. Fueled by strong demand for microprocessors, Pioneer's sales broke the billion-dollar mark in 1994, and its share of the North American distribution market rose again, to 7.3 percent. By 1995, Pioneer could boast that its stock had risen 17.4 percent a year since its IPO in 1971 and that it did more business in a single day than it had in all of 1969.

In April 1995, James Bayman succeeded Pete Heller as Pioneer's CEO and announced his intention to continue Heller's expansion and value-added services strategies: "Our strategy is to grow internally and pursue acquisitions domestically and overseas in Europe and the Pacific Rim. . . . We [electronic distributors] are no longer just logistics managers. We are information managers. . . . We can't just sell a product, we have to show our client how to use it to become more competitive." In November Pioneer-Standard's long anticipated acquisition of the remaining 50 percent of Pioneer/Technologies was finalized, and in a deal estimated at about $50 million Pioneer/Technologies officially became Pioneer-Standard of Maryland. "With our buying technologies," Bayman quipped, "we finally put to bed the longest-running rumor in the industry, a rumor 20 years running." In one fell swoop Pioneer-Standard had become the third largest electronics distributor in North America, absorbing Pioneer/Technologies' 11 branch operations in the northwestern and southeastern United States and expanding its line card of products to one of the industry's most extensive. Rumors immediately began circulating that Pioneer-Standard would soon merge with another major distributor to gain ground on Arrow Electronics and Avnet—or even attempt to merge with one of those two industry leaders itself. "As usual, there is no basis for any of the rumors," Bayman asserted, while admitting coyly, "We are very interested in expanding."

The unprecedented growth of the distribution industry in 1991–95 tailed off in 1996, and Pioneer lost its rank as the third largest North American distributor. Nevertheless, in 1996 it announced distribution agreements with RadiSys Corporation, Cisco Systems, Micron Technology, AccelGraphics Inc., Tadpole Technology, Network General, Murata Electronics, Symbios Logic, Lucent Technologies, Actel Corporation, and Cipher Systems. It also entered into an increasingly typical "remarketing" agreement with IBM, in which Pioneer-Standard would not only distribute Big Blue's computer systems but would support them by providing value-added resellers (VARs) with an umbrella of services such as sales and technical services, direct marketing services, product evaluation, financial services, and business planning. With semiconductors representing an ever larger segment of the distribution market, in 1996 Pioneer-Standard also relocated its semiconductor marketing operations to California's Silicon Valley, the heart of the U.S. high-tech industry.

Between 1991 and 1996, the industrial electronics distribution industry had grown from $9 billion to more than $20 billion, a 300 percent increase over its volume in 1986. Despite the cost of its acquisition of Pioneer/Technologies and a slowdown in industry sales, Pioneer-Standard's sales topped $1.5 billion in 1996, and in 1997 it announced new distribution agreements with U.S. Robotics, Celestica Inc., and Fairchild Semiconductor. Its implementation of Total Quality Management (TQM) principles had lifted its quality control score to the "world-class" level, and the American Society for Quality Control was citing the company's quality program as a "textbook example of comprehensive planning activity, followed by rigorous implementation, producing results." The year 1996 was the tenth consecutive year of record sales for Pioneer-Standard; since its 1971 IPO its sales had increased every year but one.

In 1997, the company strengthened its international foothold with the purchase of World Peace International, a distributor located in Taiwan. It also branched out into Europe when it acquired a stake in the United Kingdom's Eurodis Electron. Technology had continued to change at breakneck speed during the late 1990s, and major changes were on the horizon for Pioneer-Standard.

A New Name for the New Millennium

During the early years of the new millennium, Pioneer-Standard operated with two main divisions: Computer Systems Division (CSD), which was responsible for the distribution and resale of enterprise computer systems products and solutions; and Industrial Electronics Division (IED), which handled the company's electronic components distribution. Pioneer-Standard also operated Aprisa Inc., a majority owned unit that created software for the electrical components market.

A major slowdown in tech spending during this time period forced Pioneer-Standard to rethink its business strategy. As such, the company made a bold move in early 2003 and decided to sell off its IED operations to competitor Arrow Electronics Inc. in a $240 million deal. The company restructured itself to focus solely on its enterprise computer solutions business. Pioneer-Standard's shift away from its electronic roots was made obvious in September when the company adopted a new corporate moniker: Agilysys Inc. The new name was a combination of the words "agile" and "systems" and was chosen to help the company transform its image.

Agilysys's first move came later that month with the $30 million acquisition of Kyrus Corporation, an IBM retail systems and solutions provider. The deal secured Agilysys's position as the leading provider of IBM retail solutions and services to the supermarket, chain drug, general retail, and hospitality markets. The company also gained a foothold in the casino and destination resort market segments in February 2004 when it added Inter-American Data Inc. to its arsenal. According to Agilysys, its Lodging Management Systems was considered to be the hospitality industry's leading property management solution.

In May 2005, the company bought The CTS Corporation, an independent services firm providing information technology storage solutions for large corporations. It also formed a reseller agreement with EMC Corporation. Sales in the 2005 fiscal year reached $1.62 billion, an increase of 16 percent over the previous year. Net income was also on the rise, reaching $19.5 million in fiscal 2005.

With solid financial results as evidence, it appeared as though Agilysys's new acquisitions were paying off. In fact, Arthur Rhein, who was named CEO in 2002 and chairman in 2003, claimed in a July 2004 *Plain Dealer* article that 80 percent of the rooms in Las Vegas and all of the rooms in Atlantic City operated on Agilysys software. Indeed, the company had an impressive client list across several industries including the Venetian Resort Hotel Casino in Las Vegas, Duane Reade drug stores, Family Dollar stores, and the International Securities Exchange.

Although Pioneer-Standard's metamorphosis into Agilysys was a sharp departure from its roots as an electronic components supplier, the company stood on solid footing as a leading enterprise computer technology solutions provider. Management was confident that its strategy would continue to pay off in the years to come.

Principal Subsidiaries

Agilysys, Inc.; Agilysys Canada Inc.; Agilysys S.C. Inc.; Agilysys NV LLC; The Dickens Services Group, A Pioneer-Standard Company LLC; Aprisa, Inc.; Aprisa Holdings LLC; Pioneer-Standard Financial Trust.

Principal Competitors

Avnet Inc.; Ingram Micro Inc.; Tech Data Corporation.

Further Reading

"Agilysys Agrees to Acquire Kyrus," *Wall Street Journal,* September 17, 2003.

Baird, Kristen, "Setting New Standards at Pioneer-Standard," *Crain's Cleveland Business,* July 24, 1995, p. 3.

Bounds, Wendy, "Pioneer-Standard Acquires Remainder of Pioneer Technologies for $50 Million," *Wall Street Journal,* December 1, 1995.

Burke, Steven, "Pioneer: New Name, Renewed Commitment," *Computer Reseller News,* September 1, 2003.

Cohodas, Marilyn, "Siemens Teams with Pioneer," *Electronic Business Buyer,* November 1993, p. 22.

Gerdel, Thomas W., "Acquisitions Fuel Growth at Agilysys," *Plain Dealer,* July 29, 2004, p. C1.

Gomez, Henry, "Agilysys Is Slowly Rolling Out New Name," *Crain's Cleveland Business,* September 22, 2003, p. 2.

Harrison, Kimberly P., "Pioneer-Standard Electronics, Inc.," *Crain's Cleveland Business,* May 23, 1994, p. S-15.

"How They Rank," *Electronic News,* December 2, 1996.

Jackson, Tom, "Agilysys Takes First Steps in Software," *Crain's Cleveland Business,* February 9, 2004.

Levine, Bernard, "Pioneer-Standard Buys Remainder of Tech Affiliate," *Electronic News,* December 4, 1995.

McCausland, Richard, Untitled, *Electronic News,* July 26, 1993, p. 18.

"Pioneer-Standard Electronics," *Wall Street Journal,* March 3, 1994.

"Pioneer-Standard Electronics Inc.," *Wall Street Journal,* January 14, 1993.

"Pioneer-Standard Electronics Inc.: Who's News," *Wall Street Journal,* April 30, 1997.

"Pioneer-Standard Says Bookings Are Declining," *Wall Street Journal,* May 30, 1980.

"Pioneer-Standard's Centers," *Wall Street Journal,* January 24, 1991.

"Pioneer-Standard Stocks Sold," *Wall Street Journal,* January 8, 1971.

"Pioneer-Standard To Buy Some Assets of Harvey Unit," *Wall Street Journal,* November 2, 1982.

Ruston, Richard E., and John Bussey, "Semiconductor Issues Have Soared As Outlook for Prices, Orders Growth Is Seen Brightening," *Wall Street Journal,* August 27, 1984.

Savitz, Eric J., "More Than Their Name Implies: Electronic Distributors Widen Horizons," *Barron's,* June 25, 1990, p. 15.

—Paul S. Bodine
—update: Christina M. Stansell

Alberici Constructors
AN ALBERICI ENTERPRISE

Alberici Corporation

2150 Kienlen Avenue
St. Louis, Missouri 63121-5592
U.S.A.
Telephone: (314) 261-2611
Toll Free: (800) 261-2611
Fax: (314) 261-4225

Private Company
Incorporated: 1918 as J.S. Alberici Construction
   Company
Employees: 2,500
Sales: $608.1 million (2003)
NAIC: 236220 Commercial and Institutional Building
   Construction

Alberici Corporation is an employee-owned corporate parent of nearly 20 construction subsidiaries, the largest of which is Alberici Construction Company. The St. Louis-based company is diversified geographically as well as in capabilities, allowing it the potential to prosper no matter what the economic conditions. With regional offices in Ontario, Canada, Michigan, West Virginia, and Georgia. Alberici offers a full range of construction services for general contracting, construction management, and design-build projects. It also offers special construction services, including steel fabrication and erection, heavy demolition, rigging and heavy lifting, and equipment installing and relocation. Among the markets Alberici serves are automotive manufacturing, energy, food and beverage, healthcare, pharmaceutical, marine, industrial, and water/wastewater. The company also owns a massive fleet of equipment, valued at more than $100 million. Alberici is ranked in the top 50 of U.S. contractors with annual sales in excess of $600 million.

1918 Origins

Alberici Corporation was founded in St. Louis in 1918 as J.S. Alberici Construction Company by John Stanislaus Alberici, an immigrant from the wine country of northern Italy. Alberici launched the business in his mid-40s after managing the construction of a bank building in St. Louis for a New York

firm. The clients were so pleased with his work they urged him to start his own contracting business. As a further inducement he was allowed to set up shop in an extra office of The Boatmen's National Bank. J.S. Alberici Construction Company specialized in concrete contracting, and it wasn't until 1923 that Alberici traded in his horse and wagon for a truck.

In 1928 Alberici was joined in business by his 18-year-old son Gabriel, who initially attended Washington University's engineering school at night before the long hours demanded by his father proved to onerous for studies as well. The younger Alberici would eventually graduate from the American School of Welding in 1932. In the early days, however, he generally started his 16-hour days by reporting to a construction site at 3 a.m. to set it up for the day's work. On Sunday, his only day off, he and his father helped friends in the Italian district of St. Louis, known as The Hill, as they constructed their homes bit by bit, whenever they had saved enough money to buy more materials. "My father was a stern guy," Alberici told the *St Louis Business Journal,* in a 1996 profile. "I loved him but you didn't stray far from the course. He showed me how to work hard and make it into a routine."

Gabriel Alberici assumed an increasing amount of responsibility in the 1930s, especially in the area of equipment investments. The roots of the firm's $100 million fleet were planted during this period. Like his father and their immigrant friends, he loathed to borrow money. In fact, throughout its history the company took out just one loan, for $20,000, and it was repaid within the year. During the 1930s Alberici Corporation landed one of its first high-profile jobs, the $100,000 contract in 1939 to provide stonework and walkways for the Muny Opera building in St. Louis. With the profits the company was able to purchase its first crane for $2,000.

A New Generation of Leadership in 1940

The elder Alberici died in 1940, leaving the business to 31-year-old Gabriel and his younger sister Mary. A graduate of the Washington University School of Business in 1933, she forged a partnership with her brother to run the business their father had founded. Essentially he ran the outside of the company and she

Company Perspectives:

Our goal on every project we undertake is to bring owners new and unexpected value to construction services.

ran the inside, and by all accounts she maintained a tight ship. Gabriel was president of the firm, while Mary served as secretary and treasurer. A few years later, in 1946, key employees gained a stake in the business when Alberici Corporation became an employee-owned entity, with the Alberici family still retaining majority ownership. When employee-stockholders left the company or retired, they were required to sell back their stock. For the employees who did not own stock, a profit sharing plan was instituted. Not many of the stockholders left before retiring, however, as many opted to stay with the company for their entire work careers. For her part, Mary Alberici retired in 1960.

The 1950s was a period of diversification for J.S. Alberici. From the beginning the company prided itself on completing projects on time and on budget, but after a pair of projects were delayed because a local fabricator failed to deliver steel, the company in 1952 built its own fabrication plant. This would expand over time into a 200,000 square-foot facility, becoming not only one of the largest steel fabrication plants in the Midwest but one of the most sophisticated in the entire country. A year later, that capability would begin to be put to use as Alberici Corporation entered the automotive plant construction market when General Motors decided to build a plant in the St. Louis area. Later Alberici would win contracts to build facilities in St. Louis from the two other members of Detroit's Big Three automakers, Chrysler and Ford. Another new area of business begun in the 1950s was highway construction, which in the postwar era was deemed a national security issue. Both the federal and state governments invested heavily in the construction of highways. Alberici got its start in 1955 by working on the Third Street Highway that cut through the heart of St. Louis.

Diversification continued in the 1960s. A vice-president named Raymond F. Pieper recognized that air pollution control held great potential for the construction industry, at a time when the need for clean air and clean water was becoming a major concern in the United States. He began going after some projects outside of St. Louis. His first successful bid was for a retrofit for a central Illinois public service company. Next Alberici did some power plant maintenance work, which set the stage for the construction of power plants. Gaining experience incrementally, Alberici was able to develop its current expertise in the energy and water/wastewater fields.

Other developments in the 1960s included the introduction of the industry's first 16-cubic-yard capacity roll-on/roll-off dumpster container, which was used to more efficiently clean up job sites. The company also launched its first formal construction safety program. The reduction in accidents resulted in lower insurance costs. At the end of the 1960s the company moved to a new 65-acre site, large enough to accommodate future growth.

In 1976 Pieper became the first non-member of the Alberici family to be named company president. Gabriel Aberici re-

tained the chairmanship and remained actively involved in the business, still coming to work in the early morning hours and opening the office at 5:30 each day. Pieper had never worked anywhere else in his life. After graduating from Washington University with a civil engineering degree in 1949, he went to work for Alberici as a field engineer and began to work his way up the ranks of the company's hierarchy. The 1970s was also marked by the company's entry into yet another field: Marine. In 1979 J.S. Alberici landed a $212 million, 15-year project to build the Alton Lock & Dam No. 26 at the confluence of the Illinois River and Mississippi River in Alton, Illinois.

1980s Expansion

Expansion continued in the 1980s for Alberici. In 1983 it acquired General Installation Company, a mechanical contracting business that installed commercial piping and heating and air-conditioning systems. The company also began to expand geographically, opening an office in Denver and at the end of the decade a Detroit office. While the Denver office would be closed in 1990, and Alberici shied away from the Sun Belt states, where it would have to contend with competition from non-union contractors, it would enjoy strong success out of Detroit, where it landed a number of significant contracts with automakers for plants in the Great Lakes area and Canada. The company also worked on projects in Mexico through a joint partnership and looked increasingly overseas for new opportunities. In 1991, for instance, it won a $50 million contract to build more than 1,000 apartments in Israel. It was also during this period that Pieper launched a management training program, primarily to groom the company's ranks of middle managers. Alberici had enjoyed long-term stability in its management ranks, but as key members grew older it became increasingly important to make sure there would be a new generation of leaders capable of taking charge. This need was made evident in 1991 when Pieper elected to retire when he turned 65. His replacement as president was 60-year-old Edward L. Calcaterra, but 80-year-old Gabriel Alberici continued to come into the office each day. Calcaterra served as president until 1996 when at the age of 66 he too retired, albeit a year later than he had planned in order to complete some major projects. One of those younger managers groomed in the management training program was 45-year-old Robert F. McCoole, who had joined the company in the early 1980s. Several months prior to Calcaterra's announced retirement, McCoole was one of five younger executives promoted to senior vice-president who formed an executive committee intended to lead the company into the future.

Diversification helped Alberici to weather a recession in the early 1990s that in particular limited the number of major projects in the St. Louis area. Retrenchment was in order, however, and some subsidiaries were shut down or sold. General Installation, for example, was dissolved in 1994. As a result, Alberici was able to focus on its core construction business. Business began to pick up as the economy rebounded in the 1990s. Revenues totaled $333 million in 1993, then surged to $659 million in 1994, due in large measure to renovations made by General Motors, Ford, and Chrysler to Detroit plants. As the Big Three also became more global in their reach, opening plants around the world, Alberici followed them, building a Chrysler Jeep Grand Cherokee assembly plant in Argentina. Later in the 1990s it built an engine plant in Brazil as part of a joint venture project between DaimlerChrysler Corporation and BMW. In 1998 the firm began construction on an engine plant in Mexico for Ford, and in that same year began construction on a plant in Guanajuato, Mexico, for American Axle & Manufacturing. Alberici also looked to the domestic market in 1998, opening an office in Atlanta, bringing the number of regional offices to three.

Gabriel Alberici remained active in the company his father founded until 1999 when he reached the age of 90. He lived until December 2002, passing away from natural causes at his home at the age of 93, outliving his wife of 61 years by seven years. Five months earlier his 91-year-old sister Mary died from complications of pneumonia in a nursing center. Although Gabriel Alberici's son, John S. Alberici, succeeded his father as chairman of the company, the direct ties to the founding of the family business were severed. Nevertheless, Alberici continued to follow the hard-working tradition established by an Italian immigrant nearly a century earlier.

With the economy lapsing into recession in the early 2000s, Alberici was once again well served by its long-term commitment to diversification. That trend continued in the new century. Alberici Global Group GmbH was formed in 2002 as a holding company for international business, mostly performed for U.S. clients and involving a partnership with a company already working in that country. In the United States, another regional office was opened in West Virginia in 2003. Alberici Corp. launched a new business called Vertegy in 2005 to provide design, procurement, and construction consulting services for green and sustainable facilities, the outgrowth of work the company did on its new corporate headquarters that it billed as one of the "greenest" headquarters in the country.

Principal Subsidiaries

Alberici Group, Inc.; Alberici Constructors, Inc.; Alberici Industrial LLC; Gunther-Nash, Inc.; Alberici Global Group GmbH. Alberici Healthcare Constructors.

Principal Competitors

Fluor Corporation; McCarthy Building Companies, Inc.; Washington Group International, Inc.

Further Reading

Franklin, Donald E., "Pioneer In Construction Industry Here Was Generous Philanthropist; Gabriel J. Alberici, 1909–2002," *St. Louis Post-Dispatch,* December 10, 2002, p. B1.

Lerner, Howard, "Alberici Shutting Down Mechanical Contract Subsidiary," *St. Louis Business Journal,* May 30, 1994, p. 11A.

"Mary Alberici: Co-Partner In Construction Firm," *St. Louis Post-Dispatch,* June 19, 2002, p. B4.

McLaughlin, Tim, "Early To Rise Regimen Aided Alberici's Climb in Building," *St. Louis Business Journal,* January 22, 1996, p. 6A.

Miller, Patricia, "Pieper's Vision Helped Alberici See Through Polluted Air," *St. Louis Business Journal,* February 4, 1991, p. 9C.

"Still Running the Family Business," *St. Louis Commerce,* June 1, 1991, p. 6.

—Ed Dinger

Allen Canning Company

305 West Main Street
Siloam Springs, Arkansas 72761
U.S.A.
Telephone: (479) 524-6431
Fax: (479) 524-3291
Web site: http://www.allencanning.com

Private Company
Incorporated: 1926
Employees: 90
Sales: $330 million (2004)
NAIC: 311421 Fruit and Vegetable Canning

Allen Canning Company, based in the small town of Siloam Springs, Arkansas, is one of the largest private canner of foods in the world, offering a full line of canned vegetables to the retail food and food service industries, including a variety of southern vegetables. The company also does contract canning for major and private labels. It operates about a dozen plants, strategically located close to the growing fields in Arkansas, Louisiana, Mississippi, North Carolina, and Texas. Allen Canning sells its products under a dozen brand names. The Allens label offers a wide variety of beans as well as carrots, hominy, blackeyed peas, and chicken broth. The Allen name is also found on the company's Allen Italian Green Beans product line. New whole and diced potatoes and potato sticks are sold under the Butterfield label. The East Texas Fair brand is devoted to lima beans, field peas, blackeyed peas, and chick peas. Under the Freshlike brand, Allen offers a variety of vegetables, including spinach, corn, peas, and beets. The Popeye label, which features the likeness of Popeye, the venerable cartoon sailor, offers chopped and leaf spinach. The focus of the Princella, Royal Prince, and Sugary Sam labels are sweet potatoes, either cut, mashed, or candied. The Sunshine label is found on such vegetables as turnip greens, rutabagas, yellow squash, and butter beans. The Trappey's name is applied to another line of bean products, including northern beans, pinto beans, kidney beans, black beans, and navy beans, as well as sweet potatoes, blackeyed peas, and okra. The Veg-All line of products include a varied of mixed vegetable combinations and regular vegetables. Finally, Allen offers the Wagon Master brand of pork and beans. Allen Canning is headed by Rick Allen, grandson of the company's founder. A fourth generation is also employed in the executive ranks and being groomed to carry on the family business.

Canning Technique Introduced in 1800s

Canning was in fact bottling when it was first developed in the early 1800s. The idea of preserving food in a container grew out of a challenge by Napoleon Bonaparte, who knew full well that an army marched on its stomach. About the only obstacle preventing him from conquering the world, it seemed, was that the food supplies of his army and navy had a tendency to spoil. In 1895 he offered a 12,000 franc prize to anyone who could find a way to solve the problem. A French chef named Nicholas Appert was determined to win the prize and spent the next 15 years working on a way to bottle food in much the same way wine was. Through trial and error Appert discovered that if food was heated and sealed in an airtight container it did not spoil. Originally it was thought that the elimination of oxygen was the key, and half a century would pass before Louis Pasteur demonstrated that it was the growth of microorganisms that was the culprit in food spoilage. By heating the food sufficiently, Appert had succeeded in killing the bacteria and enzymes that caused spoiling, then by hermetically sealing the food in a bottle he prevented new organisms from gaining an opportunity for contamination. Appert's method was given a trial by the French Navy around 1806 and was so successful it became a military secret. But like many a good idea, it was too commercial to remain a secret and was soon learned by Napoleon's arch enemy, the British.

It was an Englishman, Peter Durand, who first used tin containers, a marked improvement over bottles, which were susceptible to breaking. The first commercial canning factory was opened in England in 1813, but a year earlier immigrant Thomas Kensett launched the first canning operation in New York City for vegetables, fruits, meats, and oysters. Over the years the canning processed remained the same, but in the beginning it was time consuming, requiring about six hours to process food in a can. By the 1860s that time was reduced to about 30 minutes, the price came down, and canned food became available to the masses.

Company is Established in the 1920s

According to company lore, Allen Canning's founder Earl Allen moved to the healthy climes of the Ozark hills of Arkansas in 1922 with his wife and five children crammed into a Model T Ford. A year later he began working in a canning operation located near Siloam Springs, established in an abandoned distillery that was no longer permitted to produce liquor after prohibition took effect in 1919. Allen became the sole owner of the business in 1926 and named it after himself. It was a tiny operation and he produced just one item during his first year: 4,000 cases of tomatoes. It was also very much a family affair from the start, as his wife and children all pitched in.

Allen Canning began to establish connections with locals growers and expand beyond tomatoes, but within a few years Allen Canning had to face the challenge of the Depression. The company managed to scrape by and survive the 1930s, which were also extremely difficult on the growers. Earl Allen established a solid reputation for his honesty in dealing with growers, forging relationships that would benefit the company for years to come. The advent of World War II in the first half of the 1940s revived the economy as well as spurred the growth of Allen Canning, which supplied canned vegetables to the military. Following the war, the United States, after a brief recession, enjoyed a decade-long period of expansion, fueled in large part by the economic activity of returning servicemen, who married and began raising the Baby Boom generation in the new suburbs. The self-service grocery store concept also came into its own as larger "super" markets became the norm and spread across the country in chains. With the expansion of retail outlets, canners like Allen Canning prospered as well. Also, during the 1940s a second generation of the Allen family took charge, as 29-year-old Delbert Allen, Sr., now led the company.

In the 1940s and 1950s Allen Canning added a wide variety of items, such as an array of beans, greens, potatoes, and blackberries. It also became one of the first companies to pack sweet potatoes, especially popular in the south, along with collard greens, turnips, blackeyed peas, and rutabaga. Another regional item Allen Canning specialized in was poke salet, made from the pokeweed, the asparagus-like shoots of which became edible in early spring. It was popular because as one of the first spring greens it served to provide relief from a common winter menu that consisted mostly of salt pork, beans, and cornbread. As people were forced to flee the Dustbowl conditions of Arkansas and Oklahoma for California during the 1930s, they brought their taste for poke salet to the West Coast, which became a prime market for Allen Canning. As the people who grew up on poke salet became to die off, however, the demand for the item dried up. More so, pokeweed wasn't grown so much as it was gathered. In the spring the company put out the word that it was ready to can poke salet and people would

bring in bags and tubs of the greens, which had to be gathered in remote locations. Not only were the eaters of poke salet dwindling, so were the people willing to gather it. Allen Canning packed its last batch of poke salet greens in the spring of 2000.

In the 1960s and 1970s Allen Canning expanded on a number of fronts. To keep up with consumer demand and accommodate its growing slate of products, the company opened more plants and began running them 24 hours a day. In 1963 it opened one of the most modern canning plants in the United States. State-of-the-art equipment would also be installed in the company's other plants to make them more efficient and improve the quality and freshness of the products. The plants were strategically located close to the fields because it was important to pack the vegetables as quickly as possible, before they began to lose nutrients. With increased capacity, Allen Canning was also able to expand into new markets. Among the new products the company added during this time were shoestring potato sticks in 1971, and in 1978 the company acquired the popular Popeye Spinach brand.

In the 1980s Allen Canning made strong inroads into the institutional market, which became an increasingly important sales channel, eventually accounting for about 35 percent of all revenues. By the middle of the decade, Allen Canning was billing itself as the world's largest private canner. It produced more than 75 products from 11 plants in Arkansas, Louisiana, Mississippi, Oklahoma, and Texas, and its products were now distributed across the United States. It was also during the 1980s that a third generation took the helm of the family business, as Delbert Allen Sr.'s son, Roderick Allen, succeeded him.

Canned Food Loses Popularity in 1990s

The canning industry had to contend with a decrease in popularity in canned foods in the 1990s. According to Debbie Howell writing for *DSN Retailing Today* in 2002, "Fresh produce, frozen food and takeout meals have made what once was considered the ultimate convenience food a dinosaur." Moreover, consumers became less loyal to brand name canned vegetables and fruits, and as a result private label products became increasingly popular. The canning industry was not in danger of disappearing, but many of the players found it difficult to make much money. The only reason sales grew over the course of the decade were price increases: unit sales steadily dwindled. Smaller companies like Allen Canning, which specialized in niche products such as Southern vegetables, fared better by being innovative to gain a competitive edge. One way Allen Canning was able to maintain sales was by adding seasonings to some of their items, spurring renewed interest.

Despite the difficult climate facing the canning industry, Allen Canning entered the 2000s looking to expand, even as rivals were looking to cut back. Birds Eye Foods sold its Veg-All brand of canned mixed vegetables to Allen Canning in July 2003. The Birds Eye brand, long associated with frozen foods, had undergone a number of ownership changes in the previous 20 years, and in 1998 was acquired by Agrilink Foods, Inc., which was involved in frozen, fresh, and canned foods. Then in February 2003, Agrilink assumed the Birds Eye name and began closing half-a-dozen plants and casting off product lines. Veg-All was as old as Allen Canning, dating back to 1926 when the

---

Key Dates:

1923: Earl Allen finds work in an Arkansas canning company.
1926: Earl Allen becomes sole owner of what becomes Allen Canning Company.
1963: Modern state-of-the-art plant is opened.
1978: Popeye Spinach brand is acquired.
2003: Veg-All brand is acquired.
2004: Freshlike brand is acquired.

---

combination of 10 vegetables was introduced with the promise of "no scrubbing, no peeling, no work!" The Veg-All products had been produced by a Birds Eye plant in Green Bay, Wisconsin that was slated to be closed. Allen Canning bought much of the facility's assets and transferred them to its plants in Arkansas and Mississippi. A year later, in August 2004, Birds Eye sold another Green Bay-based product line, Freshlike canned foods, to Allen Canning. Established in 1934, Freshlike offered a variety of popular vegetables, such as corn, carrots, green beans, peas, and beets. The Freshlike name was also found on a line of frozen vegetables, which were not part of the deal.

Not only was it clear that Allen Canning remained committed to canned vegetables despite declining popularity, it continued to be very much a family-owned and operated company. The third generation of the Allen family served as chairman of board and president of the company, while a fourth generation was actively involved. While one of the younger family members, Dave Allen, left the company to produce horror films in Hollywood, with the help of the family largesse, another, Josh Allen, became vice-president of operations while in his 20s and appeared to be well on his way to being groomed to one day carry on the family heritage.

Principal Operating Units

Allens; Allens Italian Green Beans; Butterfield; East Texas Fair; Freshlike; Popeye; Princella; Royal Price; Sugary Sam; Sunshine; Trappey's; Veg-All; Wagon Master.

Principal Competitors

B&G Foods, Inc.; ConAgra Foods, Inc.; Del Monte Foods Company; Dole Foods Company, Inc.; Seneca Foods Seneca Foods Corporation.

Further Reading

Howell, Debbie, "Canned Goods May Be Losing Customer Appeal," *DSN Retailing Today,* May 6, 2002, p. F12.

"Marketplace Southern Vegetables," *Arkansas Democrat-Gazette,* September 3, 1986.

"Open Up to Allens: The Inside Story on Canned Foods Popularity," *Restaurant Business,* March 15, 2003, p. 123.

Stogner, Alicia, "Allen Canning to Buy Birds Eye Subsidiary," *Arkansas Business,* June 23, 2003, p. 11.

Turner, Lance, "Allen Canning Buys Freshlike Business," *Arkansas Business,* April 12, 2004 , p. 11.

"Twp Canning Firms Offer Southern Spring Favorite, Poke Salet," *Toronto Star,* April 11, 1990. p. C14.

—Ed Dinger

American Italian Pasta Company

4100 North Mulberry Drive, Suite 200
Kansas City, Missouri 64116
U.S.A.
Telephone: (816) 584-5000
Fax: (816) 584-5100
Web site: http://www.aipc.com

Public Company
Incorporated: 1986
Employees: 589
Sales: $417.4 million (2004)
Stock Exchanges: New York
Ticker Symbol: PLB
NAIC: 311823 Dry Pasta Manufacturing; 422490 Other
    Grocery and Related Products Wholesalers

The largest pasta producer in North America, American Italian Pasta Company (AIPC) produces more than 220 dry pasta shapes, selling its pasta to supermarket chains, food processing companies, and foodservice companies. AIPC produces pasta for private-label brands and its own brand, Pasta LaBella. The company grew significantly through several acquisitions it completed in the early years of the new millennium. Its expansion came to a standstill in 2004, however, when the low-carb diet trend caused demand for carbohydrate-rich pasta to plummet. In 2005, the company launched an internal investigation into its accounting practices amid shareholder class action lawsuits that claimed that AIPC's officials proffered misleading financial data.

Origins

Richard C. Thompson brought an eclectic professional past with him when he founded AIPC in 1986. During the 1970s he was involved in real estate surrounding the Houston Astrodome. During the early 1980s he turned his attention to the oil and gas business, forming an exploration firm, Kinson Resources Inc., to make a living wildcatting in North Dakota. The cyclical nature of the oil and gas business, which descended into one of its deepest ruts during the early 1980s, convinced Thompson to search for a

business with fewer market fluctuations and led him to explore food manufacturing as an option. Food production sprang to mind not only because "there's always a demand for food," as Thompson once remarked, but also because North Dakota was home to a prized crop: durum. Renowned for its superior pasta-making qualities, North Dakota durum was imported by Italian companies, who converted the wheat into pasta and then exported the pasta back to the United States. Thompson decided to use North Dakota durum to start his own pasta-making company, and he began enlisting the support of financial backers. From the start, he decided to focus on producing premium-grade pasta and avoid competing against low-priced, mass-produced brands manufactured by such industry giants as Hershey Foods and Borden. "If we're going to survive," Thompson explained, "we cannot compete on price. If we do, we'll get stepped on, thrown away, chewed up, and walked over." Accordingly, Thompson devoted a considerable amount of time to researching pasta making. He spent four years in the United States and two years in Italy learning how to make pasta, searching for the method his company could use to produce superior pasta. "I want my pasta to be known as the finest in the world, bar none," Thompson declared, "including the Italians."

Aside from producing a premium brand that would limit direct competition with low-priced brands, Thompson's strategy also hinged on something else, something that would make his company a rarity among U.S. pasta producers. Most manufacturers purchased their pasta flour from commercial mills, rather than producing it on their own, but from the start Thompson preached vertical integration, striving to realize the financial benefits of owning his own flour-making facility and the greater control over quality such ownership would give him. He decided to build his production plant in Excelsior Springs, Missouri, selecting the location because of the presence of pure spring water and, more important, because of Excelsior Springs' proximity to rail lines accessing North Dakota durum. The $50 million, state-of-the-art facility began production in 1988, officially making Thompson's AIPC a participant in the growing pasta industry. At the time, pasta consumption in the United States was on the rise, a trend that would continue into the 1990s as a national passion for pasta intensified. The average American ate 17 pounds of pasta a year in 1988, up from 13 pounds a year in 1981, which translated into a $2 billion market by the time Thompson's plant began producing its first shipments. Into this market AIPC entered as a newcomer in 1988; barely more than a decade later the company would hold sway as the dominant force, ranking as the largest pasta producer in North America.

Business began on a high note when Thompson secured contracts to supply his pasta to the A&P grocery chain and SYSCO Corporation, the largest restaurant supply firm in the country. These two customers purchased the company's initial production output, pushing AIPC's first-year sales into the $20 million range, while Thompson pursued contracts with other institutional customers and began negotiations with brokers in several foreign countries. Thompson's goal was to make AIPC the first U.S. company to ship pasta to Italy, a feat that would go a long way toward legitimizing his pasta as the "finest in the world." To accomplish this objective and to give AIPC a product to increase sales domestically, Thompson invested his efforts in the creation of what he termed a "super-premium" brand, the pasta product that would drive the company's sales upward, distinguish AIPC as a premier pasta maker, and fuel expansion into foreign markets, particularly into the much-vaunted Italian market. The company's signature brand debuted in January 1990, introduced under the name Pasta LaBella. As Thompson had planned, AIPC's flagship brand stood apart from other mass-produced brands such as American Beauty and Creamette. Pasta LaBella was stocked in the deli section, away from competitors shelved on the pasta aisle, and its retail price of approximately $2.65 for a one-pound package was $1.50 more than most other American brands. Although the sales generated by Pasta LaBella accounted for only 5 percent of AIPC's revenue volume during the brand's first year, the brand attracted a wealth of new business that promised to be the beginning of more to come. The 800-store Kroger chain began stocking LaBella, as did several other large retail chains, such as IGA, Payless, Hy-Vee, and Price Chopper. Several restaurant chains replaced their Italian pasta brands with LaBella as well, but in Thompson's mind the true measure of success was LaBella's entry into the Italian market. "Everyone remembers the first company to do something," Thompson mused, "just like everyone remembers the first person to walk on the moon. But who cares about the second or third?"

AIPC's place in the annals of business history was secured in May 1990 when Thompson attended a European trade fair for food brokers. At the trade fair Thompson reached an agreement to sell LaBella through an Italian grocery store called Casa di Risparmio di Parma, making AIPC the first U.S. company to sell pasta in Italy. AIPC's historic achievement fanned excitement at company headquarters, inducing Thompson and his management team to develop ambitious plans. As negotiations were under way to sell LaBella through a 400-store distributorship in Italy, a LaBella pasta sauce was developed, slated for introduction by the end of December 1990, while LaBella olive oil and LaBella breadsticks were in earlier stages of development. By the end of 1990 sales were up 60 percent from the previous year's total, prompting Thompson to expand production capacity. He increased production capabilities at the company's Excelsior Springs plant 200 percent, giving AIPC the ability to make 150 million pounds of pasta per year.

New Management in 1991

In 1991 a host of changes swept through AIPC that few outside observers could have foreseen. According to one report, the investors who had financially helped Thompson build his Excelsior Springs plant grew worried by the end of 1990 that AIPC would not meet certain financial objectives and would fall short of reaching the new, expanded production capacity at the company's plant. In the midst of this reported anxiety, a $76 million buyout of AIPC by Hershey Foods was announced in early 1991. Thompson welcomed the deal, but the U.S. Justice Department intervened and launched an investigation into the proposed buyout. After a three-month inquiry, the Justice Department ruled against the proposed acquisition in March, stating that the union of AIPC and the second largest pasta producer in the United States would result in higher prices for consumers. In the wake of the scuttled buyout, Thompson stepped aside, vacating his posts of president and chairman of the board to make room for what industry pundits termed "professional managers." Horst Schroeder, formerly the chief operating officer for Kellogg, was named chairman of the board, and Timothy Webster, formerly AIPC's chief financial officer, was promoted to president, along with a number of other promotions that gave AIPC a revamped management team. The change in leadership was a smooth transition, without any finger-pointing at Thompson or much to suggest that Thompson's leadership had led to failure. "This is a step all entrepreneurial companies go through," explained Webster, "where the creator hands the baton to his managers." Thompson, who ranked as AIPC's largest shareholder, retained a seat on the company's board. Under the new management, however, a new business plan emerged, one that was substantially different from the philosophy espoused by Thompson. Said Webster, "Our focus is on the high-volume segments. We need to be a manufacturing-driven company until the plant [capacity] is utilized."

From 1991 forward AIPC strove to be a low-cost producer of pasta, rather than a company seeking to make the "finest pasta in the world." The new strategy sought to utilize the full strength of the company's unique manufacturing capabilities, capitalizing on the vertically integrated operations that had been established

Key Dates:

1986: Richard C. Thompson establishes AIPC.

1988: A $50 million, state-of-the-art facility in Excelsior Springs, Missouri begins production.

1990: The company's signature brand debuts under the name Pasta LaBella; AIPC becomes the first U.S. company to sell pasta in Italy.

1991: Thompson resigns as president and chairman; a new management team is elected.

1997: AIPC becomes the exclusive producer of the Mueller brand of pasta; the company goes public as the second largest pasta producer in the United States.

2000: The company acquires the Mueller's pasta line.

2001: Seven regional pasta brands are purchased from Borden Foods Corporation.

2004: The low-carb diet trend forces sales and profits to fall dramatically.

2005: AIPC launches an internal investigation into its accounting practices; shareholders file class action lawsuits against the company for filing misleading financial information.

by Thompson. Although making quality pasta had not been abandoned as a company goal (AIPC touted itself as the only pasta maker to use high-temperature drying, reportedly the best way to process wet pasta), operating as a low-cost producer had moved to the forefront of the company's pursuits. Toward this end Webster and his staff achieved encouraging results. Using aggressive marketing and citing the advantages of the company's own mill operations, Webster convinced a number of large customers to purchase their pasta from AIPC. Supplier contracts with companies such as Wal-Mart, Publix, Pillsbury, Kraft, and General Mills fostered consistent, strident financial growth, assuaging any anxiety investors might have experienced. Sales rose to $39 million in 1992 and then began increasing by at least 20 percent each year as AIPC headed toward the mid-1990s. As the company's customer base of grocery chains, restaurants, and food processing companies increased in number, pushing sales upward and stretching production capacity to its limit, a different type of AIPC took shape. The AIPC of Thompson's era had sought to distinguish itself from the established giants in the industry by producing a higher-priced, higher-quality product, but during Webster's era the pursuit of becoming a low-cost producer had developed AIPC into a giant itself. By the mid-1990s AIPC was one of the major producers with which it had avoided directly competing during the late 1980s and was well on its way toward becoming the largest pasta producer in the United States. The prospect of reaching the industry's number one position was not a "goal in and of itself," Webster noted, as the company steadily increased its market share. "But we do want to continue to grow," he added. "If it were to happen, we'd certainly have grins on our faces."

Late 1990s Expansion

By 1995 any fear of not reaching full production capacity at the company's Excelsior Springs plant had been thoroughly eliminated. The company was ready, in fact, to build a second manufacturing facility. Construction of the new plant began in 1995 in Columbia, South Carolina, with its completion lifting AIPC's production capacity to roughly 300 million pounds of pasta per year. By the end of 1996 sales had eclipsed the $100 million mark, climbing to $121 million. AIPC, by this point, was the third largest pasta producer in the United States, trailing only Hershey Foods and Borden, Inc., and it was regarded widely as the most efficient producer. Its two manufacturing plants, which made more than 80 shapes of pasta, utilized the most advanced production technology in the industry, a distinction used as a persuasive marketing tool to win new customers and one that was making it increasingly difficult for other companies to compete with AIPC on a low-price basis. The fruits of AIPC's decade-long investment in its manufacturing facilities were realized in 1997, a year that saw the company achieve great strides while its largest competitor began to retreat.

In early 1997 CPC International, a global food company that marketed 45 varieties of pasta, announced that AIPC would become the exclusive producer of its Mueller's brand of pasta, the leading brand in North America. The contract represented an extraordinary boon to AIPC's business, one that could not have been gained without its state-of-the-art manufacturing facilities. "By joining with AIPC," a CPC International senior executive remarked, "we make a leap from the oldest production technology in the industry to the newest." The addition of the Mueller's brands led to a $45 million expansion at AIPC's Columbia plant, where Mueller's was scheduled to begin production in January 1998. News of the Columbia facility expansion was followed by the announcement of a $20 million expansion at the company's Excelsior Springs plant, which had been planned for a later date but was accelerated once AIPC executives learned of their biggest rival's future plans. In mid-1997 Borden announced that it would start to close its pasta-producing plants after deciding to stop manufacturing private-label brands and pasta for the "ingredients business," which included making noodles for products such as Hamburger Helper. AIPC moved in to fill the void created by Borden's retreat, implementing an expansion program designed to increase its production capacity by 60 percent, making it the second largest pasta producer in North America.

As work was under way to increase AIPC's production capacity to more than 600 million pounds of pasta per year, the company decided to convert to public ownership. In October 1997 AIPC's initial public offering on the New York Stock Exchange raised $87 million in net proceeds, giving the company the financial resources to pay for expansion. Following the public offering, Thompson stepped forward to remark, "It's been wonderfully exciting and a dream come true. I'm a proud papa." There was good reason for Thompson's elation. "Everything looks to be going very, very well for them," one stock analyst remarked. "They continue to gain market share." In November 1997 the likelihood of further gains in market share appeared assured when AIPC announced preliminary plans for a third pasta production plant in Kenosha, Wisconsin, to be constructed through a joint venture with Harvest States. Following this exhaustive period of expansion, the company entered its tenth year of production, by which time both expansion projects at Columbia and Excelsior Springs were completed. The results were impressive. In 1998 revenues increased from $129 million to $189 million and net income swelled from $5 million to more than $15 million, both record results. On this bright note, AIPC prepared for its second decade of business, having successfully climbed the rungs of its industry to hold sway as a dominant presence in the North American pasta market.

The New Millennium

AIPC experienced marked growth in the early years of the new millennium. In 2000, the company acquired the Mueller's pasta line from Unilever PLC's Bestfoods subsidiary. This was followed by a $67.5 million purchase of seven regional pasta brands from Borden Foods Corporation in 2001. Two pasta brands from Archer Daniels Midlands were added to AIPC's holdings in 2002. As part of its strategy to bolster its European business, AIPC bought the Lensi brand from Pastificio Lensi, a small Italian pasta manufacturer, later that year. AIPC rounded out its acquisition spree in 2003 with the purchase of Martha Gooch/La Rosa, Golden Grain, and Mrs. Leepers pasta brands.

By now, AIPC enjoyed a dominant position in the North American pasta market. Its closest competitor was Barilla Holding, an Italian company that entered the U.S. market in 1996. From 2000 to 2003, revenues grew from $248.8 million to $438.8 million. Net income also rose significantly, from $27.5 million in 2000 to $42.6 million in 2003.

AIPC's success came to a sudden halt the following year. Americans began following new dietary trends led by the Atkins and South Beach diet plans. These diets were based on low carbohydrate consumption, which spelled disaster for companies in the pasta industry. Indeed, the company deemed 2004 the most challenging year in its history. As the popularity of the Atkins and South Beach diets skyrocketed, demand for pasta products fell sharply. In fact, AIPC claimed that from mid-2003 to the end of 2004, pasta consumption in North America fell by more than 100 million pounds. As a result, AIPC moved to reduce manufacturing capacity and inventory levels, as well as its workforce. During 2004, the company's employee count fell by 14 percent and operations at its Kenosha, Wisconsin manufacturing facility were suspended.

In response to the low-carb consumer craze, AIPC launched a version of low-carb pasta in February 2004. Demand for the new pasta was weak. Overall, revenue fell by 4.9 percent in 2004 and net income dropped from $42.6 million in 2003 to just $3 million in 2004.

The company faced a second challenge in August 2005 when it failed to report its third-quarter earnings due to an ongoing internal investigation into its accounting practices. Founder Richard Thompson stepped down from AIPC's board of directors that month. At the same time, shareholders filed class action lawsuits against AIPC, claiming that the company provided misleading financial information in order to inflate AIPC's share price. In September of that year, the company hired turnaround specialists Alvarez & Marsal in an attempt to revitalize the company's financial position. Although the low-carb fad appeared to be slowing down by 2005, AIPC's future remained in question. Management hoped to overcome its financial challenges and put its accounting investigation to rest in order to resume its focus on putting pasta on North American dinner plates for years to come.

Principal Subsidiaries

American Italian Pasta Company; AIPC Wisconsin, L.P.; AIPC Sales Company; IAPC UK Ltd.; IAPC Holding UK Ltd.; Pasta Lensi, S.R.L. (Italy); IAPC B.V. (Netherlands); IAPC CV (Netherlands); AIPC Finance, Inc.; AIPC South Carolina, Inc.; AIPC Missouri LLC; AIPC Arizona LLC; IAPC Italia Leasing S.R.L. (Italy).

Principal Competitors

Barilla Holding S.p.A.; Dakota Growers Pasta Company Inc.; New World Pasta Company.

Further Reading

"American Italian Pasta Co.: Seven Regional Pasta Brands to Be Brought from Borden," *Wall Street Journal,* June 5, 2001.

Bassing, Tom, "Pasta Maker Restructures After Buyout Bid Squelched," *Kansas City Business Journal,* June 14, 1991, p. 2.

Brockhoff, Anne, "Romance, Intrigue of IPOs Intoxicate Some Executives," *Kansas City Business Journal,* December 12, 1997, p. 22.

Clevenger, Brenda, "That's Not Italian," *Ingram's,* November 1990, p. 59.

Collins, Martha, "Using Their Noodles," *Ingram's,* July 1992, p. 40.

Davenport, Carol, "Richard C. Thompson, 38," *Fortune,* November 6, 1989, p. 196.

Everly, Steve, "American Italian Pasta Co. To Expand Excelsior Springs, Mo. Plant," *Knight-Ridder/Tribune Business News,* July 2, 1997, p. 7.

Levine, Joshua, "Yankee Noodles Dandy," *Forbes,* November 12, 1990, p. 310.

"Missouri Pasta Maker To Sell 5.4 Million Shares of Common Stock," *Knight-Ridder/Tribune Business News,* April 30, 1998, p. 4.

"Mueller's Pasta Line Sold," *New York Times,* October 5, 2000.

Otto, Alison, "Where Are They Now?," *Prepared Foods,* October 1991, p. 47.

Reeves, Scott, "No Fireworks, Just Pasta: An IPO with Real Growth and Actual Earnings," *Barron's,* October 6, 1997, p. 39.

Roth, Stephen, "Public Offering Poises American Italian for No. 1," *Kansas City Business Journal,* November 14, 1997, p. 3.

Stein, Mark A., "Mamma Mia!," *New York Times,* October 23, 2005.

"United States—Pasta & Noodles—Competitive Landscape," *Datamonitor Market Research Profiles,* November 1, 2004.

"USA: American Italian Pasta Outlines Strategic Plan for 2005," *Just-Food,* October 28, 2004.

Welbs, John, "Pasta Giant Expands in South Carolina To Begin Production for Mueller's," *Knight-Ridder/Tribune Business News,* April 15, 1997, p. 41.

—Jeffrey L. Covell
—update: Christina M. Stansell

American Management Association

1601 Broadway
New York, New York 10019-7406
U.S.A.
Telephone: (212) 586-8100
Toll Free: (800) 262-9699
Fax: (212) 903-8168
Web site: http://www.amanet.org

Not-for-Profit Company
Founded: 1923
Employees: 700
Sales: $129 million (2003)
NAIC: 611000 Educational Services

The American Management Association is a global, not-for-profit, membership-based management development organization. With its headquarters located in New York City, AMA offers a wide range of business education and management development programs to individuals, businesses, and government agencies, covering such topics as manufacturing, sales and marketing, human resources, communication, finance and accounting, and International management. The information is disseminated through assessments, books and other publications, seminars, conferences, forums, briefings, and online self-study courses.

1800s Origins

Although today's AMA is geared toward management-level individuals, the origins of the Association lay in the education of workers. Until the middle of the 1800s, Americans primarily learned a skill on the job from people who were doing the work already, whether it was learning how to be a printer or an attorney. Many trades had a formal apprenticeship program in which young people learned from a master, became journeymen, and eventually established their own practices and became master craftsmen themselves. Thus, traditional education and job training were kept separate, as people generally quit school to learn a trade. The combination of formal education and vocational preparation was a much later construct. The rise of industrialization, however, began to have a dramatic effect on the prevailing system, with a large number of skills superseded by technology. Many artisans were replaced by hourly employees who needed to learn very specific skills to operate the new machinery. Apprenticeships in these fields were now replaced by a makeshift combination of on-the-job technical training and some academic training added to the mix. Given that many of these new workers were immigrants it was in the best interest of employers to help them learn English as a second language and to assimilate them into the culture. In 1872 the R. Hoe Company, a printing press manufacturer, became the first company to launch the "corporation school," which combined technical and academic training. Other major companies followed the example, such as General Electric and the New York Central Railroad. The goal was not philanthropic; it was to groom better workers, people who were able to adjust to a rationalized industrialize process. In the late 1880s American industry was heavy influenced by the work of Frederick Winslow Taylor, the man with the stopwatch who became the champion of efficiency and productivity. A primary objective of the corporation schools was to train workers in the new ways of efficiency, while the offer of night classes for personal advancement and fulfillment was in large part a perk to dissuade workers from taking an interest in unionism.

In 1913, 35 of the largest corporation schools, with New York Edison company at the head, joined together to form the National Association of Corporation Schools. The influence of Taylor on management was reflected in the formal objectives of the new organization: "Corporations are realizing more and more the importance of education in the efficient management of their business. The Company school had been sufficiently tried out as a method of increasing efficiency to warrant its continuance as an industrial factor." The NACS now became a driving force in workforce education, while fighting against the idea of public scrutiny. With the entry of the United States into World War I in 1917, NACS played a role in the mobilization of industry, as did another organization, The National Association of Employment Managers, which was founded in 1918. This new group changed its name to the Industrial Relations Association of America. Following the war, the two groups merged forming the National Personnel Association in 1922. At the

Company Perspectives:

No one knows training better than American Management Association. Since 1923, the business community had turned to AMA for the practical training and business tools needed to improve individual and organizational performance and achieve bottom-line results.

time, there was a major split in the personnel management field, with one side believing that anything having to do with employees was the sole province of the personnel manager, while the other saw the personnel manager in a more supportive role.

In 1923, the Association directors met and changed the name to the American Management Association, a name that better reflected the organization's philosophy and refined mission. It was now more of a managers association than a coordinator of workers' educational programs. The Smith-Hughes Act of 1917 funded vocational education in the public school system, while technical high schools, correspondence schools, and proprietary schools also emerged to meet the needs of workers. Universities, on the other hand, aligned themselves with corporations, assuming the task of educating the aspiring management ranks. AMA's role was to provide business leaders with a chance to meet and discuss workplace concerns and practices, much of which dealt with the "human element in commerce and industry." The "human element" was little more than code for "labor relations," a term which itself was pregnant with implications. The period following World War I provided fertile soil for the rise of Socialism, resulting in a Red Scare. Poor working conditions and wage inequalities led to labor unrest and calls for unionism, which business leaders believed was spurred on by Socialists and their radical brethren.

AMA added to its scope in 1924 by absorbing the National Association of Sales Managers. Because different types of executives had different subjects to address, AMA soon created separate divisions for finance managers, production managers, marketers and the like. Each division then held a annual conference specifically designed to address the needs of its participants. The upper ranks of management met in AMA-sponsored executive meetings where big picture ideas were discussed, such as the concept of "Work Councils" and "Democracy in Industry," which embraced the notion that education for workers and democracy could ward off the threat of Socialism. After the stock market crash in 1929 and the country was plunged into the Great Depression of the 1930s, however, the AMA began to advocate progressive positions on the issues of the day. It was perhaps more a pragmatic than enlightened stance, given the mood of the country that led to the election of Franklin Roosevelt, who had the clear mandate of the public to make sweeping changes to the way business was conducted in the United States, especially in terms of labor relations. The president's "New Deal" legislation strengthened the hand of unions. The National Labor Relations Act provided workers with the right to organize and bargain as a group, and the government showed a willingness to intervene if necessary. AMA's General Management Conference became an important forum where business and government leaders could air their views. Some of the New

Deal legislation would be struck down by the Supreme Court in 1936, but by this time the AMA and business leaders realized that it made more sense to address workplace problems themselves, rather than have the government intervene.

It was during World War II, which lifted the country out of the Depression, that AMA research began to weigh in on the issue of equality in the workplace brought on by the war effort. In 1942 the AMA issued a research report that advocated the need for African Americans to be better incorporated into the work force, which had been thinned dramatically by military enlistments and the draft. The report shared best practices of AMA member companies and listed the high-skill jobs held by African Americans. It was the opportunities afforded African Americans, however limited, during World War II that served as a starting point for the Civil Rights movement in subsequent years. In 1943 the AMA issued a similar report about women production workers, urging supervisors not to confuse a woman's mechanical familiarity with mechanical aptitude, arguing that there was no essential difference between men and women in performing jobs, just opportunity. The AMA also played its part in the war effort, essentially serving as a communications conduit between the government and member companies. AMA conferences were often used as a place where new government programs could be announced and explained. Moreover, executives from AMA member companies filled key government jobs during the war. AMA's vice-president on its personnel division, Lawrence A. Appley, headed the War Manpower Commission.

Postwar Contributions

After the war, the AMA made contributions on other fronts. In 1946 the Association's annual report urged corporations to prepare more illuminating financial reports, then in 1948 the organization urged better cooperation with unions, its report arguing that "instead of reducing management's revenue producing powers, such cooperation increases them." It was also in 1948 that Appley became president of AMA, a position he would hold for the next 20 years. Under his leadership, the organization would move well beyond the research it conducted and conferences it hosted to become a leader in business training seminars. The son of a Methodist minister, Appley worked his way through college, eventually graduating Phi Beta Kappa from Ohio Wesleyan University. Along the way he worked in a cafeteria, drove a truck, served as a motorcycle policeman, and even quit for a year to save up enough money to complete his education, teaching school and working for a while as a New York City streetcar conductor. He would later teach at Colgate University and hold executive positions at Mobil Oil, Vick Chemical Company, and Montgomery Ward. Along with his stint heading the War Manpower Commission, Appley was uniquely qualified to understand the differences between workers and management, business and government, and business and academia.

Appley would write or co-author six books on management principles. It was under his leadership that AMA in 1949 began to sponsor workshop seminars that allowed managers to meet, share, and essentially educate themselves. Out of this grew other types of programs, such as continuing education courses for different professional functions, and "orientation" seminars, which essentially helped executives to gain cross-functionality by learning about other areas of their business. In 1952 AMA launched an executive training program, The Management Course, which would become a mainstay of the organization. It would consist of one-week sessions devoted to four areas— management, finance, marketing, and leadership—and focus on real-world situations.

As had been the case during World War II, the AMA continued to serve as an intermediary between industry and the government during the 1950s. After a surprise dip in the economy in 1958, the association hosted a special Economic Mobilization Conference, where President Dwight D. Eisenhower made the keynote address and top executives from the largest corporations convened with government officials to discuss recovery plans.

The AMA began expanding beyond the United States in 1961 when it opened the Management Centre Europe in Brussels. Five years later a center opened in Mexico City, followed by the Canadian Management Center in 1974, AMA-Japan in 1993, the Asia Pacific Management Institute in Shanghai in 1995, and AMA-Latin America in 1996. During the 1960s AMA centers also opened in Atlanta, Chicago, San Francisco, and Washington, D.C.

The AMA also became increasingly more concerned with publishing. The seminars it hosted led to the printing of booklets to be distributed to AMA member. Then, in 1963, the association established a book publishing division called AMACOM to produce practice-oriented management books. Appley led the way, publishing *The Management Evolution* through AMACOM in 1963. His 1956 title, *Management in Action,* would also be published by AMACOM, as would three more management books in 1969, 1970, and 1974. In 1981 Appley co-authored his last book to be published by AMACOM. AMA also launched a venue that provided a spring board for a number of unknown writers. In 1972 it founded the journal *Organizational Dynamics.*

AMA expanded in other ways during the 1960s. The Association started Operation Enterprise, a program to inform high school and college students about possible business careers. On-site training was now provided by way of programmed instruction and videotape, and briefing and seminars were created to supplement AMA conferences and workshops.

Appley retired as president in 1968, but stayed on as AMA's chairman another six years, only leaving after AMA took a major step in 1973 when it consolidated the operations of five national associations that provided management education services. AMA was then able to receive recognition as an educational institution from the Regents of the University of the State of New York.

Appley's retirement coincided with a downturn in the United States economy and a host of fresh challenges facing government and business leaders. AMA forums would become a place to discuss problems that included inflation, productivity, environmental concerns, and foreign competition. AMA reports and books suggested solutions. During the late 1970s members were concerned with becoming low-cost producers, which led to the outsourcing of manufacturing to countries with cheap labor and the roots of the service economy at home. The 1980s then brought the concept of "Quality Renaissance," an idea promoted by AMA research and AMACOM books that maintained companies could produce higher quality products at a lower cost if the quality of processes were improved. In later years AMA worked with Motorola to develop supply management seminars, which then led to AMACOM books on the subject.

Technology Embraced in 1980s

During the 1980s AMA continued to show a willingness to embrace new technology. In 1985 the Association began broadcasting its briefings and forums by satellite. AMA also championed the use of bar coding for inventory control and other uses through a number of seminars that demonstrated to managers how to take advantage of the technology. AMA seminars would also provide a venue for contemporary accounting practices such as activity-based costing. When the Internet came on the scene in the 1990s, AMA not only held seminars to show managers how to use the tool in a variety of ways, the association launched Online classes and used its Web site as a repository for dozens of multimedia self-directed training classes. AMA also combined electronic media with print, producing book and CD-ROM combinations.

The 1990s saw AMA grow on a number of other fronts. The Padgett-Thompson training organization was bought in 1991, expanding the Association's subject matter as well as geographic reach. The Growing Companies Division was launched to cater to the needs of small to mid-sized businesses. To accommodate the growth of the Association , AMA moved into new state-of-the-art facilities in the Times Square section of New York City in 1996.

In the 2000s AMA launched a new quarterly journal, *MWorld,* for members and customers. The Association's web site was also beefed up with Members-only content. In 2005 AMA broadened its reach to include the people who assisted managers when it forged an alliance with the National Association of Executive Secretaries and Administrative Assistants. NAESAA members would now be able to take advantage of AMA's classes, services, and resources. By now, more than 100,000 people around the world attended AMA seminars. All told more than 25,000 people and 3,000 organizations in some 90 countries were members of the Association.

Principal Subsidiaries

AMACOM.

Further Reading

"AMA and NAESAA Form Alliance," *OfficeSolutions,* March–April 2005, p. 12.

Fagiano, David, "AMA Expands into China," *Management Review,* March 1996, p. 5.

Jones, Bodil, "AMA Expands European Operations," *Management Review,* January 1996, p. 34.

"The Power of Management: 75 Years of Leadership for Business and Industry," *American Management Association,* 1998.

Scheid, Fred M., " 'How Did Humans Become Resources Anyway?' " paper presented at the University of Alberta in Edmonton Adult Education Research Conference, 1995.

Stone, Florence, "AMA: Building Management Excellence for 80 Years," *MWorld,* Fall 2003, p. 74.

—Ed Dinger

Amy's Kitchen Inc.

P.O. Box 7868
Santa Rosa, California 95407
U.S.A.
Telephone: (707) 578-7188
Fax: (707) 578-7995
Web site: http://www.amyskitchen.com

Private Company
Incorporated: 1988
Employees: 850
Sales: $200 million (2005 est.)
NAIC: 422420 Packaged Frozen Food Wholesalers;
    311422 Specialty Canning

Amy's Kitchen Inc. is the top producer of natural frozen foods in the United States. It sells about 60 million vegetarian meals a year. The product line spans more than 130 items, including frozen dinners, pizzas, burgers, and burritos. Shelf-stable items such as soups and salsa have been on the menus since 1999. The company has emphasized organic ingredients from the start, and was a pioneer in making packaged organic foods. Owned by the Berliner family, which is vegetarian (including the dog and cat), the young company has already employed three generations, notes *People Weekly.* Founder Andy Berliner is CEO; his wife Rachel addresses marketing and design issues; Rachel's mother has contributed copy for the packaging. The Berliner's child, Amy, whom the company is named after, has been involved from an early age. Amy's Kitchen handles all of its own packaging and production, building a 200,000-square-foot facility in Medford, Oregon to complement its 100,000-square-foot plant in Santa Rosa, California. The company even makes its own organic tofu. It also handles much of its own distribution, though middlemen sell the products as far away as the United Kingdom and New Zealand. Originally limited to health food stores, the brand's reach has taken off, reaching mainstream supermarkets, warehouse clubs, at least one school district, and even Continental Airlines. Amy's is committed to organics, preferring to use produce grown without pesticides. Where milk is used, it is rBST hormone-free (the products do not include fish or eggs). Banned substances include hydrogenated fats. A number of dishes address specific dietary concerns, such as cholesterol and sodium restrictions and gluten allergies.

Earthy Origins

Amy's Kitchen Inc. was launched in 1987 by a Petaluma, California family that believed that vegetarians needed more healthful vegetarian options on the frozen foods aisle. Andy Berliner, who had worked for an herbal tea company (San Rafael's Magic Mountain Tea), and his wife Rachel had each eschewed meat since the 1960s and grew their own food—at least until her pregnancy slowed down the gardening. They wanted to develop a business, but were unsure how to keep their healthy eating habits when their schedules were compressed by the demands of entrepreneurship.

The Berliners decided to address the lack of tasty convenience foods for vegetarians, settling upon the humble pot pie as their entrée into the frozen foods industry. Rather than mechanically separated chicken, their version of the American comfort food classic would feature organic vegetables.

Soliciting advice from friends and relations, the couple whipped up some recipes at home for a few months before launching their new business in a barn on an old dairy ranch in Sonoma County. Start-up capital of $20,000 was raised by pawning a gold watch and car and getting a second mortgage on their Victorian farmhouse, Andy Berliner told *People Weekly.* The company, incorporated in 1988, was named after their new baby.

According to *Entrepreneur,* while sales calls were made from the barn, for the first few months the Berliners farmed out production to a bakery. The veggie pot pies sold like hotcakes— soon reaching 36,000 per month. Other pie varieties, including an apple pie, were soon developed, even though the original contractor, unable to keep up with the volume, suddenly bailed out. Amy's then hastily set up its own kitchen in rented space. It would continue to handle its own manufacturing from then on.

New Markets, Facilities in the 1990s

Amy's entered the 1990s with about two dozen employees. The company made its first international sales in Canada in 1991, according to *Entrepreneur.* The business was moved to

Key Dates:

1988: Andy and Rachel Berliner of Petaluma, California, begin making Amy's vegetarian pot pies.
1995: Business is relocated to Santa Rosa.
1997: Sales are about $25 million.
1999: Amy's grocery line hits store shelves.
2001: Sales are more than $100 million.
2005: The company begins building a second plant in Medford, Oregon.

Santa Rosa, California in 1994. The new 100,000-square-foot facility cost $12 million and was formerly occupied by St. Francis Winery.

In 1996, Andy Berliner and Fantastic Foods founder Jim Rosen began building a spiritual center in Sonoma County for Science of the Soul. This group was led by Gurinder Singh, a native of India and proponent of vegetarianism. (Andy and Rachel Berliner had originally met on a spiritual retreat in India in 1979.)

The company's first frozen pizza came out in the mid-1990s. Beginning with a simple cheese and sauce pie, the line was expanded to ones with roasted vegetables and spinach and feta. Revenues were about $25 million in 1996–97, reported the *Press Democrat.* Company founder and CEO Andy Berliner later mused that he had originally anticipated reaching sales of $3 million per year.

In the late 1990s, mainstream grocery stores such as Albertson's and Publix, eager to differentiate their offerings from those of warehouse clubs, embraced the organic packaged food concept quickly. In fact, by the 1997–98 fiscal year, Amy's was deriving half of its revenues from mainstream supermarkets, reported *Frozen Food Age.* According to the journal, overall sales had increased 80 percent in a single year.

By this time, Amy's employed 400 people preparing more than two million meals per month. Amy's grocery line hit store shelves in 1999. This grew to include a range of canned soups, chili, and beans, as well as salsa and pasta sauce in jars.

Still Growing Fast in the New Millennium

A significant new product line was launched in 2001: bowls. Sales, growing at a 25 percent clip, exceeded $100 million during the year. The company was doing more of its own distribution and was upgrading manufacturing. The manufacturing process was labor-intensive, with dough kneaded by hand and pizzas, pies, and burritos assembled by hand. Sophisticated robotic machinery was installed later, however, to handle the packing. Amy's Kitchen had 700 employees. The local *Press Democrat*

gave it kudos as being a commuter-friendly workplace for doling out free bus passes and special carpool parking spots.

By 2005, Amy's Kitchen was preparing five million meals a month. Its product line had expanded to 100 items. The natural foods market in the United States was then worth an estimated $15 billion and was growing at up to 15 percent a year. Amy's held 70 percent of the organic frozen section of the market. Full-year sales were estimated to be between $150 million and $250 million. According to *BusinessWeek online,* the company had a relatively low profit margin of 3 percent. Distribution extended as far as the United Kingdom, Dubai, and New Zealand.

Building for the Future

To meet demand and save money, the company built a new $40 million, 200,000-square-foot plant in Medford, Oregon, which offered lower costs than California, and had lobbied heavily in the previous two years to try to win the new facility. Other locations in California (Modesto) and several other states including South Carolina also had been considered.

California Governor Arnold Schwarzenegger had pushed to lower the company's electricity rates—a legacy of the state's recent power crisis. The prospect of Oregon's lower worker's compensation and development costs, however, plus an ample supply of workers, proved too attractive. Proximity to Oregon's produce farmers was another selling point. The new location also gave Amy's its first direct rail access. The new plant was opening with about 350 employees.

Principal Competitors

ConAgra Foods, Inc.; The Hain Celestial Group, Inc.; H.J. Heinz Company; Homegrown Naturals, Inc.

Further Reading

Allday, Erin, "Three in Sonoma County Top Commuter-Friendly List," *Press Democrat* (Santa Rosa, Calif.), December 4, 2002, p. E1.

"The Action's Getting Hot and Heavy in Lite Frozen Food Market Segment," *Quick Frozen Foods International,* January 1997, pp. 124ff.

Baker, David R., "A Tempting Deal: Governor Promises Food Manufacturer Cheap Power to Build a New Plant in State," *San Francisco Chronicle,* October 28, 2004, p. C1.

Bosco, Maryellen, "Two Chains Forge Links to Organic Food Firms," *Supermarket News,* August 4, 1997, p. 39.

Dam, Julie K.L., and Vicki Sheff-Cahan, "Healthy Prophets: Marketing Tasty Vegetarian Dishes Has Rachel and Andy Berliner Rolling in Dough," *People Magazine,* December 18, 2000, pp. 151ff.

Davenport, Rex, "The New Healthy Foods: Fads Come and Go, But New Products Aim to Live Long Lives As Consumer Favorites," *Refrigerated & Frozen Foods,* January 2004, pp. 18ff.

Fish, Tim, "A Nice Little Niche: Successful Vegetarian Frozen Food Venture Is a Family Affair," *Press Democrat* (Santa Rosa, Calif.), February 19, 1997, p. D1.

"Growth at Amy's Is Just Natural," *Frozen Food Age,* February 1, 2002, p. 52.

Har, Janie, Harry Esteve, and Jeff Mapes, "Oregon's Governor Woos Jobs One CEO at a Time," *Oregonian* (Portland), May 17, 2004.

Hartnett, Michael, "A Natural Addition," *Frozen Food Age,* February 2001, p. 64.

Hays, Constance L., "Can Healthier Foods Help the Bottom Line? Companies Find Gains in Your Loss," *New York Times,* November 8, 2000, p. C1.

Kolodny, Lora, "Andy Berliner: Things I Can't Live Without and What I Covet," *Inc.,* July 2005, p. 64.

Landers, Meg, "Natural Frozen Food Firm Plans to Work with White City, Ore., Farmers," *Mail Tribune* (Medford, Ore.), July 28, 2005.

Loyalka, Michelle Dammon, "Amy's Kitchen: Entrée to Oregon," *BusinessWeek online,* July 15, 2005.

Mann, Damian, "Governors Battle Over California Organic Food Firm's Possible Move to Oregon," *Mail Tribune* (Medford, Ore.), April 1, 2004.

Norberg, Bob, "Amy's Kitchen to Grow; SR Frozen Food Company to Double in Size," *Press Democrat* (Santa Rosa, Calif.), December 23, 1998, p. E1.

"Over Half of Amy's Sales Come from Mass Market," *Frozen Food Age,* September 1998, pp. 16f.

Rose, Bleys W., "SR Company Lightning Rod for Business-Climate Debate; Food Processor Wants to Expand, But Can't Afford to Do It Here," *Press Democrat* (Santa Rosa, Calif.), April 4, 2004, p. A1.

Stiles, Greg, "Organic Frozen Food Maker Breaks Ground on White City, Ore., Plant," *Mail Tribune* (Medford, Ore.), August 20, 2005.

——, "Rogue Valley of Oregon Tops Organic Food Manufacturer's Wish List," *Mail Tribune* (Medford, Ore.), November 17, 2004.

Williams, Geoff, "100 Million Dollars Baked in a Pie (Management Tips from Amy's Kitchen)," *Entrepreneur,* September 2001, p. 107.

Wollman, Cynthia, "Amy's Makes Vegetarian Cooking Easy," *San Francisco Chronicle,* January 25, 2002.

"Wrapped & Handled: New Equipment Helps Amy's Kitchen Boost Productivity and Meet Demand for Up to 2 Million Meals a Month," *Frozen Food Age,* October 2004, p. 49.

—Frederick C. Ingram

Arc International

41 av du General de Gaulle
Arques
France
Telephone: +33 03 21 93 00 00
Fax: +33 03 21 38 06 23
Web site: http://www.arc-international.com

Private Company
Incorporated: 1825 as Verrerie Cristallerie d'Arques
Employees: 17,000
Sales: EUR 1. 3 billion ($1.44 billion) (2003)
NAIC: 327213 Glass Container Manufacturing; 327212
    Other Pressed and Blown Glass and Glassware
    Manufacturing; 327215 Glass Product Manufacturing
    Made of Purchased Glass

Arc International is the world's leading producer of glassware and stemware. Based in Arques, France, Arc International produces more than six million pieces per year in six production sites, including two in France, and one each in the United States, Spain, Italy, the United Arab Emirates, and China. The company's brands include the consumer brands Luminarc, Cristal d'Arques, Salviati, Studio Nova, and Mikasa, allowing the company to cover every tableware segment, from luxury to low end. The company also markets products through the Arcoroc brand, targeting the professional restaurant and catering sector. The company's U.S.-based Mikasa subsidiary, acquired in 2000, provides the group with a network of nearly 170 retail stores, and in the mid-2000s the company has begun expanding the Mikasa brand to the European market. In addition to Mikasa, Arc has taken control of its distribution operations, acquiring its distributors in France, the United States, The Netherlands, the United Kingdom, Spain, and Portugal. In 2005, the company created a new distribution joint venture for Japan in partnership with its long-term distributor there. Arc International remains controlled by the Durand family, which has been involved in the company since the late 19th century and has owned the company outright since the 1920s. Philippe Durand is company chairman.

Crystal Origins in the 19th Century

The village of Arques, in the north of France, began its association with glassmaking in the early 19th century, with the rise of demand for a new type of bottle, the "dames jeannes." Known as demijohns in English, the new bottle featured large bodies with narrow necks, and the largest were capable of holding as much as 20 and even 50 liters. Used for storing cognac and wine and other liquids, demand for the bottles quickly outstripped supply. In the 1820s, two entrepreneurs in the Artois region, near Saint Omer and Calais, decided to set up their own glassworks.

The first of these was built by Charles Carpentier in Saint Martin au Laert, and began production in 1823. Two years later, a new glassworks was built nearby in Arques, by Alexander des Lyons de Noircarme. The following year, the two sites were merged into a single company, Verrerie des Sept Ecluses. In 1869, the glassworks was acquired by another glassworks operating in Arques, and then renamed as Verrerie Cristallerie d'Arques in 1892.

Verrerie Cristallerie d'Arques was placed under the management of Georges Durand in 1897. Then just 27, Durand had already been active in the glassmaking industry, having worked for three years at another glassmaker, the Cristallerie de Sèvres. By 1916, Durand had bought Verrerie Cristallerie d'Arques outright.

Into the 1920s, the Arques glassworks remained a fairly small business focused on the French market, with just 350 employees at the end of the decade. The arrival of Durand's son, Jacques Durand, as head of the company in 1927 signaled the start of its growth into the world's leading manufacturer of glass tableware. The younger Durand recognized the potential for introducing new production methods to the French glass industry. In 1930, Jacques Durand took a trip to the United States, visiting glassmakers there. During that trip, Durand discovered new mechanical production techniques, including the use of tank furnaces. Returning to France, Durand decided to expand the Arques works, installing the company's first tank furnace, as well as three automatic presses and the first mechanical blowing machine. The investment, completed in 1933, enabled Durand to launch large-scale production, a first in the French market.

The outbreak of World War II temporarily suspended the company's expansion. Instead, the company focused its efforts on designing and developing new glass presses, which the company installed in 1947. Three years later, the company returned to the United States, bringing back a new generation glass-blowing machine. The adoption of the new production equipment and processes enabled the Arques site to become the most modern glass production site in Europe. In 1948, the company launched its first consumer-oriented brand name, Luminarc, which quickly became its flagship mid-priced brand.

JG Durand, as the company became known, also emerged as an important innovator in its own right. In 1958, the company became the first to automate the production of opaque "opal" glass, which was launched under the brand name Arcopal. Two years later, the company achieved another first, with the implementation of an automatic process for the production of stemware. Whereas elsewhere in the industry the joining of a glass bowl to its stem was still carried out manually, Durand's process made it possible for the two parts to be fused mechanically, vastly speeding up the production process while dramatically lowering the cost of production. By placing stemware on store shelves at prices far below those of its competitors, the company rapidly gained a leading share of the international market.

Durand also captured a significant share of the professional market. In 1963, the company introduced its industrial tempering process, making its glasses more resistant to breakage. This development formed the basis for the launch of a new brand, Arcoroc, dedicated to the professional restaurant and catering sectors. During the 1960s, Durand also began targeting expansion into the United States, launching sales through local distributors. In 1968, the company set up its own distribution subsidiary for the U.S. market.

International Success in the 1960s

The new subsidiary was established in large part to support the company's true breakthrough, which came at the end of the decade. In 1968, the company became the first in the world to develop a method for automating the production of lead crystal. Launched under the brand name Crystal d'Arques (Longchamps in the United States), the company's new line of crystal stemware quickly swept over the market. Whereas traditionally lead crystal stemware sold at $25 per stem, Durand's stemware boasted prices as low as $6 per stem.

The success of the Longchamps stemware line helped establish Durand as a worldwide market leader, and also contributed to

a revolution in the glassware industry in general. Whereas previously crystal tableware had been luxury items reserved for special occasions, the automation of lead crystal production placed crystal stemware within the realm of everyday consumer products.

Durand made a strategic move to back up its growing sales in the United States, launching a production subsidiary in 1979. Located in Millville, New Jersey, the subsidiary, Durand Glass Manufacturing Company, launched production in 1982. In the meantime, the company had expanded its production to Spain, acquiring, in 1980, full control of a production joint venture initially established in partnership with Saint Gobain in 1971.

Durand also expanded its brand offerings. In 1983, the company launched a high-end line, named JG Durand, to complement its existing Longchamps and Crystal d'Arques brands. By then, the company had become a truly international operation, posting more than 75 percent of its sales outside of France. The United States had become one of the country's single largest markets, accounting for 15 percent of the group's total revenues.

World Leader in the New Century

Jacques Durand remained in control of the company into the 1980s, joined by son Philippe in 1973. The younger Durand began to take over the group's direction in 1990. Nonetheless, Jacques Durand continued to lead the company until his death in 1997. In 50 years, Durand had successfully transformed the company from a small, locally focused business to the world's leading maker of glass stemware, with more than 16,000 employees and sales to more than 130 countries.

Nonetheless, the company found itself faced with growing competition as it approached the 21st century. Philippe Durand now became determined to extend the group's operation, launching a new line of porcelain items, as well as taking control of the group's distribution. Durand also sought to reposition the company's portfolio of brand names.

That latter effort led the company, in 1999, to make its first brand acquisition, of Italy's Salviati. Founded in 1856, Salviati produced high-end glassware using traditional handmade and mouth-blown techniques—taking Durand full circle, as it were. The following year, the company reached an agreement with Nanjing Glass Factory to form a distribution joint venture for the Chinese market.

The year 2000, however, marked a more significant milestone for the company. In that year, Durand reached an agreement to acquire U.S. tableware brand and retailer Mikasa for $280 million. The deal not only gave Durand control of the highly popular Mikasa and Studio Nova brands, but also the company's network of 167 Mikasa retail stores. Mikasa was founded in 1948 as American Commercial, serving as first an importer and later wholesaler of dinnerware. The company launched its own Mikasa-branded line of dinnerware in 1957. In the 1970s, the company expanded its line to include stemware and flatware, as well as gifts and other home furnishings. The expanded line supported Mikasa's entry into the retail sector, with the opening of a first outlet store in 1978.

Following the merger, Durand changed its name, becoming Arc International. The addition of Mikasa had boosted the company's sales by some $400 million. It also had transformed the

Key Dates:

1823: Charles Carpentier founds a glassworks in Saint Martin au Laert to produce "dames jeannes" bottles.

1825: Alexander des Lyons de Noircarme founds a glassworks in Arques.

1826: Both glassworks merge as Verrerie des Sept Ecluses.

1869: Verrerie des Sept Ecluses is sold to new owners.

1892: The company is renamed as Verrerie Cristallerie d'Arques.

1897: Georges Durand becomes manager of the Arques works.

1916: Georges Durand buys Verrerie Cristallerie d'Arques.

1927: Jacques Durand succeeds his father as head of the company.

1933: The company installs the first tank furnace and automatic presses in Europe.

1948: The Luminarc brand is launched.

1950: The company installs the first automatic blowing machine in Europe.

1960: The company debuts a mechanical stemware fusing system.

1968: A U.S. distribution subsidiary is opened; an automatic lead crystal production system is launched.

1971: The company forms a production joint venture with Saint Gobain in Spain.

1979: A U.S. production subsidiary is founded.

1980: The company acquires 100 percent control of a production unit in Spain.

1997: Jacques Durand dies, and Philippe Durand becomes head of the company.

1999: Salviati, in Italy, becomes the company's first brand acquisition; a distribution joint venture is formed in China.

2000: The company acquires Mikasa in the United States; the company name is changed to Arc International.

2001: The company announces the launch of production in China.

2005: Newell Cookware Europe and licenses for the Pyrex and Vitri brands are acquired.

company's geographic focus, raising the share of the United States markets to more than 50 percent of the total group sales.

In the meantime, the success of Arc's joint venture in China had encouraged the company to branch out into the production market there as well. In 2001, the company announced its intention to launch a new production facility in China. The company continued in its effort to transfer part of its production overseas. This effort came in large part in response to the increasing inroads of low-cost producers into the company's core European and U.S. markets. Yet the company's decision to step up its foreign production also came in support of its effort to target sales to the Middle East and Asian markets. In 2003, the company added a new production unit, this time in the United Arab Emirates, with the purchase of 80 percent of RAK Glass from PAK Ceramics in Ras al Khaimah.

Into the mid-2000s, Arc put into place another prong of its growth strategy, that of taking control of its international distribution operations. The company began acquiring its foreign distributors, many of which had worked with the company for several decades. In 2003, the company acquired its distributors in the United Kingdom and Spain, followed by the purchase of its four French distributors, regrouped as Arc International France in 2004. The company continued its distribution acquisitions into 2005, acquiring U.S. distributor Cardinal International and Dutch distributor Glasheinz, and forming a new joint venture with its distributor in Japan.

As it completed the consolidation of its distribution network, Arc returned its attention to developing its brand portfolio. In 2003, the company launched an effort to introduce the Mikasa brand to the European market, opening its first factory outlet stores. In late 2005, the company began negotiating with Newell Rubbermaid to acquire the Portland, Maine-based company's European business, Newell Cookware Europe, as well as the European, African, and Middle East license for the Pyrex and Vitri brands. Arc International inherited more than 170 years of glasswares history—and raised its own glass for continued growth in the new century.

Principal Subsidiaries

ARC Distribution France; Arc Glassware Nanjing (China); Arc International Middle East (United Arab Emirates); Arc International North America (United States); ARC International Tableware UK; Art Glass Manufacturer Salviati (Italy); Cardinal International (United States); Durand Glass Manufacturing Company (United States); La Vajilla Eneriz (Spain); Mikasa (United States); Vidrieria Cristalleria de Lamiaco (Spain).

Principal Competitors

Compagnie de Saint-Gobain; Owens-Illinois Inc.; OSRAM GmbH; Schott Glas; Nipro Corporation; Belopal AD; Turkiye Sise ve Cam Fabrikalari A.S.; Vereenigde Glasfabrieken N.V.; Cristaleria Peldar S.A.; Nihon Yamamura Glass Company Ltd.

Further Reading

"Arc Cuts in Europe, Grows Outside," *Glass,* November 2004, p. 316.

Bryceland, Kristen, "Raising the Glass," *HFN The Weekly Newspaper for the Home Furnishing Network,* September 18, 2000, p. 1.

"Cardinal Acquired by Arc International," *Foodservice Equipment & Supplies,* March 2004, p. 18.

Garcia, Shelly, "Durand's Dynasty," *HFD—The Weekly Home Furnishings Newspaper,* April 16, 1984, p. 1.

Harrison, Joan, "French Crystal Maker Is Enticed by Mikasa's Universal Appeal," *Mergers & Acquisitions Journal,* November 2000, p. 20.

Porter, Thrya, and Allison Zisko, "Newell Lines Up Arc to Purchase European Arm," *HFN The Weekly Newspaper for the Home Furnishing Network,* October 24, 2005, p. 36.

Zisko, Allison, "Arc International, Mikasa Create New Organizational Structure," *HFN The Weekly Newspaper for the Home Furnishing Network,* April 21, 2003, p. 26.

——, "Arc's Triumph," *HFN The Weekly Newspaper for the Home Furnishing Network,* November 15, 2004, p. 32.

——, "New Arc CEO Revamps Staff As Part of Focus on Brands," *HFN The Weekly Newspaper for the Home Furnishing Network,* April 5, 2004, p. 25.

—M.L. Cohen

Austin Powder Company

25800 Science Park Drive
Cleveland, Ohio 44122
U.S.A.
Telephone: (216) 464-2400
Fax: (216) 464-4418
Web site: http://www.austinpowder.com

Private Company
Incorporated: 1867
Employees: 70
Sales: $208.3 million (2004)
NAIC: 325920 Explosives Manufacturing

Austin Powder Company is a Cleveland, Ohio-based private company that produces a full line of industrial explosives and accessories, including detonator-sensitive and booster-sensitive emulsions and detonating cord. The company also provides blasting services in North America, and around the world through subsidiary Austin International. Other subsidiaries include Austin Star Detonator, which offers electric and non-electric detonators, and Austin Detonator, which manufactures detonators in the Czech Republic for sale in Europe and elsewhere. Austin Powder customers are served in four major industries: the quarrying industry, which uses the company blasting products and services to produce the stones needed for construction purposes as well as the glass and steel industries; surface mining, Austin Powder's original focus, which relies on blasting agents to mine coal and precious metals; the construction industry, which relies on blasting for a variety of projects, from roads to home building; and seismic exploration, for oil and gas exploration. Austin Powder's primary plants are located in McArthur, Ohio; Camden, Arkansas; Brownsville, Texas; and Valle Hermosa, Mexico. Products are distributed mostly in North America through 65 company-owned stores.

Company Origins in the 1830s

Austin Powder was founded by the five Austin brothers: Daniel, the eldest at 28; Alvin; Lorenzo; Henry; and Linus, the youngest at 15. They left their home in Wilmington, Vermont, in 1832, heading west by horse and wagon in search of a suitable place to build a black powder mill. They traveled as far as Kansas City, where they found a plentiful supply of sulfur and saltpeter, the raw materials of black powder, but a local market that was limited to the gunpowder the small population required for hunting and fighting Native Americans. Hence, the Austins returned eastward, finally settling in a part of Ohio near Akron known as Old Forge. In 1833 they built their first powder mill on the banks of the Cuyahoga River.

Akron held great potential for a powder company because the Erie canal, the Great Lakes, the Ohio Canal, and the Pennsylvania & Ohio canal provided connections to eastern markets. This meant that coal mines in the region would prosper, and they in turn would need the blasting powder the Austin brothers produced. In the beginning Austin Powder relied solely on the labor of the five Austins, who worked 12 hours a day. By the end of the 1830s they were able to increase their annual output of black powder to 72,500 pounds, but more would be needed as the Akron coal industry continued to grow. In addition, there was a need for explosives in the area for canal building, the clay mining industry, the mining of iron ore needed for the growing steel industry, quarrying, and heavy construction, as well as demand for "sporting powder" (i.e., gunpowder). In order to better serve its many customers, Austin Powder built magazines to store the explosives in Kenmore, Canal Dover, and Canal Fulton. By 1865 Austin Powder employed 20 and looked to grow even larger.

In 1867 Austin Powder acquired Cleveland Powder Company, which had been founded in the late 1850s. The deal brought 400 acres of land in what would become the industrial heart of Cleveland, where one day plants for the Republic Steel Corporation and Aluminum Company of America would be located. The second Austin Powder mill was advantageously situated close to the Ohio Canal as well as key railroads that allowed the company to ship its products both east and west. In order to take advantage of the company's position, the Austin brothers incorporated the business in 1867 to raise $300,000 for expansion. Now in his 60s, Daniel Austin became the first president; he would die in 1874 at the age of 71. The youngest of the brothers, Linus, succeeded him.

Company Perspectives:

While our black powder days are long gone, the original spirit and initiative remain as part of our corporate culture. We are pleased to be of service to our mining, construction, and seismic exploration customers in North America and throughout the world.

Austin Powder operated both the Akron and Cleveland plants until 1871, when the latter was closed and all operations were now conducted in the Newburgh Mill near Cleveland. Over the next decade business prospered in all areas, as Cleveland become an industrial powerhouse. The company employed no salesmen, but simply took orders from its customers at the beginning of the year and scheduled its manufacturing according to need. In 1884 Austin Powder drummed up some additional business by investing $10,000 and selling a magazine and keg factory to a Cleveland company that loaded shot shells, Chamberlin Cartridge Co. Austin Powder now became Chamberlin's exclusive supplier of rifle powder.

Glenwillow Facility Built in the 1890s

In 1887 the last of the five Austin brothers left the company when Linus died. He was succeed by R.T. Coleman and Austin Powder launched a new era of expansion, as it began investing in several other powder companies. But it soon reached a crossroads at the start of the 1890s: Cleveland's population center was creeping toward the Newburgh Mill, which was operating at capacity but had no place to expand, and its rifle powder mill was out of date and needed to be upgraded to incorporate new manufacturing techniques. Moreover, the Newburgh mill's close proximity to the Ohio Canal no longer held any particular advantage, due to the 11 railroads that now intersected Cleveland. Thus in January 1892 Austin Powder decided to build a new plant to produce rifle powder in the Cleveland area and relegate the Newburgh Mill to the manufacture of black powder only. A total of 1,000 acres of farmland was bought southeast of Cleveland in Glenwillow. Here mills were built to produce sporting powder, and within the year production began.

Despite downturns in the U.S. economy during the 1890s, Austin Powder expanded on a number of fronts. Branches in major cities such as Chicago, Detroit, and St. Louis were established. Coal mining still accounted for the bulk of sales, but business continued to grow in the quarry and construction industries. Sporting and rifle powder sales also were strong, prompting the 1895 establishment of Austin Cartridge Company, to produce loaded shot shells at the Glenwillow site under brand names such as Crack Shot, Club Sporting, and Champion Ducking.

Austin Powder entered the 1900s on a sad note, that of Coleman's death. It also faced a number of decisions. Both plants were producing as much powder as possible, but it was becoming obvious that given the way Cleveland was expanding the Newburgh facility would soon have to be given up. In 1904 the plant began to gear down gradually and a year later Austin

Powder's board of directors voted to invest $60,000 to double the production capacity at Glenwillow. It proved to be a difficult project to complete, going over budget by about $10,000 and taking longer than expected. This was just one aspect of a difficult stretch for Austin Powder in the early years of the 20th century. The sporting powder business was highly competitive and no longer offered much profit, and in 1907 Austin Cartridge was sold for $195,000. In that same year, production ceased in Newburgh and the facility now served only as a magazine for the next five years, after which all operations were consolidated in Glenwillow. To make matters worse during this period, labor difficulties in the coal mining industry led to a cutback in black powder purchases.

Austin Powder managed to navigate the tough times and enjoyed steady growth during the first 20 years of the 1900s mostly serving the coal industry, despite limiting its production to black powder. High explosives, in the form of dynamite, had been used in coal mining since 1870, but it was not until 1908 when the first reliable "permissible" came on the market. Nevertheless, black powder was still widely used, so that in 1923 about three times more black powder was used as permissibles. The market for explosives of all sorts was growing, and for years Austin Powder had been getting requests for dynamite from its customers. Finally, in the 1920s the company decided it had to become involved in the dynamite business and began the search for a suitable production site.

In 1930 nearly 1,200 acres of land was purchased close to the B & O Railroad near McArthur, Ohio. A year later, despite the Great Depression that gripped America, the new Red Diamond plant, named for the company's brand of dynamite, went into production and began supplying explosives to coal mines and quarries. With the entry of the United States into World War II in 1941, all of the company's production capacity at both of its plants was devoted to the war effort, turning out military ordnances such as Bangalore torpedoes, demolition charges, land mines, and flares.

After the conflict ended in 1945 Austin Powder resumed its prewar activities, but the industry was undergoing significant changes. The use of black powder declined rapidly, prompting Austin Powder to add specialized blasting supplies to its product offerings. In 1948 the company funded a research and development effort to produce detonating cord, which it began producing in Glenwillow and shipping in 1950. In that same year Austin Powder diversified further by launching its first technical training program. In 1953 Austin Powder offered its first electric industrial detonator and also expanded its Midwest presence by acquiring an Evansville, Indiana jobber, Diamond Supply. Later in the 1950s Diamond Supply was relocated to Madisonville, Kentucky, where it supplied explosives and other blasting products to mining, quarry, and construction customers in Kentucky, Illinois, Indiana, Iowa, and Missouri.

Development of a New Primer in the 1950s

The 1950s also witnessed the introduction of the predecessor to the modern ANFO blasting agents, Akremite, named for Bob Akre, who was the first to develop an explosive that used ammonium nitrate. Austin Powder was quick to recognize the importance of ANFO and was the first to develop the first true dynamite primer for the explosive. To meet the demand for the product, sold under the AL (Austin Lab) label, the company opened mixing plants throughout its markets. The introduction of ANFO could not have been timed better, given that in 1956 the Federal-Aid Highway Act was passed and the United States began building its massive Interstate highway system, which required the use of a great deal of explosives. In addition, in 1956 Austin Powder added a new customer, the Calcite Quarry of U.S. Steel in Michigan, the largest limestone operation in the world.

Austin Powder now looked to grow the market for its explosives and blasting agents by expanding geographically and drumming up business from new industries. In the late 1950s it moved into Florida, a major explosives market, and then to the Southwest where in affiliation with Midland, Texas-based Southwestern Explosives, Inc. it attracted seismic exploration customers. In the 1960s the company began serving New England as well as the Pacific Coast, and even provided a good deal of the powder used to explore the North Slope of Alaska. But by 1968 Austin Powder ceased production of black powder at Glenwillow, instead using the facilities to make blasting agents, cord, and cast boosters, as well as Bangalore torpedoes for the military. A year later the company won a military contract to provide detonating cord, which was instrumental in the creation of the Special Products area at Red Diamond. Here, in the early 1970s, the company developed water-based slurries, an explosive that, essentially, would render dynamite obsolete.

In the second half of the 1970s, Austin Powder acquired Southwestern Explosives, with branches throughout the Southwest, and Oregon's Western Explosives, which added a dozen distributors in Oregon, Washington, and California, and established Austin Powder as a national company. The Southwestern Explosives acquisition proved highly beneficial, as the Arab oil embargo led to robust growth in U.S. oil exploration. Business also was increased in the 1970s when Austin Powder's research and development efforts once again paid off, this time with the introduction of the ADP booster, the first non-electric delay device that was versatile, easy to use, and safe. The company closed the 1970s by shuttering its Glenwillow facility after nearly 90 years of operation. A new plant was opened in East Camden, Arkansas, where the production of cast boosters was now handled.

The 1980s brought more product development, with Austin Powder improving upon its slurries and work beginning on emulsions. To keep pace with the production side of the growing company, in the early 1980s Austin Powder modernized its sales force, providing better training on the new generation of products and refining the way the salesmen sought to meet customer needs. Having already become a national company, Austin Powder now looked to become an international player. In 1985 Austin International was founded, and began forming alliances, funding start-ups, and creating joint ventures around the world. In 1988 Austin Powder and Austin International formed Austin Star Detonator to manufacture a full line of electric and non-electric detonators for sale throughout the Americas.

Austin Powder, along with a score of commercial explosives companies, had to contend with federal antitrust changes. The company was charged with conspiring with competitors to fix prices and rig bids in the sale of explosives in four states between 1987 and mid-1992. Like ten companies before it, Austin Powder eventually decided not to go to trial, as the cost of litigation and the distraction was not deemed to be worth the effort. In 1996 Austin Powder pleaded guilty and agreed to pay a $7 million fine.

Austin Powder took another step in its international expansion during the 1990s. It founded Austin Detonator in August 1998 in the Czech Republic to produce detonators for sale throughout Europe as well as the Far East. Several months later, in January 1999, the start-up acquired the detonator division of Zbrojovka Vsetin, INDET A.S., a company with 45 years of experience in industrial detonators and an established customer base.

In the wake of the terrorist attacks of September 11, 2001, on the United States, Austin Powder and other explosives companies entered a new era of caution and an emphasis on security. The company became more circumspect about its operations. In September 2002, two days before the anniversary of the September 11 attacks, the company discovered that 330 pounds of explosives were missing at its Brownsville, Texas plant. The immediate fear was that the incident was related to a potential terrorist attack. It was soon learned, however, that a local man had stolen a 30-pound tube of ammonium nitrate. His goal, according to authorities, was simply to "blow it up and see what it would do." The remaining ten 30-pound tubes were attributed to an accounting error. The company's bookkeeping would attract the scrutiny of the Bureau of Alcohol, Tobacco, Firearms and Explosives (ATF), which launched an undercover operation. Agents were able to buy blasting caps stolen from an Austin Powder delivery truck and then trade them for cocaine. This led the government to dig further into Austin Powder, which would be found to have falsified records at three of its locations to cover up missing explosives. In October 2005 Austin Powder reached a plea agreement and accepted a fine of more than $1 million. In addition, the ATF permanently revoked federal explosives licenses at three Austin Powder facilities.

Principal Divisions

Austin International; Austin Detonator; Austin Star Detonator.

Principal Competitors

Dyno Nobel ASA; Orica Ltd.; Sasol Ltd.

Further Reading

"Austin Powder Celebrates 150 Explosive Years," *Pit & Quarry,* December 1983.
"Austin Powder Enters Guilty Plea to Charges in U.S. Antitrust Probe," *Wall Street Journal,* September 27, 1996, p. B7.

Bickett, Jac O., "Austin Powder's Program Is Dynamite," *Sales & Marketing Management,* August 13, 1984, p. 82.
Osborn, Claire, "Explosives Theft Solved, Officials Say," *Austin American Statesman,* September 13, 2002.

—Ed Dinger

Autobacs Seven Company Ltd.

5-6-52 Toyosu, Koto-ku
Tokyo
Japan
Telephone: +81 03 6219 8700
Fax: +81 3 6219 8701
Web site: http://www.autobacs.co.jp

Public Company
Incorporated: 1947
Employees: 4,009
Sales: ¥227.07 billion (2.12 billion) (2004)
Stock Exchanges: Osaka Tokyo London
Ticker Symbol: 9832
NAIC: 441310 Automotive Parts and Accessories Stores;
336399 All Other Motor Vehicle Parts Manufacturing;
423120 Motor Vehicle Supplies and New Parts
Merchant Wholesalers; 423130 Tire and Tube
Merchant Wholesalers

Autobacs Seven Company Ltd., Japan's leading retailer of aftermarket auto parts, has begun exporting its successful retail formula into the international market. Unlike many of its foreign counterparts, Autobacs targets the market for automobile customization and upgrades, rather than simply providing replacement parts. In Japan, Autobacs operates more than 530 stores, including nearly 350 franchised stores. Autobacs stores operate under two major formats. The original Autobacs store features one-stop shopping for a full range of auto parts, as well as repair, installation, and maintenance facilities, service stations, and automotive sales. Autobacs remains the largest part of the group's network. Since the 2000s, however, Autobacs has been expanding its second format, the Super Autobacs. These large-scale facilities, which reach up to 50,000 square feet and more, feature an extended range of products, as well as a variety of amenities—including three full-sized, 100-seat movie theaters showing first-run movies—in order to attract and retain customers in the stores. The Super Autobacs stores extend the aftermarket concept to include books, DVDs, music, apparel, gifts, and other items related to automobiles and automotive culture. The Super Autobacs format features prominently in the company's plans for international expansion; the company opened its first Super Autobacs in the United States in California in 2003. The company operates six stores in Taiwan, two in France, in partnership with Renault, and one each in Singapore, Thailand, and, since 2004, mainland China. Autobacs also has begun to roll out a third retail format in Japan, Autobacs Hashiriya Tengoku, which specializes in sales of secondhand auto parts and equipment culled from the company's primary retail network. Listed on the Osaka, Tokyo, and London Stock Exchanges, Autobacs remains controlled by the founding Sumino family and Chairman Koichi Sumino. In 2004, the company posted sales of ¥227.07 billion (2.12 billion).

Auto Parts Wholesaler in the 1940s

The automotive market in Japan took off especially following World War II. The country's fast-rising economy and its commitment to establishing its own full-fledged—and internationally competitive—automotive industry introduced a variety of new business opportunities, such as the need to develop national networks for the wholesale distribution of automotive parts. Among the entrants into this sector was Toshio Sumino, who founded his company, called Suchiro Syokai, in Fukyushima-ku, in Osaka, in 1947. Less than a year later, Sumino reincorporated his company as a limited liability company, called Fuji-Syokai Ltd.

Fuji-Syokai quickly added a retail component as well, and by the 1950s the group's retail sales formed a major part of its business. The growth of this activity was fueled by the rise of a culture of automobile customization (called ''tuning'') among a segment of the consumer market. Unlike typical automobile owners, content with merely replacing parts on their cars as necessary, tuning enthusiasts sought to upgrade and modify their automobiles, and were prepared to pay for high-end components, customized paint jobs, and the like.

Sumino's company began to cater more and more to the growing tuning market. By 1958, the company restructured, spinning off its wholesale operations into a separate company, Daiho-Sangyo Co. Ltd. In that year, the company also created

---

Company Perspectives:

Mission: Our dream is to create a paradise for car enthusiasts. Our common purpose in each country is to create a place where car-lovers can come and enjoy the one thing that brings them together, enthusiasm for cars in any form. An Autobacs store is a place where you can explore the joy of car ownership, the pleasure of customizing your vehicle, improving its appearance, or performance. Autobacs' mission is to promote the idea that the car is more than just a means of transport, and the means of expressing this in every aspect of our customers' car lifestyle. We believe that this enthusiasm is something that goes beyond borders; that exists in a similar form in all countries, and is shared by people from various cultures and languages.

---

its Drive Shop division. Over the next decade, Fuji-Syokai continued to expand its range of operations, adding automobile sales, and its own chain of service stations.

In the early 1970s, Sumino recognized a new opportunity in the Japanese auto parts aftermarket. Until then, the market remained highly segmented, meaning that customers were required to shop at one store for their tires, at another for other parts, and continue on to yet another for repairs and installation services. Sumino saw an opening for a new type of auto parts retail store in Japan, one that would offer a one-stop shopping concept to the automotive aftermarket. In 1974, the company opened its first one-stop retail store in Osaka.

The new store was called AUTOBACS, which stood for "Appeal, Unique, Tires, Oil, Batteries, Accessories, Car audio and Services." Opened in Higashi, Osaka, the first Autobacs paved the way for the company's growth into Japan's leading aftermarket specialist. The company quickly began developing its plans to extend its reach nationwide, adding franchise operations in addition to stores under its own direct management. The first Autobacs franchise store opened in Hakodate, Nakamichi in 1975.

The success of the Autobacs concept and the rapid development of the retail network soon encouraged the company to adopt its retail brand as its own, and in 1978, the company became known as Autobacs Seven Company Ltd. The following year, the company merged with its Daiho-Sangyo and Autobacs Higashi subsidiaries into a single corporation, which also became known as Autobacs Seven Co. in 1980.

International Expansion in the 2000s

Autobacs continued its rapid expansion through the 1980s. The company marked its entrance into the eastern Japanese market in 1981, with the opening of a store in Koshigaya. By the mid-1980s, the company boasted nearly 300 stores in its total network, franchisees included. These were organized along regional lines, with offices in Tokyo, Sapporo, Sendai, Nagaoya, Takamatsu, and Fukuoka. Although the group provided direction from its headquarters (moved to a nine-story purpose-built building in Osaka in 1986), the company's regional offices were encouraged to operate more or less autonomously. By then,

Autobacs had claimed the leadership in the Japanese automotive aftermarket.

Autobacs's growth suffered a setback in the mid-1980s, when a group of franchise owners decided to break away from the company and establish their own business. The defection eliminated more than 50 stores from the Autobacs network. Nonetheless, the company remained focused on expansion, with plans to expand its total network to more than 500 stores by the early 1990s. In preparation for this growth, the company turned to the stock market, listing its shares on the Osaka Stock Exchange in 1989. Four years later, the group added its listing to the Tokyo Stock Exchange as well. In 1995, in preparation for the future launch of international operations, the company opened its capital to foreign investors, adding a listing on the London Stock Exchange.

By the mid-1990s, competition in the Japanese automotive aftermarket had grown increasingly intense. To distinguish itself from its fast-growing rivals, Autobacs began emphasizing a new range of customer services. The loosening of Japanese restrictions governing the country's automobile repair sector allowed the company to begin marketing an extended range of repair services, in addition to its existing installation services.

The company also began preparing a new retail format, introducing something of an automotive aftermarket retail revolution in Japan and establishing the direction of the group's future international expansion. In 1997, the company unveiled the first of the new stores in Chiba. Called Super Autobacs, the new format featured more than 50,000 square feet of selling and repair space, set over two floors. The Super Autobacs featured more than mere auto parts. Indeed, in addition to an expanded selection of goods, including books, DVDs, music, and apparel, the large-scale stores also offered three in-house, 100-seat movie theaters showing first-run films to customers.

Autobacs began rolling out the Super Autobacs format across Japan, meeting with strong success. The format also became the company's flagship for its international expansion. The group's first target was Taiwan, where the company quickly followed the success of the first Super Autobacs with the opening of five more stores by the mid-2000s. Autobacs also entered Thailand, forming a franchising joint venture with that country's auto parts retailer Champion in 1997 to open a string of smaller format Autobacs in Thailand. The company opened its first Super Autobacs in Thailand at the end of the 1990s. In the meantime, the company expanded in Japan, acquiring a stake in the rival Auto Helloes Co. Ltd. The company acquired full control of Auto Helloes in 2002.

In 1999, Autobacs turned to Europe, reaching an agreement with French automaker Renault to form a new retail joint venture. That company, owned at 51 percent by Autobacs, opened two large-format stores in France and planned to expand the format throughout Europe through the 2000s.

Autobacs moved its headquarters to Tokyo in 2001. In that year, as well, the company launched an e-commerce-enabled web site, extending its retail reach to Japan's highly active Internet market. Also in 2001, the company announced its plans to develop its own sports car, called the Garaiya.

Key Dates:

1947: Toshio Sumino launches an auto parts wholesaling business in Osaka and then enters retailing in the 1950s.

1974: The first Autobacs auto parts store is launched in Higashi, Osaka, creating the first one-stop shopping auto parts and service store in Japan.

1980: The company formally adopts the name Autobacs.

1989: A public offering is made on the Osaka Stock Exchange.

1993: A listing is added to the Tokyo Stock Exchange.

1995: The company places shares on the London Stock Exchange ahead of the international rollout of the Autobacs retail concept.

1997: The first Super Autobacs store is launched in Chiba, Japan; the company enters Thailand.

1999: The company establishes its first European operations through a joint venture with Renault.

2003: The company enters the U.S. market with the opening of the first Super Autobacs in California.

2004: The company enters mainland China with the opening of its first store in Shanghai.

2005: The company announces plans to develop a network of up to 100 stores in China and 200 stores in the United States.

Into the mid-2000s, Autobacs focused on two new, and potentially vast, markets. The first was the United States, where the company opened a Super Autobacs in 2003. Located outside of Los Angeles, the new store, at 50,000 square feet, easily tripled the size of its nearest competitors' stores. The Super Autobacs proved an immediate success as well, posting sales of more than $9 million after its first year. The company began plans to introduce its franchise into the United States, and a future expansion of its network to as many as 200 stores.

Next, the company turned to a far different market. In 2004, the company opened its first auto parts store in China, in Shanghai, forming a joint venture, called Shanghai Autobacs Paian Auto Service Co., held at 65 percent by Autobacs. After opening a second store in China in 2005, the company announced plans to boost its Chinese franchise network to as many as 100 stores before the end of the decade. After conquering Japan's automotive aftermarket, Autobacs hoped to repeat its success on an international scale.

Principal Subsidiaries

Autobacs Seven Europe S.A.S.; Auto Helloes Co. Ltd.

Principal Competitors

Sears, Roebuck and Co.; SAM'S Club; Rite Aid Corporation; AutoZone Inc.; Advance Auto Parts Inc.; Jardine Cycle and Carriage Ltd.; Castorama France S.A.; Kohnan Shoji Company Ltd.; Pep Boys-Manny, Moe and Jack; CSK Auto Corporation; Yellow Hat Ltd.; Autoseven Company Inc.

Further Reading

"Autobacs Aims for 11% National Market Share by 1986," *Home & Auto 95,* November 1, 1985, p. 1.

"Autobacs Opening Express Shops with Gas Service," *Comline Transportation,* October 31, 1997.

"Autobacs to Open 1st Outlet in China," *Jiji,* April 27, 2004.

Bernstein, Marty, "Japanese Tuner Store Is a Major Retail Hit in California," *Automotive News,* August 2, 2004, p. 36D.

Desjardins, Doug, "Japan's Top Auto Parts Retailer Debuts in US," *DSN Retailing Today,* September 8, 2003, p. 4.

"Japan's Autobacs Seven to Expand Store Network 20%," *Asia Pulse,* June 16, 2005.

"Japan's Auto Product Market Resides in China," *SinoCast China Business Daily News,* April 30, 2004.

Matthew, Maier, "A New Mecca for Motorheads," *Business 2.0,* May 2004, p. 34.

"Renault, Autobacs to Form Auto Goods Outlets in Europe," *Japan Transportation Scan,* May 17, 1999.

Silvey, Larry, "New Japanese Parts Custom: Serious Fun," *Aftermarket Business,* May 2004, p. 8.

Willins, Michael, "Autobacs Unveils Parts, Japanese Style," *Aftermarket Business,* October 2003, p. 12.

—M.L. Cohen

Bar-S Foods Company

3838 North Central Avenue, Suite 1900
Phoenix, Arizona 85012-1906
U.S.A.
Telephone: (602) 264-7272
Fax: (602) 285-5252
Web site: http://www.bar-s.com

Private Company
Incorporated: 1981
Employees: 1,500
Sales: $400 million (2004)
NAIC: 311610 Animal Slaughtering and Processing

Bar-S Foods Company is a leading manufacturer of meat products. Although headquartered in Phoenix, the company operates four plants in Oklahoma. Brands include Bar-S, President's Pride, Jumbo Jumbos, Old World Premium, and Chuck Wagon. With annual production of 40 million pounds, it is among the 40 largest meat processors in the United States. It is also one of Arizona's largest privately owned companies.

Origins

Bar-S Foods was formed in 1981 in a management buyout of the venerable Cudahy Company meatpacking business, which dated back to 1890. General Host Corporation, a conglomerate, had acquired Cudahy in 1970 but was looking to sell it due to structural issues such as dilapidated plants and 34 demanding labor unions.

The new owners paid General Host $28 million in cash, notes, and stock for the assets, which included processing plants in Seattle and Denver and nine distribution centers. It had a half-ownership of a facility in Clinton, Oklahoma. Bar-S Foods, named after one of Cudahy's major brands, started operations with 45 employees producing ten million pounds of meat products a year. Its first day of business was August 28, 1981. The company was led by Tim Day, a former General Host executive who had been in charge of downsizing Cudahy in the 1970s.

A foodservice unit was set up in 1986. By the end of the 1980s, production was approaching 70 million pounds a year. The company spent $1.6 million to expand its 75,000-square-foot facility in Clinton, Oklahoma, by a third. Bar-S was ranked the 40th largest meat processor in the United States by product sales volume and employed about 700 people. Distribution focused on the south and west of the country, but extended as far as Alaska and Puerto Rico.

To Oklahoma in the 1990s

Based in Phoenix, the company consolidated its operations around its Oklahoma facilities in the 1990s. This area was strategically located, and chicken, beef, and pork could be sourced from surrounding states. Water and power were also relatively cheap there.

In the early 1990s Bar-S added production capacity with a new hot dog plant in Altus, Oklahoma, and another, $7 million expansion to its existing Clinton, Oklahoma, facility. The town Altus adopted a sales tax to get their plant built.

Soon after, it also relocated its Denver ham operation to Clinton, whose central location was a key factor in the move. In addition, it was impractical to expand the Denver facility due to a lack of land, the building's age, and nearby power lines. The Denver plant dated back to the 1920s. It was finally closed in 1996 and most of its remaining 200 workers were offered jobs in Oklahoma.

Altus also served as a distribution center. It was expanded within a couple of years of opening. Bar-S's total sales were about $250 million a year by the mid-1990s. It offered 396 different products, but this would be streamlined to 119 by 2004, according to the *National Provisioner*. A new 85,000-square-foot wiener and sausage plant in Lawton, Oklahoma, and a 145,000-square-foot central distribution center in Elk City both became operational in 1998.

The meatpacking industry was notorious for dangerous working conditions, but Bar-S had implemented a safety program that had cut the number of accidents nearly in half. There

Key Dates:

1890: The Cudahy meatpacking empire begins.
1923: The Bar-S meatpacking plant is built in Denver.
1970: General Host Corporation acquires the Cudahy Company.
1981: Bar-S Foods is formed in a management buyout.
1993: A hot dog plant and distribution center opens in Altus, Oklahoma.
1995: Sales are $300 million.
1996: The Denver plant is demolished.
2001: The company recalls 14.5 million pounds of products due to a listeria threat.
2005: The Altus plant is upgraded.

was an attempt made to organize a union at the Altus plant in the late 1990s, which management vigorously opposed. At the time, employees made an average of $7 an hour.

Fit to Compete After 2000

Bar-S employed about 1,350 people in Oklahoma in 1999. Sales exceeded $300 million. The company had built a considerable foreign trade with Russia, but this was hammered by the devaluation of the ruble, competition from Canada and France, and a U.S. free meat aid program. Bar-S then focused on Puerto Rico for export growth, reported an Oklahoma City paper. Other major foreign markets were Mexico, Canada, Japan, Korea, and Hong Kong.

The company weathered a public relations crisis in April 2001, when it voluntarily recalled 14.5 million pounds of processed meat and poultry products from its Clinton, Oklahoma, plant due to a listeria threat. The recall affected several foreign countries as well as the United States. The plant was subsequently closed and most of the 400 workers there laid off. Fortunately for the little town of Clinton, where Bar-S was the largest employer, the plant reopened after the source of contamination was discovered inside some packaging machinery, which was cleaned and redesigned to avoid recurrences of the problem. Listeria could cause rare but serious infections; fortunately no one reported any problems from eating Bar-S products through the course of the recall, which did not involve any of the company's other plants. Bar-S later installed state-of-the-art ozone wash and ultraviolet pathogen reduction systems from The BOC Group.

Bar-S was manufacturing more than 100 different items, including cold cuts, sausage, hot dogs, and bacon. Total production was about 400 million pounds a year and was growing as Americans embraced low-carb diets.

The Altus plant was upgraded in 2005 at a cost of $40 million. Part of the upgrade allowed the company to produce its own corn dogs. About 50 new jobs were being added there. After the expansion, Bar-S had 360,000 square feet of production space.

Bar-S had top five national brands in lunchmeat, bacon, dinner sausage, hot dogs, and corn dogs. It had done little traditional advertising, but since the early 1990s it had been investing in large color graphics to promote its brands on the side of tractor-trailers carrying its products.

A key part of the company's philosophy dealt with employee fitness. Various incentives awarded employee achievements such as losing weight or quitting smoking. Workers began the day with a series of stretching exercises at 8:15 a.m. The regimen seemed to be working, with net income increasing fivefold in ten years. Company founder, CEO, and Chairman Tim Day told the *National Provisioner,* "Superior physical and mental fitness leads to a distinct competitive advantage, making us more effective, productive, and a tougher competitor in the marketplace." Phoenix's *Business Journal* attributed Day's discipline to his three years in the Marine Corps. Day was supported by president and fellow Cudahy Company alumnus Bob Uhl, who had been Bar-S's original treasurer and vice-president of finance.

Another incentive program rewarded perfect attendance with cash awards. A human resources official told the *National Provisioner* the company had reduced employee turnover from 88 percent to 40 percent in three years. Projects in 2004 focused on reducing waste and increasing efficiency; in 2005 Bar-S was spending $50 million on capital upgrades.

Principal Competitors

Hormel Corporation; Kraft Foods Inc.; Sara Lee Food & Beverage.

Further Reading

Accola, John, "Bar-S Closing Denver Plant; Food Distributor's Move to Oklahoma Affects 200," *Rocky Mountain News,* February 10, 1996.
"Altus Backs Meat Plant," *Tulsa Tribune,* June 25, 1991, p. 4C.
"Bar-S Announces $7 Million Expansion," *Tulsa World,* July 19, 1991, p. B6.
"Bar-S in Fast Break for Foodservice Business," *Meat Processing,* November 1, 1994, p. 20.
"Bar-S Opens Depot, Facility," *Supermarket News,* June 21, 1993, p. 37.
Brus, Brian, "Bar-S Adds Jobs with $40 M Upgrade to Its Altus, OK Plant," *Journal Record,* August 11, 2005.
Caulk, Steve, "Bar-S to Close 70-Year-Old Denver Plant; Company Will Offer Most of 200 Workers Jobs in Oklahoma," *Rocky Mountain News,* May 3, 1995.

"Clinton Expansions Total $1.78 Million for 2 Firms," *Journal Record,* October 3, 1989.

"Continuing Evolution: Bar-S Foods Co. Changes with the Times, But Still Offers Only the Finest in Top-Quality Product," *National Provisioner's Meat & Deli Retailer,* October–November 2004, p. S18.

Denton, Jon, "Oklahoma Meat Producer Replaces Russia with Puerto Rico As Target Market," *Knight Ridder Tribune Business News,* April 19, 2000.

"Employees Make Bar-S Foods' Safety Program Work," *Meat Processing,* September 1, 1996, p. 35.

Ensslin, John C., "Historic Site Gone in Seconds, Explosives Demolish Bar S Plant for Stock Show Space," *Rocky Mountain News,* July 26, 1999, p. 5A.

Ford, Brian, "State Hungry for Food Processing," *Tulsa World,* January 19, 2002, p. 1.

Gonderinger, Lisa, "Exec Finds Strength in Discipline," *Business Journal—Serving Phoenix & the Valley of the Sun,* October 27, 1995, p. 38.

Jackson, Ron, "Altus, Okla., Bar-S Workers Argue Need for Union," *Daily Oklahoman,* August 21, 1998.

——, "Altus, Okla., Meat Plant Workers to Vote on Union," *Daily Oklahoman,* September 15, 1998.

Lewis, David, "Bar S Foods to Shut Down Ham Operation," *Rocky Mountain News,* June 26, 1993.

Macklin, Gary, "Bar-S Provides Images; 3KB Provides Wheels," *Refrigerated Transporter,* April 2001, p. 16ff.

McMullen, Cheryl A., "Company Weighs Recalled Meat Options," *Waste News,* April 30, 2001, p. 5.

Marks, Dawn, "Crews Search for Bacterium at Clinton, Okla., Meat Plant," *Knight Ridder Tribune Business News,* April 14, 2001.

Young, Barbara, "Profitable Production: Continuous Improvements at Manufacturing Facilities Operated by Arizona-Based Bar-S Foods Fuels the Company's Bottom Line," *National Provisioner,* February 2005, p. 4.

——, "Pursuing Excellence: Sizzling Taste Profiles, Topnotch Quality, and Low Retail Prices Keep Arizona-Based Bar-S Foods on a Course Toward Category Dominance for Its Line of Processed Meats," *National Provisioner,* February 2005, pp. 38ff.

—Frederick C. Ingram

Barden Companies, Inc.

400 Renaissance Center, Suite 2400
Detroit, Michigan 48243
U.S.A.
Telephone: (313) 496-2900
Fax: (313) 496-8400
Web site: http://www.fitzgeralds.com

Private Company
Incorporated: 1994
Employees: 4,000
Sales: $372 million (2004 est.)
NAIC: 713210 Casinos (Except Casino Hotels); 721120
   Casino Hotels; 236220 Commercial and Institutional
   Building Construction

Barden Companies, Inc., is a holding company whose subsidiaries primarily operate gambling casinos and develops real estate. The firm owns the Majestic Star floating casino in Gary, Indiana and Fitzgeralds casinos in Tunica, Mississippi, Black Hawk Colorado, and Las Vegas, Nevada. Other Barden companies include real estate developer Waycor Development Company; Barden International, which pursues business ventures in Namibia; and Barden Entertainment, which markets a video jukebox. Headed by African American entrepreneur Don Barden, Barden Companies is one of the ten largest black-owned firms in the United States, according to *Black Enterprise* magazine.

Beginnings

The different enterprises that make up Barden Companies are the brainchild of Michigan native Don Barden. Born in 1943, he was the ninth of 13 children and grew up poor on a nine-acre farm in the Detroit suburb of Inkster, Michigan. He learned the value of hard work and determination from his father, who worked at the Chrysler auto plant and repaired cars on the side, and his mother, who helped the family raise animals and grow vegetables for food. When he finished high school, Barden scraped together enough money to begin attending Central Ohio University, but he was forced to drop out after a year when funds ran low. He moved in with an older brother in

the city of Lorain, Ohio, near Cleveland, and took a series of jobs ranging from cafeteria manager to assistant to the president of a shipbuilding company. In 1966 Barden took $500 he had saved and opened a record shop called Donnie's, and also began to promote concerts, work as a disc jockey at parties, and release records on his own small label.

With record sales slow due to competition from discount department stores, in 1968 Barden sold his store and started a public relations and marketing firm. He had once briefly published a small newspaper with a partner, and now he started a weekly called the Lorain County Times. In 1971 Barden found out from a military recruiter that recruitment offices would soon be moving out of post offices into spaces of their own, and he quickly decided to buy a building and lease it to the military. After submitting a successful bid for office space, he received a $25,000 bank loan and bought the building. Two years later he sold it for $50,000, and then bought another building for $85,000 from Ohio Edison, which he leased back to the utility. By 1975 the real estate business had grown such that he was able to begin construction of a new $1 million building.

The early 1970s also saw Barden win election to the Lorain city council and start working for a Cleveland television station, where he served as host of a talk show and as a weekend news reporter. After using his political connections to ensure that 4 percent of the new cable television systems in Lorain and neighboring Elyria would be owned by minorities, he invested $2,000 in each. Two years later he sold his stakes for $200,000, and immediately began laying plans to buy cable franchises of his own. In 1981 he formed Barden Communications, Inc., which bid on cable franchises in seven cities around the United States.

Wiring Detroit For Cable in the 1980s

Barden first won the right to provide cable service to 10,000 households in his old hometown of Inkster, and after successfully connecting them on time and within budget, he was able to secure franchises in nearby Romulus and Van Buren Township. After these were established, he turned his attention to winning the franchise for Detroit, with 375,000 households. When bidding was put off until December 1982, it gave Barden more time

Key Dates:

1981: Don Barden forms Barden Communications, Inc., to win cable TV franchises.
1983: Barden wins bid to build Detroit cable system.
1988: Barden founds Waycor Development to build jail, other projects.
1993: Barden Development, Inc., formed to seek Indiana gaming license.
1994: Barden sells cable interests for $105 million, forms Barden Companies.
1996: Majestic Star floating casino opens in Gary.
1997: Barden loses bid for Detroit casino, begins working to overturn ruling.
1998: Barden International opens auto conversion plant in Namibia.
2001: Barden buys three casinos from Fitzgeralds Gaming.
2002: Barden Technologies, Barden Entertainment formed.
2004: Barden wins half of $79 million Indian tribe casino settlement.

to prepare, and he spent $500,000 to create an eight-volume proposal, which was declared the winner the following year.

Barden moved to Detroit in late 1984 and immediately began the complicated process of laying out the cable system. To help fund the massive undertaking, he partnered with Toronto, Canada-based Maclean Hunter Ltd., a conglomerate with interests in cable television, magazines, and newspapers. Maclean arranged to provide $100 million in financing, and took a 49 percent ownership stake in the system.

In 1986 the five-year wiring process began. More than 100 miles were laid underground, at a cost of $350,000 per mile, with the rest strung across utility poles for $20,000 per mile. During this time Barden sold the Romulus and Van Buren systems while he continued to expand his real estate interests, founding Waycor Development Co. in 1988 to build the $61.5 million Wayne County Detention Facility in Hamtramck. Later projects included an apartment complex in Detroit and a Department of Veterans Affairs clinic in Canton, Ohio. Another business that attracted Barden's attention was radio, and in the late 1980s he won licenses to build stations in several states. He would go on to build or acquire five stations in the Chicago, Illinois metropolitan area.

Not all of Barden's ventures were successful, however. His attempt to turn the vacant Stouffer's Northland Hotel in Southfield, Michigan into a senior citizen's housing center was abandoned after he spent $1.5 million to buy it, and another $1 million was invested in a Pontiac, Michigan savings and loan which was later taken over by the Resolution Trust Corporation.

By 1992 Barden's Detroit cable system was fully operational and had attracted 120,000 subscribers. The entrepreneur already had other projects on the drawing board including Cable Cheque, which would offer cable subscribers discounts on their bill when they purchased certain products, and a low-power cellphone-like device, which he had allocated $1 million to develop. Barden Communications now employed 332, and had taken in $91.2

million in its most recent fiscal year. In 1992 the firm was named Company of the Year by *Black Enterprise* magazine.

Move Into Gambling in 1993

In 1993 Barden partnered with St. Louis-based President Riverboat Casinos to work on obtaining a license to operate a casino in Gary, Indiana, where boat-based gaming had just been legalized. The deal was to be a 50/50 partnership, but when President began having financial problems, Barden took full control. A new company, Barden Development, Inc., was formed to oversee this new business.

In the fall of 1994 Barden sold the Detroit cable system to Comcast, Inc., after partner Maclean Hunter had been acquired by the cable giant. His take from the deal was $105 million, and he funneled some of the proceeds into his new gambling boat project, which had recently been given the go-ahead. By now Barden had also acquired a stake in University Communications, Inc., which marketed a computer-based learning and communications system to schools and corporations.

In the fall of 1995 Barden reached an agreement with Trump Indiana, Inc., to form a 50/50 joint venture called Buffington Harbor Riverboats LLC that would develop a dock, restaurants, and parking for the gambling boats each planned to operate. In June 1996 the Majestic Star Casino opened on a leased boat, which would give way the following year to a new 40,000 square foot, $50 million vessel that featured 1,550 slot machines and 70 table games. The firm sold $105 million in secured notes to fund the expansion, which included significant development in the dock area, whose cost was shared with Trump.

The year 1996 also saw a new business unit called Barden International reach an agreement with the government of Namibia to build a $15 million plant in that country to convert General Motors vehicles from the American standard left-hand drive to Namibian right-hand drive. An initial $31 million contract was signed with the Namibian government for conversion of 823 vehicles including Chevrolet pickup trucks and Bluebird buses. Barden was also named General Motors' official distributor of cars and trucks to the country. His wife Bella Marshall, an attorney who had served as Detroit's finance director, was appointed president of the new unit.

Back in the United States, Don Barden was already working on an even bigger venture. Casino gambling, as recently as the late 1970s legal only in Nevada, had lately been touted around the country as an antidote to joblessness, and in 1994 the beleaguered citizens of Detroit had voted to allow it after a casino was opened just minutes away in Windsor, Ontario, Canada. Once Michigan voters approved the plan in late 1996, Barden launched a public campaign to win one of the three permitted licenses. Competing against ten others, he made it to the semi-final round of consideration, but in November 1997 was declared out of the running. Unhappy with the decision, which awarded casinos to two major gaming companies and the Sault Ste. Marie Band of Chippewa Indians, Barden sought a new vote on the licenses, arguing that Detroit, which was more than three-fourths black, should allow at least one casino to be owned by an African American-controlled firm.

A referendum on the awarding of casino licenses was set for August 1998, and to bolster his chances Barden brought in a new business partner: superstar Michael Jackson. The pair proposed a billion-dollar casino, hotel, and theme park complex on Detroit's waterfront, and Jackson also flew with Barden to Namibia to promote his newly-opened plant there. The effort to win a license was unsuccessful, however, with Barden winning only 45 percent of the vote. Also in 1998, the entrepreneur sold the five radio stations he owned in the suburbs of Chicago.

In 1999 Barden filed a federal lawsuit against the state of Michigan and its gaming control board along with Detroit, its mayor, and its city council, which alleged that the casino selection process had unfairly given other bidders preferential treatment, but a judge ruled against him in July. Detroit's MGM Grand casino opened a week later in a $225 million temporary location, and the other two followed suit over the next year and a half. The year 1999 also saw the sale of Barden's educational software business.

Fitzgeralds Casinos Acquired in 2001

In 2000 Barden began working on a deal to buy three casinos from the bankrupt Fitzgeralds Gaming Corp., which were located in Tunica, Mississippi, Black Hawk, Colorado, and Las Vegas, Nevada. The $149 million deal was completed in December 2001, just after the September 11 terrorist attacks had devastated the travel industry, and Las Vegas in particular. Barden put up $14 million of his own funds and sold $135 million in bonds, which he raised on a ten-day tour to 40 institutional investors in 12 cities. The Tunica casino was the most profitable, being the premier gambling facility in its region, while the Black Hawk and Las Vegas properties were smaller players in their respective areas. After taking control Barden moved to diversify their workforces by hiring blacks and women for prominent jobs in each. The casinos, in particular the Las Vegas one, would be marketed increasingly to African Americans, trading on Barden's status as the first black casino owner in the United States and now the only one with a Las Vegas property.

In 2002 Barden formed new companies called Barden Technologies and Barden Entertainment. The former would develop computerized voting machines, while the latter made a video jukebox for use in bars and casinos, with initial deployment in Barden's own facilities.

In June 2003 Barden's various enterprises, now known collectively as Barden Companies, were once again chosen as Black Enterprise magazine's Company of the Year. The firm was ranked sixth on the list of top 100 industrial/service firms owned by blacks, with total revenues of $347 million (95 percent of which was now derived from gaming). In October the company was refinanced through the sale of notes worth $260 million, and the firm also boosted its credit line to $80 million.

A short time later the underperforming Las Vegas Fitzgeralds casino was incorporated as a separate entity within Barden Companies. The firm had recently spent $2.5 million on upgrades to the 638-room property, and was working on expanding the Black Hawk Fitzgeralds and adding a new blues club/restaurant, Koko Taylor's Blues Café, to the dock area of the Majestic Star Casino.

The energetic Barden was now serving as vice-chairman of finance for the presidential bid of congressman Richard Gep-

hardt of Missouri, targeting donors in the black community. He had earlier helped raise funds for the presidential campaign of Bill Clinton.

In the spring of 2004 Barden bid on a license for a horse-racing track in the Detroit suburbs, but his effort proved unsuccessful. The year also saw his Namibia operations taken over by another firm, after Barden International gave up its GM distribution contract. There had been complaints that the vehicles chosen for conversion were unsuited to the rough terrain, and some had gone unsold. Barden remained committed to seeking other investments in Namibia after the sale, however.

In 1997 the Lac Vieux Chippewa Indian tribe filed a lawsuit against Detroit's winning casino bidders that put roadblocks in the way of permanent casinos, and then in 2002 Barden had agreed to help the tribe build a casino if they won a license. They were ultimately denied one, and in 2004 agreed to settle their claims against two of Detroit's three casino owners for $79 million, to be paid out over 20 years. Barden expected to receive half the total, but when the tribe stopped making payments to him, he sued them. In October 2005 a judge awarded him $33 million, slightly less than the claimed amount.

In November 2005 Barden announced a $253 million deal to buy Trump Indiana, Inc., which owned a floating casino in Gary and a 300-room hotel. It would give Barden two gambling boats there as well as full ownership of the dockside restaurants and parking that Trump had shared with the Majestic Star. After the acquisition both vessels would be upgraded and a portion of the new one would be given over to smoke-free gaming. Barden had also recently purchased a 3.8 percent stake in Detroit's Greektown Casino, which he planned to sell to the casino's majority owners, the Sault Ste. Marie Tribe of Chippewa Indians, for $16 million.

Nearly 25 years after Don Barden entered the cable television business, the firms that made up Barden Companies, Inc., continued to grow under the leadership of their founder. The planned acquisition of Donald Trump's floating casino in Indiana would increase his gaming holdings to five properties, and Barden also appeared resolute in his goal of someday owning a gambling facility in his hometown of Detroit.

Principal Subsidiaries

Barden Development, Inc.; The Majestic Star Casino LLC; Barden Nevada Gaming LLC; Majestic Investor Holdings LLC; The Majestic Star Casino Capital Corporation; Majestic Investor Capital Corporation; Buffington Harbor River Boats LLC (50%); Waycor Development Company; Barden Entertainment, Inc.; Barden International, Inc.; Barden Technologies, Inc.; Gary New Century LLC.

Principal Competitors

Harrah's Entertainment Inc.; MGM MIRAGE; Boyd Gaming Corporation; Trump Entertainment Resorts, Inc.; Isle of Capri Casinos, Inc.

Further Reading

Amupadhi, Tangeni, ''Barden Motors Shuts,'' *Free Press of Namibia*, December 15, 2004.

Ankeny, Robert, "Barden Casino Set to Sail," *Crain's Detroit Business*, July 21, 1997, p. 1.

——, "Barden Trump Card: Experience," *Crain's Detroit Business*, February 10, 1997, p. 1.

——, "City and Barden Vie for Votes on Casinos," *Crain's Detroit Business*, July 27, 1998, p. 29.

——, "Digital Video Jukeboxes are Barden's Next Big Venture," *Crain's Detroit Business*, February 2, 2004, p. 38.

——, "Jackson's Role With Barden Unclear," *Crain's Detroit Business*, July 13, 1998, p. 20.

Bodipo-Memba, Alejandro, "Barden Gets Trump Deal," *Detroit Free Press*, November 5, 2005.

Bray, Hiawatha, "Wired for Success," *Black Enterprise*, June, 1992, pp. 134–137.

Chappell, Kevin, "Don Barden: Hitting the Casino Jackpot," *Ebony*, October, 2004.

Goodin, Michael, "Faces: Don Barden, The Barden Cos.," *Crain's Detroit Business*, February 27, 1995, p. 64.

Guest, Greta, "Barden to Get Part of Payout," *Detroit Free Press*, October 7, 2005.

Gupte, Pranay, "Detroit's Gift to Namibia," *Forbes*, October 19, 1998.

Hughes, Alan, "The House Always Wins," *Black Enterprise*, June, 2003, pp. 126–133.

Hughes, John, "Millions of Dollars, Past Successes Are Not Enough for Don Barden," *Southcoast Today*, August 24, 1997.

Hyde, Justin, "Judge Rejects Lawsuit Seeking to Stop Casinos," *Associated Press State & Local Wire*, July 22, 1999.

King, R.J., "Barden Seeks Metro Racino," *Detroit News*, April 20, 2004.

Lam, Tina, "An Unfulfilled Desire," *Detroit Free Press*, February 23, 2004.

——, "Lawyers Spar on Detroit Casinos," *Detroit Free Press*, May 2, 2002.

Lowery, Mark, "Barden Selling Detroit Cable Franchise," *Black Enterprise*, September, 1994, p. 17.

McNeil, Jr., Donald G., "Black Pioneer Answers the Call; Detroit Entrepreneur Sees 'Sleeper' Market in Namibia," *New York Times*, July 7, 1998, p. D1.

Smith, Eric L., "Barden's Excellent Adventure," *Black Enterprise*, May, 1998, p. 74.

"Timeline of Events in Detroit's History with Casino Gambling," *Associated Press State & Local Wire*, August 2, 2002.

Windsor, Shawn, and M.L. Elrick, "Investor Pursues Bid for Detroit Casino," *Detroit Free Press*, April 23, 2002.

Yerak, Becky, "Barden Buys Vegas Gaming Hall," *Detroit News*, October 23, 2001.

——, "Barden's Record in Indiana Mixed," *Detroit News*, November 17, 2002.

—Frank Uhle

Bel/Kaukauna USA

1500 East North Street
Little Chute, Wisconsin 54140
U.S.A.
Telephone: (920) 788-3524
Fax: (920) 788-9725
Web site: http://www.kaukaunacheese.com

Wholly Owned Subsidiary of Fromageries Bel
Founded: 1918 as South Kaukauna Dairy
Employees: 350
Sales: $101.9 million (2004)
NAIC: 311513 Cheese Manufacturing

Located in Little Chute, Wisconsin, Bel/Kaukauna USA is the American subsidiary of Paris-based Fromageries Bel. The company makes a variety of processed cheese products. Kaukauna spreadable cheese is packaged in cups and tubs and is available in a wide variety of flavors, from sharp cheddar to port wine. The Kaukauna brand is also found on cheese balls and cheese logs, which are offered in flavors similar to the spreadable product, and on a variety of Mexican sauces & dips, which include cheese items as well as salsa and French onion and ranch dips. In addition, the company manufactures and markets a number of brands picked up from its corporate parent, including spreadable cheese brands WisPride, Merkts, Owl's Nest, and Connoisseur; The Laughing Cow processed cheese wedges; Mini Baybel natural cheeses; and Price's pimiento cheese spreads. In addition to its Wisconsin operation, Bel/Kaukauna also operates a plant in Leitchfield, Kentucky, and a satellite sales office in Fort Lee, New Jersey.

Founding Family Immigrates to Wisconsin in the 1800s

Kaukauna Cheese was founded by Hubert Fassbender in Kaukauna, Wisconsin. His father, Peter Fassbender, was born in Prussia in 1838 and moved with his mother and stepfather to the United States in 1856, landing in New York and settling in Wisconsin. In 1862 he was married and a year later bought farmland in Outagamie county, where he and his wife raised nine children, including Hubert, the sixth in line, born in 1875. Over the years the elder Fassbender bought more land to grow a dairy operation and in 1887 built a cheese factory, with the milk coming from his own cows as well as neighboring farms. When he was 14 Hubert Fassbender began to learn the cheese making trade in his father's factory. In 1901 Peter Fassbender sold his farm to a son, Joseph P. Fassbender, and sold the factory to Hubert, who rebuilt the facility, turning it into one of the largest creameries and cheese factories in the area. Using Appleton, Wisconsin, as his main distribution point, Fassbender began shipping his product all over the country.

In 1918 Fassbender started a distribution company known as South Kaukana Dairy, which became known as Kaukauna Dairy Company, and eventually took the name of Kaukauna Cheese. When Prohibition came to an end in 1933 his distribution company handled another favorite Wisconsin product: beer. According to the Wisconsin Center for Dairy Research, Fassbender became a pioneer in spreadable cheese through his beer depot business. Known as cold pack cheese, spreadable cheese, unlike processed cheese, mixed cheeses and other ingredients together with the use of heat. It was a good way to make use of old cheese beginning to dry up and was no doubt produced by frugal people long before Hubert Fassbender began tinkering with the idea. After he had started delivering beer, tavern owners asked if he had something the patrons could wash down with that beer. The idea of the free lunch was hardly new, and cheese makers had long depended on the sale of cheese to barrooms, which offered it along with bread, ham, eggs, pickles, and the rest of the usual spread of a free lunch.

Early 1930s Introduction of "Club Cheese"

Using his extensive background in cheese making, Fassbender looked for a way to make use of excess cheese while satisfying the request of his beer customers. After some experimentation he perfected the production of cold pack cheese that could be spread at room temperature. In brief, the method combined finely ground natural cheese with whey solids, dry milk, and any number of flavorings. In 1933 he began providing the cheese to customers—taverns, clubs, and hotels—if they bought enough beer. It proved popular with patrons who nicknamed it "club cheese." According to great-nephew Gary Fessbender, interviewed by the Wisconsin Center for Dairy Research, customers after a while were more interested in Fassbender's club cheese than his beer. Thus, in 1933, Fassbender created the Kaukauna Klub brand of cold packed cheese, marketed in a gray stone crock container about four inches in diameter, using the slogan, "It spreads like butter." After first establishing the business by selling the crocks to taverns, Fassbender sold it in retail channels and gradually made it into a national brand. Other Wisconsin cheese makers followed his example and began launching their own brands of club cheese. A major reason why Kaukauna Klub had staying power was that its founder did not simply see the product as a way to make use of scraps. According to company information, he once said, "We must never waste our care nor risk the flavor of Kaukauna Klub trying to work with cheese that isn't worthy of the effort."

Kaukauna Cheese was sold to Minneapolis-based International Multifoods Corporation in 1971. Multifoods had started out as a flour milling operation, best known for the Robin Hood brand. At one point the company, along with General Mills and Pillsbury, was a member of the "Big Three" in U.S flour milling, but Robin Hood always lagged behind the others in brand recognition. In the early 1960s the company began an aggressive diversification effort into the consumer foods markets and over the next decade acquired more than 40 companies, including a number of niche-market food products companies like Kaukauna Cheese.

With the financial backing of its new corporate parent, Kaukauna Cheese in 1974 opened new facilities in an industrial park in Little Chute, Wisconsin. With more specialized equipment now at its disposal, the company would emerge during the 1970s as America's largest manufacturer of cheeseballs and cheeselogs. Then, in the 1980s, Kaukauna Cheese expanded its product offering to include a line of Mexican-style cheese dips and other sauces.

Multifoods was a billion dollar company by 1980, having enjoyed a decade-long period of strong growth. The increases continued until 1984, but disturbing signs were emerging. Nearly all of its consumer products were losing market share and only one, Kretschmer Wheat Germ, was a market leader. Multifoods lacked focus, the byproduct of an indiscriminate buying spree as well as meager brand recognition for the Multifoods name. The company now undertook a restructuring program, a selling and buying of assets that over the course of several years transformed Multifoods from a flour milling and consumer foods company into a major foodservice distribution and manufacturing company.

Regaining Independence in the Mid-1980s

One of the subsidiaries Multifoods chose to divest was the Kaukauna Cheese operations. In 1986 a Kaukauna management team, led by Robert Gilbert and private investors, formed Kaukauna Cheese Corp. to buy the business. The transaction was completed in early 1987 and Kaukauna Cheese was once again an independent company, with Gilbert serving as president and chief executive officer.

That independence lasted a decade. During that time Kaukauna Cheese made headlines by becoming the first company, in 1991, to use the all-natural fat substitute, Simplesse 100, developed by NutraSweet using a whey protein concentrate. The "light" cheese category was extremely competitive, and for several years Kaukauna Cheese's entry had experienced flat sales. The new product, called Kaukauna Lite 50, reflecting a 50 percent reduction in fat, was produced in four varieties and sold side by side with the company's other cold pack products. Other cheese makers would soon follow the company's lead and introduce their own products using Simplesse 100.

Kaukauna Cheese was doing well in the mid-1990s, generating annual sales in the $50 million range, but when it was approached by Fromageries Bel about selling the business, management listened. "I'm not going to live forever," Gilbert told the *Milwaukee Journal Sentinel.* "In life, you can't pick your moments, and this is a company we respect, they approached us, and discussions took off from there." In February 1996 the two parties announced they had reached an agreement. Fromageries Bel's New Jersey-based subsidiary, Bel Cheese USA, Inc., would purchase the assets of Kaukauna Cheese, which included a manufacturing and distribution facility in Little Chute, a retail store in the town, and a refrigerated warehouse in Neenah, Wisconsin.

Gilbert also received a contractual assurance that the operation would not be relocated. Given that Kaukauna Cheese had recently moved into a new $3.5 million plant and produced as much sales as all Bel Cheese USA products combined, there was no desire on the part of the new corporate parent to move the operations. But it was an important commitment nonetheless, given the problems Bel Cheese USA had encountered with another Wisconsin cheese spread maker, Wispride. About a year earlier Wispride's plant was closed, costing about 120 people their jobs, as Wispride production was moved to Leitchfield, Kentucky. In November 1995, Wisconsin Attorney General Jim Doyle filed suit against Bel Cheese USA, alleging that its use of the Wispride trademark, which indicated the cheese products came from Wisconsin, amounted to false advertising.

After the acquisition of Kaukauna Cheese, Fromageries Bel reorganized its U.S. subsidiary, not only streamlining the operation but eliminating the nettlesome problem with Wispride. In late 1996 and early 1997 Fromageries Bel announced a number of sweeping changes. First, the production of Wispride products was transferred to the Little Chute plant. The move was not made to settle the pending lawsuit with the state of Wisconsin, but was just an ancillary benefit. The company maintained that cost studies it conducted revealed the Wispride line would be less expensive to produce in Kaukauna's newer plant. Fromageries Bel also decided to downsize the Fort Lee, New Jersey office, making it a satellite sales office and shifting administrative positions to Little Chute. The New Jersey office and its marketing team would continue to market the Bel brands and Price's brands, while Wispride marketing would be taken over

Key Dates:

1887: Peter Fassbender builds a cheese factory in Kaukauna, Wisconsin.

1901: The factory is sold to son Hubert Fassbender, who turns it into one of the largest creameries and cheese factories in the area.

1918: Fassbender starts a distribution company known as South Kaukana Dairy, which eventually takes the name of Kaukauna Cheese.

1933: Fassbender creates the Kaukauna Klub brand of cold packed cheese, which becomes a national brand.

1971: Kaukauna Cheese is sold to Minneapolis-based International Multifoods Corporation.

1987: A Kaukauna management team completes the purchase of the business, with Robert Gilbert serving as president and chief executive officer.

1991: Kaukauna Cheese becomes the first company to use the all-natural fat substitute, Simplesse 100, developed by NutraSweet using a whey protein concentrate.

1996: Fromageries Bel's New Jersey-based subsidiary, Bel Cheese USA, Inc., purchases the assets of Kaukauna Cheese.

1997: Kaukauna Cheese undergoes substantial reorganization, and Fromageries Bel decides to rename its U.S. operations Bel/Kaukauna USA.

2002: The company acquires a number of brands from Ohio-based Lakeview Farms Inc.

2003: Bel/Kaukauna receives a major break when *The South Beach Diet* book, which became a runaway bestseller, includes a wedge of Laughing Cow light cheese and a pear as an afternoon snack in a sample meal plan.

by the Kaukauna marketing group. Moreover, the sales force of Kaukauna Cheese and Bel Cheese USA were to be integrated, resulting in staff reductions. Regional managers would now be responsible for the line of products produced by Bel Cheese USA and Kaukauna Cheese. Finally, Fromageries Bel decided to rename its U.S. operations Bel/Kaukauna USA. The head of Bel Cheese USA, Patrick Robbe, a French native, was reassigned to Paris, and Kaukauna's Robert Gilbert took over the presidency of the combined enterprise. While the changes resulted in the loss of jobs in Kentucky and New Jersey, it also meant that Little Chute would be adding about 40 production jobs, several managers, and another half-dozen clerical employees. The Little Chute plant would increase its poundage volume by about 25 percent over the previous year. "I would say that the latest round of decisions solidified our position for the future," Gilbert told Appleton, Wisconsin's *Post-Crescent*, "and shows that Fromageries Bel is fully committed to its operations in the United States."

To accommodate its enlarged business in Little Chute, Bel/Kaukauna expanded its offices and production facilities. That extra room would be needed in 2002, when the company acquired a number of brands from Ohio-based Lakeview Farms Inc. It added the Merkts and Owl's Nest cheese spread brand and several private-label brands.

Over the years Kaukauna Cheese had won an abundance of awards for its products. Under French ownership that would not change. In 2003, for example, the company's sharp cheddar cold pack cheese won first place in a countrywide contest sponsored by the Wisconsin Cheese Makers Association. In that same year, at the Wisconsin State Fair, the same product won the Governor's Sweepstakes Award.

Bel/Kaukauna received a major break in 2003 when "The South Beach Diet" book, which became a runaway bestseller, included a wedge of Laughing Cow light cheese and a pear as an afternoon snack in a sample meal plan. As a result the demand for Bel/Kaukauna's Laughing Cow wedges skyrocketed. The company could not make the product fast enough and had to expand production in its Kentucky plant and import product from France, where it originated in 1921. The logo came from the smiling cow pictures stenciled on the trucks that supplied food to French soldiers in the field during World War I. "If you are an old cheese warrior like me, this breaks your heart," Gilbert told the *Wisconsin State Journal*. "I fought and clawed for every pound I could get in this business and it breaks my heart that we aren't able to ship more." He had to be content to take advantage of the trend as much as possible while he could. "If other fads are any indication, if other diets are any indication, people will tend to slip away and fall away," Gilbert told the *Journal*. "But hopefully when they do, they are going to remember that Laughing Cow tastes great."

Principal Operating Units

Kaukauna; WisPride; Merkts; Owl's Nest; Price's; The Laughing Cow; MiniBabyBel; Connoisseur.

Principal Competitors

Kraft Foods North America, Inc.; Saputo Cheese USA Inc.; Sargento Foods Inc.

Further Reading

Boardman, Arlen, "Fromageries Bel U.S. Headquarters Moving to Little Chute, Wis.," *Post-Crescent, Appleton, Wis.,* February 5, 1997.

Imrie, Robert, "Laughing Cow's Supple Problem Not Funny," *Wisconsin State Journal,* August 19, 2004, p. E1.

Lewitt, Alan, "Kaukauna First to Use WPC-Based Simplesse," *Cheese Market News,* August 16, 1991, p. 1.

Olson, Jon, "Cheesemaker Employs 110 in Fox Valley," *Milwaukee Journal Sentinel,* February 23, 1996, p. 1.

Paulus, Karen, "Cold Pack Cheese—It's a Wisconsin Original," *Dairy Pipeline (Wisconsin Center for Dairy Research),* July 2004, p. 6.

Romell, Rick, "French Cheese Giant to Move Wispride Production to Wisconsin," *Milwaukee Journal Sentinel,* December 18, 1996.

Sharma-Jensen, Geeta, "Cheesemaker Consolidating," *Milwaukee Journal Sentinel,* February 4, 1997, p. 8.

—Ed Dinger

Belden CDT Inc.

7701 Forsyth Boulevard, Suite 800
St. Louis, Missouri 63105
U.S.A.
Telephone: (314) 854-8000
Fax: (314) 854-8001
Web site: http://www.beldencdt.com

Public Company
Incorporated: 1902 as Belden Manufacturing Company
Employees: 6,750
Sales: $966.2 million (2004)
Stock Exchanges: New York
Ticker Symbol: BDC
NAIC: 331319 Other Aluminum Rolling and Drawing;
331422 Copper Wire (Except Mechanical) Drawing;
335921 Fiber Optic Cable Manufacturing; 331491
Nonferrous Metal (Except Copper and Aluminum)
Rolling, Drawing, and Extruding

Belden CDT Inc. operates as one of the largest manufacturers of high-speed electronic cables in the United States. The company serves the electronic, electrical, and communications markets and offers wire, cable, and fiber optic products. Approximately 60 percent of sales stem from Belden CDT's North American operations, while the remaining revenues are secured in Europe and Asia. The company exited the telecommunications industry when it sold its North American communications assets in June 2004. Belden Inc. merged with Cable Design Technologies Corporation (CDT) in July of that year. The company adopted its current moniker upon completion of the deal.

Recognizing a Need in 1902

Belden was founded by Joseph C. Belden in Chicago in 1902. Belden had been working as a purchasing agent for Kellogg Switchboard & Supply Company of Chicago but was finding it difficult to locate the high-quality, silk-wrapped magnetic wire needed for telephone coils. Recognizing the need for this product, Belden, then 26, decided to go into business for himself, selling shares in the company, called Belden Manufacturing Company, to 11 investors for $25,000 in start-up capital. Belden served as the company's president until 1939.

The wiring of America was just getting underway, and Belden quickly found a market for his product. However, in order to protect itself from fluctuations in demand, the company began to expand its product line. An initial foray into supply silk-wound wire frames for ladies' hats proved less successful given caprices of fashion, and Belden quickly found two new markets—the nascent automotive and electrical appliance industries—for the company's wire products. Belden's early commitment to quality helped the company become a leading source of wiring and cables for these industries. Early customers included Thomas Edison and Lee De Forest, creator of the radio vacuum tube. By the end of the century's first decade, the company had achieved sales of $350,000.

Belden was already establishing its reputation for innovative product development, with strong research and development efforts and a quick recognition of market opportunities. The increasing use of electricity demanded better insulation capacities, and in 1910, Belden introduced its enamel insulation, marketing under the trade name Beldenamel, which would become an industry standard and open the way for such wire refinements as fine and ultra-fine magnet wire. At the same time, Belden also introduced rubber-covered wire products. The new additions to the Belden line helped the company nearly triple its sales to $900,000 by 1913.

Belden next expanded operations to include plastic manufacturing capabilities, primarily to supply bakelite housings and other products for the electrical markets. However, the outbreak of World War I provided the company's strongest growth, as Belden supplied wire and cables for such support units as motorized transport and field communications for the war effort. The company also began receiving orders from England and Russia for enameled copper wire—Belden later discovered that its products were used for developing and installing wireless radio communications, bringing the company into a new market. After the war, Belden continued to supply both the aviation and radio markets. Meanwhile, the company had a two-year backlog of orders from its domestic customers.

Company Perspectives:

Belden CDT, Inc., formed in July 2004 through the merger of Belden Inc. and Cable Design Technologies Corp., is one of the largest U.S.-based manufacturers of high-speed electronic cables and focuses on products for the specialty electronics and data networking markets, including connectivity.

When commercial radio broadcasting began in the 1920s, Belden's low tension cables, aerial wire, and magnet wire found strong demand. The company also began selling parts to jobbers in the radio industry, beginning the company's distribution arm. In the late 1920s, Belden entered another market with the development of a molded rubber plug. By then, orders for the company's expanded product line were outstripping its production capacity, and in 1928 the company opened its second plant, in Richmond, Indiana, which would later become the site of the company's Electronic Division. In that year, also, the company started producing for the automotive aftermarket. Four years later, Belden signed a distribution agreement with the recently formed National Automotive Parts Association.

Despite the Depression, Belden's diversified product line and its expansion into the replacement parts market helped the company continue to grow. In 1939, with sales of $4.9 million, and a net income of $378,000, the company went public, listing on the Midwest Stock Exchange. Joe Belden died in 1939; replacing him was Whipple Jacobs, who had started in the company's cost department as a temporary clerk earning $9.10 a week in 1914. Whipple led Belden into the World War II era, during which, Belden, already a major military supplier, converted much of its production to supply the war effort. Belden also began introducing new forms of wire insulation using such recently developed chemical compounds as vinyl, nylon, and neoprene, further expanding the Belden family of products with Beldure, Nylclad, Formvar, Beldfoil and other brand names. Belden also introduced the first solderable enamel compound, replacing its Beldenamel with the Celenamel trademark. During the postwar years, Belden continued to supply the electric product markets but also expanded into the new and growing fields of radar, sonar, and electronics. Whipple stepped down as president, and Charles S. Craigmile, who had started with the company as an electrical engineer in 1915, was named in his place.

Growth through the 1970s

Belden began its shift toward the television and data processing markets as these industries began their commercial growth in the 1950s. Belden's sales continued to grow steadily, and it continued to add capacity to its Chicago and Richmond plants. By 1965, the company's sales had grown to $53 million. In that year, Robert W. Hawkinson became the company's president. Hawkinson, who joined Belden in 1945 as an engineer after serving as a fighter-bomber captain in the Army Air Forces during the Second World War, would lead Belden through its next growth phase.

That era began in 1966, when Belden changed its name to Belden Corporation and built a plant in Franklin, North

Carolina—its first new plant since 1938. Over the next three years, the company constructed two more plants, one in Pontotoc, Mississippi, and a 170,000-square-foot site in Jena, Louisiana. The company also went on an acquisition binge, acquiring Complete-Reading Electric Company, a distributor of electrical motor parts, in 1967. The following year, Belden acquired Southern Electric Sales Company, based in Dallas, which distributed electrical wire, insulating material, and replacement parts, and Insulation & Copper Sales, a Detroit-based distributor of magnet wire, lead wire, and associated products. Capping the expansion of Belden's distribution business, which gave the company 16 warehouse distribution centers, was the 1969 stock-swap acquisition of Electrical Specialty Company of San Francisco, adding that company's electrical wire, insulating materials, industrial plastics, and shop equipment distribution facilities. Meanwhile, Belden was also expanding its production capacity, with the acquisition of General Wire & Cable Company Ltd. of Canada and that company's two manufacturing plants. At the same time, Belden moved to consolidate its research and development operations, building the company's Technical Research Center in Geneva, Illinois. Among the products Belden developed during this period was its Duofoil brand of coaxial cables for master antenna and cable television systems.

By 1970, sales had topped $100 million, and the company began listing on the New York Stock Exchange. Helping to fuel this growth was a stepping up of its activity in the automotive aftermarket, which itself was growing rapidly with the steady increases in car sales of the period. During the 1970s, the company continued to expand its production capacity, adding a 75,000-square-foot automotive aftermarket facility to its Jena plant, while adding new plants in Dumas, Arkansas, and Monticello, Kentucky. The company also moved to improve its profits by exiting the low-margin commodity market, discontinuing production of heavy wire and closing its original Chicago plant. By 1978, the company's sales had grown to $240 million, earning profits of $8.8 million.

Reemerging in the 1990s

Belden's stock price, however, had not kept pace with its revenue growth. By 1980, the company had become the target of a hostile takeover, and Belden found refuge in a merger with Crouse-Hinds Company. The following year, when Crouse-Hinds itself became a takeover target, another white knight appeared, and Belden found itself a subsidiary of Cooper Industries. Belden served Cooper as a source of cash flow to fuel Cooper's expansion into other industries; meanwhile, Belden began positioning itself toward the international market, while also expanding heavily in the booming computer industry. In 1993, Cooper spun off Belden as an independent, publicly-traded company with annual sales of $300 million.

Within three years, Belden would more than double its annual sales, a growth fueled in large part by sales of the company's network cable products. The company's international sales to Canada, Europe, and Latin America were also becoming a strong source of revenue, nearing 25 percent of annual sales by the mid-1990s. After moving its headquarters to St. Louis in 1994, the company prepared for a new string of acquisitions. In March 1995, Belden acquired American Elec-

Key Dates:

1902: Joseph C. Belden establishes Belden Manufacturing Company.
1910: Belden introduces its enamel insulation, marketing it under the trade name Beldenamel.
1939: Annual sales reach $4.9 million; the company goes public.
1966: The company changes its name to Belden Corporation.
1970: Sales top $100 million; Belden begins listing on the New York Stock Exchange.
1981: Cooper Industries buys Belden.
1993: Cooper spins off Belden as an independent, publicly-traded company with annual sales of $300 million.
2000: Belden signs a five-year $700 million deal to supply SBC Communications Inc. with copper telecommunications cable.
2004: Belden merges with Cable Design Technologies Corporation; the company changes its name to Belden CDT Inc.

tric Cordsets, based in Bensenville, Illinois, adding the $24 million company to its newly formed Cord Products Division. Two months later, Belden purchased rival Pope Cable and Wire B.V., based in Venlo, the Netherlands, for $50 million, adding that company's $112 million in annual sales and strengthening Belden's position in Europe. A year later, Belden acquired the wire division of Alpha Wire Corporation, based in Elizabeth, New Jersey, further positioning Belden to achieve a strong share of the ongoing networking products boom. It also added Cowen Cable Corporation to its arsenal. Meanwhile, Belden began preparing for expansion into the growing Asian and Pacific Rim markets, while extending its Latin American reach as well. With the new market for Internet and corporate intranet products just beginning to explode in the mid-1990s, Belden's history of quickly shifting its focus to emerging technologies and markets continued to serve the company well.

Changes in the Late 1990s and Beyond

During 1998 and 1999, the company continued to focus on strengthening its Communications division. During 1999, Belden acquired Cable Systems International Inc. (CSI), the second-largest copper telephone cable manufacturer in the United States. The addition of CSI to Belden's holdings gave it a significant advantage in the growing specialty wire and cable market. Indeed, the purchase helped Belden secure a $700 million contract to provide copper telephone cable to SBC Communications for the next five-years.

While Belden's future seemed bright, an economic slowdown began plaguing the telecommunications industry in 2001. Lower demand led to falling income and revenues. Belden responded by cutting nearly 6,000 jobs. In 2002, the company purchased Cable Design Technologies' NORCOM wire and cable division. NORCOM provided telecommunications cable in Canada and the United States. A continued turndown in the industry however, forced Belden to shutter its NORCOM facility and close down

manufacturing operations in Australia and Germany. During 2003, Belden's North American communications division reported an operating loss on $109.4 million. Overall, the company reported a net loss of $60.7 million for the year.

With its telecommunications arm stifling profits, Belden revamped its strategy and decided to jettison that portion of its business. Its exit from the telecommunications industry was made evident in June 2004 when the company sold its North American communications assets to Superior Essex Inc. Meanwhile, Belden's CEO C. Baker Cunningham had started toying with the idea of merging with Cable Design Technologies (CDT). After meeting with CDT's CEO Fred Kuznik in November 2003, the two companies hammered out the details and announced merger plans in February 2004.

CDT had been established in 1980 as Intercole Automation Inc. and went public in 1993. The company had grown throughout its short history by acquiring many companies including Northern Telecom Ltd.'s (Nortel) communication cable and network wiring products businesses. By 2004, CDT was also struggling to shore up profits and eyed the union with Belden as a lucrative alternative to going alone in the industry.

The union was structured as a stock deal with each share of Belden stock exchanged for one share in the combined company, while two shares of CDT stock were exchanged for one share of the combined company. The merger-of-equals was completed on July 15, 2004 and created one of the largest manufacturers of high-speed electronic cables in the United States.

With five operating divisions, the newly created Belden CDT Inc. stood on much stronger ground. Its Electronics division accounted for nearly 60 percent of sales while its Networking arm secured the remaining revenues. The company expected to save $35 million within two years of the merger and immediately set plans in motion to shut down plants in England, Massachusetts, and Vermont. At first glance, the merger appeared to have paid off. Sales increased by nearly 17 percent over the previous year and the company posted net income of $15.2 million. While management was optimistic about the company's prospects, only time would tell what the future had in store for Belden CDT.

Principal Divisions

Electronics; Networking; Specialty; European Operations; West Penn Wire.

Principal Competitors

Alcatel Alsthom Compagnie Générale d'Electricité; Pirelli & C. SpA; Sumitomo Electric Industries Ltd.

Further Reading

De Young, Garrett H., " 'You Must Know Your Strengths,' " *Photonics Spectra*, August 1989, p. 52.
Galarza, Pablo, "Belden Inc., St. Louis, Mo., Cashing in as Technology Lifts Wire Demand," *Investor's Business Daily*, June 16, 1994, p. A6.
"High Operating Rates Prove Boon to Belden, Wire Maker," *Barron's*, August 7, 1978, p. 39.

Manor, Robert, "Local Newcomer Soars on Market," *St. Louis Post-Dispatch*, July 11, 1994, p. 4.

Mehlman, William, "Investors Responding Slowly to Altered Belden Image," *Insiders' Chronicle*, April 6, 1979, p. 1.

Milligan, Brian, "Belden CDT Continues Rationalizing Plan Following Merger," *Cabling Installation and Maintenance*, February 2005, pp. 44–45.

Naudi, Jack, "Missouri's Belden to Sell Communications Unit to Atlanta-Based Superior Essex," *Knight Ridder Tribune Business News*, March 20, 2004.

Shabelman, David, "Belden, CDT to Merge," *The Deal.com*, February 6, 2004.

"Strong Demand Puts Belden Operations in High Gear," *Barron's*, September 25, 1972, p. 29.

Stuenkel, Gil, "Biggest Deals of 2004: The Deal: Belden Mergers with CDT," *St. Louis Business Journal*, December 10, 2004, p. 26.

"Wire and Cable Maker Belden Set to String Up an Earnings Comeback," *Barron's*, December 15, 1969, p. 26.

Zaczkiewicz, Arthur, "Belden's Growth Strategy Pays Off," *Electronic Buyers News*, February 28, 2000.

—M.L. Cohen
—update: Christina M. Stansell

Belron International Ltd.

The King's Observatory
Old Deer Park
Richmond TW9 2AZ
United Kingdom
Telephone: 44 208 332 0099
Fax: +44 020 8948 7323
Web site: http://www.belron.com

Majority Owned Subsidiary of D'Ieteren N.V.
Incorporated: 1947 as Plate Glass & Shatterprufe
 Industries
Employees: 10,000
Sales: EUR 1.12 billion ($1.5 billion) (2004)
NAIC: 811122 Automotive Glass Replacement Shops

Belron International Ltd. is the world's leading provider of vehicle glass repair and replacement (VGRR) services. The company operates a network of more than 1,300 glass replacement service centers, backed up by a mobile repair fleet of nearly 4,000 vehicles. Belron is a holding company overseeing several brand names, including the company's flagship brand Carglass, present in some 20 countries, primarily in Europe. Other brands include Autoglass (United Kingdom, Ireland, and Poland); O'Brien (Australia); Hurtigruta (Norway); Smith & Smith (New Zealand); and, since 2005, the Elite Auto Glass, Auto Glass Specialists, and GlasPro brands in the United States. Altogether, Belron operates in 27 countries; the company directly oversees its operations in 19 countries and has put into place franchise networks in nine countries. Belron also supports its VGRR operations with its own research and development arm, which has been developing a new windshield removal system in the 2000s. Belron is a subsidiary of Belgian automotive distribution giant D'Ieteren N.V., which is also a major shareholder in Avis Europe. D'Ieteren holds nearly 75 percent of Belron, which is registered in Luxembourg and headquartered in the United Kingdom. In 2004, Belron's revenues reached EUR 1.12 billion ($1.5 billion).

South African Plate Glass Specialist in the Early 20th Century

The origins of Belron lay in the South African glass and furniture industries at the turn of the 20th century. The earliest part of the group was founded in 1896 by Ernest Beardmore, who emigrated to South Africa from England and set up the Plate Glass Bevelling & Silvering Company in Cape Town. Beardmore's company specialized in decorative glass work and in producing mirrored glass. Into the new century, however, Beardmore faced growing competition, particularly from City Glass. That company had been established by Adolph Brodie, a Lithuanian native who had emigrated to England in the 1880s, before coming to South Africa in 1903. Brodie launched City Glass in 1909.

City Glass grew quickly, and overtook Beardmore's Plate Glass company. From rivals, Brodie and Beardmore quickly became friends, and toward the end of World War I decided to merge their companies in 1917. Brodie then bought out Beardmore, and brought his three sons into the business. Following the merger, the Brodies changed the name of their own company to Plate Glass Bevelling & Silvering Company. The company then began to expand into other South African markets, establishing branches in several towns.

Each of the Brodie brothers was assigned a branch, with Emmanuel Brodie operating the Cape Town branch, and Harry Brodie placed in charge of a branch in Port Elizabeth. A third Brodie brother, Jackie, was sent to Johannesburg to open a company branch there. However, as Ronnie Lubner, future Belron chairman, told *Business Times:* "Jackie's heart was never in it and the brothers came to Johannesburg to find a replacement."

Instead, the company took on Morris Lubner as a part-time agent. Lubner quickly proved himself an industrious salesman, and by 1922 had been taken on as a partner in the Johannesburg branch. Lubner expanded the operation, moving it to new premises. Lubner also was responsible for the company's first diversification, adding plywood and lumber sales in the 1920s.

A more significant diversification for the later Belron company came in the late 1920s. The Ford and General Motors companies had come to South Africa and had set up their first factories in Port Elizabeth. Emmanuel Brodie recognized an opportunity to expand the company's glass business, and convinced both U.S. automakers to purchase their windshields from Plate Glass Bevelling & Silvering. In 1927, the company set up a division specialized in the production and sale of windshields and other automotive windows.

The company began producing its first safety glass in 1931, a move driven by Harry Brodie, who went to England to acquire the manufacturing rights to the new windshield type, called Shatterproof. As Ronnie Lubner recalled in *Business Times:* ''It was an early example of built-in obsolescence, because the original design was a film of celluloid between two thin plates of glass which soon yellowed.'' The Brodies built their own factory in Port Elizabeth and began producing safety glass for the South African automotive industry, under the Afrikanerized name Shatterprufe.

Adolph Brodie died in 1934, and the company was taken over in a three-way partnership among Emmanuel and Harry Brodie and Morris Lubner. In 1940, the company decided to step up its plywood and lumber business, and bought up rival Plywoods of Parow, which became known as PG Bison. In 1947, the Brodies and Lubner took their company public, listing it on the Johannesburg Stock Exchange as Plate Glass & Shatterprufe Industries (PGSI). The company adapted to the change in safety glass technology, developing its own molding process for the new heat-toughened armorplate standard (which replaced laminated glass) in partnership with Triplex Safety Glass in England. The new glass type marked an important step into the windshield's emergence as an important structural element in modern automobile design. In 1953, the company acquired the rights to a new process for producing curved windshields.

Morris Lubner became chairman of the company after Emmanuel Brodie's death in 1961. Lubner had by then brought his own sons, Ronald and Bernard, into the business. Ronald Lubner became especially involved in PGSI's automotive glass arm. In 1958, the company developed its own laminated glass for rear windshields. In the early 1960s, the company spotted a new expansion opportunity: the vehicle glass repair and replacement, known as VGRR in the trade, the basis of the later Belron company.

In 1962, Ronald Lubner convinced his father to buy up a fast-growing glass company, Express Glass. That company posed an increasing threat to PGSI's own operation, especially in that it had established a nationally operating chain of 67 vehicle glass replacement shops. Disputes among the family owners, however, had slowed Express Glass's growth into the early 1960s. PGSI took advantage of the disagreement over the company's management direction to step in with a buyout offer in 1962.

International Focus in the 1980s

Through the 1960s, PGSI solidified its position as South Africa's leading VGRR company. By the beginning of the 1970s, the company then turned its interest toward the international market. PGSI took a first step in 1971, when it bought up the Australia VGGR group, O'Brien. Over the next decades, that brand emerged as the leader in Australia's vehicle glass market. Another early international market for the company was the United States. Rather than establishing a direct presence in the United States, however, the company entry came as an export supplier of windshields and vehicle glass for the Japanese auto industry, as it began its push into the U.S. market in the 1970s.

PGSI restructured its operations at the beginning of the 1980s, separating its plywood/wood and vehicle glass operations into two core divisions. The company then renamed its vehicle glass interests outside of South Africa as Solaglass in 1982. The following year, however, PGSI's international vehicle glass business took a big step forward when the company acquired two VGGR specialists in the United Kingdom, Windshields and Autoglass. The company kept the Autoglass brand name, developing it into the leader in the United Kingdom and in Ireland.

An important milestone for the company came in 1983, when PGSI agreed to merge its vehicle glass manufacturing operations with that of its primary glass supplier, Pilkington Glass, forming Glass South Africa. PGSI's next major growth move came in 1988, when it acquired Carglass. That business provided the company with a springboard for expansion into the Benelux market, as well as in France and Germany. In addition to its own network of VGRR service shops, Carglass had launched a mobile repair and replacement service, building up a fleet of vehicles. Carglass became the most international of the later Belron group's brands, serving as its primary brand on the European continent.

PGSI acquired full control of Glass South Africa in 1992. In that same year, South African Breweries (SAB) acquired a majority stake in PGSI itself. The Lubner family retained some 22 percent of the company as well as directional control, while the financial backing of SAB enabled PGSI to step up its expansion efforts. In 1994, the company regrouped its international VGRR businesses under a new holding company, Belron International.

The company's expansion hopes focused on the United States in the 1990s. In 1990, the company made its first effort to penetrate that market directly, founding a new subsidiary, Windshields, starting with 25 service shops. In the mid-1990s, however, the newly named Belron sought a different approach to achieving scale in the United States. In 1996, the company agreed to merge its Windshields operation into the VGRR business owned by Vistar Inc., in exchange for a 51 percent share of Vistar. The merged entity now boasted a network of more than 250 VGRR shops, and a 12 percent market share.

Belron appeared to have hit the big time in the United States by the end of the decade. In 1998, the company convinced rival U.S. autoglass group Safelite to merge the two companies' operations. Belron's stake in the newly enlarged Safelite stood

---

Key Dates:

1897: Ernest Beardmore founds Plate Glass Bevelling & Silvering Company in Cape Town, South Africa.
1909: Adolph Brodie founds City Glass in Capetown.
1917: Beardmore and Brodie merge their companies as Plate Glass Bevelling & Silvering Company.
1921: Morris Lubner becomes a partner with Brodie and opens a branch in Johannesburg.
1927: The company launches vehicle glass manufacturing for Ford and General Motors in Port Elizabeth.
1931: Laminated safety glass production is launched.
1947: The company goes public as Plate Glass & Shatterprufe Industries (PGSI).
1962: The company acquires Express Glass and becomes the leading South African VGRR group.
1971: The first international expansion, into Australia, is initiated.
1983: The company acquires the Windshields and Autoglass brands in the United Kingdom.
1988: The company acquires the Carglass brand in France and Benelux.
1990: The company establishes Windshields in the United States.
1992: South African Brewers acquire control of PGSI.
1994: VGRR operations are regrouped under the Belron holding company.
1996: The company merges Windshields into Vistar Inc.
1997: Vistar is merged into Safelite, which becomes the VGRR market leader in the United States.
1999: D'Ieteren, of Belgium, acquires a majority stake in PGSI; Belron sells its stake in Safelite.

---

at nearly 45 percent, while Safelite, with a 25 percent share of the U.S. VGRR market and sales of nearly $1 billion, emerged as the clear market leader.

In the meantime, Belron had been expanding its business elsewhere, too, buying operations in Spain and New Zealand at a total cost of $71 million. The company also entered Canada, buying up two of that country's leading VGRR specialists for $98 million.

SAB's decision to refocus its operations around a core of beverage production and hotel and leisure operations placed Belron on the market in the late 1990s. Belgium's D'Ieteren, the country's leading automobile distributor and a major shareholder in Avis Europe, bought PGSI in 1999, and then shed the group's non-auto glass operations, keeping only the Belron International business.

World Leader in the 21st Century

Soon after the D'Ieteren purchase, Belron sold off its stake in Safelite, which had begun to experience financial problems at the dawn of the 21st century. Instead, Belron turned its focus toward expanding its European presence, particularly under its Carglass flagship. As part of that effort, the company launched a series of acquisitions, such as the purchase of GTC Glaslinien

A/S in Denmark in 2001. The following year, the company acquired Darma SpA in Italy, as well as a VGRR specialist in Sweden. Then, in 2003, the company acquired Norway's Hurtigruta.

Another significant part of the group's expansion was the launch of a new Carglass franchise operation for selected markets. Greece became the first country targeted for Carglass franchises in 2001, followed by the Czech Republic, Israel, and Slovenia in 2002. By 2003, the company had added franchises in Poland (under the Autoglass name) and Serbia-Montenegro.

Belron's ambitions continued to grow toward the mid-2000s. The company added a new acquisition in Italy, buying up that country's second largest VGRR group. Belron also added to its Norwegian business that year. In 2005, the company entered the Hungarian market, forming a franchise agreement with that country's Pneutrade Service, a specialist in tire replacement.

The year 2005 marked Belron's return to the United States, and the expansion of its North American operations in general. In March 2005, Belron reached an agreement to acquire two Colorado-based companies, Elite Auto Glass Inc. and Glaspro Inc., giving the company a combined 31 branches operating in the western regions of the United States. The company next turned to Canada, buying TCG International, based in British Columbia in September 2005. In that month, as well, Belron boosted its new U.S. position with an agreement to purchase Wisconsin's Auto Glass Specialists. One month later, Belron added new operations in California through the acquisition of Windshield Pros there. By then, Belron's international network boasted more than 1,300 shops in 28 countries. With revenues of more than EUR 1.3 billion ($1.5 billion), Belron remained the world's leading VGRR specialist.

Principal Subsidiaries

Elite Auto Glass Inc. (United States); GlasPro Inc. (United States); Hurtigruta (Norway); Lebeau (Canada); O'Brien (Australia); Smith & Smith (New Zealand).

Principal Competitors

Automotive Products Ltd.; Auto Glass Specialists Inc.; Safelite Glass Corporation; Saint Gobain Sekurit Deutschland GmbH and Company KG; Glassworks Plus Inc.; Botzaris Automobiles; Highway Emergency Services Ltd.; MidAmerican Auto Glass.

Further Reading

"Belgian Takeover of Plate Glass & Shatterprufe Industries Cleared," *European Report*, November 20, 1999.
"Belron Announces a New Business-to-Business Internet Company," *Autoglass Magazine*, December 7th, 2001.
"Belron Canada Buys Canadian Glass Operations from TCG International," *Newswire.ca*, September 2, 2005.
"Belron Continues to Expand Portfolio," *Autoglass Magazine*, October 2005.
"Belron Purchases Elite," *AGRReports*, May/June 2005.
"Belron Takes Steps to Re-enter U.S. Market," *Glass Digest Magazine*, January 23, 2003.
"Belron to Acquire Auto Glass Specialists," *Autoglass Magazine*, September 2005.

"European Commission Approves D'Ieteren's Purchase of Belron," *Autonews,* December 1999.

"No One Behind AutoRestore's Wheel," *Design Week,* December 5, 2002, p. 3.

"Removing Windscreens in a Flash," *The Engineer,* June 15, 2001, p. 14.

Walker, Julie, "PGSI Raises a Glass to 100 Years of Business and Growth," *Business Times,* August 31, 1997.

——, "PGSI's Got 18% of the World's Cars Covered," *Business Times,* May 10, 1998.

—M.L. Cohen

Ben E. Keith Company

601 East 7th Street
Fort Worth, Texas 76102-5501
U.S.A.
Telephone: (817) 877-5700
Fax: (817)338-1701
Web site: http://www.benekeith.com

Private Company
Founded: 1906 as Harkrider-Morrison Company
Employees: 2,800
Sales: $1.5 billion (2004)
NAIC: 424410 General Line Grocery Merchant Whole-
      salers; 424810 Beer and Ale Merchant Wholesalers

Based in Fort Worth, Texas, Ben E. Keith Company is a distributor with two divisions: food and beer. Ben E. Keith Foods is a full-line foodservice distributor, serving more than 12,000 restaurants, hospitals, schools, and other institutional customers in Texas, Oklahoma, Arkansas, parts of New Mexico, the southern part of Kansas, and northern Louisiana through six distribution centers. Products include produce, frozen foods, meats, refrigerated foods, dry groceries, and paper goods, as well as equipment and other supplies. The unit is among the ten largest foodservice distributors in the United States. Ben E. Keith Beers is the largest independent Anheuser-Busch wholesaler in the United States and one of the largest distributors of Anheuser-Busch products in the world, selling 35 million cases a year through a network of eight distribution centers, serving 60 Texas counties. In addition, the division distributes Redhook and Kirin brewery brands. The private company is partially owned by brothers Robert and Howard Hallam, who serve as chairman and chief executive officer, and president and chief operating officer, respectively.

Early 1900s Origins

Ben E. Keith is named for Benjamin Ellington Keith, who was born in Fort Worth, Texas, in 1882. The company was founded in Fort Worth in 1906 as a produce house known as Harkrider-Morrison Company. Keith had been forced to leave school when he was just 14, driving a coal wagon at first to help out his family, but he would later attend business college and study accounting. In 1909 he became the first salesman of Harkrider-Morrison, which targeted small grocery stores. The company received shipments of fresh fruits and vegetables from the West Coast and South Texas. The train cars in which the items were transported were iced repeatedly along the way. The mix was simple: lettuce, onions, potatoes, apples, citrus, and other fresh staples. Harkrider-Morrison also carried dried fruit, very popular at a time when refrigeration was an almost unheard-of luxury. Each day the young Keith visited his customers to take their daily produce orders, returned to the warehouse, loaded a wagon, and made his deliveries. Other times he might load up the wagon with whatever he thought he could sell on the spot and make his rounds. During this period of horse-and mule-drawn wagons, deliveries outside of Fort Worth were problematic, however, due to unpaved roads that would become muddy quagmires during the rainy season. Deliveries to stores in outlying towns were delivered the next day using Railway Express company. To improve the service to these communities, the company began opening branch houses. The first, Wichita Fruit and Vegetable Company, opened in Wichita Falls, Texas, in 1910. Two years later Merchant's Fruit Company was establish in Forth Worth, close to the downtown farmer's market. West Texas would be served by the 1914 opening of a branch in Abilene, Texas, the Abilene Fruit and Vegetable Company.

Ben Keith quickly made himself an important part of the business, and his contribution was recognized in 1911 when the company changed its name to Harkrider-Keith-Cooke Company. Keith became vice-president and treasurer, and then in 1918, he bought a controlling interest when two of the owners dropped out. He now became president and general manager, but kept the name of the firm, which did not become known as Ben E. Keith Company until 1931. After taking charge he continued to open new branches, in Dallas in 1920 and in Lubbock, Texas, in 1925.

During the mid-1920s Keith became involved in the gift business when the publisher of the Fort Worth *Star-Telegram*, Amon G. Carter, asked him if he could package and ship some

Texas grapefruit—the popular Texas Ruby Red—to some New York friends. The idea proved so popular that for the next couple of years Keith shipped more grapefruit gift packages on request. This led the company in 1929 to produce a crude gift catalog. It was just a mimeographed affair, but it served the purpose. Ruby Reds and other fruit were placed in baskets made in Mexico and shipped around the country. It was Carter who urged Keith to produce a professional catalog in the 1940s. Later in the decade the catalog added items such as smoked ham, turkey, and fruitcake. It grew by word of mouth and formed the basis of the Ben E. Keith Gift Division, which by 1990 had a mailing list of 100,000 names, specialized in gourmet specialty foods, and generated $2 million in annual sales. Nevertheless, the division was discontinued later in the 1990s.

Acquisition of Anheuser-Busch Distributorship in the 1920s

Another effort launched in the 1920s by Keith would prove to have a more lasting effect on the evolution of the company. At the time, the company experienced a lull in business during the summer months, since many people maintained their own gardens and supplied themselves with fruits and vegetables, and even sold some to the local stores. In 1928 Keith paid a personal visit to Adolphus Busch in St. Louis and secured the Texas distributorship for Anheuser-Busch products. Although the introduction of Prohibition several years earlier had put Busch out of the beer business temporarily, his company distributed other products, especially ice cream syrup, as well as soft drink flavorings and a near beer product with a negligible amount of alcohol. Anheuser-Busch also offered baker's yeast and malt syrup. Salesman made sure to warn about the danger of allowing the yeast to mix with the malt syrup and water: Customers would likely end up with the problem of disposal of a batch of beer. With the repeal of Prohibition in 1933, Anheuser-Busch returned to beer brewing, and Ben E. Keith was well positioned to take advantage of the situation. Not only did it have an Anheuser-Busch franchise, it had the refrigeration facility from its produce business that was needed to store unpasteurized draught beer, which had to be stored below 40 degrees Fahrenheit.

Ben E. Keith made advances on other fronts during the 1930s. It began using the advertising slogan, "Fresh from Keith's," which was painted on the side of its delivery trucks and featured on instore posters. The company also took some tentative steps in the foodservice area, but retail remained the key channel at a time when most people ate at home. During this period frozen food storage and delivery technology were becoming available, but with the advent of World War II, some equipment was commandeered for the war effort. When the war ended in 1945, however, Ben E. Keith was quick to invest in this new sector, becoming the first Birdseye distributor in Texas.

Ben Keith died in 1959, not only leaving behind a thriving business but also a legacy of personal accomplishments. He helped in the establishment of three Texas universities and was involved in the founding of three Fort-Worth area military bases during World War I and the Carswell Air Force Base during World War II. He helped to organize the first modern citrus plant in the Rio Grande Valley, and was a founder of the Fort Worth Chamber of Commerce and served as its president. He was also a pioneer in employee relations. In 1943 his became one of the first companies in America to offer a pension and profit-sharing plan to employees.

In the early 1960s Gaston Hallam acquired a large stake in the company and in 1962 became president and assumed the chairmanship five years later. Hallam was well familiar with the operation, having worked for the company for 40 years. He started out unloading boxcars, and after he learned bookkeeping he became bookkeeper in the Dallas office, then assistant manager of the Lubbock branch. After Prohibition ended he became involved in the beer side of the business and in 1939 took over as manager of the Dallas operation. When he took charge of the company, Ben E. Keith employed 400 and generated annual sales of $40 million. When Hallam retired in 1979, the company would have 1,200 employees and sales of $350 million. One of his major contributions was to expand Ben E. Keith both within and beyond the confines of Texas. In 1966 a Shreveport, Louisiana produce company was acquired, and two years later The Panhandle Fruit Co. of Amarillo was bought to form another branch office. Ben E. Keith moved into the Arkansas market in 1972 when it established a branch in Little Rock.

A new generation of management took over in 1979 when Hallam's sons, Robert and Howard, assumed the top positions. They grew up with the company, learning the business from the ground up during holidays and summer vacations when they loaded trucks and made sales calls, among other tasks. Unlike Ben Keith and their father, who scraped together an education, they both earned law degrees from the University of Texas. By the time they succeeded their father, they were seasoned executives. Robert Hallam launched a beer branch in 1967 and Howard opened a beer branch two years later in 1969.

Shift to Foodservice Emphasis in the 1980s

The Hallam brothers took control at a crossroads in the company's history. The food division produced about $80 million in 1979, of which $35 million came from foodservice. According to *Institutional Distribution,* "It had become apparent that the game was changing. A number of major supermarket chains that had been purchasing produce from Keith put up their own refrigerated warehouses and began to source their own produce and distribute it to their stores. Obviously, opportunity for future growth at retail was limited. . . . The die was cast in 1980 when Piggly Wiggly, Keith Foods' biggest customer, announced that it was going into self-distribution." Keith Foods now directed its focus toward foodservice and in 1981 announced that it would significantly broaden its offerings beyond produce, which accounted for 75 percent of volume, in order to become a full-line foodservice house. The company's reputation in produce helped to open doors, and the service inherent in the business—daily deliveries and the development of close relationships with customers—was added to a broad-

Key Dates:

1906: The company is founded as Harkrider-Morrison Company.
1909: Ben E. Keith is named as the company's first salesman.
1918: Keith acquires a controlling interest in the company.
1931: The Ben E. Keith Company name is adopted.
1933: A beer distribution business is launched.
1959: Keith dies.
1962: Gaston Hallam is named president.
1979: Hallam retires and his sons, Robert and Howard, take charge.
1981: The company begins to focus more fully on foodservice, broadening its offerings beyond produce.
1993: The Denton beer distribution facility is expanded.
2003: Major expansion on Amarillo and Oklahoma City foodservice facilities is begun.

line approach to create an effective combination in winning accounts. Although deliveries were not made six days a week as had been the case with produce, Ben E. Keith still made deliveries far more often than the competition.

The company was also deliberate about how it expanded into foodservice, initially targeting white tablecloth restaurants, many of which were already buying produce from the company and were the type of customers that appreciated the extra service. From there Ben E. Keith targeted hospitals, schools, and other institutions. It also increased its business through strategic acquisitions, including small foodservice distributors in Little Rock and Oklahoma City, thereby extending its reach into markets in northern Texas, Oklahoma, Louisiana, Arkansas, and eastern parts of New Mexico.

Three years after making the switch to full-line foodservice, Ben E. Keith had to contend with inventory problems with small quantity items, which often led to short supplies. To address this problem the company created a redistribution system out of Fort Worth, called Keith Central Distribution (KCD). In 1984 KCD set up operations in an 18,000-square-foot warehouse. Not only would it provide low-volume items to branches, it would also ship high-volume items to fill out loads if they could be delivered cheaper than regular shipments. The program proved effective, and a large number of items were added and the warehouse space expanded to meet increasing demand.

By the start of the 1990s Ben E. Keith Food's sales reached $211 million, more than double the total sales volume when the shift to full-line foodservice began a decade earlier. The business continued to grow in the 1990s and facilities were expanded to keep up. Ben E. Keith Beer also kept pace. In July 1993 it began expanding its Denton warehouse. By now sales

had reached $50 million and the division was servicing 46 Texas counties. It ranked 37th on *Beverage World's* list of the Top 50 Beverage companies.

In the late 1990s Ben E. Keith Foods enjoyed a major growth spurt, as sales increased 50 percent over a five-year period. To keep apace with demand, the company in 2003 began to build a $20 million warehouse in Amarillo, expanding the current operation from 61,000 square feet to about 250,000 square feet. Moreover, the new site could later be expanded to 450,000 square feet. The company also began work on a 285,000-square-foot facility in Oklahoma City. Enough land was purchased to allow the operation to eventually house 800,000 square feet.

As Ben E. Keith approached its 100 anniversary, the beer division had spread to 60 Texas counties and the food division continued to expand its geographic reach. They combined to generate sales of $1.5 billion in 2004, a 12.4 percent increase over the previous year. The food unit, accounting for about $1 billion of that amount, had long since surpassed the beer business as the driving force behind the company. There was every reason to expect that Ben E. Keith would continue to enjoy strong growth for some time to come.

Principal Subsidiaries

Ben E. Keith Beer; Ben E. Keith Corporate; Ben E. Keith Food.

Principal Competitors

The Gambrinus Company; McLane Foodservice, Inc.; SYSCO Corporation; U.S. Foodservice, Inc.

Further Reading

Albright, Max, "Amarillo, Texas-Based Food Distribution Firm Sees Sales Increase," *Amarillo Globe-News,* December 2, 2003.

"Ben E. Keith Co., New Niche for Former Specialist," *Institutional Distribution,* October 1984, p. 88.

"Ben E. Keith's 10-Year Rise to Greatness," *Institutional Distribution,* August 1989, p. 59.

"Building on the Fruits of Success," *Institutional Distribution,* August 1989, p. 154.

"From Grapefruit to Texas Champagne," *Institutional Distribution,* August 1989, p. 208.

Sfiligoj, Eric, "Ben E. Keith Expansion Evidence of Big Beer Business in Texas," *Beverage World,* September 30, 1993, p. 6.

"A Sleeping Giant Stirs—The Rest Is History," *Institutional Distribution,* August 1989, p. 66.

"Turning Slow Movers into Profit Builders," *Institutional Distribution,* August 1989, p. 174.

Wiley, Elizabeth Camacho, "Ben E. Keith Foods to Build New Distribution Warehouse in Oklahoma City," *Daily Oklahoman,* November 4, 2003.

—Ed Dinger

Benesse

Benesse Corporation

3-7-17 Minamigata
Okayama
Japan
Telephone: +81 086 225 1100
Fax: +81 086 227 6112
Web site: http://www.benesse.co.jp

Public Company
Incorporated: 1955 as Fukutake Publishing Co. Ltd.
Employees: 8,081
Sales: $2.73 billion (2004)
Stock Exchanges: Osaka Tokyo
Ticker Symbol: 9783
NAIC: 611699 All Other Miscellaneous Schools and
    Instruction; 511130 Book Publishers; 541990 All
    Other Professional, Scientific and Technical Services;
    611513 Apprenticeship Training

Benesse Corporation is Japan's leading provider of private educational support services, senior care services, translation and interpretation services, and, through subsidiary Berlitz International, the world's largest provider of foreign language instruction. Education support remains the group's largest area of operation, accounting for approximately two-thirds of the group's annual sales. Benesse provides correspondence and in-class course programs for all ages—starting at six months old and extending through high school and university entrance exam preparations. The company is also Japan's leading provider of translation and interpretation services, through subsidiary Simul International. Benesse also provides call center services through Telemarketing Japan, Inc. The company's control of Berlitz International gives it operations in more than 50 countries worldwide; in the mid-2000s, Benesse has been focusing Berlitz's expansion on Asia and Europe. Japan's declining birth rate, coupled with the rise in the proportion of senior citizens in the country has prompted Benesse to develop a new line of business, providing senior citizen care services, through subsidiary Benesse Style Care Co. The company operates more than 90 senior care facilities in Japan. Listed on the Osaka and

Tokyo Stock Exchanges, Benesse Corporation posted sales of $2.73 billion in 2004. Soichiro Fukutake, son of the company's founder, serves as chairman of the board. Masayoshi Morimoto is Benesse Corporation's CEO.

Correspondence Origins in the 1950

Tetsuhiko Fukutake began his professional career as a schoolteacher, before launching his own printing business in the early 1950s. When that company failed, however, Fukutake was forced to find a new career. By then, the Japanese economy had begun its entry into an extended boom that saw the country emerge as the world's second largest industrial and financial market. A major factor in the national effort to achieve technological and industrial superiority was the high level of commitment to education. Fukutake recognized an opportunity for combining his former career as a teacher and his experience in printing and in 1955 founded his own publishing company, Fukutake Shoten, in Okayama.

Fukutake launched its first series of educational books and other study materials that year, targeting especially the junior high school segment. By the early 1960s, the company had extended its range to include the nation's high school students as well. The company enjoyed strong success with the launch of its Kansai Simulated Exams in 1962. The company later rolled out that service on a national scale in 1973, changing the program's name to Shinken Simulated Exams.

Fukutake efforts were buoyed by the steadily intensifying competition among Japanese students for the relatively few university openings, especially among the country's top universities. Educational support services soon came under demand, presenting Fukutake with new expansion opportunities. The company developed its own correspondence course programs. The first of these was launched in 1969, geared toward the high school student market. In 1972, the company added a program targeting the junior high market as well. The following year, both were rebranded, as Shinkenzemi.

Pressure on Japanese students continued to build through the 1970s. The competition among students soon extended into the elementary school level, as a population boom made future university spots rarer still. Fukutake responded to this development by launching an extension of the Shinkenzemi program, with courses designed specifically for elementary school children, in 1980.

The company responded to the youth market in other ways. In 1977, Fukutake established a new publishing division and began publishing a variety of support materials for the junior high and senior high markets. The company's extension into the elementary school segment also led the publishing division to develop specific products for that market, including the 1985 launch of a new series of dictionaries, with a Japanese dictionary and a Kanji-character dictionary specifically for the elementary grades. Tetsuhiko Fukutake died in 1986, and son Soichiro took over as the company's head.

By the late 1980s, the pressure on Japanese children to perform had become so intense that Fukutake was able to extend its Shinkenzemi concept to the preschool segment. The company continued to develop the concept, launching a new course for toddlers aged two to three in 1994. By the mid-2000s, the company had extended the Shinkenzemi program to include children as young as six months old.

New Corporate Identity in the 1990s

Japan's changing demographics, however, had by then forced the company to redefine itself. By the late 1980s, it had become clear that the country's birthrate had entered a period of serious decline; at the same time, the population in general was growing older, as people now lived longer than ever before. The drop in birthrate represented a clear challenge to Fukutake's core youth market.

In 1990, therefore, the company adopted a new philosophy, called "Benesse"—derived from the Latin "bene" and "esse," or "living well." The company now set out to expand its range of operations into other age segments, extending its educational services from a focus on scholastic achievement to a wider target of lifestyle enhancement. The change in philosophy led to a change in the company's name, to Benesse Corporation, in 1995. In that year, as well, Benesse went public, listing its shares on the Osaka and Hiroshima Stock Exchanges.

By then, Benesse had begun putting its new corporate identity into action. Language instruction and interpretation services appeared to be a natural market for the group's extension. In 1990, the company purchased a 20 percent stake in the Japanese branch of the United States' Berlitz International. That company, founded in Rhode Island in 1878, had grown to become the world's leading language education group, targeting especially the U.S. and European markets. By the late 1980s, Berlitz had come under the control of Maxwell Communications, which launched Berlitz as a public company in 1989.

The death of Robert Maxwell and the collapse of Maxwell Communications in 1991 provided Fukutake the opportunity to take control of Berlitz International itself. By 1993, Fukutake had acquired fully two-thirds of Berlitz's stock. The company then began reorienting Berlitz's focus, targeting the high-growth Asian region, where the learning of foreign languages in general, and English in particular, was experiencing a boom in demand.

Meanwhile, the company had begun to explore other areas of expansion. Magazine publishing became a natural extension of the group's publishing operations and led to the launch of titles such as Tamago Club and Hiyoko Club in 1993. The company, which had traditionally provided correspondence courses, now began investing in a new range of on-site operations. In 1994, for example, the company opened its first day-care center, called La Petite Academy, and later rebranded as Benesse Childcare Center.

The company also began investing in on-site career training, targeting specifically the growing demand for in-home nursing services (known as home helpers). In 1995, the company launched its first Home Helper training course. In that year, as well, Benesse began offering its own Home Help services program.

This led the company to extend its operations once again, into the management of senior care facilities. The first of these, Benesse Home Clara, opened in Okayama in 1997. The Clara chain grew into a national network of facilities, with more than 30 in operation by the mid-2000s. Benesse began developing other senior care facility brands, targeting different segments and price points, including the Madoka and Granny & Granda formats. In 2003, the company added a fourth brand, Aria, which featured on-site medical care as well as its own nursing capacity. In addition, in 2000, the company extended its senior services with the launch of nursing care subsidiary Benesse Care Corporation. In that year, too, Benesse added its listing to the Tokyo Stock Exchange.

Shifting Focus in the New Century

By the early 2000s, the company's educational services wing, while still the largest part of the group's operations, accounting for some two-thirds of the company's sales, appeared to have peaked. Although the division's revenues had continued to climb through the 1990s, into the mid-2000s, the division began to decline. Demographics played a dual role in the shift in the group's core market. The declining birthrate in Japan also meant that competition for entry into the country's universities was not nearly as fierce as before. Indeed, by 2009, all students wishing to enter university were expected to be assured of a place. As a result, children's motivation to study had begun to decline, which in turn placed pressure on Benesse's revenues.

Benesse continued, therefore, in its effort to diversify its base of operations. The company made a number of strategic acquisitions, such as its 1998 purchase of Simul International

---

Key Dates:

1955: Tetsuhiko Fukutake, a former schoolteacher and printer, launches Fukutake Shoten in order to publish educational materials for junior high school students.

1962: Fukutake begins publishing Kansai Simulated Exams, for high school students.

1969: The company launches the first correspondence courses for high school students.

1973: The correspondence products are rebranded as Shinkenzemi.

1977: The new Publishing Division is launched.

1980: The company extends the Shinkenzemi format to the elementary school market.

1986: Tetsuhiko Fukutake dies and his son Soichiro Fukutake takes over as head of the company.

1988: The Shinkenzemi format is extended to the preschool market.

1990: Declining demographics in Japan lead to the launch of the new "Benesse" (Living Well) corporate philosophy, repositioning the company as a provider of services to a wider array of markets.

1993: The company acquires two-thirds control of Berlitz International.

1994: The Shinkenzemi format is extended to the toddler (two- to three-year-old) market.

1995: The company changes its name to Benesse Corporation and goes public; the first Benesse child-care center is launched; "home-helper" training program and services are launched.

1997: The company opens its first senior care facility, Benesse Home Clara, in Okayama.

2000: The company lists stock on the Tokyo Stock Exchange; the new subsidiary Benesse Care Corporation is launched.

2001: The company acquires 100 percent control of Berlitz International.

Inc., the leading provider of translation and interpreter services in Japan. That company had been founded in 1965 and had first captured the attention of the national market when it provided live televised interpreter services for the 1969 Apollo 11 moonwalk. Following its acquisition by Benesse, Simul began its own diversification drive. In 2000, for example, Simul began offering temporary job placement services. This was followed by the launch of permanent job placement services in 2001. Simul also opened its own training academies, including a new school opened in Yokohama in 2004.

Benesse acquired 100 percent control of Berlitz International in 2001. Following that purchase, Berlitz stepped up its effort to shift its focus of operations from the United States and Japan to more dynamic markets, including Europe and, especially, Asia.

With the approach of the middle 2000s, Benesse began to develop an interest in expanding its own operations into the international market. As such, the company launched a subsidiary in Hong Kong in 2004. The new operation began sourcing products, including toys, tools, and other supplements for use in Benesse's Japanese operations. Yet a major purpose of the new subsidiary was to begin preparations for a later entry by Benesse into the Chinese educational support market. Similarly, Benesse established a subsidiary in South Korea in 2004, as well. Benesse hoped to reproduce its success in Japan on an international scale for the new century.

Principal Subsidiaries

AVIVA Co., Ltd.; Benesse Hong Kong Co., Ltd.; Benesse Korea Co.; Benesse Style Care Co., Ltd.; Berlitz International; Berlitz Japan Ltd.; Learn Co. Ltd.; Shinken-AD Co., Ltd.; Telemarketing Japan, Inc.

Principal Competitors

Kumon Institute of Education Company Ltd.; Eikoh Inc.; Ichishin Company Ltd.; Nagase Brothers Inc.; WAO Corporation; Jeugia Corporation; Wish Us Corporation; Shuei Yobiko Company Ltd.

Further Reading

"Benesse, Sega Toys to Sell LeapFrog Product," *Jiji,* January 21, 2002.

"Benesse to Enter Cram School Business," *Japan Weekly Monitor,* August 12, 2002.

Cropper, Carol M., "Declining Fortunes," *Forbes,* February 14, 1993, p. 14.

"Japan's Benesse Opens Regional Office in HK," *Asian Economic News,* February 17, 2004.

"Japan Correspondence-Education Provider Benesse Ties Up Chinese Firm," *Knight Ridder/Tribune Business News,* April 22, 2004.

—M.L. Cohen

Benihana, Inc.

8685 N.W. 53rd Terrace
Miami, Florida 33166
U.S.A.
Telephone: (305) 593-0770
Fax: (305) 592-6371
Web site: http://www.benihana.com

Public Company
Incorporated: 1964 as Benihana of Tokyo
Employees: 4,091
Sales: $216.8 million (2005)
Stock Exchanges: NASDAQ
Ticker Symbol: BNHN
NAIC: 722110 Full-Service Restaurants

Benihana, Inc., operates as one of the largest chains of Asian restaurants in the United States. Benihana restaurants specialize in an exhibition-style of Japanese cooking called teppanyaki. Customers sit around a communal table at which a Benihana chef slices their seafood, steak, chicken, and vegetables with lightning speed, grills their meal right in front of them, and then tosses it accurately onto their plates. The company operates 56 Benihana locations, has 22 franchised Benihana locations in 12 different countries, and also runs six Haru restaurants in New York City, eight RA Sushi restaurants, and one Doraku restaurant in Miami, Florida. Benihana of Tokyo, a private company owned by founder Rocky Aoki and his family, owns approximately half of all shareholder votes in Benihana.

Early History from Tokyo to New York

The founder of Benihana, Inc., was a 25-year-old Olympic wrestler from Japan named Hiroaki Rocky Aoki. He got his start in the restaurant business by working after school in his family's coffee shop in downtown Tokyo. His mother named the family business Benihana after a red flower that survived the bombing of Tokyo during World War II. Rocky was a scrapper, defending himself in the streets and schoolyards against bigger boys. He got hooked on wrestling, became a national university champion, and earned a place on the 1960 Olympic team. Although he did not compete because he was over his weight

limit, he did fall in love with New York when the plane stopped there on the way to the Games in Rome. That fall he left Japan for the United States.

In 1964, Aoki graduated from New York Community College's School of Hotel and Restaurant Management. During the summer he earned money driving the only ice cream truck in Harlem. The job was not easy, as he explained in an article in *Management Review*. "Every time I robbed, I get up earlier the next day and work later to make up. Every time I lose money, I get more challenge." With that philosophy, he managed to save $10,000 during the summer, which, along with a loan, was enough to start his first restaurant, Benihana of Tokyo.

Aoki's concept for his new restaurant, derived from specialty restaurants he knew of in Japan, was part entertainment and part foodservice. He wanted to offer Americans food with which they were familiar, such as chicken, steak, and shrimp, prepared in a novel setting. He chose the teppanyaki table—a stainless steel grill surrounded by a wooden eating surface—where customers could watch a knife-wielding, joke-telling chef prepare and serve their food. His parents and brothers came from Japan to help him get started.

Unfortunately, New Yorkers equated Japanese food with raw fish and were not comfortable sitting at a table with strangers. They ignored the midtown Manhattan eatery until the restaurant critic of the *New York Herald Tribune* gave it a glowing review.

Suddenly, everyone in New York, including the Beatles and Muhammad Ali, wanted to sit around one of Benihana of Tokyo's four teppanyaki tables. Within six months after the review the restaurant had paid for itself, and Aoki quickly opened another restaurant in a larger, fancier building. The new location provided the same teppanyaki-style cooking but was decorated with valuable art, Samurai armor, heavy wooden ceiling beams brought from Japan by Aoki's father, and sliding Shoji screens to provide some privacy.

1965–80: Building a Company

The Benihana concept combined reasonable prices with good food and, by preparing what was eaten right at the table, held waste to a minimum. Profits were good, and, in 1968, Aoki opened his first Benihana of Tokyo outside New York City—in downtown Chicago. That location made $700,000 in its first year and continued to be one of the company's top-earning outlets.

Between 1969 and 1972, the company opened six more of its own restaurants and licensed franchisees to open another ten. In a joint venture with the Las Vegas Hilton, the company developed Benihana Village, a 38,000-square-foot complex of restaurants, bars, and other entertainment venues. In 1972, the company grossed $12 million and the Harvard Business School selected Benihana of Tokyo as a case study of an entrepreneurial success story.

With business going so well, Rocky Aoki could devote time to his other interests, which included racing balloons and powerboats, collecting items ranging from vintage cars to slot machines, and learning backgammon. "Rocky wanted to play," Joel Schwartz, the company's president, explained in a 1989 *Forbes* article. To help oversee the chain's operations and expansion, Aoki brought in a management company, Hardwicke Cos., as a partner in 1976. The relationship lasted only four years and, in 1980, Aoki ended the partnership, paying $3.7 million to break the contract. As Rod Willis of *Management Review* explained in a 1986 article, "He [Aoki] felt the company's management style clashed with his predominately Oriental workforce, and he wanted to maintain control over each restaurant's quality." The following year Aoki settled, without admitting any guilt, a Securities and Exchange Commission charge that he had improperly traded in Hardwicke stock while serving as vice-president of Hardwicke.

The 1980s: Ups and Downs

To help pay off the debt incurred in the split with Hardwicke, Aoki decided to take part of the company public. He accomplished this by having Benihana of Tokyo (BOT) form Benihana National Corporation (BNC) in 1982 and then taking the latter company public the following year. Investors paid the Miami-based BNC $11 for a unit consisting of two common shares and a warrant to buy another at $6. With the $5.5 million raised by selling half a million of these units, BNC bought 11 restaurants from Aoki in exchange for 60 percent of the BNC common stock and $2.5 million to pay BOT's debt. Later in the year, BNC bought another three restaurants from BOT for $7 million.

In spite of the new corporate structure, Benihana of Tokyo and Benihana National Corporation remained under the management of the same group of executives. As corporate president, Joel Schwartz continued to oversee the day-to-day operation of both companies. Aoki, who served as chairman of both entities, retained 51 percent of the common stock in BNC and kept about 30 restaurants in the privately held BOT. Aoki developed new concepts for the Benihana food chain but he also continued to play hard, becoming a championship-level backgammon player and setting a world record in off-shore powerboat racing. The Double Eagle V, a 400,000-cubic-foot gas balloon, displayed the Benihana logo as it became the first crewed balloon to successfully cross the Pacific Ocean, with Aoki as one of the crew members.

One of Aoki's new concepts was Benihana National Classics, a line of Chinese gourmet frozen foods, introduced in 1984 and sold in supermarkets. Chinese cuisine was chosen when the company found that Japanese food did not freeze well. Within a year the Classics were the best-selling Oriental frozen foods in the United States, with sales in one quarter alone reaching more than $40 million and profits climbing to more than $4 million. The company's stock took off, going as high as $21.50 in 1985. In December of that year, *Restaurant and Institution* magazine named Benihana of Tokyo the most popular family-style restaurant in America. At that time, Benihana of Tokyo and Benihana National together operated or franchised restaurants in 60 locations, from Seattle to New Jersey, serving a total of 25,000 customers a day.

Benihana National's frozen food success quickly attracted the attention of major food companies. When Campbell Soup and Stouffer's began offering their own lines of Oriental frozen foods, however, Benihana could not compete. The company lost $11 million on frozen foods between 1985 and 1987 and finally sold the business, for $4.5 million, to the small company that had been producing the dinners for them.

Frozen food, however, was not Aoki's only new idea. In 1985, Benihana National opened its first seafood restaurant, The Big Splash, just north of Miami. Aoki believed the sea would be the primary supplier of food in the future, and, borrowing an idea from a Malaysian fish market, came up with the concept of a seafood marketplace/restaurant. Customers could choose from hundreds of varieties of fresh seafood, decide how they wanted it cooked, and watch it being prepared. The idea was so popular initially that a second Big Splash was opened. The seafood restaurants soon experienced difficulty, however, registering losses of $2.7 million during 1987. The wide variety of options ran completely counter to the tight focus and minimal waste of the Benihana steakhouses. At the Miami location, the majority of customers were retirees who resented the high prices and preferred to eat fish with which they were familiar. "All we sold was salmon and red snapper," Aoki told Eric Schmukler in a March 1989 *Forbes* article. The company closed its Big Splash outlets in March 1988. The 1988 fiscal year was a hard one for Benihana, as the company recorded a loss of nearly $7 million.

Despite the company's financial problems with Classics and Big Splash, the Benihana restaurants themselves were still popular. By the end of fiscal 1989, the publicly owned Benihana National Corp. reported profits of some $1.8 million on sales of

Key Dates:

1964: The first Benihana of Tokyo restaurant opens.
1968: Benihana enters the Chicago market.
1982: Benihana of Tokyo (BOT) forms Benihana National Corporation (BNC).
1983: BNC goes public.
1984: Benihana National Classics, a line of Chinese gourmet frozen foods, is introduced in supermarkets.
1994: The company enters into a licensing agreement with Campbell Soup to launch a line of frozen stir-fry kits featuring the Benihana trademark.
1995: BNC buys Aoki's 21 Benihana of Tokyo restaurants on the U.S. mainland and the U.S. rights to the Benihana trademark; Benihana, Inc., is created as part of the corporate restructuring.
1997: Nine teppanyaki restaurants are acquired from Rudy's Restaurant Group Inc.
1999: The company purchases the Haru Sushi restaurants.
2002: Benihana adds the RA Sushi Bar and Restaurant chain to its holdings.

$34 million at its 20 restaurants, with Aoki's privately held Benihana of Tokyo taking in similar revenues.

1990–94: Making a Turnaround

Rocky Aoki kicked off the new decade by opening a gallery in one of the Miami Benihana restaurants to display a portion of what was becoming known in the art world as the Rocky Aoki Collection. Having spent more than a year consolidating his diverse collections, Aoki told *Antiques & Collecting*, "I think it's a natural to have a gallery here. More than 90,000 people eat in this restaurant every year; why not provide them with something beautiful to look at, not to mention buy, if they so desire." In a 300-square-foot space that had been the restaurant's gift shop, diners could view etchings by Icarts, lamps by Tiffany and Handel, and bronzes by Remington.

The publicity about Aoki's collection helped generate business for the restaurant, and overall company revenues continued to grow. Profits, however, were less than a million dollars a year, and BNC stock fell below $1 a share. Angry at the situation, some shareholders sued. As Marilyn Alva reported in a 1992 *Restaurant Business* article, the shareholders claimed Aoki and his management team were in a conflict of interest by managing the two companies. The complainants further maintained that Benihana management had misappropriated the assets of Benihana National Corporation, passing them through Benihana of Tokyo for their personal benefit. The shareholders, however, were ultimately unsuccessful in trying to take control of the company away from Aoki.

Meanwhile, Benihana management took advantage of a health-conscious American public's growing interest in Japanese food and entertainment. With the tag line, "We have been the restaurant of the '90s since the '60s," Aoki and Schwartz instituted a major advertising campaign stressing the fact that Benihana had always offered healthful food. Soon afterward, in 1993, the Atlanta Benihana of Tokyo restaurant added an 18-seat sushi

bar and 35-seat Karaoke dining room to draw more customers on weekday nights. Despite the higher labor and food costs associated with sushi, the company reported an increase in beverage sales, and a lot of sampling of the $.99 sushi pieces by people waiting to eat at the traditional teppanyaki tables.

Learning from its experience a decade earlier, in 1994 Benihana National Corp. decided to get into the frozen food business again. This time, however, by entering into a licensing agreement with Campbell Soup Co., the company hooked up with a major marketer rather than trying to compete with the big names. The new product was a line of frozen stir-fry kits featuring the Benihana trademark. The dinners served six people and sold for about $8.00. As Peter McMullin, an analyst with Southeast Research Partners, told *Florida Review.Net,* "This time the strategy makes sense because it is linking with a high profile food company to help strengthen the distribution side and offsetting the razor-thin margins of retail by manufacturing with a low cost producer like Campbell." By the end of the fiscal year, revenues were more than $70 million, with profits up 41 percent to $2.4 million.

1995: A New Company

At the beginning of 1995, Benihana National announced that it would buy Aoki's 21 Benihana of Tokyo restaurants on the U.S. mainland, along with the U.S. rights to the Benihana trademark, for about $6.15 million. On May 16, a newly created subsidiary, Benihana, Inc., acquired the BOT restaurants and, through a merger, simultaneously acquired Benihana National. BNC shareholders received one share in the new holding company for each of their shares of Benihana National. Aoki continued to serve as chairman of the new company, with Schwartz as president.

Benihana, Inc. now owned or licensed the 43 Benihana restaurants in the continental United States along with a franchise in Honolulu. It also had the rights to develop or license Benihana restaurants in Central and South America and the Caribbean Islands. Aoki kept private his Benihana of Tokyo restaurants in Hawaii, Britain, and Thailand.

During 1995, the new company took several steps to attract more customers. Benihana introduced weekend luncheon service and, following the success in Atlanta, opened sushi bars in seven locations. The company also instituted a national Karaoke contest for its patrons. In the fall, the company opened its first smaller format unit, called the Benihana Grill, in Sacramento. At 3,800 square feet, the Grill format was less than half the size of the traditional Benihana, and enabled the company to open units in smaller locations, particularly in urban areas. Schwartz had been refining this format since 1989 as an alternative to the company's more common free-standing, special use restaurant buildings. The Benihana Grill was designed to accommodate ten to 12 teppanyaki tables, compared with the 18 tables in the typical Benihana. Analyst Peter McMullin remarked, "Initial indications are encouraging even before the grand opening. With the lower capital costs of approximately $500,000 versus a stand-alone restaurant cost of $2 million, this could become an enormous growth vehicle for Benihana."

The new hours and offerings helped increase guest counts in existing restaurants by 8.7 percent and same-store sales by an average of 7.7 percent for fiscal 1996. This rise, plus the addition of the Benihana of Tokyo restaurants and the new Benihana Grill, resulted in annual revenues of more than $81 million.

Benihana's growth came primarily from increased traffic in its existing restaurants, and the company continued to support that strategy. Early in 1996, in an effort to gain a larger share of the ethnic market, the company launched Spanish-language television advertisements in Miami and Los Angeles. In May, Benihana kicked off a two-year, $5 million ad campaign, focusing on the entertainment value of teppanyaki cooking. "We want to bring the Benihana name to a different audience," company president Joel Schwartz told *Nation's Restaurant News* in a May 6, 1996 article. "The ads show that Benihana is a place the entire family can come to and have a good time—a place they will see the chef perform and flip shrimp." Individual restaurants also developed innovative marketing techniques. A visit and meal at the Benihana in Bethesda, Maryland, for example, is one of the activities in the county's social studies curriculum for third graders learning about Japan.

The company did not depend entirely on its existing restaurants for growth. During 1996, it also signed leases for several more Benihana Grills and expanded its franchise operations, including restaurants in Bogota, Columbia, and Aruba, Netherlands Antilles. Benihana's track record of steady growth in same-store sales, rising customer count, and profitability appeared to be continuing into the late 1990s as revenues for the first half of fiscal 1997 were up more than 8 percent from the year before.

Focusing on Growth: Late 1990s and Beyond

Benihana entered the late 1990s focused on additional growth. In 1997, it acquired nine teppanyaki locations from Rudy's Restaurant Group Inc. The $20 million deal included six Samurai and three Kyoto Steak and Seafood restaurants, and eased Benihana's entrance to the Washington, D.C., Michigan, and Minneapolis, Minnesota, markets. The company also opened its first Sushi Doraku restaurant in Fort Lauderdale, Florida. That location was eventually closed in 2002 while one remained in operation in Miami, Florida. In 1999, the company purchased an 80 percent stake in Haru Holding Corporation, an operator of two sushi restaurants in New York City with a third location under construction.

In the midst of its expansion efforts, Benihana was dealt a blow in 1998 when founder Aoki resigned as chairman and CEO after being indicted for insider trading. In August 1999, Aoki pleaded guilty to four criminal counts of insider trading related to his purchases of Spectrum Information Technologies Inc. stock in 1993. Aoki was fined $500,000, received three months probation, and was barred from ever serving on the board of a public company; Aoki has remained a consultant to Benihana since leaving his post in 1998.

Despite the management shakeup, Benihana continued to forge ahead with Joel Schwartz at the helm as president and CEO. Schwartz commented on the scandal in a 1999 *Forbes* article claiming, "I thought it was a sad, unfortunate event, but it had nothing to do with the company." Shareholders and business analysts agreed with Schwartz's assessment and the company moved forward with little interruption to daily operations. As such, Benihana entered the new millennium on solid ground. New locations continued to open and in 2002, Benihana added the RA Sushi Bar and Restaurant chain to its holdings.

During the early years of the new millennium revenues increased, rising from $163.2 million in fiscal 2001 to $218.3 million in fiscal 2005. Net income fluctuated, falling in 2002, rising in 2003, and then falling off again over the next two years. Net income was $7.8 million in 2005—its lowest point since 2001. During that fiscal year, the company opened one teppanyaki, one Haru, and one RA Sushi restaurant. The company remained focused on growth and anticipated further expansion. It also launched a redesign of its teppanyaki restaurants. Locations in California and New York were refurbished with the new look and Benihana's new location in Miramar, Florida, was the first restaurant to incorporate the new design during the building process. Management was optimistic as it looked toward the future and believed Benihana was well positioned for success in the competitive restaurant industry.

Principal Competitors

Brinker International Inc.; Carlson Restaurants Worldwide Inc.; P.F. Changs China Bistro Inc.

Further Reading

Alva, Marilyn, "Very Rocky Business: Aoki Besieged by Shareholder Suits," *Restaurant Business,* February 10, 1992.

"Benihana Buying Founder Aoki's Units," *Nation's Restaurant News,* January 16, 1995, p. 14.

"Benihana Profits Rise 67% for First Nine Months of Fiscal '95," *Nation's Restaurant News,* February 12, 1996, p. 12.

"Benihana Testing Stir-Fry Kits," *Supermarket News,* October 17, 1994, p. 28.

Card, Keith A., "The Rocky Aoki Collection," *Antiques & Collecting,* November 1990, p. 36.

Hamstra, Mark, "Benihana Seeks to Expand Teppanyaki Empire With Rudy's Buy," *Nation's Restaurant News,* August 4, 1997.

Hayes, Jack, "Sushi Bar, Karaoke Boost Benihana's Midweek Traffic," *Nation's Restaurant News,* March 15, 1993, p. 50.

Kroll, Luisa, "Business As Usual," *Forbes,* November 1, 1999.

Lockyer, Sarah E., "Benihana Cooks Up Brand Refocus Plan," *Nation's Restaurant News,* February 16, 2004.

"More Ticker Tape: Benihana National Corp.," *Nation's Restaurant News,* May 29, 1995, p. 12.

"Operators Up Ante for Hispanic Markets," *Nation's Restaurant News,* January 29, 1996, p. 18.

Papiernik, Richard L., "Benihana Reports Profits Up 17% in First Quarter," *Nation's Restaurant News,* August 26, 1996, p. 12.

Peters, James, "Benihana Sees Raw Growth Potential in Recently Acquired Sushi Concept," *Nation's Restaurant News,* June 2, 2003.

Russo, Catherine, "Benihana Recovers from Frozen Foods," *Florida Review.Net,* November 17, 1995.

Schmukler, Eric, "Rocky's Road," *Forbes,* March 20, 1989, p. 80.

Schroeder, Michael, "Aoki Admits Insider Trading in Spectrum Case," *Asian Wall Street Journal,* August 25, 1999.

"Shareholders OK Reorganization Plan for Benihana Corp.," *Nation's Restaurant News,* May 15, 1995, p. 2.

Willis, Rod, "Rocky Aoki: Samurai Restaurateur," *Management Review,* May 1986, p. 17.

Zuber, Amy, "Benihana's New Ad Campaign: A Slice of Theater," *Nation's Restaurant News,* May 6, 1996, p. 16.

—Ellen D. Wernick
—update: Christina M. Stansell

Bianchi International (d/b/a Gregory Mountain Products)

27969 Jefferson Avenue
Temecula, California 92590-2609
U.S.A.
Telephone: (951) 676-5621
Toll Free: (800) 477-3420
Fax: (951) 676-6777
Web site: http://www.bianchi-intl.com;
          http://www.gregorypacks.com

Wholly Owned Subsidiary of Armor Holdings Inc.
Incorporated: 1968 as Bianchi Holster Company, Inc.
Employees: 280
Sales: $36 million (2004)
NAIC: 314911 Textile Bag Mills; 315999 Other Apparel
    Accessories and Other Apparel Manufacturing;
    316999 All Other Leather Good Manufacturing

Bianchi International, which trades under its own name and that of Gregory Mountain Products, produces an array of backpacks, holsters, and accessories for a range of markets. Bianchi began as a maker of leather holsters for police use. It developed an expertise in ballistic nylon, which it used to win business from the military as well as from sportsmen and shooting enthusiasts. Gregory Mountain Products, a legendary brand of internal frame backpacks known for their fit and durability, was acquired in 1983. Bianchi has a 70,000-square-foot facility in Temecula and another 40,000-square-foot plant in Imperial Valley, located in the midst of southern California's climbing haven. As part of Bianchi, Gregory has ventured into designing customized packs for elite military units, while remaining one of civilian backpacking's most respected brands.

Origins

Wayne Gregory began making backpacks at an early age, 14, when he was a Boy Scout eager to improve on heavy canvas rucksacks. An early head injury had kept him out of most sports, according to a profile in the scouting magazine *Boys' Life,* but he had become a hiking devotee. He also learned how to operate a sewing machine, learning what would be for him a lifelong craft of repairing and making outdoor gear.

Gregory soon became one of the first employees of the Adventure 16 camping equipment factory in San Diego, California, whose owner, Andy Drollinger, was something of a mentor to Gregory. According to *Boys' Life,* Gregory also sought advice from Dick Kelty, whose company was known for high-end performance backpacks.

An early venture, Sunbird, was launched by Gregory in 1970 to produce external-frame backpacks. This was shut down within three years, however, as Gregory grew disillusioned with the technology. External frames could support weight, but only at the cost of flexibility—a serious liability in rock and mountain climbing.

Gregory then did freelance designing for several companies in the emerging outdoor industry, including Alpenlite, Gerry Outdoors, Frostline Kits, and Snow Lion. Gregory also ran a backpacking store and in 1977 began making backpacks for sale in the back room. This time around, he focused on internal frame designs and soft packs. He developed the Gregory Active Suspension System, which allowed packs to support more weight while retaining their flexibility and comfort.

Gregory packs became highly sought after. Among the most expensive on the market, they were considered well worth the cost by the climbers who took them as far as Mount Everest. The company also made a Daypack for urban types. It sold for $70 and featured the "unique body-hugging shape" that was Gregory's specialty. Wayne Gregory was a stickler for packs that fit, eventually flying to the Appalachian Trail with a team of artisans every spring to give thru-hikers free fittings and repairs. Gregory packs were made available in different sizes to match different torso lengths. Although Wayne Gregory remained handy with needle and thread, he became an enthusiastic user of computer-aided design and manufacturing tools.

Mid-1980s Acquisition by Bianchi

Bianchi International, a maker of holsters for firearms, acquired Gregory Mountain Products, Inc., in 1983 and moved the business one hour north to Temecula, California. After selling Gregory Mountain Products to Bianchi, Wayne Gregory remained with the company to lead product design and became a vice-president at Bianchi International.

Bianchi produced holsters for pistols. Originally known for its leather holsters, the company also used other materials, such as canvas for military products. It progressed to nylon fabric and other synthetic materials, following the same pattern as the backpack industry.

John Bianchi began making pistol holsters in his garage in 1958 when he was a full-time policeman. It was incorporated as Bianchi Holster Co., Inc., ten years later and was relocated from Monrovia to Temecula, California in 1971. First working with leather, Bianchi introduced a number of holster design innovations, beginning with the thumb clasp in 1960's Model 5BH/5BHL. A popular and widely imitated shoulder holster, the Model X15, was developed for "civilian advisors" during the Vietnam Era. Other innovations included the Model 27 "Break Front" in 1970, which was designed to prevent gun removal by an attacker.

Bianchi produced its one millionth holster in 1975. In the same year, it bought Berns-Martin, which had been producing innovative fast-draw leather holsters for law enforcement since the 1930s. In 1978, company founder John Bianchi published a definitive text on holsters called *Blue Steel & Gunleather*.

The company launched a pistol shooting tournament in Columbia, Missouri in 1979 to raise the profile of the sport and enhance involvement with the shooting community. The National Rifle Association took over management of the event, dubbed the NRA Bianchi Cup Championship, in 1985.

In the 1980s Bianchi began working with woven nylon. A holster of this material called the M12 became the U.S. military's first new holster since before World War II. Bianchi subsequently developed a number of other military products of ballistic weave nylon, which was lighter and easier to maintain than leather.

The 1990s were marked by technical innovations intended to improve weapon retention in various situations. The company also improved the precise fit of nylon holsters to the equipment they carried via its new AccuMold technology. More advances in security followed in 2003, based on proprietary "Auto Retention" technology.

Growing in the 1990s

Gregory had tried its hand at the competitive tent market in the early 1990s. Backpacks, however, were where its success

lay. The company's backpack business was growing nearly 25 percent a year, an executive told the *Press-Enterprise* of Riverside, California. By 1993, Gregory packs accounted for 40 percent of Bianchi's revenues. Of Bianchi's 230 Temecula employees, 90 were dedicated to Gregory Mountain Products.

The two product lines catered to markedly different clientele. Whereas Gregory's high-end backpacks were popular with die-hard backpackers, or "pine cone eaters" as Wayne Gregory affectionately called them, Bianchi holsters were distributed through gun shops and sporting goods stores. In 1996, the fit was refined further with the new "Adjust-A-Cant" system. This was used in the Reality model, which *Backpacker* magazine editors pronounced the most comfortable backpack out there.

As new adventure sports such as snowboarding evolved, Gregory developed customized packs to suit their adherents. It even made a little fanny pack that sold for $15. (Its most expensive backpack was $400.) Gregory then had about 18 different product lines in the late 1990s. One thing the company did not make was bookbags. Although most of the five million packs made by the industry every year were destined for the schoolyard, not the summit, Gregory eschewed the low end of the $160 million market dominated by the likes of Jansport and Eastpak. It was, however, the likely leader among specialty packs, one of *Backpacking*'s editors told the *Press-Enterprise*. Wayne Gregory added that the company had at least 100 products in development.

In 1998, Bianchi International tapped Gregory's advanced suspension technology for a new line of backpacks for hunters. Gregory Mountain Products did something a little more urbane, distributing a Yahoo! branded line of courier bags and day-packs. Gregory introduced a line of crush-resistant cases in 2000. The AccuCase.range offered protection for sunglasses, CD players, GPS units, etc.

2000 and Beyond

The outdoor recreation industry had seen tremendous technical advances throughout Gregory's existence. In the military mobilization that followed the September 11, 2001, terrorist attacks on the United States, operations in the mountains and deserts of Afghanistan proved that standard Army gear lagged behind its civilian equivalent in design and performance. Military planners turned to commercial off-the-shelf (COTS) procurement to supplement outdated, heavy army materiel such as tents and clothing.

Bianchi/Gregory already had a contract to supply Special Forces with its customized SPEAR rucksack system. Designed for long-range reconnaissance missions, it had a capacity of 120 pounds and a volume of nearly 8,800 cubic inches. It also carried an ample retail price tag—$1,400. Gregory began tailoring its Denali Pro backpack to Marine Corps and Special Forces requirements. In turn, these modifications improved the civilian product.

Bianchi International had sales of $36 million a year by 2004. Armor Holdings Inc. bought the company that December for $60 million in cash. True to its name, publicly held Armor Holdings produced armor plates for military and commercial vehicles as well as body armor and security-related products

Key Dates:

1958: John Bianchi begins making pistol holsters for sale in his garage.
1975: Bianchi produces its one-millionth holster; Berns-Martin is acquired.
1977: Wayne Gregory launches a backpack manufacturing business.
1979: The Bianchi Cup Invitational International Pistol Tournament is launched.
1983: Gregory Mountain Products is merged into Bianchi International, and relocated to Temecula, California.
1984: Bianchi's ballistic weave nylon holsters replace leather ones in the U.S. military.
1998: The Bianchi Outdoors line of hunting backpacks is launched.
1999: Bianchi/Gregory wins a contract to supply Special Forces with the SPEAR backpack system.
2004: Armor Holdings Inc. acquires Bianchi International.

for law enforcement and others. These product lines were seen as complementary to those of Bianchi, particularly the military business.

Gregory continued to roll out new designs for the outdoor enthusiast using the most advanced materials of the day. One of these was siliconized nylon, which had the ability to seal up small punctures on its own. The brand had a strong sentimental appeal. One of Gregory's early packs reportedly fetched almost $3,000 from a Japanese collector on eBay. New products were in demand as well, winning more praise from expedition and backpacking experts.

Principal Competitors

American Recreation Products, Inc.; Arc'Teryx Equipment Inc.; Lowe Alpine; Mountainsmith.

Further Reading

Bianchi, John, *Blue Steel & Gunleather: A Practical Guide to Holsters,* North Hollywood, Calif.: Beinfeld Pub., 1978.

Brand, Rachel, ''EBay Drop-Off Stores Popping Up,'' *Rocky Mountain News* (Denver), June 20, 2005, p. 1B.

Crider, Jeff, ''Nylon Holster Triggers Sales Increase; Temecula's Bianchi International, Which Has Perfected a Nylon Holster That Is Replacing the Leather Varieties, Is Expecting a Good Year,'' *Press-Enterprise,* July 29, 1995, p. C1.

Endberg, Bryan, ''Gadget Guru: The Reality from Gregory Mountain Products,'' *Record* (Bergen County, N.J.), March 21, 2002.

''Great for Combat—and for Camping,'' *Business Week,* May 12, 2003, p. 12.

Gorman, Jim, ''Leader of the Packs: Backpackers Have Been Good to Eagle Scout Wayne Gregory. So Wayne Gregory Likes to Be Good to Backpackers,'' *Boys' Life,* September 2003, pp. 46ff.

Riedman, Patricia, ''Interactive: Online Brands Spread the Word with Traditional Merchandising,'' *Advertising Age,* June 15, 1998, p. 60.

Scally, Robert, ''Backpacks Carry Load of Business for Holster Maker,'' *Press-Enterprise* (Riverside, Calif.), July 18, 1993, p. G1.

Thurman, Ross, ''Anti-Gun Battles Rage, Bianchi Builds Power Packs,'' *Shooting Industry,* March 1, 1998.

—Frederick C. Ingram

Blackwater USA

P.O. Box 1029
Moyock, North Carolina 27958
U.S.A.
Telephone: (252) 435-2488
Fax: (252) 435-6388
Web site: http://www.blackwaterusa.com

Wholly-Owned Subsidiary of The Prince Group
Founded: 1997
Employees: NA
Sales: NA
NAIC: 561612 Security Guards and Patrol Services

Based in Moyock, North Carolina, close to Fort Bragg, the notoriously private company Blackwater USA bills itself as "the most comprehensive professional military, law enforcement, security, peacekeeping, and stability operations company in the world." Founded by former Navy SEALs, Blackwater is comprised of five business units. The Blackwater Training Center, the company's original focus, is one of the best facilities of its kind in the world, located on some 6,000 acres of private land. More than 50,000 law enforcement, military, and civilian personnel have trained here since opening in 1998. The center includes a number of live fire shooting ranges and tactical training facilities, like mock-ups of urban settings, a high school, and naval ship. Blackwater Security Consulting provides vulnerability assessments and risk analysis and training services, and supplies clients with mobile security teams comprised of former members of U.S. military special operations units and foreign intelligence services. Blackwater Target Systems offers indoor and outdoor shooting range target systems. Blackwater K9 maintains two facilities used to train dogs for law enforcement, the military, and commercial organizations in such areas as patrolling and the detection of explosives. The final business unit is Raven Development Group, which was launched in 1997 to design and construct the Blackwater training facility and now offers its services to government and commercial clients, capable of building an office complex in the United States as well as secure facilities in Iraq. It was in Iraq that Blackwater came to the attention of the general public after

a number of its operators were killed in a pair of well publicized incidents, which brought notice to the increasing reliance of the U.S. military on professional security firms in Iraq, Afghanistan, and elsewhere in the world.

Private Military Companies Emerge in Early 1990s

Soldiers for hire have essentially been around since man first began forming armies. While the Geneva Convention held after World War II expressly banned the use of mercenaries, "soldiers of fortune" continued to show up at hot spots around the world. With the demise of the Soviet Union an opportunity was created for a new breed of professional security companies. "At that time," according to a 2004 *New York Times'* article, "many nations were sharply reducing their military forces, leaving millions of soldiers without employment." Many of them went into business doing what they knew best: providing security or training others to do the same. The proliferation of ethnic conflicts and civil wars in places like the Balkans, Haiti and Liberia provided employment for the personnel of many new companies. The United States employed a small number of these private contractors with the 1991 Gulf War. When it was over Defense Secretary Richard Cheney hired Halliburton subsidiary Brown & Root to study how private military companies might support the military in combat zones.

Blackwater was one of dozens of a new breed of private military companies that sprung up in the 1990s in the United States and the United Kingdom. It was founded in 1997 by former Navy SEALs Gary Jackson and Erik Prince. It was Prince, one of the richest men to have ever served in the U.S. military, who furnished the financial backing and business acumen needed to launch Blackwater.

Prince was the son of Edgar D. Prince, a highly religious man who at the age of 33 in 1965 quit his job as chief engineer of a machine tools company to start his own die cast business. In 1972 Prince Corp. branched into the auto parts industry by inventing the lighted vanity visor for front-seat passengers, first offered on the 1973 Cadillac. This led to the introduction of a multitude of other car interior components and Prince Corp. enjoyed exceptional growth over the next 20 years. As he grew wealthy Edgar Prince became prominent in right wing politics, supporting like-minded candidates around the country. In 1988 he helped Gary Bauer in the establishment of the "pro-family" lobbying group, the Family Research Council.

Erik Prince followed in his father's footsteps to a large degree: devout in his religion, smart in business, and firm in his patriotism. In the late 1980s he attended a small liberal arts school, Hillsdale College, where he studied economics. He also got an education in politics, becoming one of the first interns at the Family Research Council in Washington, D.C. He then worked as a defense analyst for conservative republican Congressman Dana Rohrbacher, before becoming a White House intern for President George H.W. Bush. In a rare interview (his father scrupulously avoided the press), Prince told the *Grand Rapids Press* in 1992, "I saw a lot of things I didn't agree with—homosexual groups being invited in, the budget agreement, the Clean Air Act, those kinds of bills. I think the administration has been indifferent to a lot of conservative concerns."

Prince returned to Hillsdale and became a member of the local volunteer fire department, attending classes with his emergency radio, and sometimes startling classmates as he rushed off to fight a fire. Prince transferred to the U.S. Naval Academy but resigned, preferring instead to join the Navy and earn a commission as a lieutenant. He then became a Navy SEAL (the acronym drawn from the attack routes of sea, air, and land). According to a Special Forces officer quoted by Raleigh, North Carolina's *News & Observer,* "Prince was a first-class SEAL, he was the real deal." He would serve four years with Seal Team 8 in Norfolk, Virginia.

Erik Prince Inherits Fortune in Mid-1990s

In March 1995 Edgar Prince died of a massive heart attack, found on the floor of an elevator shortly after leaving the executive dining room at Prince Corporation headquarters. By now the automotive industry was going global and the private company faced a crossroads. The Prince family decided to sell off the automotive unit, receiving $1.35 billion from Johnson Controls Inc. A year later in 1996 Eric Prince quit the NAVY and returned home to Michigan to run the remaining family companies, which included the original die cast machine business, an airplane leasing operation, and a real estate development company. However, the 27-year-old soon found a venture that was more to his liking.

In 1997 Prince and Jackson went into business together to build a first class private military training center, believing there was an opening for such a facility as the military closed the

doors on a number of its training centers. They bought a large section of farmland in Camden and Currituck counties in North Carolina, some 25 miles from Fort Bragg. Because the large amount of peat in the area turned the water black in the drainage canals they called the company Blackwater USA. For a logo they chose a bear claw, an allusion to the large brown and black bear population in the area.

Blackwater experienced some difficulty in gaining permission from Currituck County to build its training center because officials worried that the firing ranges might disturb residents in nearby Moyock, a growing community. Instead, Blackwater turned to Camden Country where it found a more receptive hearing. What resulted would be a world class training complex. Writing for *Handguns* in 2000, Katherine Rauch took a three-day handgun course at Blackwater and offered a glimpse at the facilities: "There are steel movers and steel plates, steep Pepper Poppers and stationary steel, along with computerized pneumatic steel targets and automated paper targets. There's Simunitions complex of four buildings, with a live-fire 'Hogan's Alley' right across the 'street,' along with two all-steel shoot houses, a 1,200-yard range and a 7,000-square-foot schoolhouse dubbed 'R.U. Ready High.'... All This, plus breakfast and lunch, along with a private room (by request) in the bunkhouse complex with its own little deck overlooking one of the many ponds on the property."

The Blackwater training center was open for business in 1998, but in the early months had difficulty in drumming up much business. The company became adept, however, at keeping tabs on national and international news, then adding facilities and training programs to meet perceived needs. For example, R.U. Ready High School was built after the 1999 shootings at Columbine High School in Littleton, Colorado. It was essentially a two-story, 24-room, six-stairwell, all-steel building that allowed for the use of live gunfire inside and even the use of explosives for "dynamic entry" through the doors. R.U. Ready was used to teach law enforcement and military personnel special tactics. A catwalk across the ceiling allowed instructors to monitor students as they made their way through the building. The facility found a ready market, clients included a number of police officers who paid for the training out of their own pockets

Another event that caught the attention of Blackwater was the 2000 bombing of the destroyer *Cole* in Yemen. In response, Blackwater constructed a realistic mockup of a Navy vessel. In the fall of 2002 the company won a $35.7 million, five-year contract with the Navy to conduct two-week training sessions for Navy personnel on topics that included sentry duty, weapons use aboard a ship, and how to board, seize, and search another ship.

2001 Terrorist Attacks: A Turning Point

What led to the most significant spike in business for Blackwater were the terrorist attacks on the United States on September 11, 2001, and the ensuing events. Not only would the training facilities find more use, the company would be called on to provide trained personnel to corporations, the U.S. government, and the U.S. military. Blackwater supplied independent contractors to Afghanistan and later to Iraq when the United States invaded the country in spring 2003. Among their tasks, Blackwater personnel served as the personal guard for

Key Dates:

1997: Company is founded by two former Navy SEALs.
1998: The training facility becomes operational.
2002: Blackwater is awarded a major Naval contract.

Paul Bremer, the head of the civilian administration. The company mostly recruited by word of mouth, hiring from within the close-knit community of former SEALs, Green Berets, Army Rangers, and Delta Force Troops. As the war in Iraq settled into a long-term conflict, the demand for personnel increased and Blackwater had to branch out. Jackson told the British newspaper *The Guardian* in 2004, "We scour the ends of the earth to find professionals." The company also found recruits in the Currituck County sheriff's office, where a number of deputies went to work for Blackwater overseas, making as much money in a single month as they did in a year at home. In 2004 Blackwater made news when it recruited 60 former commandos and other members of Chile's military and flew them to North Carolina for training before deploying them elsewhere.

Modern day "free lancers" were known in international security circles as "operators." In 2004 *The Virginian Pilot* offered a glimpse of them in Iraq: "They are easy to spot in a landscape dominated by young, uniformed soldiers and the dark slender profiles of Iraqis. Operators tend to be muscled-up men in their 30s or 40s, wearing T–shirts, ball caps and wrap-around sunglasses. An automatic weapon is ever present, cradled in their beefy biceps." Operators tended to be loners who joined the military but grew bored with the regimen and frustrated by the bureaucracy and low pay. It was not the life for a married man. According to the *Virginian Pilot,* "A military husband occasionally goes off to war, but an operator is always heading somewhere dangerous. Turn down a job or two, and the phone stops ringing. Retirement and leave don't exist. . . . Operators rarely discuss their families. . . . More than just a soft spot to shield, families can doom a man in a war zone if he can't cut off his emotions."

The use of operators and the companies like Blackwater that supplied them were little known until March 4, 2004 when four Blackwater employees were leading a convoy of trucks to pick up kitchen equipment. According to the company, they were assured by men they believed were members of the Iraqi Civil Defense Corps that they would have safe and quick passage through the dangerous city of Falluja. Instead, the road was blocked, their escape route cut off, and the men were shot to death, burned, and mutilated. Their charred remains were dragged before cameras, the video broadcast around the world. In another well chronicled incident, in April 2005 six Blackwater personnel were killed when the helicopter they were riding in was shot down, apparently by rocket-propelled grenades.

The Falluja incident led to a spike in employment applications for Blackwater, fueled in large part out of a sense of revenge, but it also brought the use of private security firms by the military into public view. To critics of the practice, Blackwater became the face of the entire industry, although in reality there were scores of similar companies. Altogether they added about 15,000 men to the military forces stationed in Iraq. Critics charged that rapid growth in the private military industry was leading to inexperience and poorly trained units. Moreover, the cost of using such forces could be hidden from the public, and the personnel were not subject to the same kind of accountability as U.S. soldiers. Miscreants were simply shipped home. Given that U.S. forces were stretched thin, however, the military had little choice but to continue to rely on private contractors. Following the events in Falluja, according to *Nation* magazine, Blackwater "hired the Alexander Strategy Group, a PR firm with close ties to GOPers like [House Majority Leader Tom] DeLay. By Mid-November the company was reporting 600 percent growth. In February 2005 the company hired Ambassador Cofer Black, former coordinator for counterterrorism at the State Department and former director of the CIA's Counterterrorism Center, as vice chairman."

Blackwater continued to see training as its core mission and made major upgrades to its North Carolina facilities. In 2004 the company received permission from Currituck County to expand operations into that county, including firearms ranges, parachute landing zones, and explosives training. Later in the year Blackwater began to build a roadway through 90 acres of its property that would be suitable for training in high-speed chases (above 100 miles per hour) as well as motorcade protection against terrorist attacks.

Blackwater was again in the news in the autumn of 2005 when about 150 Blackwater men were spotted in New Orleans during the aftermath of Hurricane Katrina, which devastated the city. Not only did they—along with operators from other firms—secure government facilities, they guarded private businesses and homes. The company also lobbied in 2005 for Homeland Security contracts to train 2,000 new Border Patrol agents. Jackson testified before Congress regarding the business and made a pitch for Blackwater as a one-stop shopping solution for the government. There was every reason to believe that because of military limitations and the company's strong political ties Blackwater, despite the notoriety it had received, was well positioned to prosper in the years to come.

Principal Operating Units

Blackwater Training Center; Blackwater Security Consulting; Blackwater Canine; Blackwater Target Systems; Raven Development Group.

Principal Competitors

Smith Consulting Group; Intercon Security; DynCorp International Inc.; The Wackenhut Corporation.

Further Reading

Barstow, David, and Eric Schmitt, "Security Firm Says Its Workers Were Lured Into Iraqi Ambush," *New York Times,* April 9, 2004, p A1.
Barstow, David, "Security Companies: Shadow Soldiers in Iraq," *New York Times,* April 19, 2004, p. A1.
Connolly, Allison, "Blackwater's Best-Kept Secret: It's Founder," *Virginian Pilot,* May 3, 2004, p. A1.
Dao, James, Eric Schmitt, and John F. Burns, "Private Guards Take Big Risks, For Right Price," *New York Times,* April 2, 2004, p. A1.

Duffy, Michael, "When Private Armies Take to the Front Lines," *Time,* April 12, 2004, p. 32.

Kimberlin, Joanne, "In the Line of Fire," *Virginian Pilot,* April 15, 2004, p. A1.

Lerman, David and Stephanie Heinatz, "Military-for-Hire Companies Have Large Presence in Newport News," *Daily Press (Newport News, Va.),* April 4, 2004.

Rauch, Katherine, "Lessons From Blackwater," *Handguns,* May 2000, p. 72.

Scahill, Jeremy, "Blackwater Down," *Nation,* October 10, 2005.

Scharnberg, Kirsten and Mike Dorning, "Security Firms Find Thriving Business in Iraq, Other Danger Zones," *Chicago Tribune,* April 2, 2004.

Yeoman, Barry, "Soldiers of Good Fortune," *Mother Jones,* May 2003.

—Ed Dinger

Blockbuster Inc.

1201 Elm Street
Dallas, Texas 75270
U.S.A.
Telephone: (214) 854-3000
Fax: (214) 854-4848
Web site: http://www.blockbuster.com
Wew

Public Company
Incorporated: 1982 as Cook Data Services
Employees: 84,300
Sales: $6 billion (2004)
Stock Exchanges: New York London
Ticker Symbol: BBI
NAIC: 532230 Video Tape and Disc Rental

Blockbuster Inc. is the largest video rental chain in the world providing in-home rental, retail movie, and game entertainment. Blockbuster operates about 9,100 video stores, serving approximately three million customers each day in the United States, its territories, and 24 other nations. Founded in the mid-1980s as an alternative to small, local operations with limited video rental selection, the company grew quickly into a global chain, offering videos, DVDs, and video games in its stores as well as through an online subscription program. Viacom sold off a minority stake in the company in 1999 and sold its remaining interest in 2004. The company appeared to be in a state of flux during 2005 due to litigation surrounding its ''no late fees'' policy, lost income from extended viewing fees, a failed attempt to merge with competitor Hollywood Entertainment Corporation, and corporate raider Carl Icahn's efforts to oust CEO John Antioco.

An Immediate Hit in the Mid-1980s

Blockbuster traces its history to the formation of Cook Data Services, Inc., in 1982. This company was founded by David Cook to supply computer software services to Texas's oil and gas industry. When the industry went bust, the company was left without a strong customer base. Cook was searching for another source of revenue when his wife, Sandy, a movie fan, suggested entering the video rental business.

Cook learned that the video rental field was highly fragmented. Most stores were relatively modest family operations that carried a small selection of former big hit movies. Providing a large selection of movies required a large investment of capital, since distributors typically charged approximately $70 per tape. In addition, tapes were generally not displayed, but kept behind the counter to discourage theft, and had to be fetched and laboriously signed out to the customer. Cook saw that operations could be greatly streamlined by a computerized system for inventory control and checkout, something his software background prepared him to develop.

After Sandy Cook conducted several months of research into the video rental industry, David Cook sold his oil and gas software business to its managers and entered the movie rental business. In October 1985, Cook opened the first Blockbuster Video outlet in Dallas. With 8,000 tapes covering 6,500 titles, it had an inventory many times larger than that of its nearest competitor. In addition, tapes were displayed on shelves throughout the store, as in a bookstore, so that customers could pick them up and carry them to the front desk for checkout. A magnetic strip on each video and sensors at the door discouraged theft. Computers were used to keep track of inventory, and a laser scanning system, which used barcodes on the tapes and on members' cards, simplified and reduced the time involved in conducting transactions.

The first Blockbuster store was an immediate hit. The Cooks discovered that the public had a much greater appetite for renting video movies than anyone had previously suspected. People were interested not just in seeing hit movies they had missed in the theaters but also in a broad variety of other features.

By summer 1986, Cook had expanded the Blockbuster concept to three additional stores. To reflect the different nature of the company, Cook Data Services became Blockbuster Entertainment Corporation in June 1986. In September, the company set out to raise money for further expansion with an initial stock offering. Days before the sale was to take place, however, a financial columnist wrote a damaging article citing Cook's background in the oil industry and questioning the company's know-how in the video field. The article caused the equity offering to be canceled, and without this infusion of cash, Blockbuster began to run out of money. The company finished 1986 with a loss of $3.2 million.

In February 1987, however, Cook sold one-third of Blockbuster to a group of three investors, who were all former associates at another company, Waste Management, Inc. Wayne Huizenga had in 1972 cofounded Waste Management, which grew to be the largest garbage disposal business in the world, and served as its president and chief operating officer until 1984, when he retired. John Melk, the president of Waste Management's international division, was first to invest in a Blockbuster franchise. Joined by Donald Flynn, the chief financial officer of Waste Management, the group invested $18.6 million in Blockbuster stock.

New Management and Aggressive Expansion in the Late 1980s

With this move, Cook surrendered future control of Blockbuster, and Huizenga became the dominant voice in determining the company's future. Where Cook had envisioned growth through franchising, selling Blockbuster's name and computer system to individual entrepreneurs, Huizenga foresaw growth through company ownership of stores. In April 1987, two months after the men from Waste Management bought into Blockbuster, Cook left the company. Soon thereafter, the company's headquarters were moved to Fort Lauderdale, Florida.

By June 1987, Blockbuster owned 15 stores and franchised 20 others. With this base, Huizenga set out to transform Blockbuster into the industry's dominant player. He kept most of Cook's policies, such as store hours from 10:00 a.m. to midnight every day; a three-day rental policy, which encouraged customers to rent more than one tape at once; and a broad selection of titles. Despite conventional wisdom that the videotape rental business was heavily dependent on hits, 70 percent of Blockbuster's rental revenues came from non-hit movies, which had the added benefit of being less expensive to purchase from distributors. In addition, Blockbuster's management decided to eschew revenue from X-rated adult films, opting instead for a family environment.

With these policies in place, Blockbuster set out on a program of aggressive expansion. The company began to buy back franchised operations with the goal of 60 percent company-owned Blockbuster outlets. In addition, Wayne Huizenga began to buy up chains of video stores that already dominated their local markets, using this as a shortcut to quick expansion. In March 1987, Blockbuster bought Southern Video Partnership as part of this policy. Two months later, it purchased Movies To Go, Inc., of St. Louis, for $14.5 million.

To support its expansion, Blockbuster established six regional offices, including a distribution center in Dallas that prepared tapes to be placed in stores. By the end of 1987, Blockbuster was operating 133 stores and had become the country's fifth largest video chain in terms of revenue. Sales rose from $7.4 million in 1986 to $43.2 million that year.

Blockbuster continued its ambitious expansion program in 1988. In March, the company purchased Video Library, Inc., for $6.4 million plus stock. The following month, Blockbuster made a deal with the United Cable Television Corporation (UCTC) to open 100 franchised stores over the next two-and-a-half years. In addition, UCTC purchased 5 percent of Blockbuster's stock for $12.25 million. By November, this stake had risen to 20 percent. With 200 stores, Blockbuster had become the largest video rental chain in the country. At the end of the year, the company's number of stores had risen to 415.

In January 1989, Blockbuster finalized its purchase of Las Vegas-based Major Video, Inc., the country's fourth largest video rental chain, for $92.5 million. It also purchased Oklahoma Entertainment, Inc. The following month brought the purchase of Vector Video, Inc., and Video Superstores Master LP, which, with 106 stores, had been Blockbuster's largest franchisee. By June 1989, two years after Huizenga's takeover, the company ran 700 stores. Sales had tripled, profits nearly quadrupled, and the value of the company's stock had risen seven-fold.

Despite these gains, in April 1989, Blockbuster's efforts to buy up other chains with stock suffered a setback when an analyst at a large stock brokerage issued a report condemning what he considered to be the company's misleading accounting practices. In calculating its earnings, Blockbuster spread out the costs of purchasing video store chains and building new stores over a 40-year period, and also spread out the cost of buying large numbers of hit tapes over three years, much longer than tapes retained their value. In addition, the company relied on one-time-only franchise fees for 28 percent of its revenue. Despite this criticism, Blockbuster declined to change its accounting practices, and the company's stock price eventually regained its former level.

In November 1989, Blockbuster's largest shareholder, the United Artists Entertainment Company, announced that it would sell its 12 percent holding in the company, having previously sold its 28 franchised Blockbuster stores, in an effort to streamline its own business holdings. Worries that the video rental industry was reaching a saturation point cast doubts on Blockbuster's ability to keep opening stores indefinitely.

Foreign Expansion and Diversification in the Early 1990s

One response to this concern was to look to markets outside the United States for growth. Accordingly, original investor John Melk was dispatched to start up a British subsidiary, with the company's first foreign store to be opened in South London called the Ritz. Blockbuster's management continued to maintain that since the video ''superstore'' concept was open for anyone to copy, it needed to grab market share as fast as possible in order to exploit its ground-breaking concept. Carrying out this philosophy, the company opened its 1,000th store before the end of 1989.

To increase business, Blockbuster embarked on a $25 million ad campaign, and also undertook joint promotions with fast-food outlets such as Domino's Pizza and McDonald's. In addition, the company accelerated foreign expansion, augmenting its operations in Britain and planning for operations in Australia and the rest of Western Europe. In the United States, the chain had opened its 1,200th store by June 1990; new outlets opened at a rate of one a day.

In October 1990, Blockbuster announced plans to cooperate with Den Fujita, the company that ran McDonald's franchises in Japan, in the development and franchising of video rental stores in that country. The following month, Blockbuster made its largest acquisition to date, when it acquired Erol's, a video store chain with 200 outlets on the East Coast and in the Midwest, for $30 million, including cash, notes, and debt assumption.

Although Blockbuster continued its strong pace of new store openings in 1990, the slowing growth of the video rental industry was becoming evident. Even though the company's earnings grew an astronomical 114 percent in 1988, they contracted to a still-impressive 93 percent rate of growth in 1989, followed by a rate of 48 percent in 1990. In keeping with this trend, first quarter financial results for 1991 were disappointing. Huizenga blamed the Gulf War for keeping people interested in television news instead of rented videos. In early May, Cox Communications, one of the company's franchisers, announced that it would sell all 82 of its Blockbuster stores.

Faced with a rapidly maturing industry, Blockbuster began to expand its offerings to maintain profitability. The company began to offer video game equipment and Sega Genesis video games at some of its stores. The company considered selling audio cassettes and compact disks. Blockbuster also acquired the right to market tapes of the 1992 Olympic games.

In a further effort to encourage rentals, the company launched an advertising campaign themed "Win in a Flash,"

and made an agreement with the Showtime cable network for a joint promotion. In August 1991, Blockbuster dropped its rental price for hit movies for the first three months after their release and shortened the time they were taken out, as a further step to raise earnings. In an effort to ensure that the company would be just as good at running video stores over the long haul as it was at opening them, Blockbuster hired more senior executives with long-term experience in the retail field.

In addition to these efforts to increase earnings in the United States, Blockbuster increased its foreign efforts. Along with its operations in the United Kingdom and Japan, the company found markets in Europe, Australia, and Latin America. With 30 stores already established in Britain, Blockbuster announced in November 1991 a large expansion in that country, designed to make it the nation's number one video rental chain. Further foreign involvement came later that month, when Philips Electronics N.V., a Dutch firm, agreed to invest $66 million in the company. As a result of this partnership, Blockbuster said that it would market Philips's newly introduced interactive compact disc systems and software in its stores. Five months later, Philips purchased an additional six million shares to raise its investment to $149 million.

To streamline its corporate management, Blockbuster bought a large office building in Florida and consolidated the company's five regional offices. As Wall Street pundits continued to predict that Blockbuster's success was short-lived, and that the video rental industry would be made obsolete by new technologies, Blockbuster's systemwide sales of $1.5 billion in 1991 earned $89 million. By the end of the year, the company had opened stores in Japan, Chile, Venezuela, Puerto Rico, Spain, Australia, New Zealand, and Guam.

In further overseas expansion, Blockbuster bought Citivision PLC, the largest video rental chain in Britain, for $135 million in January 1992, anticipating that this property would provide valuable exposure in the United Kingdom, and a jumping-off point for further European growth. The company hoped that, through joint ventures, international operations would contribute a quarter of revenues by 1995. With 952 stores in nine foreign countries, Blockbuster began to intensify its efforts to expand both in products and geographically.

In October 1992, Blockbuster embarked on a series of agreements that were designed to expand the company's operations beyond its core movie rental business. Blockbuster bought Music Plus and Sound Warehouse from Shamrock Holdings, a California company, for $185 million. One month later, Blockbuster entered into an agreement with the British conglomerate Virgin Group plc to set up "megastores" in the United States, Europe, and Australia. In December 1992, the first such store in the United States opened in Los Angeles, the precursor to a network of stores that Huizenga envisioned not only renting videos, but also selling and renting music, computer programs, and games, and containing high-tech "virtual reality" entertainment arcades. The company also hoped to improve on the traditionally low profits of music retailing by adding other, more profitable products.

By 1993, the distinctive bright blue and yellow Blockbuster logo adorned more than 3,400 video stores worldwide, about one-third of them overseas. Late in January of that year, Blockbuster branched out further, paying $25 million for a one-third, controlling share in Republic Pictures, a movie and television production and distribution company based in Hollywood. Republic's most valuable asset was its film library of television shows and films, including several John Wayne movies and the hit television series *Bonanza*. In March 1993, Blockbuster also purchased 48.2 percent of Spelling Entertainment, a producer of popular television shows with a large library of past programs. Moreover, Blockbuster began construction of a prototype family entertainment center in Florida.

The Controversial Viacom Merger: 1994

With its ever-growing number of corporate activities, Blockbuster was committed to diversification as a means of ensuring its future in the entertainment industry in the face of the potential onslaught of new formats—video-on-demand and satellite TV—and the shift from rentals to lower-priced tapes. In September 1993, Huizenga's Blockbuster makeover hit full stride when the company proposed a $4.7 billion merger with media giant Viacom Inc..

Toward that end, Blockbuster invested heavily in Viacom, reportedly to help strengthen Viacom's bid to purchase Paramount Communications against rival QVC Network Inc. Viacom did win the war for Paramount, but the merger talks with Blockbuster stalled, and the move cost Blockbuster a great deal as Blockbuster shareholders lost confidence in the company and wondered if its investment in Viacom would pay off. By April 1994, Blockbuster's and Viacom's stock had tumbled dramatically.

Blockbuster's glory days appeared to be over. Insiders assessed that the company was suffering from dramatic changes in the industry. Specifically, with competition stiffening due to newly emerging formats, the video industry's meteoric growth began to level off. Moreover, there was trouble internally. The merger between Blockbuster and Viacom, though eventually effected, had been rough, and Viacom was reportedly depending heavily upon Blockbuster's cash to help pay its debts and have money for future investments.

In addition, leadership at Blockbuster seemed unstable. Wayne Huizenga ceded his leadership role in the company in September 1994 and was replaced as president by Steven Berrard, who focused on rapidly expanding the company during his year-and-a-half on the job. Amid legal entanglements involving earlier business dealings, however, Berrard left to be succeeded by Bill Fields in March 1996. Soon thereafter, Fields was named CEO as well and during his brief tenure attempted to revitalize the company's image. Specifically, he set about transforming Blockbuster's video rental stores into whole entertainment centers, selling t-shirts, toys, snacks, books, magazines, and CDs as well as selling and renting videos. Fields also oversaw the company's move from Fort Lauderdale to Dallas to be closer to its new, centralized distribution center. He also downsized the company's workforce, paring back about one-third of its senior staff and two-thirds of its overall staff before he left for a position at Wal-Mart. In 1996, in the wake of slipping sales, Blockbuster's worth was estimated at $4.6 billion with its stock worth only 50 percent of its 1993 price. Parent Viacom's stock price was 60 percent off its former high.

New Leadership and Independence in the Late 1990s

By the time John Antioco took over in the summer of 1997, Blockbuster was floundering. New releases were not making it to stores by their "street date," and the loss of so many key people with the company's move left it stumbling in basic store operations. Cash flow for the second quarter of 1997 at Blockbuster dropped a precipitous 70 percent. As a result, the chain scaled back on expansion and moved to refocus on its core business, video rentals. In late 1997, it exited the computer business, closing its PC Upgrades stores only months after acquiring the business.

Under Antioco, the company revived its old tag line, "Make it a Blockbuster Night," and sought to smooth out the problems with its state-of-the-art distribution system, which allowed it to use a customer database to determine store sites and inventory based on consumer preferences. Although the company had fallen on hard times, it still controlled 25 percent of the $16 billion a year home video market. Under Antioco, the company signed "revenue sharing" agreements with the major Hollywood studios, making them financial partners. Now instead of paying $65 for new tapes, Blockbuster paid $4 and turned over 30 to 40 percent of the rental income to the studio. In 1998, the company boasted that it had served nearly 60 million people who rented more than 970 million movies and video games. In early 1999, it continued to expand overseas, purchasing a Hong Kong video chain, and at home with the acquisition of Denver-based Video Visions and Videoland in Oregon and Washington. The chain was making money again, and its share of the home video retail market increased to 31 percent. Still, the video market was shrinking, dropping 2.6 percent in 1998 and 8.4 percent in the first half of 1999. While revenues at Blockbuster were increasing, the company was still reporting losses, of $336.6 million in 1998, for example, compared with a $318.2 million loss in 1997.

Nevertheless, Blockbuster seemed to be effecting a turnaround, when in August 1999 Viacom made an initial public offering of around 18 percent of its stock in Blockbuster; it divested its remaining shares in 2004. The initial offering raised only $465 million; clearly, investors did not take the future of Blockbuster for granted and the company needed to search for a viable business model. Toward that end, management worked on increasing Blockbuster's market share in the growing VHA/DVD tape and disc rental category. Moreover, it also made a commitment to exploring new distribution channels, such as those offered by e-commerce.

Blockbuster in the New Millennium

During the early years of the new millennium, Blockbuster's competitors included cable and satellite companies offering video-on-demand movies, online movie rental firms offering mail-order rentals, and large retailers like Wal-Mart Stores that sold inexpensive movies and games. As such, Blockbuster continued to look for ways to remain competitive in the industry while shoring up sales and profits. In 2001, the company announced that it would reduce its VHS and video game inventory by 25 percent in order to give DVDs more shelf space. The company also created DEJ Productions, an independent film acquisition and distribution subsidiary, and signed a deal to

78   **Blockbuster Inc.**

distribute DIRECTV satellite systems through its stores. Block-buster debuted on the New York Stock Exchange that year.

During 2003, the company began offering its customers an in-store subscription pass. This program was expanded in 2004 and enabled customers to rent unlimited movies for a monthly fee. The company also made several purchases, including Movie Trading Company and U.K.-based Gamestation. To compete with new online movie rental firms like NetFlix Inc., Blockbuster rolled out its Blockbuster Online subscription service, which offered DVDs delivered to customers' homes with no shipping charges. Chairman and CEO Antioco commented on Blockbuster's strategy in a July 2004 EQUIS release stating, "We realize the movie rental business alone won't give us the kind of growth we want in the future. That's why we're determined to transform Blockbuster from a place where you go to rent movies to a place where you go to rent, buy or trade movies and games, either in-store or online."

In December 2004, the company began running television ads touting its new "no late fees" policy. The new program, which eliminated daily late charges, was launched on January 1, 2005. Early that year, 47 states filed suit against the company for false advertising, claiming that customers had been charged fees for unreturned and late DVDs, videos, and games, despite the "no late fee" promotion. The suit claimed that in its advertising, Blockbuster had failed to reveal that customers who kept an item more than seven days would be charged the current selling price for the item. If the item was returned within 30 days, the customer would receive a refund, but would be charged a $1.25 restocking fee. In the end, Blockbuster agreed to pay $630,000 to settle the litigation.

At the same time, the company dropped its bid to buy its closest competitor, Hollywood Entertainment Corp., after the Federal Trade Commission delayed its ruling on the merger proposal. Corporate raider Carl Icahn—Blockbuster's largest shareholder—began to attack the company's strategy and made a play to oust several Blockbuster directors, including Antioco. In May, Blockbuster shareholders voted to appoint Icahn and two of his allies to the board. A new director's seat was created, allowing Antioco to remain chairman.

In the midst of the boardroom politics, Blockbuster's financial position came under fire when it announced in September 2005 that it would not pay a quarterly dividend for the first time since 1999. A major factor contributing to the company's financial woes was the elimination of late fees, which were responsible for approximately $250 million in operating income. Antioco stood behind the strategy, however, claiming it was crucial to Blockbuster's future success. Management expected that revenue from new and existing ventures would make up for lost income and leave Blockbuster well positioned for success in the years to come.

Principal Competitors

Hastings Entertainment Inc.; Movie Gallery Inc.; Netflix Inc.

Further Reading

Anderson, Stephanie, and Tom Lowry, "Blockbuster: The Sequel Revived," *Business Week,* September 16, 2002, p. 52.

"Big Blue Hastens Rollout of Online Subscriptions," *Executive Quote and Information Service,* July 26, 2004.

Calonius, Erik, "Meet the King of Video," *Fortune,* June 4, 1990, p. 208.

Castle, Steven, "Wayne's World," *Robb Report,* February 1993.

Carlson, Gus, "The Next Disney," *Miami Herald,* March 14, 1993, p. 1K.

Chakravarty, Subrata N., "Give 'Em Variety," *Forbes,* May 2, 1988, pp. 54–56.

DeGeorge, Gail, "Blockbuster's Grainy Picture," *Business Week,* May 20, 1991, pp. 40–41.

——, "Call It Blockbummer," *Business Week,* May 9, 1994, p. 31.

——, "The Video King Who Won't Hit Pause," *Business Week,* January 22, 1990, pp. 47–48.

——, "They Don't Call It Blockbuster for Nothing," *Business Week,* October 19, 1992.

Desjardins, Doug, "Blockbuster Drops Bid to Buy Hollywood," *DSN Retailing Today,* April 11, 2005, pp. 3–5.

——, "Blockbuster Shakes Up Board," *DSN Retailing Today,* May 23, 2005, pp. 5–7.

Engardio, Pete, and Antonio N. Fine, "Will This Video Chain Stay on Fast Forward?," *Business Week,* June 12, 1989, pp. 72–74.

Feare, Tom, "High-Tech DC; Just the Right Ticket for Blockbuster Video," *Modern Materials Handling,* October 31, 1998, p. 34.

Forest, Stephanie Anderson, "The Script Doctor Is In at Blockbuster—Again," *Business Week,* July 28, 1997, p. 101.

Govoni, Stephen J., "Blockbuster Battles the Shorts," *CFO,* December 1991.

——, "Hot Ticket," *Information Week,* August 30, 1993, p. 28.

Katel, Peter, "New Kid on the Block, Buster," *Newsweek,* January 11, 1993.

Kirchdoerffer, Ed, "Blockbuster Set to Rebuild," *Kidscreen,* October 1, 1997, p. R7.

Miller, Michael, "Coming Soon to Your Local Video Store: Big Brother," *Wall Street Journal,* December 26, 1990, p. 9.

"Not a Blockbuster Debut," *Ottawa Citizen,* August 12, 1999, p. F3.

Roberts, Johnnie L., "Chips Off the Block," *Newsweek,* February 20, 1995, p. 42.

——, "Hit the Eject Button," *Newsweek,* August 18, 1997, p. 50.

Peers, Martin, "Video Poker: At Blockbuster, New Strategies Raise Tensions Over Board Seats," *Wall Street Journal,* April 18, 2005, p. A1.

Savitz, Eric J., "An End to Fast Forward?," *Barron's,* December 11, 1989, pp. 13, 43–46.

Siklos, Richard, "Blockbuster Finally Gets It Right," *Business Week,* March 8, 1999, p. 64.

Silverman, Edward R., "Global Go-Getters," *International Business,* October 1992.

Sweeting, Paul, "B'buster Settles 'Late Fees' Claims," *Video Business,* April 4, 2005, p. 6.

"USA/UK Blockbuster Strikes from Home Base," *Sunday Times,* November 10, 1991.

Walsh, Matt, "Rent Things," *Florida Trend,* March 1993.

Whitford, David, "The Predator's Ball Club," *M,* June 1992, pp. 80–85.

"Will Big Blue Break Its Bank?," *Home Media Retailing,* September 2005, pp. 3–5.

—Elizabeth Rourke
—updates: Carrie Rothburd, Christina M. Stansell

Australian Since 1870.

Blundstone Pty Ltd.

88 Gormanston Road
P.O. Box 316
Moonah, Tasmania 7009
Australia
Telephone: +61 3 6272 3000
Fax: +61 3 6273 2780
Web site: http://www.blundstone.com

Private Company
Incorporated: 1902 as John Blundstone and Son Ltd.
Employees: 550
Sales: $60 million (2005 est.)
NAIC: 316213 Men's Footwear (Except Athletic)
    Manufacturing; 316214 Women's Footwear (Except
    Athletic) Manufacturing; 422340 Footwear Wholesalers

Blundstone Pty Ltd. is Australia's leading footwear manufacturer. Originally synonymous with its durable and comfortable boots for the farm and factory, the company developed a sense of style that made its footwear sought after in fashion centers around the world. Its distinctive elastic-sided boots became a global hit in the 1990s. The company exports to more than 20 countries. It also owns New Zealand's John Bull brand. The company is one of Tasmania's leading employers; along with the associated Cuthbertson Brothers Tanners, it has been a part of the island's economy since the late 19th century. Blundstone has renewed its commitment to the area by investing millions of Aussie dollars in equipment and training to keep its products competitive with foreign imports.

Tasmanian Origins

Blundstone has been in business since 1870, when British émigré John Blundstone began producing footwear in south Hobart on the island of Tasmania. The original address was 71 Liverpool Street. By 1892 Blundstone had moved to a new facility and was working with his son. The company became John Blundstone and Son Ltd. in 1902. The firm soon built a new two-story building on Campbell Street.

The brothers Frank and William Cane acquired the footwear business in 1921. It was sold to the Cuthbertson family, who would own it for the rest of the century, in 1932. The Cutherbertsons also owned a tannery.

Brothers James and Thomas Cuthbertson had come to the area in 1853. They originally had sailed for Melbourne, but remained where they landed in Hobart after a sickening voyage had them vowing never to go on the seas again. James Cuthbertson established a business making and importing shoes.

The company had gotten a big boost in 1914 when it began supplying the army. World War II also produced great demand for boots. After the war, Blundstone produced a line of ''Mountain Masters'' boots for farmers to wear as they tramped about the countryside. These were discontinued in the 1970s but the concept was revived and updated in 2002.

A variety of different boots was developed, including those with chemical resistant soles, waterproof boots, and those with wooden soles. Blundstone's specialty was work and safety footwear; the company pioneered steel-toed safety shoes. Dress and uniform shoes also were made. Along the way, production methods were updated to employ the latest technologies. Stitched and cemented soles were replaced by direct-vulcanized rubber soles in the 1950s, which gave way to thermoplastic soles a decade later, noted *Manufacturer's Monthly.*

The company began exporting in 1969, beginning with Papua New Guinea. The company got a new CEO in 1973, Tony Stacey, who would hold the job for about 30 years.

In 1993, Blundstone opened a small manufacturing and distribution facility in New Zealand to produce gumboots for the local market. The company had begun making gumboots, which were waterproof, injection-molded footwear, four years earlier.

A Global Hit in the 1990s

Blundstone was making about 500,000 boots a year in the early 1990s. Blundstone's elastic-sided 500s began turning up in London boutiques, following a trend for heavy footwear set by punk icon Doc Martens boots. They also were becoming popular among fashion-conscious young Aussie women. Their durability was a selling point in the global recession.

Blundstone took bold strides with fashion in the 1990s. New materials, such as blue suede and white leather, were tried. Although these did not prove to be enduring successes, they created a buzz and established Blundstone's work boots as chic, CEO Tom Stacey told *Footwear News*.

The company trod into new environs in 1992 by inviting Australian artists to ''Do Something With a Blundstone'' for a touring exhibition. Three years later, it began sponsoring a contest for contemporary art at the Queen Victoria Museum and Art Gallery.

In 1997 the company began an AUD 5.5 million program to upgrade its buildings, manufacturing equipment, and information technology. Blundstone opened a new distribution channel, the Internet, selling boots on its web site. The new technology helped make the company less isolated from the rest of the world. A training center was opened next to the main Blundstone plant. Cuthbertson Brothers Tanners also underwent an upgrade, spending AUD 2 million to install new technology.

A line of children's shoes called Blunnies (the brand's traditional nickname) was unveiled in time for the Christmas 1999 season. Children's author Alison Lester was recruited to design merchandising materials. Based on the No. 500, the tiny boots were an instant sensation around the world. A company official told *Footwear News* that the key to brand extensions such as this was authenticity. ''It's not a contrived product,'' said marketing manager Barry Smith. ''It's not the name of a tractor put on a boot made in a factory in China.'' Blunnies were made, with pride, ''down under.''

Blundstone was making 80 different types of boots. The company had started rolling out other new products, such as sandals, hiking boots, and women's safety shoes. Blundstone-branded socks and belts were also available.

Blundstone ended the 1990s with 340 employees and annual revenues of AUD 50 million to AUD 75 million. Half of this came from safety and work sales, according to *Footwear News*, and 35 percent from farming footwear. A total of 15 percent was exported to 22 countries. More than half of its exports went to retail fashion stores, where they sold for up to $125 (AUD 200)—more than twice the price down under (AUD 75 on average). By this time, the boots had caught on in the United States, Argentina, Brazil, and Italy.

The Tap Dogs, an Australian tap dancing troop that was touring the world, wore Blundstones in their energetic routines.

A herd of celebrities was hoofing them around Hollywood, and they were also a favorite of humble backpackers.

Acquiring John Bull in 2000

Blundstone's New Zealand subsidiary acquired John Bull Footwear in June 2000. John Bull had a factory in Auckland that employed more than 100 people. The company had been formed in 1934 to produce footwear for the rural market. In 1981 it was acquired by OPSM Protector; it then became the leading industrial footwear company in New Zealand.

The New Zealand gumboot operation was moved to Victoria, a suburb of Melbourne, Australia, in 2001, when the operation employed about 30 people. The Auckland factory continued to make John Bull boots.

With more women taking up industrial jobs, it seemed natural for Blundstone's designers to develop a line of boots called ''Women's Work.'' Tailored to fit women's feet, these boots were marketed in packaging featuring designs commissioned from six female Aboriginal artists. They hit the Australian market in August 2000. The design effort was led by a woman, Sharon Teuma. Teuma had previously worked in Australia with U.S. brands Colorado and Columbia, and had led Blundstone's children's shoe development. The step into ladies' footwear was more than just politically correct, an official told Melbourne's *Herald Sun*; women bought several times as many shoes as men. The first female-specific product was a multipurpose outdoor shoe.

Blundstone continued to produce new designs for both men and women. These included the unisex Mountain Master line of hiking boots (these were bundled with a special travel booklet produced by publisher Lonely Planet).

Blundstone struggled with a world leather shortage in 2001 brought on by the hoof-and-mouth crisis in Europe. Blundstone was unique among Australian footwear manufacturers in being associated with its own tannery. Most sourced their uppers premade from Asia.

Competition from cheap imports hurt sales in 2003, prompting management to consider moving production offshore. On the plus side, a severe drought had farmers sending more cattle to slaughter, increasing the Blundstone's stockpile of leather.

Blundstone was introducing new, more stylish lines into the John Bull collection. The Matador and the Warrior both had safety features as well as looks. Another new product for its namesake brand was the Blundstone Action Sandal.

In spite of the high cost of running a business in Tasmania, and pressure from low-cost foreign imports, Blundstone renewed its commitment to its home with an AUD 2 million investment in new machinery in 2004. A new automated leather cutting machine and extra molding machine were intended to make the operation more efficient, CEO Steve Gunn told *The Mercury*.

At the time of its 135th anniversary in 2005, the company's 550 employees were producing 1.5 million pairs of footwear a year at three sites, including the original Cuthbertson tannery in Tasmania. Training was a priority at the company to keep morale and quality high and turnover low.

Key Dates:

1870: John Blundstone begins making boots in Hobart, Tasmania.
1914: Army business gives Blundstone a boost.
1932: The Cuthbertson family acquires Blundstone.
1969: Blundstone begins exporting.
1989: Blundstone begins making gumboots.
1992: No. 500 boots appear in London and New York boutiques.
1993: A plant is opened in New Zealand.
1995: Blundstone experiments with materials; style establishes its work boots as a fashion concept.
1999: Children's shoes are introduced.
2000: "Women's Work" footwear is introduced; New Zealand's John Bull Footwear is acquired.
2005: As Blundstone marks its 135th anniversary, the company's 550 employees are producing 1.5 million pairs of footwear a year at three sites.

Blundstone's gumboot operation was relocated from Laverton, near Melbourne, to Hobart, Tasmania in the fall of 2005. The Tasmania government pitched in $96,000 to help move a molding machine. Steve Gunn, a former civil servant and the company's CEO since 2001, said that the ample availability of skilled workers in Tasmania was one factor in relocating the operation.

Principal Subsidiaries

Blundstone New Zealand Ltd.

Principal Divisions

Blundstone Australia; Blundstone USA; John Bull Footwear.

Principal Competitors

AirWair International Ltd.; R.M. Williams Pty. Ltd.; Redback Boot Company Pty. Ltd.

Further Reading

Allen, Nikki, "Beef to Boots Campaign Puts Best Foot Forward," *Tasmanian Country,* June 12, 1998.
——, "Blunnies Sold on the Internet," *Tasmanian Country,* September 26, 1997.
"Blundstone Buys NZ's John Bull," *Christchurch Press,* May 24, 2000, p. 23.
"Blundstone Gives Old Prejudices the Boot," *The Australian,* November 3, 1999, p. 43.
"Blundstone Gumboot Plant Relocates to Victoria, Australia," *AAP Newsfeed,* June 27, 2001.
"Blundstone Moves Manufacturing, Distribution Centre to Australia," *AsiaPulse News,* June 27, 2001.
"Blundstone Sinks the Slipper in UK," *Herald Sun,* January 22, 1992.
Brown, Terry, "Aussie Work Boots Top Fashion Item Overseas," *The Advertiser,* January 23, 1992.
Cawthorne, Zelda, "Designs for the Heart and Sole," *Herald Sun* (Melbourne), April 23, 2003, Bus. Sec., p. 29.
——, "Women of Steel Get Their Own Blunnies," *Sunday Times* (Perth), June 4, 2000.
Choy, Heather Low, "Blundstone to Stay; Boots Factory Commits to State," *Mercury* (Australia), April 27, 2004, p. 7.
Coster, P., "Fashion Strides Up to Blundstones," *Courier Mail* (Queensland), December 29, 1998, Bus. Sec., p. 25.
Coutts, Donna, "The Woman Behind the Boot," *Herald Sun* (Melbourne), March 17, 2001, p. W3.
Fyfe, Moya, "Bootmakers Face Showdown Over Environmental Licence," *Hobart Mercury,* April 25, 1996.
Geister, Wendy, "Blundstone Launches Women's Line," *Outdoor Retailer,* August 2002, p. 46.
Hart, Bob, "Forget the Socks," *Herald Sun* (Melbourne), June 14, 2003, p. W2.
Huntington, Patricia, "Down-Under Designs; Australian Boot Manufacturer Blundstone Is Expanding: Product Offering to Include a New Children's Line," *Footwear News,* February 4, 2000, p. 114.
"Ill Wind Created the Boot We All Love," *The Australian,* May 28, 2005, p. 47.
Johnston, Damon, "Boots Made for Hawkin'," *Herald Sun* (Melbourne), March 28, 2001, p. 18.
Konkes, Claire, "Boots Made for Staying," *Tasmanian Country* (Australia), September 26, 2003.
——, "Small Businesses Sink the Boot; Locals Left Out," *Tasmanian Country,*
Lamb, Eve, "Blundstone Graduates Give Unemployment the Boot," *Hobart Mercury,* May 27, 1998.
O'Leary, Wade, "These Boots Are Made for Walking to Kindergarten," *Daily Telegraph* (Sydney), November 23, 1999, p. 9.
Russell, Teresa, and Craig Donaldson, "How to Secure the CFO's Seal of Approval," *Human Resources Magazine* (Australia), May 31, 2004.
Simon, Kearney, " 'Blunny' Strides into the Art World," *Hobart Mercury,* February 24, 1995.
Sproull, Richard, "Blundstones: Bless Their Soles," *Australian,* February 15, 1999, p. 35.
"Steve Gunn, Blundstone Group Chief Executive," *Herald Sun* (Melbourne), November 18, 2002, p. 28.
Tasmania Department of Economic Development, "Blundstone Brings Gumboots Home," September 28, 2005.
Trayler, Debra, "The Sole of a Workboot," *Manufacturers' Monthly* (Australia), July 2001.

—Frederick C. Ingram

Catholic Charities USA

1731 King Street
Alexandria, Virginia 22314
U.S.A.
Telephone: (703) 549-1390
Fax: (703) 549-1656
Web site: http://www.catholiccharitiesusa.org

Not-for-Profit Company
Founded: 1910 as National Conference of Catholic
   Charities
Total Assets: $3 billion (2004 est.)
NAIC: 624000 Social Assistance

Catholic Charities USA, based in Alexandria, Virginia, is the largest private social service network, comprised of more than 1,400 social services agencies and institutions with a combined budget of more than $2 billion. CCUSA supports Catholic Charities membership through program development, training, financial help, national advocacy work, and media efforts. CCUSA is, in turn, a member of Caritas Internationalis, a confederation of 162 Catholic relief, development and social service organizations located in more than 200 countries and territories.

U.S. Catholic Charitable Work Dates to 1700s

Shortly after Christopher Columbus discovered the New World in 1492, the Catholic religion came to the United States through the activities of Spain. While the Spanish were successful in colonizing America's Southwest, Central America, and South America, what would become the United States and Canada were dominated by the Protestant English and Jesuit French, the latter concentrating on the upper reaches of North America and a settlement at the mouth of the Mississippi called New Orleans. It was here that the Ursuline Sisters from France came to open an orphanage for street girls, becoming the first formal Catholic charity in the United States. After the French were driven out of Canada during the French and Indian War of the mid-1700s, Colonial United States became a predominantly Protestant country.

Catholic numbers grew dramatically in the United States during the 1800s. In 1820 there were 195,000 Catholics and 124 Catholic parishes, located mostly in Maryland and Kentucky. But after 1820 there was a wave of Irish and German immigration, so that by 1860 there were 3.1 million American Catholics and 2,385 parishes. Most of them came to America to escape famine and poverty, and now represented the vast majority of the underclass in the United States, essentially relegated to second class citizenship because of their religion and were often shunted aside by the public institutions. As a result, the Catholics in the United States began to organize to take care of their poor, especially orphaned and delinquent children. By the end of the 1800s there were over 800 Catholic charitable institutions, mostly providing care to dependent children, the aged, and infirm. In many ways it was a chaotic collection of institutions and it became increasingly clear that a national structure was needed to bring some order to it.

In 1909 Brother Barnabas McDonald, F.S.C., a man recognized internationally for his work with orphans, abandoned children and delinquents, asked the President of Washington, D.C.-based Catholic University, Thomas Shahan, to issued a call for a meeting of everyone involved in Catholic charities. Six months later, in 1910, the National Conference of Catholic Charities, the predecessor to Catholic Charities USA, was convened, and 400 delegates from 38 cities in 24 states attended. The attendees included clergy as well as laypeople, representing a wide variety of charitable organizations serving the needs of children, the poor, and immigrants. The mission of NCCC was to help bring professional social work practices to the charities—many of which were led by the laypeople who had founded them in their communities—as well as to promote the creation of diocesan Catholic charities bureaus. NCCC also sought "to be the attorney for the poor." A 22-person executive committee was selected and Catholic University's Msgr. William J. Kerby was named the first executive secretary.

A sociologist at Catholic University dedicated to bringing Catholic values to social work education, Kerby had for many years stressed the importance of organization, and in 1908 helped promote the creation of the short-lived St. Margaret's Union, a confederation of Catholic Women's social work organizations.

82

Kerby was a self-effacing man who knew how to smooth over differences and played a key role in NCCC establishing itself as a fixture among catholic charities. During the 10 years that he serve as executive secretary, the 400 leaders of the NCCC met every other year, bringing national focus to an evolving Catholic social agenda, while urging Catholics to pursue so-called "scientific charity." Kerby was also responsible for grooming his successor, Msgr. John O'Grady, who lead NCCC for the next four decades and shaped it into a modern organization.

O'Grady was an inquisitive Irish-born man who after being ordained at the age of 23 chaffed at his assignment to the diocese of Omaha. He soon moved to Washington D.C. 1912 to continue his education at Catholic University. It was here that Kerby took him under his wing and began grooming him. O'Grady assisted Kerby in organizing the 1912 NCCC conference, including the editing of all the papers presented there. Later Kerby recruited O'Grady to help with the editing of a monthly publication, *Catholic Charities Review.* In 1915 O'Grady received a degree in labor economics and became a professor in Catholic University's Department of Sociology. The United States was soon involved in World War I and Kerby urged his protégé to wander around the Midwest to get a feel for the country. He reportedly told O'Grady, "John, this war will end someday and a huge army will be demobilized. Think of what that will mean. What it will mean so far as housing, job dislocation, problems of security, reconstruction and all kinds of problems. Go out to the Midwest and check around. Come up with some ideas." As soon as the war ended in 1918 Kerby was instrumental in having O'Grady appointed secretary of the Committee on Reconstruction for the National Catholic War Council. Shortly after finishing this assignment, he was considered to be experienced enough, despite being just 34 years of age to succeed his mentor as executive secretary of NCCC in 1920.

Far less politic than Kerby, O'Grady had already ruffled some feathers within the ranks of NCCC. In June 1919 he spoke before a meeting of the National Conference of Social work and outlined his ideas about expanding the influence of NCCC. The first step, he advocated was replacing lay volunteer leaders with professionals. The lay people objected, but had little influence on O'Grady who reportedly told a colleague, "We cannot change some of these old fellows. After I get full control, I expect to throw some of them overboard." Moreover, once O'Grady took the reins from Kerby, their relationship began to fray, as the steps O'Grady took were inherently critical of the man he replaced.

While his abrasive personality put off some people, O'Grady's ambitious nature provided a key influence on the growth of NCCC for the next four decades. When he took over

as executive secretary in 1920, there were just six bureaus. Two years later there 35, and by 1937 there 68, and by the time he retired the number reached 140. Under his guidance Catholic charities did indeed become more professional. They incorporated the practice of family casework, and an organizational structure developed that included professionally trained case workers and supervisors handling day-to-day affairs while the clergy acted as executive officers of the diocesan charity organizations.

NCCC Becomes 1930s New Deal Advocate

Under O'Grady, NCCC also began to champion social issues in the political realm. The primary catalyst was the advent of the Depression precipitated by the stock market crash of 1929. O'Grady now began to become a national voice for social reform, as NCCC and the diocesan bureaus sought to promote social legislation based upon Catholic principles. They became major backers of President Roosevelt's New Deal legislation. For example, O'Grady and NCCC played important roles in the passage of the Social Security Act in 1935 and the inclusion of child welfare provisions in Social Security. O'Grady would also help in the passage of housing legislation and become an advocate of a liberal immigration policy. Following World War II, NCCC helped in resettling displaced persons. O'Grady visited a number of internment camps and began urging the government to replace its quota system for immigration with a far more liberal policy. He would fight against the restrictive McCarran-Walter Act of 1951, despite its support from the National Catholic Welfare Conference. The law would pass, and Congress would override President Truman's veto. O'Grady's efforts were appreciated by many, however, including his superiors at the Vatican, who sent a message: "God can only reward you for your noble and courageous fight. You win even in apparent defeat."

Under O'Grady's tenure as NCCC executive secretary, the nature of Catholic charity underwent a sea change. According to Dorothy M. Brown in her book, *The Poor Belong to Us: Catholic Charities and American Welfare,* "By the end of the New Deal, Catholics in financial need were assisted primarily through public agencies. Catholics caring for the material needs of 'their own' increasingly did so from the professional ranks in the public welfare departments." Brown added, "Increasingly the poor were not 'us.' During World War II and after, many Catholics entered the expanding American middle class."

After O'Grady was replaced as executive secretary in 1961 by Msgr. Raymond Gallagher, NCCC experienced even more changes, as did the Catholic Church in the wake of the Second Vatican Council that ushered in sweeping changes to the church. The 1965 Vatican II document, *The Church in the Modern World,* exhorted the church to become more involved in the world and rededicate itself to serving the poor and disadvantaged. For charitable organizations it meant opening the doors to everyone, regardless of their faith or lack of it. Gallagher was replaced as executive secretary in 1966 by Msgr. Lawrence Corcoran, then in 1969 NCCC launched a three-year study, which would become known as the Cadre Study, to consider the organization's contemporary mission. In 1972 a report called *Toward a Renewed Catholic Charities Movement*

Key Dates:

1910: National Conference of Catholic Charities formed.
1920: Msgr. John O'Grady named executive secretary.
1935: NCCC plays role in passage of Social Security Act.
1961: O'Grady retires after four decades of leadership.
1972: *Cadre Study* refines NCCC's mission.
1986: NCCC renamed Catholic Charities USA.
1997: *Vision 2000,* an update of *Cadre Study,* is approved by membership.

was published, expressing a renewed mission to serve people in need and act as a social advocate.

Some of the outgrowths of the Cadre Study included the creation of the parish outreach program in 1973. A year later NCCC began hosting annual congresses where specific areas of concern could be discussed and policy statements drafted. NCCC then became a legislative advocate of these positions. A few of the most important statements that emerged from these congresses was housing in 1985, the feminization of poverty in 1986, pluralism a year later, and a just food system in 1989.

Name Change in 1980s

Corcoran was succeeded as executive secretary in 1982 by Rev. Thomas Harvey, who would later become the first to assume the titles President and Chief Executive Officer. During Corcoran's tenure NCCC followed up on the work established by Bishop Gallagher, resulting in major growth in the programs, budgets, and staffing of local agencies. Harvey continued that trend. In 1983 NCCC played an important role in the creation of the federal Emergency Food and Shelter Program, contributing about $130 million a year to local volunteer organizations. In that same year, NCCC published the *Code of Ethics* to lay out Catholic values and ethical standards, and to promote quality service. In 1986, NCCC became Catholic Charities USA, a name more suited to the organization's contemporary role.

In 1990 Catholic Charities USA expanded its purview when it entered into an agreement with the National Conference of Catholic Bishops to coordinate domestic disaster response on behalf of the conference. A year later Catholic Charities USA gained some national recognition when *NonProfit Times* proclaimed it to be the largest voluntary social service network in the United States. Over the years an increasing percentage of the organization's funding came from government money, as public agencies contracted Catholic Charities for services, especially its children's institutions. By 1994 contracted services accounted for 65 percent of the $2 billion budget.

After ten years of heading the organization, Harvey was replaced as president and CEO by Rev. Fred Kammer, SJ, in

1992. Under Kammer's watch, Catholic Charities USA continued to refine its mission on both the local and national levels. In 1993, following in the tradition of the *Cadre Study* 20 years earlier, *Catholic Charities USA: Vision 2000,* a three-year "dialogue" within and outside the church, was begun. One of the initiatives to grow out of that effort was the 1995 Racial Equality Project. The final report of the Vision 2000 Task Force was approved by the Board of Trustees in 1996 and a five-year effort to implement the report's plan was then put into place. In 1997 the membership of Catholic Charities USA approved the new bylaws that would accomplish these changes and the Board of Trustees was reorganized to increase representation of diocesan directors. In addition member sections were formed, including Health Care, Emergency Services, Parish Social Ministry, housing and community development, and children, youth, and family services. Two years later a report titled *In All Things Charity: A Pastoral Challenge for the New Millennium* was submitted to the National Conference of Catholic Bishops and approved.

In 2001 Rev. J. Baran Heir became the seventh head of Catholic Charities USA. He would only serve for two years before being called back to his Archdiocese by his Bishop. He would be replaced on an interim basis by Thomas A. Stefan until the board was able to conduct a search for a permanent replacement. In early 2005 Rev. Larry Snyder became president and CEO.

Catholic Charities USA continued to fulfill its mission during the 2000s. In addition to the regular work of its many agencies, it also responded to disasters, such as the hurricane that leveled the city of New Orleans in 2005. It also pursued its role as legislative advocate. It championed the need for greater availability of healthcare. It also fought to fend off privatization efforts and preserve Social Security, a program that it had been instrumental in establishing seven decades earlier. Although Catholic Charities USA had changed names and undergone a pair of revisions it remained just as viable a force in American society.

Further Reading

Berg, Brother Joseph, "Msgr. John O'Grady and Immigration," *Charities USA,* Third Quarter 2005, p. 13.

Brown, Dorothy M., *The Poor Belong to Us,* Cambridge, Mass.: Harvard University Press, 1997, 284 p.

"Catholic Charities: The American Experience," *Charities USA,* January/February 1987, p. 8.

Dolan, Jay P., "The Church and America," *Charities USA,* Second Quarter 2002, p. 27.

Reese, Thomas J. *Episcopal Conferences: Historical, Canonical & Theological Studies,* Washington, D.C.: Georgetown University Press, 1989.

Rice, Douglas, "Why Catholic Charities USA Will Fight to Preserve Social Security," *Charities USA,* Second Quarter 2005, p. 14.

—Ed Dinger

original
cewe color
einfach schöne Fotos

CeWe Color Holding AG

Meerweg 30-32
D-26133 Oldenburg
Germany
Telephone: (49) (441) 404-0
Fax: (49) (441) 404-421
Web site: http://www.cewecolor.com

Public Company
Incorporated: 1961 as CeWe Colorbetriebe
Employees: 3,829
Sales: EUR 428 million ($561 million) (2004)
Stock Exchanges: Frankfurt
Ticker Symbol: CWC
NAIC: 812921 Photofinishing Laboratories (Except One-Hour); 443130 Camera and Photographic Supplies Stores

Headquartered in Oldenburg, northern Germany, CeWe Color Holding AG is the holding company of the CeWe Color group, the leading industrial photo finisher in Europe. Through its 22 state-of-the-art photo labs in Germany, France, Denmark, the United Kingdom, Poland, the Czech Republic, Slovakia, and Hungary, CeWe Color serves large retail clients—drugstore chains as well as department stores that offer photo development services—as well as smaller customers such as photo studios and retail stores all over Europe. The company's 1,300 couriers deliver color prints to more than 42,000 points of sale in 19 countries. CeWe Color's subsidiaries Japan Photo and Fotolab own about 230 retail outlets for photo supplies in Norway, Sweden, the Czech Republic, and Slovakia. Altogether, Europe's largest photo finisher produced 3.5 billion color prints in 2004 with roughly 500 million made from digital images.

Former Naval Officer Expanding the Family Business in the 1950s

Before Heinz Neumüller, the son of a physician who worked for the German army, founded CeWe Color Betriebe in 1961, he served as a marine officer during World War II. Rather than becoming a naval officer, Neumüller wanted to study engineer-ing, but his family lacked the funds needed for enrolling him at a university in the late 1930s. Although the war cost him part of his left leg, Neumüller never lost his drive, ambition, and determination to succeed. The traits he acquired as a submarine commander during this time helped him later succeed in business: a positive attitude and high morale, thorough planning and flexibility in tactics, team spirit and leadership skills, working hard and delegating tasks to the right people, monitoring one's environment carefully, and acting promptly if necessary. After the end of the war Neumüller learned the nuts and bolts of accounting and running a company from the financial perspective as a volunteer at Schiffbau Unterweser AG, a shipbuilding company with about 600 employees in the harbor of Bremerhaven. Although he did not receive a salary, the training he received and experience he gathered proved invaluable for his future role as an entrepreneur. After he had finished his practical training in business management, he was offered a job there with the prospect of becoming CFO after two to three years. Neumüller's career took an unexpected turn, however, when he married Sigrid Wöltje, a master photographer whose father owned a reputable photo supplies store with an adjunct photo studio and photo lab in the northern German city of Oldenburg, in 1948.

When Carl Wöltje, his father-in-law, became Oldenburg's mayor in the same year, Neumüller—who had become a shareholder in Wöltje's family business—and his wife took over the task of running the store. Right from the beginning, delivering the highest possible service quality was Neumüller's foremost goal. When color photography technology was first introduced in Germany in 1951, he did not hesitate to acquire a license, create workspace, and buy the necessary equipment to offer this innovative, if expensive, new service to his customers. Neumüller and his wife and mother-in-law worked relentlessly on expanding the business, which in 1953 led to the opening of a second branch in Oldenburg. The main branch was renovated and expanded, too, and soon became the most modern photo retail store in northern Germany. In the second half of the 1950s a third Wöltje branch opened its doors in Oldenburg, and by the end of the decade the business employed more than 100 people. The photo lab in the main branch was expanded and new equipment was installed, capable of putting out 6,000 color

Company Perspectives:

The Name CeWe Color stands for both innovation and continuity. Extensive experience with management and employees, continuous and manageable growth, and continuously high profits and dividends are hallmarks of the company. As a technology leader and cost leader we have managed to substantially expand our market position. With a market share of over forty percent on average in fourteen European countries, CeWe Color is the European market leader in industrial photofinishing.

prints a day. At the same time, customer service was expanded and a sales office set up in Bremen that sold photo supplies to large customers such as industrial firms, hospitals, large archives, and public institutions.

Building Germany's Largest Industrial Photo Lab in the 1960s

The 1960s saw the introduction of ''instamatic'' compact cameras, which soon became very popular in Germany and helped turn amateur photography into a hobby for the masses. With the onset of the postwar economic boom in Germany, more and more people were able to afford cameras. Over time they were also able to travel during their increasing leisure time and, as a result, they took more pictures. Color photography, although still rather expensive, was on the rise. With these developments in mind, Neumüller took a major step that paved the way for his successful enterprise. In 1961 he founded a new company that focused solely on the photofinishing business. Taking the two initials of his father-in-law, ''C''arl ''W''öltje, he combined them to form CeWe, the name for his new company. At the time it was founded, Wöltje's photo lab had already reached a considerable size, ranking in the top-five league of photofinishers in Germany. In the first three years of CeWe Color Betriebe, Neumüller focused on modernizing and supplementing the existing equipment. To counterbalance the slowly but steadily deteriorating profit margins for color prints because of falling prices, more work processes had to be mechanized and automated. Looking into the future, Neumüller realized that state-of-the-art technology had to be combined with high volumes of processing orders and that only a photo lab of industrial dimensions would be able to compete in the long term. When the brand-new laboratory on the outskirts of Oldenburg was completed, the equipment that was moved there at first took up only a miniscule space in the 40,000-square-foot building. Therefore, it was called the ''roller skate building'' by some. In the following two years Wöltje's two photo labs in the city of Oldenburg were successively moved to the new location. Over time more buildings were added to the site: two office buildings, a shipping hall, and warehouse space. Finally, all of Wöltje's former photo processing departments were united under one roof.

As color prints increasingly replaced black-and-white prints, many small photo labs, often adjunct to inner-city photo studios or specialty stores for photo supplies, could not afford the additional personnel and special equipment necessary for color

film development and for making color prints anymore, which was much more cost-intensive. CeWe Color's new photo lab, which started operations in 1965, catered to their needs and was able to offer higher-quality development services in a shorter time for less money than if these small enterprises would have done the same work in-house. Consequently, CeWe Color's business volume began to grow. When CeWe Color opened its new lab there were 180 people working there. Just four years later, the number of employees had almost tripled along with the processed volume. Despite a massive downslide in prices for color prints, caused by competitors aiming at a larger piece of the market, CeWe Color's client roster kept growing, due to Neumüller's customer-oriented approach and high quality standard. The pressure on prices increased as new players entered the market for photo works, including mail-order companies and department stores. Meanwhile, Neumüller traveled to the United States to learn how American photofinishing labs were organized. By the end of the 1960s, CeWe Color had gained a reputation that reached way beyond the German border.

Expansion at Home and in Europe Beginning in the 1970s

For Heinz Neumüller the 1970s began with a big tragedy: His wife Sigrid, who had worked relentlessly by his side in the family business for more than 20 years, passed away. Together they had successfully established CeWe Color as a major player in photofinishing. Every little space in the ''roller skate lab'' was taken. Neumüller decided to double it. The 1970s, however, also marked the beginning of CeWe Color's external expansion—at first in Germany and its bordering states, later into many parts of Europe. While the processing facilities in Oldenburg were greatly expanded, CeWe Color successfully launched a sales offensive in The Netherlands, where a distribution network was established in 1971. One year later a new CeWe Color photo lab was set up in Munich. In 1973 CeWe Color merged with northern German photofinisher Vereinigte Color, including two processing facilities, one in Hamburg and one in Bremen, and a majority share in Union-color, another competitor with photo labs in Lübeck, Paderborn, Berlin, Cologne, and Nuremberg. The company was renamed Vereinigte CeWe Color Betriebe. Two years later CeWe Color took over two more competitors: Nordcolor based in Lübeck and Koliphot based in Nuremberg. After these transactions CeWe Color had become Germany's market leader in color-photofinishing. The company's workforce more than doubled within three years: from 700 in 1972 to 1,600 in 1975.

By 1975 CeWe Color served about 4,000 clients a day. Roughly every fifth order was shipped abroad, mainly to The Netherlands, Belgium, and France. For another ten years, however, the company worked on expanding its network of processing facilities in Germany, before it entered another country. In the late 1970s the photofinishing market stagnated and competition became stiffer. To defend CeWe Color's leading position, the company introduced one-day service for standard films in 1977. A new marketing campaign that supported photo retail stores—an important clientele for CeWe Color—was launched two years later. In the early 1980s the price for color prints once again came under massive pressure. As a result, CeWe Color's closest competitor, photofinisher Heinze, went bankrupt. Other competitors also struggled, such as Freiburg-based Fotocolor

Key Dates:

1961: Heinz Neumüller founds CeWe Color Betriebe in Oldenburg.
1964: The first industrial-scale photofinishing laboratory is built.
1973: CeWe Color merges with northern German photofinisher Vereinigte Color.
1975: After the takeover of two German competitors the company becomes Germany's market leader in color-photofinishing.
1986: CeWe Color acquires a photo lab in Paris, France.
1991: The company develops more than one billion color prints in a year for the first time.
1992: CeWe Color Holding AG is established.
1993: CeWe Color Holding AG becomes a public company.
1997: The new subsidiary CeWe Color Digital GmbH is founded.
1998: CeWe Color acquires a majority share in northern European photo specialty retail chain Japan Photo.
2001: The company takes over French competitor Konica Photo Service France.
2002: CeWe Color and German manufacturer Agfa jointly develop and market the DigiFilm concept.
2005: U.K.-based digital photofinisher Standard Photographic joins the group.

Wermbter, which was acquired by CeWe Color in 1983. The company's network of processing sites now covered most metropolitan areas in Germany. By 1984 the CeWe Color group operated seven large photo labs, putting out more than 450 million color prints per year. Three more large facilities were built in Germany in the second half of the 1980s in order to guarantee the quickest possible processing of orders from large customers such as department stores.

The year 1986 marked the beginning of CeWe Color's international expansion. To gain better access to the large markets in France, the company took a first step and acquired a color photo lab in Paris in 1986. In the following year, a modern photofinishing lab was established there. Increased efforts to win over customers abroad resulted in a growing number of orders from Austria and Switzerland, which were served by CeWe Color's branches in Freiburg and Munich. In 1987 Denmark's largest specialty photo retail chain was won as a new customer by the company's northern German subsidiary Nordcolor.

Transition to Digital Technologies in the Late 1990s

In the late 1980s, when electromagnetic imaging technologies first emerged, CeWe Color hosted a symposium about the future of classical photography. Participants agreed that the traditional way of capturing images with the help of chemicals would have a long and secure future. Asked about the future of video for amateur photography in *Bilder eines Mannes* Heinz Neumüller replied that he could not imagine that paper prints would totally disappear one day and that people would be content to carry a monitor around. For another two decades his

prediction proved accurate. While digital imaging technologies were refined, CeWe Color focused on further growth in the markets that suddenly opened up with the fall of the Berlin Wall. After the reunification of Germany in 1990, another large processing facility was built in Dresden to serve the eastern part of Germany as well as the first customers in Poland. To raise more capital for new acquisitions, the company was reorganized under the umbrella of a new holding company, CeWe Color Holding AG, in 1992. Company founder Heinz Neumüller became head of the newly established advisory board, a position he held until his retirement in 1998. In the following year the company went public. Throughout the 1990s and into the new millennium CeWe Color conquered new markets by means of new distribution networks, new processing facilities, or joint ventures in many parts of Europe, including the Czech Republic and Poland, Belgium, Slovakia, Romania, Slovenia, Croatia, Lithuania, the United Kingdom, and the Ukraine. In 1998 the company acquired a majority share in northern European photo specialist retail chain Japan Photo Holding Norge AS, with 32 outlets in Norway and Denmark.

By the late 1990s digital imaging technology had made significant progress and early generations of pricey digital cameras were available to consumers. In 1997, when the Internet was just emerging as a new distribution channel for business, a new subsidiary, CeWe Color Digital, was founded to explore business models and develop innovative technologies and services based on digital imaging. When the company set up a first digital terminal in Oldenburg, there were an estimated 30 digital cameras in the whole city of roughly 150,000 inhabitants. By 1999 the company offered delivery of images on CD-ROM and had its first version of an Internet platform for use by its clients as well as by consumers, called "Photoworld," up and running. Consumers were able to send in their digital images via the Internet and pick up paper prints at the photo shop of their choice two days later. A major breakthrough followed in February 2002, when CeWe Color and the German film and photo equipment manufacturer Agfa presented the jointly developed "DigiFilm-Maker," a terminal where—with the push of a button—image data were transferred to a CD that was then sent to a photo lab for development, to the Photo Marketing Association (PMA) in Orlando. By the end of 2002, CeWe Color had installed roughly 2,400 such terminals in photo specialty stores. Many other large photofinishers, such as Kodak, later adopted the new technology.

A Winner of Market Consolidation After 2000

While digital photography gained momentum, the photofinishing market in Europe underwent a massive consolidation. Although hobby photographers took more pictures with their digital cameras, they deleted many of them and did not order as many paper prints. The terrorist attacks of September 11, 2001 in the United States, as well as an unfavorable economic climate in Western Europe, caused a lasting downturn in tourism. The photofinishing industry, a highly seasonal business that made a considerable part of its sales from developing vacation pictures, suffered as a result. The German market for color prints diminished from five billion in 2001 to 3.7 billion four years later. In addition, large drugstore chains initiated a ruinous price competition that drove many photo specialty stores into bankruptcy or out of photofinishing. Consequently, 20 out of 42 large processing facilities were closed down, reducing total industry capacity by one third. Kodak, one of CeWe Color's major competitors, abandoned the European photofinishing market altogether. In 2001 CeWe Color began to close down older and smaller processing facilities, but expanded sites closer to growth markets, for example, in Slovakia and in the Ukraine. Nonetheless, the company's net profits plummeted, in part caused by restructuring efforts and high investments in new equipment for digital processing. CeWe Color answered by raising prices. Although the company had gained a significant market share—about 45 percent in Germany and roughly 40 percent in Europe—it remained to be seen if this measure would find lasting acceptance in the marketplace.

It was in 2002 when digital photography turned into a mass market. The future impact of the transition from film-based to digital photography on the photofinishing industry, however, seemed to be open at that time. On the positive side, costs for processing digital images were lower than for processing films. In addition, CeWe Color's photo-enhanced products, such as T-Shirts and aprons, stickers and calendars, mugs and mouse pads, and its innovative ''photo books''—customer-designed photo albums that included text added by customers over the Internet, printed on high-quality paper, and bound into books offered through CeWe's Internet portal—seemed to catch on with consumers. On the negative side, while digital orders grew rapidly, the volume of traditional photo development business dropped more significantly than expected. In a stagnating market, a new round of price wars with major competitor Fuji, resulting in lower prices for digital prints, seemed likely. One major promise of CeWe Color's executives for the future lay in the increasing popularity of the photo cell phone or ''cameraphone''—little mobile phones with photo capabilities. If future generations of consumers still wanted some of their digital images printed on paper or organized in albums, if they still sent them to a lab or printed them out at home, or if they got used to just looking at them on mobile phones, computers, or TV screens, remained to be seen. By 2005, Germany and France remained CeWe Color's most important markets, but the Eastern European countries promised the highest growth rates for the future.

Principal Subsidiaries

CeWe Color AG & Co. OHG (Germany); CeWe Color S.A.S. (France); CeWe Color Danmark A.S. (Denmark); CeWe Color Nederland B.V. (Netherlands); CeWe Color Belgium S.A.; CeWe Color AG & Co. OHG (Austria); CeWe Color Fotoservice AG (Switzerland); CeWe Color Sp. z.o.o. (Poland); Fotolab a.s. (Czech Republic); Fotolab Slovakia a.s.; CeWe Color Magyarország Kft. (Hungary); Japan Photo Holding Norway A/S; Japan Photo Sverige AB (Sweden).

Principal Competitors

Fuji Photo Film Europe GmbH; Spector Photo Group N.V.; Color Drack GmbH; Fotolabo Club GmbH.

Further Reading

''CeWe Color fuerchtet keinen Preiskampf,'' *Börsen-Zeitung,* September 2, 2003, p. 11.

''CeWe Color will 2005 zurueck ins 'normale Fahrwasser,' '' *VWD Wirtschaftsnachrichten,* March 14, 2005.

''German CeWe Color Starts Operations in Four Countries in Eastern Europe,'' *SeeNews,* October 4, 2005.

''On the Horizon: Digital Retail Markets General Sessions Look at Cameraphones, In-Camera Editing, and Printing Opportunities,'' *Digital Imaging Digest,* April 2005, p. 4.

''Photographic Firm Has German Buyer,'' *Birmingham Post,* November 1, 2005.

Pieper, Claas, ''Schlummernde Bilderflut,'' *Spiegel,* May 28, 2005, p. 78.

''Rein ins kalte Wasser—aber bitte lächeln,'' *Börse Online,* July 11, 2002, p. 23.

—Evelyn Hauser

China National Cereals, Oils and Foodstuffs Import and Export Corporation (COFCO)

11/F, Tower A, COFCO Plaza
No. 8 Jian Guo Men Nei Avenue
Beijing 100005
China
Telephone: +86 10 6526 8888
Fax: +86 10 6527 6028
Web site: http://www.COFCO.com.cn

Government-Owned Company
Incorporated: 1952
Employees: NA
Sales: $2.2 billion (2004)
NAIC: 424410 General Line Grocery Merchant
Wholesalers

China National Cereals, Oils and Foodstuffs Import and Export Corporation (COFCO), is one of China's state-owned foodstuffs import and export holding companies, including rice and other grains, edible oils, sugar, brewing products, fruits, vegetables, and the like. The former state agency has embraced its corporate status through a drive to develop itself into a world-leading diversified conglomerate. As such the company is involved in a variety of food manufacturing businesses, including a Coca-Cola bottling franchise; the production of premium quality chocolate and other snack foods through subsidiary Shenzhen Le Conte; wines and spirit, primarily through its market-leading Great Wall brand. Yet COFCO has diversified beyond the food and beverage industry to include real estate, through Hong Kong-listed subsidiary Top Glory International, which includes the Sanya Yalong Bay development, Hong Kong Top Glory Tower, Beijing COFCO Plaza, Beijing Capital Paradise, and the Gloria International Hotel Group, among others in its property portfolio. COFCO entered the insurance and finance industries in the early 1990s, and groups these operations under its COFCO Financial division. COFCO's finance business operates especially through two insurance joint ventures, Aviva-COFCO and Aon COFCO. The

company has announced its intention to expand its financial operations to account for as much as one-third of its total business by the end of the 2000s. COFCO also controls Hong Kong-listed COFCO International, which directly controls a number of COFCO's foods-related businesses, and serves as a vehicle for foreign investors to acquire a stake in the state-controlled parent. Under managing director Zhou Mingchen, the company has adopted a strategy calling for it to double in size by 2010 and toward that end has adopted the world's largest company, General Electric (GE), as its corporate model.

State Grains Agencies in the 1950s

COFCO's origins reached back to the early years of the Chinese Communist revolution, when the new government took control of the country's agricultural sector, including and especially its foodstuffs exports, which provided much needed foreign currency for the country's struggling economy. In 1952, the government organized a number of specialized state-owned agencies, including China Oils Export Corporation, China Foodstuffs Export Corpation, and China Cereals Export Corporation.

During the 1960s, the government began merging its state-owned agencies toward a single, centralized operation. This process began with the creation of China China Cereals and Oils Export Corporation, which was then merged with China Foodstuffs Export Corporation in 1961 to form the China Cereals Oils and Foodstuffs Import & Export Corporation. The company's change in focus reflected the country's growing dependence on foodstuffs imports to feed its ever-growing population. In 1965, these activities were grouped together under a single body, China National Cereals Oils and Foodstuffs Import & Export Corporation, or COFCO. The company became an important component of the Chinese government, and especially during the hardships of the 'Great Reform' era.

By the beginning of the 1980s, a new Chinese government had initiated a new era in China, gradually re-opening the country to capital reforms, and foreign investments and operations. COFCO became an early participant in this movement, founding

Key Dates:

1953: Chinese government forms several export-oriented state trade agencies, including China Oils Export Corporation, China Foodstuffs Export Corporation, and China Cereals Export Corporation.

1961: Government begins centralizing foodstuffs trade, creating China China Cereals and Oils Export Corporation, which merges with China Foodstuffs Export Corporation to form the China Cereals Oils and Foodstuffs Import & Export Corporation.

1965: Changes name to China National Cereals Oils and Foodstuffs Import & Export Corporation, or COFCO.

1980: Company opens first international subsidiary in New York.

1990: Le Conte chocolate production joint venture is formed.

1992: Launch of new diversification strategy and acquisition of Top Spring (foodstuffs) and Top Glory (real estate) in Hong Kong.

1998: China Foods becomes COFCO International.

1999: COFCO International goes public on Hong Kong exchange.

its first international subsidiary, COFCO New York Co. Ltd., in the United States, in 1980. Into the second half of the decade, COFCO began preparing its transformation from a state-owned trade agency to a full-fledged corporation. That process was completed in 1988, when COFCO, although still owned by the Chinese government, adopted a corporate structure.

Into the early 1990s, COFCO carried out a restructuring of its operations, redeveloping itself into a nationally operating network of subsidiaries and branch offices. The company also pushed through reforms in the agricultural sector, instituting modernized production techniques, and improving the quality of its grains and other products in order to support its future efforts on the export market.

Diversified Conglomerate in the 1990s

The arrival of Zhou Mingseng as the company's managing director in 1992 became a new milestone for the company, as Zhou initiated a new diversification strategy for the company. As part of this effort, the company targeted several sectors for its expansion. Food manufacturing became a natural extension for the company, and included the founding of Shenzhen Le Conte Foodstuff Co, Ltd. Le Conte launched production in 1991, becoming the first in China to manufacture European style premium chocolates. By 1995, Le Conte was China's leading chocolate brand. The company later grew into one of the Asia's largest producers of chocolates. That company later branched out into candy production in 2000, and snack foods in 2003.

COFCO expanded into Hong Kong in the early 1990s as well, buying up majority control of Top Spring Development Ltd., a company initially founded in 1977. COFCO then began redeveloping Top Spring into a food processing business, transferring a number of its own food and beverage production businesses. In 1994, COFCO renamed Top Spring as China Foods Holdings Ltd., which then joined its parent in a joint venture with an edible oil processor in Shenzhen, on the Chinese mainland.

By then, COFCO had launched a new direction in its diversification strategy. In 1993, the company targeted the real estate market, and acquired another Hong Kong-based company, which was renamed Top Glory International Group Company. Top Glory developed into one of COFCO's major branches, with real estate and property development holdings including COFCO Plaza in Beijing, the Top Glory office complex in Hong Kong, and the Sanya Yalong Bay project. Top Glory was later listed on the Hong Kong stock exchange, becoming COFCO's first public subsidiary.

China Foods Holdings also developed into another major COFCO company, particularly after its acquisition of Eastbay Oils and Fats Industries in Guangzhou in 1997. In 1998, the Hong Kong-based subsidiary acquired a 25 percent stake in China Great Wall Wine Co., the leading wine producer in China. In that year, China Foods adopted the new name of COFCO International. COFCO then transferred more of its business interests to COFCO International, including operations in edible oils, wine and beverages and soybean oil. Following its expansion, COFCO International went public in 1999, listing on the Hong Kong Stock Exchange. At that time, COFCO announced its intention of building COFCO International into the primary conduit for foreign investment capital into China's booming foods industries. The listing of COFCO International also came as part of an overall restructuring effort by COFCO to transform itself into a fully publicly listed corporation in the future. This restructuring also came as part of the Chinese government's announcement that it intended to reduce the number of state-owned companies from 189 to just 44 into the new century.

The Chinese General Electric of the 21st Century

COFCO began developing a new wing for its diversified operations. For this effort, the company sought inspiration from General Electric (GE), the world's largest corporation, which derived some 40 percent of its annual revenues from its operations within the financial sector. COFCO itself began developing a finance wing, starting in 1993 with the acquisition of an insurance business based in New Zealand, which was renamed as Peng Li Insurance. In 1994, the company established two new subsidiaries, COFCO Capital Corporation, based in the United States, and Ceroilfood Finance Ltd. based in Hong Kong. In 1996, the company added a futures business, COFCO Futures Company, based in Beijing, which became one of the top ten futures brokers in China.

COFCO targeted the mainland insurance market for its next financial sector expansion, after the Chinese government began allowing insurance brokerage activities in 2000. For this effort, the company teamed up with foreign partners, eager to make their own entry into the vast Chinese market. In 2003, the company announced it had formed a joint venture with insurance giant Aviva to establish an insurance company in Guangzhou in 2003. That company, Aviva-COFCO, which also represented the first entry of a foreign insurance company in China, quickly developed ambitions to become a major player in the country's insurance market, and began plans to expand into new markets.

Developing its financial wing became a key part of COFCO's growth strategy. As *Business Daily Update* quotes Zhou: "All the top 50 multinational companies in the world have businesses in finance sectors, which provides us good incentives to put more resources in this emerging financial sector," said Zhou. "It is a must for COFCO to enhance its presence in the finance sector if we want to hit our target by 2010—doubling our net assets, which stood at 12.1 billion yuan (US$1.5 billion) in 2001." As part of its strategy, COFCO added a new financial partner at the end of 2003, when it created a new joint venture with AON Corporation, launching its first insurance subsidiary in the Shanghai market.

COFCO meanwhile became a central vehicle for the Chinese government's efforts to streamline its unwieldy and inefficient network of state-owned corporations. In 2004, for example, COFCO carried out the acquisition of China National Native Produce and Animal By-Products Import and Export Co (China Tuhsu). Later that year, the company acquired a 37 percent stake in Xinjiang Tunhe Investment Company Ltd., followed by the 2005 purchase of a 59.63 percent stake in Shenzhen Baoheng (Group) Company Ltd. These acquisitions were also seen as playing a part in the run up to COFCO's own future public offering. COFCO meanwhile set its sights on remaining one of China's top ten corporations, and becoming an international heavyweight as well.

Principal Subsidiaries

BNU Corporation; Ceroilfood (New York) Inc.; Ceroilfood Finance Ltd.; China Great Wall Wine Co., Ltd.; China National Liangfeng Grain Import & Export Company; COFCO (Hong Kong) Ltd.; COFCO (Singapore) Ltd.; COFCO Capital Corporation; COFCO Dalian Import & Export Company; COFCO East China Co., Ltd.; COFCO Oils & Fats Holdings Ltd.; COFCO Shandong Cereals & Oils Import & Export Company; COFCO Shandong Peanut Imp. & Exp. Co., Ltd.; COFCO Shanghai Cereals & Oils Import & Export Company; COFCO Shanghai Import & Export Company; COFCO Shenzhen Trading & Co., Ltd.; COFCO Wines & Spirits Co., Ltd.; COFCO Wuhan Import & Export Company; COFCO Wuhan Meat Products Ltd.; COFCO Yantai Winery Co., Ltd.; COFCO Zhuhai Industries Co.; East Ocean Grains and Oils (Zhangjiagang) Co. Ltd.; Eastbay Oils & Fats Industries (Guangzhou) Co., Ltd.; Euro-China Trading Corporation GmbH; Great Ocean Oils and Grains Industries (Fangchenggang) Co., Ltd.; Hochu Trading Co., Ltd. (Hong Kong); Huaxia Winery Co., Ltd.; Laiyang LuHua Fragrant Peanut Oil Co., Ltd.; North Sea Grains and Oils (Tianjin) Co. Ltd.; Pangthai (Qinhuangdao) Flour Co., Ltd.; Shenzhen COFCO Industries Co., Ltd.; Shenzhen Huaxiahong Wines & Spirits Co., Ltd.; Shenzhen Le Conte Foodstuff Co., Ltd.; Southseas Oil & Fats Ind. (Chiwan) Co., Ltd.; Tian Ding International Trading Co., Ltd; Top Glory (Australia) Pty Ltd.; Top Glory (London) Ltd.; Top Glory Enterprises (Canada) Ltd.; Xiamen Haijia Flourmill Co., Ltd; Yellow Sea Grains and Oils (Shandong) Co. Ltd.; Zhengzhou Haijia Food Co., Ltd.

Principal Competitors

Xiamen Cannery; Hangzhou Wahaha Group Corporation; Fujian Cereals, Oils and Foodstuffs Import and Export Group Corporation; Wuhan Zhongbai Group Company Ltd.; First Investment and Merchant Company Ltd.; Anhui Huangshan Foreign Trade Corporation; Jiangsu Cereals, Oils and Foodstuffs Import and Export (Group) Company; Shaanxi Cereals, Oils and Foodstuffs Import and Export Corporation.

Further Reading

"Aviva-COFCO Ambitious to Become Leading Life Insurer in China," *Alestron*, November 23, 2005.

"China's Market Orientation Still Depends on Centralized Purchases," *Milling & Baking News*, October 10, 1995., p. 46.

"Chinese Firm Seeks More Market Share," *Business Daily Update*, November 10, 2003.

"COFCO Buys 59.63% of Shenzhen Baoheng for US$94.43 Mn," *Business Daily Update*, January 7, 2005.

"COFCO Buys Xinjiang Tunhe for CNY 410 Mn," *Alestron*, June 20, 2005.

"COFCO Consolidates Great Wall Wine Brands," *People's Daily Overseas Edition*, April 8, 2003, p. 2.

"COFCO Eager to Shift into Finance Sector," *Business Daily Update*, December 2, 2003.

"COFCO Prepares for Listing," *News Express*, September 21, 2004, p. 1.

"COFCO Ready for China Tuhsu Takeover," *China Daily*, May 31, 2004.

"COFCO Restructuring Xinjiang Tunhe," *Asia Africa Intelligence Wire*, July 11, 2005.

"COFCO Sets Dedicated Food Arm in Motion," *South China Morning Post*, February 1, 2001.

"COFCO to Build Logistics Centre in Southeastern China," *Alestron*, July 28, 2005.

"Dispute Over Famous Wine Brand," *Asia Africa Intelligence Wire*, February 21, 2005.

"Food Giant Marches to New Beat," *China Daily*, January 6, 2003.

Lim, Wendy, "COFCO Intl Keeps Focus on Growth," *FWN Select*, July 2, 2002.

O'Neill, Mark, "COFCO Wants to Copy GE Strategy," *South China Morning Post*, February 28, 2004.

Sito, Peggy, "COFCO Beefs Up Stake in HK-Listed Subsidiary," *South China Morning Post*, February 5, 2003.

"State Traders' Merger Process Underway," *China Daily*, July 14, 2004.

—M.L. Cohen

Cimentos de Portugal SGPS S.A. (Cimpor)

Rua Alexandre Herculano 35
Lisbon
Portugal
Telephone: +351 21 311 81 00
Fax: +351 21 356 13 81
Web site: http://www.cimporgroup.com

Public Company
Incorporated: 1976
Employees: 5,706
Sales: EUR 1.37 billion ($1.73 billion)(2004)
Stock Exchanges: Lisbon
Ticker Symbol: CIM
NAIC: 327310 Cement Manufacturing; 327320 Ready-Mix Concrete Manufacturing; 327331 Concrete Block and Brick Manufacturing; 444190 Other Building Material Dealers; 484110 General Freight Trucking, Local; 488510 Freight Transportation Arrangement; 488991 Packing and Crating; 551112 Offices of Other Holding Companies

Formerly a state-owned business, Cimentos de Portugal SGPS S.A. (Cimpor) is the Iberian region's leading producer of cement and related products, including concrete, aggregates and mortar. Cimpor has also asserted itself as a rapidly growing player in the international cement market, building up key positions in Spain, Mozambique, Angola, Morocco, Egypt, South Africa, Tunisia, Brazil and, since late 2005, Cabo Verte. In Portugal, the company is the clear market leader, with a 58 percent share of the national market. The company also holds top positions among the top five in each of its other markets, including the number three spot in Brazil. Cimpor's total installed capacity tops 24 million tons per year. The company operates three cement plants in Portugal, along with 66 concrete plants and backed by 16 aggregate quarries, among other operations. The company operates 15 more cement plants among its international holdings. Together, Cimpor's foreign holdings account for nearly 60 percent of its revenues. Into the 2000s, Cimpor's domestic production continued to account for some 50 percent of its operations, down from 100 percent just a decade earlier. The group's strong strategic position has made it an attractive takeover target from its larger global competitors. If Cimpor was previously protected by the Portuguese government's 'golden share' (which successfully ended a takeover attempt at the beginning of the 2000s) Cimpor is now 100 percent publicly owned, and therefore remains a potential target. The company is listed on the Lisbon Stock Exchange. In 2004, Cimpor posted sales of EUR 1.37 billion ($1.73 billion).

Nationalized Cement Company in the 1970s

Founded in 1976 as a result of the nationalization of the Portuguese cement industry, Cimpor built on foundations established in the late nineteenth century. The first element of the later national cement giant appeared in 1873, with the founding of Companhia Mineira e Industrial do Cabo Mondego. That company became the first in Portugal to install a vertical oven for the production of cement in 1884. Another important element of the later Cimpor was founded in 1890, with the construction of a plant in Alhandra. That plant became the first in the country to produce artificial cement using the Portland cement method. The Alhandra plant launched production in 1894, marketing its cement under the Tejo brand. In 1912, the Alhandra company adopted the Tejo name as its own, becoming Cimentos Tejo.

Alhandra was by then an important center for the Portuguese cement industry, and included another plant, built in 1904 by the Araujo Rato company. Another company, Compagnie des Ciments du Portugal, founded in 1906, represented the entry of foreign investors into the country.

By 1913, Portugal's total cement production had already topped 3,600 tons. In that year, also, the Alhandra plant became the first in the country to switch over to the dry production process (the last of the later Cimpor's wet process production plants was phased out only in 1985). By the end of the First World War, Portugal's total cement production had topped 8,000 tons per year.

A new company joined the Portuguese cement industry, when Henrique Araujo Sommer founded Empresa de Cimentos de Leiria in 1919, and began constructing that company's first cement complex in Maceira in 1920. The new plant was the first purpose-built dry process cement plant in Portugal and the launch of production at the site in 1923 single-handedly tripled the country's total production, which topped 26,500 tons that year. The Maceira site also built the country's first modern rotary kiln, with a daily output capacity of 220 tons.

Cimentos de Leiria was merged into Cimentos Tejo in 1925. That year, the Maceira site launched production at Portugal's first horizontal kiln. The new facility, and further investments in the industry enabled the country's total output to near 90,000 tons by the end of the decade.

In the 1930s, the Sommer family emerged as the dominant force in Portugal's cement industry. In 1934, the family acquired control of Cimentos Tejo, including the Cimentos de Leiria operation. In that year also, Henrique Araujo Sommer acquired the Araujo Rato cement company, giving the Sommer family the leading position in the national cement industry.

The Sommer-controlled cement group continued to grow, modernizing and expanding its production plant. The group also acquired another cement producer, Favrica da Matola in 1944, and began building a new plant in Dondo starting in 1945.

Following the Second World War, shortages in domestic production led the government to lower tariffs on cement imports. This resulted in a drop in domestic prices. At the same time, new competitors had begun to emerge in the industry in the 1950s. In 1950, a new facility for the production of white cement was established in Pataias, forming the basis of the Cibra company. The government too began to invest in the sector, with the Ministry of Public Works backing the creation of a Fábrica Cimento da Sociedade Técnica de Hidráulica in Alhandra for the production of asbestos-cement pipes. The Ministry of Defense, at the same time, launched Companhia de Carvoes e Cimentos do Cabo Mondego in 1950.

Cimentos de Leiria continued to expand its own operations. At the end of the 1950s, the Alhandra site added a new 167.5-meter kiln, then the world's largest, with a production capacity of more than 500,000 tons per year. The following year, the Cimentos Tejo operation installed the world's largest rotary kiln for the period. By the end of the 1960s, Cimentos de Leiria controlled more than half of Portugal's total cement production.

Two new cement companies were established in the early 1970s. In 1972, Cinorte was established and began constructing a plant at Souselas. The following year, another new company, Cisul, began construction of its plant at Loulé.

The 1974 revolution, which saw the end of some 50 years of dictatorship in Portugal, led to the new government's taking control of much of the country's industry. The nationalization of the cement sector came in 1975. Under that legislation, the government took control of Cimentos de Leiria, Cimentos Tejo, Cinorte, Cisul, Sibra, Cabos Mondego and Sagres, all fully owned by Portuguese interests, as well as the Portuguese share of another company, Secil, Companhia Geral de Cal e Cimento. The following year, these companies were merged together to form a single company, CIMPOR – Cimentos de Portugal EP.

International Cement Leader in the New Century

Cimpor operations included its newest production site, at Souselas, which came online in 1975. The government-owned company continued to expand that facility, opening two more production lines. The third line at Souselas, with a capacity of one million tons/year, began production in 1982. Cimpor also began shifting its factories from a reliance on coal as a fuel source, adapting the plants to run on oil. This program was completed in 1983. Two years later, the company shut down the last of its wet process production lines, completing its shift to the more fuel-efficient dry process method.

Portugal's admittance into the European Union in 1986 signaled the start of a new era for the country's cement industry. The Portuguese government made a commitment to privatize the cement industry in the early 1990s. As part of that effort, Cimpor was converted to limited liability status in 1991, becoming Cimpor-Cimentos de Portugal S.A. In that year, also, the company launched a new ready-mix business, creating subsidiary Precimpor. In 1992, the company's operations in Maceira and Pataias were hived off into a separate company, Cimentos Maceira e Pataias (CMP).

In the run-up to privatization, Cimpor recognized that in order to become competitive in a deregulated market it would have to expand its operations beyond Portugal. The company took its first step internationally in 1992, buying 97.7 percent of Spain's Corporacion Noroeste S.A. The purchase of Noroeste gave Cimpor control of two cement plants and a number of ready mix plants, with a total cement production capacity of 1.3 million tons, and a 4 percent share of the Spanish market. At that time, the company announced its plans to increase the share of international sales to 50 percent of its total sales.

Cimpor's privatization began in 1994, when the Portuguese government sold 20 percent of the company to the public. In that year, the company continued its drive to boost its foreign holdings, acquiring a 51 percent stake in Cimentos de Moçambique, which, with three cement plants, was that country's largest cement operation. While the Mozambique market remained quite small, the lack of infrastructure in the country suggested strong growth possibilities in the future. Back in Europe, meanwhile, Cimpor became one of 33 European cement companies fined for forming a price-fixing cartel.

Cimpor next expanded into North Africa, acquiring 55 percent of Asment Temar, which operated a cement plant between that country's two principal markets of Casablanca and Rabat. That 1996 purchase was accompanied by the sale of a new tranche of Cimpor's shares, representing another 45 percent of the company. The following year, the company moved into the Brazilian market, acquiring two companies, Cisafra, and the cement division of Serrana Group. These purchases gave the company approximately 5 percent of the Brazilian cement market.

Key Dates:

1975: New Portuguese government nationalizes the cement industry.

1976: Seven nationalized cement companies are merged to become Cimpor.

1992: Cimpor acquires first international cement operations in Spain.

1994: The first stage of Cimpor's privatization is completed, reducing government's position to 80 percent.

1994: Cimpor acquires the cement business in Mozambique.

1996: Government completes second stage of privatization process, reducing government stake to 35 percent.

1997: Cimpor enters the Brazilian market.

1998: Government completes third stage of privatization, reducing its holding to a 'golden share' of 10 percent.

1999: The company acquires Brennand Group cement business in Brazil, becoming the third-largest cement producer in that market.

2000: Government deploys golden share to block takeover of Cimpor; Cimpor acquires Amreyah Cement Company in Egypt.

2001: Government sells remaining 10 percent stake to Teixeira Duarte.

2003: Lafarge's cement operations in southern Spain are acquired.

The third stage of Cimpor's privatization was completed in 1998, reducing the government's stake to a 'golden share' of just 10 percent—giving the government the right to veto a potential takeover of the company. In the meantime, Cimpor continued its own acquisition drive, buying up Société des Ciments de Jbel Oust, the second-largest cement producer in Tunisia. The following year, the company returned to Brazil, buying up three cement companies belonging to the Brennand Group. That acquisition, at a cost of more than $500 million, boosted Cimpor to the number three position in Brazil, with a 10 percent share of the total cement market there.

By 2000, Cimpor's international growth, and the strong positions it held in its selected markets, had brought it to the attention of the rapidly consolidating multinational cement industry. The company found itself at the center of a bidding war, launched by Holcim, of Switzerland, and joined by France's Lafarge. Cimpor's independence appeared in doubt—until the Portuguese government deployed its golden share to veto any acquisition of Cimpor. When the government sold off its remaining stake in 2001, it did so to Portuguese group Teixeira Duarte, which became Cimpor's single-largest shareholder.

Assured of its independence, at least for the time being, Cimpor returned to its expansion drive. The company added

operations in Egypt in 2000, buying Amreyah Cement Company, and adding its 2.4 million ton capacity. In 2002, Cimpor entered South Africa, buying up 33 percent of Natal Portland Cement Company. Later that year, the company took control of Natal through its purchase of Lafarge's own 33 percent stake in Natal. Lafarge provided the source for other Cimpor acquisitions, including its Cimento Brumado operation in Brazil, and, for EUR 225 million, its cement operation in southern Spain in 2003. This latter acquisition boosted the group's Iberian Peninsula capacity to 9.7 million tons.

By 2005, Cimpor had completed two more acquisitions, of 49 percent of Nova Cimangola, in Angola, and 86.65 percent of Cimento Cabo Verde. With a total capacity of more than 24 million tons, Cimpor had raised itself to the upper levels of the global cement industry. The company expected to continue its expansion in the new century, boosting its production while adding new international acquisitions.

Principal Subsidiaries

Societé des Ciments de Jbel Oust; Cimentos de Mozambique SARL; Amreyah Cement Company.

Principal Competitors

Lafarge S.A.; Guizhou Cement Factory; Tata Sons Ltd.; CRH plc; Supercemento S.A.I.C; Beijing Yanshan Cement Plant; Grupo Empresarial Maya S.A. de C.V.; Cementos Apasco S.A. de C.V; Holcim Ltd.; HeidelbergCement AG; Taiheiyo Cement Corporation.

Further Reading

"Cimpor Takeover of Cimento Brumado for Euro 92.5 Million," *European Report*, May 22, 2002.

"Cimpor to Merge Foreign Assets," *Business News Americas*, January 7, 2003.

Claasen, Larry, "Cimpor Takes Over Holdings of Natal Portland Cement," *Africa News Service*, October 23, 2002.

"Lafarge Announced the Conclusion of an Agreement for the Sale of Cement Assets to Cimentos de Portugal SGPS SA (Cimpor) for Euro 225 Million," *Pit & Quarry,* January 2003, p. 55.

"Lafarge Out of Cement Privatisation: Portuguese Firm Left in the Race for One of the Three Plants on Offer," *MEED Middle East Economic Digest*, July 4, 2003, p. 19.

"Lafarge to Sell Cement Assets in Southern Spain to Cimpor for Euro 225 Million," *PR Newswire*, November 13, 2002.

"Morocco: Portuguese Company Invests in Cement," *InfoProd*, February 12, 2004.

"Portugal Sets Cement Offer for May," *Privatisation International*, May 1, 1998.

"Portuguese M&A Cemented in Domestic Market," *Acquisitions Monthly*, January 2001, p. 60.

Wise Peter, "Cement Group is a Vital Ingredient in the Global Mix," *Financial Times*, August 21, 2001, p. 22.

——, "Cementing Its Overseas Standing," *Financial Times*, June 29, 2001, p. 2.

—M.L. Cohen

CIT Group Inc.

1211 Avenue of the Americas
New York, New York 10036
U.S.A.
Telephone: (212) 536-1211
Web site: http://www.citgroup.com

Public Company
Incorporated: 1908 as Commercial Credit and Investment
   Company
Employees: 6,000
Sales: $46.7 billion (2004)
Stock Exchanges: New York
Ticker Symbol: CIT
NAIC: 522220 Sales Financing; 522290 Other
   Nondepository Credit Intermediation

CIT Group Inc. is one of the nation's leading specialty and commercial finance companies. It specializes in lending, leasing, and financing for small- to mid-sized companies. CIT is an expert in some of the more arcane aspects of corporate borrowing, using intimate knowledge of its client companies to arrange successful deals for equipment leasing, factoring, lending for acquisitions and expansion, and credit management. The company's clients include more than 700,000 companies, with specializations in the transportation industry, the apparel industry, and the construction equipment industry. CIT operates across North and South America, in Europe and the Pacific Rim. The company was a subsidiary of RCA and then Manufacturers Hanover Bank in the 1980s, after being a freestanding public company for many years. CIT went public again in 1997. It was briefly owned by Tyco International Ltd. in 2001 and then was spun off to the public again in 2002.

Early Years

CIT began life with a longer name, the Commercial Credit and Investment Company. It was founded in St. Louis in 1908 by businessman Henry Ittleson. Ittleson was first interested in financing receivables for area companies. Receivables are cash amounts due a company from its customers or other companies with which it does business. With managing cash flow some-times a problem for small businesses or those in certain industries, a third-party financial company like Commercial Credit and Investment may be welcome to step in. So from its very earliest years, CIT was involved in this kind of behind-the-scenes commercial financing. After working in the St. Louis area for a few years, Ittleson significantly expanded the business by signing an agreement with the automobile maker Studebaker in 1915. Commercial Credit and Investment became the nation's first specialized financer of wholesale and retail automobile sales. With this move to a nationwide business, Commercial Credit moved its headquarters to New York City. It also changed its name to Commercial Investment Trust, and became known thereafter by the initials C.I.T.

In 1924, C.I.T. sold stock to the public and was listed on the prestigious New York Stock Exchange. By that year it had assets of almost $50 million and 600 employees. It continued its focus on automobile financing, in 1933, buying Universal Credit Corporation, the financing subsidiary of the Ford Motor Company. C.I.T. explored other forms of industrial financing as well. Lending money and financing equipment leases to companies too small to attract big banks was a profitable niche in the overall financial services industry. C.I.T. incorporated a new subsidiary, CIT Financial Corporation, in 1942, to focus on industrial financing. The company was also long involved in a financial service called factoring. Factoring is when a financial services company buys a manufacturer's invoices at a discount. C.I.T. would pay cash for the discounted invoices, and then proceed to collect the owed amount. Factoring is deeply embedded in the apparel and textile industries in the United States, and C.I.T. was a major player from early on. The company had several subsidiaries involved principally in factoring. In 1964, C.I.T. combined its factoring units into a new subsidiary called Meinhard-Commercial Corporation. At the same time, it maintained another factoring company called William Iselin and Co. By the end of the 1960s, C.I.T. poured more of its energies into factoring as well as into financing of industrial equipment leases. It began to diminish its automobile financing business.

Subsidiary Company in the 1980s

C.I.T. was a publicly listed company from 1924 until 1980, when it was acquired by the electronics giant RCA. RCA was a

```
┌─────────────────────────────────────────────┐
│              Company Perspectives:            │
│                                               │
│   Leasing and lending solutions. See it with CIT. │
└─────────────────────────────────────────────┘
```

pioneer in both radio and television, and it had many patents on electronic devices, from transistors and semi-conductors to improved vinyl records. It had been one of the country's leading high-technology companies since the 1920s, but by the mid-1970s, when it passed out of the hands of its founding family, the company began to flounder. Between the mid-1970s and the early 1980s, RCA bought into many non-electronic industries in an attempt to diversify. Such diversification was common in the 1970s, which was the era of many conglomerate companies that sold everything from carpet tiles to automobile parts. RCA acquired the frozen foods company Banquet and the rental car company Hertz, and then in 1980 bought up C.I.T. A new RCA president in 1981 vowed to sell off the company's noncore businesses, and in 1984 RCA sold C.I.T. to the Manufacturers Hanover Bank.

Manufacturers Hanover was the country's fourth largest bank at that time, with $62 billion in assets. It paid $1.5 billion for C.I.T. According to the banking industry journal *American Banker* (November 25, 1983), Manufacturers Hanover was willing to pay a steep price for C.I.T. because it liked the financial services company's "hold on the national middle market." C.I.T. was in a high-growth, high-margin niche. RCA was willing to let C.I.T. go not only because the electronics company was returning to its core business but because it had not been able to make money out of C.I.T. RCA had taken on too much debt in acquiring C.I.T., and even though C.I.T. contributed half of RCA's net income of $223 million in 1983, cash flow had not been enough to offset debt. So both RCA and Manufacturers Hanover seemed pleased with the sale.

In 1986, C.I.T. changed its name to simply the CIT Group. The next year, Manufacturers Hanover senior executive vice-president Albert Gamper, Jr., became chairman and chief executive of the acquired company. In the mid-1980s, CIT was a leader in so-called asset-based financing, and was one of the largest U.S. companies in industrial and commercial financing. It targeted companies with sales from $1 million to $250 million, a vast and growing market of small- to mid-sized firms often too small or too risky to attract other lenders. By that time, CIT had approximately 100 offices around the United States, and handled roughly 50,000 accounts. The company prided itself on its knowledge of its core market of small businesses. It was able to charge from 1 to 2 percent more than regular bank lenders by doing so-called asset-based financing. This means CIT gave out loans secured by a lien on assets, which could be accounts receivable, inventory, or even things like trademark and franchise rights. CIT also continued to provide factoring and traditional commercial financing.

But Manufacturers Hanover sold a majority stake in CIT to a Japanese bank three years later. By 1989, Manufacturers Hanover had dropped from the nation's fourth largest bank to the seventh largest, and its financial condition had weakened as a result of troubled loans to foreign countries. Manufacturers Hanover's foreign debt problems dated back to the early 1980s, before it purchased CIT. In 1989, it sold 60 percent of CIT to the world's largest bank, Tokyo-based Dai-Ichi Kangyo Bank. Dai-Ichi Kangyo paid $1.4 billion for control of CIT and a small portion of Manufacturers Hanover stock. Manufacturers Hanover was then able to put cash in its reserves in case it lost out on some of its dicey loans. This was the largest investment in a U.S.-based financial services company ever made by a Japanese bank.

Changes in the 1990s

CIT Group continued to be run by CEO Albert Gamper through the change in parent company. The early to mid-1990s was a period of great growth and change at CIT. The company went from being a fairly narrowly focused financial services company into one with a broad range of subsidiaries. The company added divisions, sold or merged some units, and grew in assets from about $9 billion in the late 1980s to $19 billion by 1997.

CIT Group opened two new units in 1991, an equity investment firm and a credit finance division. The credit finance division was acquired as Fidelcor Business Credit Corp., and its new owner changed the name to CIT Credit Finance. The next year, CIT branched out in another new direction, debuting a new division, CIT Consumer Finance, in order to offer home equity loans. Then in 1994, the company made another acquisition, taking on Barclays Commercial Corp. This new company was merged with CIT's existing commercial services unit, and the combined subsidiary became the leading factoring company in the U.S. market. CIT had been involved in factoring for a long time, and now was finally in a dominant position within this specialized industry. Factoring had low growth potential, but according to an interview with CEO Gamper in *Chief Executive* (June 1997), it gave the company "phenomenal return." So by 1995, CIT Group had a more diverse mix of financial services in its stable, from commercial to consumer lending. The company had also stretched itself geographically to reach more of the U.S. market. The year 1995 was a record year for CIT Group, with earnings at $225 million and $17 billion in assets. That year its original parent company, Manufacturers Hanover (which had changed its name to Chemical Banking), sold an additional 20 percent of CIT to Dai-Ichi Kangyo. The Japanese bank then owned a full 80 percent of CIT Group.

Manufacturers Hanover had merged and changed its name to Chemical Banking, and in 1996 it underwent another transition as it merged with Chase Manhattan. Chase Manhattan wanted to get rid of its 20 percent stake in CIT Group. So this portion was sold to the public in 1997, and CIT Group became a public company on the New York Stock Exchange for the second time in its history. The initial public offering went well, as the company was seen as a consistently strong earner. In 1998, the company made a secondary offering, which reduced its Japanese parent company's stake to roughly 44 percent.

Acquisitions and New Ownership in the 2000s

CIT Group continued to do well in the late 1990s, with record earnings of $339 million in 1999. That year the company made a significant purchase, swallowing a giant Canadian commercial finance company, Newcourt Credit Group, Inc. Newcourt was founded in the mid-1980s by a young accountant, and by 1999 it

Key Dates:

1908:	The company is founded in St. Louis.
1915:	The company becomes the nation's first automobile credit corporation.
1924:	The company goes public on the New York Stock Exchange.
1942:	CIT Financial Corporation subsidiary is founded.
1980:	The company is acquired by RCA.
1984:	The company is sold to Manufacturers Hanover Bank.
1986:	The name is changed to CIT Group Inc.
1989:	Sixty percent of CIT is sold to Dai-Ichi Kangyo Bank.
1997:	The company goes public for the second time.
2001:	The company is acquired by conglomerate Tyco International.
2002:	The company is spun off to the public for the third time.
2005:	The company names a new CEO.

had grown to be counted as the second largest commercial finance company in the world. It had many large clients, such as Lucent Technologies and Dell Computer, whereas CIT Group specialized in smaller and lesser known client companies. Newcourt's stock began to falter in the late 1990s, apparently because investors feared it had been an overly aggressive lender, and its founder put the company up for sale. CIT Group snapped up the Canadian company in a stock swap valued at approximately $4.2 billion. The deal was finalized in November 1999, resulting in a new firm with more than $50 billion in assets, revenue of some $2.2 billion, and earnings expected at more than $500 million. That same year, CIT also acquired another factoring company, Heller Financial Inc., with assets of about $435 million.

The Newcourt deal was the biggest acquisition CIT Group had made. Although the company had diversified and expanded through the 1990s, it had not been an aggressive buyer like some of its competitors, particularly GE Capital Corp. According to a profile of CIT in *Business Week* (June 24, 2002), the company had seemed less flashy than others in its industry, as its CEO "struggled to interest investors in a slow-growing company that lent to businesses such as trucking and forest products in the tech-crazed '90s." The Newcourt acquisition broke the slow-growth pattern, and it precipitated difficulties that led to CIT itself being sold.

Just before the deal with CIT was finalized, Newcourt took a writedown of $1 billion, and as a result CIT's share price dropped by 50 percent. By early 2001, CIT Group's stock was still languishing. Investors were apparently somewhat wary of the company's loans backed by securities, as in the early 2000s this kind of loan was seen as too risky. With Newcourt and its loan profile seen as having two strikes against it, CIT seemed to be struggling. In March 2001, the New Hampshire conglomerate Tyco announced it was buying CIT Group in a deal worth some $9.2 billion. Tyco International Ltd. was known for its ADT brand security systems and for its electronics component business. Once a rather staid industrial company, Tyco had begun growing quickly through acquisitions, making four major purchases in the four months before it announced the CIT deal. Tyco apparently thought it was getting CIT for a bargain price, given its low recent performance. But CIT was still something of an odd choice for Tyco to make, as financial services was clearly outside Tyco's core business and area of expertise.

Perhaps the naysayers were right. CIT Group was under Tyco's umbrella only for about a year. By early 2002, Tyco's stock price was in a steep slide as rumors hit Wall Street about accounting regularities and suspicious payments to its director, Dennis Kozlowski.

Tyco's declining reputation had damaged CIT Group's ability to borrow, and in February 2002 Tyco announced that it would sell the financial company within the next few weeks. When it failed to find an immediate buyer, Tyco spun CIT Group off to the public. Tyco had hoped to sell CIT for $10 billion, but spun it off for about $4.6 billion. The public offering took place in July 2002, and CIT Group was once again a stand-alone public company. At almost the same time, the Securities and Exchange Commission announced that it was investigating Tyco. (Tyco's chief executive, Dennis Kozlowski, was sentenced to jail in September 2005 and ordered to pay fines of $167 million for his part in financial wrongdoing at his company.)

This was a rocky time for CIT Group. The Tyco story was one of the biggest scandals of the early 2000s, and CIT was inevitably tarnished by its short stay in Tyco's realm. The company had posted its first loss before Tyco spun it off, and it took some time before CIT was profitable again. But after losses in 2002, the company was in the black in 2003 with a substantially rebuilt reputation. CIT sold off some of its loans investors deemed riskiest, and it had gone after the kind of small business client it knew best. In late 2003, CIT bought the factoring business of GE Financial, making it the biggest U.S. factoring business by far. CIT looked for solid small-capitalization companies, of the sort that others neglected but that CIT had long made its core clientele. Also in 2003, the company chose Jeffrey Peek as president. He became chief executive officer in 2005, when Albert Gamper, who had led the company since 1987, retired. CIT made several acquisitions in 2005, broadening its portfolio to include an educational lending group and a healthcare financing group. At a time when there was some speculation that CIT might again be for sale, its new CEO proclaimed instead that the company would acquire others. The company predicted strong earnings growth in 2005. Under new leadership, CIT reorganized its business, aligning divisions by industry they served, rather than by financial product. The company launched a new investment banking division, while continuing to investigate divesting itself of some units. The company was avowedly in a growth mode as it entered the middle to late 2000s.

Principal Subsidiaries

CIT Capital Finance; CIT Commercial Finance; CIT Equipment Finance; CIT Small Business Lending Corporation; CIT Specialty Finance; Education Lending Group, Inc.

Principal Divisions

Commercial Finance; Specialty Finance.

Principal Competitors

GE Capital Corporation; AIG Inc.

Further Reading

"American Pie," *Chief Executive,* June 1997, p. 36.

"Better Than a Loss," *Fortune,* October 31, 1983, p. 7.

Brick, Michael, "Tyco's Deal to Buy CIT Turns Heads," *New York Times,* March 14, 2001, p. C1.

Forde, John P., "Hanover Foresees Bright Earnings," *American Banker,* November 25, 1983, p. 1.

Hahn, Avital Louria, "CIT's Peek Hitting Acquisition Trail," *Investment Dealer's Digest,* July 26, 2004, pp. 10–12.

"Heller Financial in Deal with CIT Group," *New York Times,* October 5, 1999, p. C6.

Johnson, Arthur, "The Dealer Folds," *Canadian Business,* August 27, 1999, p. 6.

Kite, Shane, "All Left Feet in CIT, Newcourt Dance?," *Asset Sales Report,* June 21, 1999, p. 2.

Kruger, Daniel, "Near-Death Experience," *Forbes,* January 12, 2004, pp. 70–72.

Kulikowski, Laurie, "Capital One, CIT Win 'Outperformer' Ratings from CIBC," *American Banker,* August 2, 2005, p. 2.

Lindenmayer, Isabelle, "CIT Embraces Another Low-Risk Consumer Line," *American Banker,* January 6, 2005, p. 1.

Norris, Floyd, "CIT Shakes Off Tyco's Leash, But Its First Day Is Bumpy," *New York Times,* July 3, 2002, p. C7.

O'Brien, Timothy, "CIT to Acquire Newcourt in Stock Swap," *New York Times,* March 9, 1999, p. C2.

O'Connor, Colleen Marie, "CIT Gets Green Light, Tyco Comes Under Fire," *IPO Reporter,* June 17, 2002, p. 1.

Quint, Michael, "Japanese Making Biggest Deal Yet with a U.S. Bank," *New York Times,* September 19, 1989, p. A1.

Rieker, Matthias, "Out from Tyco's Shadow," *American Banker,* July 10, 2002, p. 19.

Sloane, Leonard, "Talking Business with Wingfield of CIT Group," *New York Times,* December 9, 1986, p. D2.

Sorkin, Andrew Ross, "Market Place," *New York Times,* July 1, 2002, p. C2.

Sorkin, Andrew Ross, and Alex Berenson, "To Stem Crisis, Tyco Is Moving Fast to Shed Finance Unit," *New York Times,* February 6, 2002, p. C1.

Sundaramoothy, Geeta, "CIT Angles for More Deals," *American Banker,* August 2, 2004, pp. 1–2.

——, "CIT, Steadier, Eyes Deals to Buttress Its Core Lines," *American Banker,* February 12, 2004, p. 1.

——, "Progress Report," *American Banker,* August 23, 2005, pp. 1–2.

Timmons, Heather, "CIT Goes Public with $850M Offering," *American Banker,* November 14, 1997, p. 9.

Timmons, Heather, and William Symonds, "The Anti-Kozlowski Treatment," *Business Week,* June 24, 2002, p. 132.

—A. Woodward

CMGI, Inc.

1100 Winter Street, Suite 4600
Waltham, Massachusetts 02451
U.S.A.
Telephone: (781) 663-5001
Fax: (781) 886-4884
Web site: http://www.cmgi.com

Public Company
Incorporated: 1968 College Marketing Group
Employees: 4,100
Sales: $1,06 billion (2005)
Stock Exchanges: NASDAQ
Ticker Symbol: CMGI
NAIC: 511210 Software Publishers; 523999
    Miscellaneous Financial Investment Activities

CMGI, Inc., provides technology and e-commerce solutions that assist businesses to market, sell, and distribute their products and services. Through its subsidiaries, ModusLink and SalesLink, CGMI provides targeted solutions including supply chain management and web-based distribution and fulfillment. In addition, the company's venture capital affiliate, Ventures, invests in a range of technology companies. CMGI offers a variety of services and solutions, including inventory management, sourcing, manufacturing, configuration and assembly processes, EDI solutions providing direct connections with customer information technology systems, e-commerce, order management, customer service and supply chain design, and consulting. CMGI also offers marketing and distribution services, entailing fulfilling orders for promotional and collateral products by assembling and shipping the items requested. In addition, the company provides print on demand solutions, product and literature inventory control and warehousing, reporting, research and analysis, shipments, billings, back orders, and returns. The company serves a broad array of clients, such as software publishers, hardware manufacturers, telecommunications companies, broadband and wireless service providers, and financial institutions. The company's global reach includes operations in the United States, Canada, United Kingdom, the Netherlands, Hungary, France, Singapore, Taiwan, China, Malaysia, and Ireland.

Beginnings

CMGI, Inc., was founded in 1968 as College Marketing Group by Glenn and Gail Mathews who aimed to sell lists of college courses and names of college faculty to textbook publishers. In 1986, David Wetherell assumed control of the small direct marketing company in a leveraged buyout, renamed it CMG Information Services, and took it in a new direction—cyberspace. The company went public in 1994, selling 1.2 million shares at $8 each. That same year, with $900,000, the company created Booklink Technologies, one of the world's first commercial web browsers, enabling customers to select and purchase textbooks. Wetherell sold the browser to America Online in exchange for 710,000 shares of its stock, valued at $70 million. In 1995, the company used the proceeds to launch the world's first Internet-only venture capital firm, @Ventures, to fund and nurture promising new technology businesses. As a result, Wetherell began investing in fledgling Internet firms including Blaxxum Interactive, Lycos, and Ikonic.

Company Expands into Cyberspace in the 1990s

The company formed a second venture fund, @Ventures II, with $60 million in 1996 and expanded its Internet reach by investing in ThingWorld.com, Silknet Software, Premiere Technology, Vicinity, and GeoCities. In the same year, the company created two Internet-focused majority-owned companies, Engage (Internet marketing) and NaviSite (e-business outsourcing). In 1997, @Ventures invested in various web-oriented firms, including Ventro Corporation (formerly Chemdex), Speech Machines, Reel.com, PlanetAll, Softway Systems, and KOZ.com. CMG also launched Planet Direct, a developer and distributor of wired and wireless customer portal services, and Adsmart, an online advertising network (now part of Engage Media). CMG forays into the Internet arena caught the attention of Microsoft and Intel, both of which took just under a 5 percent stake in the company in 1997. With CMGI's expanding portfolio of Internet firms, the Internet incubator company sought to become a fully developed Internet and operating development firm.

In 1998 the company formed @Ventures III, a $282 million capital venture fund geared toward expanding investments in Internet and technology companies. CMGI contributed 20 percent to the fund with the remaining 80 percent capitalized by outside limited partners. The fund invested in a range of enterprises, including MyFamily.com, Promedix, ONElist.com, Furniture.com, Hotlinks, Asimba.com, Virtual Ink, RagingBull, WebCT, Visto.com, MotherNature.com, Critical Path, and Tickets Live. The company's partnership with the Sumitomo Corporation helped boost CGMI's Internet business in the rapidly expanding Japanese market. The company also acquired Accipiter, an ad serving technology platform, and merged it into Engage Technologies, its Internet marketing firm. In addition, by merging its acquisitions of InSolutions and OnDemand Solutions into its subsidiary, SalesLink, the company believed it could strengthen its e-commerce and fulfillment offerings.

Aggressive Adds to its Internet Holdings

CMGI took six of its Internet companies public in 1999, among them Critical Path, Silknet Software, and Ventro Corporation. It also made five strategic sales, including GeoCities to Yahoo! and Raging Bull to AltaVista. Among the Internet firms added to CMGI's portfolio in 1999 were Oncoiogy.com, Snapfish, Spotlife, Vcommerce Corporation, Gamers.com, Dormania.com, FindLaw, Boatscape.com, Mondera.com, Idapta, Hotlinks, AuctionWatch.com, Radiate, CarParts.com, PlanetOutdoors.com, Exp.com, BizBuyer.com, Productopia, eCircles.com, OneCore.com, and NextMonet.com. The company also announced a $100 million initiative to build and launch iCAST, a new majority-owned operating company focused on Internet broadcasting. The company's goals for iCAST included offering users a highly interactive environment with a downloadable desktop entertainment application, syndicated and original audio and video content, self-publishing tools, instant messaging, news feeds, and the ability to communicate or connect with entertainers.

In addition, the company's flurry of acquisitions and mergers in 1999 included buying out I/PRO, a leader of world wide web traffic verification and analysis, and Adknowledge, a provider of web marketing services. CMGI merged the two enterprises into Engage as wholly owned subsidiaries. These acquisitions and mergers, together with the $500 million acquisition of AdForce, a web ad management company, and the $11.3 million purchase of Flycast, an Internet advertising network, helped to boost CMGI's position and services in the online marketing and advertising field. CMGI further expanded its Internet service offerings with the acquisition of 1stUp.com,

an Internet advertising provider. The company also acquired Activerse and Tribal Voice, merging these providers of instant messaging and interactive communication solutions under the Tribal Voice name. CMGI bolstered its e-commerce and fulfillment services with the acquisition of ExchangePath (formerly 1ClickCharge), an online payment solution provider, and folded ZineZone and Signature Networks into iCast to expand its online entertainment offerings.

On March 18, 1999, moreover, the company joined the Nasdaq 100. In June, it bought an 83 percent stake in search engine AltaVista from Compaq, then filed to take it public. The IPO, however, was delayed when the Nasdaq proved erratic, and finally withdrawn in 2001 with the plunging markets. In October the company completed the initial public offering for NaviSite, selling 5.5 million shares at $14 each. In December, CMGI launched CMGI Solutions, a new majority-owned operating company focused on providing e-business solutions. During 1999, shareholders received a boost when CMGI formed a direct share program allowing shareholders to participate in IPO's of CMGI companies. The firm also jettisoned part of its past after selling its lists and database services unit CMG Direct. In addition, the company set up @Ventures B2B Fund to focus on business-to-business Internet investments.

In early 2000, the company continued to expand its holdings with new mergers and acquisitions. The company's various @Venture funds invested in a variety of Internet and technology firms, such as TheRealm, Corrigo, Alibris, Ironmax, The EC Company, Dialpad.com, Tvisions, OneMediaPlace, Dejima, Gofish.com, MobileLogic, AnswerLogic, Industria Solutions, NextOffice.com, FoodBuy.com, Half.com, and Knowledge First. The company also sold several firms, including Silknet Software to Kana Communications, Half.com to eBay, and eGroups to Yahoo! At the same time, CMGI acquired Adsmart and together with Flycast merged it with Engage. The company further acquired yesmail.com, an outsourcer of permission email marketing technologies and services, and added online auctioneer uBid. CMGI acquired e-commerce software developer Tallan Inc. for $920 million and merged it with CMGI Solutions, the company's e-business software firm. In October, CMGI Solutions subsequently adopted the Tallan name after the Irish-Gaelic word meaning "talent." CMGI also merged Raging Bull, an online financial community, into AltaVista, creating additional search engine services. It invested $1 billion into the formation of @Ventures Technology Fund, focusing on web enabling technologies. The company also expanded its investing through partnerships that included CGMI Asia with a unit of Pacific Century Group; wireless broadband Internet service provider SoftNet Zone with SoftNet Systems, Cisco Systems, Compaq, and Nokia; and Internet profiling services company CMGion with Compaq, Novell, and Sun Microsystems. In November as the markets began to decline, CMGI announced it was spinning off iCAST, exiting the entertainment portal business, and 1stUp.com, exiting the Ad-support Internet access field.

Collapse of the Internet Bubble: CMGI Restructures

By the time of the crash of the Internet bubble, CMGI's portfolio included more than 70 Internet companies. The company's stock that once traded at $160 a share in January 2000 fell to below $2.00 a share by September 2001. The company reported a fourth quarter net loss for 2001 of $1.27 billion,

Key Dates:

1968: Company founded as College Marketing Group.
1986: David Wetherell assumes control of firm in leveraged buy out.
1994: Company goes public, selling 1.2 million shares at $8 each.
1995: Company forms world's first Internet-only venture capital firm, @Ventures.
1999: Company joins Nasdaq 100.
2002: Company restructures, spinning off many of its Internet holdings.
2004: Joseph C. Lawyer becomes CMGI's new president and CEO.

nearly double its net loss in the same quarter the year before. CMGI chairman and chief executive David Wetherell, who had bought the firm in 1986, said the company would pursue a strategy of spinning off underperforming and non-strategic assets in order to focus on core profitable businesses.

As a result, the company ceased funding the operations of NaviPath, the interest access provider, and sold its webcasting firm Activate.com to Loudeye Technologies Inc. It sold its online advertising assets to BlueStreak, a marketing firm, and spun off other firms, including Furniture.com, instant message service PowWow, investor site Raging Bull, and Internet Profiles Corporation. In September 2002, CMGI also divested itself of Internet marketing firm Engage, and sold NaviSite, Inc. to ClearBlue Technologies, a manager of a nationwide portfolio of carrier-neutral data centers. In addition, the company divested its debt and equity interests in Signature SNI, Inc. in November. At the end of the 2002 fiscal year, CMGI's net loss totaled $524.9 million.

The company continued to restructure its operations in 2003, exiting the technology professional services business. In March, it sold both email acquisition and retention services provider Yesmail, Inc., to InfoUSA for cash and Tallan, Inc., to an investor group led by Tallan's management team, including President and Chief Executive Officer Peter Bourdon. In April 2003, Overture Services, Inc., acquired AltaVista for $60 million in cash and 4,274,670 shares of Overture common stock. For fiscal year 2003, the company narrowed its net loss to $216.3 million, about half its net loss for the previous year.

Recovery in the Early 2000s

By 2004, CMGI had weathered the worst of the Internet crash. In May, the company's wholly-owned subsidiary, SalesLink, expanded its supply chain management operations into Eastern Europe by opening a new operating facility in Miskoic, Hungary. The new facility added to the company's other locations in Ireland and The Netherlands. In August, the company acquired Modus Media, which it folded into its supply chain management business, SalesLink. The combined businesses were reorganized as ModusLink with the SalesLink marketing distribution services business continuing under the SalesLink name. CMGI announced the appointment of a new president and chief executive officer in August. Joseph C. Lawyer took over the post from George A. McMillan, who oversaw the

company's restructuring from an Internet operating and development firm to a global integrated solutions provider. Lawyer came from RR Donnelley's (RRD), where as vice-president he diversified RRD's holdings by pursuing growth in emerging markets, international start-ups, and acquisitions.

In a further sign of recovery and renewed expansion, the company's subsidiary, ModusLink, expanded its Utah operations in August 2005 by opening a new facility in West Valley. The expansion stemmed from increased demand for ModusLink's supply chain solutions within the technology market. The new facility provided a broad range of forward supply chain services, such as supply chain design and consulting, just-in-time materials planning and procurement, inventory management, assembly and packaging, and fulfillment to client's distribution centers, retail partners, and end users. ModusLink also opened a facility in Bron in the Czech Republic, offering clients a low cost infrastructure and strong transportation grid, enabling products to be shipped to and from key distribution points for final delivery to countries in Europe or outside the region to the Americas or Asia. For the 2005 fiscal year, the company reported net revenue of $1.1 billion, an increase of $672.3 or a 169 percent increase over 2004. CMGI attributed the improved performance largely to the acquisition of ModusLink, which provided significant financial benefits driven by its global supply chain services business. In October 2005, CMGI announced that its WebCt Inc. unit was being acquired by education software maker Blackboard Inc. for $180 million in cash. The parties expected the transaction to close by the end of the year or in early 1996, pending regulatory approval.

Principal Subsidiaries

ModusLink Corporation; SalesLink Corporation.

Principal Competitors

Internet Capital Group Inc.; Optiant Inc.; Redprairie Corporation.

Further Reading

"CMGI Solutions Renamed as Tallan," *Business Wire*, October 25, 2000.
"CMGI to Acquire Tallan: Company to Merge with CMGI Solutions to Deliver Innovative E-Business Applications to Global 2000 Customers," *Cambridge Telecom Report*, February 21, 2000.
"CMGI to Acquire Tallan for $920 Million," *InfoWorld*, February 21, 2000.
Fusco, Patricia, "CMGI Picks Up 1stUp," *Internetnews.com*, September 28, 1999.
Ginty, Maura, "CMGI Adds Flycast to its Cache of Online Ad Firms," *Clickz.com*, September 30, 1999.
——, "CMGI, Pac Century Aim for Asia," *Internetnews.com*, September 24, 1999.
Mehler, Mark, "Roll 'Em Up, Buy 'Em Out, Rawhide," *Sm@rt Reseller*, February 21, 2000.
"Tallan Unveils Strategic Services Unit," *Business Wire*, October 25, 2000.
"US Financial Network: Ebay Closes $2.6 B Skype Acquisition and CMGI says Blackboard to Buy WebCt Unit," *Presswire*, October 17, 2005.

—Bruce P. Montgomery

COGNEX®

Cognex Corporation

One Vision Drive
Natick, Massachusetts 01760-2059
U.S.A.
Telephone: (508) 650-3000
Fax: (508) 650-3333
Web Site: http://www.cognex.com

Public Company
Incorporated: 1981
Employees: 746
Sales: $202 million (2004)
Stock Exchanges: NASDAQ
Ticker Symbol: CGNX
NAIC: 334513 Instruments and Related Product
Manufacturing for Measuring, Displaying, and
Controlling Industrial Process Variables; 334111
Electronic Computer Manufacturing; 334119 Other
Computer Peripheral Equipment Manufacturing

Based in Natick, Massachusetts, Cognex Corporation is a leading global supplier of machine vision systems, which give computers the power of sight. In addition to its East Coast headquarters and other U.S. locations, Cognex's operational base includes sites in Europe, Japan, and Southeast Asia. Cognex's clients hail from a number of industries, including aerospace, automotive, consumer products, healthcare, packaging, pharmaceuticals, and semiconductor manufacturing. The company offers a comprehensive lineup of industrial-grade machine vision products, including vision sensors, PC vision systems, hand-held and fixed-mount code readers, and surface inspection systems. As of late 2005, semiconductors accounted for 27 percent of Cognex's business, followed by factory automation (57 percent), and surface inspection (16 percent). Outside of its initial success in the semiconductor and electronics OEM business, Cognex considers its foray into general factory automation as one of the most important events in its history.

Cognex's products are used to automate different aspects of the manufacturing process. As the company explains, its sys-tems "automatically identify products, inspect for defects, gauge part dimensions, and guide robotic equipment—at up to thousands of parts per minute. ... In a typical application, a Cognex machine vision system captures an image of the part to be inspected through a video camera. The system then analyzes the image and generates an answer about it, such as whether a part is defective. This information then can be sent to other equipment in the manufacturing line, including a robotic arm that will remove a bad part from the process."

Pioneering Machine Vision: The 1980s

Cognex, which draws its name from the phrase "Cognition Experts," was established by Dr. Robert J. Shillman, a lecturer in human visual perception at the Massachusetts Institute of Technology (MIT). Prior to receiving his doctorate from MIT, Dr. Shillman earned undergraduate and graduate degrees in electrical engineering from Northeastern University and taught computer science at Tufts University.

According to the April 1999 issue of *Electronic Business,* Shillman was "deeply dissatisfied" with life in the academic world. Psychotherapy revealed that he wanted to be two things: an entrepreneur and an entertainer. Using research from his dissertation at MIT, in 1981 Shillman invested $87,000—his life savings, which he earned by restoring classic cars and fixing up apartment buildings—to start Cognex in a 1,000-square-foot office.

Over the years, Shillman has built a culture that prizes humor and allows him to entertain others. When asked about his emphasis on humor, he once explained that it is an effective way of increasing morale, addressing rumors, and breaking down barriers between workers, whom he affectionately calls "Cognoids." In addition to instituting a policy that made Halloween Cognex's official holiday—and required all employees to work in costume—Shillman became known for wearing wild costumes throughout the year and engaging in complicated practical jokes. A *Fortune* article noted that Shillman once gave out cash bonuses of up to $10,000—in moneybags from a Brink's truck. He awards 15-year employees with trips to one of the world's seven wonders, and engages in a Three Stooges routine to welcome new hires. Cognex's 2002 annual report was a *Mad Magazine* parody, with Shillman appearing on the cover as Alfred E. Neuman. The

102

Company Perspectives:

I started Cognex because I wanted to work each day in a particular type of company—one that had smart, energetic people who enjoyed what they were doing, who liked to have goals and to accomplish those goals. And I wanted a physical environment that reflected the culture of the company, which I wanted to be dynamic. I also wanted to work for a company where the management would tolerate, or better yet, seek out outspoken and assertive people like myself who don't care about office politics but who care deeply about doing the right thing for customers. Well, I couldn't find such a company, so I had to create it.—Cognex Founder Dr. Robert J. Shillman, Electronic Design, February 2, 2004

company even has its own corporate anthem, which Shillman leads with the backing of an employee rock band.

Shillman launched Cognex with the help of Bill Silver and Marilyn Matz, two graduate students from MIT's Artificial Intelligence Lab, luring them to summer jobs with free bicycles and the prospect of interesting work. Silver and Matz remained with Cognex long-term, earning pioneer status along with Shillman. Matz eventually became senior vice-president of engineering for Cognex's Modular Systems Division, and Silver became senior vice-president of research and development and chief technology officer.

In the February 2, 2004 issue of *Electronic Design,* Silver explained that youthful idealism and risk-taking were key elements in the company's early success, remarking: "We saw a problem people wanted solved, and we were crazy enough to do it. We had our share of good luck too. Had we known how hard it would be, who knows if we would have given it a try?"

Cognex initially set its sights on developing custom machine vision systems and installing them for clients. The company quickly made its mark by releasing an industrial optical character recognition (OCR) system called DataMan in 1982. According to Cognex, DataMan was an industry first and had "the capability to read, verify, and assure the quality of letters, numbers, and symbols in industrial environments." The new system was first used by a typewriter manufacturer to ensure correct key placement. After securing its first customer, the company's growth was aided by capital investments of more than $5 million.

According to the company, when DataMan successfully read its first character, employees celebrated with champagne. So began a tradition of celebrating important milestones with a bottle of the sparkling beverage. After employees autographed the label, these special bottles were added to Cognex's "Wall of Fame." Following the introduction of DataMan, Cognex introduced its Checkpoint 5500 Automatic Visual Tester in 1984, which was used for detecting assembly errors on circuit boards.

After helping to form the machine vision industry, Cognex soon found itself in an increasingly competitive environment, with roughly 100 players vying for a share of the market. Developing custom machine vision systems was a costly propo-

sition. In addition to significant operating losses, Cognex ran into technical difficulties with some of its early installations. For example, a system developed for American Cyanamid performed correctly in the company's lab, but had problems on the shop floor in Puerto Rico. Cognex was forced to take a loss on the project and refund American Cyanamid's money.

For reasons such as these, the company shifted gears in 1986. Allan Wallack, a manager from Digital Equipment Corp., was hired as Cognex's chief operating officer. Wallack helped to change the company's focus from custom systems to the development of standardized machine vision hardware and software for the original equipment manufacturer (OEM) market. Cognex reasoned that technically adept OEMs—especially those in industries like semiconductors, which rely heavily on machine vision technology—could then tailor these standardized products to meet their specific needs.

In tandem with its new approach, Cognex unveiled two new products. The first was Cognex 2000, which the company described as "the world's first machine vision system built on a single printed circuit board." The second was a software application called Search, which had the capability to "locate patterns in images very quickly and accurately."

By the mid-1980s, Cognex was quickly establishing a position of industry leadership. Leading firms provided development funds to Cognex for the development of much needed technology. For example, General Motors' Delco Electronics division gave Cognex $500,000 to develop a system for inspecting circuit boards with surface mounted devices (SMDs).

Cognex turned its first profit in 1987. The following year, the company's revenues totaled $10.6 million and net income reached $2.4 million. At this time, approximately 33 percent of total sales came from OEMs in the $600 million semiconductor industry. This focus required Cognex to do a growing amount of business with Japanese firms, which held attributes like quality and punctuality in high regard.

Initially, Cognex worked with Japanese firms through a distributor named Marubeni Hytech Ltd. Dr. Shillman eventually began traveling to Japan, however, to forge direct relationships and learn more about Japanese business practices. His efforts were met with success. As the November 13, 1989 issue of *Electronic Business* explained, quality improvements at Cognex resulted in tighter delivery schedules and shorter response times, and helped the company to secure significant business from the Japanese.

In late 1988 Tokyo-based Seimitsu Co. Ltd. agreed to purchase Cognex's machine vision systems at a rate of about 50 per year. This was followed by a $9 million agreement with Shinkawa Ltd. in the spring of 1989, which some observers considered the largest contract in the machine vision industry's history. The company expected that the percentage of its sales attributable to Japanese companies would increase from 14 percent in 1988 to more than 20 percent in 1989.

Cognex ended the 1980s on solid footing. The company went public in 1989 at $1.38 per share. Sales reached $15.9 million that year, with net income of $3.7 million.

Key Dates:

1981: MIT professor Dr. Robert J. Shillman invests $87,000 to start Cognex.

1982: The company releases an industrial optical character recognition (OCR) system called DataMan.

1986: Cognex begins focusing on the development of standardized machine vision hardware and software for the original equipment manufacturer market.

1987: The company turns its first profit.

1989: Cognex goes public.

1990: Dr. Robert Shillman is named Entrepreneur of the Year by *Inc.* magazine.

1994: Cognex introduces its Windows-based Checkpoint system, which can be implemented by nontechnical employees.

1995: Cognex acquires Portland, Oregon-based Acumen Inc., a wafer identification technology firm.

1996: Cognex purchases Alameda, California-based Isys Controls, a manufacturer of high-performance surface inspection systems.

2000: Cognex buys Komatsu Ltd.'s machine vision business, Epsom, U.K.-based Image Industries, and the surface inspection business of Kuoppio, Finland-based Honeywell International.

2001: Amidst an industry downturn, Cognex announces its first major layoff since 1985.

2004: Jim Hoffmaster is named company president, becoming the first employee other than Dr. Shillman to hold the title.

2005: Cognex acquires Duluth, Georgia-based DVT Corporation for approximately $115 million.

2006: Cognex celebrates its 25th anniversary.

Focused Growth: The 1990s

The 1990s began on a high note. Cognex saw its stock price triple only a year after its initial public offering. In the March 5, 1990 issue of *Metalworking News,* Fechtor, Detwiler & Co. analyst M. Ronald Opel forecast that Cognex would see its net income grow at an annual rate of 25 to 35 percent during the first years of the decade. At 25 percent, Opel explained that the company held a commanding share of the U.S. merchant electronics manufacturing machine vision market (not including companies that manufactured their own systems), and that Cognex was "the only machine vision company thus far to have achieved substantial profitability."

Another positive development occurred in 1990 when Dr. Shillman was named Entrepreneur of the Year by *Inc.* magazine. With Cognex in good condition, COO Allan Wallack left the company to pursue other opportunities. He was replaced by Neil R. Bonke, who previously served as president of General Signal Corp.'s Xynetics division. At this time, the company's products ranged from the Cognex 1500 system to higher-end applications such as its 2000 and 3000 series. Starting at $20,000, Cognex's systems required engineers to be knowledgeable in the C programming language.

Cognex ended 1990 with sales of $23.5 million. That year, the company's net income surged 76 percent, reaching $6.5

million. Milestones at Cognex during the early 1990s included a patent for VC-1, a dedicated vision chip, in 1991. That same year, the company unveiled the Cognex 4000, a full-capability machine vision system for VME bus computers. In 1993 the Cognex 5000 marked the first advanced vision system for PC/AT bus personal computers. Finally, the company introduced its Windows-based Checkpoint system in 1994. Priced at $23,900, the point-and-click machine vision system could be implemented on assembly lines by nontechnical employees.

Heading into the second half of the 1990s, Cognex began to actively acquire other businesses. In 1995 the company acquired Portland, Oregon-based Acumen Inc., a wafer identification technology firm. This was followed by the purchase of Alameda, California-based Isys Controls, a manufacturer of high-performance surface inspection systems, in 1996. Cognex acquired Mayan Automation, a manufacturer of low-cost surface inspection systems, in 1997, followed by the machine vision business of Allen-Bradley Inc., a division of Rockwell Automation, in 1998.

A number of important product rollouts occurred at Cognex during the mid-1990s. In 1996 the company introduced the acuReader/2Dm, a PC plug-in Data Matrix 2D code reading solution. The following year Cognex unveiled PatMax, a fast, highly accurate, high-yield object location technology. Finally, a high-speed, compact industrial machine vision camera called the CVC-1000 was introduced in 1998.

The Cognex Surface Inspection Systems Division was formed in late 1997. Based in Alameda, California, it was established to develop and market high-speed, camera-based inspection systems to end-users in the plastics, metals, paper, and nonwoven materials sectors. The company ended 1999 with revenue of $152.1 million and net income of $30.4 million.

Acquisition and Expansion: 2000–05

The new millennium brought new developments at Cognex. In May 2000, the company bought Komatsu Ltd.'s (Japan) machine vision business for $11 million, with additional performance-dependent payments of up to $8 million. During the same month, the company purchased Epsom, U.K.-based Image Industries, a manufacturer of vision sensors. The purchase made Cognex a leading supplier in the United Kingdom. In 2000, the company also acquired the surface inspection business of Kuoppio, Finland-based Honeywell International.

New products during 2000 included the acuReader III, Checkpoint II, and SMD4 machine vision systems, as well as the SmartView web inspection system and the In-Sight 2000 machine vision sensor. According to Cognex, its In-Sight line helped it to expand into the realm of factory automation. In 2001 the company introduced the In-Sight 1000 and In-Sight 3000 industrial machine vision sensors. Equipped with Ethernet ports, the sensors were suited for a range of industrial applications.

Jim Hoffmaster became Cognex's chief operating officer in 2001, a difficult year in the company's history. As overall economic conditions soured in late 2001, exacerbated by the terrorist attacks of September 11, the electronics and semiconductor segments began to decline. This prompted Cognex to announce its first major layoff since 1985. In addition to cutting 25 unfilled positions and contractor jobs, the company let 60 regular employees go. The workforce reduction, which was expected to save the company $6.5 million, affected Cognex's Modular Vision Systems Division and included 30 positions at the company's headquarters. Despite the workforce reduction, the industry downturn still impacted Cognex; in 2002 the company lost $6 million on revenues of $114 million.

Cognex made two additional acquisitions in 2003. That year, the company purchased the wafer identification business of Siemens Dematic AG, as well as the ID code reading business of Aachen, Germany-based Gavitec AG. By 2003 Cognex served the Asian market from offices in Japan, Korea, Singapore, and Taiwan, and through partnerships with Chinese firms. In August of that year, the company announced plans to open an office in Shanghai to directly serve the burgeoning Chinese market. Cognex marked the year's end by reaching a significant milestone: the sale of its 200,000th machine vision system, marking $1.5 billion in cumulative revenue since 1981.

Cognex's revenues reached $202 million in 2004. That year, Jim Hoffmaster was named company president, becoming the first employee other than Dr. Shillman to hold the title. Shillman remained chairman and CEO. Cognex's total number of system shipments exceeded 275,000 in 2004, representing cumulative revenue of more than $1.9 billion since 1981. With 207 patents and more than 100 additional patents pending, Cognex had devoted more than 500 "man-years" to the development of its vision systems. At this time, the company employed nearly 700 workers, affectionately known as "Cognoids," some 200 of whom worked outside of North America.

In late 2004 Cognex formed two new teams in its Modular Vision Systems Division with a goal of devoting resources to new markets for machine vision technology, namely early vision technology adopters with strong growth potential. One new team was focused on expert sensors, which included sensors for monitoring admission to restricted areas, while another concentrated on identification products. The latter area involved technology for reading two-dimensional bar codes, which were being adopted by manufacturers in the automotive, electronics, aerospace, and defense sectors. Two-dimensional bar codes are capable of encoding more than 1,000 characters of data, and are useful for tracking and tracing parts.

In May 2005 Cognex announced that it had acquired one of its main rivals, Duluth, Georgia-based DVT Corporation, for approximately $115 million. The acquisition gave Cognex access to a network of more than 150 industrial distributors worldwide who were trained to support and sell machine vision products. In particular, the distribution network would help Cognex to expand its market for low-cost vision sensors.

As Cognex prepared to mark its 25th anniversary in 2006, the future appeared to hold nearly limitless potential. As Bill Silver explained in the February 2, 2004 issue of *Electronic Design:* "We have hardly begun to scratch the surface of machine-vision applications and technology. We have examples in the world of human vision that are so far in advance of anything we can make with machines, that I don't expect us to catch up in my lifetime or my children's."

Principal Subsidiaries

Cognex Finland Oy; Cognex International Inc. (France); Cognex Germany Inc.; Cognex Ltd. (Ireland); Cognex Benelux (Netherlands); Cognex UK Ltd.; Cognex KK (Japan).

Principal Divisions

Modular Vision Systems; Surface Inspection Systems.

Principal Competitors

KLA-Tencor Corporation; Orbotech; Robotic Vision Systems, Inc.

Further Reading

Autry, Ret, "Cognex," *Fortune,* August 13, 1990.
Braham, Lewis, "What. Me Worry?," *Business Week,* May 12, 2003.
Donlin, Mike, "The Incredible Shrinking Vision System," *Computer Design,* July 1993.
"Cognex," *Boston Business Journal,* February 11, 1991.
"Cognex Aims Resources at Future," *Solutions—for People, Processes and Paper,* March 2004.
"Cognex Acquires DVT," *Robotics World,* May 2005.
"Cognex Acquires Machine Vision Business of Komatsu," *Robotics World,* May 2000.
"Cognex, Avalon Join Forces," *Nonwovens Industry,* March 1999.
"Cognex Buys Image to Create Strong Vision Team," *Packaging Magazine,* May 18, 2000.
"Cognex Entering ATE Market," *Electronic News,* October 22, 1984.
"Cognex Expands to China," *Nonwovens Industry,* August 2003.
"Cognex Hits Milestone," *Nonwovens Industry,* December 2003.
"Cognex Ships 300th SmartView System," *Solutions—for People, Processes and Paper,* May 2003.
"Cognex to Reduce Workforce," *Nonwovens Industry,* November 2001.
Fraone, Gina, "Mavericks," *Electronic Business,* April 1999.
Fusaro, Dave, "Machine Vision Project: Delco Commits $500,000," *American Metal Market,* January 6, 1986.
"How to Succeed with Machine Vision," *Quality,* December 2004.
Kerr, John, "Cognex: Breaking into Japan: Small U.S. Companies Show How It's Done," Natick, Mass.: Cognex Corp., November 13, 1989.
Kilbane, Doris, "Cognex Brings In-Sight to Machine Vision: Machine-Vision Technology Continues to Reinvent the Production Process, and In-Sight Systems Put It Within Everyone's Reach," *Electronic Design,* February 2, 2004.
"Machine and Plant Floor News: Cognex Launches Machine Vision Systems for Key Industries," *Manufacturing Automation,* August 2000.
"Machine Vision Sensors Have Ethernet," *Test & Measurement Europe,* June 2001.
Mayersohn, Norman S., "The Eyes Have It," *Chief Executive,* November 1999.
Mula, Rose, "Selling to the Competition Pays Handsomely for Cognex," *Electronic Business,* February 5, 1990.
"Nyuck, Nyuck, Nyuck. (Robert Shillman, CEO, of Cognex, a Software Firm, Uses Humor to Motivate Employees)," *Fortune,* March 31, 1997.
Rossi, Cathy, "With Cognex in Good Shape, Wallack Moves On," *Metalworking News,* March 5, 1990.
Slutsker, Gary, and Ruth Simon, "The Vision Thing," *Forbes,* December 10, 1990.

''Success Story: Cognex Milestones,'' *Electronic Design,* February 2, 2004. Available from http://www.elecdesign.com/Articles/Index .cfm?ArticleID = 7251.

Testa, Justin, ''A Broader Vision for Industry Pioneer,'' *Test & Measurement World,* March 2005.

''Vision 'Measures' Up: Cognex Chief Says Vision Is a Viable Solution to Quality Needs,'' *Quality,* August 2005.

''Vision Ventures,'' *Electronic News,* February 8, 1999.

Woods, Wilton, ''Machine Vision,'' *Fortune,* June 27, 1994.

—Paul R. Greenland

Cole National Corporation

4000 Luxottica Place
Mason, Ohio 45040
U.S.A.
Telephone: (513) 765-6000
Fax: (513) 765-6249

Business Segment of Luxottica S.p.A.'s North American Retail Group
Incorporated: 1930 as National Key Company
Employees: 9,330
Sales: $1.2 billion (2003)
NAIC: 446130 Optical Goods Stores

Once an optical retailer with nearly 3,000 outlets in the United States, Canada, and the Caribbean, Cole National Corporation was acquired by Italy's Luxottica S.p.A. in 2004. Luxottica proceeded to fold Cole's operations into its North American Retail Group, and while Cole's holdings (such as Pearle Vision) continued to thrive, the Cole structure was dissolved. Over the course of its history, Cole National had dabbled in specialty retail ventures ranging from key cutting services to children's toys to cookie-baking to shoe repair and watchbands. Optical retail, however, began to play a large role in the company's strategy in 1996 when it acquired Pearle Inc. in a deal that made it the second-largest optical retailer in the United States. In 2004, at the time of the Luxottica acquisition, the company operated as a leading provider of vision care products and services—including managed vision care programs—and personalized gifts through its Things Remembered stores.

Early History

Company namesake and guiding light Joseph E. Cole was born in Cleveland in 1915, the youngest of nine children. He started his retail career with Cleveland's National Key Company in 1935 at the age of 20. He left National Key nine years later to establish the key division of Curtis Industries, another Cleveland business.

Cole's first key shop was set up in the parking lot of a local Sears, Roebuck & Co. store that same year. By the end of the decade, Cole had built his little sideline into America's second-largest key retailer. The self-made entrepreneur was coronated "king of keys" in 1950, when he acquired National Key and Curtis' key division, the industry's two top players. The newly unified firm took the name of its larger constituent, National Key. (Although National Key was founded in 1932, Cole National claimed 1944 as its inaugural year.)

Joe Cole's key-selling concept was predicated on the idea that keymaking was a highly specialized, service-oriented business. While mass retailers wanted a share of this segment's high profit margins, they did not want to deal with the equally high level of training, service, and inventory control it demanded. Cole leased space from such leading department stores as Sears, Roebuck and Co., Montgomery Ward, and Kresge's. He then installed key-making machines, trained store employees to cut keys, and oversaw the operations' complex 3,000-unit inventory. While Cole neither manufactured keys nor owned stores, Cole found a profitable niche in providing its services to customers and retailers.

A company executive would later characterize Cole's counters as "an oasis of service in a sea of self-service." The tiny selling areas emerged as the most productive areas—in terms of profits per square foot—in some stores. During the 1950s, the company expanded into the manufacture and sale of key chains and jewelry, and launched a while-you-wait shoe repair division.

Public Offering Leads to Growth in the 1960s

The explosion of automotive and home sales in the postwar era made expansion of the replacement key industry virtually inevitable. Less than a decade after assuming the helm of National Key, Joe Cole increased sales fourfold, from $2.33 million in 1950 to $10.52 million in 1959. When the firm went public that year, it sold out its entire offering in one day. The Cole family retained a 25 percent stake in their company, which by that time was netting over $635,000 annually.

The company used the proceeds of its initial public offering to fund an acquisition spree in 1960. Over the course of that single year, the firm purchased Fairfield Publishing, a greeting-card company; Shore Manufacturing, a novelty business; and Masco Optical. Having thus diversified from its base in keys—and in recognition of its leader—the company was renamed Cole National Corp. in 1960.

That same year, Cole tested a new concept in optical retailing, establishing an eyewear counter within space leased from a Detroit Montgomery Ward store. This venture was based on the same concept as the company's key business. Company strategists recognized that mass retailers had the traffic, but not the expertise, to run such an operation. Masco Optical became the foundation of a chain of optical counters that numbered over 150 locations by the end of the 1960s. Optical centers had become Cole National's largest division by 1964, contributing about half of annual sales.

Although CNC retained a focus on retailing, it also diversified into manufacturing during the 1960s. It acquired Sterling Industries, a Cleveland manufacturer of aluminum, steel and plastic products in 1961, thereby winning an exclusive contract with Welcome Wagon. In 1966 Cole National merged with Susan Crane, producers of giftwrap, and acquired the Gene Upton Co., manufacturers of self-adhesive metal letters and numbers. Two years later it acquired Manco, Inc., a manufacturer of Topps and Everbest brand watchbands. The Manco purchase included Canadian, British, and Japanese retail outlets. Griffon Cutlery Corporation, a marketer of manicure tools, was added to the roster in 1969. These acquisitions more than quadrupled Cole National's sales to over $40 million, but also invited speculation from analysts that the company had overextended itself. In 1970, in fact, the retail conglomerate's profits declined by half.

The company's acquisitive push also got it into trouble with the Federal Trade Commission in the mid-1960s. Cole National had purchased Independent Lock Co., a 45-year-old manufacturer of locks and key blanks with about $14 million in annual sales, early in 1964. In 1967, however, the government compelled Cole to sell the business, which would have nearly doubled CNC's annual sales.

Reorganization in the 1970s–80s

Although Joseph Cole brought in new presidents to help him run the company beginning in the 1960s, he retained defacto control of his firm as its chairman and chief executive officer. In the face of declining profits in the 1970s, son Jeffrey A. Cole convinced his father to bring a group of young MBAs like himself into upper management. According to a 1980 article in Forbes, the "young turks ... managed to rid the company of its poorer diversifications, prevent Joe Cole from making any more bad moves and get the company back to its special service orientation." Both the Canadian retail operations and a distribution business were put on the auction block. In spite of (or perhaps because of) the divestments, annual revenues rose by nearly 50 percent, from $106 million in 1976 to $158 million in 1980. One survivor of the cutbacks was Things Remembered, the chain of mall-based gift shops that specialized in monogrammed and engraved items. Established in 1967 by Cole National, the chain had expanded to 280 shops in 38 states by 1980.

In 1984 Kohlberg Kravis Roberts and Co., an investment firm, took Cole National Corp. private through a leveraged buyout. The outsiders took a managerial approach typical of the investment-house "reorganizations" of the 1980s. They sold off Cole's Craft Showcase chain in 1984 and the Original Cookie Company stores in 1985. In 1987 a group led by Jeffrey Cole took on more debt to regain control of the retail conglomerate. They created a holding company, CNC Holding Corporation, and kept the firm private until 1994.

During the early 1980s, CNC had made what has been called "its highest-profile deal" with the 1981 acquisition of Child World Inc., which then ranked second only to Toys-R-Us among toy supermarket chains. By 1985, when the parent sold 18 percent of the Child World subsidiary to the public, the chain boasted over 100 stores in 21 states under the Child World and Children's Palace names. However, a late 1980s retail slump, combined with intense competition from Toys-R-Us and a $300 million-plus debt load, crippled the subsidiary chain. While Jeffrey Cole struggled to sell off the business—in 1990 a potential acquirer failed to secure financing—Child World incurred a massive $192 million loss on sales of $830 million.

Cole's woes concerning Child World were compounded when the chain was one of seven toy stores named in a 1990 federal lawsuit brought by the Consumer Product Safety Commission. Nonetheless, CNC was finally able to sell the subsidiary to a coalition of former Toys-R-Us executives. Instead of cash, Cole traded $60 million in long-term debt for $30 million in short-term debt. While Cole had been able to negotiate a $157 million price tag for the stores in 1990, it was clearly not in a strong bargaining position by this time. The divestment slashed Cole's annual sales from over $1.25 billion in 1990 to $425 million in 1991. Within a year of the exchange, Child World's new owners were forced to file for bankruptcy and liquidate the entire chain.

That deal left CNC with three retail divisions: Things Remembered gift shops; Cole Key; and Cole Vision. Cole's Vision group, along with much of the eyewear industry, had enjoyed double-digit annual growth in the 1980s. By the early 1990s Cole Vision ranked third among the United States' largest eyewear chains, and its more than 750 outlets contributed about half of the company's sales. Although annual increases in eyewear sales fizzled to just 1 percent by that time, CNC expressed confidence that aging baby boomers would be buying many pairs of glasses and contacts after the dreary economy reheated in the mid-1990s. In fact, the company expanded its eyecare business into the managed healthcare market in the early years of the decade, establishing benefits contracts with labor unions, insurance companies, health management organizations, and other large groups.

CNC also converted hundreds of its Cole key counters in department stores into "Gift Centers" that resembled the successful Things Remembered shops. The growing emphasis on giftware prompted expansion of the concept into a "superstore" format and the addition of personalized soft goods such as shirts on a test basis.

After incurring back-to-back net losses in 1990 and 1991, Cole National's profits multiplied steadily, from $5.5 million in 1992 to $24.7 million in 1994. Sales increased as well, from $428.1 million to $528.1 million over the same period. Most of that increase came from expansion; same-store sales increased by 8.2 percent in 1993 and 3.5 percent in 1994. An aggressive growth plan fueled the acquisition or establishment of 235 new retail locations in 1994.

That same year, Cole National returned to the public arena with a 6.5 million share offer, the proceeds of which were used to reduce persistent leveraged buyout (LBO) debt. The reborn firm's "first" annual report enumerated several corporate goals, including debt reduction, increased earnings growth, and (re)doubling sales to over $1 billion by 2001.

Changes in the Late 1990s and Beyond

In 1996, CNC made a decisive move to strengthen its Cole Vision unit when it acquired Pearle Inc. The deal secured the company's position as the second-largest optical retailer in the United States but proved to be difficult to integrate. CNC integrated the Pearle Vision retail centers into its Licensed Brands unit, which was operating Sears Optical, Target Optical, and BJ's Optical Stores. Pearle Vision and Cole Licensed Brands had vastly different business models and catered to different types of customers. Pearle Vision generally tapped into an upscale clientele looking for eyeglasses in one hour, while CNC's outlets were geared towards moderate income customers, had a centralized lab, and offered private label frames. Costs associated with the acquisition as well as increased competition began to stall profits.

As such, CNC was forced to rethink its strategy. In order to shore up earnings, it split its business into two divisions in early 2000. Meanwhile, CNC had shuttered 402 gift stores located in Sears department stores in 1998 and purchased the managed vision-care benefits division of Metropolitan Life Insurance Co. in 1999.

During the early years of the new millennium, CNC worked to combat a sluggish economy while advances in corrective laser eye surgery potentially threatened sales of eyeglasses and contacts. However, the company's optical retail and leading managed vision care business made it an attractive target for

larger companies looking to expand their optical holdings. Sure enough, CNC caught the eye of two international firms. Italy-based Luxottica S.p.A. and Moulin International Holdings Ltd. of Hong Kong began their battle for CNC in 2004.

Luxottica first offered $401 million for CNC in 2003. Moulin counter offered in April 2004, coming in with a $419 million bid just before shareholders met to approve the Luxottica offer. Moulin lost its footing trying to secure financing for the deal, leaving Luxottica in a position to seal the deal with a $495 million offer. The Federal Trade Commission gave its approval in September, enabling CNC and Luxottica to finalize the union in October. CNC headquarters were moved to Mason, Ohio, and the majority of its operations were consolidated under Luxottica's Retail division—the future of Things Remembered remained uncertain due to Luxottica's focus on its optical businesses.

As a member of Luxottica's Retail group, CNC held an enviable position in the eyewear industry. Often referred to as the 800-pound gorilla by independent eyewear retailers, Luxottica owned optical retailer Lenscrafters Inc. and considerably strengthened its optical empire when it acquired CNC. Luxottica had also acquired Sunglass Hut and OPSM Group in 2001 and 2003 respectively and had become the leading distributor of optical and sun products in North America and Asia Pacific as a result of its strategic purchases. By adding CNC's Managed Vision Care to its arsenal, Luxottica also secured a position as the second-largest administrator of U.S.-managed vision programs used by corporations, government entities, and health insurance providers.

In 2005 the absorption of Cole's holdings into the Retail Group was complete and Cole National ceased to exist as a separate entity. Luxottica's future success depended on the successful integration of these different companies. In fact, CNC's Pearle Vision and Lenscrafters, both consolidated under the arm of Luxottica Retail, were referred to by a *Crain's Cleveland Business* journalist as the Pepsi and Coke in the eyeglass frames world. With such similarities, Luxottica's future strategy would no doubt include initiatives to differentiate the two retail brands.

Principal Competitors

Eye Care Centers of America Inc.; National Vision Inc.; U.S. Vision Inc.

Further Reading

Cochran, Thomas N., "Offerings in the Offing: Cole National," *Barron's*, April 4, 1994, p. 46.

"Cole National Accepts Luxottica's Final Offer," *Ophthalmology Times*, August 15, 2004.

Fisher, Christy, "Eyewear Sales Slow," *Advertising Age*, March 9, 1992, p. 46.

Funk, Nancy M., "Child World Posts Huge Loss," *Cleveland Plain Dealer*, March 30, 1991, p. E1.

——, "Cole Unit Struggles in Tough Climate for Retailing," *Cleveland Plain Dealer*, December 9, 1990, pp. E1, E3.

Gleisser, Marcus, "Cole National Reports Lower Retail Sales," *Cleveland Plain Dealer*, January 10, 1995, p. C4.

Gomez, Henry, "Merger May Focus Pearle Vision, Lenscrafters Stores," *Crain's Cleveland Business*, August 9, 2004, p. 5.

Hagan, John F., "Area Firm Linked to Hazardous-Toys Suit," *Cleveland Plain Dealer*, August 21, 1990, p. B1.

Hardin, Angela Y., "Refocusing Cole Given Wary Eye by Moody's," *Crain's Cleveland Business*, May 31, 1999.

——, "Underpaid Pollock Ready to Rally Cole," *Crain's Cleveland Business*, May 22, 2000.

Harrison, Joan, "Luxottica's Buy of Cole Hits as Sector Perks Up," *Mergers and Acquisitions*, March 2004.

"Key Maker Cole Sharpens Its Vision," *Business Week*, January 15, 1966, pp. 84, 86.

Koff, Stephen, "Child World Closing All Toy Stores," *Cleveland Plain Dealer*, July 14, 1992, p. G1.

Rose, William Ganson, *Cleveland: The Making of a City,* Cleveland: World Publishing Co., 1950.

Seilberg, Jaret, "Luxottica Passes Hurdles to Win Cole," *TheDeal.com*, September 27, 2004.

"Service at a (Stiff) Price," *Forbes*, February 4, 1980, p. 84.

Van Tassel, David D., and John J. Grabowski, *The Encyclopedia of Cleveland History,* Bloomington, Ind.: Indiana University Press, 1987.

—April D. Gasbarre
—update: Christina M. Stansell

Companhia Brasileira de Distribuiçao

Avenida Brigadiero Luiz Antonio 3142
Sao Paulo, Sao Paulo 01402-901
Brazil
Telephone: (55) (11) 3886-0421
Fax: (55) (11) 3886-7686
Web site: http://www.grupopaodeacucar.com.br

Public Company
Founded: 1948 as Doceira Pao de Açúcar
Employees: 63,484
Sales: BRL 15.3 billion ($5.22 billion) (2004)
Stock Markets: Sao Paulo; New York
Ticker Symbols: PCAR3; CBD
NAIC: 443111 Household Appliance Stores; 443112
 Radio, Television and Other Electronics Stores; 45211
 Supermarkets and Other Grocery (Except
 Convenience) Stores

Companhia Brasiliera de Distribuiçao (CBD), much better known as Grupo Pao de Açúcar or simply Pao de Açúcar, vies with the Brazilian subsidiary of French-based Carrefour S.A. for the title of largest retailer in Brazil, operating more than 500 hypermarkets, supermarkets, and stores that specialize in furniture and electronic and home-appliance products. It has a close partner in a rival of Carrefour, Casino Guichard-Perrachon S.A.

Development of a Retailing Empire: 1948–89

Valentim Dos Santos Diniz, a Portuguese immigrant, arrived in Brazil in 1929. He established a pastry shop named Pao de Acucar (Sugarloaf) in Sao Paulo in 1948. By the end of 1952 he had added two branches, and in 1959 Pao de Açúcar acquired another chain, and with it, its first supermarket. There were 11 stores in 1965. The following year the enterprise added its first store outside Sao Paulo, in Santos.

Pao de Açúcar established the first Brazilian around-the-clock, 24/7 supermarket in 1969, in Sao Paulo. At this point it had 55 stores. The following year it was the first Brazilian retailer to open a store abroad, in Lisbon. In 1971 the chain opened the first Brazilian hypermarket, called Jumbo, selling a variety of goods as well as food products. That year it also introduced its own private-label brands, beginning with a detergent, and launched auto dealerships and auto-parts stores under the Pao de Açúcar name.

Pao de Açúcar acquired a travel agency in 1972 and a second one in 1974. In 1973 it opened a Jumbo in Luanda, Angola, and acquired the Carisma supermarket chain in Belém. The company opened Nell's, a restaurant chain, in 1974, and acquired the CompreBem supermarket chain, consisting of 15 supermarkets in the states of Pernambuco and Paraíba, in 1975. This raised the number of its stores to 100. The following year the enterprise acquired Electroradiobraz, consisting of 26 hypermarkets, 8 supermarkets, and 16 department stores. With the acquisition of three chains in 1978, Pao de Açúcar now had 236 stores. The following year it introduced Minibox, a chain of no-frills stores for low-income shoppers, with a limited number of items and very competitive prices. At one point there were more than 300 Minibox units.

Pao de Açúcar began the 1980s by opening Sandiz, a department-store chain, and launching Superbox, a big food discount chain. In 1981 it merged the eight chains of the retail division of Grupo Pao de Açúcar into Companhia Brasileira de Distribuiçao (Brazilian Distribution Company). Three more chains were acquired in 1983. The group had 657 units in 1985, 170 of them in greater Sao Paulo. In terms of sales, it was the largest nationally owned private enterprise in Brazil. By the end of 1986 there were 50 Pao de Açúcar stores in Portugal, making it the 22nd-largest enterprise in that country. In 1987 the company introduced First Express, a joint venture with Shell Brazil Ltda. that placed convenience stores within Shell's service-station properties. It sold the Sandiz department-store chain in the same year. Also that year, the company built a $15-million supermarket in Moscow. By 1988 the Pao de Açúcar group consisted of 22 enterprises with 55,000 employees and $2.1 billion in annual sales. It had stores in all but five Brazilian states. And in 1989 yet another chain—Extra—was introduced. This was a hypermarket chain offering a large variety of both food and nonfood products.

All was not well, however, within Pao de Açúcar's Diniz clan. The founder, now 74, had yielded day-to-day management of the group to the eldest of his six children, Abílio. His

Company Perspectives:

The company's mission is to ensure the best shopping experience to all our customers, in each of our stores.

privileged position was resented by Valentim's two younger sons, Alcides and Arnaldo. The Sandiz sale, which was Alcides' work and opposed by his father, brought in $60 million, some of which went to the children, but it left Alcides still unhappy. In 1988 he surrendered his 8 percent holding in the group to his father. In terms of liquid net worth, this amounted to $21 million, but in an attempt to keep peace within the family, Valentim awarded Alcides land, two enterprises, and cash that was valued in total at $120 million.

Retrenchment and Recovery in the 1990s

A severe economic recession forced Pao de Açúcar to restructure its operations in 1990, a year in which it lost $60 million. The enterprise was so short of ready cash that it was in arrears of its taxes and its payments to suppliers. Abílio Diniz went to London and offered the enterprise to the investment bank Morgan Grenfell & Co. Ltd. for $400 million but was able to attract only half that as a counteroffer. To save itself from bankruptcy, Pao de Açúcar borrowed $120 million from banks and sold its headquarters building—dubbed the "Glass Palace"—for $55 million. It closed many stores (including the Jumbo and Minibox chains), fired workers, and disposed of its noncore businesses. The number of outlets dropped to 233, the number of employees from 45,000 to 18,000, and the group fell to second place in Brazilian retailing, behind the French company Carrefour. By late 1992 Arnaldo Diniz, the youngest son, was ready to defect and sell his share of the family holding company, but he rejected the amount offered. The net worth of this holding company, Pao de Açúcar S.A. Indústria e Comércio, had fallen by about half because of Brazil's hard times. The dysfunctional family was again in the news in 1993, when Abílio persuaded his father—over his mother's objections—to turn over enough of his shares to give him 51 percent majority control. The sale that year of Supa, the group's Portuguese branch, brought in $300 million and allowed Abílio to buy out Arnaldo and two of his three sisters.

By this time the Brazilian economy had recovered, and Pao de Açúcar had regained its stride. The Extra hypermarket chain, pursuing a policy of aggressive price cutting, was accounting for nearly a quarter of the group's revenues. In 1994 Pao de Açúcar equaled the peak revenue of $2.3 billion that it had attained five years earlier, although the number of its units had now fallen to 216. In 1995 it introduced the first electronic supermarket in Brazil, Pao de Açúcar Delivery, which became Internet-accessible the following year. As CBD, the group went public in 1995, selling $112.1 million worth of preferred shares on the Sao Paulo stock exchange. Two years later, CBD became the first Brazilian retailer with a listing on the New York Stock Exchange, raising $172.5 million by selling preferred American Depositary Receipts—the equivalent of shares.

The Minibox format was reintroduced in 1998 as Barateiro (Cheap), the name of a chain, Rede Barateiro de Supermercados,

that had recently been acquired by the group. Also that year, the group introduced, in Sao Paulo, Pao de Açúcar Kid's, an educational supermarket. In 1999 Pao de Açúcar acquired two chains and leased three more. During the year Casino Guichard-Perrachon S.A., a French-based giant multinational retailer, paid more than $1.3 billion for about 21.3 percent of CBD's voting capital, plus debentures convertible within five years into a potential maximum of 40 percent of the voting capital. The money was earmarked to help Pao de Açúcar continue making acquisitions and to service its BRL 1.5 billion ($692 million) of debt.

"This is not the fall of the last Brazilian supermarket operator," Abílio Diniz told Geoff Dyer of the *Financial Times*. "We will continue to be a Brazilian company controlled by Brazilians." He said that the principal advantages would be technological, plus access to a global system of sales. Casino—a principal rival of Carrefour in France—was used to operating in markets that were extremely concentrated and competitive, and it had a large line of its own private-label products, a field in which Diniz acknowledged that Pao de Açúcar was deficient. Casino also had lessons for its new Brazilian partner in the fields of efficient operation of distribution centers and operating such other retail formats as convenience and discount stores.

Challenges of the 21st Century

Pao de Açúcar's acquisitions helped increase the group's annual revenues to $3.2 billion. It was the first food chain to keep many of its stores open around the clock and the first to popularize its own brand of food items. The stores in Sao Paulo's better neighborhoods carried gourmet treats in the bakery sections; those in the city's Japanese and Jewish neighborhoods included ethnic fare. Yet the company was still left second to Carrefour's Brazilian subsidiary and apprehensive of the looming presence of Wal-Mart Stores Inc. In 2000 it closed the gap on Carrefour by adding 80 stores, most of them from five chains that it acquired. And the next year it purchased ABC Supermercados S.A. in the state of Rio de Janeiro, thereby adding another 26 stores. In 2002 Pao de Açúcar acquired the Sé Supermercados chain—60 stores in 16 cities of Sao Paulo state—for BRL 250 million (about $85 million). These additions enabled Pao de Açúcar to pass Carrefour in sales volume but increased its debt-to-equity ratio to 50 percent, compared to only 15 percent after selling stock shares and debentures to Casino.

In 2003 Diniz relinquished his position as chief executive officer of the group, assuming instead the supervisory post of chairman of the board. He passed over Ana Maria, the oldest of his four children and vice-president of operations, selecting as his successor Augusto Marques da Cruz, administrative vice-president and chief financial officer.

Pao de Açúcar made another major transaction in late 2003 by forming a joint venture with Grupo Sendas S.A., operator of 106 stores in Rio de Janeiro. Once the largest supermarket chain in Rio, Sendas had fallen on hard times and was operating in the red and having difficulty paying its suppliers. Pao de Açúcar added its own Rio stores to those of Sendas and turned Sendas into a low-priced chain similar to its own CompreBem in Sao Paulo, reducing the number of items sold, selling one of the two Sendas distribution centers and its fleet of refrigerated trucks, but also providing a large infusion of funds for modernization.

Key Dates:

1948: Valentim Dos Passos Diniz establishes the Pao de Açúcar pastry shop in Sao Paulo.
1959: Pao de Açúcar opens its first supermarket.
1971: Pao de Açúcar opens the first Brazilian hypermarket, called Jumbo.
1981: The group's eight retail chains are merged into Companhia Brasileira de Distribuiçao.
1989: Introduction of the Extra hypermarket chain, which becomes the group's largest.
1997: CBD becomes the first Brazilian retailer with a listing on the New York Stock Exchange.
1999: French retailer Casino takes a large stake in the enterprise.
2002: Additional acquisitions allow Pao de Açúcar to regain its rank as top Brazilian retailer.
2005: Pao de Açúcar's five retail chains have a total of 553 stores.

Pao de Açúcar entered, in 2004, in an agreement with Banco Itaú S.A.—Brazil's second-largest private bank—to establish Financeira Itaú CBD S.A. The partnership was aiming to issue 9.3 million credit cards by 2014 to retail shoppers such as Pao de Açúcar's own customers. It also intended to offer other products, such as insurance and real-estate loans.

Casino raised its equity stake in Pao de Açúcar in May 2005, and took 50 percent of the common shares of a holding company that would partly own the enterprise. Casino and Diniz would have equal membership on the boards of both bodies. The complex arrangement included Casino's payment of BRL 1 billion (about $400 million) for 60 Pao de Açúcar real-estate properties. The infusion of funds was expected to enable the enterprise to pay down its debts and fund an expansion program aimed at opening 160 more stores in the next four years.

In August 2005 Pao de Açúcar unexpectedly announced that Cruz would be leaving the company. Although neither he nor Diniz would speak candidly about the circumstances, the Brazilian business magazine *Exame* reported that associates of Cruz said that Diniz had continually interfered with Cruz's administration of the enterprise, and that Casino was dissatisfied with the profits—even though net income increased by 51 percent between 2002 and 2004. A committee headed by Ana Maria Diniz was said to have narrowed the choice of Cruz's successor to six, with the final decision to be made by her father.

Pao de Açúcar had five retail chains in 2005, with a total of 553 stores operating in 13 states. The largest, in terms of units, was Pao de Açúcar, with 185 stores. It had a neighborhood supermarket format and was aimed at higher-income consumers with a cosmopolitan lifestyle. CompreBem had 177 supermarket stores. It was aimed at working women and emphasized low prices and fresh produce and meat. Sendas, with 66 stores, was very similar to CompreBem. By far the largest chain, in terms of

selling space, was the Extra hypermarket chain, offering a large variety of food and nonfood products at competitive prices. Extra's 75 stores had 578,208 square meters of selling space, or about half of the total in the group. Extra Electro (the successor to Electradiobraz) had 50 stores. It specialized in electronic and home-appliance products but also sold furniture and bazaar items.

Pao de Açúcar's gross revenues came to BRL 15.3 billion in 2004, or $5.22 billion, based on the average value of the currency in relation to the U.S. dollar during the year. Of this sum, Extra accounted for almost half (48 percent), followed by Pao de Açúcar, CompreBem, Sendas, and Extra Electro. The net revenue (less taxes and returns) was BRL 12.57 billion ($4.29 billion), and the net profit BRL 369.83 million ($126.22 million). Although net revenue was up 18 percent from the 2003 total, Pao de Açúcar fell behind Carrefour's subsidiary, Carrefour Comércio e Indústria Ltda., in sales.

Principal Subsidiaries

CBD Technology Inc.; Golden Auto Posto Ltda.; Sé Supermercados Ltda.

Principal Operating Units

CompreBem; Extra; Extra Electro; Pao de Açúcar; Sendas.

Principal Competitors

Casas Bahia Comercial Ltda.; Carrefour Comércio e Indústria Ltda.

Further Reading

"Agora tudo vai ser diferente," *Exame,* August 24, 1988, pp. 99–100.
Blecher, Nelson, "Como Abilio manteve seu poder," *Exame,* May 25, 2005, pp. 50–53.
Carvalho, Denise, and Nelson Blecher, "Troca de comando," *Exame,* August31, 2005, pp. 54–55.
"Cidao dá exemplo," *Exame,* October 14, 1992, p. 69.
Correa, Cristiane, "Dois lados de un casamento," *Exame,* November 10, 2004, pp. 62–64.
Dolan, Kerry A., "Outmuscling Wal-Mart," *Exame,* May 10, 2004, pp. 80–81.
Dyer, Geoff, "Casino takes stake in Brazilian store chain," *Financial Times,* August 11, 1999, p. 22.
Katz, Ian, "Clicking for Groceries," *Business Week,* May 8, 2000, p. 20.
Netz, Clayton, and Joaquim Castanheira, "As liçoes que o abos,p traz," *Exame,* April 12, 1995, pp. 44–50.
Ogier, Thierry, "The Handoff," *Latin Trade,* July 2003, p. 52.
Rosenburg, Cynthia, "A empresa de *um rosto só*," *Exame,* April 18, 2001, pp. 47–56, 58.
Samor, Geraldo, "French Retailer Casino to Boost Its Stake in a Brazilian Grocer," *Wall Street Journal,* May 5, 2005, p. B8.
"Sócia, esposa, mae e guerreira," *Exame,* February 3, 1993, p.45.
Whitefield, Paul, "Casino boosts Brazilian interests," May 4, 2005, TheDeal.com.

—Robert Halasz

Companhia Siderúrgica Nacional

Avenida Fario Lima 3400
Sao Paulo, Sao Paulo 04538-132
Brazil
Telephone: (55) (11) 3049-7100
Web site: http://www.csn.com.br

Public Company
Incorporated: 1941
Employees: 10,207
Sales: $3.9 billion (2004)
Stock Exchanges: Sao Paulo; New York
Ticker Symbols: CSNA3; SID
NAIC: 331111 Iron and Steel Mills; 331112
  Electrometallurgical Ferroalloy Product
  Manufacturing; 331419 Primary Smelting and
  Refining of Nonferrous Metals (Except Copper and
  Aluminum)

Companhia Siderúrgica Nacional (CSN) is the second-largest steel producer in Brazil. Its fully integrated manufacturing facilities turn out a broad line of steel products, including slabs, hot- and cold-rolled plates, sheets, and coils, plus galvanized and tin-coated steel products for the distribution, packaging, automotive, home-appliance, and construction industries. It produces about half of all galvanized-steel products sold in Brazil and much of the nation's tin-mill products, which are used in packaging containers. More than one-fourth of the company's sales come from exports. CSN is a vertically integrated company that owns its own iron ore, generates most of its own electricity, and has a stake in the ownership and/or operation of the rail and port facilities it uses. It has been described as the most cost-competitive steel producer in the world.

Government-Run Behemoth: 1941–92

Steel production in Brazil began in the 1920s and was dominated by a company established with Luxembourg and Brazilian capital. With war clouds gathering over Europe prior to World War II, Brazilian leaders became concerned about securing its supplies of steel, so essential to manufacturing in this period. About 70 percent of the nation's rolled-steel products were still being imported. An effort in 1939 to obtain financing—in exchange for equity—from the United States Steel Corporation for an integrated steel mill foundered under opposition from Brazilian nationalists, especially the army. President Getúlio Vargas next invited German industrialists to make an offer. This had the expected effect of catching Washington's attention, and in 1940 the U.S. Export-Import Bank pledged $20 million in financing. Savings banks and pension funds provided half of the initial capital. The Brazilian treasury purchased all the common stock not subscribed to by the public, and for all practical purposes Companhia Siderúrgica Nacional (National Steel Company), founded in 1941, became a government-owned and -operated company.

A virtually uninhabited site about 75 miles west of Rio de Janeiro had already been selected for the plant. Volta Redonda was built from scratch as a paternalistically run company town that also served as CSN headquarters. The company operated the schools and the only hospital in the city. It built and maintained houses for the workers and charged rent well below market value. A 2.5-mile spur was built to link the plant to an existing railway line that carried iron ore from the state of Minais Gerais and imported coal—needed to make coke for the blast furnaces—arriving at Rio de Janeiro's port. A hydroelectric plant, completed in 1948, was intended to meet the mill's large power needs.

Steel production began in 1946 and, 20 years later, production had reached about 1.4 million metric tons of ingot steel a year, or about one-third of Brazil's output, which had recently been enhanced by the opening of two other large integrated steel mills. Employment was now about 14,000. On a number of occasions, the government ordered CSN to sell its goods at below-market prices in order to combat inflation, regardless of the effect on the company's own bottom line. It also encouraged the company to borrow money abroad, then used the money to meet its own needs.

CSN in the 1970s was, besides, being engaged in steelmaking, dealing commercially in raw materials and supplies, tin, zinc, manganese, and ferroalloy requirements, and transporting.

Its capacity was raised to 1.6 million metric tons of steel a year in 1974 and 2.4 million tons in 1977. It had foreign offices in New York and Japan and sales of 27 billion cruzeiros (about $930 million) in 1979. This was a boom decade for Brazilian steelmaking, with the nation vaulting from 18th to 7th place in world production, and with CSN in the lead.

During the 1980s, by contrast, more steel mills came online in Brazil while national demand stagnated. Moreover, the Brazilian government set steel prices 40 percent below the world price to help other domestic industries, depriving CSN of perhaps $7 billion in potential revenue. The enterprise suffered the first strike in its history in 1984; during the next six years, there were 11 more. The worst was in 1988, when three workers were killed by soldiers. Although CSN's production of ingot steel rose from 3.3 million metric tons in 1984 to 4.1 million tons in 1988, a severe downturn in the Brazilian economy contributed to a fall in production to 3.4 million tons in 1989 and only 2.7 million tons in 1990. As a result, CSN lost over $1 billion that year on revenue of only $1.76 billion, and it had a debt of $2.6 billion.

During that year Roberto Procópio Lima, Jr., was appointed president of CSN and charged with preparing what the Brazilian business magazine *Exame* called an "obese elephant" for privatization. He reduced the bloated work force of 23,800 by 7,000 despite the combination of a 31-day strike and arson that cost the company hundreds of millions of dollars. He also cracked down on management, dismissing 545 executives. Lima also took on the networks of suppliers, transporters, and subcontractors that were draining CSN of badly needed funds. By encouraging competition, he reduced these costs by 40 percent. All contracts with third parties were reviewed. To break the power of the 23 trading companies conducting two-thirds of CSN's export sales, Lima contracted 20 other companies.

Privatized, Sprawling Giant: 1993–2000

Sales fell still further in 1991 because the adoption of lower import duties subjected CSN to stronger competition from foreign steelmakers. In addition, Brazilian steel sales were suffering from a world economic recession and the fall of the Soviet Union, which had been a big buyer. Even so, the company was able to reduce its debt by $1 billion and to register small profits in 1991 and 1992. CSN was sold at auction in 1993. The purchaser was Valepar S.A., a consortium in which one of the principal partners was the Vicunha textile group. Other members of the consortium included state-owned Companhia Vale do Rio Doce (CVRD), Brazil's biggest mineral company; Banco Bradesco S.A, Brazil's largest privately owned bank; and Previ, the pension fund run by state-owned Banco do Brasil

S.A., Brazil's biggest bank. Some 12 percent of the enterprise was set aside for CSN's employees.

CSN produced a record 4.6 million metric tons of ingot steel in 1993 and achieved a profit of $70 million, its largest ever. The fewer but more productive 15,000 workers enjoyed a real increase in wages of 30 percent over 2 years. A six-year modernization program estimated to cost $900 million was adopted, including construction of a thermoelectric plant to meet future power needs. However, Lima left the enterprise in early 1994, since he did not have backing from the new owners, who carved up the administration into areas that they individually controlled. Without a strong hand at the rudder, CSN postponed plans for the new power plant and a decision to dismiss 4,000 workers over 3 years, an action deemed necessary to keep the enterprise competitive in controlling expenses. Despite another record profit, the company's return on its liquid net worth was much lower than that of its main privatized rivals, Usinas Siderúrgicas de Minas Gerais S.A. (Usiminas) and Acesita S.A.

This period of indecision ended in 1995, when one of the large shareholders withdrew from the consortium and Vicunha's chief executive, Benjamin Steinbruch, became CSN's chairman of the board. A young, dynamic, and extremely ambitious entrepreneur, Steinbruch acquired, in 1996, a 7 percent interest in newly privatized Light Servicios Eletricidade S.A., the main power distributor in the state of Rio de Janeiro and was chosen to be the utility's chairman. CSN also purchased interests in several hydroelectric plants. The following year Valepar paid in excess of $3 billion to purchase the Brazilian government's stake in CVRD, with Vicunha as the lead partner. Steinbruch now controlled both companies as well as Vicunha. CVRD was the world's largest producer and exporter of iron ore, and the largest diversified mining company in the Americas. Moreover, it owned about 10 percent of CSN itself. "Bringing CSN and CVRD together made very good sense," Steinbruch told Jonathan Wheatley of *Business Week* in 2000. "Both have mining interests, both have steel, both have logistics. It gave us the chance to bring together three sectors in which Brazil is very competitive."

Steinbruch appointed a woman, Maria Sílvia Marques Bastos, to be CSN's chief executive officer at the end of 1998. During that year the company took 51 percent of a joint venture with Germany's Thyssen-Krupp Stahl A.G. to build GalvaSud, a galvanizing plant in Brazil, mainly for the auto sector. It was completed in 2000 in Porto Real City, Rio de Janeiro. CSN also built a joint-venture cold-rolled strip mill and galvanizing plant for civil construction and home appliances in Araucária City, Paraná.

By 1999 Brazil had fallen into another of its intermittent economic crises, forcing the nation to devalue its currency, the real. The devaluation made it more difficult for CSN to make payments on the $800 million in dollar-denominated debt that Steinbruch had incurred to make acquisitions. He sold CSN's stake in Light in 2000. And, since he had fallen out with Bradesco and Previ, he sold CSN's stake in Valepar to them on the last day of 2000. At the same time, Bradesco and Previ sold their Valepar stakes in CSN to Vicunha for BRL 1.5 billion ($773 million) in debentures. They also won the right to buy iron ore from CSN's own mines at their option.

New Century, New Challenges

Now more firmly in Steinbruch's hands, CSN was *Exame*'s enterprise of the year in 2001. The 238-mw thermoelectric power plant, using as fuel CSN's own industrial gases, was completed in late 1999 in Volta Redonda and was supplying 60 percent of the company's needs. During 1999–2000 two hydroelectric plants—Itá and Igarapava—in which CSN held a stake came on line. With the completion of these projects, CSN became one of the few Brazilian enterprises to generate not only enough electricity to meet its own needs but to sell to others. The company's considerable investment in infrastructure and logistics was also bearing fruit. A rehabilitated rail line in which CSN had taken a stake was bringing in, on time, a supply of low-cost iron ore to Volta Redonda from the company's Casa de Pedra mine in Minais Gerais. Coal and coke were being sent by the railroad to the mill from the port of Sepetiba, Rio de Janeiro, where CSN held a share in the operating concession for the coal and container terminals. Another rail line in which CSN held an interest brought limestone and dolomite from its Arcos mine to the mill. The steel plant itself had been modernized at a cost of $1.5 billion.

The enormous gain in productivity yielded bonuses for CSN's now-reduced work force of about 9,000 to 10,000. In return, they were held to a code of ethics. In order to combat corruption, the purchasing office was moved from Volta Redonda to Sao Paulo. An incentive program that included stock options attracted not only well-qualified engineers and other technical personnel—always a company strength—but also commercially adept executives. About two-thirds of CSN's 617 women were working in the steel mill, traditionally a masculine venue. It had been discovered that women were better than men at details such as detecting flaws in metal sheets. The company's president also provided a feminine touch; since she didn't like the workers' uniforms, she promoted a competition that resulted, by electronic vote, in a different choice. (In 2002, however, Steinbruch assumed the presidency as well as the chairmanship of CSN.)

Privatized CSN did not please everybody, however. After the company reduced its commitment to Volta Redondo—selling the hospital, for example—attention turned to its woeful environmental record. For more than half a century CSN had tossed industrial waste into the river that supplied the metropolitan region, resulting even in genetic deformities in children. Gases spewed out by the mill's chimneys were held responsible for compromising the immune systems of the population in general. Landfills contained solid wastes. CSN agreed to spend BRL 180 million (about $60 million) on 133 projects. The company installed a system installed to convert industrial gases for cogeneration, sold the solid waste for pavement, and filtered the liquid waste. Local residents remained unhappy, however. CSN owned almost 20 percent of the land in Volta Redonda and, under Steinbruch, fenced in several community soccer fields, closed an environmental reserve, and repossessed areas mostly used by retired mill workers to grow vegetables.

CSN purchased bankrupt Heartland Steel Inc. of Terre Haute, Indiana, in 2001 for $55 million plus the assumption of its $19 million in debts. It was renamed CSN LLC. The purpose of the acquisition was to gain a foothold in the United States, sending excess slabs of steel to Heartland's cold-rolling mill for conversion to value-added products. Steinbruch explained to Nelson Blecher of *Exame*, "Our major strategy is to make CSN a multinational. We have to compete in the world market as an equal in order to stay in business. That is the challenge."

Widely honored for its efficiency and low cost of production, CSN also earned a reputation as a cash cow for its shareholders—especially for Vicunha Siderúrgica S.A., which now owned 46.5 percent of CSN. The financing of Vicunha's buyout of its partners was met from CSN's profits; in fact, in 2000–01 CSN paid out more in dividends than it collected in profits. This created new financial pressures that Steinbruch met by selling half of CSN's majority stake in the Itá power plant in 2001. He sold its interest in the smaller of its two rail lines in 2003. He also proposed, in 2002, a merger with the Corus Group, the British-based second-largest steelmaker in Europe. The deal foundered, with each party blaming the other. It would have created the fifth-largest steelmaker in the world, with Corus holding the larger share but assuming $2.66 billion in debt from CSN.

Corus had been tempted to merge with CSN in part because of the prospect of gaining access to cheap iron ore from the huge Casa de Pedra mine. China's voracious appetite for iron ore to feed its steel mills was driving up prices for the mineral and thereby helping to improve CSN's bottom line. The company made itself self-sufficient in tin by acquiring Cia. Metalic Nordeste, owner of a tin mine and smelter, in 2002 and purchased a half-share in Lusosider S.A., a Portuguese manufacturer of galvanized metal products and tin plate, in 2003. In 2004 CSN enjoyed its best year ever, earning $855 million on revenues of $3.9 billion. That year it purchased Thyssen-Krupp's share of the GalvaSud plant. CSN produced 5.6 million metric tons of crude steel in 2004, 17 percent of Brazil's output. Nevertheless, it lost its longstanding leadership in steel output and revenue in 2003, when Gerdau S.A. merged with Aços Minas Gerais S.A. to form Gerdau Açominas S.A. Vicunha Siderúrgica S.A. held 40.5 percent of the company in 2005, having recently sold a 6 percent stake to a government development agency.

Principal Subsidiaries

Cia. Metalic Nordeste; CSN Energia S.A.; CSN Panama S.A. (Panama); CSN Steel Corporation (United States); GalvaSud

S.A.; Indústria Nacional de Aços Laminados S.A.; Lusosider Projectos Siderúrgicos S.A. (Portugal; 50%).

Principal Competitors

Companhia Vale do Rio Doce S.A.; Gerdau S.A.; Usinas Siderúrgicas de Minas Gerais S.A. (Usiminas).

Further Reading

Baer, Werner. *The Development of the Brazilian Steel Industry.* Nashville: Vanderbilt University Press, 1969.

Benson, Todd, "Brazil's Steel Giant and Its Company Town Are on the Outs," *New York Times,* May 17, 2005, p. C4.

Blecher, Nelson, "O brilho do aço," *Exame,* July 11, 2001, pp. 42–52, 54, 56.

Brooke, James, "Brazil Shakes Up Its Steel Industry," *New York Times,* May 28, 1990, p. 29.

Correa, Cristiane, "A major isputa do mercado brasileiro," *Exame,* August 31, 2005, pp. 42–45.

Dieguez, Consuelo, "O futuro em jogo," *Exame,* February 20, 2002, pp. 56–58.

Goulart, Rubeny, "Eles agora querem usar black-tie," *Exame,* September 30, 1992, pp. 42–44.

——, "Feudos de aço na usina," *Exame,* May 10, 1995, pp. 74–75.

Kandell, Jonathan, "The CVRD Factor," *Institutional Investor,* October 1997, pp. 191–92, 195–96.

Kepp, Michael, "The Billion-Dollar Woman," *Latin Trade,* September 1999.

Pfeiffer, Margarida O., "Arms of Iron and Steel," *Latin Trade,* July 2005, p. 66.

Smith, Tony, "Deal to Take Over Brazilian Steel Maker Falls Apart," *New York Times,* November 14, 2002, pp. W1, W7.

Vassallo, Cláudia, "Um negócio quase perfeito," *Exame,* August 21, 2002, pp. 86–92.

Wheatley, Jonathan, "Twilight of a Latin Mogul?," *Business Week,* June 28, 2000, p.

—Robert Halasz

Confluence Holdings Corporation

111 Kayaker Way
Easley, South Carolina 29642
U.S.A.
Telephone: (864) 859-7518
Toll Free: (800) 59-KAYAK
Fax: (864) 855-5995
Web site: http://www.confluencewatersports.com

Private Company
Incorporated: 1998
Employees: 300
Sales: $60 million (2005 est.)
NAIC: 336612 Boat Building; 339920 Sporting and
    Athletic Goods Manufacturing

Confluence Holdings Corporation, which trades as Confluence Watersports Company, is one of the leading producers of canoes and kayaks in the world. Confluence addresses various segments of the paddlesports market through its various brands: Wilderness Systems, Mad River Canoe, Voyageur, Wave Sport, Watermark, Perception, Dagger, and Mainstream. Formed from the amalgamation of numerous smaller companies around the United States, the company has consolidated its manufacturing near Greenville, South Carolina, the home turf of industry builder Perception, Inc., which was considered the first to successfully sell rotomolded plastic kayaks.

Wilderness Systems Origins

Andy Zimmerman and John Sheppard formed kayak manufacturer Wilderness Systems, Inc., in 1986. According to *Nation's Business,* they had both worked at Casa Bique, a furniture business in High Point, North Carolina owned by Zimmerman's family but wanted to try their hand at something a little less pedestrian. They began in a shed in Zimmerman's backyard, making boats—and selling them—one at a time. The two managed sales of $160,000 the first year.

Ten years later, the company was *Canoe & Kayak* magazine's favorite kayak manufacturer, employing 100 people at a

60,000 square foot plant. Annual sales reached $10 million in the mid-1990s as the kayak industry experienced dramatic growth. In 1996, the governor of North Carolina pronounced it "Entrepreneurial Company of the Year."

After beginning with fiberglass, or composite, kayaks, around 1992 Wilderness Systems began using plastics to create inexpensive kayaks that prompted many new users to take the plunge into paddlesports. In the late 1990s, the company came out with a polyethylene plastic-hulled trimaran for salt water sailing.

Confluence Formed in 1998

Wilderness Systems merged with Mad River Canoe in June 1998; Confluence Holdings Corporation was created as a holding company, while the two brands continued to operate as separate entities. Westbury Partners of New York became its largest investor. American Capital Strategies Ltd., a publicly traded buyout and mezzanine fund based in Maryland, began providing financing in September 1998; it later converted debt to equity.

Mad River had been formed in Vermont in 1971 by Jim and Kay Henry and then employed about five dozen people. Mad River's high-end canoe business complemented Wilderness Systems' kayaks. Mad River brought with it Voyager Ltd., a producer of paddles and accessories.

In the winter of 1999/2000, Mad River moved its administrative headquarters to North Carolina. Wilderness was adding 30,000 square feet to its Trinity, North Carolina facility for a total of about 150,000 square feet. Mad River's manufacturing operation, which employed 40 people making 5,000 canoes a year, remained at two factories in Waitsfield, Vermont for another year or two. Wilderness invested $500,000 in the Vermont plants in an effort to turn them around.

Confluence acquired another kayak maker, Wave Sport, in 1999. Like other companies in its peer group, Wave Sport had been launched out of its founder's residence. Chan Zwanzig had started the business in the small town of Oak Creek, Colorado in 1987. Wave Sport specialized in stubby, maneuverable kayaks called "rodeo boats" intended for whitewater. Confluence relocated its production to North Carolina. Wave Sport was making about 5,500 kayaks a year.

By 2000, Confluence was the world's third largest canoe and kayak manufacturer, with annual sales of $30 million and 200 employees. It had a 200,000 square foot facility in Randolph County, North Carolina, but the next year nearly doubled its space through an expansion. Confluence's new CEO Bill Medlin told the *Greensboro News & Record* the US kayak market, which sold 500,000 units a year, had plenty of room to grow. However, by 2002 the company was cutting the number of employees from about 270 to less than 200 as sales stalled in a slowing economy. A debt burden from its merger was also a factor. The Mad River plant in Vermont, which had been making about 35 percent of Confluence's total production of 10,000 boats a year, was closed. Savings were earmarked to develop new products.

By mid-2003, Confluence was hiring again and ramping up production to three shifts due to unprecedented demand. The company had already taken on yet another CEO, John Bergeron. Confluence was on its way to making 77,000 canoes during the year, up 28 percent from the previous year, Bergeron told the *Greensboro News & Record*. Independent stores accounted for three-quarters of sales.

Confluence Acquires Watermark in 2005

Confluence took a quantum leap forward by buying industry leader Watermark Paddlesports Inc. in 2005. American Capital invested another $19 million in Confluence Holdings to support the acquisition. This brought American Capital's total investment in Confluence to $61 million. Confluence also made a divestment during the year, selling its WindRider line of trimarans to the newly formed Windrider, LLC of Minnesota. Like Confluence, Watermark was itself an assemblage of a number of pioneering watersports companies, including Dagger, Perception, and Mainstream kayaks; Harmony accessories; and AT (Adventure Technology) paddles. It had been formed in Atlanta in the late 1990s.

Dagger Canoe Company was formed in 1988 by a group of four whitewater paddlers led by Joe Pulliam. By the mid-1990s, the fast growing enterprise had about 60 employees and was expanding its Midtown, Tennessee, facilities for a second time, to more than 50,000 square feet. Its product line of two dozen plastic watercraft was distributed as far as Europe, Australia, and Japan. Towards the end of 1994, Dagger acquired Maryland's Valley Mill Boats, the leading producer of advanced

whitewater racing boats using advanced composites technology. It had been formed by whitewater canoeing champion Andy Bridge.

Dagger itself was acquired by Watermark in 1998. Its founder, Joe Pulliam, remained president. Watermark had also acquired Perception, Inc., one of Dagger's main rivals. Perception, based in Easley, South Carolina, had been formed in the early 1970s by Bill Masters, who had worked summers as a river guide while studying at nearby Clemson University. He began making his own kayaks while still a student, beginning with a $50 investment in supplies.

Perception was credited with expanding the kayaking market by pioneering the production of low-cost, rotational molded plastic kayaks in 1977. In 1984, he started another company, Aquaterra, to produce touring kayaks, but this was eventually merged into Perception, Inc. Masters received a number of accolades for his entrepreneurship and innovation. Jim Clark became Perception's president after it was acquired by Watermark, while founder Bill Masters remained on board as an advisor. At the time, Perception was selling 50,000 boats a year.

In 2001, most of Dagger's business was relocated to Watermark Inc.'s facility in Easley, South Carolina (a small composite manufacturing operation remained in Tennessee). By this time, Watermark had added Islander sit-on-top kayaks and Mainstream, a value-priced line, to its holdings.

Watermark also diversified, acquiring the Yakima and Rhode Gear brands of vehicle racks for bicycles, skis, and other recreational equipment, including kayaks. Yakima, then based in San Diego, California, had once supplied Perception with kayak hardware.

Another couple businesses were acquired in 2001: snowshoe manufacturer SnoWalkers and the Sospenders floatation device. Watermark in the following two years to bring its disparate brands together. In the process, 18 of its 450 US employees were let go. An executive told *Bicycle Retailer* the company was concerned with streamlining operations in an uncertain economy.

At the same time, its Perception brand was bringing its revolutionary new Airalite technology to the market. It offered composite-type performance with the durability of plastics.

The brands were divided into Watermark Boat and Watermark Gear. After its boat business was acquired by Confluence in 2005, Watermark relocated the rest of its operations from California to Oregon; the company was then renamed Yakima Products, Inc.

The merger of Confluence and Watermark's paddlesports unit in 2005 formed probably the largest producer of canoes and kayaks in the world. Its closest rival was the watercraft business of Johnson Outdoor, Inc., which included Old Towne Canoe Company and a handful of other brands.

Principal Subsidiaries

Confluence Watersports Canada, Inc.

Principal Divisions

AT Paddles; Dagger; Harmony; Mad River Canoe; Mainstream; Perception; Wave Sport; Wilderness Systems.

Principal Competitors

Johnson Outdoors Inc.

Further Reading

"American Capital Invests $19 Million in Combination of Two Leading Kayak Manufacturers," *PR Newswire,* May 18, 2005.

"Atlanta's WaterMark Acquires Perception, Inc. and Dagger Canoe Co.," *PR Newswire,* June 26, 1998.

Becker, Denise, "Kayak Manufacturer to Expand; A $750,000 Community Development Grant Will Allow Confluence Watersports to Connect with Archdale Sewer System," *Greensboro News & Record,* June 27, 2001, p. B7.

Brumley, Mark, "Kayak Maker Lays Off 69 Workers in Trinity," *Greensboro News & Record,* April 24, 2002, p. B8.

——, "Kayak Manufacturer Follows River of Dreams," *Greensboro News & Record,* Special Sec., January 28, 2001, p. 9.

"Canoe Firm to Expand Its Roane Facilities," *Knoxville News-Sentinel,* July 26, 1994, p. C2.

"Company Moves Headquarters; Production to Stay in Waitsfield," *Associated Press Newswires,* November 17, 1999.

Confluence Watersports Company, "Company History," Easley, South Carolina: Confluence Watersports Company, 2005.

Craver, Richard, "Randolph County, N.C.-Based Sports Equipment Manufacturer Says It's Rebounding," *Knight-Ridder Tribune Business News,* August 28, 2001.

"Dagger Canoe Co. Sold," *Knoxville News-Sentinel,* July 7, 1998, p. C6.

Delaney, Ben, "Watermark Cuts Jobs: Some At Yakima," *Bicycle Retailer,* May 1, 2003, p. 11.

——, "Yakima Bought by Watermark, A Top Water Sports Company," *Bicycle Retailer,* August 1, 2001, p. 13.

DeLozier, Stan, "Roane Kayak Maker Leaving; Dagger Plants Going to South Carolina," *Knoxville News-Sentinel,* October 31, 2001, p. C1.

Gray, Tim, "Rapids Transit," *Business North Carolina,* May 1, 2002, p. 50.

Hindo, Brian, "Tug-of-War," *BusinessWeek,* November 8, 2004, p. 12.

Holman, Kelly, "Confluence Buys Watermark," *TheDeal.com,* May 20, 2005.

Kimbrough, Pat, "Trinity, N.C.-Based Canoe Maker to Hire 41 in Preparation for Business Boom," *Knight-Ridder Tribune Business News,* July 7, 2003.

Lipsher, Steve, "North Carolina Company Buys Colorado-Based Kayak Manufacturer," *Knight-Ridder Tribune Business News,* April 30, 1998.

McClellan, Matt, "Mergers Form Top Kayak Firms," *Plastics News,* August 9, 2004, p. 14.

"Mad River Canoe Merging with Kayak Maker," *Associated Press Newswires,* October 7, 1998.

Moody, Robin J., "WaterMark Changes Name, Sells Off Division," *Business Journal of Portland,* May 13, 2005.

Opdahl, Cristina, "Splashmasters: Paddlers Who Set the High-Water Mark," *Outside,* April 2002, p. 96.

Rizzo, Russ, "Canoe, Kayak Sales Create 41 Factory Jobs," *Greensboro News & Record,* June 20, 2003.

Seccombe, Jane, "Paddlespot Products Makers Merge Into Confluence Holding," *Greensboro News & Record,* October 8, 1998, p. B6.

"World's Largest Maker of Kayaks Has the Masters' Touch," *PR Newswire,* July 1, 1998.

Williams, Kelly, "White-Water Wonders (Wilderness Systems Inc. Becomes Top Manufacturer of Kayaks in the U.S.)," *Nation's Business,* May 1, 1997, p. 17.

Wilson, Amy, "Paddle Away," *Money,* March 1, 2004, p. 141.

—Frederick C. Ingram

Corel Corporation

1600 Carling Avenue
Ottawa, Ontario K1Z 8R7
Canada
Telephone: (613) 728-0826
Fax: (613) 728-9790
Web site: http://www.corel.com

Private Company
Incorporated: 1985 as Corel Systems Corporation
Employees: 769
Sales: $126.7 million (2002)
NAIC: 511210 Software Publishers

Corel Corporation offers personal productivity software used by millions of customers in 75 countries across the globe. As one of the top ten packaged software brands in the world, Corel provides software in four major market segments including PC graphics, office-productivity, digital image editing, and natural-media painting and illustration. Its products include WordPerfect Office Suite, CorelDRAW Graphics Suite, Corel Painter, Paint Shop Family, and Corel DESIGNER Technical Suite. Vector Capital Corp. acquired Corel in 2003.

Origins

Corel is the offspring of Michael Cowpland, a high-energy entrepreneur and Ottawa celebrity who is credited with founding two of Canada's most successful high-technology ventures: Corel and the earlier Mitel. Cowpland was born in Sussex, England, in 1943 and received his bachelor of engineering degree from Imperial College in London. In 1964 he emigrated to Canada. There, he earned a master's degree and a Ph.D. at Carleton University while working as a research and development engineer at the respected Bell-Northern Research Ltd.

Cowpland worked at Bell-Northern with Terry Matthews, a friend who also had emigrated from the United Kingdom. In 1973 the pair left Bell to form a new venture dubbed Mitel (an abbreviation for Mike and Terry Electronics). They launched the tiny company with the hope of creating a device that could translate the pulses generated by rotary dial telephones into the tones created by touch-tone phones. Laboring in Cowpland's garage in Ottawa, the pair achieved their goal and went on to build one of Canada's most successful private telecommunications products companies.

Cowpland and Matthews realized stunning success with Mitel during the 1970s and early 1980s, doubling sales of its advanced telephone switching equipment every year for ten straight years. The darlings of the Canadian investment community, Cowpland and Matthews grew rich. In the early 1980s they began to chase new markets by diversifying into various digital technologies, and the pair seemed to have the Midas touch when most of those projects took off.

All seemed to be going well until the mid-1980s. Mitel posted revenues of CAD 343 million in 1984, in fact, by which time the company was employing more than 5,000 workers in ten plants around the world. It was in 1984, though, that Mitel's diversification effort suddenly began to look like a miscalculation. Significantly, Cowpland and Matthews fell behind schedule on the development of a state-of-the-art phone switch called the SX-2000. When computer giant IBM tired of the delay and shopped elsewhere for the technology, Mitel was faced with plant overcapacity, cost overruns, and a CAD 50 million research-and-development tab. Mitel began losing money, and Cowpland and Matthews were compelled to sell the enterprise to British Telecom. Still, both founders walked away with millions in cash.

Undeterred, Cowpland viewed the sale of Mitel as an opportunity to pursue the development of technology that was of greater interest to him at the time and to escape a job that had become an administrative burden. In 1985 he dumped CAD 7 million of his own money into a new venture, which he named Corel. His initial goal was to develop a better laser printer that could be used with personal computers. He found that it was too difficult to compete in that market with low-cost Asian manufacturers, however, and quickly shifted his strategy. Corel soon became a value-added reseller of computers, selling complete systems geared for desktop publishing tasks.

Cowpland scrambled during his first few years to find a role for Corel in the marketplace. He eventually added optical disk-drives to his desktop publishing system lineup and then started marketing local area networks. Considering the hefty start-up investment, sales grew tepidly—to about CAD 6.6 million during 1988—and for a few years, Cowpland seemed the consummate fallen star. "The first couple of years were the most challenging as we were trying to find the right niche, but I think that is typical of any new company," Cowpland recalled in the June 1992 *Profit.* "It's almost impossible to come up with the ideal concept right out of the starting gate," he added.

Debut of Corel's Graphic Software in 1989

While he pushed his value-added hardware, Cowpland labored behind the scenes on what became a pet project: the creation of software that offered better design and layout capabilities than were offered by leading applications of the time. To that end, he hired a crack software development team that he allowed to work relatively autonomously. Before the end of the decade, the team had developed a graphic arts software package that would become the standard for the PC-based desktop publishing industry. In 1989 Corel unveiled its cutting-edge Corel-DRAW software program. CorelDRAW, significantly, was the first graphics application to incorporate into one package all of the major graphics functions: illustration, charting, editing, painting, and presentation.

CorelDRAW was an instant success, which was surprising given the fact that Corel had never mass-marketed anything, much less a software application. Cowpland's savvy marketing strategy, however, eventually earned him almost as much respect in the software community as did CorelDRAW. Cowpland plowed millions of dollars into an aggressive sales campaign. Specifically, he bucked the industry norm by marketing CorelDRAW heavily in Europe and Japan. Most software companies at the time started out focusing almost solely on English-speaking consumers. Furthermore, as CorelDRAW became more popular, Cowpland refused to adhere to the convention of selling different versions of the program one after the other. Instead, Corel developed and simultaneously sold multiple versions of CorelDRAW, each of which was tailored for a select market niche.

Corel's rapid-fire product development and marketing effort quickly boosted its bottom line. Indeed, sales (roughly 80 percent of which were attributable to CorelDRAW) rose to CAD 36 million in 1990 and then to CAD 52 million in 1991, while net income increased to a solid CAD 7 million. Going into 1992, Corel was employing about 250 workers and had shipped nearly 300,000 of its CorelDRAW packages to more than 40 countries. CorelDRAW was becoming increasingly popular with customer groups such as children, artists, architects, and business owners, among others. In short, CorelDRAW allowed users to create anything from T-shirt designs to corporate logos

and technical drawings. Using a computerized pencil, or drawing from 12,000 programmed images, users could create an endless array of color illustrations, designs, and drawings.

As Mitel had, Corel reflected the insatiable drive of its founder. Cowpland had established his name in the Canadian business scene with Mitel, but his remarkable success with Corel revived his fame in his home town, where he "replaced Pierre Trudeau as Ottawa's most-watched celebrity," according to *Canadian Business Magazine.* In Ottawa, Cowpland was known as much for his persona as his business success. He raced around the city in flashy sports cars and generally made no apologies for his wealth. He and his wife built a massive new home that included a ten-car underground garage and two squash courts and was designed to mimic the look of Corel's gold-colored headquarters.

Cowpland's no-holds-barred, unemotional business style was mirrored more clearly on the tennis court, where he was known as an aggressive contender driven to win at any cost. Evidencing that drive was Cowpland's relationship with longtime tennis partner Ed Hladkowicz, the tennis pro at a club that Cowpland bought during his Mitel days. Cowpland hired Hladkowicz to work for Corel, and Hladkowicz became a manager in the company's systems division. Meanwhile, the two friends continued what became a 20-year run of regular tennis matches. Then, one day in 1992, Cowpland coldly and abruptly eliminated the systems division and sent Hladkowicz packing. A week later he phoned the stunned Hladkowicz to arrange a time to play tennis (the two eventually did resume their association).

Although Cowpland was criticized for his callous treatment of employees, few could dispute the success of his philosophy in the business arena. Cowpland prided himself on making quick decisions and moving briskly to capitalize on new opportunities. During the early 1990s Corel introduced a string of CorelDRAW programs geared for entry-level users, intermediates, and advanced buyers. Those introductions helped Corel to capture a hefty 55 percent share of the global market for drawing and illustration software products. The resulting revenues rose to CAD 90 million in 1992, CAD 140 million in 1993, and then to CAD 226 million in 1994, while net income increased to nearly CAD 45 million.

Corel's success in 1993 and 1994 blasted critics, who claimed that Cowpland's downfall was imminent. Based on what they believed was a saturated market as well as Cowpland's history at Mitel, a number of investors began shortselling (betting against) Corel stock in 1992 in anticipation of an earnings slide. Instead, the company's earnings climbed rapidly in the wake of new product introductions and an improved balance sheet. Impressively, Cowpland had managed to grow Corel without taking on any debt. By 1994, in fact, Corel had virtually no long-term debt. Furthermore, Cowpland still owned an equity stake in the company of about 20 percent by 1995, giving him an estimated net worth of $200 million.

By 1994, though, it could be argued that Corel was relying too heavily on a single product line geared for a market niche that was becoming saturated. So, after shipping nearly one million CorelDRAW programs in 15 different languages, Cowpland began looking for a new avenue to growth. In 1994

Key Dates:

1985: Dr. Michael Cowpland founds Corel as a systems integration company.
1989: CorelDraw is launched after two years of code development.
1991: CorelSCSI is launched.
1992: CorelDraw 3 debuts, representing the beginning of the modern full-featured graphics suite.
1995: CorelDraw 6 is launched simultaneously with Windows 95, becoming the first major 32-bit application available for the new operating system.
1996: Novell Inc.'s WordPerfect division is acquired.
1999: WordPerfect Office 2000 is released; sales of CorelDraw reach ten million copies.
2000: Merger plans with Inprise/Borland Corporation are scrapped; Cowpland resigns; Microsoft buys a 20 percent stake in the company.
2001: Corel sells its Linux business.
2003: Vector Capital Corp. acquires Corel.
2004: The company purchases Jasc Software to bolster its graphics software line.
2005: Corel celebrates its 20th anniversary.

the company launched an ambitious initiative to branch into four new markets: consumer CD-ROMs, office suites (or "bundles" of productivity software), video-conferencing, and computer-aided design (CAD). Production of CD-ROM games and educational products was a top priority; Corel planned to launch 30 titles in 1995 and an additional 50 each following year. Corel planned to tap its established network of distributors in 60 countries to vie with venerable Microsoft in the $1 billion CD-ROM consumer market.

Creating its CD-ROM products in cooperation with Artech Digital Entertainments, Inc., Corel launched several CD-ROM products in 1995, including an electronic coloring book called "Blue Tortoise," a Marilyn Monroe photo compilation, a movie database, and collections of card and board games. At the same time, it continued to enhance its CorelDRAW line and to chase the other market categories it had targeted in 1994. For example, it announced plans to begin shipping a CAD software application called CorelCAD, which was designed to help homebuilders and people doing home renovations. Cowpland expected that effort to generate sales of $50 million annually by 1998. Likewise, Corel introduced a video-conferencing system early in 1996 called CorelVideo that was designed to operate efficiently on local area network systems.

Acquisition of WordPerfect in 1996

Critics wondered why Cowpland would take on so much risk by simultaneously jumping into industries in which he had little or no prior experience. Their concern was no doubt heightened early in 1996, when Corel stunned the software community by agreeing to purchase Novell Inc.'s vaunted WordPerfect division in a transaction valued at $124 million. WordPerfect word processing software was a leader in the massive word processing market. The deal also included Quattro Pro, a lead-

ing spreadsheet software, and the PerfectOffice application suite of productivity software. The surprising purchase was expected to more than triple Corel's annual revenue base.

The WordPerfect purchase vaulted Corel from a major niche player to a software industry contender in a business dominated by operating system powerhouse Microsoft: "Corel Feels Bold with WordPerfect Deal; CEO Has Glass House, But He Throws the First Stone at Microsoft," read the headline in the February 11, 1996 *Wall Street Journal.* By purchasing WordPerfect, Cowpland threw down the proverbial gauntlet, positioning his company to go toe-to-toe with Bill Gates's behemoth Microsoft. The acquisition marked the beginning of a new era for Corel. From 1996 onward, Cowpland's success with Corel would be measured by his ability to beat Bill Gates at his own game.

In the wake of the signal WordPerfect acquisition, Corel braced itself for the intense media scrutiny fueled by Cowpland's bid to break Microsoft's hegemony. The company continued its practice of relaunching CorelDRAW approximately every 13 months, recording consistent market success with its tried and true graphics product. In 1999, when CorelDRAW 9 was released, sales of Corel's mainstay product line reached ten million copies, a milestone achieved during the tenth anniversary of the product's release that testified to the one enduring strength supporting Corel. The company's success in posing as a legitimate threat to Microsoft's formidable position in business productivity software, however, was considerably less certain.

Corel's Java-compatible version of WordPerfect was tailored for compatibility with a variety of platforms, including Windows 95 and 98, Windows NT, Windows 3.1x, Macintosh, Unix, and Linux. In 1998 the company released WordPerfect Suite 8 with Dragon NaturallySpeaking, giving users speech-enabled word processing. A year later, Corel released WordPerfect Office 2000, but neither version catapulted the company to the rarefied heights for which it clamored. Corel lost $30 million in 1998 on $246 million in revenues and posted a $16 million profit on declining revenues of $243 million in 1999. To be fair, the company was pursuing an ambitious goal, one that could not be realistically achieved by the decade's end.

Changes in the New Millennium

The true measure of Cowpland's success remained to be determined in the inaugural decade of the 21st century. Corel made a positive start to its determinative decade by announcing an important merger. In February 2000, the company made public that it had signed a definitive merger agreement with Inprise/Borland Corporation, a transaction valued at $2.44 billion. The union of Inprise/Borland, a leading provider of Internet access infrastructure and application development tools and services, and Corel represented a pivotal step toward reaching Cowpland's goal. In a February 7, 2000 Corel press release, Cowpland stressed the importance of the merger's effect on Corel's advances with the Linux operating system, which was capable of running on a wide range of hardware. "With Inprise/Borland's leadership in the software development community and Corel's Linux desktop operating system and productivity applications," Cowpland said, "we have an extraordinary opportunity to reach all facets of the exploding Linux market."

If the merger reached fruition, Inprise/Borland was to be organized as a wholly owned subsidiary of Corel. Based on 1999 figures, the two companies would generate more than $400 million in revenues. Although the company's graphics and business productivity software was developed for a variety of platforms, much of its future success—particularly its success in wresting market share from Microsoft—hinged on the popularity of the Linux operating system. Toward this end, Cowpland's hopes were buoyed by the announcement that the Linux operating environment was expected to grow at a compound annual rate of more than 25 percent through 2003, according to International Data Corporation, an industry research organization. Whether or not such growth could inject Corel with muscle it needed to combat Microsoft remained to be determined in the years ahead.

Cowpland's grand plan failed to come together when the merger deal with Inprise/Borland was called off in 2000 as Corel's profits and share price continued to fall. In June, the company was forced to eliminate 350 jobs as part of a $40 million cost-cutting effort. Two months later, Cowpland resigned amid an ongoing insider trading investigation led by the Ontario Securities Commission. The charges were eventually settled in 2003. Cowpland was forced to pay fines and was barred from serving as a director of a public company for two years. Chief technology officer Derek J. Burney was tapped to take over as Corel's new president and CEO. Under his leadership, the company realigned its business structure into three major products groups: Creative Products; Business Applications; and Linux products.

Corel received a much-needed cash infusion in October 2000, when Microsoft agreed to invest $135 million in Corel. During the next two years, Corel attempted to regain its financial footing. In 2001, the company sold its Linux desktop operating system business in order to strengthen its focus on its WordPerfect and CorelDRAW products. In 2002, Corel tried to gain a foothold in the XML software market when it acquired SoftQuad Software in a $16.6 million deal. Despite its efforts to enter new markets, Corel was unable to shore up profits and found itself in a precarious financial position.

During 2003, California-based Vector Capital Corp. acquired Microsoft's interest in Corel for $12.9 million (Microsoft had lost more than $100 million on its Corel investment). Later that year, the private equity firm made a play for Corel, offering $1.05 per share, or approximately $97.6 million, for the company. The deal was approved by shareholders in August of that year.

Under new ownership, the company streamlined its product offerings and focused on its three major products: CorelDRAW, WordPerfect, and Corel Painter. In 2004, the company purchased Jasc Software to bolster its graphics software line, which included CorelDRAW and Corel Painter. By honing in on the home and small office consumer segment, Corel hoped to bolster sales.

Corel celebrated its 20th anniversary in 2005. Although the changes Corel had faced in the early years of the new millennium were swift and dramatic, it appeared as though the company was on the right track for the first time in years. Both revenue and profits had started to climb slowly, indicating Corel's strategy was paying off.

Principal Competitors

Microsoft Corporation; Adobe Systems Inc.; Quark, Inc.

Further Reading

Aragon, Lawrence, "Caution: Stories Graphic in Nature: CEO Mike Cowpland's Plan to Diversify into Publishing and Video-Conferencing Could Lead His Corel to the Heart of Palookaville," *PC Week,* September 4, 1995, p. A10.

Bagnall, James, "Corel Good Example of New Wave of Business," *Ottawa Citizen,* January 10, 1994, p. A9.

——, "Corel Marketing Machine Goes Formal; Software Star Offers Big Reward for Top Artist," *Ottawa Citizen,* August 10, 1995, p. C6.

Doyle, T.C., "Targeting the SMB—Corel Perfects Turnaround," *VARbusiness,* March 21, 2005.

Duros, Sally, "New President, Cash Buoyed Troubled Corel," *B to B,* October 23, 2000.

Gallit, Peter, "Corel Seeks Buyer," *eWEEK,* March 24, 2003.

Hatter, David, "The Fastest Finalists: Drawing on Innovation," *Profit,* June 1992, p. 32.

Holloway, Andy, "Corel: Rest in Peace," *Canadian Business,* September 15, 2003, p. 13.

Kainz, Alana, "Corel Decides To Spread Its Software Bets Around; Company Moves Aggressively into New Markets," *Ottawa Citizen,* October 8, 1994, p. E1.

——, "Corel's No. 2 Executive Abruptly Quits on High Note," *Ottawa Citizen,* December 21, 1993, p. C8.

——, "Corel Up, Up and Away; Firm To Unseat Cognos As No. 1 in Software," *Ottawa Citizen,* December 24, 1994, p. H12.

King, Laura, "Corel Accepts $96M Offer from Vector," *Daily Deal,* June 9, 2003.

Oberbeck, Steven, "Novell Finally Gets Monkey Off Back," *Knight-Ridder/Tribune Business News,* February 1, 1996.

"Stitch in Time," *PC Week,* September 11, 1995, p. A5.

Sutcliffe, Mark, "Racquet Scientist," *Canadian Business,* June 1995, p. 62(5).

Sutton, Neil, "Corel Gets Back to Its Roots," *Computer Dealer News,* November 5, 2004.

Tamburri, Rosanna, "Corel Feels Bold with WordPerfect Deal; CEO Has Glass House, But He Throws the First Stone at Microsoft," *Wall Street Journal,* February 11, 1996, Sec. 2, p. 2.

Tillson, Tamsen, "Corel Inside Out," *Canadian Business,* Spring 1997, p. 58.

Urlocker, Michael, "Corel Has Last Laugh," *Financial Post,* July 11, 1992, p. 10.

—Dave Mote
—updates: Jeffrey L. Covell, Christina M. Stansell

Country Kitchen International, Inc.

801 Deming Way
Madison, Wisconsin 53717
U.S.A.
Telephone: (608) 833-9633
Fax: (608) 826-9080
Web site: http://www.countrykitchenrestaurants.com

Private Company
Incorporated: 1939
Employees: 10,810
Sales: $234.9 million (2004 est.)
NAIC: 722110 Full-Service Restaurants

Country Kitchen International, Inc. (CKI) operates a chain of about 170 Country Kitchen restaurants that are located in 26 states. The firm owns about three dozen of the sites, with the rest held by franchisees. Country Kitchen restaurants are well known for their breakfasts and feature burgers, steaks, chicken, and more contemporary fare as well. Some units also incorporate a Breadeaux Pizza outlet and offer delivery. The firm's primary customers are blue-collar families, and its meals are priced higher than fast food but a notch below casual dining chains. Most sites are freestanding locations, but some are found in strip malls, travel plazas, and hotels. The company has been owned since 1997 by top franchise owner Chuck Myers.

Beginnings

The origins of Country Kitchen International date to 1939, when Bill Johnson and Bill Goodman pooled $400 in savings and opened a storefront restaurant in Cincinnati, Ohio. Under the name Country Kitchen, they served hamburgers for five cents and steak sandwiches for a dime. Johnson, who had grown up in Kentucky and quit school in the eighth grade, had learned the business as a teenager while working at a hamburger stand. His philosophy was to "treat folks special," and that, and the good food he served, led the restaurant to quickly become a popular destination for hungry customers.

In 1942 a second location was opened, and during World War II business boomed as the restaurants fed a steady stream of war plant workers. During the 1940s several more Country Kitchen restaurants were added, and in the 1950s the firm responded to the growing popularity of drive-ins by offering its own version of "eat in your car" service. In 1958 Johnson decided to franchise the concept, and in the next few years Country Kitchens began to open around the United States. Franchise fees were relatively modest, and owners of the firm's restaurants were often "mom and pop" entrepreneurs who wanted to run a business of their own.

In 1968 Country Kitchen Restaurants, Inc. and Northwest Franchise merged to form Country Kitchen International (CKI), and the firm's stock later began trading publicly. In 1972 the corporation's revenues hit $2.8 million, but as expansion ramped up they rose to nearly $6.6 million by 1976, with earnings of more than $1 million. The company's locations had by now evolved into 24-hour coffee shops, with breakfast items like omelets and pancakes served around the clock.

Sale to Carlson Companies in 1977

In 1977 CKI was acquired by Carlson Companies, Inc., a privately owned conglomerate whose holdings included several retail firms, Radisson Hotels, and the TGI Fridays restaurant chain. New owner Curtis Carlson was a hard-driving entrepreneur who sought growth in his properties, and over the next several years the Country Kitchen chain continued to expand, reaching a peak of 340 locations by the end of the decade. Its base of operations was now located in Minneapolis, where Carlson was headquartered.

During the late 1970s sales stagnated as the U.S. economy hit a downturn and the company's restaurants saw increasing competition from fast-food and casual dining chains. Over the next several years a number of underperforming locations were closed.

In 1983 McDonald's and Red Barn restaurants veteran Richard Hohman was named president of CKI as it was folded into Carlson's new Hospitality Group, and he quickly began working to improve the bottom line. A variety of measures were taken to standardize operations and boost sales outside the chain's breakfast stronghold, and alcoholic beverages were added to some locations. CKI also established a new national advertising media fund, which offered rebates to franchisees

---

Company Perspectives:

Country Kitchen is where our guests feel like they're coming home, the food is always fresh, the smiles stretch a country mile, and breakfast can be anytime of the day.

---

who spent money on local ads. Although they were required to spend 1.5 percent of sales on advertising, audits by the firm had found that they often did not meet this obligation.

During 1985 revenues for the entire system reached $153 million, up 5.5 percent from the year before, and 16 new restaurants were opened while only nine closed. In 1986 the chain had a total of 246 outlets, three of which were owned by the company and the rest by franchisees. They were spread out over 20 U.S. states and two Canadian provinces, with about two-thirds found in Minnesota, Wisconsin, and Iowa.

The year 1986 saw the company launch a new print, radio, and television marketing campaign that used the tagline, "The Country's Calling You." CKI customers were typically working-class families, and the ads stressed the food's reasonable prices and country-style taste, as well as the firm's hospitality.

In October of 1986 CKI rolled out a new menu that emphasized breakfast items as well as lunch and dinner choices like calico bean soup and fried chicken. It was optimized to be easier to prepare for restaurant cooks (who were now proving difficult to hire and retain), and some recently added trendy items were eliminated to focus on classic fare. Restaurant designs were now being updated as well, with seating capacity increased and interiors revised to feature homespun prints and pastel colors.

In 1987 Carlson unveiled a new budget lodging concept called Country Inn that featured a Country Kitchen restaurant and a limited service hotel. The first unit opened in Minneapolis in the spring, but afterward most Country Inn hotels were built without restaurants. An agreement had earlier been reached with a hotel firm called Dillon Inn Co. that had begun to add Country Kitchen restaurants to a small number of its properties as well.

As it sought to upgrade the brand, CKI now began moving beyond the "mom and pop" franchisees of earlier years to look for operators willing to open multiple restaurants in a particular geographical area, as well as to sub-franchise units for the parent firm. Deals of this type were soon struck in Colorado and Texas, with others under consideration. The firm charged a franchise fee of $25,000 plus a 5 percent royalty on gross sales and 3.5 percent for local and national advertising. Total development costs of a new restaurant were put at between $750,000 and $850,000. Sales had now increased each year for five years running, and the firm's new menu had helped boost the average check total by 61 cents to $3.50.

In 1989 CKI head Richard Hohman died of cancer at the age of 56, and his place was taken by Frank Steed. Under Steed the firm's headquarters staff was trimmed by a third and menu items were made more spicy and flavorful, while new dishes like Shrimp Scampi and Fajitas were added. Food in the family dining category was seen by many as somewhat bland, with the lack of seasonings and spices attributed to the large proportion

of senior citizens who were customers. With the baby boomer generation now starting to age, the firm began adapting to their more adventurous dining choices. New desserts and seasonal menu specials also were added in an attempt to lure in new customers, some of which (including a $9.95 USDA choice steak) cost more than the firm's typical entrée maximum of $5.95. The new menu was advertised with the tagline, "American Favorites, Yesterday and Today," and cash sales incentives were offered to waitstaff who sold the most desserts. Some franchisees were now beginning to grumble that too many changes were being made for them to keep up with, however.

Franchising Extending to Puerto Rico in 1991

In 1991 the company announced that ten franchised restaurants would be added in Puerto Rico, with one opened in a Travelodge hotel in November and another in a closed Wendy's restaurant at San Juan International Airport several months later. Systemwide sales were $178 million for 1991, although the number of units now stood at slightly more than 230. The firm had sold or de-licensed more than 70 restaurants over a three-year period, which did not meet its new operating standards, and as a result per-unit sales were up.

In 1992 CEO Frank Steed left the company to head the Bonanza steakhouse chain, and his position was taken by TGI Fridays vice-president Curtis Nelson. Efforts to improve performance were ongoing, and the firm soon unveiled a new restaurant design that resembled a country farmhouse complete with dormer windows, a porch, and red awnings. The company was striving to carve out a niche for its restaurants as an improvement over fast food but a cheaper alternative to casual dining restaurants like Olive Garden and Red Lobster.

In 1994 CKI opened its first restaurant in a truck stop, in Wyoming, added a 220-seat outlet in Jakarta, Indonesia, and signed an agreement to convert 19 Captain Pancake restaurants on Long Island into Country Kitchens. The year also saw introduction of a new child-themed promotion, "CK Junction," which used activities like coloring books and posters of a train engineer bear character.

Growth continued over the next several years, with the restaurant total sliding back up to 250 by 1996. In January 1997 the firm named a new president, Charles Foster, who had most recently been a vice-president at TGI Fridays. In March he announced plans for further expansion at the firm's annual franchisees' meeting, while some of the company's restaurants began offering prepackaged take-home meals to go.

Sale to Kitchen Investment Group in 1997

In the summer of 1997 Carlson Companies agreed to sell Country Kitchen International to its largest franchise owner, Kitchen Investment Group, Inc. of Madison, Wisconsin. Headed by 20-year franchisee Charles Myers, Kitchen Investment Group owned 35 restaurants and sub-franchised 22 others. Like company founder Bill Johnson and recent owner Curt Carlson, Chuck Myers was a born entrepreneur, having formed a vending machine business in high school and then become the owner of a Country Kitchen restaurant at the age of 21, after which he built up a chain of the restaurants in Wisconsin and Illinois.

Key Dates:

1939: Bill Johnson opens the first Country Kitchen restaurant in Cincinnati.
1942: The second restaurant is opened; others follow.
1958: Johnson begins selling franchises.
1968: A merger with Northwest Franchise creates Country Kitchen International.
1977: Carlson Companies acquires the firm.
1983: The new president, Richard Hohman, begins efforts to revitalize the chain.
1997: Top franchisee Charles Myers buys the company from Carlson.
2003: Cobranding with Breadeaux Pizza brings new delivery and takeout options.
2005: The company begins developing the Peppermill Grill casual dining concept.

Myers knew the business well, and he immediately began working to reorganize the firm in a way that made sense to franchisees. The 100-item menu was made more upscale without compromising the basic value its customers expected, while a new tagline, "It's Different in the Country," was added. Food ordering had heretofore been fragmented, and it was now consolidated with a single source. To improve employee recruitment and retention, the firm's training process also was streamlined.

In 2000 CKI redoubled its promotional efforts with a new television ad campaign that touted the firm's "Real Meals" as a better alternative to fast food, and launched a line of $4.99 bread bowl lunches that were guaranteed to be ready in five minutes or less. For 2000 the system, still with about 250 restaurants, had sales of $223 million.

Over the next year the company continued to expand its menu to include more upscale choices like lobster ravioli and stir-fry dishes, and boosted the frequency of special meal promotions from four per year to six. In 2002 a new Wisconsin Cheese Skillets menu was introduced that was a co-promotion with the Wisconsin Milk Marketing Board.

The same year saw CKI begin trying to position itself as a national brand with the "Taste of America" promotion that featured regional dishes from around the country. The firm also sent cease-and-desist letters to about 350 restaurants that used the words "country kitchen" somewhere in their name, but were not franchisees. Many of the small restaurants affected had been in business for years, and some changed their names, while others ignored the warning. In the summer, one of the firm's major Ohio franchisees went out of business, causing the closing of a number of restaurants there.

In 2003 CKI unveiled a new logo and also reached a cobranding agreement with Breadeaux Pizza of Missouri to offer the latter firm's pizza in its restaurants and for home delivery. The company was again shrinking, and the number of locations dipped below 200, with all non-U.S. operations now shut down or sold.

In the fall of 2005 CKI announced the development of a new concept called Peppermill Grill. A casual dining restaurant that served alcoholic beverages, its dishes would be seasoned by "Flavor Ambassadors" who brought an array of spices and a large peppermill to the table. Décor would evoke the flavor of a spice marketplace. The firm integrated the idea into one of its Country Kitchen sites during the year, and began preparations to open a prototype restaurant in Madison in 2006. After the menu and other details were finalized, it would be available to franchisees for integration into their existing restaurants, for full conversions, or to build new outlets.

More than 65 years after its first restaurant opened, Country Kitchen International, Inc., continued to offer quality food at an affordable price to customers in its stronghold of the Upper Midwest and around the United States. Since its acquisition in 1997 by veteran franchisee Chuck Myers, the chain had shrunk in size as it sought to standardize operations and fend off fierce competition. The firm had high hopes for its new Peppermill Grill concept, which was set to debut in 2006.

Principal Competitors

Shoney's, Inc.; Denny's Corporation; The Restaurant Company; CBRL Group, Inc.; VICORP Restaurants, Inc.; IHOP Corporation; Bob Evans Farms, Inc.; Golden Corral Corporation.

Further Reading

Bain, Laurie, "Carlson Plays to Win," *Restaurant Business,* June 10, 1987, p. 161.

Carlino, Bill, "Country Kitchen Picks Up Speed with 'CK Junction,' " *Nation's Restaurant News,* September 19, 1994, p. 37.

——, "Country Kitchen Revamps Menu to Broaden Appeal," *Nation's Restaurant News,* February 3, 1992, p. 7.

Cebrzynski, Greg, "Country Kitchen Expands Menu, Marketing," *Nation's Restaurant News,* December 10, 2001, p. 8.

——, "Country Kitchen Keeps Promos Rolling, Unveils New Logo," *Nation's Restaurant News,* May 26, 2003, p. 14.

——, "Country Kitchen Seeks Nationwide Status with 'Taste of America' Promo," *Nation's Restaurant News,* July 15, 2002, p. 14.

"Country Kitchen," *Nation's Restaurant News,* May 8, 2000, p. 130.

Creasey, John, "Country Kitchen Cooks New Marketing Strategy," *Nation's Restaurant News,* March 24, 1986, p. 3.

Farkas, David, "Good-Bye Coffee Shops," *Restaurant Hospitality,* August 1, 1991, p. 126.

Merrill, Ann, "Carlson Hospitality Worldwide Gets Out of the Country Kitchen," *Star-Tribune Newspaper of the Twin Cities,* July 24, 1997, p. 1D.

Mills, James, "Country Kitchen Owner Is Expanding the Restaurant Chain," *Capital Times & Wisconsin State Journal,* February 29, 2004, p. C1.

Rhein, Elizabeth, "Country Kitchen: Coming on Strong," *Restaurant Business,* September 20, 1986, p. 88.

Richgels, Jeff, "Country Kitchen Cookin' Up New Image," *Capital Times,* May 1, 1998, p. 1C.

Romeo, Peter, "Hohman Dies at 56: Country Kitchen CEO," *Nation's Restaurant News,* June 26, 1989, p. 26.

Seligman, Bob, "Country Kitchens Aims to Spice Up Menu Offerings in Bid for Bigger Market Share," *Nation's Restaurant News,* April 9, 1990, p. 38.

Walkup, Carolyn, "Country Kitchen: Cooking Up a Global Future," *Nation's Restaurant News,* March 29, 1993, p. 62.

—Frank Uhle

The David J. Joseph Company

300 Pike Street
Cincinnati, Ohio 45202
U.S.A.
Telephone: (513) 419-6200
Fax: (513) 419-6222
Web site: http://www.djj.com

Wholly Owned Subsidiary of SHV Holdings, N.V.
Incorporated: 1920
Employees: 1,100
Sales: $5 billion (2005 est.)
NAIC: 421930 Recyclable Material Wholesalers

The David J. Joseph Company (DJJ) is widely recognized as America's oldest and largest scrap iron and steel company. With more than $5 billion in sales and $600 million in assets, DJJ is also one of the largest scrap metal companies in the world. The company provides procurement services for scrap consumers, ferrous and nonferrous scrap trading and processing, international scrap and substitutes marketing, ferro-alloy and nodular and foundry pig iron trading, mill services, rail services, industrial scrap services, and railcar lease, purchase, sale, and finance. DJJ operates as a subsidiary of Netherlands-based SHV Holdings, N.V.

Early History

The company's history can be traced back to the mid-19th century, when German immigrant Joseph Joseph started a textiles business in Cincinnati. Swept up in the industrial revolution, the founder launched a scrap iron business in 1885. The railroad and construction industries helped increase demand for steel—and in turn boosted the scrap business—throughout the late 19th century.

Known in the late 1800s and early 1900s as the Joseph Joseph & Brothers Company, the family business diversified vertically and horizontally. The Indiana Rolling Mill Co. subsidiary was eventually merged into Republic Iron & Steel, a leading steelmaker in the early 20th century. The founder also created the Railway Supply Company and the Ohio Falls Iron Company.

Although each of the founder's five sons earned positions in management, it was the youngest who rose to the top. David Joseph first started working at the scrap brokerage in 1897 at the age of 11. The future company namesake rejoined the firm in 1905 after earning degrees from the Franklin Institute and Harvard University. He advanced to leadership of scrap operations by the time he was 30. Following the 1920 dissolution of Joseph Joseph & Brothers, the David J. Joseph Co. was formed to pursue the scrap iron business.

The development of the open-hearth furnace in the early 1900s both improved the quality of steel and encouraged consumption of scrap metal. Although steel manufacturers used "home scrap" from their own operations, the burgeoning auto industry's voracious appetite drove the expansion of the purchased scrap business.

Nonetheless, the scrap business remained a risky proposition ruled by the cyclical dictates of supply and demand. Scrap dealers played the odds, stockpiling material when prices dropped and selling when demand drove prices up. Scrap collection grew so efficient that an analyst for American Metal Market characterized the market as "demand-driven," asserting that "scrap is bought, not sold." A 1995 company publication noted that DJJ dealers occasionally "resorted to barter, taking finished steel in the attempt to make a profit." Given the structure of the industry, DJJ evolved into a brokerage. It established contracts with steelmakers that required the firm to find scrap supplies to meet steelmakers' needs.

Surviving the Great Depression/War Years

The speculative nature of the scrap iron business was exacerbated by the Great Depression, which in the United States shut down more than half of the capacity for steel production. According to a company history, David Joseph did not let the national financial crisis stand in the way of a good deal. The 1933 purchase of 16,000 Southern Railroad railcars and engines is an oft-cited case in point. DJJ shipped a whopping 625,000 tons of scrap to Great Britain four years later. Large, risky transactions such as this helped DJJ rebound in the mid-1930s.

DJJ's close ties to the railroad business developed into an enduring, but lesser-known, segment of the family company.

Railcars were an abundant source of scrap steel. DJJ's railcar scrapping developed proprietary burning equipment for wood-lined boxcars. The firm not only scrapped railroad equipment, it also refurbished railcars. Some of these were drafted for use in a company-owned fleet that transported scrap across the country; others were sold or leased to railroads and businesses. This auxiliary operation eventually developed into DJJ's Railroad Equipment Division, which had facilities in Illinois, Nebraska, Colorado, Tennessee, Florida, Kentucky, Virginia, Georgia, Texas, and Utah by the late 1980s. This division maintained a fleet of nearly 10,000 general-purpose railcars by the mid-1990s.

By the early 1940s DJJ was generally acknowledged to be America's largest scrap iron broker; it also ranked as a top scrap iron and steel exporter. David J. Joseph, Jr., joined the family firm in 1938 and assumed the presidency in 1945. In contrast to his father, the Yale alumnus was better known for his managerial techniques than his trading prowess. DJJ expanded with the steel industry throughout the postwar era.

A New Parent Company for DJJ in 1975

The Joseph family divested ownership of its namesake company to SHV Holdings, N.V. of The Netherlands in 1975. SHV was a worldwide global trading conglomerate with interests that included wholesaling and energy. David J. Joseph, Jr., accepted the presidency of SHV's North American Holding Corporation and remained in that capacity for seven years. He retired in 1982.

James R. Breth was elected to DJJ's presidency in 1980. He had started as a broker in one of the firm's southern offices, advancing to office manager in 1960. He became vice-president of trading in 1976. In 1986, the veteran trader was elected chairman.

Technological advances and structural changes in the steel industry benefited DJJ in the 1980s and early 1990s. Just as open-hearth furnaces had changed the face of the steel industry at the dawn of the 20th century, the development of the electric-arc furnace in the 1960s spurred another revolution. The electric-arc furnace used scrap iron and steel—instead of the traditional mix of iron ore, limestone, and coke—to make a limited range of steel products. Compared with conventional integrated mills, the "minimills" that evolved around electric-arc furnace technology were faster, more efficient, more versatile, and more productive than their dominant counterparts. At the same time, steel mills striving for increased efficiency reduced their production of "home scrap," thereby raising their need for purchased scrap. Thus, even as U.S. steel production declined in the late 1970s and early 1980s, demand for purchased scrap iron and steel increased.

The minimill segment of the steel industry fit well with DJJ's own decentralized strategy. Its regional markets and emphasis on autonomy echoed DJJ's corporate culture. DJJ had the foresight to forge close ties with two of the most important minimills in the United States, Nucor Corp. and Florida Steel Corp. Established in 1967, North Carolina-based Nucor had grown into the largest and most profitable producer in the minimill sector. DJJ enjoyed valuable exclusive brokerages with Nucor and Florida Steel.

DJJ's internal technological advances created efficiencies and improved profitability as well. Perhaps most noteworthy was the company's information system that linked company traders, and technology facilitated the coordination of orders and supplies.

Global Expansion in the 1980s and Early 1990s

The vast majority of DJJ's post-World War II business was conducted domestically, but in recognition that the United States was the world's largest exporter of scrap, the company reentered international markets in 1985 and created an international division two years later. With the support of its globally influential parent, DJJ expanded its geographic reach through exports to Canada, Mexico, and overseas markets. In 1993, DJJ expanded railcar leasing, repair, and remarketing into Mexico through a joint venture with Servicios Financieros Quadrum S.A.

DJJ also expanded through acquisition in the late 1980s and early 1990s. After a six-year hiatus, the company reentered the nonferrous segment of the scrap business with the purchase of United Iron & Metal Co., a Baltimore firm. The 1991 acquisition of Frank H. Nott Inc., a private, family-owned company founded in 1887, further expanded DJJ's nonferrous activities.

Two publicized attempts to expand DJJ's processing activities through acquisition were inexplicably aborted, however. In 1992, the company initiated the $18 million purchase of three southern scrap yards from Proler International Corporation. The deal was abandoned within months of its announcement with no public explanation. Less than a year later, the proposed acquisition of Ferrous Processing & Trading Company, a major Detroit-area scrap yard, fell through. Later in 1993, DJJ was able to acquire two ferrous scrap shredders from the bankrupt CF & I Steel Corporation.

Although DJJ's processing operations remained limited in the early 1990s, the company was not sheltered from the environmental pitfalls of this aspect of the scrap business. Scrap processing entails handling and disposition of the hazardous byproducts of everything from automobiles to medical equipment. As a result, it is regulated by state and federal environmental and worker safety agencies. In 1993, DJJ's Tampa, Florida, scrap yard discovered two cancer therapy devices containing radioactive material. (Both components were found before any harm was done.) DJJ also has been involved in a Tampa-area Superfund cleanup ordered by the U.S. Environmental Protection Agency. These events dramatically illustrated some of the risks associated with the scrap industry.

DJJ got a new leader in 1992, when Louis F. Terhar, Jr., advanced to president and chief executive officer. Terhar had

Key Dates:

1885: Joseph Joseph launches a scrap iron business.
1921: The company is renamed the David J. Joseph Co.
1975: The Joseph family divests ownership of its namesake company to SHV Holdings, N.V.
1987: DJJ creates an international division.
1996: Western Metals Recycling L.L.C. is created.
1998: The company forms River Metals Recycling L.L.C.
2000: The DJJ Metals Group and Gemini Recycling Group L.L.C. are launched.

been with DJJ a scant three years. James Breth stayed on as chairman.

Industry analysts were divided over the prospects for the domestic and international scrap markets in the mid-1990s and beyond. Some predicted that rising global minimill capacity and production would fuel scrap steel shortages. That was good news for scrap dealers, who anticipated higher prices. Other analysts, however, forecast that rising scrap prices would simply revitalize the more traditional integrated production methods. Given the support of its parent, its historical performance, and its strong ties to the minimill sector, DJJ's position appeared impervious to market shifts.

DJJ in the Late 1990s and Beyond

DJJ made several key moves in the late 1990s and early years of the new millennium that solidified its position in the scrap metal industry. During 1996 the company formed Western Metals Recycling LLC when it merged its processing facilities in Plymouth, Utah, and Englewood, Colorado, with those of Atlas Steel Inc. Two years later, the company partnered with Newell Recycling Company to create Trademark Metals Recycling LLC, a processing company based in Tampa, Florida. Later that year, DJJ added Klempner Brothers Inc. and the River City Baling and River City Shredding yards in Louisville, Kentucky to its arsenal. River Metals Recycling LLC was formed as a result of the deal.

DJJ also worked to bolster its railcar leasing business during this time period. In November 1998, the company bought FerroQuadrum, S.A. de C.V., a large railcar leasing and repair firm based in Mexico. DJJ believed the purchase would strengthen its transportation services division, which benefited from a North American rail system that stretched from Montreal, Canada, to Mexico City.

By now, sales had surpassed $2 billion. DJJ continued to forge partnerships as it entered the year 2000. It joined with Ferrous Processing & Trading Co. of Detroit, Michigan, to create Gemini Recycling Group LLC The venture gave DJJ a strong foothold in Detroit, one of the largest scrap producing areas in the country. Gemini was established as a full-service company that processed, transported, and sold scrap metal for manufacturers who produced scrap metal as a byproduct.

In September 2000, the company formed DJJ Metals Group, which was established to oversee the marketing of metal sales including aluminum, copper, brass, nickel, and stainless.

DJJ's Trademark Metals Recycling group installed a new mega-shredder at its Tampa Port in Florida in 2002. The new shredder was much more efficient and had the capacity to produce up to 30,000 tons each month—double the capacity of the old shredder.

During 2002, River Metals Recycling installed the world's first online bulk scrap analyzer at its Newport, Kentucky facility. In September 2004, the second Gamma-Tech Crossbelt Metal Analyzer went online in Louisville, Kentucky. DJJ had worked with Gamma-Tech since the late 1990s to develop the new analyzer, which after several rounds of testing was able to accurately determine the chemical makeup of scrap grades.

DJJ's actions during the last five years had left it on solid ground. It remained the largest scrap broker in the United States with 11 offices, and by 2005 sales had moved past the $5 billion mark. DJJ planned to continue to strengthen its ferrous brokerage, ferro-alloy, metals, processing, and rail operations in the future. As the leader in its industry, The David J. Joseph Company appeared to be well positioned for success in the years to come.

Principal Divisions

Ferrous Brokerage; Ferro-Alloy; Metals Group; Processing; Rail Equipment Group; Services.

Principal Competitors

Commercial Metals Company; Metal Management Inc.; Philip Services Corporation.

Further Reading

"David J. Joseph Co. Celebrates Centennial," *American Metal Market*, January 10, 1986, p. 17.

"David J. Joseph to Expand in Kentucky," *Metal Bulletin*, July 27, 1998.

Hemmer, Andy, "Today's Joseph a Quasi-Commodities Exchange Scrap-Metal Giant Hits $2 Billion in Revenue," *Business Courier*, October 31, 1997, p. 21.

Kosdrosky, Terry, "Scrap-Metal Companies Forge Joint Deal," *Crain's Detroit Business*, March 27, 2000, p. 37.

Kruglinski, Anthony, "DJJ's McMillan: A Good Time for Selling and Profit-Taking," *Railway Age*, August 1995, p. 10.

Marley, Michael, "Clues to 'Hot' Scrap Uncovered," *American Metal Market*, April 14, 1993, p. 2.

——, "No Scrap Shortage Foreseen," *American Metal Market*, October 26, 1994, p. 2.

——, "World Scrap Shortage Seen; Supply Tightness and Higher Prices May Not Ease," *American Metal Market*, March 23, 1995, p. 1.

Monk, Dan, "Recent Acquisition Bolsters Joseph's Position," *Business Courier*, November 27, 1998.

"Processing Venture Formed," *American Metal Market*, March 13, 1998.

"Volatile Scrap Market Predicted," *American Metal Market*, July 15, 1988, p. S26.

Worden, Edward, "Exec Foresees 'Crunch' Due to Prices," *American Metal Market*, April 4, 1995, p. 9.

——, "Joseph to Buy Klempner Bros.," *American Metal Market*, July 20, 1998.

Wulff, Stephen W., "Scrap's Quality Now Major Concern," *American Metal Market*, December 7, 1989, p. 14.

—April Dougal Gasbarre
—update: Christina M. Stansell

dba Luftfahrtgesellschaft mbH

Terminalstrasse West, Terminal 1 Modul A
85356 München Flughafen
Germany
Telephone: +49 89 97 59 15 00
Fax: +49 89 97 59 14 73
Web site: http://www.dba.de

Private Company
Incorporated: 1978 as Delta Air Regionalflugverkehr
  GmbH & Co.
Employees: 760
Sales: DEM 265 million ($160.9 million) (2005 est.)
NAIC: 481111 Scheduled Passenger Air Transportation

Dba Luftfahrtgesellschaft mbH (dba) is one of Germany's leading regional airlines. About four million people each year fly dba, which was expanded by a quarter in 2005 when it took over the operations of another German carrier, Germania Express. The airline operated a fleet of about 30 aircraft in late 2005, with plans to more than double the fleet and to go public. Originally established in 1978, dba was acquired by British Airways plc (BA) in 1992 to take over its German operations.

Origins

The initials "dba" go back to Deutsche British Airways, or Deutsche BA, the U.K. airline's operation in the internal German market. British Airways PLC had operated routes between Berlin and cities in West Germany since World War II. To satisfy a government mandate to wind down its Internal German Services (IGS) following the country's reunification, BA transferred its business to a new mostly German-owned enterprise.

Created as a shell in 1991, Deutsche BA was 49 percent owned by British Airways, with three German banks (Commerzbank, Bayerische Vereinsbank, Berliner Bank) owning the rest. The new airline began operations on July 1, 1992, using the assets of recently acquired Delta Air Regionalflugverkehr GmbH & Co.

Delta Air had been operating a fleet of nine Saab 340s and one Dornier 228 on a regional network based in Friedrichshafen, plus two additional hubs in Stuttgart and Bremen. Delta Air was owned by Switzerland's Crossair AG and industrialist Friedrich von Bohlen und Halbach.

Delta Air had been launched in 1978 by Alfred Scholpp as a tiny commuter airline connecting Friedrichshafen to Stuttgart and Zurich with a de Havilland Twin Otter. It also ran charter flights. Switzerland's Crossair bought a 25 percent stake in 1982 and began a strategic partnership as the fleet was upgraded with Fairchild Metroliner II aircraft, notes *Flight International.* These were replaced with the Saab 340s in 1986, when Crossair supplied new capital to raise its shareholding to 40 percent.

Delta Air then developed a considerable business supplying feeder traffic to Deutsche Lufthansa AG, the flag carrier, which accounted for up to 40 percent of its revenues. Delta Air ran into some turbulence in the 1980s but had recovered its profitability by the time it was acquired by BA. Passenger count was growing rapidly, up to 225,000 in 1991, as the airline developed new routes to the former East Germany. Revenues were about DEM 60 million ($35 million) and the airline had 190 employees.

Renamed Deutsche BA Luftfahrtgesellschaft GmbH, the airline grew rapidly at first but would be unable to post a profit for more than a dozen years. By 1995, Deutsche BA's network stretched as far as the Baltics; as a German airline, it could fly into countries its British parent could not, an executive told *Flight International.* Turnover for fiscal 1994–95 was about DEM 450 million; passenger count was up to 1.75 million.

Although a dozen or so carriers were operating within Germany as its domestic market was liberalized, by the late 1990s the competition was largely a two-way race between Lufthansa, which had a 70 percent market share, and dba, with 20 to 25 percent. Dba was gaining market share, however, at the cost of profitability, analysts told the Swiss daily *L'Agéfi.* Deutsche BA managing director Carl Michel complained that Lufthansa was unfairly pricing its flights below its operating costs on routes where it competed with dba.

Deutsche BA remained in the red into 2001 amid intense price competition from a new crop of domestic low-cost carriers and intruders from abroad. Its fares slipped as low as DEM 88 ($93) as it fought to maintain market share. As Deutsche BA developed into a low-cost carrier, British Airways, which had acquired dba's remaining shares in April 1998, sought to sell it off to focus on its own full-service network.

Relaunching as dba in 2002

British budget carrier easyJet, seeking to complete its European network, acquired an option to buy Deutsche BA in 2002 but abandoned the purchase several months later after failing to win support of the German pilots' union. By this time, Deutsche BA had 800 employees, one quarter of them pilots, and a fleet of 16 Boeing 737 aircraft flying about three million passengers a year. In spite of a reported 40 percent market share on domestic routes, dba had yet to make a profit. It lost DEM 60 million on revenues of DEM 264 million in the fiscal year ended March 2003.

Other airlines, such as German charter operator TUI, showed interest in acquiring Deutsche BA. In June 2003, however, it was sold to textiles and airline entrepreneur Hans Rudolf Woehrl via the Nuremberg-based investment group Intro Verwaltungsgesellschaft for a token DEM 1, plus a quarter share of future profits for three years. BA also agreed to cover about DEM 70 million in projected losses and lease expenses for the remainder of the year. If BA had simply shut down Deutsche BA, it would have had huge social costs under German labor law, *Airfinance Journal* noted.

The airline was now called dba Luftfahrtgesellschaft mbH, or simply dba. German rail operator Deutsche Bahn sued the company, claiming that the moniker caused confusion with its own initials. A court ruled that the names and industries involved were sufficiently distinct to avoid this problem, and noted that other well-known German businesses like Deutsche Bank and Daimler Benz also had similar initials.

As the company headed toward recovery under new ownership, employees accepted a 20 percent pay cut. The new chairman, Whoerl, also instituted a number of other cost-saving measures including refinancing aircraft, he told *Dow Jones*. While cutting back on expenses, he also expanded dba's operations, including adding new service to London in direct competition with its former owner. It also soon added service to Hanover from its Munich base.

By the end of 2005, dba had lined up feeder agreements with several international airlines, including Emirates and the U.S.

carrier Delta Air Lines. Part of the plan was to make dba more attractive to the lucrative business travel market, and these connections increased its convenience.

Profitable in 2005

Dba achieved its first profit in the fiscal year ended March 2005. Revenues were about DEM 279 million, with a net profit of DEM 1.7 million. The airline carried three million passengers during the year and expected to carry four million in 2005–06.

At the end of the 2004–05 fiscal year, dba took over the operations of Germania Express (Gexx), the budget airline set up in June 2003 by charter group Germania Fluggesellschaft mbH. Gexx operated a fleet of a dozen Fokker 100s on 15 routes and had annual revenues of DEM 130 million. The acquisition gave dba a couple of new destinations within Germany (Bremen and Frankfurt), extended its reach into Europe, and increased its annual passenger count from three million to four million, making dba Germany's third largest carrier after Lufthansa and fast-growing rival Air Berlin GmbH & Co. Luftverkehrs KG. Soon after, Gexx owner Hinrich Bischoff became dba's majority shareholder, but he quit his stake a year later.

Dba successfully worked a new channel of distribution in the summer of 2005. The grocery store chain Aldi Sued sold more than a half million one-way tickets for DEM 50 each. As demand grew, so did dba's fleet, which reached 29 aircraft by September 2005. The airline had immediate plans to raise the fleet to add another half-dozen planes as it made a bid to be the market leader on flights within Germany.

Dba increased its capacity still further by placing a large order with Boeing Company in November 2005. It was buying 40,737 jets for delivery beginning in 2008, an order worth more than $2 billion at list prices. Dba was making plans for an initial public offering to finance some of the new planes. One key step, reported *Dow Jones Newswires,* would be changing the company's corporate type from GmbH to AG in the 2006–07 fiscal year.

Principal Competitors

Air Berlin GmbH & Co. Luftverkehrs KG; Deutsche Lufthansa AG; Germanwings; Hapag Lloyd Express.

Further Reading

''L'Allemagne, champ de bataille entre Lufthansa et Deutsche British Airways,'' *L'Agéfi,* April 1, 1997.
Boles, Tracey, ''EasyJet, the Low-Fare Airline, Gave Up Its Option to Buy the Loss-Making Deutsche BA,'' *The Business,* March 23, 2003.
''British Airways Buys Its Way into Germany's Domestic Market,'' *Aviation Europe,* March 26, 1992, p. 1.
Bulkeley, Andrew, ''German Airlines Make Connection,'' *TheDeal.com,* February 21, 2005.
''Deutsche BA Consortium Takes 100% Stake in Delta Air,'' *Airline Business,* May 1, 1992, p. 20.
Done, Kevin, ''TUI in Exploratory Talks on Deutsche BA,'' *Financial Times* (London), March 23, 2003.

Eberle, Matthias, "DBA and Gexx to Merge at End of March (Gexx gibt Flugbetrieb in Hande der DBA)," *Handelsblatt,* February 17, 2005, p. 10.

Flottau, Jens, "BA Sheds Deutsche BA," *Aviation Week & Space Technology,* June 9, 2003, p. 38.

——, "Low-Cost Climate Grows in Germany," *Aviation Week & Space Technology,* September 9, 2002, p. 44.

Genger, Jenny, and Ileana Grabitz, "Deutsche Bahn Loses Court Case Against DBA," *Financial Times Deutschland,* June 23, 2004, p. 7.

"German dba to Become Market Leader on Destinations Inside Germany," *German News Digest,* September 12, 2005.

"German dba Scores Big with Discount Tickets in Aldi Stores," *German News Digest,* July 28, 2005.

"Hans-Rudolf Woehrl Gives Up Majority Stake in DBA (Gexx-Eigner Bischoff sichert sich Mehrheit beim Billigflieger DBA)," *Die Welt,* March 18, 2005, p. 15.

Jeziorski, Andrzej, "Challenging Germany's Goliath—Deutsche BA," *Flight International,* May 24, 1995, p. 42.

Lea, Robert, "BA in a Dogfight with German Arm It Sold Off," *Evening Standard,* November 5, 2003, p. 34.

Marray, Michael, "Heading for the Altar: Dba's Take Over of Germania Express's Network Could Be a Marriage Made in Heaven and Start the Transformation of Germany's Low-Cost Market," *Airfinance Journal,* March 2005, pp. 19ff.

Preuschat, Archibald, "dba will ihre Expansion über die Börse finanzieren," *Dow Jones-VWD Unternehmen Deutschland,* November 14, 2005.

——, "German Airline Dba Plans IPO to Finance Expansion," *Dow Jones International News,* November 14, 2005.

Ray, Susanna, "Germany's Dba Hopes for Black 2004 After 11 Years in Red," *Dow Jones International News,* July 9, 2003.

"Restructuring Plans Ahead of Schedule at DBA (DBA liegt bei der Sanierung uber Plan)," *Handelsblatt,* March 3, 2004, p. 15.

"Rise of Germany's Third Largest Airline (DBA wird drittgrosste deutsche Airline)," *Boersen-Zeitung,* February 19, 2005, p. 11.

—Frederick C. Ingram

Deb Shops, Inc.

9401 Blue Grass Road
Philadelphia, Pennsylvania 19114
U.S.A.
Telephone: (215) 676-6000
Fax: (215) 698-7151
Web site: http://www.debshops.com

Public Company
Incorporated: 1932
Employees: 3,700
Sales: $303.78 million (2004)
Stock Exchanges: NASDAQ
Ticker Symbol: DEBS
NAIC: 448120 Women's Clothing Stores

Deb Shops, Inc., operates retail clothing stores that supply its young, trendy shoppers with moderately priced fashions. Its main brand, DEB, serves primarily junior-sized women between the ages of 13 and 18, offering coordinated sportswear, dresses, coats, shoes, lingerie, and accessories, most under private labels. By 2005, there were 314 DEB stores, mostly in the East and Midwest; 140 of these offered plus-sized clothing, and 17 of the DEB stores had Tops 'N Bottoms departments. Deb Shops also operated 17 stand-alone Tops 'N Bottoms stores, and three CSO outlet stores. Members of the company's founding families control about 68 percent of Deb Shops stock. The company is known for its fashion-forward yet budget-conscious appeal, lean inventories, and aversion to debt.

Early History

In 1932, Philip Rounick and Aaron Weiner opened their first store in Philadelphia, Pennsylvania. JOY Hosiery offered customers a wide variety of hosiery and foundations at reasonable prices. In 1939, nylon stockings came on the market and JOY Hosiery added them to its stock.

The 1940s saw the regulation of nylon use, as it was required for parachutes and other equipment for World War II. The government also regulated how much fabric could be used in clothing and banned the use of zippers and other metal fasteners. Despite nylon's limited availability, JOY Hosiery was able to obtain enough product to continue to stay in operation.

After the war and into the 1950s, JOY grew steadily, opening new stores in various Philadelphia neighborhoods. As restrictions were lifted on clothing manufacturing, a much wider selection became available. JOY reduced its offerings of lingerie and began selling moderately priced sportswear. The merchandise mix rapidly became 50/50, and remained so through the 1950s.

1960s and 1970s: A New Focus

Marvin Rounick, Philip's son, joined the company in 1961. In 1965 Warren Weiner, Aaron's son, came on board. During the 1960s the suburbs around Philadelphia grew rapidly as families moved out of the core city. To serve their shopping needs, developers built malls and shopping centers. JOY tested those waters by opening suburban stores in shopping malls; their new concept provided a bigger store and a larger selection of merchandise. The 1960s also saw the introduction of pantyhose, which eliminated the need for garter belts. With the growth of the women's movement, many young women stopped wearing girdles or bras. As a result, hose and lingerie became a smaller part of JOY's merchandise mix. It was also during this period that young people became a larger part of the consumer base, and the unisex look began to develop.

One thing that occurred during this time greatly influenced the company's financial strategy. "We had some financial problems," president and CEO Marvin Rounick recalled in a 1986 article in *Chain Store Age Executive*. "And the banker who handled us retired and a new banker came in to replace him. We went to him for money and he told us we weren't a good credit risk." When the company nearly folded after their bank dropped them, Rounick vowed to keep the company debt free.

In the early 1970s the younger Rounick and Weiner took a more active role in the company's management and made three decisions that changed the company completely. First, they closed most of the original neighborhood stores and quickly opened larger units in shopping malls. Second, they concentrated on sportswear and dresses for the junior customer and eliminated merchandise in other sizes. Merchandise ranged from peasant tops and skirts in the early 1970s to the "Annie Hall" look of men's suits and ties. By 1975, the company had sales of $9.5 million and earnings of $400,000.

In the late 1970s, the company acquired DEB, a New Jersey junior apparel chain. Marvin Rounick was named president and chief executive officer in 1979.

The 1980s

Deb Shops began the 1980s with 59 stores. Within two years, it had 121 stores, sales were more than $70 million, and earnings were up to $5.5 million. Warren Weiner rejoined the company in 1982, having left in 1975, and was named executive vice-president and treasurer. The following year the company went public, raising nearly $27 million. According to a 1983 *Forbes* article, the funds went for spending money for Rounick, his brother Jack, and Weiner, the major shareholders in the company. "We were wealthy before," Rounick said in the article. "It's just that now we can spend it." Deb Shops had no debt and expansion continued to be paid for from its working capital.

The company's target was primarily young women, 13 to 21 years old, with a small number of customers in their 20s and 30s. Rounick was successful because of his pricing strategy and tight inventory. He sold his dresses and other apparel at low-to-mid prices, below those of more upscale, designer clothing, and cut the prices immediately if an item was not selling after two weeks. If the sale prices did not move the item, he shipped it to one of the company's CSO (Chain Store Outlet) stores where it was sold at a steep discount. The fast movement of the stock meant customers could expect up-to-date, trendy merchandise. That freshness, combined with inexpensive prices, attracted young shoppers.

Despite the company's success, Rounick realized he had to make some adjustments to his marketing strategy in response to

changing demographics: Predictions forecast that by 1990, there would be 14 to 15 percent fewer women aged 14 to 24. Unlike many of its competitors, Deb did not abandon its specialization in junior customers looking for moderately priced clothes. Rounick's answer was to market junior as a size, not an age group. Under this strategy, the company would follow customers as they grew up, serving both teens and their mothers. Accordingly, in 1983 the company started selling basic as well as trendy junior clothing.

In addition to offering a wider variety of styles, the company made some decorating changes to attract older shoppers: Its green, white, and purple color combination became purple, raspberry, and white; and lower pile purple carpeting replaced the stores' purple shag. Gone, too, were the enclosed storefronts. Instead, windows were installed to show the merchandise and draw customers in.

Another part of Rounick's marketing strategy was to encourage add-on shopping by selecting merchandise that was coordinated with something else in the store. DEB displayed its merchandise in coordinated, layered groupings, complete with accessories. As Willard Brown, an analyst with First Albany, told *Chain Store Age Executive* in a 1986 article, "Every top is coordinated with every pair of pants; and if you buy the top and pants, then they have a handbag that goes with them, too. So every time Rounick sells one piece of merchandise, he's put himself into the position to sell another piece."

The marketing changes worked. Within two years, customers at DEB stores, while still concentrated in a 13 to 25 age group, ranged in age up to 40, and sales in 1985 increased to $147.1 million.

The company was opening between 30 and 40 new stores a year, with most in regional shopping centers in major metropolitan areas. As these malls increased their rents, however, Deb began looking to mid-sized markets and secondary markets adjacent to a major town. The company also started opening stores in less expensive strip shopping centers. "They [strip center stores] are not doing the same business as the malls," Rounick explained in *Chain Store Age Executive,* "but because of the reduced costs we found we can make money in the first year." By 1989 the company had stores in 67 strip centers. Stores ranged in size from 5,000 to 10,000 square feet, with the average store occupying 6,000 square feet.

The movement into strip centers was only one cost-cutting effort the company initiated during the last part of the 1980s. The women's clothing business in general softened, and sales dropped. The reason appeared to be customer dissatisfaction with what the designers offered them. In 1987, Deb's profit margin dropped as customers waited for markdowns and sales before buying.

Rounick's response was to improve inventory control in order to cut costs and to sell more clothes at full price. In 1988, Deb expanded its warehouse space to 280,000 square feet and installed a computer-controlled sorting and distribution system. The new distribution system and the company's point-of-sale merchandise data system helped managers analyze and respond to what customers were buying. Inventories arrived at the stores twice a week and store displays were changed each week.

Key Dates:

1932: JOY Hosiery, precursor of DEB Shops, opens in Philadelphia.
1975: Revenues are $9.5 million.
1980: The company has 59 stores.
1982: Sales are $70 million; the company has 121 stores.
1983: The company raises $27 million in an IPO.
1985: Sales are $147 million.
1992: Sales are $230 million.
1994: The company posts its first net loss.
1996: Plus sizes are added to certain DEB stores.
1997: The company returns to profitability after renewed focus on juniors.
1999: The web site is launched.
2004: Online ordering capability is added to the web site.

Although the company continued to mark down slow-moving merchandise, there was less of it. As a result of cost cutting, although sales for 1988 were down 2 percent to $194 million, earnings increased 15 percent to $13.7 million. During 1988, Deb expanded beyond the Midwest, opening stores in Washington, Oregon, and California, and ended the year with 316 stores in operation.

In 1989, the company continued to expand, using its own capital to open 31 new stores. It also began increasing its private-label business in order to improve its profit margins. Its profitability and $71 million in equity was very attractive. According to an August 14, 1989 article in *Barron's,* there were rumors that Milton Petrie, who owned the competing Petrie Stores Corporation and more than 15 percent of Deb stock, might attempt a hostile takeover of Deb. Nothing came of it. For the year, the company set record net sales of $202 million and reached its peak earnings of $17.6 million.

Trying New Things in the 1990s

During the early part of the decade, Deb continued to expand, opening DEB stores in Colorado, Idaho, New Mexico, Oklahoma, and Texas. The company also acquired Tops 'N Bottoms, a New York chain selling name-brand clothing for young men and women at moderate prices. In addition to the smaller (2,300 to 3,400 square feet) stand-alone stores in the chain, the company opened Tops 'N Bottoms departments in several DEB stores. The number of stores operated by the company peaked in fiscal year 1992, with 373 open as of January 31, 1993. That year also saw the company's highest sales, $229.5 million. But earnings fell by 18 percent.

In 1993, Deb introduced its private-label credit card, which also served as a mechanism to contact customers by direct mail. The company opened 11 new stores, but saw sales decline by 4 percent. Sales continued to decline, even with reduced costs as underperforming stores were closed. In 1994 the company opened eight new stores and had a net loss for the first time. In April that year, management spent $16.8 million in cash to buy back the block of stock owned by Petrie Stores Corporation. With that acquisition, insiders, including Martin and Jack

Rounick and Warren Weiner, owned 75 percent of the company stock.

Sales continued to drop in 1995 and the company opened only one new store while closing 33 DEB units and one Tops 'N Bottoms store. Rounick introduced shoes into 200 DEB stores to generate new business and stimulate sales. That move added approximately $4.6 million to sales for the year, but continued customer resistance to offerings in women's clothing resulted in total sales of only $176.7 million and an earnings loss of $4.2 million.

On October 20, 1995, the company bought Atlantic Book Stores for $4.47 million. "The apparel industry has seen a downturn in the last three to five years, and one of the strategies to stem the tide of our decline is to diversify," Deb's chief financial officer Lewis Lyon told the *Philadelphia Inquirer.*

Martin Simon, who was 72 when he sold his company to Deb, had started his book business around 1980 by selling used books to department stores. At the time of the sale, the Atlantic Books chain consisted of 14 stores. Three were full-service warehouse stores, between 12,000 and 26,000 square feet large. These specialized in remainder books at greatly discounted prices while also offering bestsellers, new titles, and magazines. The Atlantic Book Warehouse stores were located in Montgomeryville, Pennsylvania; Cherry Hill, New Jersey; and Dover, Delaware. The other 11 stores were located in resort towns along the coasts of New Jersey and Delaware. These units were much smaller, between 1,000 and 2,000 square feet, and sold primarily remainder books and some new titles.

Deb indicated that it planned to expand the chain by adding warehouse stores in high-traffic areas. Because of the warehouse concept, the company did not anticipate any direct competition with other discount chains such as Waldenbooks, Barnes & Noble, and Borders.

In its apparel business, Deb announced that it was shifting from its all-junior concentration. By April 1996, the company expected to introduce plus sizes into one-third of its stores. Up to 19 DEB stores were to be converted to plus size stores called DEB PLUS and about half of the Tops 'N Bottoms departments in DEB stores would become plus size departments.

Deb Shops' diversification efforts appeared to build on the company's responsiveness to demographic changes and its retail operations and distribution expertise. The fact that the company was debt free and had more than $51 million in cash at the beginning of 1996 gave it some measure of flexibility and staying power as it made its changes.

Renewed Focus in 1996

Probably the company's most important strategic move in the mid-1990s was returning its focus to the junior market. "We found you couldn't cater to the teenage customer and the older customer in the same shop," chief financial officer Lewis Lyons explained to the *Philadelphia Inquirer* regarding a renewed emphasis on teen fashions.

Lyons told a financial forum covered by *WWD* that the more feminine styles of the latter 1990s were easier to deliver to teens than the grunge look. In December 1995, Deb Shops had hired former Petrie Stores Corporation. CEO Allan Laufragben as its chief merchant to help keep it on top of teen fashion trends.

Teenage girls were a relatively attractive segment of the apparel market due to their increasing spending power, lack of expenses, and passion for clothes. Their numbers also were increasing faster than other segments of the population. There was no shortage of competitors in this market, however, ranging from other specialty retailers to giant discount department stores.

Deb Shops closed 100 underperforming stores as it regained its footing. Said Lyons, many had originally been opened to produce top line growth to satisfy Wall Street's expectations. The company was also remodeling stores and opening new ones. The model store was 5,000 to 6,000 square feet with annual volume of at least $1 million.

The company's cash horde sustained it through the lean times. After losing about $11 million in three years, Deb Shops returned to profitability in fiscal 1997 with a net income of $6.6 million on sales of $205 million. There were a couple of great years before the next economic slowdown. By fiscal 1999, net income was up to $24.5 million on sales of $270 million.

A number of specialty apparel retailers did not survive the turmoil of the 1990s. One of them was rival Petrie Retail. Deb Shops acquired nine of the bankrupt chain's stores in February 1998.

Deb Shops launched a web site in January 1999. It was limited to descriptions of select merchandise at first (originally prom dresses), but added online ordering capability in February 2004.

Beyond 2000

Deb Shops was fast becoming a national presence. It opened 23 new stores in 2001, though the annual pace soon slacked off to half that.

Deb Shops decided to focus on its expanding core business and sold Atlantic Books back to its founder, Mark Simon, in the fall of 2001. The deal was worth $5 million; the chain then had annual sales of $18 million at its 11 stores.

Sales were $318 million in the 2002 fiscal year, and slipped to about $300 million a year in the 2003 and 2004 fiscal years. After a half-dozen years of success, the chain was hit by a slowing economy, lousy weather, and some poor fashion choices, according to *Chain Store Age.* The company was still making money, however, and was able to remain debt free. Net income rose 40 percent to $18 million in fiscal 2005. By this time, Deb Shops had 323 locations (including six Tops 'N Bottoms stores and three CSO outlets).

Principal Subsidiaries

Joy Shops, Inc.

Principal Operating Units

DEB; Tops 'N Bottoms.

Principal Competitors

Charlotte Russe Holding, Inc.; Gap Inc.; Hot Topic Inc.; Limited Brands, Inc.; Target Corporation; The Wet Seal, Inc.

Further Reading

Angrist, Stanley W., "So Far, So Good," *Forbes,* October 24, 1983, p. 144.

Belden, Tom, "Philadelphia Retailer Deb Shops Under Fire for Stock Options Plan," *Philadelphia Inquirer,* May 30, 2003.

——, "Philadelphia-Based Retailer Keeps Up with Target Teenage Demographic," *Philadelphia Inquirer,* July 3, 2001.

Bergen, Jane, "Thriftiness, Flexibility Mark Survivors Among Small Philadelphia Merchants," *Knight Ridder/Tribune Business News,* November 30, 1996.

Brammer, Rhonda, "Sizing Up Small Caps: Down, But Not Out," *Barron's,* January 30, 1995, p. 19.

"Bubble Gum By Night, Apple Pie By Day," *Chain Store Age Executive,* May 1986, pp. 35–39.

Byrd, Jerry W., "Philadelphia's Deb Shops to Buy Atlantic Book Shops, Inc.," *Philadelphia Inquirer,* October 23, 1995.

"Deb Shops a Trendy Competitor: Retailer's Fresh Fashion and Low Prices Woo Young Shoppers," *Chain Store Age,* November 2003, pp. 44f.

Milliot, Jim, "Atlantic Books Sells for $5 Million," *Publishers Weekly,* December 24, 2001, p. 11.

——, "Founder Buys Back Atlantic Books," *Publishers Weekly,* October 29, 2001, p. 9.

Slovak, Julianne, "Companies to Watch," *Fortune,* January 1, 1990, p. 89.

Tanaka, Wendy, "Retailers Tweak Inventories in Hopes Producing a Merry Holiday Season," *Philadelphia Inquirer,* November 26, 2004.

Von Bergen, Jane M., "Demographics Prove Right for Two Philadelphia-Based Retailers," *Knight Ridder/Tribune Business News,* November 18, 1999.

Warner, Susan, "Especially Amid Economic Downturns, Teen Market Glitters for Retailers," *Philadelphia Inquirer,* December 19, 2000.

Wyatt, Edward A., "Looking Good: Deb Shop Fashions a Neat Gain in Earnings," *Barron's,* August 14, 1989, pp. 15, 17.

Young, Vicki M., "Deb Shops' Fountain of Youth," *WWD,* December 16, 1999, p. 10.

—Ellen D. Wernick
—update: Frederick C. Ingram

DELACHAUX

Delachaux S.A.

BP 152, 119 Avenue Louis Roche
Gennevilliers
F-92231 Cedex
France
Telephone: +33 01 46 88 15 00
Fax: +33 01 46 88 15 01
Web site: http://www.delachaux.fr

Public Company
Incorporated: 1902
Employees: 2,045
Sales: $505.9 million (2004)
Stock Exchanges: Euronext Paris
Ticker Symbol: DELX
NAIC: 332999 All Other Miscellaneous Fabricated Metal
Product Manufacturing; 238910 Other Specialty Trade
Contractors; 335311 Power, Distribution, and
Specialty Transformer Manufacturing

Delachaux S.A. is a diversified industrial company grouped around three primary divisions: Railroads; Conductic; and Special Products. The company, based in Gennevilliers, France, is one of the world's leading producers of railway equipment, primarily through subsidiary Railtech. The group's railway operations include welding, track maintenance, and electrification systems, and, since the group's acquisition of Pandrol in 2004, is the world's leading producer of rail fastening systems. Following that acquisition, Delachaux's Railroad division represents nearly 65 percent of the group's total sales of EUR 400 million ($500 million) in 2004. The Conductic division produces systems and equipment for transferring energy and data for applications such as cranes and other lifting equipment, "people movers," including trams, trains, amusement rides, and the like, as well as equipment for the production of fiber-optic cables and other special cables. Under Special Products, Delachaux groups its production of chrome (the company is the world leader in this segment) as well as magnets and magnetic systems, specialty steels, and plastic injection systems. Delachaux has long had an international presence, and foreign sales account for 82 percent of the group's total revenues. The company is listed on the Euronext Paris Stock Exchange. The founding Delachaux family, through its holding Sogrepar, nonetheless controls nearly 67 percent of company shares, and nearly 80 percent of the group's voting rights. Francois Delachaux, grandson of the founder, is the group's chairman.

20th-Century Industrial Success

Clarence Delachaux founded a business in Saint Ouen, France in 1902, based on an aluminothermic welding process developed in Germany. Delachaux adapted the process for the production of overhead electrical lines for tramways. The company's production played a role in the boom of the tramway market in France in the early years of the century. Most of the country's major cities developed their own tramway system, using aerial electrical lines as an energy source.

Delachaux soon recognized the opportunity for diversifying the company's operations. As the aluminothermic welding process required special metals and alloys, Delachaux itself launched production of not only pure metals, but also alloys, into the years leading to World War I. Delachaux supported this operation by building its own foundry. The company developed its own specialty metals, including its "Infatigable" (Tireless), which remained a core company product into the next century.

As World War I drew to a close, Delachaux began preparations to lead the company into new directions. In 1917, the company purchased a 20-hectare lot in Gennevilliers, which became the company's base of operations by 1920. The company built a new factory and foundry and began producing special high-resistance steels.

The growth of the French automobile industry, then in its first expansion phase, encouraged Delachaux to adapt its production to enter the new market. In 1925, the company launched production of molded steel wheel hubs and centers. In the meantime, the company had successfully extended its other operations, adapting its production for the railroad industry—which became a core industry for the company—and also for use in construction cranes and related equipment. These activities formed the basis for the company's Conductic division. At

138

Company Perspectives:

Resolutely focused on its business of strong technological competence, the Delachaux group has confirmed itself year after year as a leading international player in its markets and has a presence on five continents.

the same time, the company continued to add to its range of railway expertise, adding the production and welding of railroad rails, as well as the production of overhead supports and rail attachment systems, and the production of rail welding machinery and other rail maintenance equipment.

In the years leading up to World War II, Delachaux also became a major producer of chrome, among its other specialty steels operations. The company became a prominent supplier of chromium metals to the United States, playing a significant part in enabling the country to build up its strategic metal supply prior to the war.

Clarence Delachaux died in 1941. The company remained in the family, however, as son Philippe Delachaux and his brothers took over the business. By the end of World War II, the company had shifted much of its production to focus on providing traction systems for industrial equipment, as well as the production of wheel hubs for the agricultural market. The company also had taken its first steps into the international market, establishing a factory in Barcelona, Spain in 1942. By the 1950s, the company had added operation producing systems and equipment for injection molding, which, with the development of the plastics industry, represented a strong area of growth.

Divisional Structure in the 1960s

By the early 1960s, the company had become a successfully diversified industrial operation. The growth of each of its core production areas encouraged the company to restructure in 1963, regrouping its production operations into dedicated divisions. These included Railway, including the company's various operations for the railroad industry, not only in France but in foreign markets as well. Other divisions were formed for the company's electrical energy transfer systems and magnetic lifting and conveyance systems operations, and for its metals production, primarily focused on the production of pure chrome metal and specialty steels business.

Into the mid-1970s, Delachaux sought further growth, especially on an international scale. A major step forward in the group's ambitions came in 1976, with the acquisition of Insul 8 Corporation. Based in California, Insul 8 had pioneered the market for protected conductor systems for use in cranes and similar equipment in the 1950s. By 1961, Insul 8 had added a production subsidiary in the United Kingdom. By the 1970s, Insul 8 was also present in Canada and Australia. The addition of Insul 8, and then, in 1979, of U.K.-based Protected Conductors Limited, established Delachaux as a leading producer of these systems.

Francois Delachaux, the oldest grandson of the company's founder, took over as CEO in 1977. The younger Delachaux

prepared to lead the company into a new period of expansion in the mid-1980s. As part of that effort, the company went public in 1985, listing on the Paris Stock Exchange's Secondary Market. The Delachaux family nonetheless maintained control of the business. Into the mid-2000s, the family's shareholding remained at nearly 67 percent, while controlling nearly 80 percent of the company's voting rights.

Delachaux began expanding through acquisitions in the late 1980s and through the 1990s. In 1987, for example, the company acquired Enrouleur Electrique Modern—Matériel Industriel Cefilav, which specialized in producing electrical power supply and transfer systems for mobile engines. The company also boosted its rail welding business by acquiring Aluminothermique, also based in France.

Acquisitions formed a part of the company's continuing effort to branch out internationally. In 1989, the company entered Portugal, buying a minority share in that country's Porsol. The group also moved into Germany that year, establishing a distribution subsidiary for that market. In 1991, the company reinforced its presence in Spain through the purchase of Fecoinsa.

International Industrial Company in the 2000s

As it entered the 1990s, the company carried out a new restructuring of its businesses. In 1991, the company created Railtech International as the holding company for its railway-related operations. The following year, the company continued its restructuring, creating its Conductic Division, including the Insul 8 business and the company's other industrial conductor systems businesses.

The company's acquisitions continued into the mid-1990s as well. In 1992, the company acquired 85 percent of Italy's MEC, a specialist in magnetism systems. The following year, Delachaux merged MEC with its Italian distribution subsidiary, Sofint, creating MEC Delachaux Italie. The company next acquired Godderich International, a conductors specialist, in 1994, and then returned to Italy in 1995, buying up majority control of that country's Comes, which specialized in conductor and connection systems.

Through the end of the decade, Delachaux maintained an interest in expanding its international operations. The company targeted growth in the Asian region, particularly in the railway sector in markets such as India and Thailand. In 1995, the company also entered China, forming the Han-Fa joint venture to begin production and distribution of conductor systems. Delachaux's share of that joint venture stood at 50.5 percent.

Delachaux continued to build up market share into the mid-2000s, particularly through a regular series of acquisitions. In 1999, for example, the company bought Stedef, a maker of flexible fasteners for railways, and then Drivecon, which produced electronic controls for electric motors. In 2002, the company bought Métal Forme Technologie (MFT), based in France, a specialist in the production of high-pressure iron and steel.

For the most part, the company's acquisitions had remained relatively minor; the MFT purchase added just EUR 15 million to the group's sales. At the end of 2003, the company launched a more ambitious takeover, paying EUR 242 million in cash and

Key Dates:

1902: Clarence Delachaux founds a business using the aliminothermic welding process to produce overhead lines for the tramway market.
1920: Delachaux moves to a new production site in Gennevilliers and adds production of specialty steels.
1925: Delachaux begins producing wheel hubs.
1942: The company opens a factory in Barcelona, Spain.
1963: The company reorganizes into a divisional structure.
1976: The company acquires Insul 8 in the United States, as well as production facilities in the United States, Canada, the United Kingdom, and Australia.
1985: Delachaux goes public on the Paris Stock Exchange's Secondary Market.
1987: The company acquires Enrouleur Electrique Modern—Materiel Industriel Cefilav and Aluminothermique in France.
1991: Delachaux restructures its railway operations under Railtech International.
1992: Delachaux restructures its conductor businesses under Conductic Divison; MEC in Italy is acquired.
2003: The company acquires Pandrol, the world's leading producer of elastic fastener systems for the railway market.
2005: International sales account for more than 80 percent of Delachaux's sales.

assumed debt to acquire Pandrol. Based in the United Kingdom, Pandrol had captured the world leadership position in the production of rail fastening systems. Pandrol was especially strong in the elastic fastenings segment, claiming some 40 percent of the world market.

The integration of Pandrol into Delachaux represented a significant step in the company's development. The addition of the new operation boosted Delachaux's annual revenues by more than one-third, topping EUR 387 million (pro forma) for 2003, and EUR 400 million by the end of 2004. The company's railway division, historically at the group's core, once again became the major part of the company's business, accounting for more than 64 percent of sales. The company also had become firmly international in focus, posting more than 80 percent of its sales from outside of France. After more than a century, Delachaux had established a prominent name as an international industrial player.

Principal Subsidiaries

Comes - Italia S.R.L.; Csa Italia; Delachaux Conductique; Delachaux Conductique; Delachaux GmbH (Germany); Delachaux Metal Inc. (United States); Delachaux Metaux; Delachaux Systemes D'injection; Ets Raoul Lenoir; Han-Fa Electrification Co. Ltd. (China; 50.5%); Insul 8 Australie Pty. Ltd.; Insul 8 Corporation Canada; Insul 8 Corporation (United States); Matweld Inc. (United States); Mec Delachaux S.R.L. (Italy); Railtech (UK) Ltd.; Railtech Australia Ltd.; Railtech Boutet USA Inc.; Railtech Calomex (Mexico); Railtech China; Railtech Contracting Corporation (United States); Railtech International; Railtech Porsol (Portugal); Railtech Schlatter Systems (Rss); Railtech Slavjana (Czech Republic); Railtech Stedef (Usine De Douai); Railtech Stedef Thailande Co. Ltd.; Railtech Sufetra-Tranosa; Railweld (Canada); Railweld; Tamaris Industries.

Principal Competitors

Robert Bosch GmbH; Unio S.A.; Seiko Epson Corporation; Faurecia; Egyptian Company for Metallic Construction / Metalco; Metalurgica Gerdau S.A.; MAN Nutzfahrzeuge AG; W.C. Heraeus GmbH; Revdinskiy Steel and Wire Works Joint Stock Co.; Hydro Aluminium A.S.

Further Reading

''Delachaux Integrates Pull Recognition,'' *Port Development International,* March 2000, p. S13.
''Delachaux monte en puissance dans le ferroviare,'' *Les Echos,* May 3, 2005.
''Delachaux se recentre sur le ferroviare avec Pandrol,'' *Les Echos,* May 4, 2004.
''Delachaux: acquisition du Groupe Pandrol,'' *Boursier.com,* July 7, 2003.
''Pandrol Sold to Delachaux,'' *International Railway Journal,* December 2003, p. 2.
Salak, John, ''Delachaux Eyes Chrome Foothold in US,'' *American Metal Market,* May 8, 1984, p. 3.

—M.L. Cohen

Dualstar Entertainment Group LLC

3760 Robertson Boulevard
Culver City, California 90232
U.S.A.
Telephone: (310) 553-9000
Fax: (310) 553-9190
Web site: http://www.mary-kateandashley.com

Private Company
Incorporated: 1993
Employees: 220
Sales: $1.2 billion (2004 est.)
NAIC: 551112 Offices of Other Holding Companies;
315999 Other Apparel Accessories and Other Apparel
Manufacturing; 511120 Periodical Publishers

Dualstar Entertainment Group LLC is the holding company for the entertainment and retail assets of twin actresses Mary-Kate and Ashley Olsen. The Olsen twins have been big-name entertainers since infancy, when they shared a role as the baby on the ABC family comedy show *Full House*. They are considered the most financially successful child stars Hollywood has ever seen. Dualstar began as the twins' corporate entity, handling their licensing, contracts, and entertainment projects. The company has evolved into a significant lifestyle retailer, along the lines of the Martha Stewart Living empire, with a popular web site, a magazine, dozens of books, music recordings, and movies, and mary-kateandashley-brand apparel, cosmetics, bed and bath products, furniture, school supplies, and fragrances. The company's goods are geared toward so-called "tween" girls, those between the ages of five and 12. This group has been a vibrantly growing demographic in terms of money spent, and the mary-kateandashley brand has been a top seller in this market. Dualstar markets many of its products exclusively through Wal-Mart stores, again paralleling the Martha Stewart connection with K-Mart. The brand has a global presence, with strong markets in the United States and in Great Britain, Australia, and Japan.

Television Stardom in the 1980s

Mary-Kate and Ashley Olsen, the principals of Dualstar Entertainment, were born on June 13, 1986. Before they reached a year old, they were earning money as television stars. The twins must have had pleasing looks even as newborns, and at five months old they were chosen for a part on a new ABC show called *Full House*. The twins shared one role, that of Michelle Tanner. By the time they were three, Mary-Kate and Ashley were being heavily promoted as the soul of the show.

When the twins were three years old, they were introduced to entertainment attorney Robert Thorne. Thorne took over negotiating the girls' *Full House* contract, and got them a raise from just above the industry standard to what they seemed to deserve based on their importance to the show. Thorne was then instrumental in seeing potential beyond entertainment contracts, to making a lifestyle company out of the sisters' popularity. In an interview with *Hollywood Reporter* (October 12, 2001), Thorne delineated a difference between "building the celebrity into something grand on the one hand and building it into a brand on the other." At first, Thorne concentrated on building up the Olsen twins' celebrity. In 1993, the Olsen family and Thorne set up Dualstar Entertainment as a legal vehicle for the girls' enterprises. At that point, Thorne claims he had not envisioned the girls as a brand. As their manager, he arranged for their first video (called *Our First Video*) to debut when the twins were six years old. This was the first of more than 40 videos the girls made as they grew up. By 1993, the twins were among the most popular celebrities in the United States. Celebrity popularity is actually somewhat scientifically tracked, according to something called a "Q score." The Q score measures both name recognition and how favorable an impression an audience has of the subject. The Olsen twins ranked very high on their Q score, on par with beloved actor Michael J. Fox and the iconic star of the 1970s show *Happy Days*, Henry Winkler, who played "The Fonz." So even after *Full House* ended its eight-year run in 1994, the girls continued to draw the admiration of American fans. They starred in a movie called *It Takes Two* in 1995 for Warner. The movie brought in some $19 million in ticket sales, netting the girls $1.6 million. In home video sales, *It Takes Two* brought in roughly $75 million, and was one of the top-selling Warner Home Video titles in the family category.

At age ten, the twins released their first book, followed by many more in several series. The young girls were the fictional stars of juvenile mystery books such as *The Case of the Candy Cane Clue* and *The Case of the Mall Mystery.* Later they expanded into more teen-oriented series, again about twins, called *So Little Time.* With these books directly tied to other movies or home videos, the Olsen twins had sold some 29 million books by 2001.

Dualstar purveyed the twins' talent after *Full House* in a new show on ABC called *Two of a Kind* in 1998. *Two of a Kind* lasted only eight months, but it was popular in re-runs, especially in England. *Two of a Kind* was also popular in re-runs on the Fox Family channel, as was all the other Olsen material. In a profile of the girls in the *Hollywood Reporter* (October 12, 2001), the writer referred to the Fox Family channel as jokingly known within the television industry as the ''Mary-Kate and Ashley Channel,'' because the Olsens were ubiquitous on it. Their television material included *Adventures of Mary-Kate and Ashley,* which were half-hour mysteries, and later an animated show called *Mary-Kate and Ashley IN ACTION!* A later show was called *So Little Time.* All of these television shows and home videos had books tied to them, and sometimes music recordings and videos as well. The girls also continued to star in made-for-the-big-screen movies such as *Passport to Paris* in 1999.

From Celebrities to Lifestyle Brand in the 1990s

Robert Thorne initially pushed the Olsen twins' fame hard, but he claimed that at first he did not see beyond promoting their images. Around 1998, Thorne's vision shifted, and he imagined the girls becoming the kind of living brand other female stars embodied, such as Oprah Winfrey and Martha Stewart. Both the Oprah Winfrey and Martha Stewart enterprises were significantly cross-marketed, with television, books, magazines, and in Winfrey's case, movies. The audiences who identified with one aspect of these powerful female figures were apparently ready to follow the star into branded goods. The Olsen twins were beacons to the ''tweener'' or ''tweens'' demographic, which was a rapidly growing market by the late 1990s. According to a marketing group quoted in *Fortune* (July 8, 2002), spending on tweens had

grown at an annual rate of as much as 15 percent since the early 1990s. By 2001, total spending on that age group in the United States had reached $264 billion. So it was no wonder that the Olsen twins could sell approximately $800 million in retail sales, across many categories, in the early 2000s.

In 2001, Dualstar began moving beyond home video and other entertainment vehicles into branded apparel and domestic goods. Dualstar came out with a mary-kateandashley line of girls' clothing, Mary-Kate and Ashley dolls (licensed to Mattel), and a new magazine, also called *mary-kateandashley.* All the mary-kateandashley brand products were developed in-house by Dualstar, with close oversight from the twins, rather than being licensed products developed outside the company. By this time, Dualstar had grown to employ more than 200 people, at offices in New York, Los Angeles, and London. The company made a profit of close to $50 million, according to CEO Thorne, who also claimed that the company would come close to rivaling Martha Stewart's sales ($1.4 to $1.6 billion retail in the early 2000s) within the next few years.

Giant retailer Wal-Mart carried the mary-kateandashley line in 2001 with apparel, footwear, cosmetics, jewelry, and accessories. The brand initially sold very well, and some Wal-Marts developed a store-within-a-store to showcase the mary-kateandashley selections. According to Dualstar's own figures, mary-kateandashley was the fastest-growing line in girls' fashion, and the largest girls' book franchise and celebrity doll franchise. Dualstar quickly followed up the apparel and accessories lines with bedding and bath lines. These were licensed to WestPoint Stevens and sold exclusively through Wal-Mart stores. According to *Home Textiles Today* (June 4, 2001), some 95 percent of girls in the mary-kateandashley brand key demographic were involved in choosing their own bedding and bath products. Although tween girls were too young to have much buying power on their own, they were a powerful force in getting adults to spend money on them. Both licenser WestPoint Stevens and Dualstar thus had great hopes for the new home goods line.

The Olsen twins were closely involved with Dualstar's business arrangements, though they were still only teenagers and had to take time away from both corporation and acting jobs in order to meet their tutor, study, and take exams. They conferred with Thorne by phone several times a day, and had face-to-face meetings every few weeks. Thorne claimed that he talked to the girls about business decisions before talking to the Olsen parents. The girls had an unusual amount of power for people their age, employing hundreds of people and making multiple millions of dollars for themselves. ''They hire; they don't get hired,'' Thorne told *Hollywood Reporter* in the aforementioned article.

Global Push in the 2000s

By 2002, the British edition of *PR Week* (November 1, 2002) claimed that mary-kateandashley was the ''number one girl's brand in the U.S.,'' and the brand was on its way to being a juggernaut in Great Britain as well. The Jackie Cooper PR company launched an extensive campaign, building up British girls' awareness of the Olsens, who had long been shown in re-runs in the United Kingdom. The Olsens landed in England in April to do press appearances. Their clothing lines were sold in the United Kingdom at the chain George at Asda. (George at Asda is part of Asda, a British subsidiary of Wal-Mart.) The mary-kateandashley product launch won an award in the United Kingdom for the broad amount of media coverage the brand and the Olsen twins secured. The clothing line sold some £2 million worth of goods in just a few months.

By 2003, Dualstar's fashion lines were doing close to $1 billion in worldwide sales. The clothing and accessories lines were sold at Wal-Marts across the United States and in Canada, and other major retailers carried mary-kateandashley in Mexico, the United Kingdom, France, Australia, and New Zealand. The company planned to bring the brand next to Germany and Japan. The Olsens starred in a new Hollywood film in 2004, called *New York Minute,* and then brought out a new line of fragrance. The perfumes, called Mary-Kate and Ashley One and Mary-Kate and Ashley Two, were sold in many retail locations other than Wal-Mart. The two perfumes were best-sellers in the months after their introductions, selling better than all other women's scents on the market except for Elizabeth Taylor White Diamonds. Coty Beauty U.S. handled the U.S. distribution of the scents. The move into perfume seemed to mark something of a coming-of-age for the girls, who were just about to turn 18, and had matured from ''cute little girls to beautiful young women,'' according to the women's fashion journal *WWD* (May 21, 2004). By 2004, Dualstar licensed some 50 different categories of products, from books to videos to socks to eau de toilette. Total retail sales for Dualstar were estimated at $1.2 billion for 2004. The twins still focused on entertainment, however. In 2003, they moved from acting to producing, signing a deal with ABC Family to executive produce a television pilot called *Carly Shows It All,* which would feature teen actors.

In January 2005, the Olsens bought out their longtime manager and Dualstar CEO Robert Thorne. This left the twins, now 18 and college students at New York University, as sole owners of Dualstar. Thorne's place at Dualstar was taken by Diane Reichenberger. Reichenberger had long experience in retail and fashion, having worked in management at Levi Strauss & Co., Joe Boxer Corp., The Gap, and other clothing companies. Reichenberger immediately oversaw a relaunch of the mary-kateandashley brand in some international markets. Reichenberger saw the brand as still in a formative stage, with much opportunity both abroad and domestically.

Thorne's replacement by fashion veteran Reichenberger seemed to symbolize a new era at Dualstar. The mary-kateandashley brand was still geared toward girls aged five to 12, but the Olsens were now college students. All their entertainment projects had highlighted the purity and fun of the twins, but by 2005, something of a darker side emerged, as celebrity gossip detailed Mary-Kate Olsen's eating disorder. Again the obvious parallel for Dualstar seemed to be with Martha Stewart, who lived on as a brand even as her personal life became less than wholesome when she was sentenced to prison. Thorne had moved the Olsen twins beyond celebrity, into a more corporate identity as a lifestyle brand. Dualstar was sure that the mary-kateandashley brand could prosper even as its namesakes were no longer the adorable children they had once been. The brand certainly had demonstrated remarkable staying power, continuing to grow as the girls moved from toddlerhood through their teen years. With a strong sales record and the staunch backing of the world's largest retailer, Wal-Mart, Dualstar seemed likely to be in a good position even as the twins aged into womanhood.

Principal Competitors

Carter's, Inc.; Gap Inc.; The Walt Disney Co.

Further Reading

David, Grainger, ''The Human Truman Show,'' *Fortune,* July 8, 2002, p. 96.
''Girl Power,'' *Hollywood Reporter,* October 12, 2001, p. S-5.
Hueso, Noela, ''High Visibility,'' *Hollywood Reporter,* October 12, 2001, p. S-68.
Klepacki, Laura, ''Mary-Kate and Ashley Scents Deliver Brisk Sales,'' *WWD,* May 21, 2004, p. 8.
Lazaro, Marvin, ''WPS, Wal-Mart Target Tweens with Twin Label,'' *Home Textiles Today,* June 4, 2001, p. 1.
''Olsen Twins and Dual Star Entertainment,'' *B&T Weekly,* April 28, 2005.
''PR Week Awards,'' *PR Week,* November 1, 2002, p. 32.
''Robert Thorne: The Attorney, Manager and Agent for Mary-Kate and Ashley,'' *Hollywood Reporter,* October 12, 2001, p. S-20.
Schiller, Gail, ''Reichenberger Is New Dualstar CEO,'' *Hollywood Reporter,* March 10, 2005, p. 5.
Song, Sora, ''Thank Goodness They're Not Triplets,'' *Time,* September 26, 2005, p. 89.
Spalding, Rachel Fisher, ''What's in a Name,'' *Hollywood Reporter,* October 12, 2001, p. S-2.
Sporich, Brett, ''Olsens Take on Star-Maker Role,'' *Hollywood Reporter,* November 14, 2003, p. 4.

—A. Woodward

Real Italian. Real *Fast.*®

Fazoli's Management, Inc.

2470 Palumbo Drive
Lexington, Kentucky 40509
U.S.A.
Telephone: (606) 268-1668
Fax: (606) 268-2263
Web site: http://www.fazolis.com

Wholly-Owned Subsidiary of Seed Restaurant Group Inc.
Incorporated: 1990
Employees: 7,400
Sales: $370.1 million (2004 est.)
NAIC: 722211 Limited-Service Restaurants

Fazoli's Management, Inc., is the operator and franchiser of the Fazoli's Italian fast-food restaurant chain. One of the most popular and fastest growing restaurant concepts in the country by the late 1990s, Fazoli's grew rapidly in its relatively short history. The company operates and franchises over 380 restaurants throughout 32 states. Fazoli's is owned by Seed Restaurant Group Inc. (SRG). SRG chairman and CEO Kuni Toyoda owns 40 percent of the company.

The Early Years

Although the Fazoli's restaurant concept was created in 1989, Fazoli's Systems, Inc., was actually formed in 1990, when the chain consisted of just five restaurant locations in Lexington, Kentucky. At that time, the restaurants were owned and operated by Jerrico Inc., which was also the parent company of the Long John Silver's seafood restaurant chain. Jerrico decided to focus solely on developing Long John Silver's, however, and Fazoli's was put up for sale. Entrepreneur Kuni Toyoda—Jerrico's Asian franchise vice-president—joined forces with Japan-based Duskin Co. Ltd. and purchased the tiny restaurant chain. They formed Seed Restaurant Group Inc. to own and manage the enterprise, and Fazoli's Systems, Inc. became its subsidiary.

When Toyoda acquired the Fazoli's chain, the restaurants were selling a pretty equal mix of pizza and pasta items. Toyoda decided that it would be almost pointless to compete in the well-established pizza industry, especially because Fazoli's did not offer home delivery. Therefore, Fazoli's began phasing out pizza and instead focused mainly on its pasta selections. Toyoda upgraded the ingredients that Fazoli's used, while also making changes such as the creation of larger portions and a shift toward cooking the pasta more firmly (known as "al dente").

The early 1990s marked a trend toward health consciousness in the United States. Grocery store shelves were lined with "fat free," "low fat," and "reduced fat" alternatives to most popular items, and Toyoda realized that he could capitalize on this trend with the Fazoli's concept. In the August 1995 issue of The Lane Report, he noted, "Pasta is here to stay, simply because the Italian segment is the most popular ethnic segment. Pizza used to dominate, but now people are so used to eating pasta. They know what good pasta is." He began marketing Fazoli's as a more healthful alternative to the traditional fast-food menu of burgers and fried foods.

Toyoda also promoted Fazoli's as an affordable alternative to most full-service casual restaurants. Each Fazoli's restaurant featured an ample, comfortably decorated dining room where the manager was likely to be seen serving patrons hot breadsticks as they ate. Dine-in customers were treated to an unlimited supply of the breadsticks, as well as free drink refills. A typical individual check at Fazoli's was under $4, while a family of four could usually eat there for less than $15. For those prices, each customer was buying six to eight ounces of food, whereas most hamburgers were only two ounces.

Fazoli's soon began opening more restaurant locations, focusing at first on gaining a presence in small- and medium-sized towns. For one thing, real estate prices were usually lower in such areas, and the healthful, low-cost Fazoli's concept appealed to their residents. Fazoli's also benefited from the fact that its restaurant set-up was flexible enough to allow the company to purchase other failed restaurant buildings and convert them, rather than having to actually build all of its new structures.

From the start, the new company placed a great emphasis on customer service. New employees were required to complete a one-week training seminar, while store managers underwent a five-week program. Rather than focus most of its attention and resources on adding restaurants and increasing in size, Fazoli's focused instead on making sure each of its locations was able to properly represent the company's principles. According to Toyoda in a 1998 issue of *Kentucky Business Viewpoint:* "We could grow faster, but we don't want to grow fast. . . . It takes time to develop competent general managers that really understand Fazoli's system. We tend to focus more on service."

Rapid Expansion in the Mid-1990s

Within a couple years, however, the chain was, in fact, expanding rapidly. By 1992, the company had grown to include over 35 Fazoli's restaurants. It almost doubled that figure in 1993 by adding 25 additional locations, giving Fazoli's a total count of 62 restaurants throughout the states of Kentucky, Florida, and Indiana. Of those, 53 were company-owned and none were franchised.

Not only did the company expand quickly in terms of the number of restaurant locations, it also exponentially increased the amount of sales that each location achieved each year. When Toyoda took over the operations of Fazoli's in 1990, the average unit volume for each of the five restaurants had been about $500,000 per year. Within five years, that figure had increased to around $1 million per year. This made expansion quite easy financially, because start-up costs ranged from $150,000 for conversions to $500,000 for newly constructed buildings. At those costs, most locations could turn a profit in the first year of operation.

Fazoli's expanded its prototype unit as well, from 2,800 square feet and 100 seats, to over 3,000 square feet and 140 seats. This helped each unit handle higher volumes of dine-in business. In 1994, the company's takeout orders represented only 30 percent of its total sales. Most of the restaurant's business was done in its dining room, with about 60 percent of it taking place during the dinner hours.

In early 1994, the company brought aboard Toyoda's former boss at Jerrico—Ernest Renaud—as a marketing vice-president and special consultant. Renaud, who was already a board member of Fazoli's parent, Seed Restaurant Group, had actually done a lot of the start-up work on the Fazoli's chain in its early years. Along with Toyoda, he set out to help the young enterprise compete with the other players in the fast-food Italian niche, including market-leader Sbarro and Pizza Hut's Fastino's concept. A goal was set to open at least 120 Fazoli's units by 1996.

In late 1994, Fazoli's began testing the potential for food court and strip mall versions of its restaurants to achieve success. This move may have come about as a means of competing with Sbarro, which operated most of its units within shopping malls. Fazoli's knew, however, that its strength was in its freestanding restaurants, and it therefore continued to expand mainly in that area. The company posted 1994 sales of $59 million.

By mid-1995, the company had grown to include 112 units in 120 states. Of those, only 30 were franchised. In the June 19, 1995 issue of *Business First—Louisville*, however, Ernest Renaud stated that the vast majority of new units in the coming years would be operated by franchisees. This would help the company offset the cost of start-ups, as each franchisee would pay a one-time $25,000 fee for Fazoli's rights, in addition to all start-up costs and 5 percent of the restaurant's gross annual sales each year.

In August 1995, Fazoli's made headlines when Nation's Restaurant News published its "Second 100 Chains" rankings, based on growth in three different areas. Fazoli's was ranked third in the area of systemwide sales growth, second in the growth of company-owned units, and first in the growth of franchised units. At year's end, the chain was composed of 164 Fazoli's restaurants, each of which generated an average of $964,000 in annual revenue.

Continued Success in the Late 1990s

Within a year, Fazoli's units numbered 214 in 23 different states throughout the country. Meanwhile, in a surprising move, Seed Restaurant Group introduced a new Italian restaurant concept called Bella Notte in 1996. According to Toyoda in a 1998 issue of *Kentucky Business Viewpoint*, "We try to duplicate Trattoria, the neighborhood, casual restaurant in Italy where people go to have fun over great quality food." While some may have felt that the company was potentially diluting its market base and creating competition for Fazoli's, Seed did not see it that way. Bella Notte would be pricier than Fazoli's, with an average individual check double that of its older sibling. In reality, the new entry would more appropriately serve as competition for such established Italian restaurants as the Olive Garden chain.

Entering 1997, the company was altering its market strategy slightly as it moved into bigger cities. Its most recent entries into larger markets dictated that the company needed to change its advertising strategy in order to maintain the sales volume it had achieved in smaller locales. Regional television advertisements surfaced. The company knew that it was important for things such as the Fazoli's tagline—"Real Italian. Real Fast."—to be in the public eye and permeate the potential consumer's awareness.

Toyoda invested himself mainly in his employees, however. In a January 21, 1997 article about him in *Nation's Restaurant News*, he contended, "To be a success in a people-driven industry like ours, you definitely have to take care of your people." Not only did he ensure that the company operated on its founding principles of open communication, idea sharing, teamwork, and excellence, but he also actually invested in his employees. Toyoda offered half of his 50 percent ownership of the company to his management team. (The other 50 percent was owned by Duskin Co. Ltd.)

Key Dates:

1989: The Fazoli's restaurant concept is created.
1990: Fazoli's Systems, Inc., is created.
1993: By now, there are 62 restaurants throughout the states of Kentucky, Florida, and Indiana.
1995: The Fazoli's chain is composed of 164 Fazoli's restaurants, each of which generate an average of $964,000 in annual revenue.
1997: Fazoli's opens its 300th restaurant.
1999: The company opens its first restaurant in Utah.
2004: Dietitian Elizabeth Somer is hired to help develop healthy low-calorie dishes.
2005: Fazoli's eliminates the trans fat found in its breadsticks.

Corporate management also began offering each of its restaurant units incentives for maintaining a high level of customer service. Each month, a "mystery shopper"—that is, a customer who actually reports back to the company about the level of service received—visited Fazoli's restaurants on multiple occasions. Any unit that received scores of 90 or higher three times within a month received bonuses for all of its employees.

In late 1997, and early 1998, Fazoli's received more accolades within the industry. *Restaurant Business* released its list of top 50 growth chains in July 1997, and Fazoli's was ranked seventh overall. The company also received a number seven ranking in terms of sales increases, and a number 13 ranking with regard to increases in number of units. The following March, *Restaurants and Institutions* ranked quick-service restaurant chains on multiple attributes; Fazoli's came out on top in overall rankings, as well as in the areas of value and service. Fazoli's also ranked second to Starbucks in the atmosphere rating, and third in cleanliness—just barely behind Starbucks and Bruegger's Bagel Bakery.

In December 1997, Fazoli's opened its 300th restaurant. As the company entered 1998, Toyoda began announcing that some time in the near future, the company would be going public in order to fund a true nationwide expansion campaign—a public offering had failed to materialize due to unfavorable market conditions. In 1999, Fazoli's announced that it had signed 150 franchise agreements to open 150 new restaurants by 2004 in Texas, Utah, Nevada, and Georgia.

Fazoli's in the New Millennium

Fazoli's entered the new millennium on solid ground. Forty franchise restaurants opened their doors in 2000 in new markets including Las Vegas, Washington DC, and Minneapolis-St. Paul. Twenty-eight franchise locations were launched the following year. The company's strong growth led to a deal with McDonald's Corp. in 2002. The nonbinding agreement was structured as a joint venture to open up to 30 Fazoli's in three U.S. markets. The deal also gave McDonald's the option to buy Fazoli's at a later date. McDonald's, which was struggling to shore up earnings, hoped its investment in the Fazoli's chain would bolster its bottom line. Meanwhile, Fazoli's eyed its

union with McDonald's as a way to further expand its burgeoning restaurant chain. McDonald's changed its strategy in 2003, however, and decided to end the venture.

Popularity of low-carb diets such as South Beach and the Atkins diet forced Fazoli's to rethink its menu strategy during this time period. In early 2004, the company launched its Smart Italian marketing campaign which featured eight menu items with eight grams of fat or less. The company's culinary and research development division also worked to create new menu items featuring more vegetables and protein. Later that year, the company hired dietitian Elizabeth Somer to help develop healthy low-calorie dishes.

In 2005, the company announced it was eliminating the trans fat found in partially hydrogenated oil from its breadsticks. According to the company, trans fat was created artificially by bubbling hydrogen gas through vegetable oil in a process called partial hydrogenation. Scientific studies demonstrated that trans fat could raise cholesterol levels and increase the risk of heart disease. As such, many food manufacturers began looking for ways to reduce or eliminate trans fat from their products.

Fazoli's became the first quick-service chain to promote zero trans fat menu offerings in a print and television advertising campaign. An ad that ran in the March 31, 2005, edition of *USA Today* claimed Fazoli's offered over 50 entrees with zero grams of trans fat. Chief concept officer Greg Lippert explained the strategy in an April 2005 *Nation's Restaurant* news article claiming, "Our intent is to position Fazoli's as a health-friendly alternative to quick-service brands offering fried food. . . . For the most part we're accomplishing this change without changing our menu."

The low-carb craze ate into company profits during 2003 and 2004 and Fazoli's experienced declining same-store sales. While revenues appeared to be on the upswing in 2005, the company began to develop a smaller store format that would be found in strip malls. The 2,800 square feet prototype was slated to debut in Summer 2005. Management believed the smaller, less expensive store concept would allow the company to continue its expansion in the years to come.

Principal Competitors

Noble Roman's Inc.; Sbarro Inc.; YUM! Brands Inc.

Further Reading

Baldwin, Amy, "Fazoli's Opens 300th Restaurant, Plans National Expansion," *Lexington Herald-Leader*, December 10, 1997.
"Blast Off," *Restaurant Business*, July 1, 1997, p. 43.
Brim, Risa, "McDonald's, Fazoli's End Joint Venture," *Knight Ridder Tribune Business News*, December 16, 2003.
Clancy, Carole, "Fazoli's Cooks Up Bay Area Expansion," *Tampa Bay Business Journal*, July 12, 1996, p. 1.
Coeyman, Marjorie, "Making it Simple," *Restaurant Business*, January 15, 1997, p. 40.
Cooper, Ron, "Fazoli's Adding Two Restaurants, Sees More Growth," *Business First—Louisville*, June 19, 1995, p. 9.
"Fazoli's Cuts Trans Fat," *Restaurant Business*, May 1, 2005, p. 56.
"Fazoli's Parent to Open New Italian Dinner House," *Nation's Restaurant News,* July 22, 1996, p. 2.
"Fazoli's," *Restaurant Business*, July 1, 1996, p. 78.

''Fazoli's Tests Food Court, Strip Malls,'' *Nation's Restaurant News*, November 28, 1994, p. 2.

''Full-Service Winners vs. Quick-Service Winners,'' *Restaurants and Institutions*, March 1, 1998, p. 68.

Hayes, Jack, ''Kuni Toyoda,'' *Nation's Restaurant News*, January 21, 1997, p. 214.

——, ''Pronto! Fast-Serve Italian Niche Swells,'' *Nation's Restaurant News*, March 14, 1994, p. 1.

Howard, Theresa, ''Fazoli's: Like Going Home to Mom's,'' *Nation's Restaurant News*, May 16, 1994, p. 62.

——, ''Trend to Cut Trans Fat Gets Boost from Fazoli's Ads,'' *Nation's Restaurant News*, April 11, 2005, p. 1.

Kass, Mark, ''On the Menu: Drive-Through Pasta, Pizza?,'' *Business Journal Serving Greater Milwaukee*, May 13, 1995, p. 3.

''Move Over Pasta,'' *Chain Leader*, February 2004.

''Second 100 Chains Ranked by U.S. Systemwide Sales Growth,'' *Nation's Restaurant News*, August 21, 1995, p. 62.

Thorn, Bret, ''Valentino G. Mennitto: Fazoli's Chef Gets Bold With Italian Food,'' *Nation's Restaurant News*, September 13, 2004, p. 42.

Walter, Grady, ''Area Restaurateurs Replicate Success through Franchising,'' *Lane Report*, August 1995, p. 20.

Wood, Campbell, ''The Seed Restaurant Group—Flourishing Italian Style,'' *Kentucky Business Viewpoint*, Second Issue 1998, p. 15.

—Laura E. Whiteley
—update: Christina M. Stansell

Finlay Enterprises, Inc.

529 Fifth Avenue
New York, New York 10017
U.S.A.
Telephone: (212) 808-2800
Fax: (212) 557-3848
Web site: http://www.finlayenterprises.com

Public Company
Incorporated: 1911 as Seligman & Latz
Employees: 6,000
Sales: $923.6 million (2005)
Stock Exchanges: NASDAQ
Ticker Symbol: FNLY
NAIC: 448310 Jewelry Stores; 551112 Offices of Other
  Holding Companies

Finlay Enterprises, Inc., is the leading operator of leased jewelry departments in the United States, with sales of $923.6 million in fiscal 2005. Unlike competitors such as Zale Corporation, Finlay operates few self-standing retail locations. Instead, the company chiefly operates fine jewelry departments in leased spaces in stores owned by 16 major and independent host store groups. The largest share of Finlay's 962 U.S. departments are located in stores in The May Department Stores Co. group, which acts as host to 481 Finlay departments. Another top Finlay host is Federated Department Stores, Inc., which hosts 113 Finlay departments. Finlay expected to lose 194 of its locations as a result of Federated's acquisition of May in 2005. As a result, the company pursued new growth avenues, which included the purchase of Carlyle & Co. Jewelers, a regional chain with 34 stores in the southeastern region of the United States.

Business Organization and Relationships

The practice of leasing jewelry departments is widespread in the department store industry, a relationship that provides benefits to both lessor and lessee. Jewelry is a specialized industry with costs and factors that lie outside of the typical department store's core base of clothing and home furnishings. Department stores are able to avoid the high costs associated with retail jewelry, such as slow, typically one-year inventory turns and expensive inventory maintenance. Lessees such as Finlay provide management expertise, marketing, merchandising, purchasing, employee hiring, training and payroll, inventory control, and security, as well as specialized relationships within the fragmented jewelry industry, while providing department store customers with the attraction of a fine jewelry department.

Finlay and other jewelry department lessees benefited from this relationship by avoiding the high investment costs of establishing and maintaining company-owned retail locations. By avoiding stand-alone formats, new Finlay departments were generally profitable within one year of opening. Finlay departments also enjoyed the enhanced reputation and customer traffic of a department store, and marketing could be tied in with the host's storewide promotions. Finlay also benefited from a reduced credit risk, as department stores generally assumed the risk of extending and collecting the credit for Finlay sales. Net sales usually were remitted to Finlay on a monthly basis, whether or not the host store had collected on the sale.

Finlay's leases ranged from one to five years and provided for rents based on the level of sales; rents typically ranged from 10 to 15 percent of sales. Finlay enjoyed long-term relationships with most of its host stores; 19 of its 26 store groups leased Finlay departments for more than five years, representing nearly 80 percent of Finlay annual sales, and 13 had relationships with Finlay lasting longer than ten years, representing nearly 65 percent of Finlay's revenue. Part of Finlay's growth was tied into the expansion of its host store groups. In the period from 1990 to 1995, for example, Finlay added 121 departments through the opening of new stores in its host groups' chains. Consolidation trends in the department store industry also aided Finlay's growth. As department stores featuring jewelry departments of Finlay's competitors were absorbed by industry giants such as May and Federated, Finlay's relationships with these groups often allowed the Finlay department to take over as lessee.

These lease relationships, however, exposed Finlay to certain risks. The closing of a department store meant the loss of Finlay's leased location and a corresponding loss of revenue. Consolidation—such as Federated's acquisition of R.H. Macy

& Co. in 1994, which operated its own department stores—could lead to the termination of Finlay's leases. Finlay also faced the risk that a department store group would decide to assume operation of their own jewelry departments. Finally, Finlay remained exposed to losses presented by the bankruptcy of its host chains.

In addition to its domestic leased jewelry department business, Finlay operated France's largest leased jewelry operations since its 1994 acquisition of Société Nouvelle d'Achat de Bijouterie (Sonab), which included 104 locations in leading French stores such as Galeries Lafayette and Nouvelles Galeries. In 1994, Finlay also began test operations of a chain of company-owned outlet stores, called New York Jewelry operations, which had grown to seven locations by 1996.

Company Origins: A Giant Without a Name

Founded in 1911 as Seligman & Latz, the company's original focus was the operation of beauty salons, also under a lease arrangement with department and specialty stores. Jewelry sales were soon added to the company's portfolio, and by 1942, the company opened its first leased Finlay Fine Jewelry department. By 1960, Seligman & Latz operated in more than 50 locations, generating nearly $170 million in revenues.

Yet the company remained essentially nameless with the general public, which tended to identify the company's beauty salons and jewelry departments with the stores in which they operated. For much of its history, the company's emphasis was on its beauty salons and products, which later included the Adrien Arpel line of cosmetics, skin care, and related products. Toward the mid-1970s, with annual revenues shrinking to $160 million, the company's focus began to shift. Jewelry sales began to represent the fastest growing share of revenues.

In 1978, jewelry provided less than $75 million of Seligman & Latz's $208 million in revenues. Four years later, Seligman & Latz's revenues swelled to $304 million; much of this growth was provided by the company's Finlay division, which had doubled in size, to $145 million in sales. The beauty division, meanwhile, had grown more slowly during this period, from $133 million in 1978 to $159 million in 1982. Together, the two divisions operated in more than 100 leading department store and specialty groups in ten countries, with Macy's providing the largest—13.8 percent—of the company's revenues, closely followed by Associated Dry Goods, May, and Gimbel Bros. Profits, however, had been shrinking. Net income, which had neared $5 million in the mid-1970s, slipped to barely more than $1.5 million by 1980.

Despite its low profile, in stark contrast to its luxury goods-oriented business, Seligman & Latz began to attract the attention of investors. The company seemed ripe for a takeover, in fitting with the flurry of corporate takeovers that marked the 1980s.

Leveraged Buyouts and a Public Offering in the 1980s

In February 1984, Seligman & Latz reached agreement with City Stores Company and its subsidiary, Diversified Investments, Inc., which would merge the two companies under the Seligman & Latz name. The company faced a difficult year, stemming from a conversion to a new inventory system that forced Seligman & Latz to stop shipments for a full year, an increase in shrinkage from theft, and the loss of several key managers. At the same time, Seligman & Latz had fallen behind the industry in sales per square foot. Underfinanced, the company was having difficulty maintaining inventory in an industry in which broad selection played a key role in sales. The company's problems were further exacerbated by a general slump in the jewelry industry and its slow recovery from the recession of the early 1980s. When Seligman & Latz, despite revenue gains to $342 million, posted a loss of $2.2 million for the year, City Stores balked on the merger agreement.

Yet the company had already attracted the attention of another group of investors. As early as 1982, Harold Geneen, former chairman of ITT, had presented David Cornstein with Seligman & Latz's annual report and asked Cornstein how he would run the company. Cornstein, whose involvement in the leased jewelry business reached back more than 20 years, and whose Tru-Run Inc., a jewelry and watch repair company, had outlets in 80 stores, identified many of Seligman & Latz's key problems.

Geneen and Cornstein began to seek financing and in 1985 structured a leveraged buyout (LBO) of Seligman & Latz for $42 million, including $1 million of Geneen's private funds. A chief investor in the LBO was Transcontinental Services Group N.V., with financing arranged through Manufacturer's Hanover Trust, Phoenix Mutual Life Insurance, and Banker's Life and Casualty. The new owners took Seligman & Latz private.

Under President and CEO Cornstein, the company was restructured as a holding company, SL Holdings, which now included Tru-Run Inc. The new management posted rapid improvements in the Finlay division, doubling store sales to $1,000 per square foot and boosting Finlay's annual revenues to $265 million in 1987 and to $315 million in 1988. The number of Finlay outlets also grew, from 460 in 1985 to 525 in 1988. Meanwhile, the beauty division, which had grown to nearly 1,000 locations, continued posting $5 million annual losses.

In 1988, Cornstein and Geneen engineered a buyout of the company's jewelry division, in a deal worth $217 million, with financing arranged through Westinghouse Credit Corporation. As part of the restructuring, Seligman & Latz's beauty division, including Adrien Arpel, was sold to Regis Corporation in Minneapolis for $17 million. The company, now specialized in jewelry, was renamed Finlay Enterprises, Inc.

By the start of the 1990s, Cornstein and Geneen began to make plans to take Finlay public, in part to help ease the debt load carried over from the buyout. In 1991, Finlay attempted an

---

Key Dates:

1911: Seligman & Latz is created as an operator of beauty salons.

1942: The company opens its first leased Finlay Fine Jewelry department.

1960: By now, Seligman & Latz operates in more than 50 locations and generates nearly $170 million in revenues.

1985: Harold Geneen and David Cornstein structure a leveraged buyout of Seligman & Latz for $42 million.

1988: Cornstein and Geneen engineer a buyout of the company's jewelry division; the division is renamed Finlay Enterprises Inc.

1993: Thomas H. Lee organizes a buyout of Finlay.

1994: Societe Nouvelle d'Achat de Bijouterie (Sonab) is acquired.

1995: Finlay goes public.

1997: Zale Corporation's Diamond Park Fine Jewelers business is purchased.

2005: Carlyle & Co. Jewelers is acquired; the company loses 194 locations as a result of Federated's acquisition of May.

---

initial public offering (IPO) of five million shares, including one million shares of stock held by company principals, to raise up to $125 million. But the recession of the period and steep sales drops across the industry, coupled with Cornstein's and Geneen's sale of their own stock, scared off investors. The company was forced to back down from the IPO. Shortly afterward, Geneen retired from the company.

In an effort to recapitalize the company after Westinghouse exited the financial services market, Cornstein approached Thomas H. Lee, whose Boston investment company had funded the growth of Snapple. In 1993, Lee organized a buyout of Finlay, taking 28 percent of the company and, with Desai Capital Management Inc.'s 32 percent share, gaining control of Finlay Enterprises.

The new owners moved to expand the company, acquiring Sonab in 1994 from Galeries Lafayette and launching the first test location of New York Jewelry Outlet. The following year, Lee and Desai took Finlay public, selling 2.62 million shares for a net of $30 million. By then, Finlay operated nearly 800 locations, including its French stores, for 1994 revenues of $552 million. With its strong French base, the company began to look toward a deeper penetration of the European market. In March 1996, Finlay signed an agreement to lease seven departments in the 89-store, U.K.-based Debenhams department store chain. Expansion into other countries was expected to follow. With its long-term lease relationships with leading department store chains, strengthening promotions, and rising revenues, Finlay was likely to maintain its glittering position in the U.S. jewelry industry and make a name for itself as well.

Challenges in the New Millennium

Finlay entered the late 1990s and early years of the new millennium on solid ground. In 1997, the company acquired Zale Corp.'s Diamond Park Fine Jewelers business in a $65 million deal. The purchase included 185 leased jewelry locations and added Dillard's, Parisian, and Marshall Field's department stores to Finlay's growing roster. In 1998, the company consolidated its 25 processing centers and opened a new state-of-the-art distribution center, which was designed to improve productivity.

In 1999, Finlay announced plans to divest its international business in order to focus on its domestic operations. The company secured its position as the leading operator of leased jewelry departments in 2000 when it agreed to buy most of the assets of Jay B. Rudolph Inc., which included 57 locations in Dayton's, Hudson's, and Bloomingdale's chains.

During this time period, the department store industry remained highly competitive and many store owners began consolidating operations and closing locations. Finlay's lease structure left it in a vulnerable position and sure enough, the company began to feel the pinch of these industry trends. In 2003, May announced plans to close 32 Lord & Taylor locations and two Famous-Barr stores. In all, the closures would spell out a loss of approximately $20 million in sales for Finlay. In 2004, the company lost its contract with Federated-owned Burdine's, which included 48 locations. The move came as Federated decided to consolidate certain operations and rebrand many of its locations with the Macy's name.

Finlay was dealt a significant blow in 2005 when Federated announced its plans to unite with May later that year. The merged company would realign many of its stores under the Macy's name, and Macy's generally operated its own jewelry departments. In one fell swoop, Finlay lost 194 of its locations. "We are disappointed that our total store base will be reduced," claimed CEO Arthur Reiner in an October 2005 *National Jeweler* article. "However, our core business remains solid and we will intensify our ongoing efforts to add new sources of growth to our business." Indeed, Finlay's plans for the future included expanding and strengthening its current host store business, adding new host store locations, and growing its business through strategic acquisition. The company's dedication to this strategy became evident in May 2005 when it purchased jewelry store operator Carlyle & Co. Jewelers in a $29 million deal. The purchase signaled Finlay's departure from its traditional leased operations by adding 34 stores in the southeastern United States to its arsenal. Although May's union with Federated dulled the company's outlook for fiscal 2006, Finlay's management believed that it had a solid business plan in place and was confident the company would continue to shine for years to come.

Principal Subsidiaries

Finlay Fine Jewelry Corporation; Finlay Jewelry, Inc.; Finlay Merchandising & Buying, Inc.; Sonab Holdings, Inc.; Sonab International, Inc.; Société Nouvelle D'Achat de Bijouterie - S.O.N.A.B. (France); eFinlay, Inc.

Principal Competitors

Helzberg Diamonds; Signet Group plc; Zale Corporation.

Further Reading

Beres, Glen A., "Macy's Brand Extension Squeezes Market for Regional Chains, Finlay," *National Jeweler,* June 16, 2004, p. 8.

Braverman, Beth, "Finlay Buys Carlyle & Co. for $29 Million," *National Jeweler,* June 16, 2005.

"Finlay Braced to Lose 194 Doors in Merger," *National Jeweler,* October 3, 2005.

Furman, Phyllis, "Glittering Jeweler Re-emerges in Big IPO," *Crain's New York Business,* September 16, 1991, p. 3.

——, "No-Name Jeweler Now Pursuing the Spotlight," *Crain's New York Business,* June 12, 1995, p. 1.

Grant, Peter, "Geneen and Friend Shine with Gold," *Crain's New York Business,* December 19, 1988, p. 1.

Kletter, Melanie, "Finlay to Acquire Operator of Leased Jewelry Departments," *Women's Wear Daily,* February 11, 2000, p. 14.

Metz, Robert, "A Low-Keyed Concessionaire?," *New York Times,* March 26, 1981, p. D6.

Springsteel, Ian, "Diamonds in the Rough," *CFO: The Magazine for Senior Financial Executives,* September 1995, p. 29.

Trachtenberg, Jeffrey A., "Good As Gold?," *Forbes,* May 20, 1985, p. 62.

"Zale to Sell Fine Jewelry Operations for $65 Million," *New York Times,* September 5, 1997, p. 3.

—M.L. Cohen
—update: Christina M. Stansell

Foster Wheeler Ltd.

Perryville Corporate Park
Clinton, New Jersey 08809-4000
U.S.A.
Telephone: (908) 730-4000
Fax: (908) 730-5315
Web site: http://www.fwc.com

Public Company
Incorporated: 1927
Employees: 6,723
Sales: $2.7 billion (2004)
Stock Exchanges: NASDAQ
Ticker Symbol: FWLT
NAIC: 54133 Engineering Services; 23499 All Other
    Heavy Construction

Foster Wheeler Ltd. is an international company overseeing a wide range of engineering and construction enterprises in more than 30 countries across the globe. The company is organized into two business groups: The Global Engineering & Construction (E&C) Group and The Global Power Group. Through its subsidiaries, Foster Wheeler offers design, engineering, construction, manufacturing, project development and management, research, and plant operations services. The company serves the refining, upstream oil and gas, Liquefied Natural Gas and gas-to-liquids, petrochemicals, chemicals, power, pharmaceuticals, biotechnology, and healthcare industries. With nearly 70 percent of revenues stemming from operations outside of the United States, Foster Wheeler moved its legal headquarters to Bermuda in 2001; operational headquarters remained in New Jersey.

Company Origins

Although Foster Wheeler was incorporated in 1927, the origins of the enterprise date several decades earlier to the founding of two manufacturing companies: Wheeler Condenser & Engineering Company and Power Specialty Company. In 1891, Wheeler Condenser and Engineering Company was created with offices in New York City and a plant in Carteret, New Jersey. Its steam condensers, pumps, and heat exchangers were bought primarily by the power and marine industries. During the Spanish-American War the U.S. Navy contracted with the company for condensers for a number of vessels, beginning what would later be a long and important relationship for Foster Wheeler with the armed forces. In the ensuing years, the Wheeler Condenser & Engineering Company became a primary equipment supplier to the growing electrical utility industry.

Power Specialty Company, founded in New York City in 1900, followed a pattern of growth similar to that of Wheeler Condenser & Engineering. The company began by marketing waterworks equipment but was soon designing and manufacturing boiler components in its Dansville, New York, plant. Primarily building superheaters, Power Specialty also expanded to serve the new electrical power industry.

Like Wheeler Condenser & Engineering, Power Specialty developed an affiliation with the armed forces early in the company's history. During World War I, the company used its engineering expertise to design an advanced marine boiler for the U.S. Merchant Marines. In the 1920s Power Specialty diversified its operations by entering the industry of petroleum refinery equipment—designing and manufacturing—including crude oil distillation units and fired heaters.

In 1927 the two companies merged, forming the Foster Wheeler Corporation, and established their headquarters in New York City. The same year, a former Power Specialty office in London was incorporated as a Foster Wheeler subsidiary. In 1928, Foster Wheeler Limited (Canada), another former Power Specialty office, was incorporated, with a manufacturing plant and offices in Ontario, Canada. Two years after the merger, the New York Stock Exchange offered Foster Wheeler common and preferred stock.

Early Expansion

The new corporation's first goal was expanding its product line, which was initiated through the production of feedwater heaters, evaporators, and cooling towers. The company also acquired the D. Connelly Boiler Company in 1931, enabling them to design and produce all steam generator system components. Foster Wheeler had another burst of expansion during World War II, when engineering expertise and manufacturing were in demand from the armed forces.

The establishment of Foster Wheeler France, S.A. in 1949 opened an era of international expansion for Foster Wheeler. Operations were begun in Milan in 1957 with the organization of Foster Wheeler Italiana, S.p.A., Foster Wheeler Iberia was established in Madrid in 1965, and Foster Wheeler Australia Pty. Ltd. was established in Victoria, Australia, in 1967. The company also created a subsidiary to handle international construction.

Challenges in the Late 1950s

Although the company was expanding internationally, several engineering crises hurt Foster Wheeler's reputation and bottom line in the late 1950s and early 1960s. Former corporation president Frank A. Lee told *Forbes* writer Geoffrey Smith, "When you're talking about a 600-megawatt boiler that looks like a 14-story apartment house, and some tubes begin to rupture, you're talking about a tremendous amount of money. A couple of those a year and you're going to be in a loss position. And that's what happened. We had quite a few engineering problems in our boiler business—and an image problem in the market." Foster Wheeler's revenues dropped, and the company even operated at a loss in 1957 and 1963.

Over the next several years, the company gradually regained a good reputation in the boiler manufacturing business. Those earlier setbacks, however, caused Foster Wheeler to adopt a conservative attitude toward growth. Rather than expand into new business areas where the company lacked expertise, such as the growing field of nuclear energy, Foster Wheeler expanded geographically, selling products and services in regions where it could confidently establish a foothold.

Although Foster Wheeler was more cautious in buying out companies in the late 1960s and 1970s than many competitors, the corporation did acquire several subsidiaries that eventually composed the core of its industrial and environmental group. The first, Fritz W. Glitsch and Sons, Inc. (renamed Glitsch International, Inc.), manufactured fractionating equipment and pressure vessels and was obtained in 1967. In 1973, the company acquired Ullrich Copper, Inc. This subsidiary produced bus bar and copper extrusions used in electrical switch gear and motor-control centers, and specialty copper components used in rapid-transit systems and computers. In 1976, another major subsidiary was

obtained: Thermacote Welco Company, a distributor of welding supplies, including welding rod and wire, connectors, electrode holders, safety goggles, and brazing materials.

Reorganization and Profitability in the 1970s

Beginning in 1974, the company embarked on a significant reorganization plan. Foster Wheeler Corporation became a holding company, and Foster Wheeler Energy Corporation became the major operating company in the United States. Its responsibilities were later divided, with Foster Wheeler USA Corporation handling the process plants and project direction duties, and Foster Wheeler Energy Corporation the energy equipment operations. Other subsidiaries were created to improve the operating efficiency of the company's engineering and construction group, including Foster Wheeler Constructors, Inc., which handled project construction; FW Management Operations, Ltd., which provided management and plant operating services and trained staff for industry; Foster Wheeler Development Corporation, which provided contract research and development services; and Foster Wheeler Petroleum Development Ltd., which provided storage and shipping terminals, equipment for offshore gas and oil drilling, wellhead recovery and piping systems, and field development services.

Foster Wheeler's conservative strategy apparently paid off. Despite the drop in refinery construction after the oil embargo of 1974, the company's share price quadrupled from 1974 to 1979 and the return on equity steadily increased; while other companies were hard pressed to keep up with rampant inflation, Foster Wheeler was earning 19.3 percent.

Foster Wheeler's large backlogs and substantial cash reserves made the corporation a prime target for takeover. In 1979, McDonnell Douglas seemed poised to attempt a takeover, having bought 4.9 percent of Foster Wheeler's common stock. Corporation president Frank Lee, however, was adamant in his refusal to consider a takeover.

Foster Wheeler developed several technological advances that contributed to the company's high standing in the industry. For example, in 1980 the energy equipment group designed and constructed the first private industry fluidized bed steam generator fired by coal in the United States. They also created a unique cyclone design for their circulating fluidized bed boiler, a design that increased heat transfer, enabled a quicker start-up, reduced space requirements, and lowered maintenance costs.

Slowdown in the 1980s

In the late 1970s and early 1980s, Foster Wheeler benefited greatly from the boom in oil and utility power industries, achieving excellent profit margins in their contracts. The industry's heavy overbuilding, however, resulted in a substantial reversal in the 1980s. Foster Wheeler's profits slumped, as indicated by a period of several years when dividends on common stock were held at 11 cents per share. The company's backlog, generally a reliable predictor of future revenues, lingered at approximately $1 billion through the mid-1980s.

To lessen its reliance on the sagging oil and power utility industries, Foster Wheeler developed subsidiaries in new indus-

Key Dates:

1891: Wheeler Condenser and Engineering Company is created.
1900: Power Specialty Company is founded in New York City.
1927: The two companies merge to form Foster Wheeler Corporation.
1949: Foster Wheeler France S.A. is established.
1967: Fritz W. Glitsch and Sons, Inc. is acquired.
1974: The company embarks on a significant reorganization plan; Foster Wheeler Corporation becomes a holding company.
1987: Foster Wheeler moves headquarters to Clinton, New Jersey.
1994: Enserch Environmental Corporation is purchased.
1997: Glitsch International, Inc. is sold.
1999: Foster Wheeler files Chapter 11 bankruptcy at its Robbins Resource Recovery facility in Illinois.
2001: Company headquarters are moved to Bermuda for tax purposes.
2004: The Securities and Exchange Commission approves an equity-for-debt exchange offer, allowing the company to sell outstanding debt in exchange for ownership in the company and thereby cutting its debt by $437 million.
2005: The company's stock begins trading on the NASDAQ.

tries, including Foster Wheeler Power Systems, Inc., and Foster Wheeler Environmental Services, Inc. Foster Wheeler Power Systems built, owned, and operated waste-to-energy plants, recycling and composting plants, and cogeneration facilities. The company had some experience to draw on in this area, having built the first waterfall mass-burning refuse boiler in the United States. Foster Wheeler Environmental Services handled hazardous waste management and later became the holding company of the subsidiaries Foster Wheeler Enviresponse, Inc., which offered environmentally related regulatory, technical, design, and remediation services, and Barsotti's, Inc., which offered asbestos abatement services.

Foster Wheeler also reacted to the economic downturn of the early 1980s by selling real estate properties and underperforming subsidiaries. In 1988 Conergics Corporation was sold to Phillips Industries, Inc., for $43.2 million, and in 1989 TANCO Corporation bought Forney Engineering Company for an undisclosed sum. The proceeds were used to strengthen Foster Wheeler's ventures into waste-to-energy and hazardous waste management.

In 1987 Foster Wheeler moved headquarters to Clinton, New Jersey, after nearly 25 years in Livingston, New Jersey; the same year, Foster Wheeler became the object of another takeover attempt. Asher B. Edelman seemed determined to have the company, stating that if the board of directors would not consider his offer, he would appeal directly to the stockholders. Although he garnered stock holdings of nearly 12 percent, the company rejected his offer. Edelman backed down, reducing his holdings over several months until they reached 4.9 percent.

Steady Growth in the 1990s

The company's traditional businesses, particularly its engineering and construction enterprises, were revitalized in the early 1990s. The company's backlog grew from the steady $1 billion mark of the 1980s to $3.47 billion by 1992. Foster Wheeler received several international contracts for oil refinery construction or modernization, including an upgrading project at three Saudi Arabian oil refineries with an estimated final cost of $4 billion, refinery work in France worth approximately $50 million, and an $80 million joint venture in the Soviet Union for materials and engineering for a new refining unit. In addition, the reconstruction in Kuwait after the Gulf War provided some refinery work for Foster Wheeler.

Although most of the company's new business had come from international contracts, particularly in Europe and Asia, Foster Wheeler anticipated a surge of refinery work in the United States due to new federal clean-air legislation that required many refineries to upgrade their facilities by 1995. Other business areas also seemed to be improving in the early 1990s, as indicated by Foster Wheeler's first order for a large central station steam generator in several years. The general outlook for Foster Wheeler in the early 1990s seemed good. The company's book value per share had been rising steadily, from $12.79 in 1988 to $15.13 in 1991. Despite a recession, Foster Wheeler's revenues increased 20 percent in 1991, and the growing backlog of business suggested a continued rise in revenues.

Along with increased oil refinery renovation, the company expected to see demand for utility construction to rise with the economic recovery in the United States in the mid-1990s. Domestic business for Foster Wheeler, however, grew more slowly than many analysts had predicted. With pressure from energy companies, legislators pushed back compliance dates mandated by the Clean Air Act. Therefore, the massive improvements to oil refineries Foster Wheeler was anticipating were delayed. Utility construction also did not materialize with the economic recovery. Apparently, supply had so outstripped demand in the United States in the late 1980s that even the warming economy did not require new plant construction.

Nevertheless, Foster Wheeler's international presence benefited the company in the mid-1990s. With environmental concerns growing in Europe, the demand for improvements to refineries and coal-burning plants increased, offering opportunities to Foster Wheeler's engineering and construction group. With offices in Singapore and Thailand, the company was well positioned to take advantage of the Asian economic boom. In 1993 the company signed new contracts with China to build two 600-megawatt boilers, and in 1996 it signed a $200 million contract with the Philippines to build a polyethylene plant.

Foster Wheeler reorganized in 1993, incorporating its environmental group into its engineering and construction group. The following year the company acquired Enserch Environmental Corporation. By merging it with its Environmental Services Division to form Foster Wheeler Environmental Corporation, Foster Wheeler created the largest full-service environmental services company in the world. The acquisition of Optimized Process Designs in 1994 provided Foster Wheeler with the means to provide engineering and construction to the hydrocarbon processing industry.

In 1995 the company expanded further both internationally and domestically. It acquired the power-generating company Pyropower from the A. Ahlstrom Corporation, bringing Foster Wheeler operations into Finland, Poland, and Japan. The $207.5 million deal also expanded Foster Wheeler's operations in the former Soviet Union. The same year the company bought a Texas-based supplier of sulfur-recovery equipment, TPA, Inc.

The analysts' predictions of booming contracts for Foster Wheeler came to fruition in the mid-1990s. The company's backlog of unfilled orders rose from 2.5 billion in 1992 to $5.1 billion in 1994. By 1996, that number stood at a record $7.1 billion. Much of the increase came from Foster Wheeler's international business, which accounted for approximately 70 percent of new bookings in 1996. Revenues and net earnings had grown commensurably throughout the mid-1990s. The company's revenues of $2.3 billion in 1994 had almost doubled to $4.0 billion in 1996, and net earnings had risen from $65 million in 1994 to $82 million in 1996. In 1997 Foster Wheeler reorganized its pharmaceutical and fine chemicals unit. As part of the engineering and construction group, the unit accounted for 42 percent of that group's operating revenue in 1996. Later in 1997, the company sold Glitsch International, Inc., a supplier of mass transfer systems and chemical separations equipment. The company received $250 million cash for Glitsch, which had revenues of $300 million in 1996. Foster Wheeler sold its Koch Engineering unit later that year.

The outlook for Foster Wheeler in the late 1990s seemed bright. Its strong international presence stood to gain from the rising energy needs of developing nations in Latin America and Asia, particularly in China. The company also anticipated new projects for its energy equipment group from the increasingly privatized power-generating industry in Europe. During 1999 the company signed a contract to design Vietnam's first oil refinery.

Overcoming Problems in the Late 1990s and Beyond

Despite the appearance of a bright future for Foster Wheeler, the company began to experience problems at its Robbins Resource Recovery facility in Illinois during the late 1990s. The state government repealed Illinois' retail rate law, which had allowed Foster Wheeler to build the Robbins facility and receive subsidies from the local government. In essence, the law allowed Foster Wheeler (and other waste-to-energy plants) to charge utilities higher rates. The utilities, in turn, received tax breaks to make up for the higher charge. Foster Wheeler was then expected to eventually pay the state the difference between the two rates, but with zero interest.

Foster Wheeler claimed it would have never built the plant without the retail rate law in place and filed suit against the state in an attempt to reinstate the law. From 1997 through 1999, the company took $235 million in charges related to costs at the Robbins facility. The company's stock price dropped significantly as a result, down from $45 in April 1997 to approximately $14 per share in August 1998. By 1999, the company opted to file Chapter 11 bankruptcy protection for the plant. It

also launched a major companywide reorganization plan that called for the closure of several plants and 1,600 job cuts.

The restructuring continued into the early years of the new millennium. During 2000, it combined the operations of its Power Systems and Energy Equipment divisions. In 2001, the company's legal headquarters were moved to Bermuda and Foster Wheeler officially adopted the Foster Wheeler Ltd. corporate moniker. At this time, nearly 70 percent of its business stemmed from its international operations and the move to Bermuda enabled the company to avoid paying taxes on income earned outside of the United States. Most of the company's main offices, however, remained in New Jersey.

The company posted a net loss of $309.1 million in 2001 and its financial position continued to weaken due to a slowdown in the energy sector. At the same time, company debt was growing at a rapid clip due to cost overruns on unprofitable projects. By 2001, debt had climbed to $2.4 billion. With a negative cash flow since the late 1990s, many analysts began to speculate that bankruptcy may be in Foster Wheeler's future.

Newly elected Chairman and CEO Raymond Milchovich immediately began to trim costs in 2002 by jettisoning noncore businesses and consolidating operations. In 2004, the Securities and Exchange Commission approved an equity-for-debt exchange offer, a plan that allowed the company to sell outstanding debt in exchange for ownership in the company. Overall, the exchange offer cut the company's debt by $437 million. To avoid future cost overruns, Milchovich also created a Project Risk Management Group that was charged with the task of reviewing proposals and new contracts to determine their financial benefits or weaknesses. In June 2005, the company's stock began trading on the NASDAQ.

By now, Foster Wheeler appeared to be on the road to recovery with two main business segments: Engineering & Construction and Global Power Group. An expected upturn in building contracts in the oil, gas, and chemical industries bode well for the company. With its debt under control and solid strategy in place, the company hoped to win lucrative contracts that would lead to success and profitability in the years to come.

Principal Divisions

The Global Engineering & Construction (E&C) Group; The Global Power Group.

Principal Competitors

Bechtel Group Inc.; Fluor Corporation; Halliburton Company.

Further Reading

Biswas, Soma, "Foster Wheeler Might Not Survive," *Daily Deal,* April 25, 2002.

Carvlin, Elizabeth, "SEC Accepts Foster Wheeler's Plan to Exchange Debt for Incinerator Ownership," *Bond Buyer,* August 6, 2004.

"A Comeback for Foster Wheeler?," *Business Week,* August 8, 1988.

Doherty, Jacqueline, "Survivor," *Barron's,* January 31, 2005, p. 17.

"Foster Wheeler Reorganizes Drug Unit," *The Record,* March 28, 1997, p. B3.

"Foster Wheeler Sells Unit for $250M Cash," *The Report,* June 28, 1997, p. A9.

Geiselman, Bruce, "Lost Subsidy Means Foster Wheeler Loss," *Crain's Chicago Business,* September 22, 1997, p. 46.

Halpern, Steve, "Investors Eye China," *Knight Ridder/Tribune News Service,* November 19, 1993.

Hardman, Adrienne, "All Pumped Up," *Financial World,* May 11, 1993, p. 30.

Knapp, Kevin, "A Village's Hopes Going Up in Smoke with Incinerator," *Crain's Chicago Business,* August 10, 1998, p. 4.

Kuhn, Susan E., "The Best Capital Goods Stocks to Buy Now," *Fortune,* April 4, 1994, pp. 33–34.

Smith, Geoffrey, "No Hiding Place," *Forbes,* September 3, 1979.

"Swelling Backlog Sets Stage for a Surge in Earnings," *Barron's,* August 19, 1991.

—Susan Windisch Brown
—update: Christina M. Stansell

Franke Holding AG

Dorfbachstrasse 2
Aarburg
Switzerland
Telephone: +41 062 787 31 31
Fax: +41 062 791 30 37
Web site: http://www.franke.com

Private Company
Founded: 1911
Employees: 7,500
Sales: CHF 1.63 billion ($1.32 billion) (2004)
NAIC: 332322 Sheet Metal Work Manufacturing; 332999
    All Other Miscellaneous Fabricated Metal Product
    Manufacturing

Franke Holding AG is one of the world's leading producers of kitchen and related systems and equipment, including washroom and sanitary facilities systems. Franke products span the range of customer sectors, including the household and semi-professional market, and the professional restaurant, catering, and hospitality sectors. Among other customers, the company is a leading supplier of kitchen and other systems for McDonald's restaurants worldwide. Franke's operations are grouped around three core divisions: Kitchen Systems, including the group's historical production of sinks, as well as water tap and waste treatment systems, food preparation surfaces and work tops, and the like; Washroom and Sanitary Facilities, including paper towel and soap dispensers, toilet paper holders, as well as toilets, shower installations, and sinks for the consumer, commercial, professional and industrial markets; and Franke Coffee Systems, grouped around subsidiary Franke Kaffeemaschinen AG, which develops and manufactures coffee machines for the professional and semi-professional markets. Based in Aarburg, Switzerland, Franke has expanded to include more than 85 companies throughout Europe, North and South America, Asia, and Africa. The privately held company is led by Michael Pieper.

Sink Success in the 1930s

Franke started out as a small sheet metal plant, founded by Hermann Franke in 1911 in Rohrschach, Switzerland. Franke struggled throughout his first decade in business, however, in large part because of materials shortages brought on by the outbreak of World War I in 1914. The difficult economic climate in Switzerland continued to plague Franke's business into the next decade. Yet the growth of Switzerland's economy, stimulated by its liberal banking policies, in the 1920s offered new opportunities for Franke's business. The company began focusing its production on the construction sector, producing its first sanitary systems and fittings such as skylights and window frames. Another product line, tops for ovens, brought the company into the kitchen as well.

By the 1930s, Franke had begun to explore new materials as well, leading the company eventually to specialize in the production of stainless steel equipment. The 1930s also marked the emergence of a new core operation, that of the production of kitchen sinks, launched in 1931. This activity played a major role in the company's growth into not only a leading producer in Switzerland, but on a global level as well. By the end of the century, the company claimed to have produced more than 50 million kitchen sinks.

Into the 1930s, however, Franke remained a small business, with just ten employees. In the middle of the decade, the company moved to larger facilities in Aarburg. Franke then began developing a new generation of sink, a fully welded and smoothed sink. The company successfully launched the new sink type in 1937.

The end of the decade presented new difficulties for the company, however. Founder Hermann Franke died in 1939. With son Walter Franke taking the leadership, the company then faced into the outbreak of World War II. Once again, the company was faced with severe materials shortages. Yet the difficult conditions led the company to branch out again, and during the war years Franke began producing a more complete range of kitchen and sanitary equipment.

Fast-Food Expansion in the 1970s

By the end of the war, the company had grown to include more than 100 employees. The first stirrings of the postwar European economic boom encouraged the company to invest for future growth, with expanded production facilities and a

Company Perspectives:

Ours is a permanent quest for perfection, one to which we lend all our strength, intelligence, imagination, passion, heart and soul. Here is a summary of our core values: Leadership: We are among the pioneers in our industry and strive to achieve a leading position. Performance-oriented: We invest a great deal in the quality of our business processes and the skills of our employees.

Solution expertise: We continuously develop appropriate time-to-market solutions. Quality: We are committed to delivering Swiss quality. Our appliances function longer, more precisely and more reliably than the industry average.

Proximity to customers: We help customers find solutions, which makes us an important contributor to the achievement of their goals. Innovation: We continually surprise and delight with innovative solutions that set the standard for our industry. Values: Our appreciation of quality and performance is all-embracing. It encompasses—but is not limited to—the quality, functionality, design and performance of our products. Quality comes out in all that we do.

steadily expanding range of products. By 1949, the company had more than doubled its payroll and had launched production of entire kitchen systems. Sinks remained a central point in the group's production, and the Franke name became associated with the most advanced sink design developments.

The construction boom occurring across Europe, as the continent rebuilt and modernized its cities following the war, presented still greater growth opportunities for Franke into the 1950s and 1960s. Demand for sanitary installations and systems was particularly high, as that market evolved rapidly in the postwar years. Private, in-house bathrooms, showers, and toilets now became the norm in many markets where previously they had been unavailable; public and communal washroom facilities also were modernized. The rapid growth of the sector led Franke to develop a dedicated Washroom and Sanitary Equipment product group into the 1950s. By the end of the decade, the company's product offering spanned the complete range of washroom equipment and fittings.

Meanwhile, the construction boom occurring elsewhere in Europe, and the strong demand for the company's state-of-the-art kitchen and washroom equipment, attracted Franke's expansion interest. The company began adding its first international components in the 1950s, starting in Germany in 1955. Over the next decades, the company added operations throughout Europe, entering Italy in 1963 and France in 1964, among other markets. By the early 1970s, the company had added 12 foreign subsidiaries. During this period, the company expanded strongly, boosting its number of employees from 750 at the start of the 1960s, to more than 2,500 into the 1970s.

A major milestone in the company growth came in 1972. When McDonald's began to expand its restaurant empire into Europe, it turned to Franke to provide much of its kitchen equipment. The company's relationship with McDonald's quickly expanded, and the company became a major provider to the fast-

food giant worldwide. The company's expertise in this area also brought it contracts from many of McDonald's competitors, including Burger King. Nonetheless, McDonald's remained one of the company's largest customers, accounting for a significant portion of the group's annual sales—nearly 20 percent into the 2000s.

Coffee Equipment Extension in the 1980s

Franke added the production of colored enamel-coated sinks in 1973, in part to accommodate shifting consumer trends. The company also responded to the needs of the professional and commercial markets, developing its so-called compact sink system. Introduced in 1979, the compact sink system added to Franke's standing as one of the world's leading sink producers. By then, the company was under the direction of Willi Pieper, a friend and business partner of Walter Franke, who took over the company after Franke's death in 1975.

Under Pieper, the company's growth continued. In the early 1980s, the company became interested in expanding beyond its kitchen and sanitary systems operations. The company's target fell on the promising professional coffee machine sector. Always strong in its European base, the sector was undergoing something of a revolution in the United States, where the appearance of the first Starbucks in the early 1980s inspired a new appreciation for gourmet coffees.

In 1984, Franke acquired century-old coffee machine producer Augsberger. The company's intention was to redevelop its new subsidiary, now called Franke Kaffeemaschinen AG (later known as Franke Coffee Systems in English), into a producer of high-end, high-tech coffee machines. The rapid success of this subsidiary led the company in 1988 to restructure its operations into several core divisions, including Kitchen Systems, Washroom and Sanitary Facilities, and Coffee Systems.

The restructuring prepared Franke for a new period of strong growth. Led by Michael Pieper, son of Willi Pieper, who took over as group CEO in 1989, the company began transforming itself into a truly global operation. Over the next decade and half, the company entered most of the major world markets. By 2005, the company counted some 85 subsidiaries worldwide. Acquisitions formed a major role in the group's expansion. In 1990, for example, Franke expanded in the United Kingdom through the £8 million purchase of Carron Phoenix.

Global Leader in the New Century

The collapse of the Soviet system and the newly liberalized markets in Eastern Europe presented a fresh opportunity for growth close to home. Franke began expanding into the Central and Eastern European markets through the 1990s and into the 2000s. The company turned to Poland, in 1993, establishing a subsidiary in Warsaw. Franke also entered Russia that year, and then established operations in Hungary in 1994. Closer to home, the company established a dedicated subsidiary for the Portuguese market in 1995.

Yet Franke's expansion continued beyond Europe. In 1995, the company entered mainland China, establishing a presence in what was soon to become the world's fastest growing economy. In 1997, Franke boosted its presence in South America, launching a local subsidiary in Brazil.

Key Dates:

1911: Hermann Franke opens a sheet metal workshop in Rohrschach, Switzerland.
1931: Franke launches production of sinks.
1936: The company moves to Aarburg and opens a larger production plant.
1939: Hermann Franke dies and son Walter Franke takes over as head of the company.
1950: The Washroom and Sanitary Equipment division is launched.
1955: The company launches its first international expansion, into Germany.
1972: The company begins contract manufacturing for McDonald's.
1975: Willi Pieper takes over the company after the death of Walter Franke.
1979: The compact sink system is launched.
1984: The company acquires Augsburger and enters production of coffee systems.
1993: The company enters Poland and Russia.
1999: The company acquires full control of a Chinese joint venture.
2002: W&S Sutton in the United Kingdom is acquired.
2004: The company acquires ESI in the United States.
2005: The company acquires AquaRotter from Grohe.

Further international growth led the group into Bulgaria in 2000 and Thailand in 2002. The company also acquired a presence in South Africa, through its purchase of City Metal Products (CMP), formerly part of Boumat Ltd. The addition of CMP, renamed as Franke South Africa, placed Franke as the leading manufacturer and distributor of sinks and sanitary products in that country. In 1999, the company bought out its joint venture partner in China. The following year, it established a new subsidiary in Makati City, in the Philippines.

By the beginning of the 2000s, Switzerland, which had accounted for more than 40 percent of the group's sales a decade earlier, had been reduced to just 15 percent. For the new century, the company launched a restructuring operation in order to focus on just three core divisions: Kitchen Systems, including its washroom and sanitary business; Contract Manufacturing, for McDonald's and others; and Coffee Systems. As part of its restructuring, the company sold off parts of its diversified operations, which included industrial technology and automotive equipment. In 2003, the group's restructuring included the sale of its bathroom furniture subsidiary in a management buyout.

The streamlined group now launched a new series of acquisitions in order to boost its core operations. Franke's Coffee Systems division proved particularly active in its bid to acquire scale. In 2001, the division acquired KAMA Kaffeemaschinen & Service, based in Worb, Switzerland. The following year, the company moved into the top ranks of coffee machine producers, buying up Germany's Bremer. In 2003, the coffee systems division moved into The Netherlands, buying up KO-ks Benelux B.V. This was followed by an entry into the United States in

2004, with the purchase of ESI, based in Seattle. That subsidiary was renamed as Espresso Specialists Inc.

Other acquisitions included Niggemann Food Service Technik in Bochum, Germany, acquired in 2000, boosting the group's contract manufacturing operations for the fast-food restaurant market in Germany and Europe. The company moved into Denmark at the end of 2001, acquiring that country's A/S Panda Stal, a manufacturer of sinks. Although a small company, at just EUR 3 million in sales, the Panda purchase provided Franke with a beachhead for further expansion in the Nordic market.

In 2002, Franke took the leadership position in the European stainless steel sanitary product market through its acquisition of W&G Sissons Ltd. The purchase of W&G Sissons, which also gave the company operations in Belgium, followed on the company's decision to form a new dedicated Washroom & Sanitary Equipment division as a subdivision of its Kitchen Systems division in 2002.

Franke returned to the acquisition drive in 2004, buying up 49 percent of Italy's Faber Group. Specialized in the production of hoods and extraction systems for ovens and stoves, Faber claimed a position among the global top three in that category, with production plants in nine countries, and sales of more than EUR 250 million. In 2005, Franke bought up full control of Faber.

The company turned to South Africa, buying water heater manufacturers Supa Heat Geysers and the Geyser Company, gaining a market share of more than 35 percent in that country. By October 2005, Franke had reached an agreement to acquire AquaRotter, a subsidiary of Grohe based in Germany. As it neared the end of its first century, Franke had grown from a small sheet metal workshop into a leading globally operating company.

Principal Subsidiaries

Espresso Specialists Inc. (United States); Franke (Thailand) Co., Ltd.; Franke Douat Ltda. (Brazil); Franke France S.A.S.; Franke Kitchen Systems (Pty) Ltd. (South Africa); Franke KS International; Nortesco Inc. (Canada); NIRO-Plan AG.

Principal Competitors

DHS-Dillinger Huette Saarstahl AG; Aktiengesellschaft der Dillinger Huettenwerke; Independenta S.A.; Permasteelisa S.p.A. (Italy); Huta Florian S.A. (France); Scott Company of California Inc. (United States); Karl Steiner AG; Teich AG.

Further Reading

"Franke Acquires Espresso Specialists," *Tea & Coffee Trade Journal,* November 20, 2004, p. 100.
"Franke Coffee Systems Acquires ESI," *Gourmet Retailer,* November 11, 2004, p. 14.
"Franke Grows Outside Home Market," *Neue Zuercher Zeitung,* June 2, 1999, p. 13.
Murphy, Colum, "Swiss Kitchen Maker Eyes 50 Percent Market Share in Thailand by 2006," *Bangkok Post,* June 5, 2003.
Strauss, Karyn, "Franke's Japanese Subsidiary Begins Operation," *Hotels,* March 2005, p. 70.

—M.L. Cohen

Gardenburger, Inc.

15615 Alton Parkway, Suite 350
Irvine, California 92618
U.S.A.
Telephone: (949) 255-2000
Toll Free: (800) 459-7059
Fax: (949) 255-2010
Web site: http://www.gardenburger.com

Public Company
Employees: 172
Sales: $48.6 million (2004)
Stock Exchanges: OTC
Ticker Symbol: GBUR
NAIC: 311412 Frozen Food Specialty Manufacturing;
    422219 Other Grocery and Related Products
    Wholesalers

Gardenburger, Inc., headquartered in Irvine, California, produces meat alternative products and branded veggie burgers. Its frozen grain and soy-based meat replacement and meat analog products are sold to retail grocery, foodservice, club store, and natural foods outlets. Once the nation's leading wholesaler of vegetarian hamburgers, Gardenburger met a series of challenges in the early years of the new millennium. Intense competition as well as increasing popularity of protein and meat-based diets, including South Beach and Atkins, caused sales to plummet. The company filed for Chapter 11 bankruptcy protection in 2005 and planned to emerge as a private entity.

The Founding of Wholesome & Hearty Foods: 1981–85

The history of Gardenburger's meatless burger goes back to 1981, when the company's founder, Paul Wenner, created the first version of it at his Garden House Restaurant in Greshom, Oregon. As he explained in his cookbook, *Garden Cuisine,* Wenner became a dedicated advocate for meatless foods as a result of their beneficial effect on him. He suffered from asthma and tuberculosis in his youth, but his health began improving when he limited his diet to all natural, meatless foods, and

initiated a program of vigorous exercise. Thereafter, when he was in his 20s, he started teaching cooking classes in college, focusing on health issues as well as methods of preparing foods. He subsequently opened both his Garden House Restaurant and his own cooking school.

At the Garden House Restaurant, with a fair amount of ingenuity and some leftover rice pilaf, Wenner patted together and grilled the veggie burger that would eventually become the signature product of Gardenburger, Inc., although with its ingredients much changed. Wenner's original version also used mushrooms, rice, onions, oats, and low-fat cheeses.

Despite the success of his burgers, Wenner could not keep his restaurant open. Oregon entered a recession soon after he started in operation, and the economic downturn forced him to close his doors in 1984. Wenner continued to make his patties, however, selling them to a widening circle of local stores. The growing demand for them encouraged him to found his wholesale business, Wholesome & Hearty Foods, Inc., which he incorporated in 1985.

Early Promise Giving Way to Bottom Line Difficulties: 1986–94

Wenner gradually built his business up, creating other meat analog recipes and adding them to his line of foods. He was tapping into a fat-free, health food market that was rapidly growing as a health-conscious America was becoming increasingly receptive to low-fat, low-cholesterol foods. His prospective customers included reluctant vegetarians, people who had to give up eating meats not so much by choice as by dangerous cholesterol levels or other dietary concerns. The trick was to create passable look- and taste-alike substitutes for old American favorites such as hamburgers and hot dogs.

In 1986, to help publicize his foods, Wenner reentered the retail market with a small cafeteria outlet at a natural foods trade convention, but he never again went into the restaurant business. He sought to extend his food line and customer base, which he managed to do with a fair degree of success, and in 1992 was confident enough to take the company public. At that time sales had reached $6.9 million, and the company was realizing a small net profit, but it soon became apparent that in its growth Wholesome & Hearty had hit a plateau. Although revenues were growing, their rate had slowed, and the company's earnings were stagnating. In particular, 1994 was a very disappointing year. The company's stock dropped to less than $10 a share, down from as much as $14.50 in the previous year. Moreover, the company had a very low market profile and was simply limping along, generally outside much public notice. It was clear that Wholesome & Hearty needed some fresh thinking.

Expansion, Change, and Calculated Risks Under Hubbard: 1995–98

Significant changes made in an effort to improve the company's image and to bolster sales and profits began in 1995, when Lyle Hubbard took the operating reins of the company as CEO. He came over from Quaker Foods, where he had worked for 15 years and had acquired a reputation as an imaginative innovator as head of Quaker's $500 million convenience-food division.

Hubbard was given carte blanche. Although founder Wenner stayed on as the senior chairman and as chief creative officer, a rather unique title, he stepped aside to give full operational control to Hubbard. It was a change that almost immediately brought positive results, for in 1996 revenues grew by 10 percent, with sales of $39.63 million.

More of a business risk taker than Wenner, in that same year Hubbard began an expansion move with the acquisition of two companies: Gorilla Foods, Inc. and Whole Food Marketing, Inc. Wholesome & Hearty Foods purchased the former, a southern California-based distributor of specialty foods, including Wholesome & Hearty Foods' products, for $350,000 in cash. Gorilla Foods was a manufacturer and distributor of wheat protein-based meatless foods, including a frankfurter called the GardenDog. Hubbard acquired it for 240,000 restricted shares of Wholesome & Hearty's common stock and $68,750 in cash. At the time, the common stock, trading at $6.875 per share, was worth $1.65 million, but it was to be held in escrow before being distributed to Gorilla's stockholders if the sale of its gluten products met negotiated threshold targets.

The expansion was almost immediately complemented by moves to improve the company's efficiency. To reduce costs and boost sales, Hubbard and his staff decided to stop manufacturing a few products with a sluggish sales record, notably the company's breakfast sausage and faux hot dogs. These were dropped from its line in 1997. Steps were then taken to improve the sales volume of the remaining line of foods.

The first was a move to refurbish the company's image. Hubbard oversaw the company's name change to Gardenburger in October 1997, a change designed to enhance the company's

marketing profile. It brought no objections from stockholders, who saw the impact potential of the new name, one that could stick in customers' minds. It was a vital first step in achieving Hubbard's primary goal, to turn Gardenburger's signature burger into a household name, accepted not only as a health item but as a regular staple.

The second step was to launch a major advertising campaign, one that started with print but moved on to radio and television, most notably with a spot on the much-ballyhooed, final episode of *Seinfeld,* the very popular situation comedy, which aired in May 1998. The campaign was first designed and managed by a team at Hal Riney & Partners, a San Francisco firm with a very good reputation for producing creative ads that greatly improved brand-name recognition. The campaign involved putting $17 million into Gardenburger's 1998 advertising budget, an increase of 300 percent over the previous year. It was clearly a monumental risk for a company that in the previous year had only logged $56.8 million in sales. At a cost of $1.5 million, the *Seinfeld* spot alone ate up almost 10 percent of that inflated budget. It seemed a justified expense, however, for sales immediately picked up, and by the end of its 1998 fiscal year, Gardenburger's volume of sales climbed to more than $100 million, almost doubling. The campaign's success led Gardenburger to change its advertising account to Rubin Postaer & Associates after the three principal members of the original Riney team went to work for that firm.

By the end of 1998, the company had become the nation's leading wholesaler of vegetarian burgers, holding a 41 percent share of the market in the frozen, meat-analog burger category, rated as a $132 million business. The company's chief competitor, Worthington Foods, a larger company with a more varied line of products, trailed behind Gardenburger at a 30 percent market share. The increased sales were very encouraging and, among other things, prompted the company to add five new products to its growing line.

Gardenburger had to contend with some niggling problems, however. From 1996 to early 1999, the company faced some public relations and marketing difficulties when it was subjected to a nationwide boycott instituted by PCUN (Pineros y Campesinos Unidos del Noroeste), Oregon's farm workers' union. In 1992, PCUN had begun a boycott of all NORPAC products, including FLAV-R-PAC and Westpac frozen fruits and vegetables, because of NORPAC's reputed and documented ill treatment of farm laborers. Since Gardenburger had been buying and continued to buy farm produce from NORPAC, in 1996 PCUN added Gardenburger's own products to its boycott list. Facing mounting pressure from advocacy groups that had taken up PCUN's cause, after three years Gardenburger was finally forced to terminate its contractual arrangements with NORPAC. It did so on April 23, 1999, and PCUN immediately suspended its boycott of the company's products.

More important, despite the great increase in sales in 1998, the company continued to suffer bottom line problems. These began in 1997. Although Gardenburger's sales volume in that year rose to $56.84 million, an increase of almost 45 percent over the previous year, its increased operating expenses produced a net loss of $2.06 million. In 1998, when, driven by the ad campaign, sales increased by almost 76 percent, the net loss ballooned to $14.35 million. Growing sales simply could not compensate for increasing costs, not in the short run at least. Hope still ran high for the long run, however, especially in light of the tremendous increase in volume in 1998.

Bottom Line Realities Leave the Future Uncertain: 1999–2000

Yet the situation worsened in 1999, when, alarmingly, sales dropped back down by 40 percent, to $60.11 million, and operating losses, more than doubling, rose close to $30 million. That was bad news in a year in which the company had taken measures to ensure that it could meet the projected sales volumes based on the figures from 1998. Its most important expansion step was to move its production base to a new facility in Clearfield, Utah, a 120,000-square-foot plant three times the size and product capacity of its old plant in Portland.

When it became obvious that the projected sales volume increase was not going to materialize, the company closed its old plant, leaving only its headquarters and research facility in Portland. It also began cutting back on some of its more aggressive expansion plans and marketing strategies.

By the second quarter of 1999, Gardenburger's net loss had grown to $10.5 million. At that time, in July, Hubbard commented, "We are changing our business model on a go-forward basis to emphasize near-term profitability over aggressive market growth."

In September 1999, from change-of-control policy agreements filed with the Securities and Exchange Commission (SEC), it appeared that Gardenburger might go on the auction block, but by the close of the year it had not been sold. At the time of the SEC filing, Gardenburger's CFO Richard Dietz claimed that the company was not being prepared for sale, but,

when asked, he also refused to divulge whether the company was pursuing a merger with another company. That led to speculation and rumor about Gardenburger's fate. Even so, the company had reason to hope that its future prospects might improve, thanks to developments such as the Food and Drug Administration's October 1999 approval of claims that soy protein foods reduce the risk of coronary disease and the growing concern with obesity as a national and even a global problem, an issue widely publicized in the media in the early months of 2000.

Continuing Problems: 2001–05

Scott C. Wallace came on board as president and CEO of Gardenburger in early 2001; Hubbard had resigned in August 2000. The former CEO of Mauna Loa Macadamia Nut Corporation was charged with rejuvenating the company's bottom line and immediately set a strategy in place to shore up sales and increase market share. In an attempt to diversify from its veggie burger roots, Gardenburger launched an array of new products, including meatless chik'N Grill patties, meatballs, ribs, and a ground beef alternative. In 2002, it added meatless sausage patties, breaded cutlets, and pizza nuggets to its product line.

Despite the company's efforts, Gardenburger continued to lose ground against competing brands, including Morningstar Farms and Boca Burger. These brands were owned by Kellogg Company and Kraft Foods Inc., respectively. These companies had larger advertising budgets and as a result, commanded more shelf space in grocery stores.

The company's debt continued to climb and in 2001 its stock was delisted from the NASDAQ. In 2003, a management buyout group that included Wallace made a $4.5 million offer to take Gardenburger private. The deal failed to reach fruition and the company was left on its own to manage its turnaround strategy.

Gardenburger closed its Portland office in 2003 and moved company headquarters to Irvine, California. By now, sales had fallen to $49.4 million and the company continued to post losses. Intense competition as well as increased popularity of protein and meat-based diets such as Atkins and South Beach ate away at Gardenburger's bottom line. Nevertheless, the company was determined to recapture its lost market share. Gardenburger introduced a line of meatless frozen entrees in 2004 and black bean chipotle and sun-dried tomato basil wraps the following year. Its veggie burger also was added to cafeterias in the New York City school district. In March 2005, the company formed a partnership with Blimpie International Inc. to offer Gardenburger GardenFresh and Santa Fe subs in its franchised restaurants.

With $40.2 million in debt, falling sales, and growing losses, Gardenburger was forced to file for Chapter 11 bankruptcy in October 2005. Founder Paul Wenner commented on the filing that month in an *Oregonian* news article claiming, "It's a very sad story." In that same article, Seth Tibbott, president of vegetarian food company Turtle Island Foods, commented, "Gardenburger was a historic company—I'm sad to see them struggle. It points out the difficulty faced by the little guy in this big corporate world." Indeed, many analysts speculated that

Gardenburger's fate may have followed a much different path if the company would have orchestrated a sale to the likes of Kraft or Kellogg in the late 1990s. Although the future remained uncertain for Gardenburger, the company hoped to successfully emerge from Chapter 11 as a private entity.

Principal Competitors

ConAgra Foods, Inc.; Kellogg Company; Kraft Foods Inc.

Further Reading

Brinckman, Jonathan, "Gardenburger Heads for Private Control," *Oregonian,* October 15, 2005.

Colker, David, "Gardenburger Blames Carb Fears for Chapter 11," *Los Angeles Times,* October 16, 2005.

DeSilver, Drew, "Flipping Focus of Gardenburger," *Seattle Times,* July 1, 2001, p. D1.

Dwyer, Steve, "A Lean, Mean Meatless Machine," *Prepared Foods,* October 1998, p. 12.

Hill, Jim, " 'Seinfeld' Finale Will Serve As Gardenburger's Entree," *Oregonian,* March 3, 1998.

"Gardenburger Inc.—Creating Healthy Diets for New York City School Students," *Market News Publishing,* March 29, 2005.

Love, Jacqueline, "Gardenburger's Coming Out Party," *Oregonian,* May 10, 1998.

"Management Team Makes Offer to Buy Gardenburger," *Deseret News,* August 20, 2003.

Pollack, Judann, "Gardenburger: Lyle Hubbard," *Advertising Age,* June 28, 1999, p. S2.

Rose, Michael, "Gardenburger, Inc. Goes After Hamburger Lovers," *Business Journal-Portland,* October 24, 1997, p. 8.

——, "Is Sale Next for Burger Boys?," *Business Journal-Portland,* September 10, 1999, p. 1.

Wenner, Paul, *Garden Cuisine,* New York: Simon & Shuster, 1997.

—John W. Fiero
—update: Christina M. Stansell

Glaces Thiriet S.A.

Zone Industrielle
Eloyes
France
Telephone: +33 03 29 64 64 64
Fax: +33 03 29 64 64 44
Web site: http://www.thiriet.com

Private Company
Incorporated: 1973
Employees: 2,550
Sales: EUR 290 million ($350 million) (2004)
NAIC: 311520 Ice Cream and Frozen Dessert Manufacturing; 445110 Supermarkets and Other Grocery (Except Convenience) Stores; 445299 All Other Specialty Food Stores; 311412 Frozen Specialty Food Manufacturing; 311411 Frozen Fruit, Juice, and Vegetable Processing

Glaces Thiriet S.A. is the third largest manufacturer of ice cream in France, trailing only multinational giants Unilever and Nestlé. The company is also France's leading manufacturer of frozen pastries and other desserts. Yet Thiriet also has built up a presence among that country's top frozen food retail specialists, with more than 150 stores located throughout France offering nearly 1,200 frozen food items. Most of the items sold in Thiriet stores feature the company's own brand names, including Thiriet and Prelande. Thiriet also carries a number of brand names, typically from the high-end bracket and not commonly found in the larger supermarket channel. In addition to its retail store network, Thiriet is present in France's frozen foods home delivery segment. In support of these operations, the company operates a fleet of more than 400 trucks, backed by a network of 75 distribution centers and staffed by a 1,000-strong sales force. Thiriet's home delivery sales are preordered through the company's 30-page catalog. Founded by Claude Thiriet in the early 1970s, Glaces Thiriet remains a privately held, independent company.

From Baker to Ice Cream Maker in the 1960s

The Thiriet family operated a bakery in the village of Eloyes, in the Vosges region of France. In 1966, Claude Thiriet, then just 22 years old, joined his mother at the bakery, where he began producing his own ice cream, in addition to the bakery's breads and pastries. Thiriet's ice creams quickly gained a reputation for their high quality, attracting customers from throughout the region.

Thiriet's reputation soon reached the attention of the country's wholesalers and growing distribution companies. France was then undergoing a revolution in its retail sector. Traditionally based on small, locally oriented and independently owned grocery shops, the retail sector had begun a shift toward the rapidly growing supermarket format. By the early 1970s, the country had seen the opening of the first hypermarkets—combining the supermarket and department store formats—as well. Whereas the smaller grocers had only limited shelf space and focused on basic foods, the supermarket format provided the space for an extensive variety of items, including expanded frozen foods sections. Attracted by the high quality of Thiriet's ice creams, the wholesalers encouraged the bakery to invest in larger-scale production for the supermarket sector.

The supermarket format favored the emergence of a small number of large-scale retail groups operating on a regional and then national scale. The development of these supermarket groups transformed the French foods sector. On the one hand, the larger companies possessed greater purchasing power, enabling supermarkets to compete with lower pricing. Contracts with the larger supermarkets also enabled food production companies to invest in expanding their own production capacity, while also stimulating the growth of a production channel dedicated to the supermarkets' private-label sales. On the other hand, as the retail sector entered into a steadily tightening consolidation, producers were confronted with a shrinking number of outlets for their products. The large-scale supermarket groups featured only a limited number of brands within each product category on their shelves—losing a spot on a supermarket's shelf spelled potential disaster to the food producers. As a result, the large-scale distribution groups came to dominate the food producers as well as the retail channel.

Key Dates:

1966: Claude Thiriet, 22 years old, joins the family bakery in Eloyes and begins producing ice cream.

1973: Thiriet forms Glaces Thiriet S.A. and specializes in production of ice cream; the company begins sales to the retail sector and launches its own home delivery operation.

1980: The company builds a national brand through a concessions network; production of frozen pastries and desserts is launched.

1985: The first Thiriet frozen foods store is launched.

1990: The company expands frozen foods production and packaging.

1995: The company continues expansion, completing its range to feature more than 1,000 frozen food products.

2000: The company builds a state-of-the-art logistics platform.

2001: A EUR 38 million expansion program is launched.

2002: The company opens a new logistics platform in Donzère in the Drôme region.

2004: Home delivery service is launched in Luxembourg and part of Belgium.

2005: The company opens a new logistics platform serving the southwest region.

Thiriet recognized the opportunities offered by placing its products into the supermarket sector. In 1973 the family decided to specialize in the production of ice cream, and formed a new company, Glaces Thiriet. Yet Claude Thiriet remained wary of the retail industry, and instead of devoting the new company to the production of its ice cream, decided to enter the direct retail sector as well, developing its own home delivery operation. In this way, the company was able to maintain a degree of independence.

The home delivery market had long been an important retail channel in France, and especially in the country's rural and agricultural regions. These areas remained underserved by the larger distribution groups, which focused their expansion efforts on the country's metropolitan areas. A number of companies came to specialize in home delivery, typically operating truck-stores and making the rounds of customers' homes. The appearance of freezers as common home appliances in the late 1960s and early 1970s created a new market for frozen foods, and a number of companies established specialized frozen food home delivery services.

Thiriet launched its own catalog, and invested in its own fleet of refrigerated trucks, providing deliveries of customer orders. The company also developed its own sales staff in support of its home delivery operation, serving the Lorraine region. The success of both its wholesale and home delivery business led Thiriet to step up its production in the mid-1970s. In 1975, the company moved to the outskirts of Eloyes, building a new factory to support the growing demand for its ice cream. Through the rest of the decade, Thiriet focused on expanding the geographic reach of its ice cream brand, establishing con-

cession partnerships throughout the country. By 1980, Thiriet had become a national ice cream brand.

Retail Network in the 1980s

Into the 1980s, the company began expanding its product line, adding a line of frozen pastries and desserts. The company continued to distinguish itself by the high quality of its products; by the end of the 1990s, the Thiriet brand held the number three spot in the ice cream category (trailing only food products giants Unilever and Nestlé) and the number one position in frozen desserts.

A major factor in the growth of the Thiriet brand was its decision to expand its retail operation in the mid-1980s. The company opened its first retail store in 1985, offering its ice creams and desserts, as well as a limited range of other food products. The success of the company's retail division convinced Thiriet to expand that business starting from 1990. As part of that expansion, the company began diversifying its production, building up a more complete range of frozen food items under the Thiriet name. In addition to basic products, such as bulk vegetables, meats, fruits, and the like, the company created its own research and development team, charged not only with maintaining quality levels, but also with developing new prepared foods recipes.

By the mid-1990s, competition in the frozen foods sector had intensified. Thiriet faced competition not only from the supermarket groups, which by then had come to dominate the national grocery market, but also from rivals such as Picard, which, like Thiriet operated in both the home delivery and retail stores segments, Gel 2000, a retail specialist, and Agrigel, the leading home delivery specialist. In order to boost its position, Thiriet decided to engage in a massive investment program in the mid-1990s. The company expanded its range of goods, boosting its catalog to more than 1,000 items. Yet Thiriet remained true to its roots—more than one-third of its products fell under the frozen dessert category.

As part of its investment drive, Thiriet stepped up the pace of its new store openings. By the middle of the 2000s, the company numbered more than 150 stores. At the same time, the group's home delivery business had continued to deepen its penetration of the French market. Supporting the company's expansion was the establishment of a network of some 75 distribution centers. The company also built up a network of logistics platforms, including at its home base in Eloyes, but also serving the Sarthe, Aube, and Rhone regions.

International Interest in the 2000s

Thiriet continued building up its national infrastructure into the mid-2000s. As part of this effort, the company earmarked some EUR 38 million in new investments starting in 2001. This led to the construction of a new 12,000-square-meter logistics platform in Donzère, serving the Drôme region. In 2002 and 2003, the company added new distribution centers in Dainville and Petit Forêt, followed by the opening of a logistics platform in Moutauban-La Bastide St. Pierre in 2005 to provide support to the company's southwest region operations. In that year, as well, the company boosted its distribution network to 75 centers, adding distribution centers in Mezieres and Albi.

While building up its own national presence, Thiriet had long been interested in the international markets as well. The company extended its reach to France's overseas possessions, establishing a store in Guadeloupe, as well as two stores on the island of Reunion. The company also teamed up with international partners to introduce its ice cream and pastry products to other markets. In Switzerland, for example, the company formed a partnership with Agemo, which extended the company's distribution and home delivery operations into the French- and German-speaking regions, and also opened a Thiriet store in Switzerland. The company also added sales in Japan, The Netherlands, Korea, Morocco, and Portugal. In 2004, the company extended its operations to Luxembourg and parts of Belgium, providing home delivery operations there.

By 2005, Thiriet held a solid place as France's third largest manufacturer of ice cream and leading producer of frozen desserts. The company also had established itself as the country's second largest frozen foods retailer, with 150 stores throughout France. Thiriet, which remained privately held and controlled by founder Claude Thiriet, also retained its interest in seeking out new partners to aid in building its brand on the international market. Thiriet looked forward to a tasty future in the new century.

Principal Competitors

Carrefour S.A.; Etablissements E. LeClerc S.A.; ITM Entreprises S.A.; Groupe Auchan; Rallye S.A.; Toupargel-Agrigel S.A.; Maximo.

Further Reading

Ambrosi, Pascal, "Thiriet engage 38 millions d'euros d'investissement sur trois ans," *Les Echos,* October 8, 2001.

Davis, Mary B., and Joan Schatzberg, "Regrouping in Freezer Center Segment As Fierce Competition Rivets France," *Quick Frozen Foods International,* January 2000, p. 80.

"Glaces Thiriet (651e) élargit sa gamme," *L'Expansion,* November 8, 2001.

Vercesi, P.M., "Le bel appétit de Claude Thiriet," *BREF Online,* March 2002.

—M.L. Cohen

Groupama S.A.

8-10 rue d'Astorg
Paris
F-75383 Cedex 08
France
Telephone: +33 1 44 56 77 77
Fax: +33 1 44 56 72 74
Web site: http://www.groupama.com

Private Cooperative
Incorporated: 1900 as Caisses d'Assurances Mutelles
    Agricoles
Employees: 33,000
Sales: EUR 12.8 billion ($14 billion) (2004)
NAIC: 524113 Direct Life Insurance Carriers; 524114
    Direct Health and Medical Insurance Carriers; 524126
    Direct Property and Casualty Insurance Carriers

Groupama S.A. is France's second largest insurance group, with total assets of more than EUR 70 billion and annual revenues from premium income of nearly EUR 13 billion ($13.5 billion) in 2004. Groupama is a mutual insurance company, with more than four million members in France, and operations in the United Kingdom, Spain, Portugal, Italy, and Hungary. In the mid-2000s, Groupama also has begun a drive to expand into the Asian insurance market, with operations in Hong Kong, mainland China, and Vietnam. Groupama provides a full range of insurance products, and also offers reinsurance products, asset management, and related banking services. Groupama's organizational structure remains highly local in nature—the group operates through more than 7,000 independent, local offices, regrouped under 3,000 local branch operations. These in turn report to 11 regional mutuals, which in turn report to the group's national organization. Since the early 2000s, Groupama has been reducing its number of regional mutuals, previously 23 in number, to just nine. On a national level, Groupama operates through three structures: Groupama National Federation, which represents its members and acts as a coordinator of group strategy; Groupama S.A., which operates the group's insurance business as a limited liability company; and Groupama Holding company, owned by the group's regional offices, as the shareholding entity in Groupama S.A. Groupama traditionally focuses on France's large rural and agricultural market, which remains the group's core market. The group's products are available to nonmembers, however. In order to minimize the risk of over-exposure to the French market, Groupama has developed a strategy of international expansion for the 2000s. As part of that strategy, the group expects to go public as early as 2006.

Farmers' Mutual Assistance in the 1840s

The democratization of much of Europe in the 19th century stimulated the growth of new models for the financial industry. Whereas previous banking and insurance models had been oriented in large part toward the wealthy, the rise of new social strata, including a new industrial working class, a rapidly growing middle class, and a fully emancipated agricultural population, introduced the need for products and organizations. The creation of "friendly societies" in England in the late 18th century pointed the way toward the development of a mutual aid and cooperative movement that quickly spread across Europe.

By the end of the first half of the decade, a growing number of France's farmers had recognized the potential for grouping together to provide their own insurance against crop failures, the death of livestock, farm accidents, and other specific issues faced by the agricultural community. The first insurance cooperative was founded in the Isère region in 1840, and was created specifically in order to provide fire insurance for its member farmers. The mutual movement quickly swept across France, and developed a variety of other insurance products created specifically for the country's rural, agricultural population. The development of this network of locally controlled mutual assistance groups occurred more or less spontaneously, with as yet no central coordination to speak of.

The new "mutuelles" soon became an important facet of French farming life. By the beginning of the 1890s, France counted more than 550 across the country. The development of the cooperative movement in general, and of the farmers' insurance market, was aided and encouraged by the French government, which began introducing legislation toward the end of the

Company Perspectives:

Groupama's guiding principles: Local presence. The mutual's elected representatives and Group staff are in close contact with customers on the ground, and present throughout France, listening to the needs of members and customers. They act to find genuine solutions. Responsibility. Responsibility is both individual and collective and functions at every level of the organisation. It goes beyond legal responsibility and expresses a vision of the insurance business that includes preventive actions. Solidarity. Assisting each other is at the heart of a mutual's mission—sharing resources to come to the aid of people who have suffered a loss or an accident. Solidarity is well thought out and combines both financial and human solidarity.

century. In 1900, the government passed legislation governing the farmers' mutuals. Under this legislation, a new body was created, called the Caisses d'Assurance Mutuelles Agricoles, or AMA, to provide centralized oversight to the sector. The mutuals themselves remained local and more or less autonomous in their operation.

The financial crises in the 1930s led the French government to force a consolidation of the banking and insurance industries. The move toward nationalized industries became particularly strong following World War II, when the French government nationalized much of the insurance sector, creating a small number of large-scale companies, including GAN, AFF, and UAP.

During this period, the AMA, too, emerged as a full-fledged corporate entity, becoming the heart of what has been described as a network of "capillaries." Local mutuals, while remaining independent, were grouped along regional lines. The regional bodies, some 23 in number, then provided representation to their farmer-members for decisions taken by the AMA. Local mutuals were typically operated on a part-time basis, often by a village priest or schoolteacher, who then received a commission on sales of the group's insurance products. This close proximity—and often intimate knowledge—of the local market enabled the AMA to become the agricultural community's leading provider of life insurance by the 1960s.

The AMA had by then begun expanding beyond its original focus on providing farmers' risk insurance. Laws passed by the French government, starting in the late 1920s, had begun to put into place a system of social security, protecting workers and their families in case of sickness or death, and by providing maternity leave and retirement security. The social security system was expanded to include not only farm employees, but the farmers themselves, and sparked the development of what was called the "social insurance" system.

By the early 1960s, the AMA sought to branch out from its focus on farmers' insurance. In 1963, the group's membership voted to allow the AMA to begin providing other insurance products, such as automobile and home insurance. In 1972, the AMA created a new entity, Soravie, and began marketing its own life insurance products as well. The group's highly developed local network, operated by salespeople who also held prominent roles in their communities, allowed the AMA to become a leading local insurance provider in France and one of the top insurance groups overall. The expansion into new products also allowed the group to attract clientele from beyond its core agricultural market.

The AMA became one of the first in France to offer traveler's assistance insurance, launching SOS-AMA in 1975 to provide roadside assistance to its members. In 1981, the AMA placed SOS-AMA into a joint venture with another mutual group, creating Mutuaide. The AMA then took full control of Mutuaide in 1990.

In the late 1970s, the AMA entered a new market, founding a reinsurance subsidiary, Sorema. The reinsurance operation, created in 1978, also exposed the mutual to the international insurance market for the first time. As part of the development of Sorema, for example, the company established an office in New York, placing its subsidiary closer to the world financial market.

In the meantime, the French government had been preparing to privatize much of the nationalized insurance sector. In the late 1970s, a number of government-controlled insurance bodies had been allowed to list their stock on the Paris Stock Exchange. In 1986, the government announced its intention to privatize all ten government-owned insurance companies, allowing them to reincorporate as limited liability companies the following year. The privatization effort accompanied the launching of a deregulation effort in the insurance and financial markets in general. The AMA responded to the changing market by restructuring itself from a federation of local businesses into a more unified organization. The group then adopted a single brand name, Groupama, in 1986.

International Growth for the New Century

With competition rising at home, Groupama began developing an interest in international expansion into the 1990s. The company's target turned first to the European market. For this, the company targeted the more developed financial markets, establishing a subsidiary in Switzerland, for example. In 1995, Groupama entered the United Kingdom, paying £83 million to acquire Lombard Insurance. That company had been formed in 1993 from a management buyout of the U.K. operations of U.S.-based Continental. Lombard was renamed as Groupama UK following the acquisition.

Into the late 1990s, however, Groupama was described as a "minnow" in France's insurance market, with a distant fifth place behind its fast-growing, publicly listed competitors. Groupama held several key positions in the French insurance sector, including a 63 percent share of the agricultural risks market, and an 80 percent share of the market providing insurance to agricultural cooperatives. The company attempted to attract a wider and more diversified client base; in 1995, Groupama opened up its membership to nonagricultural policyholders for the first time. Nonetheless, the rural market remained the dominant source for the company's revenues, with towns of population of 10,000 or less accounting for 70 percent of group revenues.

The merger of longtime mutual insurance rival AXA with UAP in 1997 created the dominant player in the French insur-

Key Dates:

1840: The first farmers' mutual insurance group, providing fire insurance, is formed.
1900: The French government establishes AMA as the central farmers' mutual body.
1963: AMA begins diversifying products, adding automotive insurance, etc.
1972: Life insurance operations are launched.
1975: The roadside assistance subsidiary, SOS-AMA, is launched.
1978: The Sorema reinsurance subsidiary is launched.
1980: SOS-AMA is merged into Mutuaide.
1986: The AMA network is regrouped under the single Groupama brand name.
1990: The company acquires full control of Mutuaide.
1995: Membership is opened to nonagricultural policyholders; Lombard Insurance in the United Kingdom is acquired.
1998: Groupama acquires GAN and becomes the number two French insurance company.
2002: Plus Ultra in Spain is acquired.
2003: The company receives a license to sell insurance in China.
2004: The company opens its first Chinese branch, in Chengdu.
2005: The company receives a license to expand product offerings in Vietnam; Groupama UK acquires Clinicare.

ance market and forced Groupama to launch an effort to build its own scale, and especially to diversify its client base. The company attempted to buy up Athena, another French insurer, in 1997, but lost the bid to AGF.

Groupama had better luck in 1998, when the French government announced that it was going to complete a long-awaited privatization of its GAN (Groupe des Assurances Nationales) insurance operation. Groupama joined the bidding, against rival Swiss Life. Despite GAN's larger size, Groupama won the bid, adding GAN's $8.7 billion in revenues and four million clients. The addition of GAN catapulted Groupama to the number two position in the French insurance market. At the same time, GAN's client base proved complementary to Groupama's, helping it to achieve a greater diversity of customers.

With its position in France secured, Groupama was able to turn its attention to developing an international presence. In the beginning of the 2000s, the company decided to revise its foreign strategy and refocus its expansion effort on the one hand to developing its business in southern Europe, as well as entering the Asian market. As part of that strategy, the group announced its decision to sell off its U.K. and Swiss subsidiaries in 2001. Poor market conditions forced the company to put these sales on hold, however. Although the Swiss operation was finally sold by 2005, the U.K. operation had in the meantime made substantial progress in gaining market share, and its sale was put on hold indefinitely. Instead, in October 2005, Groupama backed its U.K. subsidiary's expansion with the acquisition of Clinicar, a specialist in the healthcare insurance sector.

Groupama, which had already established a subsidiary in Spain, boosted its presence in the market in 2002 when it acquired Spanish insurer Plus Ultra Generales. Groupama then merged its existing business in Spain into Plus Ultra's, forming Groupama Plus Ultra. That company claimed a spot in the top ten nonlife insurers in Spain, and in the top 20 in the country's overall insurance market.

Groupama also had begun to explore expansion in Asia. The group set up a subsidiary in Vietnam, and began providing agricultural insurance there. In January 2005, Groupama's Vietnamese subsidiary, struggling to achieve profitability in its narrow market, was granted a license to offer an expanded range of insurance products there. In 2003, Groupama received a license to sell insurance products in China, leading to the establishment of its first branch office in Chengdu in 2004. By 2005, Groupama had opened four offices in China.

As mid-decade approached, Groupama began preparing for a public offering. As part of this process, the group had begun streamlining its organization, reducing the number of regional offices from 24 to just nine, and its number of local offices from more than 10,000 to just 7,000. Groupama also created a new administrative structure, establishing a holding company, Groupama Holding, for its business operations, known as Groupama S.A. After more than 150 years as a mutual insurance group, Groupama hoped to go public as early as 2006.

Principal Subsidiaries

Assuvie; Caisse Fraternelle d'Épargne; Caisse Fraternelle Vie; Cofintex Luxembourg Reinsurance; Compagnie Foncière Parisienne; Gan Assurances Iard; Gan Assurances Vie; Gan Eurocourtage Iard; Gan Eurocourtage Vie; Gan Italia S.p.A.; Gan Italia Vita; Gan Outre-mer Iard; Gan Patrimoine Insurance; Gan Portugal Seguros; Gan Portugal Vida; Gan Prévoyance; Gan UK plc; Groupama Assurance-Crédit; Groupama Banque; Groupama Biztosito (Hungary); Groupama General Insurances CL (United Kingdom); Groupama Holding; Groupama Holding 2; Groupama International; Groupama Plus Ultra (Spain); Groupama Protection Juridique; Groupama S.A.; Groupama Transport Insurance; Groupama Vie; Günes Sigorta (Turkey); Luxlife Insurance (Luxembourg); Mutuaide Assistance; Rampart Reinsurance (United States); Scepar Investments; Sepac; Silic.

Principal Competitors

Confederation Nationale du Credit Mutuel; AXA Group; Banque Federative du Credit Mutuel; Credit Lyonnais; MAAF; MAIF.

Further Reading

Anker, Guy, ''Groupama Sets Out to Treble Its Business,'' *Post Magazine,* March 31, 2005.
Buliard, Fabien, ''Groupama Plans Listing in 2006 to Boost Expansion,'' *Insurance Day,* November 21, 2003.
''Does Floatation Suggest a Groupama Sea Change?,'' *Post Magazine,* September 22, 2005.
''French Insurance Giant Groupama Keen on China,'' *Asianinfo Daily China News,* December 31, 2001.

Groom, Brian, "Globalisation Shakes Groupama Rural Idyll," *Financial Times,* August 27, 2004.

"Groupama Facing Acid Test in China," *SinoCast China Financial Watch,* September 21, 2005.

"Groupama Opens Chengdu Branch," *SinoCast China Business Daily News,* October 27, 2004.

"Groupama souhaite grossir avant peut-être d'aller en bourse," *L'Expansion,* March 23, 2005.

Jack, Andrew, "Groupama Emerges from Obscurity," *Financial Times,* July 2, 1998, p. 32.

Kielmas, Maria, "Groupama Buys GAN," *Business Insurance,* July 13, 1998, p. 17.

Rouse, Lynn, "Clinicare Deal Offers Groupama PMI Boost," *Post Magazine,* October 20, 2005.

Swift, Jonathan, "Groupama Looks at UK Acquisitions," *Post Magazine,* September 22, 2005.

Tieman, Ross, "A Gaelic Response to Keeping Your Customers Local," *Financial Times,* November 16, 1999, p. 20.

—M.L. Cohen

Hansen Natural Corporation

1010 Railroad Street
Corona, California 92882-1947
U.S.A.
Telephone: (951) 739-6200
Fax: (951) 739-6210
Web site: http://www.hansens.com

Public Company
Incorporated: 1990
Employees: 293
Sales: $180 million (2004)
Stock Exchanges: NASDAQ
Ticker Symbol: HANS
NAIC: 312111 Soft Drink Manufacturing

A descendant of a venerable California juice maker, Hansen Natural Corporation went from bankruptcy case to NASDAQ darling by focusing on innovation in the beverage marketplace. The company offers natural sodas, juices, smoothies, teas, sports drinks, Blue Sky branded carbonated beverages, and the Junior Juice line of products for toddlers. The company launched its Monster energy drink in 2002 and sales have since doubled. In 2005, *Forbes* magazine ranked Hansen Natural number one on its annual list of the 200 Best Small Companies in the United States.

A Sunny Beginning

"Hansen's Fruit and Vegetable Juices" first appeared in southern California in 1935. Assisted by his three sons, Hubert Hansen started the business in Los Angeles selling fresh, unpasteurized fruit juices. Hollywood film studios provided his first clients. That company became Hansen's Juices, later known as The Fresh Juice Company of California, Inc. The plant it opened in Los Angeles in 1946 was used until operations were moved to a new plant in Azusa, California, in 1993.

This company's fresh juice line included orange, carrot, apple, strawberry, and banana juices, as well as blends. By this time, Hansen's Juices was firmly established in the West and was shipped to the East Coast and Hawaii as well. Some of its

35,000 gallons of juice produced per week was marketed by an Illinois company, and some was shipped overseas, reported the *Los Angeles Times.*

One of Hubert Hansen's grandsons, Tim Hansen, formed his own, separate fruit juice business in 1977: Hansen Foods, Inc. He obtained a license to use the family name as a trademark. The new company, also based in Los Angeles, specialized in pasteurized, shelf-stable juices, particularly apple. It was known for innovation in combining flavors as well as in marketing. Hansen Foods branched out into Hansen's Natural Sodas in 1978. These featured all natural ingredients.

Hansen's sales reached an estimated $50 million in the mid-1980s. Sales failed, however, to climb sufficiently to repay financing for a new factory, and the company filed for bankruptcy in 1988. California CoPackers Corporation (doing business as Hansen Beverage Company), based in Hawaii, subsequently acquired the Hansen's brand name in January 1990.

Annual sales reached $13.7 million that year and rose to $17.1 million the next. Hansen, always known for using cans, introduced its first glass bottle in the summer of 1991. At this time, Harold C. Taber, Jr., was serving as president and CEO of the company, then based in Brea, California.

Creation of Hansen Natural Corporation in 1992

An investment group including Rodney Sacks, who would become CEO, bought the money-losing company on July 27, 1992. The investors felt that the brand's longevity and name recognition would be worth banking on and that its niche was just opening up in the market. Aside from Sacks, a corporate lawyer from South Africa, other new management talent included Taber, a 27-year Coca-Cola veteran. Investors included British industrialist Hilton H. Schlosberg, who became vice-chairman and president, and friends and family members. Hansen Natural Corporation went public at the same time, listing on Nasdaq. The company soon seemed to evidence a turnaround. Revenues reached $21.3 million in 1992.

Hansen employed about a dozen people at the time. Since Tropicana had acquired the Hansen factory in the bankruptcy, the company now outsourced most of its operations, even turning to

Company Perspectives:

The mission of Hansen Beverage Company is to satisfy consumers' needs for superior quality and great tasting, healthy, natural and functional beverages. Our beverages will be positioned as an upscale brand and will often be marketed at a premium to competitive mainstream products.

flavor consultants for new formulations. Independent companies blended the drinks and shipped them to independent bottlers.

Pint-sized, bottled iced teas, lemonades, and juice drinks came out in the early 1990s. These competed in the ''New Age'' drink category, which also included alternatives to traditional cola drinks such as flavored water and iced tea. What defined the category was the public perception of these drinks as relatively healthy. Hansen's heritage was perceived as particularly healthy. Its labeling began to proclaim, for example, ''California's original clear natural soda.''

Industry leaders such as Coca-Cola and Pepsi fought for a share of this segment, the fastest growing part of the $50 billion a year soft drink market. Coca-Cola introduced Nordic Mist, and Pepsi offered Crystal Pepsi as an alternative. Snapple's drinks quickly came to dominate this $1 billion category. It sold $232 million worth of iced tea in 1992. Its advertising and marketing budget that year—$30 million—exceeded Hansen's total revenues, noted the *Los Angeles Times*. Some analysts, however, believed that Hansen's long-term interests were best served by a focus on keeping costs down. They felt that the company was less likely to ''crash and burn'' in the event of a price war. Hansen embarked on a major expansion into the Midwest in 1993, introducing a multiserve, 23-ounce glass bottle to its packaging mix.

New Age drinks were faddish and in July 1994 Hansen introduced a line specially branded to appeal to young consumers. Equator drinks initially debuted in Southern California. They came in 16-ounce cans (a 24-ounce version also was tried) wrapped in environmentally conscious imagery and copy. By not packaging the drinks in glass bottles, they could be sold in more locations, such as gyms and swimming pools where risk of breakage might be considered a hazard. To capture the loyalty of younger consumers, the traditional Hansen's brand, which was identified with older drinkers, was not featured on the packaging. The first flavors were Blue Raspberry Creation Iced Tea, Cosmic Mango Iced Tea, Black Cherry Eclipse Lemonade, Heavenly Strawberry Banana Juice Cocktail, and Guava Berry Earthshine Juice Cocktail. A portion of the proceeds from each can sold went to Earth Day USA.

A ''Smoothie'' Return to Profitability in 1996

Hansen Natural lost nearly $3 million in 1994 and 1995 ($1.4 million in the latter). The debut of its Smoothie drinks late in 1995 carried high hopes. They proved to be a lifesaver. In their first nine months on the shelves, the Smoothie line brought in one-third of the company's revenues; one in every five cases sold contained Smoothies. Hansen Natural was able to report income of $357,000 in 1996.

Smoothies were available in 11.5-ounce cans and 11.5-ounce glass bottles. Although inspired by the smoothies found in fresh juice bars, Hansen's were not formulated as thick so that they could be bottled. Some smoothies had herbal additives ginseng and taurine, a meat-derived amino acid featured in many Asian ''energy'' drinks. Radically redesigned packaging helped Hansen's products stand out on store shelves. Smoothies were sold in distinctive fluted bottles.

The smoothies were more than a new product. They signaled a new innovative spirit at the company, Sacks told the *Business Press/California*. Previous national product launches had failed since they were too similar to what Snapple already had in stores—that is, iced tea, lemonade, and juice cocktails.

Another shot in the arm, Hansen's ''functionals'' came out in early 1997. This category was defined as drinks bought primarily for health benefits. They typically included extra vitamins. This trend had already been established in Europe, where they first caught the attention of Sacks. Similar, often syrupy, concoctions had been popular in Asia for more than 30 years and constituted a $3 billion market there.

Hansen's energy drinks were lightly carbonated. They were packaged in skinny 8.2-ounce cans, offering a more manageable serving for an energy drink. Each can retailed for about $2, whereas sodas cost 60 cents. They offered ''an immediate boost whenever you need it the most.'' Part of the pitch was naming the drinks not for their flavoring, but for the benefits they touted. An antioxidant (''anti-ox'') variety fought aging. Yet another pitched ''stamina.'' Finally, ''D-Stress'' was intended to enable the drinker to relax.

Some wondered whether the U.S. Food and Drug Administration would eventually regulate this category more strictly, but since the drinks were marketed as food, not as drugs promising any specific medicinal benefits, they fell out of that agency's purview. Hansen labeled the amounts of different herbs and additives in its drinks to enhance its credibility and to advise people with allergies. Although the company always had avoided adding caffeine to its drinks, and even formulated its iced tea to be decaffeinated, it was added to some of the functional drinks for the purposes of stimulating metabolism.

Bullfighting in the Late 1990s

Hansen had ventured into Great Britain in 1994, but found the market unwelcoming. It also failed to differentiate its products sufficiently. Its subsidiary there, Hansen Beverage Company (UK) Limited, stopped operating at the end of 1997. Back home, Hansen faced some competition on its own turf from Red Bull, an Austrian company that virtually owned the $500 million European market for functional drinks. Speaking to a local newspaper, Sacks characterized Red Bull as a one-product company.

Another advantage credited to Hansen was that its drinks tasted comparatively good. The company also had an established distribution network. Hansen pitched its functional drinks heavily, giving out free samples and setting up literature centers in grocery stores. Convenience stores and liquor stores were among the first to sell the new beverage, but they were soon joined by a variety of retailers. The ''new'' Hansen received much praise

<table>
<tr><td colspan="2">**Key Dates:**</td></tr>
<tr><td>**1935:**</td><td>Hubert Hansen and sons begin selling juice in Los Angeles.</td></tr>
<tr><td>**1977:**</td><td>The founder's grandson, Tim Hansen, establishes the fast-growing Hansen Foods, Inc.</td></tr>
<tr><td>**1988:**</td><td>Hansen Foods succumbs to debt load in Chapter 11.</td></tr>
<tr><td>**1992:**</td><td>Rodney Sacks and others acquire the company, and list Hansen Natural Corporation on the NASDAQ.</td></tr>
<tr><td>**1996:**</td><td>After two years of losses, the company again posts a profit.</td></tr>
<tr><td>**1997:**</td><td>The ''functionals'' line energizes Hansen's sales and share price.</td></tr>
<tr><td>**1998:**</td><td>The company relocates to Corona, California, from Anaheim.</td></tr>
<tr><td>**2000:**</td><td>Blue Sky Natural Beverage Co. is acquired.</td></tr>
<tr><td>**2002:**</td><td>Monster, Hansen's new energy drink, is launched.</td></tr>
<tr><td>**2004:**</td><td>Sales have more than doubled in two years, reaching $180 million.</td></tr>
</table>

from analysts for finding its own niche on the ''cutting edge'' rather than competing directly with the larger players.

In 1997, three-quarters of the company's sales came from California. The success of the functionals line helped Hansen sell more of its other products out of state. Earnings were $1.3 million on revenues of $43 million. The next year, functional drinks accounted for a quarter of Hansen's sales of $54 million, and the company's earnings doubled. Within a year of the introduction of the functionals line, the company's share price nearly quadrupled, to $6. The nutrient-enhanced beverage category of New Age drinks increased more than fourfold in 1998.

Hansen Natural relocated from Anaheim to Corona, California in January 1998. Its headquarters and warehouse shared a 65,000-square-foot building. It was developing the DynaJuice blended fruit drink, which contained 15 vitamins and minerals. This was first in a line of ''Healthy Start'' products for supermarket chains.

In April 1999, Brio Industries Inc. of British Columbia agreed to market Hansen's products throughout Canada. More than 18,000 venues were to be offered opportunities to sell the drinks. Because of the vastness of territory and its lack of name recognition up north, Hansen planned to introduce its products gradually there. The company had worked previously with a small Toronto-based distributor. As Canadian law forbade adding any type of vitamins to drinks, some reformulations were in order.

Revenues were expected to reach $64 million in 1999. Hansen had signed distribution agreements with Dr. Pepper and 7-Up and secured a national product introduction through 7-Eleven convenience stores. The company was planning to bring out a nutritional boxed drink for children as well as a ''super smoothie.'' Also forthcoming were Signature Soda gourmet carbonated drinks made with cane sugar and clover honey. Sacks sought to differentiate the brand on nutrition, not taste. ''What we're trying to do is sell people something that's honest—something that will do something for their bodies,'' he told one California business journal.

Success in the New Millennium

Hansen Natural experienced marked success during the early years of the new millennium. The company bolstered its holdings with two major purchases and also launched a new product that would dramatically increase its revenues. On the acquisition front, the company acquired Blue Sky Natural Beverage Company in 2000. Founded in 1980, the Santa Fe, New Mexico-based company sold nearly $6.5 million of natural soda in 1999. Hansen then added the Junior Juice brand to its arsenal in 2001.

Its most significant move, however, was the launch of its Monster energy drink in 2002. The company spent heavily to market the drink—nearly $1 million a year—in an attempt to pull market share away from competitor Red Bull. With a tagline of ''Unleash the Beast,'' the drink was a departure from the company's natural offerings. Monster contained high levels of caffeine and sugar and was sold in large black cans with neon claw marks. The product secured several extreme-sport sponsorships, enabling it to capture 18 percent of the $2 billion a year energy drink market. Red Bull continued to dominate with a 50 percent market share, but Hansen's energy drink sales grew by 162 percent in 2004, which was more than three times the rate of Red Bull.

In just two years, sales more than doubled to $180 million and net income skyrocketed to $20.4 million. The company's stock had traded as high as $108 per share, up from $4 in 2002. Hansen's recent success had catapulted it into the upper echelon of small business. In fact, during 2005 the company was positioned at the top of the *Forbes* list of the 200 Best Small Companies in the United States, a ranking based on several criteria, including growth over the past five years, recent sales, net income, stock price, price-to-earnings ratio, and market value.

With new competitors, including PepsiCo and Coca-Cola, entering the energy drink scene, Hansen was forced to stay on top of its game to maintain its sales growth. As such, Hansen bolstered its energy drink line by adding the Joker and Rumba energy drinks to its lineup, as well as Monster Assault, which was found on store shelves with the words ''declare war on the ordinary'' printed on a black and gray can.

Despite the significant growth of the energy drinks segment, an August 2005 *Barron's* article claimed, ''Energy drinks could well prove to be a passing fad.'' With this category accounting for nearly 70 percent of Hansen's sales, the company was indeed subject to changes in consumer demands. Nevertheless, Hansen Natural was confident the company was on track for success in the years to come.

Principal Subsidiaries

Hansen Beverage Company; HEB.

Principal Competitors

Cadbury Schweppes plc; Ferolito, Vultaggio & Sons; PepsiCo, Inc.; Coca-Cola Inc.

Further Reading

Ascenzi, Joseph, ''Hansen Inks Deal to Pop into Canada,'' *Business Press/California,* April 26, 1999, p. 1.

——, "Hansen Natural Squeezes Profits from Fruit-Based Health Drinks," *Business Press/California,* June 22, 1998, p. 17.

Berkman, Leslie, "Pick-Me-Up for the Bottom Line: Beverages That Claim To Energize (or Tranquilize) the Drinker Have Boosted Sales and Profits at Hansen Natural of Corona," *Press-Enterprise,* September 6, 1998, p. H1.

"Corona, California Beverage Maker Aims To Take 'Energy' Drinks Nationwide," *Press-Enterprise,* September 6, 1998.

"Drinking to Your Health—Literally," *Convenience Store News,* July 12, 1999.

"Hansen Hoping for a Smoothie Ride," *Orange County Register,* May 5, 1996.

Herrera, Paul, "Corona Firm Tops Forbes List," *Knight Ridder Tribune Business News,* October 15, 2005, p. 1.

Jabbonsky, Larry, "What the Heck Is a New Age Beverage?," *Beverage World,* September 1991, p. 42.

Johnson, Greg, "Juice or Soda, Company's Assets Increasingly Liquid," *Los Angeles Times,* Bus. Sec., June 1, 1993, p. D8.

——, "Liquid Assets: Hansen Natural Corp. in Anaheim Seeks To Expand Its Market," *Los Angeles Times,* Bus. Sec., May 28, 1993, p. D1.

Khermouch, Gerry, and Theresa Howard, "Herbal Elixirs Creating a Buzz, But May Also Awaken Feds, Execs Worry," *Brandweek,* November 2, 1998, pp. 8–9.

McKay, Betsy, "The Organic Myth," *Wall Street Journal,* December 26, 2002, p. A9.

Palmeri, Christopher, "Hansen Natural," *Business Week,* June 6, 2005, p. 74.

Sfiligoj, Eric, "Hansen's Branches Out Beyond California by Mixing Its Packages To Match All Tastes," *Beverage World,* September 30, 1993, p. 18.

——, "It's Bad to Be a Fad, Figures Taber, So Hansen's Is No Age, Not New Age," *Beverage World,* December 31, 1994, p. 1.

——, "Rail-ly Quick Change," *Beverage World,* October 1993, p. 80.

Tan, Kopin, "Buzzed to the Max: Why This Drink Is Scary," *Barron's,* August 1, 2005, pg. 20.

Trager, Cara, "Stirring Up Soft Drinks," *Beverage World,* September 1991, p. 48.

—Frederick C. Ingram
—update: Christina M. Stansell

Henry Boot

Henry Boot plc

Banner Cross Hall
Sheffield
United Kingdom
Telephone: +44 0114 255 5444
Fax: +44 0114 258 5548
Web site: http://www.henryboot.co.uk

Public Company
Incorporated: 1886
Employees: 462
Sales: £84.2 million ($156.30 million) (2004)
Stock Exchanges: London
Ticker Symbol: BHY
NAIC: 236220 Commercial and Institutional Building
Construction; 236115 New Single-Family Housing
Construction (Except Operative Builders); 236116
New Multi-Family Housing Construction (Except
Operative Builders); 236117 New Housing Operative
Builders; 236210 Industrial Building Construction;
237110 Water and Sewer Line and Related Structures
Construction; 237210 Land Subdivision; 237310
Highway, Street, and Bridge Construction; 237990
Other Heavy and Civil Engineering Construction;
532120 Truck, Utility Trailer and RV (Recreational
Vehicle) Rental and Leasing; 532412 Construction,
Mining and Forestry Machinery and Equipment
Rental and Leasing; 611513 Apprenticeship Training

Henry Boot plc is one of the United Kingdom's oldest and most well-known construction firms—in part because of the company participation in building the famed Pinewood Film Studios in Buckinghamshire. Once one of England's top home-builders, Boot has refocused itself for the new century along two primary lines of operation: property development and land management, the group's largest division, through subsidiaries Henry Boot Developments and Hallam Land Management; and commercial and industrial construction, through Henry Boot Construction UK. The company sold off its homebuilding division and other noncore operations in a major restructuring completed in 2004. Boot's property development business operates on a national scope, with regional offices in Sheffield, Manchester, London, Bristol, and Glasgow. Boot's construction wing focuses on England's northern regions, and targets contracts including prisons, schools, hospitals, and road-building. This latter activity includes the group's participation in the Road Link (A69) Holdings consortium. The company also operates a plant hire subsidiary, Banner Plant Ltd. The founding Boot family remains active in the company, with E.J. Boot serving as group managing director into the mid-2000s. The company is listed on the London Stock Exchange. In 2004, turnover topped £84 million ($156 million).

Pushcart Beginnings in the 1880s

Henry Boot founded his own building business in 1886 in Sheffield, in the north of England. Boot, who was 35 years old at the time, started out in business with a simple pushcart. The building market, especially the homebuilding market, had been expanding rapidly in the late 19th century. The rapid industrialization of the company, especially in major northern cities such as Sheffield, stimulated demand for housing from the fast-growing army of workers, as well as the rising middle class. At the same time, the building society movement had become a national phenomenon. Formed expressly to assist society members in building their own homes, building societies benefited from a series of legislation, providing a more stable financial base for their operations. In the late 19th century, the majority of building societies were of the ''permanent'' type, and rather than contributing directly to members' homebuilding projects, the societies had begun issuing mortgages. The availability of mortgages placed home construction within the reach of a far larger population than ever before.

Boot profited from the buoyant market, expanding his business from a one-man affair to become a major local building group. Later joined by son Charles Boot—leading to the adoption of Henry Boot & Sons as the company's name—Boot built up a stable of some 20 horses and carts into the 20th century. By the outbreak of World War I, the company had begun the shift to motorized transport, and already counted six trucks in 1914. By the end of the war, the company had more or less retired its horse-drawn fleet.

Company Perspectives:

Henry Boot is committed to the continuous review and improvement of its group operations and its client focus strategy. Within this culture are included the principal areas of quality assurance, safety, environmental responsibility, information technology and human resource development.

Charles Boot took over the direction of the company in the early part of the century and led it on an even greater expansion. (Henry Boot died in 1931.) The company had taken an early interest in competing for public housing as well as public works and infrastructure projects, including road-building, bridge-building, and the like. The company also contributed greatly to the British war effort, competing for and winning a large number of construction contracts for the military. Examples of the group's projects during the war included a seaplane base in Calshot, an airport in Manston, the American Army Rest Camp and Hospital in Southampton, and the Chepstow military Hospital. The company distinguished itself by its ability to complete its projects quickly, and within the space of a single year built more than 1,000 buildings for the military, as well as 50 miles of roads and sewers.

International Group in the 1920s

By then, too, Boot had expanded its range of operations to include joinery, plumbing, and painting services. The company also entered the manufacture and distribution of building materials for the general construction market. This activity enabled the company to reduce its own cost of materials, while ensuring their supply for the group's ongoing construction projects, even into the difficult years of the late 1920s and early 1930s. The production and sale of building materials also helped protect the company from cyclical downturns in the construction industry.

The interwar period saw Boot emerge as a top British and European construction company. The company's first move into the international market came soon after the war, when the French government turned to England for assistance in rebuilding its devastated towns and villages. Boot set up its own office in Paris and competed successfully for a large number of contracts. Boot quickly sought expansion on a European scale. The company went public in 1920 and began competing for contracts across Europe. Boot participated in an impressive number of large-scale infrastructure projects, including the building of harbors, subways, and water, sewage, and drainage systems.

The company set up additional offices in Barcelona, Spain and in Athens, Greece. The latter office oversaw a massive £10 million project (at the time, one of the largest in Europe) involved in modernizing Athens' infrastructure, as well as installing drainage and irrigation systems in a massive land reclamation project for agricultural use. Launched in 1927, the project, which was temporarily suspended after the German occupation of Greece during World War II, was completed only in 1952.

Boot also enjoyed other triumphs in the prewar period. In 1936, the company became one of the driving forces behind the construction of Pinewood Studios—based on a design developed by Charles Boot himself—in an effort to challenge the growing dominance of the Hollywood production studios. Built on a 100-acre site in Buckinghamshire, Pinewood Studios provided the base for the British film industry's emergence as one of the world's film centers.

Meanwhile, Boot's domestic homebuilding construction enjoyed an unprecedented boom period. By the outbreak of World War II, the company had completed some 80,000 homes, including more than 50,000 for England's local building authorities.

Boot once again turned its construction and engineering operations to work for the British military effort. Among the group's projects during the war years was its participation in the construction of the harbors used for the launch of the D-Day invasion in 1944. Following the war, the company became a major partner for the United Kingdom's steel and coal industries, and also developed a specialty in railroad engineering and construction. The company continued as manufacturer, establishing a dedicated joinery operation, while its homebuilding operations continued to flourish. Joining the company, and later becoming its head, was Hamer Boot.

The boom years of the British economy during the 1950s and 1960s gave way to a slowdown in the mid-1970s. Boot responded by turning its attention toward its international growth. For this, the company departed from its European base to begin competing for projects elsewhere in the world. The company launched operations in Hong Kong in 1976, where the group became responsible for the construction of the city's Mass Transit Railway System, as well as for building the Kowloon-Canton railroad extension. Elsewhere in the Asian region, the company took on a £120 million railway project in Singapore, and also extended its operations to Malaysia. Through the end of the 1970s and into the 1980s, Boot added projects in Saudi Arabia and Jordan, as well as in Nigeria.

Refocused for the New Century

The economic slowdown of the 1970s, and the United Kingdom's lapse into an extended recession, caught up to Boot in the early 1980s. With its domestic market shrinking, the company suffered a number of setbacks internationally as well. The company's profit began to decline, and Boot was frustrated in efforts to boost its foreign operations to compensate. As a result, the company was forced to restructure its operations for the first time. This process, led by Hamer Boot's son E.J. (Jamie) Boot, led to the company's exit from its joinery business in 1986. Two years later, the company sold off its railroad engineering operation as well.

Continued difficulties in the late 1980s and early 1990s encouraged Boot to streamline its operations still further. In particular, the company abandoned its international operations to return its focus wholly on the domestic British market. The newest restructuring effort enabled the company to restore its profit growth through most of the 1990s. Yet the primary motor for the company's growth during this period and into the beginning of the 2000s was its young property development business.

Key Dates:

1886: Henry Boot starts his own building business with a single pushcart in Sheffield.

1920: Boot goes public and opens an office in Paris, launching construction projects on the European continent.

1926: Boot establishes a dedicated joinery manufacture operation.

1936: Charles Boot, son of Henry Boot, designs Pinewood Studios, built by the company.

1950s: Railroad engineering operations, which become a company specialty, are established.

1975: Operations are expanded to the Far East, with a contract to build a Mass Transit System for the city of Hong Kong.

1986: The company restructures its operations, selling off the joinery business.

1988: The company sells off the railroad engineering operations.

1990s: The company begins property development and land management operations.

2002: The company engages in a new restructuring to refocus on property development and land management, and sells off most of the construction division.

2003: The company sells off the homebuilding division to William Bowden.

2005: Profits grow as the restructuring is completed.

Boot continued to win high-profile projects into the late 1990s, such as the construction of a new building for the Birmingham Symphony Orchestra, completed in 1999. The slackening of the British construction market again in the late 1990s, a result in part of the tightening of the government's planning approval process, intensified competition in the market and brought a drop in Boot's own profit growth.

The new market situation forced Boot to review its operations once again, and in 2002 the company launched its latest round of restructuring. As part of that process, the company decided to sell off the higher-risk, but higher-margin divisions of its construction operations, in a management buyout completed that year. In 2003, Boot's restructuring continued with the sale of its homebuilding division to William Bowden for £48 million.

By the end of 2004, Boot's profile had changed rather dramatically. Although the company maintained a construction division, these operations had been greatly reduced, and fo-

cused on the lower-risk commercial and industrial markets. Instead, Boot's center of gravity had shifted firmly to its property development and land management arm, which had played a minor role in the group's operations just a decade earlier. Although the company's sales had shrunk back, from more than £110 million in 2003 to slightly more than £84 million in 2004, the group's profits rebounded strongly, representing some 19 percent of revenues.

The "new-look" Henry Boot plc returned to revenue growth by 2005. The company's prospects for the immediate future appeared bright as well, aided by a number of prominent property developments, such as the 350,000-square-foot Ayr Central complex in Ayr. That structure, expected to be opened in March 2006, was already leased at more than 70 percent by mid-2005. After nearly 120 years in operation, Henry Boot remained a prominent name in the United Kingdom's building market.

Principal Subsidiaries

Banner Plant Ltd.; Hallam Land Management Ltd.; Henry Boot Construction (UK) Ltd.; Henry Boot Developments Ltd.

Principal Competitors

Taysec Construction Ltd.; AMEC plc; Barratt Developments plc; Persimmon plc.

Further Reading

Cole, Cheryl, "Henry Boot Forced to Sell Off Division," *Birmingham Post,* April 2, 2003, p. 19.

Creasey, Simon, "Boot's New Polish," *Property Week,* September 12, 2003, p. 109.

Faint, Martin, "Boot's Future Is Bright," *Birmingham Post,* April 7, 2005, p. 19.

"Henry Boot Developments Will Open Ayr Central in Kyle Street, Ayr, in March, Anchored by an 80,000 sq ft (7,432 sq m) Debenhams," *Property Week,* August 12, 2005, p. 65.

"Henry Boot Kick-Starts Profit After Reshuffle," *Contract Journal,* April 13, 2005.

Leitch, John, "Henry Boot Looks to Sell Housebuilding Division," *Contract Journal,* February 12, 2003, p. 3.

"New-Look Henry Boot Unveils 'Robust' Interim Performance," *Contract Journal,* September 29, 2004, p. 10.

"Putting the Boot In," *Property Week,* October 10, 2003, p. 118.

"Restructure Results in Boost for Henry Boot," *Contract Journal,* September 28, 2005, p. 12.

"The Signs Still Looking Good for Henry Boot," *Yorkshire Post,* September 22, 2005.

—M.L. Cohen

Home Box Office Inc.

1100 Avenue of the Americas
New York, New York 10036
U.S.A.
Telephone: (212) 512-1000
Fax: (212) 512-1182
Web site: http://www.hbo.com

Wholly Owned Subsidiary of Time Warner Inc.
Incorporated: 1972
Employees: 2,000
Sales: $3 billion (2004)
NAIC: 513210 Cable Networks; 512110 Motion Picture
& Video Production

Home Box Office Inc. is the leading pay-TV network in the United States. With both HBO and Cinemax in its coffers, the company has a subscriber base of approximately 39 million and sales of more than $3 billion. As a subsidiary of Time Warner Inc., HBO's programming includes original series, HBO Films presentations, Hollywood movies, documentaries, concerts, and championship boxing. More than 16 million subscribers in 50 countries outside the United States watch HBO programming, including the hit series *The Sopranos, Curb Your Enthusiasm,* and *Entourage.*

1970s Formation

Home Box Office was founded by Time Inc. in 1972 to offer cable television service. As a subsidiary of Time, HBO bought the rights to recent films and transmitted them to local systems via satellite and microwave relays. Its service was distributed by the local cable operators, typically costing subscribers $6 a month, of which HBO received $3.50. HBO management initially regarded the company as an editorial marketer, selling its programming the way Time sold magazines.

HBO grew slowly in its first years, as the nascent cable industry struggled to get off the ground. Cable was hampered by market fragmentation, lack of infrastructure, and tough federal regulations, some of them sponsored by the major television networks, which feared that cable could eventually steal much of their audience and revenue.

During the mid-1970s the cable industry laid the groundwork for rapid growth: It expanded its infrastructure through such populous areas as New York City and the suburbs of Boston, won a series of court victories that removed many federal restrictions, and won rate increases from local governments. Pay-TV customers, those buying additional cable services such as HBO, grew from 50,000 in 1974 to about 1.5 million in 1978. HBO won greater latitude in pursuing customers in 1977 when a federal ruling lifted restrictions on the choice of movies and sports available on pay-TV. HBO quickly became one of the primary engines driving the growth of the cable industry. Cable systems operators hooked up thousands of people for basic services who were primarily interested in getting HBO.

HBO made its first profit in 1977. It lost tens of thousands of customers in 1978, however, as a result of a move by its chief rival, Showtime, which was challenging HBO head-on for the cable film audience. During this time, Showtime's parent, Viacom, had struck a deal with Teleprompter, the largest cable systems operator in the United States, which resulted in Teleprompter's customers receiving Showtime instead of HBO.

Nevertheless, HBO worked diligently on its programming, lining up enough films to make it the premiere pay-TV outlet for commercial films. It also began its *On Location* comedy series and *The Young Comedians Show,* one of the first television forums for comedians such as Robin Williams and Paul Ruebens (Pee-Wee Herman).

In 1978 Time spent $145 million to buy American Television & Communications Corp., then the second largest cable systems operator in the United States, hoping a large number of its 675,000 customers would subscribe to HBO. HBO continued to expand, and as it did it was able to pay higher prices per film than its competitors, winning better films and more subscribers. In fact, its financial resources allowed it to purchase a block of 40 MGM/United Artists films all at once, paying about $35 million. HBO also began investing in the preproduction financing of movies in exchange for exclusive pay-TV rights. This prebuying was risky; HBO was paying in advance for the rights

Company Perspectives:

Home Box Office continues its strategy of investing in original programming, interweaving it with theatrical films from its existing long-term studio output agreements. It aims to increase subscription revenues as well as maximizing content sales, including syndication and DVDs.

to movies that might prove unpopular. Moreover, the practice angered movie studios, which felt that HBO was intruding on their turf, and some of them began looking for a way into the cable TV industry. Some studios warned that HBO would drive many film studios out of business and control the film industry. Although such fears eventually proved unfounded, they demonstrated the depth of concern attached to a new medium whose ultimate potential remained a mystery.

In 1980 HBO introduced a second channel called Cinemax. This channel was priced lower than HBO and was geared to compete with Viacom's Showtime. Viacom would later charge that Cinemax was priced below cost as a way to drive Showtime out of business.

The Competitive 1980s

By 1982 HBO had 9.8 million subscribers, nearly 50 percent of all pay-TV subscribers, and earned $100 million on sales of $440 million. In fact, HBO was about three times as big as its nearest competitor, Showtime. This size advantage contributed to HBO's bottom line. For example, it paid about $1.4 million for the hit film *Raging Bull,* or about 15 cents per subscriber. Although Showtime paid less for the film, $1 million, that figure worked out to more than 30 cents per subscriber. When *Star Wars* went on the block in 1982, HBO matched a Showtime offer of $1 per subscriber, but insisted on price concessions on less popular films made by Twentieth-Century Fox.

At the end of 1982 HBO worked out a deal with Columbia Pictures and CBS to create Tri-Star Pictures, the first major new U.S. film studio in 40 years. Each company was to contribute up to $100 million to the venture, and HBO received the pay-TV rights. By 1983 HBO, with 13.4 million subscribers, was producing made-for-television movies and working on its own original comedy programs. While some industry observers wondered if HBO would become the fourth major noncable television network, the growth of the cable industry as a whole slowed dramatically beginning in 1984. Part of the cause was lingering infrastructure problems. New cable systems had not yet been built in major markets such as Chicago, Philadelphia, Detroit, and Baltimore. Other causes for the cable slowdown were rising cable rates at a time when more and more consumers owned videocassette recorders and could rent their own films. Finally, HBO had also become complacent in negotiating contracts, while competitors moved quickly. As a result, HBO's share of the pay-TV market slipped from 50.4 percent in June 1983 to 48.1 percent in June 1984, while its profit margins began eroding.

Parent company Time Inc. responded by forcing out HBO chairman Frank J. Biondi, replacing him with Michael J. Fuchs. Fuchs cut HBO's staff by 125 employees and embarked on a

$20 million advertising campaign, overseen by the New York firm Batten Barton Durstine & Osborn, to polish HBO's image. He also renegotiated contracts with Columbia Pictures and Tri-Star for the broadcasting of films and cut expense accounts and other costs.

As a result of the contract renegotiations, HBO gave up exclusive rights to many films. Rival Showtime, meanwhile, was trumpeting its new policy of showing films exclusively or not showing them at all. Previously, both the two firms had shown some films exclusively, but shared many others. As a result of its new policy, Showtime won exclusive rights to several popular films. HBO management was angered, feeling that they already had learned that exclusive rights cost more than they were worth and that Showtime's move had increased the prices of acquiring even limited rights. Showtime's strategy also pushed HBO into negotiating for exclusive rights for more films than it otherwise would have done. Some industry analysts felt that the price of buying films for pay-TV should be decreasing, since the popularity of videocassette recorders had lowered their worth.

Despite the cable television slump, HBO had 14.6 million subscribers in 1985 and sales of about $800 million. Early the following year it began to scramble the signals it used to broadcast its programming to cable-system operators. Until then anyone with a satellite dish could tune in HBO for free.

Continuing to stock its film library, HBO bought the rights to 125 Warner Brothers films for five years for $600 million in 1986, also buying the rights to 72 films by MGM/UA Entertainment for four years. The following year, it bought the rights to 85 Paramount Pictures films over a five-year period.

In 1989 Viacom filed a $2.4 billion antitrust lawsuit against HBO. Viacom's Showtime subsidiary alleged that HBO was trying to put it out of business by intimidating cable systems that carried Showtime, as well as by trying to corner the market on Hollywood films to prevent rivals from showing any. The suit attracted wide attention, generating negative publicity for the cable industry at a time when the U.S. Congress was considering the re-regulation of cable. Part of the reason the antitrust charges attracted so much attention was because they were being delivered by former top HBO employees; Frank J. Biondi had gone on to become Viacom's president and chief executive officer, while Showtime's president, Winston H. Cox, was also a former HBO executive. The lawsuit would not be settled until the early 1990s.

In the meantime, hoping to branch out, HBO announced plans for a 24-hour all-comedy channel. Stand-up comedy was experiencing a popularity boom in the United States, and polls of cable subscribers showed enthusiasm for the idea. HBO's The Comedy Channel began with six million subscribers in November 1989, though industry analysts felt it would need 20 million to attract enough advertising to survive. Some critics offered harsh appraisals of The Comedy Channel's fare, citing in particular the way HBO strung together excerpts from stand-up routines, sitcoms, and movie clips rather than longer, more substantial comedic pieces, and many cable operators were resistant to offering Comedy Channel at all. HBO moved quickly to entice them into buying ownership stakes as incen-

Key Dates:
1972: Time Inc. creates HBO.
1980: HBO introduces a second channel called Cinemax.
1982: HBO works out a deal with Columbia Pictures and CBS to create Tri-Star Pictures, the first major new U.S. film studio in 40 years.
1989: Viacom files a $2.4 billion antitrust lawsuit against HBO.
1990: HBO and Viacom merge The Comedy Channel and HA! to form the Comedy Central channel.
1991: The company announces that it will convert HBO and Cinemax to multichannel services.
1992: The Viacom lawsuit is settled out of court.
1997: HBO receives 90 nominations for Emmys—the first time a cable network has garnered more nominations than any broadcast network.
1999: *The Sopranos* debuts.
2002: Chris Albrecht is named chairman and CEO.
2004: HBO wins a record 32 Emmy awards.

tive to get the new channel wider availability. Comedy Channel suffered another setback when Viacom's HA! began broadcasting old sitcoms in their entirety, eschewing Comedy Channel's practice of showing excerpts. Most industry analysts believed that only one of the channels would survive. Many cable operators did not sign up for either, waiting to see which would get more support.

HBO invested heavily in advertising to win subscribers to its new and existing services, spending about $38 million in 1990 alone. Both Comedy Channel and HA! were struggling, however, and in a surprise move, HBO and Viacom agreed to merge them into Comedy Central late in 1990. This shared channel, Comedy Central, would eventually go on to experience great success, producing several popular original comedy shows of its own.

HBO's legal challenges were not over, however. During this time, Broadcast Music Incorporated (BMI), a performance-rights society, sued HBO over the rates it was paying for the use of BMI-protected music. The suit was settled in January 1991 when HBO agreed to raise the rate it paid for its blanket license to 15 cents per subscriber per year, up from 12 cents.

One of the most common complaints subscribers had about pay-TV channels was that they all tended to show the same films at the same time; once a person had seen the film, there was nothing on TV to watch. As the cancellation rate for HBO was about 4 percent a month, or about 850,000 of its 17 million subscribers per year, this lack of options was believed to be an important factor. To hang on to subscribers, HBO announced in 1991 that it would convert HBO and Cinemax to multichannel services. Each network would broadcast different programming simultaneously on three different channels. Many cable systems had no extra channels to offer, but HBO management hoped new technologies would expand the number of channels available. Because the company had to wait for fiber-optic lines to be installed and data-compression techniques to become more widely available, however, some industry observers estimated

that it would be three to five years before these multiple channels were widely available.

In August 1992 the Viacom suit was finally settled out of court, having cost both sides tens of millions of dollars in legal fees. Time Warner, HBO's parent company, agreed to pay Viacom $75 million and to buy a Viacom cable system in Milwaukee for $95 million, $10 million more than it was worth at the time, according to the *Wall Street Journal.* Time Warner agreed to more widely distribute Showtime and The Movie Channel on Time Warner's cable systems, the second largest in the United States. The two sides also agreed to a joint marketing campaign to try to revive the image of cable, which was again in a slump; HBO had lost about 300,000 subscribers in 1991, leaving it with a total of 17.3 million.

In the late 1980s and early 1990s many analysts predicted the end of pay-TV. Competition from advertiser-supported basic cable channels and pay-per-view options threatened an HBO already weakened by the popularity of home video rentals. HBO, however, fought back on several fronts. CEO Michael Fuchs began an aggressive marketing campaign and continued to expand the availability of multiplexing around the country. He expanded the company's ventures outside its traditional enterprises, taking on sports licensing, such as the licensing of the World Cup logo. In addition, HBO moved into foreign pay TV markets and began selling original HBO productions for foreign theatrical and home video distribution.

An Early 1990s Turnaround

Several of these strategies soon showed results for HBO. The company's foreign pay TV ventures proved highly successful and helped maintain profits. Foreign distributions were booming by the mid-1990s. Outside ventures, such as sports licensing, grew quickly, accounting for 28 percent of revenues in 1993, up from 1 percent in 1982. On the home front, aggressive marketing and multiplexing were apparently behind the mild boost in subscribership in 1992. Membership continued to rise; in 1993 the subscriber base increased by one million to 24.7 million.

Competition for exclusive rights to Hollywood films subsided in the early 1990s, bringing down licensing costs by 20 percent. The end of the bidding wars helped raise HBO's profits: In 1992 operating profits were up by 10 percent, to $215 million, and they rose the next year as well, to $230 million. The tides had begun to turn for HBO, which in 1993 provided 8 percent of Time Warner's pretax profit.

Having rebounded somewhat from its slump in the late 1980s, HBO needed to maintain its momentum. In 1994 Jolie Solomon of *Newsweek* assessed the situation, noting that CEO Fuchs "must stay ahead of the multimedia revolution, especially the technology that will create home-video jukeboxes. His strategy is to make HBO a powerful brand name, signaling high quality on the cutting edge." To that end, Fuchs upped the company's advertising and focused increasing amounts of HBO's time and budget on original productions, including movies, specials, and series. Because HBO did not need to attract and keep advertisers, it could take on subjects in its original productions that networks would not touch, such as *Barbarians at the Gate,* a 1993 movie critical of R.J.R. Nabisco.

Fuchs's competitive, aggressive, and some said antagonistic management style, however, was not popular among all board members and shareholders, and he was replaced as CEO in 1995 by Jeffrey L. Bewkes. Having served HBO for years as an executive, Bewkes moved into the top position smoothly. With a more cooperative managerial style, especially with fellow subsidiary Warner Brothers, Bewkes continued Fuchs's general strategy of creating original programming and promoting HBO as a high-quality brand. In fact, in 1997 he spent an impressive $25 million to promote that brand, a figure that did not include the advertising budget for specific programs.

The company's efforts at original programming gained momentum in the late 1990s. In 1997 HBO received 90 nominations for Emmys, marking the first time a cable network had garnered more nominations than any broadcast network. Moreover, HBO was only narrowly beaten by NBC for the most Emmy awards won. Praise from critics was on the rise as well, particularly for the channel's original series, such as the comedy *The Larry Sanders Show* and the drama *Oz*. In 1999, HBO inked a deal with Twentieth-Century Fox and secured exclusive rights to its films for another ten years.

By the late 1990s, HBO had held its own against those threats to pay-TV against which other top competitors were still struggling. The Starz! and Showtime movie networks were both trailing HBO with fewer than half their subscribers. The satellite market had matured by 1998, however, and HBO could no longer rely on that market boom for increasing its subscriber base. Thus, although HBO had long outlasted predictions of its demise, it still faced many challenges as it approached a new century.

Success in the New Millennium

HBO entered the new millennium on solid ground thanks to its original programming efforts. More than $1 billion was spent on its programming budget at this time, and nearly half of that was allocated toward original programming. This budget strategy had catapulted HBO well ahead of its competitors. In fact, over the past few years several HBO shows had exploded, reaching iconic status. The hit series, *The Sopranos,* was considered to be the most successful series in cable television history. Other shows, including *Sex and the City* and *Six Feet Under,* were also highly popular. HBO won 20 Primetime Emmy awards in 2000, and the company was adding new subscribers to its base at a steady clip. By now, HBO was seen in 90 percent of the United States' 27 million premium television households.

While HBO was cranking out popular shows and miniseries, including *Band of Brothers,* its parent company was working on a blockbuster deal of its own. In 2001, America Online joined forces with Time Warner in a hotly contested, highly publicized $106 billion mega-merger. The new company was named AOL Time Warner (Time Warner dropped AOL from its name in 2003).

In 2002, HBO chairman Bewkes was tapped to head up Time Warner along with Don Logan. HBO veteran Chris Albrecht was named his successor. HBO's good fortune continued under Albrecht's leadership. The company was one of the most profitable units in the Time Warner empire and in 2004

sales surpassed $3 billion for the first time. HBO hit a brief snag in 2003 when *Sopranos* lead actor James Gandolfini sued the company, attempting to break his contract. In a highly publicized battle, Albrecht threatened to pull *The Sopranos* off the air. In the end, Gandolfini returned to work during his contract negotiations and the show was broadcast as planned.

In 2003, HBO reigned above all other networks at the annual Emmy ceremony, receiving 18 awards. It won a record 32 Emmys the following year. The trend continued in 2005 when it took home 27 awards. Along with its lineup of original series, HBO's Film business segment continued to produce highly acclaimed original movies, including *My House in Umbria, The Life and Death of Peter Sellers,* and *Iron Jawed Angels.* In 2005, the company partnered with New Line Cinema to acquire Newmarket Entertainment's distribution business.

Several new shows were slated to debut in 2005, including *The Comeback, Rome,* and *Unscripted.* Cable channel A&E signed a contract with HBO that year, paying $2.5 million per episode to air *The Sopranos* starting in 2006. The company also partnered with the Public Broadcasting Service (PBS) in a deal that allowed PBS to air three original HBO films.

By now, HBO stood as the most-watched pay-service in the United States. It held an enviable position among its competitors but realized that fickle U.S. consumers could quickly change its fortunes. In the years to come, the company would have to create unique original programming to rival its hit shows like *Sex and the City* and *The Sopranos* (which was rumored to be ending in 2006/2007). HBO management was confident, however, that its strategy would continue to pay off and that its programming would entertain subscribers for years to come.

Principal Competitors

The NBC Television Network; Showtime Networks Inc.; Starz Entertainment Group LLC.

Further Reading

"AOL Time Warner: End of a New Era," *Wall Street Journal,* July 19, 2002.

Beatty, Sally, "HBO Marches into Battle," *Wall Street Journal,* July 18, 2001.

——, "Pay TV: Unconventional HBO Finds Its Own Success Is a Hard Act to Follow," *Wall Street Journal,* September 29, 2000.

Berger, Warren, "At 25, Excellence and Big Budgets for a Late Bloomer," *New York Times,* November 9, 1997.

Block, Alex Ben, "Shoot-Out Time in Pay TV," *Forbes,* September 22, 1986.

"Cable-TV Dangles New Lures," *Business Week,* December 1, 1973.

"Can a New Chief Change the Picture at HBO?," *Business Week,* October 29, 1984.

Carter, Bill, "HBO to Give 3 New Films for Viewing on Public TV," *New York Times,* January 10, 2005.

Cox, Meg, "Time Warner's HBO, Broadcast Music Settle Suit Over Performance Rights," *Wall Street Journal,* January 11, 1991.

Gubernick, Lisa, "Time Heals All," *Forbes,* May 23, 1994, p. 241.

"HBO's Boss of Bosses," *Broadcast,* July 4, 2003.

"How HBO Dominates Pay-TV," *Business Week,* September 20, 1982.

King, Thomas R., "HBO to Offer Multiple Choice for Tuning In," *Wall Street Journal,* May 9, 1991.

Kneale, Dennis, "HBO Vows to Stick with Comedy Channel and Seek Operators Willing to Buy Stake," *Wall Street Journal,* March 6, 1990.

Lindsey, Robert, "Home Box Office Moves in on Hollywood," *New York Times Magazine,* June 12, 1983.

"A New Shooter in Tinseltown," *Newsweek,* December 13, 1982.

"Pay-TV: Even HBO's Growth Is Slowing," *Business Week,* July 9, 1984.

"Pay-TV: Is It a Viable Alternative?," *Forbes,* May 1, 1978.

"Pay TV's Lazarus Act," *Forbes,* March 1, 1993, pp. 14–15.

"The Race to Dominate the Pay-TV Market," *Business Week,* October 2, 1978.

Roberts, Johnnie L., "Time Warner, Viacom Settle HBO Suit, Clearing a Cloud from Cable's Horizon," *Wall Street Journal,* August 21, 1992.

Solomon, Jolie, "What Michael Fuchs Wants You to Know," *Newsweek,* May 30, 1994, pp. 60–61.

Stevens, Elizabeth Lesly, "Call It Home Buzz Office," *Business Week,* December 8, 1997, pp. 77, 80.

Trachtenberg, Jeffrey A., "Changing Reels," *Forbes,* May 20, 1985.

——, "Mea Culpa, Mea Culpa," *Forbes,* December 16, 1985.

Waters, Harry F., "Can HBO Change the Show?," *Newsweek,* May 23, 1983.

——, "Talk About a Running Gag," *Newsweek,* May 29, 1989.

—Scott M. Lewis
—updates: Susan Windisch Brown,
Christina M. Stansell

Hubbell Inc.

584 Derby Milford Road
Orange, Connecticut 06477
U.S.A.
Telephone: (203) 799-4100
Fax: (203) 799-4205
Web site: http://www.hubbell.com

Public Company
Incorporated: 1905 as Harvey Hubbell Inc.
Employees: 10,600
Sales: $1.99 billion (2004)
Stock Exchanges: New York
Ticker Symbol: HUBB
NAIC: 335931 Current-Carrying Wiring Device
   Manufacturing; 351210 Residential Lighting Fixture
   Manufacturing

Hubbell Inc. produces electrical equipment for commercial, telecommunications, lighting, utility, industrial, and consumer markets. With manufacturing divisions and global subsidiaries in North America, Puerto Rico, Mexico, Italy, Switzerland, and the United Kingdom, Hubbell produces items such as lighting fixtures, outlet boxes, wire and cable, insulators and surge arrestors, and voice and digital signal processing components. For many decades, Hubbell maintained a modest and unassuming profile, manufacturing the important products invented by its founder, Harvey Hubbell II; one correspondent for *Forbes* admonished his readers in 1977 that "unless you are reading this on safari, there is probably a Harvey Hubbell invention within six feet of you right now." The company had remained strongly focused on such products until the 1960s, when it embarked on a diversification program. During the early years of the new millennium, Hubbell has been dedicated to the technology of generating, transmitting, and utilizing electrical energy.

The Early Years

Hubbell bears the name of inventor and businessman Harvey Hubbell II. Born in Connecticut in 1859, he graduated from high school and began working for companies that manufac-

tured marine engines and printing machinery. During this time, he accumulated several ideas for new inventions, and in 1888 he set out on his own, opening a small manufacturing facility in Bridgeport, Connecticut. Hubbell's first product was taken from his own patent for a paper roll holder with a toothed blade for use in stores that sold wrapping paper. This cutter stand became a tremendous success; it was a common feature of retail stores that used wrapping paper in the early 1900s and remained in wide use into the late 20th century.

Hubbell also designed and built a series of new and improved machine tools during his early years in business. In the early 1890s, he began to consider the opportunities presented by Edison's new electric light bulb, and the fruits of his work would secure both the future of his company and his place in history. On a visit to New York City, Hubbell happened upon a penny arcade, featuring several electrically operated games that, although popular with customers, caused maintenance headaches. Every day, the janitor had to detach each of the power supply wires for the games from separate terminals in the wall so that he could move them and sweep the floor underneath. After he was done, he faced the tedious task of reconnecting the wires, making sure that each one went into the proper terminal—the consequence of not doing so being a short circuit. Watching the janitor gave Hubbell the idea for an electrical plug in which the wires were permanently attached in their proper sequence, so that devices could be easily detached and reattached to their power sources. Hubbell built a prototype, which he tested with the help of the janitor, and later patented it. The two-pronged electrical plug that became standard for electrical appliances is a direct descendant of this innovation. In 1896 Hubbell patented a light bulb socket with an on/off pull chain, another invention in use to this day.

In 1901 Hubbell published a 12-page catalogue that listed 63 electrical products of his company's manufacture, and four years later he incorporated his enterprise as Harvey Hubbell, Inc. In 1909 the company began constructing a four-floor factory and office building that would become the first building in New England made of reinforced concrete.

As electricity became the power source of choice in the United States, Hubbell's company did its best to keep up. Its

---

Company Perspectives:

The Combination of these—commitment to the industry, diversification of product and market, a continuing tradition of quality, partnership with the independent electrical distributor, and the experience of accomplishment in research and development—have forged Hubbell Incorporated's exceptional records of growth. The same comprehensive corporate capability will expand Hubbell's growth in the commercial, telecommunications, lighting, utility, industrial, and consumer markets of the future.

1917 catalogue was 100 pages long and listed more than 1,000 electrical products, including 277 different types and sizes of light bulb sockets. One important product was a toggle light switch, which Hubbell had invented to replace the old two-button switch. A line of 288 heavy-duty ''Presturn'' products marked the company's entry into industrial electrical products. In the 1920s, the company produced a line of low-voltage devices for use by farmers who had not tapped into higher-voltage urban electrical grids. Also during this time, Hubbell developed a device that locked streetlamp and household light bulbs firmly in place, filling a need in cities where new trolley cars were producing vibrations that loosened bulbs and caused them to fall out of their sockets.

Harvey Hubbell died in 1927 and was succeeded as president of the company by his son, Harvey Hubbell III. The 26-year-old Hubbell had been trained as an electrical engineer and was already at work for the family firm. Under Harvey Hubbell III, the company went public in 1936, a timely move considering that, during the later years of the Great Depression, some employees occasionally had to accept company stock in lieu of pay. He also proved his business acumen by establishing a network of independent distributors to help market and disseminate the company's products, a system that would help offset the low profile that, traditionally, the company has kept.

During World War II, much of the company's capacity was devoted to manufacturing electrical components for the military, including battery-charging systems for the M-4 Sherman tank. Hubbell also opened a plant in Lexington, Kentucky, in part to meet demand for its military products and also because its original factory in Connecticut was considered vulnerable to air attack.

Postwar Expansion and Diversification

After the war, Harvey Hubbell Inc. shifted its focus back to making products for the civilian economy. It custom designed and produced electrical devices for the luxury ocean liner United States, which was launched in 1952 and required electrical wiring that would resist the corrosive effects of salt air while fitting into narrow stateroom partitions. At the end of the 1950s, the company began to ponder the benefits of diversification. Until that point, Hubbell had been a conservative company with a reputation for making high-quality products that sold for higher-than-average prices. Its narrow range of products, however, limited opportunities for growth and left it vulnerable to

cyclical ups and downs. Even with its strong desire to diversify, however, Hubbell chose its targets carefully and did not stray far from its field of expertise. In 1962 it acquired Kellems, a Connecticut-based manufacturer of mesh grips, cord connectors, and wire management products. In 1963 it bought Grelco, an English company that made industrial controls, the California-based Shalda Lighting, and the Chicago-based Ralco Manufacturing. Hubbell later merged Grelco into its British subsidiary, Harvey Hubbell Ltd. In 1966 Hubbell purchased Euclid Electric, which it later renamed Hubbell Industrial Controls. The following year, Harvey Hubbell Ltd. acquired Watford Electric & Manufacturing, solidifying its presence as a producer of industrial controls in Great Britain.

Continued Growth in the 1970s and 1980s

Harvey Hubbell III died in 1968 and was succeeded as CEO by George Weppler, who became the first non-Hubbell to run the company in its 80 years of existence. Under Weppler, the pace of Hubbell's acquisition campaign was maintained. In 1969 the company acquired Kerite, a Connecticut-based manufacturer of high-voltage electrical cables used mainly by utility companies and railroads. The next year, it acquired Steber Lighting to augment its light fixtures business. In 1972 Hubbell entered the telecommunications equipment field when it purchased Pulse Communications, a Virginia-based manufacturer of voice and data signal processing components. Also that year Hubbell acquired Southern Industrial Diecasting. Moreover, the company established a presence in South America with its Brazilian subsidiary, Harvey Hubbell do Brasil, after acquiring H.K. Porter do Brasil in 1973 and Metal-Arte Industrias Sao Paolo in 1974.

Weppler was succeeded by Robert Dixon in 1975. Dixon had spent 12 years studying electrical and mechanical engineering in night school and was a firm believer in Hubbell's odyssey through diversification and expansion. ''If we had stayed only in the wiring business, our numbers would look better but we wouldn't be as strong,'' he told a *Forbes* correspondent in 1982, adding, ''I even question whether we'd still be independent.'' Under Dixon, Hubbell acquired Hermetic Refrigeration, a Phoenix-based re-manufacturer of air conditioning compressors, in 1976. In 1978 it purchased Ohio Brass, which made insulation and surge arrestors for high-voltage electrical equipment, as well as mining equipment. In 1981 the company spun off Harvey Hubbell do Brasil, and picked up Arrestor, an American manufacturer of switch, junction, and outlet boxes and electrical fittings.

By this time, Hubbell's diversification had produced mixed results. On the one hand, the company's original wiring and light fixture business accounted for a disproportionate share of profits into the 1980s, a sign that acquired companies were not proving terribly lucrative despite the fact that Hubbell had made few outright missteps. On the other hand, Hubbell generated record profits every year from 1961 to 1983. In 1961, the company posted a relatively modest $22 million in sales; by 1981 sales had reached $445.8 million. Robert Dixon retired as CEO in 1983 and was succeeded by Fred Dusto, who presided over the final acquisitions of Hubbell's long spree: Miller Lighting and Killark Electric Manufacturing, both purchased in 1985. In 1986 the company shortened its name to its current form.

Key Dates:

1901: Harvey Hubbell publishes his first catalogue.
1905: Harvey Hubbell, Incorporated is established.
1909: The company builds its first factory.
1927: Harvey Hubbell dies and is succeeded at the helm of the company by Harvey III.
1968: George Weppler chairs the company and quickens Hubbell's pace of acquisitions.
1972: Hubbell enters the telecommunications equipment field.
1986: Harvey Hubbell Inc. shortens its name to its current form.
1994: A.B. Chance Industries Co., Inc. is acquired.
1998: Hubbell purchases Sterner Lighting.
2002: The company adds LCA Group to its holdings.

The 1990s

Dusto retired in 1987 and was succeeded by George Ratcliffe, who had once served as the company's chief counsel. Under Ratcliffe, Hubbell spent aggressively on upgrading and automating its capital equipment as well as on research and development. This reinvestment produced profit margins higher than those of its competitors during the 1980s, as the company was able to cut labor costs and also sell innovative products that commanded relatively high returns. Hubbell also made further acquisitions during this time. In 1991 it purchased Westinghouse's Bryant Electric division, which made wiring devices for industrial applications. In 1993 Hubbell acquired Hipotronics, a manufacturer of high-voltage cables and test and measurement equipment, and E.M. Weigmann and Co., Inc., a manufacturer of industrial enclosures.

Hubbell continued to add to its roster of companies those that performed well in its core lighting operations. Recognizing that electricity's central role would not be diminished in the coming years, Hubbell's electrical equipment empire spanned across the globe and across applications. Because no alternative power source even remotely threatened to challenge electricity, Hubbell's strategy was sound, as its acquisitions provided for stable long-term growth.

In March 1994, Hubbell purchased A.B. Chance Industries, a powerful presence in the electrical utility sector with a number of products such as overhead and underground distribution switches, fuses, cutouts, insulators, and safety equipment. Hubbell's next acquisition was in 1996, when it bought Gleason Reel Corporation, an industrial-grade electrical cable producer. In September 1997, Hubbell acquired Namar/Wirecon, a leading producer of self-contained electrical switches and receptacle tools used in the manufacture of prefabricated housing and recreational vehicles. Buoyed by its new operations, Hubbell's sales soared from $832.4 million in 1994 to $1.38 billion in 1997. Even more impressive was the company's profits, which increased from $66.3 million in 1993 to $130.3 million in 1997.

The year 1998 witnessed several key acquisitions. On November 17, Hubbell announced its impending purchase of Sterner Lighting, a designer and manufacturer of specification-grade outdoor lighting fixtures, as well as custom lighting products. Sterner's wares could often be found in indoor sports arenas. This producer of light fixtures for corrosive and hazardous locations complemented Hubbell's existing businesses. Sales kept rising through 1998, as Hubbell achieved more than $169 million in profit. Other acquisitions completed in 1998 and 1999 included: Chalmit Lighting based in Glasgow, Scotland; Tennessee-based Chardon Electrical Components; and Haefely Test AG of Switzerland.

At the close of the century, Hubbell's four key divisions remained centered on lighting and its application in a variety of spheres. With manufacturing facilities in Canada, Mexico, Puerto Rico, Singapore, the United Kingdom, and the United States, Hubbell had grown considerably beyond its humble origins. Joint ventures in Germany, South America, and Taiwan, as well as sales offices in Asia, Mexico, and the Middle East, rounded out Hubbell's far-flung operations.

Hubbell in the New Millennium

During the early years of the new millennium, Hubbell remained focused on strengthening its core operations. It made several acquisitions, including Hawke Cable Glands Ltd., which was based in the United Kingdom, and Cooper Power Systems Inc.'s pole line hardware segment. One of its more significant purchases was completed during 2002. In April of that year, Hubbell added U.S. Industries Inc.'s domestic lighting group, LCA Group, to its arsenal in a $250 million deal. The purchase proved beneficial for both parties. U.S. Industries was in the midst of a cost reduction program and needed to shed businesses unrelated to its core bath and plumbing operations. Hubbell jumped at the chance to buy the unit, which had secured $575 million in sales in 2001. Management believed the addition of LCA would prove lucrative and expected sales in its lighting products segment to climb to more than $800 million as a result of the deal. Overall, sales during 2002 increased by 21 percent over the previous year.

During this time period, the company shed several businesses that had proved unprofitable in the long term. With the sale of The Kerite Company, Hubbell exited the insulated cable business. In 2000, the company jettisoned its WavePacer DSL business after determining it could not effectively compete with large telecommunications firms in this market. Hubbell also was forced to cut costs as the economy began its slowdown during 2001. As such, the company reduced its work force, paid down debt, and reduced its inventories and capacity.

Hubbell's efforts appeared to pay off. Net income increased by 72 percent over the previous year in 2002. Sales and profits continued to climb in 2003 as well as 2004. During 2005, the company continued work on controlling costs and shed nearly 6 percent of its work force. A slowdown in nonresidential construction—one of Hubbell's key markets—as well as high oil prices that affected freight and utility costs proved challenging in 2005. Nevertheless, Hubbell stood on solid ground with Electrical, Power, and Industrial Technology as its three main operating segments.

Although Harvey Hubbell II is not widely remembered today, his inventions were instrumental in facilitating and disseminating the pioneering work of more famous inventors such as Edison and Westinghouse. Similarly, the company that Hubbell founded has labored for more than a century without widespread recognition for the company's name or products. Nevertheless, the success of its products, which people use and rely upon daily, left Hubbell well positioned for profitability in the years to come.

Principal Subsidiaries

Artesanias Baja, S.A. de C.V. (Mexico); Dual-Lite Manufacturing Inc.; GAI-Tronics Corporation; Gleason Reel Corporation; Haefely Test AG (Switzerland); Harvey Hubbell Caribe, Inc.; Hipotronics, Inc.; Hubbell Building Automation, Inc.; Hubbell de Mexico, S.A. de C.V.; Hubbell Inc. (Delaware); Hubbell Industrial Controls, Inc.; Hubbell Lighting, Inc.; Hubbell Ltd. (United Kingdom); Hubbell Power Systems, Inc.; Hubbell-Taiwan Co., Ltd. (50%); Progress Lighting, Inc.; Pulse Communications, Inc.; Hubbell Canada L.P.

Principal Competitors

Catalina Lighting Inc.; Cooper Industries, Inc.; Thomas & Betts Corporation.

Further Reading

"Analysts' Ratings: Electric Components," *Professional Investor Report,* April 25, 1997.

Chandler, Douglas, "Hubbell Lighting Buys Sterner Lighting," *Electrical Wholesaling,* December 30, 1998.

"Crossed Currents," *Forbes,* July 5, 1982.

Hannon, Kerry, "Live Wire," *Forbes,* November 14, 1988.

"Harvey Hubbell, Harvey Hubbell," *Forbes,* August 1, 1977.

"Hubbell Closes Purchase of LCA," *Wall Street Journal,* April 29, 2002, p. B6.

"Hubbell Inc.," *Milwaukee Journal Sentinel,* February 1, 1996, Bus. Sec.

Second Century of Solutions, Orange, Conn.: Hubbell Incorporated, 1988.

Varnon, Rob, "Job Losses Bring Gains at Hubbell," *Knight Ridder Tribune Business News,* July 20, 2005.

"Wall St. Roundup: Hubbell, Inc.," *Wall Street Transcripts,* February 6, 1995.

—Douglas Sun
—updates: Rebecca Stanfel, Christina M. Stansell

Hyperion Solutions Corporation

5450 Great America Parkway
Santa Clara, California 95054
U.S.A.
Telephone: (408) 744-9500
Toll Free: (800) 286-8000
Fax: (408) 588-8500
Web Site: http://www.hyperion.com

Public Company
Incorporated: 1991
Employees: 2,500
Sales: $702.6 million (2005)
Stock Exchanges: NASDAQ
Ticker Symbol: HYSL
NAIC: 511210 Software Publishers

Headquartered in Santa Clara, California, Hyperion Solutions Corporation is a leading developer of business performance management software, which helps businesses to gather, organize, and analyze business data; determine corporate performance; and then improve that performance through the use of modeling and planning. According to the company, it is the only industry player to offer business intelligence and financial management applications in one system. Through a network of approximately 600 partners, Hyperion serves a base of some 10,000 customers in 45 countries worldwide. These include the likes of Allstate Insurance, Braun, Coca-Cola, FIAT, H & R Block, Hyatt, Novartis, Staples, Toyota Motor Sales USA, and Yale University.

Establishment and Growth: The 1980s

Hyperion Solution Corporation's roots stretch back to 1981, when Marco Arese and Bob Thompson established International Management Reporting Services Inc. (IMRS). During its early years, the company was based at 1033 Washington Boulevard in Stamford, Connecticut. According to Hyperion, the release of IMRS's flagship product, Micro Control, "defined a new market by delivering multinational financial reporting on personal computers."

A native of Milan, Italy, Arese made a sizable start-up investment in Hyperion and played a central role in developing the company's international operations. Prior to starting Hyperion, Arese earned an M.B.A. from the University of California at Berkeley and worked for Citibank in Milan and London, where he designed financial reporting software. He then established a software company called Fienco SpA, which focused on PC-based treasury management systems.

Cofounder Thomson served as Hyperion's president and CEO, ultimately retiring from the company's board in August 1998. Before his role at Hyperion, Thomson worked in the management and technical ranks for Citicorp, Citibank, Rank Xerox, and Dolby System Labs. After leaving Hyperion, he relocated to Bermuda and became a "business angel" on the U.S. East Coast and in Scotland.

In addition to Micro Control, IMRS's early products included a data collection application called FinalForm, which companies used to automate and consolidate the collection of data from remote locations. With a license price of $40,000, FinalForm helped companies to streamline their financial operations and improve the efficiency of inventory management, sales reporting, and tax recording and preparation.

IMRS ended the 1980s by acquiring New York-based Corporate Class Software Inc., a subsidiary of Bridgewater, New Jersey-based Hoechst Celanese that produced a complementary line of management reporting software called FASTAR (Financial Application Solution to Analysis and Reporting). At the time of the acquisition, Micro Control and FASTAR were the leading software applications in their category, used by the likes of Unilever USA, Warner Communications Inc., and McDonald's Corporation. Each application cost about $75,000. The acquisition pushed IMRS's sales to $20 million and saw the consolidation of development, sales, and support. At this time James Perakis served as IMRS's president and the company had about 400 corporate customers and some 5,000 installations.

In 1989 IMRS also released a new Windows-based financial reporting application called OnTrack, which was instrumental in that it allowed novice users to generate corporate and financial reports by using a mouse and clicking on hypertext links. Compatible with Micro Control, the new program was priced

---

Company Perspectives:

Hyperion Solutions Corporation is the global leader in Business Performance Management software. With Hyperion you can collect, organize and analyze data—then distribute it throughout your enterprise using a rich, unified workspace that makes business performance management easier and more powerful than ever before. Hyperion solutions can help you drive performance improvements by better aligning goals with metrics, increasing your operational efficiency and becoming more comfortable with the integrity of your numbers.

---

at \$35,000. IMRS ended its 1989 fiscal year with sales of \$12 million.

Market Leader: The 1990s

By the early 1990s IMRS was growing at a healthy clip. In fact, the company had been recognized for four consecutive years as one of the fastest growing private companies in the United States by *Inc.* magazine. After subleasing an additional 9,200 square feet at its 1600 Summer Street Stamford location in 1990, the company moved forward with a major relocation, subleasing 73,558 square feet of space in Stamford's Long Ridge Office Park. The new facility, located at 777 Long Ridge Road, allowed IMRS to consolidate its headquarters with the company's Washington Boulevard location, which was being used for training. By this time, the company had grown to include a staff of 280 employees.

IMRS continued its expansion efforts by opening three new regional offices in 1991. Devoted to sales and support, the new sites included a Canadian office in Calgary, as well as locations in St. Louis and Philadelphia. With a total of 15 offices worldwide, including 11 in the United States, the company's revenues reached \$34 million in 1991, up from \$24 million in 1990. IMRS ended the year by going public. The company completed its initial public offering on October 25, raising approximately \$40 million that it planned to use for debt reduction and future expansion.

By this time IMRS had added an application called Treasury Control to its product lineup and had named its flagship software, which held 85 percent of the financial-consolidation software market, Hyperion. With the launch of its Hyperion Financials line, IMRS set its sites on the client-server financial reporting software market in early 1995. Unlike its main market, the client-server sector was home to a number of established competitors, including Lawson Software, Platinum Software, and PeopleSoff. At this time, IMRS changed its name to Hyperion Software Corporation.

In 1998 Hyperion was acquired by Arbor Software Corporation. The newly merged firms adopted the name Hyperion Solutions Corporation. Arbor was established in 1991 by Bob Earle and Jim Dorian, two pioneers in the field of business analysis software. Prior to the acquisition, the company had unveiled its flagship online analytical processing (OLAP) software in 1992, generating sales of \$1.1 million. By 1995 Arbor

had gone public and was listed on the NASDAQ. In 1997 Arbor made its first acquisition when it purchased Orlando, Florida-based Appsource, which had developed an OLAP presentation and viewer tool.

With an estimated value of \$780 million to \$1.3 billion, the merger resulted in the company relocating its headquarters to Sunnyvale, California. Jim Perakis was named chairman of the new enterprise, and Arbor Chairman and CEO John Dillon was named CEO. Stock ownership was divided so that Arbor investors held a 40 percent stake in the company and Hyperion shareholders held a 60 percent share.

Following the merger, Hyperion Solutions had about 1,800 employees in 26 countries who served a customer base of some 4,000 organizations in 40 countries. Its clients, which included Adobe Systems, Allergan, and Kraft Foods, hailed from a variety of industries, including consumer goods and services, healthcare, information technology, education, insurance, telecommunications, government, banking, transportation, and retail.

Hyperion proceeded to integrate its products and sales forces following the merger. As of late 1998 the company offered four main products to its customers. These included a presentation and reporting tools set called Hyperion Tools; an OLAP server called Essbase; the Hyperion Enterprise tool for financial consolidation and reporting; and a budgeting analytic program called Hyperion Pillar.

In early 1999 the research firm International Data Corp. issued a report citing Hyperion as the market leader in analytic applications, with a share of 18 percent. The report also placed Hyperion at the head of the market for financial-related analytic applications, with a share of 36 percent. Around this time Hyperion spun off its decision support arm as Appsource Corp., the name it had operated under before Arbor purchased the company in December 1997.

While the Hyperion-Arbor merger created the industry's largest business intelligence software enterprise, wide-ranging integration issues followed. This especially was the case with the company's sales force, in that teams that once competed against one another (and downplayed the other side's products) were now in a position to promote the offerings of both companies.

By mid-1999 Hyperion had experienced a sequential drop in quarterly revenue, as well as a decline in its stock price. A number of executives resigned, and Hyperion fired CEO John Dillon and Vice-President of Worldwide Sales William Binch, citing "problems with their 'expectation management and forecasting,'" according to the May 4, 1999, issue of *Computergram International.*

In its May 10, 1999 issue, *Computergram International* noted that "the company's inability to successfully execute a post-merger strategy appears to have caused a level of dissension within virtually every aspect of the organization. The conservative Hyperion failed, and is still failing, to gel with the more dynamic and performance-oriented Arbor. And one year on since the deal was first announced the combined Hyperion Solutions looks in only slightly better shape than when the operation was being run as two separate organizations.''

Key Dates:

1981: Marco Arese and Bob Thompson establish International Management Reporting Services Inc. (IMRS) in Stamford, Connecticut.

1982: IMRS releases its flagship financial reporting product, Micro Control.

1989: Following the acquisition of New York-based Corporate Class Software Inc., sales reach $20 million and corporate customers number 400.

1990s: Early in the decade, IMRS is recognized for four consecutive years as one of the fastest growing private companies in America by *Inc.* magazine.

1991: IMRS goes public.

1995: IMRS changes its name to Hyperion Software Corporation.

1998: Hyperion is acquired by Arbor Software Corporation; the merged firms adopt the name Hyperion Solutions Corporation and establish headquarters in Sunnyvale, California.

2001: Hyperion cuts 400 jobs and implements other cost-saving measures.

2003: The company acquires The Alcar Group and Brio Software Inc.

2005: *Information Age* dubs Hyperion Essbase as ''one of the 10 most influential technology innovations of the last 10 years.''

After Dillon was fired, CFO Steve Imbler was named interim CEO. He ultimately was replaced by Jeffrey R. Rodek, who assumed the role of both chairman and CEO. Prior to joining Hyperion, Rodek was president and worldwide chief operating officer of Ingram Micro Inc., a Hyperion board member, and also a 16-year executive with Federal Express.

Moving past its operational troubles, in 1999 Hyperion acquired Sapling Corporation, a developer of enterprise performance management software, for $15.5 million. The acquisition helped Hyperion to stave off competition from SAP AG and Oracle Corporation. Hyperion renamed Sapling's main products and added Hyperion Performance Scorecard and Hyperion Business Modeling to its product lineup. Hyperion ended the 1990s with fiscal year 1999 sales of $424.9 million. In addition, for the second consecutive year Deloitte & Touche and Joint Venture: Silicon Valley Network named the company to the 1999 Silicon Valley Technology ''Fast 50'' for being one of the valley's fastest growing technology firms.

Web/Enterprise Focus: The 2000s

Hyperion began the new millennium by introducing Hyperion Planning and Hyperion Financial Management, two Web-based packaged financial applications. In 2000 the company also partnered with WebTrends Corporation to provide its customers with integrated e-business analysis solutions. This was accomplished by integrating Hyperion business analysis applications with WebTrends' Commerce Trends solution.

Hyperion also joined the XBRL Project Committee, a coalition of some 30 software, government, and accounting firms that was formed to promote extensible Business Reporting Language as a free, open standard for financial reporting. According to an April 6, 2000, *Business Wire* release, XBRL sought ''to help organizations easily distribute financial information in any format, including HTML documents for the Web, printed financial statements, EDGAR filing documents for the Securities and Exchange Commission (SEC), or other specialized reporting formats such as credit reports or loan documents.'' These developments came at a time when users were demanding sophisticated Web-based tools.

In addition to competition from industry heavyweights like Microsoft, Hyperion was challenged by stagnant revenues and declining economic conditions. In response, the company tightened its belt to weather the storm. This resulted in a 15 percent workforce reduction (400 jobs), a hiring freeze, travel restrictions, and cutbacks in capital spending. In addition, Hyperion indicated that it would focus its workforce around its profitable products. One analyst noted that the company had created confusion in the marketplace—and within its own sales force—by introducing too many products, and that Hyperion would do well to eliminate resource-draining, underperforming products.

Hyperion ended its 2001 fiscal year with sales of $528 million, compared with $492 million in 2000. It reported a net loss of $31.1 million, however, compared with net income of $30.6 million in fiscal 2000. On a positive note, the company returned to profitability during the fourth quarter, reporting net income of $1.8 million despite a tough economic climate.

Following similar developments by competitors like SAP AG, Oracle Corporation, and PeopleSoft Inc., in September 2001 Hyperion announced that it would make its business intelligence and data warehousing products available enterprise-wide by 2004. This move would give executives a broader top-level view and make it easier for departments and business units to share information. In October, Godfrey Sullivan was named as Hyperion's president and COO; Jeffrey Rodek remained chairman and CEO. Prior to joining Hyperion, Sullivan served as CEO of marketing software developer Promptu Corporation.

In 2002 Hyperion saw its revenues fall to $492 million. The company was profitable for the year, however, with net income of $15.7 million. Hyperion received a license revenue boost during the fourth quarter when it gained 235 new customers who contributed 44 percent of license revenue. Among the new customers were Citigroup, Motorola, and Northrop Grumman. Attributing to Hyperion's success was the introduction of new products, including its Hyperion Business Performance Management Suite.

Heading into 2003, Hyperion was on solid footing. As accounting scandals at companies like Enron ushered in new accountability standards for the corporate sector, the company stood to benefit by increased sales of its reporting software. In a January 24, 2003 interview with the *America's Intelligence Wire*, CEO Jeffrey Rodek noted a 13 percent year-over-year increase in Hyperion's software business and remarked that the company's balance sheet was ''the strongest ever.''

Hyperion's business performance management line was bolstered significantly with the April 2003 acquisition of Skokie, Illinois-based The Alcar Group, a developer of financial modeling software, followed by the $142 million acquisition of Santa Clara, California-based Brio Software Inc. By October Hyperion was working to integrate Brio's products into its own lineup, giving Hyperion the ability to offer business intelligence software; Hyperion's Business Intelligence Platform was released in 2004.

A number of important developments occurred in 2004. In response to more stringent corporate governance standards, the company split the role of chairman and CEO. Jeffrey Rodek became executive chairman, and Godfrey Sullivan assumed the role of president and CEO. The company also unveiled Hyperion Essbase 7X, calling it "the most dramatic innovation in analytics since the company pioneered OLAP technology in 1992."

In August, Hyperion cut 50 jobs as it moved more software development offshore. According to an August 18, 2004, *Knight Ridder/Tribune Business News* article, the move was upsetting to workers, some of whom had just completed a questionnaire for *Fortune* magazine's "100 Best Companies to Work For" list only days before. Despite strong financial performance, the company insisted the move was necessary for it to remain competitive. Hyperion CEO Godfrey Sullivan ended the year by announcing that the company had set aside $1 million to offer employees $5,000 toward the purchase of environmentally friendly cars (those with fuel economy of at least 45 miles per gallon).

Hyperion started 2005 on a sour note as it was sued by two other companies for patent infringement. The first suit was filed by HyperRoll Israel Ltd., claiming that the Hyperion Essbase 7X OLAP server infringed on two of its patents. Stamford, Connecticut-based OutlookSoft Corp. also filed two infringement suits against Hyperion related to patents for its Everest application.

In early 2005 Hyperion acquired Razza Solutions Inc., which bolstered its capabilities in the area of business performance management software. The company ended fiscal year 2005 with record revenues of $702.6 million, up 13 percent from $622.2 million in 2004. Hyperion's net income spiked 52 percent, reaching $66.7 million.

Hyperion continued to release new business performance management products in 2005. The company's Hyperion System 9 offered users one system with a business intelligence platform and financial management applications.

A major highpoint in the company's history also occurred in 2005 when *Information Age* dubbed Hyperion Essbase as "one of the 10 most influential technology innovations of the last 10 years," according to an August 16, 2005, *M2 Presswire* release. In the publication's 10th anniversary issue, *Information Age* editor Kenny MacIver remarked: "Hyperion Essbase was the multi-dimensional database that put online analytical processing on the business intelligence map. It has spurred the creation of scores of rival OLAP products."

Principal Competitors

Business Objects S.A.; Cognos Inc.

Further Reading

Bartholomew, Doug, "A Broader View for IMRS," *Informationweek,* February 20, 1995.

"California-Based Software Firm Hyperion Solutions Cuts Stamford, Conn., Jobs," *Knight Ridder/Tribune Business News,* August 18, 2004.

Callaghan, Dennis, "Business Intelligence Goes Enterprisewide," *eWeek,* September 17, 2001.

Callaghan, Dennis, "Product Strategizing Key to Hyperion—Company Plans Business Strategy Review, Focus on Profitable Offerings," *eWeek,* May 28, 2001.

"Company Splits CEO, Chairman Roles for Better Governance," *Compliance Reporter,* July 26, 2004.

Ferranti, Marc, "IMRS Debuts Windows-Based Financial Reporter," *PC Week,* October 30, 1989.

Hindo, Brian, "Drive Green and Get Some Green," *Business Week,* December 13, 2004.

"Hyperion Acquires Razza," *Asia Africa Intelligence Wire,* January 26, 2005.

"Hyperion and Webtrends Partner to Offer Integrated E-business Analysis Solutions," *Business Wire,* March 6, 2000.

"Hyperion Announces Cost Cutting Measures," *PR Newswire,* May 16, 2001.

"Hyperion Buys Financial Modeling Vendor Alcar," *eWeek,* April 4, 2003.

"Hyperion Buys Sapling for Enterprise Performance Software," *Computergram International,* May 19, 1999.

"Hyperion Details Brio Integration," *eWeek,* October 28, 2003.

"Hyperion Essbase Named As Top Ten Technology Innovation of the Decade by *Information Age* Magazine," *M2 Presswire,* August 16, 2005.

"Hyperion Fires CEO and Head Salesman As Merger Falters," *Computergram International,* May 4, 1999.

"Hyperion Hit with Patent Infringement Suit," *Client Server News,* January 24, 2005.

"Hyperion Joins Global Initiative to Launch Open Standards for Web-Based Financial Reporting," *Business Wire,* April 6, 2000.

"Hyperion Named a 1999 Silicon Valley Technology 'Fast 50' Company," *Business Wire,* September 22, 1999.

"Hyperion Ousters Shift Focus to IBM," *PC Week,* May 17, 1999.

"Hyperion Reports Fiscal Fourth Quarter and 2001 Results," *PR Newswire,* July 26, 2001.

"Hyperion Reports Record Fourth Quarter and Full Fiscal Year 2005 Financial Results," *Business Wire,* July 21, 2005.

"Hyperion Reports Solid Fiscal Fourth Quarter and 2002 Results," *M2 Presswire,* July 26, 2002.

"Hyperion Solutions—CEO Interview," *America's Intelligence Wire,* January 24, 2003.

"Hyperion Solutions' Customers Endorse Merger; More Than Two-Thirds of *Fortune* 100 Using Hyperion's Best-in-Class Products and Worldwide Services," *Business Wire,* August 24, 1998.

"Hyperion Spins Off Appsource; Goes for MS OLAP Space," *Computergram International,* February 9, 1999.

"Hyperion Trims Staff, Expenses," *Silicon Valley/San Jose Business Journal,* May 18, 2001.

"IDC: International Data Corporation Names Hyperion Solutions the Analytic Applications Revenue Leader," *M2 Presswire,* February 2, 1999.

"IMRS Acquires Competitor," *PC Week,* October 23, 1989.

"IMRS Buys Developer of FASTAR Software," *PC Week,* October 23, 1989.

"IMRS Expands, Files with SEC for Stock Offering," *Fairfield County Business Journal,* September 30, 1991.

"IMRS, G.E. Expand Office Space in Stamford," *Fairfield County Business Journal,* September 10, 1990.

"Ingram Micro President and COO Accepts Top Post at Hyperion Solutions Corp.," *PR Newswire,* October 12, 1999.

Khasru, B.Z., "OutlookSoft Files Patent Claims Against Hyperion," *Fairfield County Business Journal,* February 7, 2005.

"M&A Impact: Hyperion Still Suffering Indigestion Post-Arbor," *Computergram International,* May 10, 1999.

Mulqueen, John T., "Arbor Takes Root with Hyperion—Software Companies Branch Together to Create Budding Corporation," *InternetWeek,* June 1, 1998.

Pallatto, John, "Program Helps Automate Collection, Consolidation of Data from Remote Sites," *PC Week,* June 28, 1988.

Songini, Marc, "Buyouts Surge Among Data Analysis Vendors: Hyperion, Business Objects Acquire Rivals; Further Consolidation Expected," *Computerworld,* July 28, 2003.

——, "Hyperion's Challenge: Convince Users It's Growing," *Computerworld,* April 23, 2001.

Spiegler, Eric, "IMRS Will Use $40 Million from IPO to Pay Down Debt," *Fairfield County Business Journal,* November 4, 1991.

Stableford, Joan, "IMRS Leases 73,500 Square Feet in Stamford Relocation," *Fairfield County Business Journal,* July 15, 1991.

Stoll, Marilyn, "Aerospace Firm Revamps Its Tax-Recording System," *PC Week,* August 1, 1988.

"Technology Briefing Software: Hyperion to Buy Brio Software," *New York Times,* July 24, 2003.

Willett, Shawn, "After the Merger: Targets Products, Channels—Hyperion Gets Integrated," *Computer Reseller News,* September 21, 1998.

—Paul R. Greenland

IdraPrince, Inc.

670 Windcrest Drive
Holland, Michigan 49423
U.S.A.
Telephone: (616) 394-8248
Fax: (616) 394-1250
Web site: http://www.prince-machine.com

Wholly Owned Subsidiary of Idra Presse S.p.A.
Incorporated: 1965 as Prince Machine Corporation
Employees: 220
Sales: $42 million (1999 est.)
NAIC: 333513 Machine Tool (Metal Forming Types)
   Manufacturing

A subsidiary of Italian corporation Idra Presse SpA, IdraPrince, Inc. is North American's largest maker of die casting equipment, used mostly in the automotive industry. In addition to being a full-service provider to Ford Motor Company, General Motors Corporation, and DaimlerChrysler AG, IdraPrince also serves the auto industry's Tier I suppliers (companies that sell finished components to automakers) and Tier 2 suppliers (companies that sell items to Tier 1 suppliers). Products include the Revolution Two Platen machine, offering a number of innovations in die casting machine technology; cold chamber die cast machines, large units designed to make items such as engine blocks, transmission cases, gear boxes, clutch housings, and dashboards; hot chamber machines, appropriate for producing zinc, lead, and magnesium castings; and liquid metal squeeze cast systems, used to inject molten aluminum into a casting die. Other products include software to monitor the process of die casting; temperature controllers; vacuum systems to remove air and gases from a die; and a range of hydraulic presses. The company is also capable of producing custom-built die casting machines and assembling turnkey automated casting systems. In addition, IdraPrince services, rebuilds, and upgrades die casting machines. The company maintains its headquarters in Holland, Michigan.

Founding the Company in the Mid-1960s

IdraPrince was founded in 1965 by 33-year-old Edgar Prince, who quit his job as the chief engineer of Buss Machine Works in Holland, Michigan, in order to start his own die cast business—one that would reflect his deeply held religious beliefs. Holland, Michigan contained one of the largest concentrations of Dutch-Americans in the country, a community that adhered to the Calvinist values of the Christian Reformed Church. Prince also applied these values to Prince Machine, which later became part of Prince Corporation. His operations were always closed on Sundays and he flew his salespeople home to their families almost every night on a fleet of company planes. One of his chief lieutenants, John Spoelhof, who joined Prince in 1969, explained in a 1991 interview the company's philosophy: "We don't apologize for our Christianity. We have a unique opportunity in the business world to let our light shine. . . . We're not standing on a soapbox, but our walk and talk . . . will show to others that Christianity is important."

Although he wanted his business to offer a positive image about his religion, Prince shunned the limelight. He could have received a great deal of attention, given that he became a philanthropist as his wealth grew, contributing money to schools and colleges and playing a key role in the revitalization of downtown Holland. Prince also became a player in politics, albeit in the background, becoming a major contributor to Republican candidates around the country and to the Christian conservative movement. He helped religious right leader Gary Bauer establish the Family Research Council, a "pro-family" lobbying group. Prince gave one interview around 1980, felt he was misquoted, and refused to speak to the press again. The Prince family and Prince personnel also were guarded about his life. Hence, there was little known about Edgar Prince beyond his business success.

Early 1970s Switch to Car Components

A major turning point for Edgar Prince came in 1972 when his company moved beyond making custom machine tools for the die cast industry, a highly cyclical business, and became an automotive original equipment manufacturer. In that year Prince Corp. invented the lighted vanity visor for front-seat passengers,

192

first used in the 1973 Cadillac. It would be the first of countless interior items Prince sold to carmakers, which soon began to regard Prince Corp. as a model supplier. According to *Forbes,* "The carmakers appreciated Prince for his willingness to back his gadgets with his own development money. With a product prototype in hand, Prince's salesmen would put it in some cars and then ask the carmakers' representatives to try it for the weekend." Says Chrysler's [David] Swietlik, [procurement manager for large cars]: "Prince comes in saying, 'You don't know you want this yet.'" *Forbes* noted, "Over the years Prince created dashboard cup holders, movable armrests, illuminated visor mirrors that automatically adjust to external lighting, a garage door opener button mounted on a sun visor." *Fortune* offered its own take on the company: "Around the auto industry, Prince is infamous for its tight-knit culture and aggressive selling. 'Swarming the customer' is the way McKensey & Co.'s Glenn Mercer describes it. Prince makes three-dimensional prototypes as well as CAD/CAM printouts when it presents a new design, and prides itself on beating deadlines. Adds Mercer: 'They make it difficult for somebody to say no.'" The company became especially adept with electronics, recognizing early on that electronics would become increasingly important in cars. Rather than just making parts, Prince integrated electronics, and was especially good at packaging it in trim, in order to create very profitable value-added components.

By the early 1980s die cast machines were superseded by the auto interior parts business and Prince Corp. enjoyed a major growth spurt. Employment grew from less than 600 people in 1980 to more than 4,500 in 1995. In addition, sales grew from $30 million in 1982 to more than $300 a decade later. About two-thirds of that amount came from the sale of interior auto components. All told, about three-quarters of all revenues came from the "Big 3" automakers. Along the way, Prince developed a long-term goal: to become the first partsmaker capable of supplying an entire car interior, from roof to door to floor trimmings and instrument panel. It was a lofty goal, one that would be complicated by the globalization of the auto industry. As the Big 3 automakers opened plants around the world, they expected suppliers to follow suit and establish their own global footprints. How to finance such a major expansion was a challenge for a private company like Prince Corp. But events would intervene in 1995 to change the course of the company's history.

According to *Forbes,* "After finishing lunch on Mar. 2, 63-year-old Edgar Prince left the executive dining room at his Holland, Mich.-based business and took the elevator up to his office. When the elevator doors opened, Prince was dead on the floor, felled by a massive heart attack." Prince had already delegated a great deal of authority to Spoelhof, who had for several years been handling the company's day-to-day affairs, so the company was well positioned to carry on without its founder. More so, it had virtually no debt and was generating

about $500 million a year in sales. But not only did the Prince family face paying sizable estate taxes, it also had to contend with the need to raise a lot of money in order to become a global supplier to its customers. In the view of *Forbes'* Marcia Berss, writing several months after Prince's death, the family was left with three choices: "Borrow a huge amount of money, go public or sell out. Of the three, the latter looks like the quickest solution and perhaps, from the family's point of view, the easiest and most lucrative."

There was no lack of suitors for the business, so that it came as no surprise, therefore, when in July 1996 Prince Corp. sold the Prince Automotive unit to Milwaukee-based Johnson Controls Inc. for $1.35 billion. The Prince family retained Prince Machine, which would become IdraPrince, as well as two other companies, Lumir Corp. (the family's real estate operation) and Wingspan Leasing, which leased airplanes. Prince's son, Erik D. Prince, who was in his late 20s, took charge of the family businesses, including Prince Machine and its 225 employees.

Like his father, the younger Prince was a devout Christian, astute businessman, staunch patriot, and somewhat sensitive. He attended a small liberal arts school, Hillsdale College, and became one of the first interns at the Family Research Council in Washington, D.C. He also undertook intern stints with U.S. Representative Dana Rohrabacher and the White House. He next attended the U.S. Naval Academy, but resigned before graduating. Instead, he joined the Navy, earned a commission as a lieutenant, and became a SEAL—and one of the richest men ever to serve in the U.S. military. He spent four years as a SEAL before leaving in 1996 to return home and attend to family business. In was also in 1996 that he started a professional security firm and bought 6,000 acres of land in North Carolina to build a major training facility. The company became a haven for former SEALs, Army Rangers, and Delta Force Troops, many of whom had been stationed in nearby Fort Bragg. It was called Blackwater USA, an allusion to peat-colored water in that region of North Carolina as well as the nighttime missions undertaken by military divers. Blackwater was in little demand until the terrorist attacks of September 11, 2001, on the United States, and it did not receive much attention (nor did Erik Prince) until the Iraq war. Blackwater was one of about 20 private security firms supplying personnel to serve in the war zone. The role of these private contractors, regarded by some as little more than mercenaries, garnered public attention in April 2004 when four Blackwater men were murdered in the Iraqi city of Fallujah. The gruesome treatment of their corpses was videotaped and shown on television around the world. As a result, a light was turned on the military's new outsourcing of security work, Blackwater USA, and the company's very private backer, Erik Prince.

Erik Prince served as chairman of Prince Machine until 2000, although he was more interested in launching Blackwater and building an elite training center than in the manufacture of die cast machines. One major step taken during his tenure was the 1998 acquisition of Zeeland, Michigan-based Quality Process Controls (QPC), the addition of which expanded Prince's plastic processing capabilities, allowing the company to better serve die cast companies on a global basis. QPC products included high-temperature oil circulating systems, portable process water chillers, and mold die water temperature regulators.

Key Dates:

1965: Edgar Prince founds Prince Machine Corp. to custom build machine tools.
1972: Prince invents the lighted vanity visor and begins producing car interior components.
1982: Sales reach $30 million.
1995: Edgar Prince dies.
1995: Prince Automotive is sold, leaving Prince Machine as a die cast machine company.
2000: Idra Presse SpA acquires the company, renamed IdraPrince, Inc.
2001: The company merges with Idra North America.
2002: Rights are acquired to the rheocasting process developed by the Massachusetts Institute of Technology.

Sale of Prince Machine in 2000

But just as Prince Automotive was sold to a larger company because of globalization, Prince Machine soon experienced a similar fate. In August 2000 the business was sold to a rival firm, Idra Presse of Brescia, Italy, which manufactured and marketed die casting machines and automated work stations around the world, mostly to automakers but also to consumer electronics and household appliance manufacturers. With the addition of Prince Machine, Idra Presse became the largest supplier of die casting equipment in the world. Prince Machine was renamed IdraPrince, Inc., and then in January 2001 was merged with Idra North America.

Now better able to serve customers on a global basis, IdraPrince began to further develop its capabilities in the early 2000s. In July 2002 it won the worldwide licensing rights to a new rheocasting process developed at the Massachusetts Institute of Technology. In rheocasting a liquid metal, like aluminum, solidifies in a die. It also could be combined with squeeze casting to produce fiber composite materials. IdraPrince looked to use the technology to improve upon existing cold chamber die casting machines and to design new machines.

In February 2003, IdraPrince unveiled a new cold chamber aluminum and magnesium die casting machine product line, featuring a new design that reduced the required floor specification for a die cast machine by more than 30 percent. In addition, the units had less mechanical components, which in turn reduced the amount of required maintenance. The company also was working on a new injection system, which adopted a so-called "No Pipe/NoHose/No Leak" design philosophy. All external hydraulic pipes and hoses were either eliminated or designed to be leak free. The "S2" injection system completed its production trial in early 2004. Around the same time, the year-long production trial was completed on the company's innovative Revolution 2-platen, small footprint, die cast machine. Over the next year IdraPrince grew the Revolution product line to include six models with die locking forces that ranged from 900 tons to 4,000 tons.

With the backing of its Italian corporate parent, and still benefiting from the culture established by its American founder, IdraPrince had the products, personnel, and reputation needed to prosper on the global scene for many years to come.

Principal Subsidiaries

QPC Systems, Inc.

Principal Competitors

Alumasc Group Plc; Gibbs Die Casting; Productivity Technologies Corporation.

Further Reading

"Auto Supplier with an Attitude," *Fortune,* September 5, 1994, p. 60.
Berss, Marcia, "Life After Death," *Forbes,* October 23, 1995, p. 144.
Brennan, Mike, "Johnson Controls Buys Prince Automotive to Create Giant Auto Parts Firm," *Detroit Free Press,* July 19, 1996.
Connolly, Allison, "Blackwater's Best-Kept Secret: Its Founder," *Virginia-Pilot,* May 3, 2004, p. A1.
"Edgar Prince: Giant Loss, Giant Legacy," *Grand Rapids Press,* March 3, 1995, p. A1.
Gardner, Greg, "JCI Buys Itself a Prince," *Ward's Auto World,* August 1, 1996.
Harger, Jim, "Prince Corp. Will Continue to Prosper," *Grand Rapids Press,* March 4, 1995, p. A1.
Luymes, Robin, "Quiet Giant: Prince Corp. Emerges," *Grand Rapids Business Journal,* July 15, 1991, p. 1B.
Martin, Norman, "The Shy Prince," *Automotive Industries,* March 1, 1997, p. 84.
Plumb, Stephen E., "Prince Corporation Teams Stresses Old Fashion Virtues," *Ward's Auto World,* August 1993, p. 40.
Sabo, Mary Ann, "More Jobs May Come with Prince Sale," *Grand Rapids Press,* July 19, 1996, p. A1.

—Ed Dinger

Interface, Inc.

2859 Paces Ferry Road, Suite 2000
Atlanta, Georgia 30339
U.S.A.
Telephone: (770) 437-6800
Toll Free: (800) 336-0225
Fax: (706) 882-0500
Web site: http://www.interfaceinc.com

Public Company
Incorporated: 1973 as Carpets International of Georgia, Inc.
Employees: 5,006
Sales: $881.67 million (2004)
Stock Exchanges: IFSIA
Ticker Symbol: NASDAQ
NAIC: 31411 Carpet & Rug Mills; 31321 Broadwoven Fabric Mills; 325131 Inorganic Dye & Pigment Manufacturing

Interface, Inc., is a leading producer of commercial carpets. It also makes other types of flooring for work and home. Originally a manufacturer and distributor of carpet tile, Interface has expanded its presence in the commercial and institutional interiors industry. Carpet tiles, uniform floor covering modules that are easier to maintain and replace than broadloom carpet, continue to underlie Interface's business, proving popular in office design because of their flexibility in redecoration and easy removal and replacement for rewiring and other repair work. These modular carpet systems—marketed under the brand names Interface Flooring Systems and Bentley in the United States, and Heuga in Europe—are used primarily in commercial and institutional settings. Interface is also a leading producer of interior fabrics for open plan office furniture systems and other applications. These are sold under the Guilford of Maine, Chatham, Intek, and Camborne brands. Interface is also involved in specialty chemical production. Interface currently controls about 40 percent of the international carpet tile market.

Early History

Interface was founded in 1973 by Ray C. Anderson, who would remain the company's chairman and chief executive officer into the late 1990s. Before founding Interface, Anderson had been working as a research manager for Milliken & Co., a privately owned textile firm. On behalf of Milliken, Anderson was sent abroad to research the technology for manufacturing carpet tiles in preparation for Milliken's prospective entry into that field. While visiting Carpets International plc (CI), a large British company specializing in carpet, Anderson was introduced to a process called "fusion bonding." Anderson immediately recognized the potential of this process for producing carpet tiles, as well as the huge market for carpet tile in the United States that had not yet been tapped. In 1973 he quit his job with Milliken & Co. in order to start his own business.

Interface first appeared as a joint venture with CI, called Carpets International of Georgia, Inc. (Cl-Georgia). Of the initial seed money for the company, $750,000 (half of the total) came from CI, the rest from Anderson and various backers mostly from his hometown of West Point, Georgia. The new company produced its first piece of carpet on New Year's Eve, 1973. On its first day of operation, CI-Georgia had only 15 employees, including Anderson. The company's first year of operation was a financial disaster. It lost $400,000 on sales of just over $800,000. Skyrocketing prices for petrochemicals, an important raw material in the carpet industry, were a large part of the problem. These price increases were the result of the 1973 oil embargo, and the recession that ensued.

On the other hand, the company's association with an established firm like CI gave it several advantages. The most important of these was access to advanced technology. CI was able to provide cutting technology superior to that of companies like Milliken, saving the company 10 percent on the cost of yarn. Other technology was made available that enabled CI-Georgia to develop special bonding equipment. This equipment made it possible to install carpet tiles without glue, bonding the four-ply carpet fibers to a fiberglass backing. These contributions, along with the beginning of the office building boom, helped CI-Georgia triple its sales to $2.4 million by the end of 1975. The company also turned its first profit that year.

Company Perspectives:

Interface will become the first name in commercial and institutional interiors worldwide through its commitment to people, process, product, place and profits. We will strive to create an organization wherein all people are accorded unconditional respect and dignity; one that allows each person to continuously learn and develop. We will focus on product (which includes service) through constant emphasis on process quality and engineering, which we will combine with careful attention to our customers' needs so as always to deliver superior value to our customers, thereby maximizing all stakeholders' satisfaction. We will honor the places where we do business by endeavoring to become the first name in industrial ecology, a corporation that cherishes nature and restores the environment. Interface will lead by example and validate by results, including profits, leaving the world a better place than when we began, and we will be restorative through the power of our influence in the world.

During the second half of the 1970s there was tremendous growth in the white-collar segment of the U.S. economy. About 800,000 office jobs per year were created between 1975 and 1980, causing huge demand for office furnishing. It was during this period that modular carpet systems became extremely popular among office managers and interior designers. Carpet tiles allowed designers to install floor coverings that were pleasing to the eye, while at the same time were easy to remove and replace, whether for cleaning, redecorating, or accessing wiring beneath the floor. By 1978, Interface's sales had reached $11 million.

In the early 1980s CI began to face fierce competition from a flood of broadloom carpet being imported into the United Kingdom. Meanwhile, the American joint venture continued to grow, with sales swelling to $57 million in 1982. As CI continued to flounder, the American firm took over 10 percent of CI's equity in the company, and changed its name to Interface Flooring Systems, Inc. The two companies continued to move in opposite directions. While Interface's sales leaped again in 1983, to $80 million, CI teetered on the edge of bankruptcy. In order to avert receivership for CI, Interface concocted a plan to provide a $4 million loan convertible to 41.3 percent future equity in CI. The agreement also gave Interface the option to purchase another 8.8 percent of CI shares for about $2.3 million through 1987, the year the loan was due. Interface also went public for the first time in 1983, selling its shares over-the-counter. The company raised $14.4 million in its initial offering.

Growth through Acquisitions in the 1980s

Interface purchased CI's carpet tile division for $8.4 million in 1984, giving Interface entry into the European market for the first time. This transaction gave Interface ownership of CI's Illingworth and Debron brands of carpet. Around the same time, Interface acquired Carintusa Inc. from CI, for $440,000. Carintusa, the sole U.S. distributor of woven English-broadloom carpet manufactured by CI, was based in Los Angeles. In the same period, Interface also acquired Chemmar Associates, Inc.,

merging it with its Interface Research Corporation subsidiary. Chemmar was the licensor of Intersept, the antimicrobial agent developed for hospital carpets. Aided by these acquisitions, Interface's sales climbed to $107 million for 1984. By that time, after only 11 years of existence, Interface already controlled about 30 percent of the growing U.S. carpet tile market. This figure put the company in a virtual tie for the lead in market share with Milliken & Co., Anderson's former employers.

In 1985 Interface exercised its option to convert its CI promissory note, acquiring 41.3 percent of CI. The company's overseas business began to pick up around this time as well, particularly in oil-rich Middle Eastern countries. As the 1980s progressed, Interface began to diversify beyond carpets into related industries. The company purchased Guilford Industries for $97 million in 1986. Guilford was a textile company that specialized in fabrics for office furniture systems, including cubicle dividers, walls, and ceilings. This acquisition gave Interface the ability to market complete office furnishing packages, an idea that proved to be appealing to designers both domestically and abroad. Interface also began to expand its specialty chemical operations that year. Two Georgia-based companies, Rockland Corporation and React-Rite, Inc., were acquired on the last day of 1986, for a combined total of about $4 million. With the addition of these two companies, Interface improved its ability in polymer chemistry, essential to the further development of its Intersept program.

Interface swallowed up what was left of CI in 1987. CI's remaining debt was then paid off, and its broadloom carpet business sold. By this time, CI's name had been changed to Debron Investments plc. For 1987, Interface reported sales of $267 million, nearly double the previous year's figure. During that year, the company's name was changed to Interface, Inc., and Interface Flooring Systems, Inc., was retained as the name of the company's North American carpet tile subsidiary. Interface became the undisputed world leader in carpet tiles in 1988, with the acquisition of Heuga Holdings B.V., a Dutch company with sales of more than $200 million. Heuga was one of the world's oldest manufacturers of carpet tiles. Interface had been trying to acquire the company since about 1983, when it was first put up for sale by the 13 children of Heuga's founder. At that time, Interface was not able to complete a deal. The company that did buy Heuga was subsequently acquired by Ausimont N.V., a firm that was not interested in the carpet tile business. From Ausimont, Interface purchased not only Heuga but Pandel, Inc., another wholly owned subsidiary. Heuga contributed manufacturing facilities in the Netherlands, the United Kingdom, Canada, and Australia. Pandel's U.S. plant produced carpet tile backing and mats. That company recorded sales of $10 million in 1987. The acquisition of Heuga expanded Interface's international business enormously, gaining the company contracts with a number of major British firms, as well as such prominent Japanese companies as Hitachi, Tokyo Marine, and Nomura Securities. It also helped Interface further diversify into residential carpet tile sales, which had accounted for about a quarter of Heuga's European business. With the addition of Heuga, the company's revenues jumped dramatically once again, reaching $582 million.

In early 1990 Interface acquired the assets of Steil, Inc., based in Grand Rapids, Michigan. Steil had for several years been the exclusive U.S. distributor of Guilford's open line panel and upholstery fabrics. Later that year, the company invested in Prince Street Technologies, Ltd., a producer of upper-end broadloom carpet. Prince Street, based in Georgia, received a loan from Interface in exchange for the right to acquire an equity interest. Interface generated $623 million in revenue in 1990.

More than Carpet in the 1990s

Sales shrank for the first time in the company's history in 1991, largely due to the recession in the global economy. In that year, Interface generated net income of $8.9 million on sales of $582 million. During 1991, Interface Service Management, Inc. (ISM), was formed in conjunction with ISS International Service System, Inc., a Danish firm specializing in facility maintenance. The creation of ISM enabled Interface to provide its customers with a more integrated interior system in which all of its furnishing needs could be supplied by one source. In Europe the company launched a similar project, in which independent service contractors were licensed to provide maintenance services. These contractors operated under the name IMAGE (Interface Maintenance Advisory Group of Europe). Interface also reorganized its corporate structure in late 1991. The company's operations in Asia and the Pacific Islands were unified under a new holding company, Interface Asia-Pacific, Inc. Interface Europe, Inc., was also formed, merging Interface International, Inc., which had controlled operations in the United Kingdom, with the holding company that owned Heuga and its various European subsidiaries.

By 1992, Interface's antimicrobial chemical Intersept was being used in over a dozen product categories, including paints, wall coverings, ceiling tiles, carpet, fabrics, and coating materials. The marketing of Intersept was assisted by the formation of The Envirosense Consortium, a group of companies that used Intersept in the manufacture of a variety of products. The Envirosense program was initiated as a response to increasing

cases of and concern over building-related illnesses and other health concerns associated with indoor work atmospheres. Interface's sales rebounded somewhat in 1992. Sales for the year were $594 million. Net income increased by over 37 percent, to $12.3 million.

In January 1993 Interface announced that it had acquired the low-profile access flooring system of Servoplan, S.A., of France. The acquisition, through the company's U.S. and French subsidiaries, included all patents, know-how, and production equipment relating to this flooring system. Interface had previously marketed the Servoplan system in North America alone, and the positive response of its customers led the company to seek worldwide control of the system's manufacture and distribution. At the time of the acquisition, Anderson indicated that the system would be sold under the name Intercell.

The following month, Interface announced another acquisition. The company's Guilford of Maine subsidiary had acquired the fabric division assets of Stevens Linen Associates, Inc., a leading producer of panel and upholstery fabric for office furniture systems. Another acquisition occurred in June 1993, when Interface bought Bentley Mills, Inc., a manufacturer of designer-oriented broadloom carpet used for commercial and institutional settings.

New Directions for the Mid-1990s

In the mid-1990s, Interface's chairman and CEO Ray C. Anderson emerged as an outspoken advocate of sustainability, a concept that included environmental and social responsibility. Under the influence of Anderson's crusading efforts on behalf of sustainability, the company shifted strategy, aiming to redirect its industrial practices without sacrificing its business goals. Anderson, who served as co-chair of the President's Council on Sustainable Development, wrote a book entitled Mid-Course Correction, in which he discussed his own awakening to environmental concerns and commitment to changing a business not traditionally allied with the environmentalists. Anderson was called the ''Eco CEO'' by Metropolis magazine.

In 1996, Charlie Eitel was named president and chief operating officer of Interface. This allowed Anderson, who remained chairman and CEO, to pursue the ecological issues that had become so important to him. Under Eitel, the company began leveraging its market share with a sales approach he called ''mass customization,'' which facilitated rapid delivery of a wide variety of patterns, in colors selected by the customers. The owned and aligned providers of carpet and installation and other services became known collectively as the Re:Source Solutions Provider Network, and Interface began bundling installation, maintenance, reclamation, and other services with carpet sales, promoting this strategy with the slogan ''This Carpet Comes Installed.'' Carpet adhesives and other chemical applications began to be sold under the IMAGE brand name. Intercell became part of Interface Architectural Resources, a larger effort to integrate wiring and heating, ventilation, and air conditioning under the comprehensive facility solutions that Interface offered. Under Eitel, Interface branched out into a seemingly unrelated activity: motivational seminars. These sessions originated as ''Why?'' conferences for promoting social bonds with designers and other customers, and the positive response to these conferences led to the formation of "one world learning," a wholly owned subsidiary dedicated to fostering organizational development through activities and discussion.

In its quarter-century of activity, Interface had grown into a billion dollar corporation, named by *Fortune* as one of the "Most Admired Companies in America" and the "100 Best Companies to Work For." With the exception of the recession year of 1991, the company was able to increase its sales every year since its founding. In the first decade of the new century, Interface would likely be able to continue this pattern of expansion, primarily by introducing its products to a wider range of commercial customers in Asia and continental Europe. In addition, Interface's specialty chemical operations seemed poised for continued growth, as public attention to occupational health increased, and the potential hazards of higher technology in the office environment, came under closer scrutiny.

In an attempt to penetrate the health care and education markets, which generally rejected carpet in favor of hard surface floorcovering, Interface introduced Solenium in 1999. Made from PTT (polytrimethylene terepthalate), a polymer developed by Shell Labs, Solenium was a dense, lightweight material that, according to the company, combined the design, comfort, sound absorption of carpet with the practicality of hard flooring. Solenium incorporated Intersept, the company's patented antimicrobial preservative. It was pitched to hospitals and schools as an alternative to vinyl tile flooring.

The company continued to make strides in developing earth friendly fabrics for carpets and cubicle coverings. A polylactic acid-based biodegradable fiber developed with Dow and Cargill was rolled out in 2000. It was made from corn. Other innovations cubicle fabric made from recycled soda bottles

In thinking about the life cycle of its products, Interface came up with a new way of selling carpet: via a lease. The company offered to install, maintain, and eventually recycle carpet tiles for a monthly fee. The concept was slow to catch on. In its own facilities management, Interface found that when they did wear out, the company only had to replace 10–20 percent of carpet tiles at once, rather than entire floors.

Post-2000 Recession and Recovery

Charlie Eitel left the company in 1999. The company's chief financial officer, Dan Hendrix, became CEO in 2001. Anderson retained the title of chairman. It was a difficult time for management and staff. Interface was making its way through a prolonged recession carrying a $400 million debt load. The company cut hundreds from its work force of 7,000 in 2000 and 2001.

There were acquisitions and divestments as Interface focused on its core business. Interface bought Chatham Manufacturing, which made fabrics for furniture, from CMI Industries in 2000. Interface divested its access flooring business in 2004. The company's total sales fell below $1 billion, partly a result of the sell-offs.

Interface continued to trudge towards its 2020 goal of reaching "Mount Sustainability." In 2004, the company reckoned it was a third of the way there. In a long article in the journal *Quality Progress,* Anderson compared the quest for sustainability to the previous one for quality: "It's not as though business was previously on an anti-quality kick, but when quality with a capital Q took hold, it became the battle cry for business. You would be left behind if you didn't get on board."

Anderson answered business skeptics thus: "Our costs are way down. That dispels one myth that sustainability costs. Our products are the best they've ever been," he told the *Calgary Herald.* Looking to nature for inspiration, the company had just brought out a new line of carpet tiles based on random patterns found on a forest floor (the earthy tones helped camouflage tracked-in dirt). He also cited employee motivation and the goodwill of the marketplace. In fact, Anderson credited the concept of sustainability with sustaining the company through the worst market conditions it had seen in 30 years. He was thinking of more than just goodwill; Anderson had long compared business endurance to survival in nature.

Anderson appeared extensively in the Canadian documentary *The Corporation,* flailing businessmen such as himself as "plunderers" of natural resources. The visibility invariably attracted critics, including Canada's *National Post,* which ran a couple of columns questioning whether any real environmental progress had been made at Interface.

Anderson replied that over the ten years the sustainability initiative had been in place, reduction of waste alone produced enough savings ($262 million) to pay for whole program. The company had slashed greenhouse gas emissions by more than half, and had cut usage of fossil fuels, water, and landfill while planting thousands of trees to offset the environmental impact of its air travel. While Interface had its fans among socially-conscious investors, the company itself had not shown a profit since 2000. It posted a net loss of $55.4 million on sales of $881.7 million in 2004.

Principal Subsidiaries

Bentley Mills, Inc.; Bentley Prince Street, Inc.; Camborne Holdings Ltd. (United Kingdom); Interface Americas Holdings, LLC; Interface Americas, Inc.; Interface Americas Re:Source Technologies, LLC; Interface Architectural Resources, Inc.; Interface Asia-Pacific Hong Kong Ltd.; Interface Australia Holdings Pty Ltd.; Interface Europe B.V. (Netherlands); Interface Europe, Ltd. (United Kingdom); Interface Fabrics, Inc.; Interface Fabrics Canada, Inc.; Interface Fabrics Finishing, Inc.; Interface Fabrics Marketing, Inc.; Interface Fabrics Guilford, Inc.; Interface Fabrics Elkin, Inc.; Interface Flooring Systems, Inc.; Interface Flooring Systems (Canada), Inc.; Interface Global Company ApS (Denmark); Interface Heuga Singapore Pte. Ltd.; Interface Leasing, Inc.; Interface Overseas Holdings, Inc.; Interface Real Estate Holdings LLC; Interface Research Corporation; Interface Securitization Corporation; Interface Teknit, Inc.; Interface Yarns, Inc.; InterfaceFLOR, Inc.; Pandel, Inc.; Quaker City International, Inc.; Re:Source Americas Enterprises, Inc.; Strategic Flooring Services, Inc.

Principal Divisions

Modular Carpet; Bentley Prince Street; Fabrics Group; Specialty Products.

Principal Competitors

Asahi Kasei Corporation; BASF AG; Beaulieu of America LLC; The Dow Chemical Company; Mohawk Industries, Inc.; Shaw Industries, Inc.

Further Reading

Anderson, Ray S., ''Climbing Mount Sustainability,'' *Quality Progress,* February 1, 2004, p. 32.

——, *Mid-Course Correction: Toward a Sustainable Enterprise, The Interface Model,* Atlanta: Peregrinzilla Press, 1998.

Anderson, Ray S., ''A Hard-Headed Business Case for Sustainability,'' *National Post,* July 18, 2005.

Anderson, Ray S., Charlie Eitel, and J. Zink, *Face It: A Spiritual Journey of Leadership,* Atlanta: Peregrinzilla Press, 1996.

Basu, Moni, ''Conservation Connection: Carpet Giant Weaves Earth-Friendly Policies,'' *Atlanta Journal-Constitution,* June 12, 2002, p. F1.

Birchfield, Damon, ''Sustainability—Totally Floored—The CEO Who Plans to Change the World,'' *Management Magazine* (New Zealand), August 2, 2002, p. 44.

Conlin, Michelle, ''From Plunderer to Protector,'' *BusinessWeek,* July 19, 2004, p. 60.

Foster, Peter, ''Heaven Can Wait,'' *National Post,* July 2, 2005.

——, '' 'I Am a Corporate Sinner': Who Is Ray Anderson?,'' *Financial Post,* June 25, 2005.

Hagerty, James R., ''Carpet Maker Aims to Win Over Schools and Hospitals,'' *Wall Street Journal,* June 3, 1999, p. B10.

Hoogeveen, Nate, ''Reinventing Industry,'' *Business Record,* April 10, 2000, p. 22.

''Interface's Premium: The Tiles That Bind,'' *Financial World,* August 7, 1984, pp. 81–82.

Kinkead, Gwen, ''Green CEO,'' *Fortune,* May 24, 1999, pp. 190–200.

Lappen, Alyssa A., ''Carpet Tile King,'' *Forbes,* April 17, 1989, pp. 60–64.

Lee, Shelley A., ''Magic Carpet Ride,'' *Business Atlanta,* October 1992, pp. 111–19.

Neuwirth, Robert, ''The Eco CEO,'' *Metropolis,* July 1998, pp. 69–73, 103–04.

Sanchez, Mark, ''Nature Is Model for Firm's Recycled-Materials Product,'' *Grand Rapids Business Journal,* February 24, 2003, p. B6.

Sandberg, Jared, ''Mystery Underfoot: The Dizzying, Ugly, Reliable Office Carpet,'' *Wall Street Journal,* January 29, 2003, p. B1.

Toneguzzi, Mario, '' 'Green' CEO Dreams of Saving the Earth,'' *Calgary Herald,* September 16, 2005, p. D3.

Turkel, Tux, ''Fabric Woven with Vision of Sustainability,'' *Portland Press Herald* (Maine), September 15, 2002, p. 1F.

—Mark Swartz
—update: Frederick C. Ingram

ITT Technical Institute **ITT**

ITT Educational Services, Inc.

13000 North Meridian Street
Carmel, Indiana 46032
U.S.A.
Telephone: (317) 706-9200
Fax: (317) 706-3040
Web site: http://www.ittesi.com

Public Company
Incorporated: 1968
Employees: 6,200
Sales: $617.8 million (2004)
Stock Exchanges: New York
Ticker Symbol: ESI
NAIC: 611210 Junior Colleges

ITT Educational Services, Inc., is a private, postsecondary education provider, with 80 colleges operating in 30 states. The colleges, called ITT Technical Institutes, offer technology-focused, career-oriented programs that lead primarily to associate's and bachelor's degrees. There are five schools available at ITT Technical Institutes, including: Information Technology; Drafting and Design; Electronics Technology; Business; and Criminal Justice. ITT's total enrollment is approximately 40,000, and its students attend classes year-round. ITT Educational remains the largest provider of technical education in the United States, despite fending off a very public criminal investigation into its attendance records led by the Department of Justice in 2004.

1960s: Building the Business

The business that was eventually to become ITT Educational Services began as part of Howard W. Sams and Co. Inc., an Indianapolis-based publisher of technical training manuals and textbooks. Sams had been in the publishing business for almost 20 years when it decided to try its hand at running a private trade school. It established its first school—Sams Technical Institute—in Indianapolis in 1963. The institute, which taught electronics, consisted of 28 students. Sams acquired two more schools in 1965 and 1966: Teletronic Technical Institute, of Evansville, Indiana; and Acme Institute of Technology, Inc., in Dayton, Ohio. A fourth school also was opened in Fort Wayne, Indiana, during that time period.

In October 1966, Howard W. Sams and Co. was purchased by ITT Corporation, a large, New York-based conglomerate. Two years later, ITT Corporation incorporated its private school subsidiary as "ITT Educational Services" and established its headquarters in Indianapolis. ITT's first president was William D. Renner, who had previously been the vice-president of training for Howard W. Sams.

In 1968, with the backing of its capital-rich parent, ITT Educational embarked upon an ambitious plan for expansion that led to a flurry of acquisitions. By the end of the year, the company had acquired seven new schools located in Chicago, St. Louis, Boston, New York City, and Hempstead, New York. This brought the total number of schools in the ITT system to ten. The company began working toward standardizing the materials and lesson plans used in the various schools' courses by establishing curricula committees.

In 1969 ITT Educational entered the foreign market when it acquired Ecole de Gaulle, a Paris-based system of five schools focusing on vocational, business, commercial, and trade training. To hold and manage its international operations, the company established the subsidiary ITT Educational Services-Europe. Meanwhile, ITT continued to add to its domestic school system at a breakneck pace. Between February and early September of 1969, it acquired ten business and technical schools, scattered through Ohio, Michigan, Washington, Idaho, Illinois, Minnesota, and Washington, D.C. It also opened two new schools in Bethesda and Annapolis, Maryland. Both the new schools operated under the name "ITT Business Institute."

1970s: Leadership Changes

ITT Educational started the new decade with a series of transitions in its leadership. Late in 1969, the company's first president, William Renner, relinquished the position he had assumed only the year before. He was replaced in 1970 by Burton Sheff. But in May of 1972, Sheff resigned, and ITT was once again leaderless. Sheff was replaced by Neil R. Cronin, who also stayed with the company for a short time.

In 1974, however, ITT found a leader with a greater staying power: Richard McClintock. McClintock, who had been employed by ITT Corporation and its subsidiaries since 1957, had served previously as the company's comptroller and treasurer. Upon taking the helm in 1974, he immediately set about implementing new administrative structures and procedures. Two of his first initiatives were to establish an executive committee for the company and to begin establishing curriculum advisory committees for each region.

The year 1973 marked an important milestone in ITT's growth. That year, the company became a part of the Federal College-based tuition grant and loan programs, which had until then been reserved only for traditional colleges and universities. Acceptance into these programs allowed ITT to offer its students a full range of college loan and grant programs. This meant that attending an ITT school became a viable option for a new pool of students—those who needed federal financial aid to pay for schooling.

1980s: Adding New Divisions

After expanding its school system so rapidly in the late 1960s, ITT had spent much of the 1970s refining it. By the end of the 1970s, the company had significantly pared down the bulky system by selling or phasing out various schools, including ones in Boston, Akron, Toledo, New York, and Bethesda, Maryland. In 1980 the total number of schools was down to 21.

In 1981, however, the company began a period of controlled growth, implementing several new expansion initiatives. One of the first was the creation of a new division designed to target individuals who were already employed in the business world, but who wanted to improve existing skills or learn new ones. The new division, named the Business Division, opened its first school in Indianapolis in the spring of 1982. More schools of the same type followed—in Chicago, Los Angeles, Tampa, and Arlington, Texas.

Three years later, ITT created still another division: Employer Services. The Employer Services Division worked directly for businesses, training their employees in word processing. The division's services were offered originally at ITT locations in Indianapolis, Chicago, Houston, and El Segundo, California. Shortly after the division was formed, however, it expanded its services to temporary staffing by merging with a Los Angeles-based provider of interim personnel.

The company also grew via its old, tried-and-true method of adding new schools in new locations. Between 1981 and the end of 1985, more than a dozen new ITT facilities opened in Florida, California, Indiana, Texas, Tennessee, Utah, and Colorado.

In October 1984, ITT's ten-year leader, Richard McClintock, died. The company's executive committee took over day-to-day governance of the operation until a new president could be appointed, and in September 1985, the position was filled by Rene Champagne. Champagne had spent 16 years in various high-level administrative positions with Kendall Company, a subsidiary of Colgate-Palmolive. Immediately prior to joining ITT Educational, he had served as the executive vice-president and chief operating officer of Continental Pharma Cryosan Inc., a healthcare company.

The mid-1980s brought changes to ITT's Employer Services Division. In 1985 the division announced that it was closing the training and temporary staffing operations in Indianapolis, Chicago, Houston, and Los Angeles. Two years later, the Employer Services Division broadened its services by offering both temporary and permanent technical staff placement. In 1988, however, the entire division was sold to Olsten Corporation.

In 1986 the company's Resident Division took steps to become more unified and standardized. The schools operating under the Resident Division, which were those that offered technical programs such as electronics and HVAC, were renamed "ITT Technical Institutes." The Resident Division itself also was rechristened to correspond to the schools' new name, becoming the ITT Technical Institutes Division.

1990s: Ownership Changes and Rapid Growth

The early 1990s marked a turning point in ITT's evolution. In 1992 the company unveiled the Vision 2000 plan, a strategy for changing the way it was perceived. Since its formation in the 1960s, ITT institutes had been viewed primarily as "trade schools." Under the Vision 2000 initiative, however, the company planned to make the institutes more like actual colleges by offering more bachelor's degrees. In addition to this repositioning, Vision 2000 called for aggressive geographic expansion and the addition of new curricula. ITT's new goal was to have a network of 80 technical colleges located across the country, serving more than 45,000 students, by the year 2000.

ITT immediately took steps toward achieving its newly articulated goals. By the end of 1993, four new schools had been opened and plans were under way for three more. The company also had added several new degree programs to its offerings, including a bachelor of applied science in hospitality management, a bachelor of applied science in industrial design, and a bachelor's degree in electronics engineering technology. By the end of 1994, ITT Educational was operating 54 schools in 25 states. Of the more than 20,000 students it served, approximately 70 percent were enrolled in electronics-engineering technology and related programs.

In December 1994, ITT's parent company, ITT Corporation, spun off 17 percent of ITT Educational in a $20 million initial

Key Dates:

1963: Textbook publisher Howard W. Sams opens Sams Technical Institute in Indianapolis, Indiana.
1966: Sams is purchased by New York-based ITT Corp.
1968: ITT incorporates its education subsidiary as ITT Educational Services.
1981: ITT creates its new Business Division.
1984: Employer Services Division is created.
1992: ITT initiates Vision 2000, a growth strategy plan aimed at offering more degree programs and adding more colleges to the system.
1994: Parent company ITT Corporation spins off 17 percent of ITT Educational in a public offering.
1998: ITT Corp. is purchased by Starwood Hotels and Resorts Worldwide Inc.; ITT introduces its information technology program.
1999: Starwood sells off all remaining ITT Educational stock in a public offering.
2004: Federal investigators raid company headquarters and ten ITT campuses.
2005: The Department of Justice drops its criminal investigation.

public offering, still retaining majority ownership of 83 percent. The goal of the spinoff, according to ITT Educational President Rene Champagne, was to raise the company's visibility among investors. "The main reason we decided to do the public stock offering was that we were a moderate sized company in a $23 billion-a-year corporation. We were getting lost in the corporate complex," he said in a June 1995 interview with the *Indianapolis Star*. "Most people in the investment community were not aware of who we were." Less than a year after the spinoff, ITT Corporation itself announced a sweeping reorganization. During the restructuring, the giant conglomerate split into three publicly held companies. ITT Educational was a part of the new public company that continued to be called ITT Corporation.

In 1995, ITT took another step toward repositioning its "schools" as "colleges" when it established a Graduate Division at its Indianapolis ITT Technical Institute. The first degree offered by the Graduate Division was a master's in project management. The coursework and class schedules in the program were designed to appeal to adults who wanted to complete an advanced degree while working full-time.

Early 1998 brought yet another shift at the corporate level for ITT. In February, its parent company, ITT Corporation, was acquired by New York-based Starwood Hotels and Resorts Worldwide Inc. From the time of the acquisition, ITT Educational knew that change was in the offing. Starwood made it immediately clear that it had no interest in maintaining an educational subsidiary that did not fit with its core businesses of hotels and gaming. In June, Starwood sold 13 million shares of ITT Educational stock, reducing its ownership in the company from 83 to 35 percent. Then in an early 1999 public offering, the company sold the remainder of its ITT Educational stock, making ITT an independent, stand-alone company for the first time in its history.

Despite the ownership upheavals of the 1990s, ITT had continued to steadily add new colleges and new programs to its system. By spring of 1999, the company had 67 ITT Technical Institutes operating nationwide. It was also in the middle of rolling out an important new information technology program: Computer Network Systems Technology (CNST). ITT first introduced CNST at three locations in 1998, with plans to add it to 13 more schools in 1999. The program—which focused on areas such as computer network systems, programming, and Web development—was so well received, however, that the company decided to introduce it at 27 locations, rather than the 13 originally planned.

ITT Educational finished up 1999 with record revenues of $316.4 million, an 8.6 percent increase over 1998. Student enrollment was up by approximately 3.2 percent over the previous year. Enrollment increases were particularly noticeable in the schools offering the company's new CNST program; schools offering that program increased their total student enrollment as of December 31, 1999 by 7.8 percent over December 31, 1998.

ITT Educational in the New Millennium

As ITT prepared to enter the new millennium, it was placing increasing emphasis on its information technology (IT) program. The rapidly growing IT industry was in dire need of qualified workers, and demand was expected to increase in the coming years. ITT planned to capitalize on that demand. "We are focused on repositioning our company to meet the demands of the 'new economy' for more graduates in information technology," Champagne said in a January 21, 2000 press release. He added: "The IT program is serving an important catalyst for future growth."

The company planned to continue rapidly rolling out the IT program to the remainder of its schools in 2000. According to a January 21, 2000, press release, an additional 16 schools were expected to begin offering the program during the first quarter of 2000. Additional schools were scheduled to begin offering the program in each of the three remaining quarters of 2000, to complete the rollout by the end of the year. It was expected that with ITT's new focus on information technology and the continued rollout of the CNST program to its schools, enrollment and revenues would increase in the coming years.

Indeed, revenue jumped to $347.5 million in 2000, an increase of nearly 10 percent over the previous year. The company's new IT program rollout was a success; more than 13,000 students had enrolled since its inception. The company also partnered with Cisco Systems Inc. to create the Cisco Networking Academy, a short-term 24-week training course designed to teach students how to build computer networks. ITT Educational began to offer online programs in 2001 that would result in a bachelor's degree in Technical Project Management for Electronic Commerce. A second program in Cyber Security was launched in June 2002.

The increased demand for IT specialists, a slowing U.S. economy, and higher unemployment rates (displaced workers often went back to school) left ITT Educational well positioned for additional growth during this time period. In 2002, the company announced a new ten-point plan designed to ensure the company met its goal of operating 100 colleges with $1 billion in revenues by 2010. The company outlined its new strategy in its 2002 and 2003 annual reports, reporting that its initiatives included: increase enrollment; establish new locations; open new learning sites to handle growth at existing sites; offer more bachelor's degree programs at its colleges; develop new degree offerings in various technology fields; research and develop nontechnology degree programs; increase the number on online degree programs; create hybrid programs that utilize both traditional classroom instruction and online classes; seek international growth; and evaluate potential opportunities of nondegree programs of study.

During 2002, the company posted record results. Its earnings per share increased by 34.3 percent over the previous year and both revenues and net income continued to climb. The company was named to the *Forbes* 200 Best Small Companies list for the third consecutive year in 2002. Enrollment increased by 13.6 percent in 2003 as revenues and net income continued climbing to record levels.

Sure enough, ITT Educational's new ten-point strategy appeared to be paying off. Revenue, net income, and enrollment increased again in 2004 despite a very public investigation into the company's records regarding student attendance, grades, and job placement figures. In February 2004, federal investigators working for the U.S. Department of Justice raided company headquarters and ten of its campuses. At that time, the company disclosed that the Securities and Exchange Commission as well as the California Attorney General had been investigating the company since October 2002. In addition, shareholders filed suit against the company, claiming that it falsified its records in order to receive student financial aid from the federal government—aid that made up nearly two-thirds of the company's revenue—and that company officials had financially benefited from ITT Educational's inflated stock price by selling shares between 2002 and 2004. President and chief operating officer Omer Waddles stepped down amid the investigation and was replaced by Kevin M. Modany.

ITT Educational breathed a sigh of relief in June 2005 when the criminal investigation led by the Department of Justice was dropped after it found no wrongdoing by the company or its executive team. While the government continued its investigation into certain campuses and employees, ITT Educational cooperated with the investigation, releasing more than one million documents to investigators.

Overall, the charges proved costly to the company. After the raid in February 2004, ITT Educational lost $1.3 billion in market value as its share price fell hard. The firm also was forced to spend heavily on internal investigations and legal fees. Nevertheless, company management continued to forge ahead with its growth strategy. With enrollment and revenues on the rise, ITT Educational appeared to be well positioned for success in the years to come despite its legal woes.

Principal Competitors

Apollo Group Inc.; Corinthian Colleges Inc.; DeVry Inc.

Further Reading

Andrews, Greg, "Fast-Growing School Biz Plans IPO, Faster Growth," *Indianapolis Business Journal,* December 5, 1994, p. 3.
——, "ITT Paid for Feds' Aggression," *Indianapolis Business Journal,* July 4, 2005, p. A1.
——, "ITT Spin-Off at Top of Class," *Indianapolis Business Journal,* November 25, 1996, p. 1A.
——, "Raids at ITT Dim Outlook for Star Performer," *Indianapolis Business Journal,* December 27, 2004, p. 32.
Francis, Mary, "Tech Institute Places Itself on the Cutting Edge," *Indianapolis Star,* March 2, 1999, p. D1.
"ITT's President Quits As Feds Probe Records," *Grand Rapids Press,* July 13, 2004.
Lieber, Tammy, "ITT Looks to Future Despite New Ownership, Lawsuits," *Indianapolis Business Journal,* November 16, 1998, p. 9.
McKimmie, Kathy, "School Biz," *Indiana Business Magazine,* February 1, 2002.
Pulley, John L., "Justice Department Ends Inquiry into ITT Educational Services," *Chronicle of Higher Education,* July 8, 2005, p. A23.
Smith, Bruce, "ITT Educational Services Is Ahead of the Pack," *Indianapolis Star,* June 14, 1995, p. F01.
Taylor, Jeffrey, "The New America: ITT Educational Services Inc.," *Investor's Business Daily,* April 7, 1995, p. A6.
Wall, J.K., "ITT Keeps Focus Amidst Probe," *Indianapolis Star,* May 9, 2005.

—Shawna Brynildssen
—update: Christina M. Stansell

Jacuzzi Brands Inc.

777 South Flagler Drive, Suite 1100 West
West Palm Beach, Florida 33401
U.S.A.
Telephone: (561) 514-3838
Fax: (561) 514-3839
Web site: http://www.jacuzzibrands.com

Public Company
Incorporated: 1915 as Jacuzzi Brothers, Inc.
Employees: 5,929
Sales: $1.34 billion (2004)
Stock Exchanges: New York
Ticker Symbol: JJZ
NAIC: 326191 Plastics Plumbing Fixture Manufacturing;
333911 Pump and Pumping Equipment
Manufacturing; 332913 Plumbing Fixture Fitting and
Trim Manufacturing

Jacuzzi Brands Inc. operates as a leading manufacturer and distributor of bath and plumbing products, including whirlpool baths, spas, showers, sanitary ware, and bathtubs. The company also offers professional grade drainage, water control, commercial faucets, and various other plumbing products to customers in residential, commercial, and institutional markets. Jacuzzi has several brands in its arsenal, including its namesake, Sundance, Zurn, and Astracast. The company is the originator and one of the world's largest manufacturer of whirlpool baths, with which its name has become synonymous. Jacuzzi was founded in 1915 and remained a family owned and operated company until 1979 when it was bought by Kidde Inc. The latter company was subsequently purchased by the huge British conglomerate Hanson plc, which later spun off a number of its American subsidiaries as U.S. Industries (USI). USI sold off many of its businesses during the early years of the new millennium and changed its name to Jacuzzi Brands in 2003.

Company Origins in the Early 20th Century

Jacuzzi was founded by seven brothers who emigrated from Italy to California in the early 1900s. Engineers by trade, the brothers produced a variety of aviation-related innovations in-cluding a pitched propeller developed for the American government and the first enclosed cabin monoplane, which was used to carry mail and passengers for the U.S. postal service. According to certain accounts, the Jacuzzis' mother was unhappy with the risks involved in aviation and asked her sons to work on something more down to earth. The Jacuzzi Brothers family firm began to design hydraulic pumps and eventually became one of the world leaders in the engineering and production of agricultural pumps used for irrigation.

The Invention of the Whirlpool Bath in the Late 1940s

The company's hallmark product, the Jacuzzi whirlpool bath, was invented in the late 1940s as a personal project of one of the second generation of Jacuzzi company managers, Candido Jacuzzi. Candido's son Kenneth, stricken with rheumatoid arthritis, had been receiving hospital hydrotherapy treatment and, as Kenneth would later relate in *People Weekly,* "as good Italian parents do, my folks thought more is better." A team of Jacuzzi engineers were put to work to develop a home version of the hydrotherapy pump. The result was the J-300, a small portable pump that could be placed in a bathtub to create a soothing hydromassage. In 1956, Jacuzzi began marketing the therapeutic device to hospitals and schools, developing a small but solid niche in the surgical supplies market. Kenneth, who continued to battle the physical challenges of rheumatoid arthritis, went on to found his own successful software company and the Jacuzzi pump that was invented for him achieved its own fame as the plaything of celebrities.

By the mid-1950s the privately owned Jacuzzi Brothers was being run by the second generation of Jacuzzis. In addition to its market-leading agricultural pumps and the J-300, the company patented and produced a large variety of products that made use of their expertise in hydraulic technology, including water jet propulsion motors for a growing recreational motor boat industry as well as swimming pool equipment and a wind machine that helped protect crops from frost.

In 1968, Roy Jacuzzi, a member of the third generation of Jacuzzis to work for the company, graduated from college with a degree in industrial design and joined the family firm as head of the research division. Searching for new applications for the company's products, Roy struck upon the idea of marketing the J-300 hydrotherapy device to the growing leisure and fitness market. In order to create enough room to accommodate a more relaxing soak, Roy developed and patented the first bathtub with a built-in whirlpool system. Dubbed the Roman Bath, this unit made it unnecessary to place a portable pump into the tub, allowing the bather the full interior of the tub in which to enjoy the hydromassage. The self-contained unit was marketed as a replacement for the standard bathroom tub and could be used with or without the hydromassage feature. Although, by his own admission, the senior generation of Jacuzzis thought he was "a little weird," Roy set out to create a market for the Roman Bath by displaying it at country fairs and housing trade shows.

By 1970 sales of the built-in whirlpool bath were promising enough to justify the introduction of a larger model, the Adonis, and within two years the company was manufacturing a two-person unit, dubbed the Gemini, available in a wide range of colors and styles. The Gemini line was followed by even larger models called spas, which were produced complete with filters and water heaters to obviate the necessity of filling and emptying them with every use. The laid-back culture of California in the 1970s turned out to be the perfect launching ground for the leisure-oriented product and by the middle years of the decade owning a "Jacuzzi" had become a symbol of the mellow California lifestyle. With the endorsement of high-profile movie stars, sales of the units took off and soon the whirlpool bath division was Jacuzzi's biggest profit maker. As the sole supplier of the patented system, the Jacuzzi brand name was synonymous with the whirlpool baths. Although Candido Jacuzzi, the conservative inventor of the original J-300 pump, was reportedly embarrassed about their sybaritic associations, the company's whirlpool baths and spas, and the Jacuzzi name, became identified with indulgent relaxation.

Bought by Kidde Inc. in 1979

In 1976 Jacuzzi moved its corporate headquarters from Berkeley to Walnut Creek, California. By the late 1970s, thanks both to sales of whirlpool baths and the growing export market for the company's irrigation pumps, Jacuzzi Brothers sales reached about $90 million. The company, which by then employed about 100 members of the Jacuzzi family, became the subject of family disagreement, however, and in 1979 the privately owned firm began to look for a buyer. After merger talks with Textron broke down, Kidde Inc., a conglomerate that manufactured products ranging from consumer appliances to hydraulic cranes, bought Jacuzzi Brothers for about $70 million.

Under Kidde, Jacuzzi lost most of its family-run quality as many family members left the firm. The notable exception was Roy Jacuzzi, who remained in charge of the company's whirlpool bath division. Although only a tiny part of Kidde's huge operations, both of Jacuzzi's main product lines, agricultural pumps

and whirlpool baths, continued to thrive. The company was operated as two separate subsidiaries: Jacuzzi Brothers, with headquarters in Little Rock, Arkansas, manufactured pumps and pumping equipment for use in agriculture and swimming pools; and Jacuzzi Whirlpool Bath, run out of Walnut Creek, California, manufactured the company's renowned jetted baths as well as a variety of more conventional bathroom faucetry and equipment.

For both Jacuzzi subsidiaries foreign sales showed particularly strong growth. The company's water pumping equipment was in great demand in the developing countries of Central America, which were looking to develop small, efficient irrigation systems. In 1984 the company signed an agreement to become Nicaragua's sole supplier of water pumping equipment, although the subsequent American-imposed trade embargo on Nicaragua meant that products had to be shipped via the company's Spanish and Canadian branches. The European market for whirlpool bath and bathroom fixtures began to take off in the 1980s and Jacuzzi's presence in Italy and Spain assured the company a strong showing in this area. By 1987, Jacuzzi's whirlpool products alone were garnering some $57 million in sales.

Through the 1980s the trend in both America and Europe was for bathrooms to get larger and bathroom fixtures to be designed for appearance as well as function. Jacuzzi's product line expanded to dozens of models available in a huge assortment of colors and with a variety of optional features. Some options available on the more luxurious models included the "Water-Rainbow" waterfall-like fill spout, programmable massage jets, underwater lights, and built-in mirrored vanity cases. Roy Jacuzzi was personally responsible for designing many of the features of the new product lines; by 1987 Roy held 160 patents for innovations in whirlpool design and technology.

Acquired by Hanson in 1987

In late 1987, the huge British conglomerate Hanson PLC bought out Kidde Inc. and its 100 subsidiaries, including Jacuzzi, for $1.7 billion. One of Hanson's first moves in its reorganization of the acquired businesses was to appoint Roy Jacuzzi as president and CEO of Jacuzzi Inc., an umbrella company headquartered in Walnut Creek that was to control the management of both the pump and filter products of Little Rock-based Jacuzzi Brothers and the bathroom and whirlpool products of Jacuzzi Whirlpool Bath. The newly organized company employed a workforce of 1,843 and had annual revenues of about $160 million.

Under Hanson Jacuzzi continued its international expansion and its new product introductions. Chief among the company's innovations in the 1990s was the development of the J-Dream steam shower system. With the J-Dream, Jacuzzi hoped to transform the nature of showering as the whirlpool bath had transformed bathing. The shower system, available to accommodate either one or two users, featured molded seats, programmable hydrotherapy jets, multifunction shower heads, and steam therapy as well as luxurious options such as built-in CD players, cascade waterfalls, and waterproof concealed closets to store bathrobes and towels.

Spun Off As U.S. Industries in 1995

Although Jacuzzi remained solidly profitable through the early 1990s, Hanson decided to sell off a number of its American businesses to raise cash for further British acquisitions. Although analysts speculated that Jacuzzi, with its widely recognized brand identity, would be spun off as an independent public company, it was decided that 34 of Hanson's American holdings would be rolled together as a unit to be called U.S. Industries (USI), a public company with a listing on the New York Stock Exchange. Other companies that were to join Jacuzzi as part of U.S. Industries included well-known brands such as Farberware Cookware, Tommy Armour Golf, Rexair Vacuum Cleaners, and Ertl Toys.

The year after the spinoff operating income for Jacuzzi Inc. rose to $55 million on revenues of $332 million. Almost 80 percent of this revenue was contributed by the company's bath products, including whirlpool baths, spas, shower systems, and non-jetted baths. The remainder came from sales of the water systems and swimming pool equipment that had been the foundation of the company since its early years. In April 1996 this segment was strengthened with the purchase of Haugh's Products Ltd., a leading Canadian manufacturer of above-ground swimming pools and equipment with estimated annual sales of more than $11 million.

As Jacuzzi entered the final years of the 1990s international sales appeared to be the major arena of future growth for the company. By 1996 international markets, including Europe, South America, the Middle East, and the Pacific Rim, accounted for about 46 percent of Jacuzzi's sales and analysts predicted that this sector would increase into the next century as the popularity of large, elaborate bathrooms spread worldwide. Plans for a new facility in Singapore that would manufacture products specifically designed for Asian consumers were under way in 1997 and promised to deliver a significant new share of this market.

Streamlining Operations Leading to a Name Change in 2003

While Jacuzzi worked to strengthen its market share in the late 1990s, USI struggled to shore up positive financial results and was burdened with major debt. The company was forced to rethink its strategy in order to cut costs and reduce its growing debtload. As such, the company set plans in motion to streamline its operations. Beginning in early 2000, USI launched a series of selloffs that would dramatically reshape the company.

One of its most significant divestitures came later that year when Citicorp's venture capital firm Vectura Holdings L.L.C. agreed to buy its Diversified division in a $600 million deal. USI retained an 18.6 percent interest in the division, which included a host of different companies, such as Garden State Tanning, Leon Plastics Inc., EJ Footwear Corporation, Lehigh Safety Shoe Company, Huron Inc., Bearing Inspection Inc., Bilt Best Products Inc., Native Textiles Inc., and Jade Technologies Singapore Ltd.

USI continued to shape itself into a plumbing and bath products concern over the next two years by selling its lawn and garden and lighting businesses. The company jettisoned its Ames True Temper landscaping tools business, Spear & Jackson, SiTeco Lighting, Lighting Corporation of America, and Selkirk Group. Overall, nearly $600 million in assets was sold. Company headquarters were moved from New Jersey to West Palm Beach, Florida, in 2002 as part of its cost reduction program.

When the dust settled on USI's streamlining efforts, Jacuzzi stood as one of its major holdings. The final step in USI's transformation was the adoption of the Jacuzzi Brands name for its corporate moniker in 2003. Jacuzzi was one of the top 25 most recognizable brands in the world and company management hoped to capitalize on its status. Later that year, Jacuzzi Brands formed a partnership with home improvement retailer Lowe's, which put the Jacuzzi product line in nearly 900 stores across the United States.

At first glance, the company's strategy appeared to pay off. Sales and profits were on the rise in 2004 and Jacuzzi controlled 24 percent of the domestic market, with competitors American Standard and Kohler trailing behind it. Trouble proved to be lurking around the corner, however, and in May 2005 the company hired investment firm Lazard Freres & Co. to look into strategies that would improve shareholder value. Once again, Jacuzzi Brands began selling assets to improve its bottom line. Majority interests in vacuum cleaner subsidiary Rexair Inc. and sanitary ware manufacturer Eljer Plumbingware Inc. were sold that year.

By this time, Jacuzzi and Zurn—the company's major plumbing brand—were the two largest divisions in its arsenal. Analysts began to speculate that one of the brands would be sold. Zurn's operations proved successful but costs were climbing at the Jacuzzi division. Chief Operating Officer Donald Devine, slated to take over the CEO position later in the year, was fired just before the company announced significant losses in the third quarter of 2005. Alex Marni, president of the plumbing division, was named Devine's successor. While management worked to stabilize Jacuzzi Brand's earnings, the future of one of the most recognizable brands in the world remained up in the air.

Principal Subsidiaries

Asteria Company; Astracast GmbH (Germany); Astracast plc; Bathcraft Inc.; BB Investments Ltd.; Eljer Industries, Inc.; Eljer Plumbingware, Inc.; Gatsby Spas, Inc.; Jacuzzi Brands, Inc.; Jacuzzi do Brasil Industria e Commercio Ltda. (Brazil); Jacuzzi Europe SpA; Jacuzzi France S.A.S.; Jacuzzi Inc.; Jacuzzi (Chili) S.A.; Jacuzzi Investments Ltd.; Jacuzzi Singapore Pte

Ltd.; Jacuzzi UK Group plc; Jacuzzi Universal S.A. (49%); Jacuzzi Whirlpool Bath, Inc.; Jacuzzi Whirlpool GmbH (Germany); JBI Holdings Ltd.; JUSI Holdings, Inc.; KLI, Inc.; Les Aeliers de la Motte S.A.; PH Property Development Company; Redmont, Inc.; Rexair Holdings, Inc.; Rexair, Inc.; Silverdale Ceramics Ltd.; Spring Ram Bathrooms plc; Spring Ram Corporation Overseas Ltd.; Stainless Steel Products Ltd.; Sundance Spas, Inc.; The Spring Ram Corporation plc; USI American Holdings, Inc.; USI Atlantic Corporation; USI Canada Inc.; USI Capital, Inc.; USI Mayfair Ltd.; USI Overseas Holdings Ltd.; USI Plumbing plc; USI Properties, Inc.; Val Industria e Commercio Ltda.; Zurco, Inc.; Zurn Industries Ltd.; Zurn Industries, Inc.; Zurn Pex, Inc.

Principal Competitors

American Standard Companies Inc.; Kohler Co.; Moen Inc.

Further Reading

Adelson, Andrea, "Jacuzzi Whirlpool Creator to Oversee Hanson Unit," *New York Times,* January 14, 1988, p. D2.
Byrne, Harlan S., "Making a Splash," *Barron's,* August 2, 2004.
"Candido Jacuzzi, Pooling His Talent, Made the Hot Tub and His Name Part of the American Home," *People Weekly,* October 27, 1986, p. 92.
Circelli, Deborah, "Jacuzzi Parent Firm Moves Headquarters to West Palm Beach, Fla.," *Knight Ridder Tribune Business News,* August 3, 2002.
Hall, William, "More Bubbles for Jacuzzi," *Financial Times,* December 5, 1994, p. 10.
Heerwagen, Peter, "USI Sells Diversified," *North Valley Business Journal,* February 1, 2000.
"Jacuzzi Brands Inc.," *Wall Street Journal,* May 10, 2005.
"Jacuzzi Maker Changing Its Name," *Palm Beach Post,* June 5, 2003.
Muller, E.J., "Jacuzzi," *Distribution,* October 1985, pp. 41–43.
Nathanson, Ari, "Jacuzzi Jettisons Sinking Subsidiary," *Buyouts,* June 6, 2005.
Pare, Terence P., "A Tale of a Tub," *Fortune,* June 6, 1988, p. 245.
Power, Gavin, "Hanson Spins Off U.S. Units," *San Francisco Chronicle,* February 23, 1995, p. D1.
Tartakoff, Joseph M., "Is Jacuzzi for Sale?," *Knight Ridder Tribune Business News,* July 26, 2005.
——, "Jacuzzi Ditches COO, Posts Large Quarterly Earnings Loss," *Knight Ridder Tribune Business News,* August 12, 2005.
"U.S. Industries Sells Unit," *Wall Street Journal,* March 27, 2000.

—Hilary Gopnik
—update: Christina M. Stansell

James Avery Craftsman, Inc.

Harper Road
Kerrville, Texas 78029
U.S.A.
Telephone: (830) 895-1122
Fax: (830) 895-6601
Web site: http://www.jamesavery.com

Private Company
Incorporated: 1965
Employees: 1,300
Sales: $80 million (2005)
NAIC: 339911 Jewelry (Except Costume) Manufacturing

James Avery Craftsman, Inc., is a private company based in Kerrville, Texas, that designs, manufactures, and sells jewelry, primarily Christian in theme. All told, the company offers about 1,100 designs and 14,000 different pieces of jewelry, sold through 40 company-owned stores located in Texas, Georgia, Oklahoma, and Colorado; 200 independent retailers; mail-order catalogs; and an Internet site. The mostly family owned company is still headed by its founder, Homer James Avery, well into his 80s, assisted by sons Paul and Chris Avery.

Founder Turns to Jewelry Design After World War II

James Avery was born in 1920 in Milwaukee, Wisconsin, the son of a teacher and an insurance agent, who grew up attending a Presbyterian church. By the time he joined the service during World War II and became an Army bomber pilot he was what he called a "defensive agnostic." He retained a certain level of spirituality, however. He wore an amulet made from the horn of an animal, given to him by an African native who said it would protect Avery from "boom-boom"—anti-aircraft fire. He managed to survive 44 missions over Germany, a feat not easily accomplished without injury. The charm also would presage his eventual career.

Married during the war, Avery returned home and went to college, majoring in industrial design at the University of Illi-

nois and earning a bachelor of fine arts degree in 1946. He then became an industrial design teacher at the University of Iowa, then at the University of Colorado in Boulder. While teaching a class in applied design at Colorado, Avery tried to provide some variety for his students, who had grown weary of making furniture and silk screening fabrics, by looking to jewelry. He learned the rudiments of jewelry making from a library book.

By this time Avery's marriage was on the rocks. After returning from a trip with his sons to visit his parents in Chicago, he found a note from his wife asking him to call her lawyer. The breakup of his marriage caused Avery to take stock of his conduct in his marriage, which was punctuated by alcohol and stormy fights, and at the behest of his mother he visited an Episcopal minister in Boulder. His agnosticism gave way to a rekindled faith, strengthened by his natural interest in the kind of ritual and symbolism offered by the Episcopal church. In 1951 he made his first cross, inspired by a Southwestern Pueblo Indian Cross that he came across in a Denver store. Some of the college students were attracted to the cross and asked if he would make one for them. "I just charged for the metal I had to buy," he told the *Houston Chronicle* in a 1988 profile, "but then I saw how moved they were, and realized that this is important in life—to give meaning to others."

Founding the Company in 1954

During this period Avery met a 19-year-old sophomore, ten years younger than he was, Sally Ranger, who came from Kerrville, Texas. When Avery's divorce was finally settled, he married her in 1953. The couple then moved to Minnesota so he could pursue a master's degree. His inability to complete a required French class, however, derailed his plans, and lacking money they were forced to move to Kerrville and live with Sally's mother. Unsure what to do with his life (he even thought about driving a beer truck to make a living), Avery decided to go into business after his mother-in-law offered him the use of her two-car garage as a design studio. Thus, in 1954, James Avery built a workbench and fashioned a sign to hang on the garage; it read "James Avery Craftsman" and featured a candelabra logo. Both the name and image would remain part of the company thereafter. Avery was not entirely sure what kind of craft he would actually pursue, but he settled on religious symbolic jewelry, although for a while he dabbled in a number of knickknacks as well.

Avery was a novice in every way. "I wasn't a jeweler. I didn't know anything about jewelry," he told the *Dallas Morning News* in a 2000 interview. "I was out here in the country. I got a sign out on a farm road that says, 'Jewelry, 1 mile.' I mean, how dumb can you get. . . . I didn't know anything about stones; I couldn't tell a piece of glass from a diamond." He managed to sell a couple of pieces out of the garage, but the first break he received was when his mother-in-law took over the commissary at a local summer camp and began selling some of Avery's jewelry, which at the time was mostly Christian symbols such as crosses, fish, doves, and lambs. The items were simple, uncluttered, and sincere—and to many it would be the best work he ever did.

The campers who bought Avery's jewelry wrote to order more jewelry after they returned home and spread the word about the country artisan, and he gradually built a reputation. During his first year in business he sold $5,500 worth of jewelry, followed by $7,500 in 1956. He outgrew the garage and built a studio and house close by. It was also in 1957 that Avery hired his first employee, Fred Garcia, and produced his first catalog, 16 pages long, offering 39 items. The business continued to enjoy steady growth, spreading statewide through an assortment of retail outlets, including clothing boutiques and church gift shops. In 1965 it was incorporated as James Avery Craftsman, Inc. and by 1967 had once again outgrown its facilities. Avery secured a Small Business Administration loan, bought 20 acres of land, and built a corporate headquarters, studios, and workshops.

By the start of the 1970s the company employed 35 people and generated $400,000 in annual sales, but the business was in clear need of an executive to take it to the next level. Avery found it in Chuck Wolfmueller, a Kerrville native who in 1971 was working on his master's degree in business at the University of Texas. For a term project Wolfmueller analyzed James Avery Craftsman and made suggestions on how to improve production. Avery was so impressed with the paper that he hired the 23-year-old Wolfmueller in May 1971. As an example of how disorganized the company was, when he took over James Avery Craftsman the company was still filling 1970's Christmas orders.

Wolfmueller initiated a number of changes. First, he updated the equipment, and then took steps to make the company more vertically integrated. A machine shop was built to furnish necessary tools and dies, and a chain-making factory was estab-

lished. In the first year the company saw an increase in sales of 40 percent, solidifying Wolfmueller's reputation as a boy genius. Avery was known to be harsh with his own children, but took a different approach with Wolfmueller, who quickly learned how to present ideas that Avery could embrace and make his own. One of those ideas was for James Avery Craftsman to open its own retail stores. The first was established in North Dallas in 1973 and was decorated in a manner that would be followed by subsequent stores: stucco walls, wall sconces, oriental carpets, and old trunks and wardrobes scattered about. In that same year, the company expanded on its secular product line. The Dallas operation was far from an immediate success, yet the company opened a second store in southern California, followed by another in Laredo, Texas. Finally, the concept took hold in Houston, where a store generated $400,000 in 1975. A year later a San Antonio outlet opened and did even better. Business was so strong that the company had to postpone opening further stores until the manufacturing operation was able to keep up with demand.

"Even as the legend of James Avery grew," wrote *Texas Monthly* in 1991, "his private life began to diverge from his public image. The catalyst was Carmen Espinoza." She started out working on the assembly line but caught the attention of Avery, who moved her to the showroom. He began having an affair with Espinoza, then divorced his wife and left her and their four sons to marry Espinoza and move to Laredo, where the company established a retail store and he set up a small factory. Avery periodically flew back in a single-engine airplane to keep tabs on the business, which was being run in his absence by Wolfmueller and his ex-wife, who controlled half the stock. She would remarry and move away, at which point Avery gave up on the struggling Laredo operation and moved back to Kerrville with his second wife. Sally then sold back her share of the company in 1979, a year after tragedy struck the family. According to the *Dallas Morning News,* one of their sons "committed suicide on Father's Day, 1978. Stephen, who was 19, suffered from schizophrenia that began manifesting itself shortly after his father left home in 1971."

James Avery Craftsman launched a catalog sales division in 1980 and mailed its first seasonal catalog. The catalogs had the added effect of driving traffic to the retail stores, which were now expanded to Oklahoma. Business also increased when the Gemstone Department was added in 1983. As a result of the changes, sales that totaled $1.5 million in 1975 grew to $14.3 million in 1985. Wolfmueller became president of the company and Avery, now 64 years of age, decided to put the business up for sale. Not satisfied with the only bid he received, $5 million, he asked Wolfmueller if he was interested in a management-led buyout. A plan was developed that would give Wolfmueller and six other managers ownership of the company if they met certain sales and profit goals. They would then be awarded bonuses to buy the company's stock over time, allowing Avery to retire. The seven managers signed on in May 1986, each paying $50,000 to complete the initial stock payment. Although the retail operation would greatly expand during this period, including a move into Georgia, the plan would soon be derailed as a result of another affair Avery had with a woman, Sylvia Flores, who came to the company as a part-time typist while in high school but was 32 years old in the summer of 1987 when people in the office began to suspect that something was going on between her and Avery.

Key Dates:

1954: James Avery begins crafting jewelry in a Texas garage.
1957: Avery builds a studio and hires his first employee.
1965: The business is incorporated as James Avery Craftsman, Inc.
1973: The first retail store opens.
1980: The catalog sales division is launched.
1983: The Gemstone Department opens.
1988: The first retail store opens in Georgia.
1994: Specialty Charm catalog is introduced.
2003: A web site is launched.
2005: The first Colorado store opens.

He separated from Carmen and began to express misgivings about fulfilling the buyout plan, anticipating that his divorce from Carmen would prove expensive.

Early 1990s: A Period of Notoriety

Discontent within the company reached a head in the summer of 1989. Avery turned on Wolfmueller, insisting that he be more decisive and lose weight. (Avery, a fitness fanatic, preferred trim employees.) Wolfmueller responded with a lengthy memo that in essence suggested that it was time Avery practice what he preached, referencing the passage in the employee handbook that ''a person not adhering to the company's moral standard could be dismissed.'' A day after submitting the memo to Avery, Wolfmueller was asked to resign. He promptly filed a $12.3 million lawsuit against Avery, Sylvia Flores, and the company, and Avery responded with a counterclaim. Two more managers resigned, followed by a third who refused to sign a statement releasing Avery from the buyout plan. Wolfmueller's lawsuit went to trial in 1990. It was a well publicized case, filled with embarrassing details of Avery's personal life, far from consistent with his public image as a Christian craftsman. To the surprise of many, on the eve of the trial Avery and Carmen reconciled, and she sat in court each day in support of him. The question at hand was the legality of the buyout plan, and in the end a jury awarded Wolfmueller $15,000 for the buyout plan and $360,000 for the invasion of his privacy, because his office desk had been broken into and the contents examined without his consent. That amount would be reduced to $29,000. Within a matter of days, Avery and Carmen were divorced; she received a settlement worth $5 million. Wolfmueller vowed to appeal the jury's decision, but several months later he reached an undisclosed settlement with Avery.

Avery made an effort to reconcile with his five sons, giving them each 4,000 shares of stock. His youngest son Paul, a former horticulturist, joined the business and would oversee retail operations. He was followed by brother Chris, an anesthesiologist by training, who became company president. In April 1991 their father would marry a fourth time. He met his new wife, Estela, a registered nurse 30 years his junior, at a fundraising event at a Catholic school.

Under Paul Avery's leadership, James Avery Craftsman introduced corporate governance policies, granted more power to executives, and insisted that a succession plan be put into place. James Avery remained involved in the company, but day-to-day decisions were made by Paul and the company's chief financial officer, Mark Hogeboom, a former executive with Zale Corporation. Primarily, James Avery oversaw design and never entertained further plans to retire.

Despite the unwanted publicity of the Wolfmueller trial, James Avery Craftsman continued to grow during the 1990s and into the new century. In 1994 the company produced its first specialty charm catalog. A fourth jewelry workshop was opened in Comfort, Texas, in 1998. Another workshop opened in 2001, this one located in Hondo, Texas. Although other companies were quick to embrace the Internet, James Avery Craftsman held back, not because it was opposed to the technology, but because the manufacturing operation could not keep up with current demand from catalogs and retail outlets. It was not until 2003 that a company web site was launched. In 2005 James Avery came full circle in a way. In July of that year James Avery Craftsman opened a retail store in Denver, located in the state where he first learned the craft of jewelry making from a library book.

Principal Divisions

Catalog Sales; Gemstone Department.

Principal Competitors

Zale Corporation; Signet Group plc; Wal-Mart Stores, Inc.

Further Reading

Allee, Sheila, ''Jewel in the Hill Country,'' *Houston Chronicle,* September 8, 1985.
Cornell, George W., ''Sharing Faith Through Symbolism,'' *Dallas Morning News,* March 18, 1989, p. 42A.
Forgrieve, Janet, ''Jewelry Maker Returns to Colo.,'' *Rocky Mountain News,* July 22, 2005, p. 4B.
Harris, Joyce Saenz, ''Craftsman's Drive for Perfection Is Burnished by Faith and Failings,'' *Dallas Morning News,* August 22, 2000.
Rubin, Dana, ''God's Jeweler,'' *Texas Monthly,* January 1991, p. 86.
Thiruvengadam, Meena, ''Craftsman Finds His Calling in Making Religious Symbols,'' *San Antonio Express-News,* June 10, 2005.
Watts, Leslie, ''Jeweler Offers Gems of Advice on What Looks Best,'' *Houston Chronicle,* October 20, 1988, p. 4.

—Ed Dinger

JCDecaux

les vitrines du monde

JCDecaux S.A.

17 rue Soyer
Neuilly sur Seine
France
Telephone: +33 01 30 79 79 79
Fax: +33 01 30 79 77 91
Web site: http://www.jcdecaux.com

Public Company
Incorporated: 1964
Employees: 6,933
Sales: EUR 1.63 billion ($2.06 billion) (2004)
Stock Exchanges: Euronext Paris
Ticker Symbol: DEC
NAIC: 541840 Media Representatives

JCDecaux S.A. is one of the world's top three specialists in outdoor advertising (number two worldwide and number one in Europe) and the only group covering all three of the primary outdoor segments of billboards, public transport, and urban street furniture. Decaux claims the world leadership position in the urban furniture segment, a market invented by the company in the 1960s; it is also number one in European billboard advertising and holds the world leadership position in the airport advertising sector, with contracts are 155 airports. More than half of the group's revenues of EUR 1.6 billion ($2 billion) in 2004 came from its urban furniture operations—which involves the installation of bus stops, benches, public toilets, kiosks and the like, which also serve as the support for advertising. Decaux holds street furniture contracts, which often range from eight to 20 years, in some 36 countries. Large-size billboards are the company's second-largest market, accounting for 27 percent of sales. Decaux operates nearly 200,000 panels in 29 countries. Transport advertising makes up 19 percent of group sales, backed by 157,000 panels and contracts with 155 airports in 20 countries. France remains the company's single-largest market, accounting for 34 percent of sales; altogether, Europe accounts for 87 percent of company revenues. Decaux is also present in North America and in Asia. The company is listed on the Euronext Paris stock exchange and is led by co-CEOs Jean-Francois and Jean-Charles Decaux, sons of company founder Jean-Claude Decaux.

Inventing an Advertising Market in the 1960s

Jean-Claude Decaux was just 18 years old when he launched a small business placing advertising signs and billboards along France's roadsides in the late 1950s. Called up for military service, Decaux managed to avoid being sent to fight in Algeria and instead continued to run his company while completing his military service at Bourget.

Decaux's company remained a small affair into the early 1960s, in a market long dominated by just three companies: Avenir, Giraudy, and Dauphin. The future of Decaux's business appeared even more uncertain as pressures began to rise to ban the placement of billboards along France's growing road and highway system. By 1964, that pressure led to the enactment of legislation, under then finance minister Valéry Giscard d'Estaing, restricting the use of billboard advertising.

With the urban billboard market controlled by the industry's big three, Decaux's company faced collapse. Yet Decaux had been developing an idea that would enable him to skirt the new restrictions and at the same time slip past his larger competitors. Decaux's idea was simple. He created his own range of street furnishings, starting with bus stops, which he then offered at no charge to municipal governments. In return, Decaux received an exclusive 20-year contract and the right to sell advertising space for the bus stop's wall panels. A typical bus stop shelter held six panels.

Decaux signed on his first customer in 1964, when the city of Lyons contracted with the company to install a network of bus shelters in the city. The company easily signed up advertisers for its bus stop panels, to the extent that the shelters rapidly paid for themselves. In the meantime, Decaux was not merely content with providing the shelters. The company also recognized the need for incorporating both aesthetic and functional design concepts, making the shelters not only comfortable for users but also an attractive part of the urban setting. The company also showed itself committed to maintaining the cleanliness and good condition of its shelters and quickly gained a national reputation for the high-quality of its street furniture.

Company Perspectives:

The inventor of the "street furniture" concept in 1964, the JCDecaux Group is the only company worldwide to focus exclusively on outdoor advertising and develop activities in all three segments: street furniture, billboard, and transport advertising.

JCDecaux's entry into Paris, where it received its first contract in 1972, underlined the group's arrival as a major force in the country's exterior advertising market. In the meantime, the company had continued to develop its furniture designs, adding new features such as public telephones in partnership with the French telephone service PTT. In 1972, the company also launched its Citylights information panels. In 1976, JCDecaux's partnership with the city of Paris was extended with a new series of contracts, giving the company more or less exclusive control of the city's street furniture market through the end of the 1990s.

Decaux expanded rapidly throughout France, duplicating its successful formula in all of the country's major urban markets. The company's commitment to design and innovation led it to work with noted designers and architects. At the same time, the company's built up a work force dedicated to cleaning and maintaining its fixtures, an effort not lost on the French public. As a result, the company met with little resistance as it expanded throughout the country.

During this time, JCDecaux made its first moves into the international market. As the recognized inventor of the street furniture sector, JCDecaux claimed a long head start on its competitors. This fact helped the company expand its sphere of operations into Belgium and Portugal in the 1970s. In 1982, the company established its first operations in Germany, which quickly became one of its top markets. The company entered the United Kingdom in 1989, and by the end of the 1990s it had expanded throughout most of the rest of Europe. Jean-Claude's eldest son, Jean-Francois Decaux, led much of the group's expansion in Northern Europe, setting up first the group's German operations and later establishing the London office.

JCDecaux also sought new markets within the urban furniture sector. Jean-Claude Decaux, who lay at the origins of what some called the company's 'obsession' with cleanliness, turned his attention to France's notorious *pissoirs,* the often unsanitary public toilet facilities then in place around the country. JCDecaux set out to design a new type of public toilet capable of automatically cleaning itself after each use. With support from friend and then mayor of Paris Jacques Chirac, JCDecaux secured its first public toilet contract in Paris in 1980.

The company launched a new product in 1981, an electronic bulletin board for city councils for posting messages and other information. JCDecaux's interest in automation also led to the launch of its automatic scrolling billboards, called Seniors. These billboards allowed for the potential for multiple advertisement on a single site. In this way JCDecaux, which in the meantime had captured some one-third of France's exterior advertising market, now positioned itself in opposition to the proliferation of billboards in France.

Going Global at the Turn of the Century

JCDecaux's grip on the French street furniture market continued to tighten through the 1990s. By then, the company controlled the market for advertising columns, called Morris columns, in France. In 1992, the company began extending the functionality of its columns, installing telephones, or recycling bins and the like in the fixtures.

In 1994, JCDecaux launched a new generation of automatic public toilet, now made handicap-accessible. The new toilet provided the company with its first entry into the United States, as it gained a contract with the city of San Francisco. Nonetheless, through most of the decade, the company's expansion efforts remained focused on the European market in general and France in particular. In 1997, the company debuted its new Infobus system, installing real-time bus traffic information panels in its bus shelters. JCDecaux's full-fledged move into the United States came in 1998, when the company landed its first major contract with the Simon Properties Group, an operator of shopping malls.

In the meantime, JCDecaux had begun to face challenges back home. In the early 1990s, Jean-Claude Decaux had been convicted for providing funding for a Belgian politician's election campaign. (The company defended itself by noting that this was a common practice at the time.) In the late 1990s, the company once again came under criticism, this time for its contracts, considered by many to be abusive. Indeed, many of the company's contracts contained clauses calling for their automatic renewal with no possibility of a public tender for other bidders. The criticism led the city of Paris in 1998 to end the company's virtual monopoly on the city's street furniture market, opening up its tender process for the first time.

At the same time, the rest of the exterior advertising world had been undergoing a consolidation phase. JCDecaux now found itself faced with a smaller number of far larger competitors. In the meantime, throughout its existence, the company had remained resolutely family-controlled and had relied solely on organic expansion for its growth. By the end of the 1990s, as Jean-Claude Decaux began to transfer control of the business to sons Jean-Francois, based in London, and younger brother Jean-Charles, who had become responsible for the group's southern European operations, the company recognized that it needed to join the consolidation drive.

Decaux's first target was U.K. rival More Group, the U.K. leader in the outdoor furniture sector. The company offered some BP 475 million for More Group but was ultimately thwarted in its bid by fast-growing Clear Channel Communications. Instead, JCDecaux decided the time was right to extend its own operations. In 1999, the company paid the equivalent of $900 million to acquire the outdoor advertising operations of Havas Media, including its control of European billboard leader Avenir and major U.K. outdoor group Mills & Allen, among others. The addition of Avenir also established JCDecaux as the world leader in the airport advertising market.

The purchase transformed JCDecaux from a company focused on the street furniture sector to one with leading global positions in all three of the major exterior advertising segments.

Key Dates:

1957: Jean-Claude Decaux forms a small billboard advertising business.
1964: Decaux invents the urban street furniture market and receives first contract that year, for the city of Lyons.
1972: Decaux wins contract for the city of Paris and begins European expansion.
1980: Company launches first automatic toilets in Paris.
1989: Operations in United Kingdom are launched.
1994: Company places first automatic toilets in the United States in San Francisco.
1999: After acquisition of outdoor advertising division of Havas Media, which includes Avenir, JCDecaux becomes leading billboard advertiser in Europe and world's leading airport advertiser.
2001: Decaux goes public on Euronext Paris Stock Exchange.
2004: Company receives first street furniture contract in Japan, in Yokohama.

The acquisition doubled JCDecaux in size, placing the company in the top three worldwide.

By the 2000s, Jean-Claude Decaux had ceded direction of the company to his sons. In 2001, the Decaux brothers decided the time was right to list the company on the stock market, in order to gain access to funding for its further expansion. The company's timing was unfortunate, coinciding with a global stock market slump. Nonetheless, JCDecaux went ahead with its public offering, listing on the Paris Stock exchange that year.

Into the mid-2000s, JCDecaux continued its tradition of innovation. In 2001, the company became the first to launch plasma-based airport screen displays. In 2002, the company borrowed a leaf from experiments elsewhere in Europe, notably in Amsterdam, launching fleets of self-service, advertising-supported bicycles in Vienna, Austria, and then in two cities in Spain. The following year, the company launched closed circuit television programming for Aeroports de Paris.

JCDecaux also added to its global operations. In 2001, the company made a new acquisition, of Gewista in Austria. The following year, the company added Afichage Holding and DSM, specialized in billboard media and transport advertising. The company's U.S. operations received a significant boost when the company won the street furniture contract with the city of Chicago.

Into the mid-2000s, JCDecaux targeted growth in the Asian region. In 2004, the company added its first operations in Japan, winning a contract to provide street furniture to the city of Yokohama. The following year, in partnership with Mitsubishi, JCDecaux won a new 20-year contract to provide bus shelters to the city of Nagoya. JCDecaux had also entered the Chinese market, forming a joint venture to gain a contract to provide exterior and interior advertising in two Shanghai airports.

The year 2005 held a setback for the company when the contract for the city of New York (acknowledged as one of the world's most important outdoor advertising contracts) was awarded to a smaller Spanish rival. Still, JCDecaux remained in position as one of the world's leading outdoor advertising companies in the new century.

Principal Subsidiaries

JCDecaux Asia Pte Ltd (Singapore); JCDecaux Australia; JCDecaux Deutschland/Aribus Citymedia (Germany); JCDecaux do Brasil, Ltda. (Brazil); JCDecaux North America (United States); JCDecaux Pearl & Dean Ltd (Hong Kong); JCDecaux Salvador S.A. (Brazil); JCDecaux UK; MCDecaux Inc (Japan).

Principal Competitors

Clear Channel Communications, Inc.; Infinity Broadcasting Corporation; Viacom Inc.; Lamar Advertising Company; Cumulus Media, Inc.; Prismaflex International; ARBOmedia AG.

Further Reading

Arnold, Martin, "JC Decaux Bids to Cross Border," *Financial Times*, September 19, 2002, p. 26.

Crawford, Anne-Marie, "Three Hours with the Brothers Decaux," *AdAgeGlobal*, April 2001, p. 36.

Douglas, Torin, "How Decaux Saved Outdoor From Being Just a Wallflower," *Marketing Week*, September 23, 2004, p. 21.

Fox, Justin, "Media Giants Cry 'Gimme Shelter,'" *Fortune*, April 15, 2002, p. 64.

"JC Decaux fais ses premiers pas au Japon," *Le Figaro*, November 10, 2004.

McArthur, Alistair, "Writing on the Wall for Billboard Firm," *Evening News*, October 27, 2005, p. 7.

Meignan, Géraldine, "JCDecaux, citadelle assiégée," *L'Expansion*, April 26, 2001.

Minder, Raphael, and Ashling O'Connor, "JC Decaux May Face Rough Time on the Streets After IPO," *Financial Times*, June 22, 2001, p. 27.

Toscer, Olivier, "Decaux les secrets du roi de la rue," *Nouvel Observateur*, November 10, 1999.

—M.L. Cohen

Jelly Belly Candy Company

1 Jelly Belly Lane
Fairfield, California 94533-6741
U.S.A.
Telephone: (707) 428-2800
Toll Free: (800) 323-9380
Fax: (707) 423-4436
Web site: http://www.jellybelly.com

Private Company
Incorporated: 2001
Employees: 800 (est.)
Sales: $125 million (2004 est.)
NAIC: 311340 Nonchocolate Confectionery
    Manufacturing

Jelly Belly Candy Company is a privately-owned candy company based in Fairfield, California, best known for its gourmet Jelly Belly jelly beans available in 50 official flavors, including such exotic flavors as chocolate pudding, pina colada, buttered popcorn, toasted marshmallow, and café latte. Other jelly bean products include sugar-free Jelly Belly candies; Sports Beans, which contain carbohydrates and electrolytes to aid athletes; and Bertie Bott's Every Flavor Beans, a Harry Potter-licensed line of jelly beans with such flavors as booger, dirt, ear wax, and vomit. The company has also created its version of the M & M candy-coated chocolates called JBz, which are available in a dozen flavors, including chocolate banana, chocolate marshmallow, chocolate cherry, and chocolate cappuccino, Other Jelly Belly confections include candy corn, which the company has been producing for more than 100 years, chocolate Dutch mints, gummi bears and wiggle worms, licorice pastels, chocolate cherry pectin drops, and Jordan Almonds. Jelly Belly also offers the JB line of gumballs. In addition to its Fairfield plant, Jelly Belly maintains a North Chicago plant and a state-of-the art distribution center in Pleasant Prairie, Wisconsin. It also operates three retail stores in California as well as stores in the visitor centers at the Fairfield and Pleasant Prairie facilities.

Company Origins in the Mid-1800s

While the Jelly Belly was not invented until the 1970s, the company that bears the candy's name traces its roots to a pair of brothers, 22-year-old Gustav and 19-year-old Albert Goelitz, who immigrated to the United States in 1867 from Germany, joining an uncle who had come 30 years earlier and settled in Illinois. It was here that Albert learned the candy making trade, and in 1869 he bought an ice cream and candy shop in Belleville, Illinois, and began producing his own handmade candy. He was soon joined by his younger brother who would pack the confections in a horse-drawn wagon and sell them to surrounding communities. The business prospered, the two brothers both married and began raising families, and eventually their sons learned the candy business and became involved with the Goelitz Brothers Candy Company.

Goelitz Brothers survived the depression of 1873 but were not as fortunate 20 years later when the United States experienced another round of the periodic economic upheavals that struck the country in the 1800s. The Panic of 1893 that ushered in a deep four-year depression ruined the brothers, who were forced to sell their candy business. Gustav was emotionally devastated by the turn of events and died at the age of 55 in 1901. Albert, on the other hand, went to work for another company selling candy on the road until he died at the age of 80.

The sons of Gustav Goelitz carried on the candy making tradition. In 1898 Adolph Gustav and his friend William Kelley established Goelitz Confectionery Company in Cincinnati. They were soon joined by Gustav, Jr., and Herman Goelitz. The Goelitz Confectionery Company specialized in the new "butter cream" candies, which included candy corn, the invention of which was attributed to George Runninger of the Wunderle Candy Company. It was a difficult confection to produce because at the time the three different colors—white, orange, and yellow—had to be produced by hand. This meant that workers, known as "stringers," had to carry buckets with 45 pounds of hot candy and while walking backwards pour it into long, steaming trays of kernel-shaped molds. Three colors meant three grueling passes. Goelitz stuck with candy corn longer than anyone in the industry, becoming the oldest manufacturer of the treat. Although Goelitz would also produce chocolates, peppermints, and licorice, it would be the butter creams, especially candy corn, that sustained the company over the next few decades.

In 1901 William Kelley's cousin, Edward Kelley became the bookkeeper and eventually married one of the Goelitz sisters, thus creating a blood tie between the family partners. The company thrived and after a decade had outgrown its Cincinnati plant. A new operation was now established in North Chicago, which enjoyed the benefit of good rail service. Several years later the harmony of the family business was disrupted. After each of the family members had a chance to head the company, there was a split. Gustav, Jr., quit the candy business entirely, while Herman relocated to the San Francisco area to start his own company, The Herman Goelitz Candy Company, which also began to produce candy corn. Because candy was very much a regional business at the time, there was no confusion in the public mind about two companies called Goelitz.

For almost 60 years the two Goelitz candy concerns pursued parallel existences. They both survived the Great Depression of the 1930s, a time that saw nearly 900 candy manufacturers go out of business in a single year. Candy corn was the salvation of both companies, despite the price dropping from 16 cents a pound in the 1920s to less than nine cents a decade later. It was during the 1930s that another family became involved in the business when Herman's daughter Aloyse married Ernest Rowland, who became the head of Herman Goelitz Confectionery. As was the case with most industries in America, World War II revived the business of both Goelitz candy companies. Consumption of candy skyrocketed, especially among servicemen, and candy companies, whose production was curtailed by sugar rationing, sold everything they could make. After the war, Americans continued to satisfy their sweet tooth, as demand increased by 60 percent.

Third Generation Takes Over in 1960s

A third generation took over the California and Illinois Goelitz candy concerns in the 1960s, with cousins Herman Rowland in charge in the former and William Kelley in the latter. Both heavily dependent on the sale of candy corn and other butter creams (mellocremes), they were equally threatened by an increase in competition in candy corn, which led to an erosion in prices. Matters grew so bad, Rowland told Rachel Barron of *East Bay Business Times*, "We would go downtown to the post office a couple times a day looking for checks to be able to cover payroll." Rowland was advised by a banker to sell out. Instead, he chose to expand and looked to diversify the product lines. In 1972 he was driving with his parents to Las Vegas trade show, and were inspired by the desert landscape to create a candy that featured a cool mint crème center, covered in dark chocolate and encased in a candy shell. The result was

Chocolate Dutch Mints, the first chocolate candy produced by the California company.

The introduction of Chocolate Dutch Mints was a good first step, but the existence of both the California and Illinois companies were soon threatened by the surge in sugar prices in 1975. Many candy companies tried to hold off buying sugar until prices fell but couldn't hang on long enough and went out of business. Kelley shuttered the North Chicago plant for several weeks and managed to wait out the crisis, while Rowland took on debt to buy sugar and stay afloat. Both managed to survive the biggest threat faced by the family candy business since the Panic of 1893. Little did either of the cousins know that their darkest hour would soon be followed by the dawning of a new and even more prosperous era.

In 1975 in California Rowland was approached by David Klein, a driver for a candy distributor who had harbored a lifelong dream of making a "Rolls Royce" version of the lowly jelly bean, which in fact enjoyed a long history. A jelly center formula of sorts reportedly dated back to Biblical times, a descendent of the Middle Eastern confection, Turkish Delight. The shell coating came from the panning process developed in France in the 17th century to produce Jordan Almonds. In America the two processes came together in the 1800s resulting in the creation of the modern day jelly bean, which became a staple of the glass jars of penny candy found in every general store. It would not be until the 1930s that the jelly bean began its close association with the Easter holiday. When Klein approached Rowland, Herman Goelitz Candy Company was already producing jelly beans and in the 1960s had made miniature jelly beans favored by then-California Governor Ronald Reagan, who consumed the candy as a way to quit smoking cigarettes.

Klein's idea was to make jelly beans with natural ingredients, such as fruit purees and citrus oils. Rowland agreed to take on the project, and in the summer of 1976 the company developed the first eight flavors of what became known as Jelly Belly jelly beans, including root beer and cream soda, flavors never before found in jelly beans. To enhance the sensation, the flavors were mixed into both the center of the bean and the shell. Another change was the way they were packaged: bags of individual flavors rather than mixed together. It was a winning combination with the public, and consumption of the gourmet jelly beans began to grow. Because it was a premium product, Jelly Belly could command a higher price and distance itself from the rest of competition, which was selling jelly beans as a low-margin commodity product. Moreover, the company began getting requests for Jelly Belly from overseas customers in 1977, which set the stage for export development.

Demand for Jelly Belly became so high that the California plant could not keep up. It was at this point that Rowland turned to his cousin in Illinois and the two family companies began working together to produce the Jelly Belly, although they retained their independent status. The extra production capacity would be sorely needed after Reagan began his run for the presidency in 1980. During the campaign Reagan was photographed eating Jelly Belly jelly beans, and he told how he maintained a fondness for jelly beans even after he quit smoking. Some 7,000 pounds of Jelly Belly jelly beans, which had become closely associated with Reagan's persona, were report-

Key Dates:

1869: Goelitz Brothers Candy Company is founded by Gustav and Albert Goelitz.
1893: Goelitz Brothers are forced out of business.
1898: A second generation founds Goelitz Confectionery Company.
1922: Herman Goelitz breaks away to start The Herman Goelitz Candy Company in California.
1976: Jelly Belly jelly beans are introduced to the public.
2001: Goelitz Confectionery Company and The Herman Goelitz Candy Company merge to form the Jelly Belly Candy Company.

edly sold and consumed during his 1981 inaugural ceremonies. The candy was then made available at cabinet meetings and offered to visiting foreign dignitaries, ensuring ongoing publicity for the brand. In 1983 President Reagan even sent Jelly Belly jelly beans as a surprise gift for the astronauts on the Challenger space shuttle mission that included the first American female astronaut, Sally Ride. The Jelly Belly fad became so intense that the California and Illinois plants had to operate around the clock, and retailers had to place their orders two years in advance.

Mid-1980s' Plant Expansion

Even as the media attention waned, Jelly Belly jelly beans remained popular, so much so that in 1986 Herman Goelitz Candy Company built a new factory and headquarters. Not only was the extra capacity needed to produce more jelly beans, the company by now had also become the first American candy maker to produce gummi bears and gummi worm candies, and a number of other gummy items would follow.

From the mid-1980s until the mid-1990s, the sister Goelitz companies enjoyed an annual growth rate of 15 percent compounded. To keep up, in 1992 the Fairfield facility was doubled in size. It also became a popular tourist destination, as some 175,000 people a year would tour the plant by 1995. Most of them bought a lot of the products at the visitor center store, the popularity of which prompted the California company to expand into retail, opening the first Jelly Belly factory outlet store in 1996 at the Factory Stores at Nut Tree in Vacaville, California. The North Chicago plant also maintained a store, but the operation was not as sophisticated as the Fairfield operation. In 1996 22 acres of land was acquired in Pleasant Prairie, Wisconsin, a 25-minute drive from North Chicago, where a new plant and visitors center was to be built. The site would eventually increase to 50 acres.

Combined sales for the sister companies cracked the $100 million mark in the late 1990s, 70 percent of which came from Jelly Belly. To further exploit the brand name and differentiate itself from the competition, the Goelitz companies began printing Jelly Belly on every bean in 1997, using white food coloring and a special tray and printing machine capable of labeling 20,700 beans each minute. Sales finally fell off somewhat in 1999 and competition increased, prompting a decision to postpone the building of the Wisconsin plant. Instead, $10 million was invested in a much-needed distribution center, which opened in Pleasant Prairie in August 2001, while extra production capacity was found at the two existing plants.

In April 2001 the Goelitz sister companies merged into a single corporation, the Jelly Belly Candy Company. It was a move that made sense on several levels. Two independent companies sharing the Goelitz name confused both consumers and the industry, and by taking the Jelly Belly name the families were building on a very recognizable brand. Jelly Belly would gain even more exposure later in 2001 when for the first time it received a TV brand campaign.

Jelly Belly continued to develop new flavors and new confections. In 2002 it introduced Bertie Bott's Every Flavor Beans, a product based on a candy featured in J.K. Rowling's *Harry Potter* book series. A year later the company unveiled the candy-coated chocolate line called JBz. With sales reaching $125 million in 2004, Jelly Belly appeared poised to enjoy ongoing growth, eventually requiring the construction of a new plant on its Wisconsin property.

Principal Competitors

Brach's Confection, Inc.; The Hershey Company; Mars Inc.

Further Reading

Barron, Rachel, "How Sweet It is for Jelly Belly's Rowland," *East Bay Business Times,* July 26, 2004.
"Goelitz Companies To Merge And Become Jelly Belly Candy," *Professional Candy Buyer,* September 2000, p. 13.
"Herman Goelitz Candy Company, Inc.," *Gourmet Retailer,* December 2000, p. 62.
Pacyniak, Bernard, " 'All Aboard,' " *Candy Industry,* August 2001, p. 22.
Slater, Pam, "Maker of Jelly Belly Candy Takes Retail Leap with California Store," *Sacramento Bee,* October 10, 1996.
The Sweet Life: A Centennial Celebration of Goelitz Candymakers, Fairfield, Calif.: Herman Goelitz, 1998.
Thompson, Stephanie, "Jelly First Jam," *Advertising Age,* August 13, 2001, p. 4.
Tiffany, Susan, "Herman Goelitz's Sweet Fortunes Overflow," *Candy Industry,* June 1998, p. 22.

—Ed Dinger

Jennie-O Turkey Store, Inc.

2505 S.W. Willmar Avenue
Willmar, Minnesota 56201
U.S.A.
Telephone: (320) 235-2622
Toll Free: (800) 621-3505
Fax: (320) 231-7100
Web site: http://www.jennieoturkeystore.com

Wholly Owned Subsidiary of Hormel Foods Corporation
Incorporated: 1952
Employees: 7,000
Sales: $1 billion (2005)
NAIC: 112330 Turkey Production; 311615 Poultry
    Processing; 422440 Poultry and Poultry Product
    Wholesalers

Jennie-O Turkey Store, Inc. is the largest turkey processor in the world, processing more than one billion pounds of turkey each year for sale in more than two dozen countries. Formed by the 2001 merger of Jennie-O Foods, Inc. and The Turkey Store Company, both owned by Hormel Foods Corporation, Jennie-O Turkey Store offers an unrivaled selection of traditional and value-added turkey products. Its product line spans 1,300 different items, including whole birds, ground turkey, sliced meat, and hot dogs. In addition to its nine processing plants, the company has 140 farms, eight feed mills, and four hatcheries.

Origins

Jennie-O Turkey Store, Inc.'s history begins with Minnesotan Earl B. Olsen. After running a creamery, he branched out into turkey production and bought his first processing plant, the Farmer's Produce Company, in February 1949. The availability of cheap grain made it a good time to start the business, he later said. In the fall season, the operation processed 1.5 million pounds of turkey, although it was only New York dressed; that is, only the feathers were removed.

Other poultry and dairy products were discontinued as the company focused on turkey. In 1951, it came out with a nine-pound raw turkey log for military kitchens called Tur-King.

This was followed by further-processed products for the home consumer. In 1953, the company switched to eviscerated turkey rather than New York dressed.

Olsen's business grew quickly in the 1960s. Olsen successfully lobbied to sell birds in Europe. The company had introduced the Jennie-O brand name for the further processed products in 1953. It was a reference to Earl Olsen's daughter. The company itself was renamed Jennie-O Foods in 1971. Olsen's son Charles became company president in 1974.

Jennie-O built a new plant and headquarters near its existing Willmar, Minnesota facility in 1973. In the early part of the decade, the company consolidated vertically with the addition of the Merrifield Feed Mill acquired from the Peavy Company. It also bought a number of smaller turkey farms. The 1980s were also a decade of growth and development. Jennie-O helped pioneer the turkey hot dog phenomenon in 1984.

Acquired by Hormel in 1986

Hormel Foods Corporation added Jennie-O to its stable of international food brands in 1986. The price was not reported, but an analyst told the Minneapolis *Star-Tribune* that it was likely between $70 million and $100 million. It had revenues of about $155 million for 1986 and employed 1,800 people.

Charles Olsen was succeeded as Jennie-O's president by James Reith in 1989. Still more growth followed. Jennie-O bought West Central Turkey's facility in Pelican Rapids, Minnesota in the early 1990s. It built a new plant in Montevideo, Minnesota in 1996. By the end of the decade, the company had eight plants in Minnesota and was processing nearly 900 million pounds of turkey a year.

Jennie-O counted itself the top turkey processor in the United States in 2000, processing more than 800 million pounds of turkey. Its sales were $700 million a year. Jeff Ettinger, a corporate attorney, became Jennie-O's president and CEO in 2000.

2001 Merger with The Turkey Store Company

Hormel Foods brought another turkey processor under its wing in February 2001, buying Wisconsin-based The Turkey

Store Company for $334.4 million. According to the *Mergers & Acquisitions Journal,* it was Hormel's largest acquisition to date. Its operations were combined with Jennie-O Foods, and the new Jennie-O Turkey Store brand was rolled out in April 2002.

The Turkey Store Company's origins dated back to 1922, when Wallace Jerome (then just 13) of Barron, Wisconsin started hatching turkeys. Jerome's business was greatly expanded in the 1940s, when he opened his own hatchery and acquired a new barn for processing.

In 1950 Wallace bought the J.B. Inderreiden Canning Company factory and outfitted it to produce oven-ready birds. The operation was dubbed Badger Turkey Industries. Wallace bought out rival Peter Fox Sons three years later, converting its facility to another hatchery. Badger Turkey Industries was renamed Jerome Foods Inc. in 1964.

Wallace Jerome's son, Jerry, joined the company in 1974 and became president in 1980. In 1984, the company introduced The Turkey Store brand. An employee stock ownership plan was established in 1988, although it remained controlled by the Jerome family. The *Milwaukee Journal* noted that the company had 1,800 employees in the city of Barron, Wisconsin, which had a population of only 3,000.

The company stopped selling whole turkeys in 1996. It was renamed The Turkey Store Company in March 1998. The company began looking for a buyer since the Jerome family's younger generation was not interested in running it, CEO Jerry Jerome told the *Milwaukee Journal-Sentinel.*

At the time of its acquisition by Hormel in 2001, The Turkey Store Company was the sixth largest turkey business in the United States, with annual sales of $309 million and 2,500 employees. Company CEO (and chairman since 1999) Jerry

Jerome held the same roles at the combined company after the merger, while his counterpart from Jennie-O, Jeff Ettinger, was president and chief operating officer.

A ''New Recipe for Living'' in 2002 and Beyond

The combined company began with sales exceeding $1 billion, 70 percent from the old Jennie-O operations, and an 18 percent share of the $5.5 billion turkey market, according to the *Mergers & Acquisitions Journal.* The merger was a nice fit; The Turkey Store had specialized in fresh boneless and ground turkey, while Jennie-O concentrated on processed products.

According to the *National Provisioner,* turkey consumption in the United States had more than doubled since 1975 but was flat since the mid-1990s. The founders of Jennie-O and The Turkey Store had done much to make turkey an all-year item. With per capita consumption of turkey (18 pounds per year) one-third that of pork and one-fourth that of chicken, there was room for growth. Exports also were becoming more important, and the company was experiencing double-digit growth overseas. Jennie-O was pitching turkey as the perfect white meat protein source for a healthy lifestyle, or ''the new recipe for living,'' in its advertising.

Through Jennie-O, which then provided one-quarter of its revenues, Hormel was applying the same formula to turkey that it had to pork, developing new packaged products for the consumer. (It also had large deli, foodservice, and commodity trades.) To fight a trend toward lower turkey consumption in the United States, new product development under the Jennie-O brand accelerated after the merger. The company's So Easy entrées featured fully cooked dishes such as pot roast, pasta alfredo, and barbeque.

A new product in 2004 greatly simplified the art of roasting a whole bird for Thanksgiving. Jennie-O came out with a new Oven Ready turkey that could be baked without thawing. The giblets were already removed. By promising consistent results for everyone, including time-strapped or inexperienced chefs, it reduced the holiday culinary challenge to the realm of convenience foods, observed *Stagnito's New Products Magazine.* A need to cut slits in the cooking bag, however, was designed in to the product. "Consumers don't want to be completely excluded from the culinary preparation, especially a traditional holiday meal, and venting the turkey allows them to feel they are still in touch with the product they serve," said a Jennie-O executive. The Oven Ready turkey took two years to develop. It was made possible by innovative packaging featuring a proprietary Fool-Proof poly cook-in bag produced by Curwood of Oshkosh, Wisconsin.

Jennie-O was producing more than one billion pounds of turkey a year, sold in 1,300 different products. Distribution extended to a dozen foreign countries, including Canada, Mexico, Korea, Japan, and Russia. The company employed 7,000 people at seven plants in Minnesota and one in Wisconsin.

Hormel's turkey division was the goose that laid the golden egg in 2005. Its operating profit was up 73 percent to $136 million. This was the first time turkey outperformed Hormel's refrigerated and grocery businesses. Jennie-O head Jerry Ettinger was named Hormel's CEO in September 2005.

Principal Divisions

Retail; Deli; Foodservice; Commodity.

Principal Operating Units

Willmar/Spicer; Pelican Rapids; Melrose; Montevideo; Faribault; Barron.

Principal Competitors

Cargill, Inc.; ConAgra Foods, Inc.

Further Reading

Baar, Aaron, "BBDO Talks Turkey in New Ads," *ADWEEK Midwest Edition,* May 13, 2002, p. 10.

Dahm, Lori, "Turkey Made Easy: Jennie-O Turkey Store Brings Convenience to Thanksgiving," *Stagnito's New Products Magazine,* October 2004, pp. 28ff.

Daykin, Tom, "Hormel Gobbles Up Turkey Store for $334 Million," *Milwaukee Journal Sentinel,* January 24, 2001, p. 1.

Harrison, Joan, "Hormel Finds a Great Fit in Its Acquisition of the Turkey Store," *Mergers & Acquisitions Journal,* March 2001, p. 16.

"Jerome Gobbles Up Barron," *Milwaukee Journal,* December 2, 1990, p. D2.

Martin, Kathryn, "Curwood Flies Away with Award for Its Innovative Oven-Ready Frozen Turkey Carrier Bag," *Food Engineering,* April 2005, p. 17.

Merrill, Ann, "New Leader of Hormel's Jennie-O Unit Has Lots of Experience in Talking Turkey," *Star Tribune* (Minneapolis), February 18, 2001, p. 1D.

St. Anthony, Neal, "Hormel to Buy Willmar-Based Jennie-O Foods," *Star-Tribune* (Minneapolis), December 8, 1986, p. 1A.

Smith, Rod, "Jennie-O/Turkey Store Merger to Take Turkey 'Around the Calendar,'" *Feedstuffs,* January 29, 2001, p. 3.

Webb, Tom, "Turkey Sales Strong for Hormel Foods," *Saint Paul Pioneer Press,* November 24, 2005.

Young, Barbara, "Turkey Triumph: Hormel Foods' Creative Approach to Big Bird Product Development Solidifies the Position of Its Jennie-O Turkey Store Division As a Global Marketshare Leader," *National Provisioner,* December 2003, pp. 10+.

—Frederick C. Ingram

Johnny Rockets Group, Inc.

26970 Aliso Viejo Parkway, Suite 100
Aliso Viejo, California 92656
U.S.A.
Telephone: (949) 643-6100
Fax: (949) 643-6200
Web site: http://www.johnnyrockets.com

Private Company
Incorporated: 1986
Employees: 5,640
Sales: $190 million (2005 est.)
NAIC: 722110 Full Service Restaurants

Johnny Rockets Group, Inc.'s (JRG) restaurants offer American nostalgia with a menu of basic American food, served in a 1940s-style diner complete with an open chrome kitchen, a chrome and black formica counter, red vinyl seats, and counter-top jukeboxes that play old tunes for a nickel. Each year, the company serves up more than 22 million hamburgers to its guests in nearly 170 restaurants in 30 states, in countries around the world, and on Royal Caribbean cruise lines. The restaurants' signature items are four hamburgers: The Original, a hand-shaped hamburger; The Double, with two patties, cheddar cheese, and a special sauce; #12, with cheddar cheese and red, red sauce; and St. Louis, with bacon, Swiss cheese, and St. Louis sauce. The balance of the menu consists of several ''classic'' sandwiches, such as a BLT, a hot dog/chili dog, American fries, chili, and a few other items. Malts and shakes are hand-dipped and come with an extra serving on the side in the mixing canister, just like the old diners used to do. Beverages include Coca-Cola flavored with cherry, chocolate, lemon, or vanilla. Apple pie, baked fresh on the premises, is available with ice cream or Tillamook cheddar cheese and is served with a small paper American flag.

Founding the Company on a Dream

Ronn Teitelbaum founded Johnny Rockets in 1986, at the age of 46, after selling his successful, Beverly Hills-based chain of fine men's clothing stores. Although he had no experience in the restaurant business, it had been his dream to own and operate a 1940s-style diner. Teitelbaum's restaurant reflected the nostalgia he felt for his own childhood memories of the 1940s, such as the friendliness and the cleanliness of old-time diners, but his idea also coincided with a surge in retro dining concepts.

Teitelbaum took a year and a half to plan his first Johnny Rockets burger and malt shop, using the same attention to detail that he gave to his men's clothing business. Teitelbaum sought to recreate the hamburger of his childhood memories. He cooked hamburgers with a number of seasoning combinations until he found the right flavor. A favorite employee story exemplified the extremes Teitelbaum took to attain perfection in every detail. After Teitelbaum had eaten a delicious tuna fish sandwich at a Los Angeles restaurant, he returned to the restaurant with a flashlight after hours and looked in the dumpster for an empty tuna can to see which brand the company used.

Teitelbaum's $250,000 restaurant project encompassed an 844-square-foot malt shop with 20 red vinyl stools. Skeptical friends and restaurant business consultants thought that the small-scale concept could not succeed. They assumed that peak meal times would require too long a wait and that the shop could not maintain an adequate level of business during slow business hours, between lunch and dinner, and late at night. In addition, the high-fat menu, with hamburgers, fried potatoes, and ice cream shakes, did not fit the stereotype of the Californian's preference for salad and pasta.

The moment Johnny Rockets opened on chic Melrose Avenue in Los Angeles, customers filled the restaurant, and a line of 30 customers formed at the door. The wait staff, dressed in white, 1940s-style soda jerk uniforms, mixed malts on 30-year-old spindle mixers (which required frequent repair) and supplied nickels to customers to play the vintage countertop jukeboxes. Instead of using a machine that would squeeze the juices from the fresh ground beef, kitchen staff hand-patted hamburgers and cooked them to order. The burgers were served wrapped in paper on a cardboard plate. Outside the restaurant, above the smooth white exterior, a 1940s-style logo blazed, ''Johnny Rockets,'' in yellow neon on a red and blue lighted background. On its first day of business, June 6, 1987, Johnny Rockets stayed open until 5:00 a.m. to serve all of the day's customers.

Company Perspectives:

Johnny Rockets was founded on the belief that everyone deserves a place where they can escape today's complicated world and experience the food, fun and friendliness reminiscent of feel-good Americana. On June 6, 1986, the first Johnny Rockets opened on trendy Melrose Avenue in Los Angeles, offering its guests fast, friendly service, a simple menu, great food and fun.

Attracting a panoply of Los Angeles residents of all ages, the restaurant sustained a continuous flow of customers in the days that followed. Business hours spanned from 11:00 a.m. to 12:00 midnight except Fridays and Saturdays, when the shop stayed open until 2:00 a.m. The high turnover cycled at approximately every 30 minutes. Johnny Rockets served 600 to 700 customers per day, involving around 19 percent takeout sales. With customers spending more than $5.00 each, revenues reached $1 million the first year.

Within the first year of operation Johnny Rockets grew into a small chain with franchises and company-owned stores. In the Los Angeles area, restaurants opened in Westwood, Sherman Oaks, and Beverly Hills. Franchises in Atlanta and San Francisco resulted when interested parties approached Johnny Rockets to license the concept. Johnny Rockets restaurants also opened in Minneapolis and Chicago. In an article in the October 24, 1988, *Nation's Restaurant News,* Teitelbaum attributed the success of Johnny Rockets to his own inexperience in the restaurant business, stating, "I didn't know it was impossible to do over $1 million in 20 seats. I didn't know people wouldn't line up at midnight for a hamburger, fries, and a malt."

With intentions to further expand the chain Teitelbaum sought to protect the Johnny Rockets trade dress. The company won the first of its trademark-related cases in New York in August 1989. Despite the objections of Teitelbaum, the Johnny Rock-it bar and grill opened in New York City in early 1989. Teitelbaum contended that the value of the Johnny Rockets name was undermined, and he supported that view with the deposition of a prospective franchisee reluctant to open a Johnny Rockets restaurant in New York because of concern that the similar name would cause confusion. Trademark infringement precedents helped win a federal injunction that prevented the lounge from using "Johnny" or "rock" in its new name. The company also filed suit against Suzy Q's diners in Winnipeg, Manitoba, for trade dress violation.

Johnny Rockets expanded internationally, capitalizing on the appeal of American popular culture abroad. Teitelbaum used a business connection from his clothing business to open a Johnny Rockets restaurant in Tokyo in September 1989. City Centre Restaurants, which operated a variety of casual dining chains in London, opened a Johnny Rockets there in 1990. In addition, a prospective franchisee approached the company to open a Johnny Rockets in Melbourne, Australia, which went into development at this time. By June 1992 the company had expanded to 28 stores in the chain, with six company-owned units and 22 franchises.

The Johnny Rockets dining concept found many believers, including Lloyd Sugarman. Originally senior vice-president of Johnny Rockets, Sugarman acquired ownership of the first San Francisco restaurant, a 42-stool location in the Marina, as well as franchise rights to the San Francisco Bay area. Sugarman boosted growth in northern California with two new shops in the summer of 1992, while negotiations for locations in San Jose, Santa Rosa, and Fisherman's Wharf in San Francisco progressed.

Sugarman attained the Fisherman's Wharf location with some difficulty, but it would set a significant precedent for the company. The city of San Francisco did not allow fast-food restaurants at Fisherman's Wharf, in an effort to retain the historical integrity of the area. The city did allow a Johnny Rockets malt shop, however, as cooked-to-order hamburgers and made-to-order shakes differed from fast-food restaurants, with precooked sandwiches to be available upon request and dispensed premixed shakes. The issue defined the market niche that Johnny Rockets occupied, between fast-food and casual dining restaurants. That niche served customers who had grown weary of fast food, who wanted full service and an inexpensive, fresh-cooked meal. Johnny Rockets accommodated that customer base with quick food preparation, but further distinguished itself with wait people who were known to suddenly break into song and dance routines using ketchup bottles as microphones. Johnny Rockets' wait staff learned as many as nine dance routines, to old songs on the countertop jukeboxes such as "Great Balls of Fire" and "Respect."

Expansion and Leadership Changes in the 1990s

In mid-1992 the company opened a new burger and malt shop every three to four weeks. The chain expanded in southern California with new stores in Encino and Agora Hills in August 1992. New franchises opened around the United States, in Miami; Baltimore; Scottsdale, Arizona; Sunriver, Oregon; and Burlington, Massachusetts. Unit-level sales averaged $850,000 annually with only 20 to 26 seats. Expansion of the chain required experienced leadership in franchise development, and Ray Cabana, formerly of Taco Bell and Kentucky Fried Chicken, became president in June 1992. Teitelbaum remained chairman and CEO.

Growth at Johnny Rockets meant the company confronted challenges to its identity. Teitelbaum set a new precedent for the Mexican government's acknowledgement of international franchise law after an imitation of Johnny Rockets appeared in Cancun, Mexico. The company won the case and government officials shut the place down at gunpoint, just in time for the debut of Johnny Rockets in Mexico City in April 1993. Another situation occurred two days before the grand opening of a Johnny Rockets restaurant at West Edmonton Mall, the world's largest shopping mall at that time, in Alberta, Canada. McDonald's of Canada obtained an injunction to prevent the opening. The agreement between McDonald's and the mall owner, Triple Five, stated that no other fast-food restaurant in the Phase II area could serve hamburgers, except in the food court. Johnny Rockets used the Fisherman's Wharf store as an example of the company's identity as a full-service restaurant. In June an Alberta Court dismissed the argument by McDonald's of Canada, which identified Johnny Rockets as a fast-food restaurant, and lifted the injunction.

Key Dates:

1987: The first shop opens on Melrose Avenue in Los Angeles.
1989: A period of rapid expansion ensues, including a Johnny Rockets in Tokyo.
1995: The company is under new ownership by Carpenter Investment and Development Corporation.
1998: The 100th Johnny Rockets unit is opened in the Georgetown area of Washington, D.C.
1999: Michael Shumsky is named CEO.
2000: Founder Teitelbaum dies of brain cancer.
2005: The company's 175th restaurant opens for business.

Teitelbaum's ambitions to expand the Johnny Rockets chain prompted negotiations with Carpenter Investment and Development Corporation (CIDC), whose primary activities involved hotel and shopping center development. CIDC would aid the growth of Johnny Rockets with its knowledge of city centers and shopping malls, as well as its affiliations with shopping malls and with the Hilton and Hyatt hotels. In June 1994 CIDC agreed to acquire a majority interest in Johnny Rockets International, as the company was called then. Internal disputes at Johnny Rockets slowed the transition to CDIC ownership, however. Rockets Holding Inc., which formed to handle the acquisition, had to negotiate separate terms of sale with Teitelbaum and Alfred M. Bloch, another majority stock owner.

In the immediate interim Johnny Rockets continued to grow and succeed. When Johnny Rockets won the 1994 Golden Chain award from *Nation's Restaurant News,* the company encompassed 63 units, including five in Australia, three in Mexico, and one each in Japan, England, and Canada. Customer checks averaged $6.50 per person. Rare changes to the menu involved the addition of a peanut butter and jelly sandwich to the children's menu and the addition of a vegetarian burger, the Streamliner, to the regular menu. In April 1995 Johnny Rockets signed an agreement to place a restaurant on the main floor of the casino at the Hilton Casino Resort in Reno, Nevada. The menu included breakfast to accommodate all night and early morning gamblers. Internationally, new stores opened in Kuwait and in the United Arab Emirates in 1995.

CIDC completed its acquisition of Johnny Rockets in November 1995 and named the new company Johnny Rockets Group (JRG). JRG held a 95 percent ownership, with the balance owned by Teitelbaum and a group of small investors. The majority investors included Patricof & Company Ventures, Inc. of New York with $12.5 million invested, General Motors Pension Fund with $10 million, Center Partners of New York with $6 million, as well as CSK Ventures, Tokyo, and CIDC. A total investment of $44 million involved $25.6 million paid to previous investors, $12 million for expansion, and $4.4 million to acquire five franchises.

New ownership was followed by a time of turbulent changes in leadership. With the formation of JRG, Teitelbaum remained on the board of directors and became the company's creative consultant. JRG hired Jeffrey Campbell, former CEO and chair-man of Burger King, as the new CEO. Cabana retained the title of CEO, although he reported to Campbell until he eventually resigned. Campbell resigned in July 1996 because of disagreements over strategy, in regard to the pace of development of new stores, and management, in regard to whether to franchise or open company-owned units. Glen Hemmerle became president of JRG in February 1997. He brought retail experience with Pearle Vision, Crown Books, and Athletes Foot, but no restaurant experience. Hemmerle's strong customer orientation led to the addition of a hot fudge sundae, lemonade, and a hot dog/chili dog to the menu.

Hemmerle became president during a surge in expansion. The earlier internal disputes slowed long-term growth, with only two restaurant openings from 1995 until February 1997, compared with 20 restaurants from mid-1994 into 1995. In addition, some restaurants closed, such as the Sherman Oaks, California store, because of the 1994 earthquake, and the Laguna Beach, California store, because of the 1997 floods. Some stores in Australia closed as well, because of poor locations chosen by subfranchisees. Finally, in February 1997 JRG opened four new malt shops, in Miami, Boston, Memphis, and Birmingham.

JRG opened a total of 14 stores in 1997 and 1998 with the assistance of $15 million in venture capital that the company received in spring 1997. JRG sought to develop company-owned stores in three kinds of locations: neighborhood outlets that would attract local residents, unusual locations like the casino at the Reno Hilton, and high-traffic shopping areas. The company preferred mall locations near movie theaters, because it combined two distinctly American inventions—the diner and the movies. New stores in 1998 included openings at Providence Place Mall in Rhode Island and at Downtown Plaza Mall in Sacramento, a 2,200-square-foot store next to the movie theaters. In October 1998 JRG opened its 100th unit, in historic Georgetown in Washington, D.C. In addition, after four years in development, a Johnny Rockets opened in Beirut, Lebanon. The restaurant's interior was constructed in London, shipped to Lebanon, and snapped together at the site. The interior could be relocated if necessary.

In May 1999 Hemmerle suddenly resigned, and JRG immediately replaced him with Michael Shumsky, former president of Sonic Restaurants, a 2,000-unit drive-in restaurant based in Oklahoma City. JRG chose Shumsky because of the similarity of the Johnny Rockets and Sonic restaurant concepts and Shumsky's experience in franchise development. Shumsky would provide needed leadership, as JRG had decided to grow through franchises rather than through company ownership, as well as stability, with Shumsky's agreement to a five-year contract.

Strategy and Identity in Focus in 1999

Shumsky intended to focus on brand development, store-level operations, and market development. Although same-store sales increased 6 percent during the fiscal year ended May 2, 1999, systemwide sales showed lower-than-expected revenues as some larger stores did not attain the same customer appeal as small, intimate stores. In addition, Shumsky found that JRG did not have a store prototype, and he planned to develop one based on the smaller units, which seated from 20 to 65 customers. New stores would be located in areas where Johnny Rockets malt shops already existed, mainly California, Florida, and New York, at an average cost of $575,000. Shumsky prepared JRG for new development with two new positions, regional vice-presidents of the eastern and western United States. Shumsky hired Pamela Britton, from Cinnabon, for the east, and Barry Cook, from Sonic Restaurants, for the west.

To sharpen the Johnny Rockets brand identity, an art program was undertaken. David Willardson, known for his posters for the movies *American Graffiti* and *Raiders of the Lost Ark,* produced ten oil paintings that featured Johnny Rockets' signature menu items, as well as its logo. The paintings then replaced some of the older pictures that hung at Johnny Rockets restaurants.

JRG cooperated with Warner Brothers in a movie promotion for the animated feature film, *The Iron Giant,* during the summer of 1999. The storyline of the movie centered on a single mother employed as a wait person at a 1950s-style malt shop. For the first three weeks after the movie's release, Johnny Rockets wait staff gave a comic book or cassette tape to each child customer. The promotion involved the sale of Johnny Rockets promotional items at Warner Brothers retail outlets, including t-shirts, sweatshirts, and caps with the Johnny Rockets logo in embroidery. A compact disc of old tunes from Johnny Rockets' jukeboxes, such as ''Stand By Me'' and ''Under the Boardwalk,'' was also among the company's promotional items.

With more than 120 restaurants in 25 states, Washington, D.C., and seven countries, JRG's plans for expansion in late 1999 involved 35 new units. Johnny Rockets' franchisee in Mexico opened a new store in Cancun in August and planned another for that city. In November 1999 Johnny Rockets signed a deal to become the first branded restaurant chain to be located on a passenger cruise ship. An agreement with Royal Caribbean International placed a 259-seat Johnny Rockets malt shop on the pool deck of its new cruise ship, *Voyager of the Seas,* in May 2000.

Johnny Rockets in the New Millennium

Founder Ronn Teitelbaum lost his battle with brain cancer in September 2000. His dedication to the business lived on at company headquarters and JRG worked diligently to preserve Johnny Rockets' position in the restaurant industry. As such, the company found itself on solid ground during the early years of the new millennium. JRG's strategy at this time was to close 13 unprofitable stores, turn seven corporate stores into franchise units, move company headquarters from Irvine to Aliso Viejo, and cut executive staff in order to trim costs. JRG also began focusing on product quality and employee training. The company opened a restaurant at Cedar Point Amusement Park in Sandusky, Ohio, in 2001. It also bolstered its cruise line business, opening its fifth cruise ship-based restaurant on Royal Caribbean International's *Mariner of the Seas* in 2003.

In all, CEO Shumsky had put JRG on track to open 25 new stores a year. While the company worked to open new corporate stores as well as franchise units, it began to embark on a creative advertising campaign. In order to raise brand awareness and bolster sales, JRG used product placement in the 2005 movie *The Island* and an episode of *Queer Eye for the Straight Guy.* It also worked to keep the atmosphere in its restaurants fun and entertaining. In May 2004, it celebrated the 100th anniversary of the hamburger with a month-long celebration at its restaurants. On June 3, 2005, the 175th Johnny Rockets opened its doors.

In late 2005, JRG announced plans to launch a new menu design in all of its restaurants. The move was significant—it was the largest redesign of the Johnny Rockets menu in JRG's history. The new menu included an image of a jukebox and photos of the restaurant's most popular food, including its Rocket Double hamburger, its shakes, and its fries. Shumsky commented on the new menu in a November 2005 company press release, claiming, ''The new design reflects our continued commitment to providing guests with a unique and quality dining experience.''

Indeed, Shumsky's strategy over the past several years was paying off. In 2005, estimated sales reached $190 million and were expected to climb further in 2006. Industry analysts speculated that the company may be poised for an initial public offering, an acquisition, or a sale. Regardless, Johnny Rockets appeared to be positioned for future success. Management was confident that in the years to come customers around the world would continue to enjoy the food and dining experience that inspired Ronn Teitelbaum to open the first Johnny Rockets restaurant in 1986.

Principal Competitors

Carlson Restaurants Worldwide Inc.; Red Robin Gourmet Burgers Inc.; The Steak 'n Shake Company.

Further Reading

Acle Chasko, Ana, and Raul Ruberia, ''At Johnny Rockets, Entertainment Costs a Nickel,'' *Miami Herald,* December 11, 1994, p. 4.

Apodaca, Patricia, ''Venture Capital Financing Nearly Doubles,'' *Los Angeles Times,* September 17, 1997, p. 10D.

Ballon, Marc, ''Johnny Rockets Names Shumsky As New CEO,'' *Los Angeles Times,* May 27, 1999, p. 6C.

Barnes, Tom, and Dan Fitzpatrick, ''Pittsburgh Unveils Plans for Retail Development at Heart of City,'' *Knight-Ridder/Tribune Business News,* October 5, 1999.

Battaglia, Andy, ''Johnny Rockets's Success Takes Off; Chain Launches 100th Unit,'' *Nation's Restaurant News,* October 12, 1998, p. 102.

Beck, David, L., ''Johnny Rockets Knows Its Burgers,'' *San Jose Mercury News,* September 29, 1995, p. 53.

''Campbell Resigns Johnny Rockets Prexy, CEO Posts,'' *Nation's Restaurant News,* August 5, 1996, p. 156.

Correa, Tracy, ''Fresno, Calif, Shopping Center To Add Restaurants, Retailers,'' *Knight-Ridder/Tribune Business News,* August 18, 1999.

Glover, Kara, ''Investor Group Acquires Johnny Rockets,'' *Los Angeles Business Journal,* November 6, 1995, p. 10.

Greenberg, Herb, ''What's Mickey Drexler Doing When He's Not Running Gap? He's Got His Mind and Lots of Money on Johnny Rockets,'' *San Francisco Chronicle,* September 6, 1996, p. E1.

Hardesty, Greg, ''Irvine, Calif.-Based Johnny Rockets Embarks on New Marketing Campaign,'' *Knight-Ridder/Tribune Business News,* June 18, 1999.

——, ''Retro-Look Restaurant Chain Changes Leadership at Key Stage,'' *Knight-Ridder/Tribune Business News,* May 25, 1999.

Hernandez, Greg, ''Johnny Rockets To Drop Art Used in Rival Ruby's Chain,'' *Los Angeles Times,* June 23, 1999, p. 6C.

"Investors Finalize Majority Buyout of Johnny Rockets," *Nation's Restaurant News,* November 6, 1995, p. 2.

Jennings, Lisa, "Johnny Rockets Relaunches Plan for Growth After Sales Take Off," *Nation's Restaurant News,* August 29, 2005.

"Johnny Rockets Debuts in Hilton," *Nation's Restaurant News,* April 3, 1995, p. 11.

"Johnny Rockets Investor Ignites Unit Expansion," *Nation's Restaurant News,* June 20, 1994, p. 2.

Johnson, Greg, "Noshing on Nostalgia Is Big with Consumers and Developers," *Los Angeles Times,* February 4, 1996, p. 1.

Lipson, Larry, "Dine Beat: New Links in Chains," *Los Angeles Daily News,* July 10, 1992, p. L45.

Lockwood Tooher, Nora, "Proposed Providence, RI, Mall Announces Names of Its Restaurants," *Knight-Ridder/Tribune Business News,* April 29, 1998.

Loyie, Florence, "Johnny Rockets Restaurant Finally Blasts Off; Diner Rockin' at West Edmonton Mall After Court Lifts Injunction Sought by McDonald's," *Edmonton Journal,* July 16, 1993, p. B3.

Luna, Nancy, "Playing Catch-Up," *Orange County Register,* August 26, 2004.

——, "Ready for Its Close-Up," *Orange County Register,* August 9, 2005.

Martin, Richard, "Hot Johnny Rockets Lifts Off; Newest Entry in Rock 'n' Roll Diner Revival," *Nation's Restaurant News,* February 2, 1987, p. 1.

——, "Johnny Rockets Founder Sues To Oust Prexy, Break Sale Block," *Nation's Restaurant News,* October 10, 1994, p. 2.

——, "Rockets' Kingpin Oust Teitelbaum; Boardroom Shakeup Rocks Chain," *Nation's Restaurant News,* November 7, 1994, p. 1.

——, "Ronn Teitelbaum: Riding on His Own Set of Rules," *Nation's Restaurant News,* September 19, 1994, p. 178.

Mehegan, Sean, "From Burger King to Rockets' Man," *Restaurant Business,* March 1, 1996, p. 118.

Montgomery, Christine, "Take Rockets Back in Time: Food, Decor from the 1950s," *Washington Times,* April 8, 1999, p. 6.

"The Old Fashioned Corner Malt Shop Comes of Age," *San Francisco Chronicle,* June 24 1992, p. B3.

"Ronn Teitelbaum, Johnny Rockets Founder, Dies at 61," *Nation's Restaurant News,* September 25, 2000.

Spector, Amy, "Johnny Rockets Taps Shumsky To Succeed Hemmerle As CEO," *Nation's Restaurant News,* June 7, 1999, p. 4.

Tannenbaum, Jeffrey A., "Hamburger Chain Hopes Buyout Will Hasten Growth," *Wall Street Journal,* January 12, 1996, p. 12.

Telberg, Rick, "Guts, Determination Key to Success as Restaurateur," *Nation's Restaurant News,* October 24, 1988, p. F46.

—Mary Tradii
—update: Christina M. Stansell

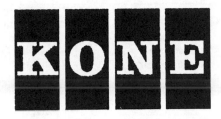

KONE Corporation

Keilasatama 3
FIN-02150 Espoo
Finland
Telephone: (358) 204 751
Fax: (358) 204-75-4496
Web site: http://www.kone.com

Public Company
Incorporated: 1910
Employees: 33,021
Sales: EUR 2.9 billion ($3.4 billion) (2005)
Stock Exchanges: Helsinki
Ticker Symbol: KNEBV
NAIC: 333921 Elevator and Moving Stairway
Manufacturing

KONE Corporation is the world's fourth largest elevator company. It provides installation, modernization, and maintenance of elevators, escalators, and automatic doors. The company operates approximately 800 service centers in 40 countries across the globe and its customers include builders and building owners, designers, and architects. During 2004, KONE set plans in motion to split itself into two separately listed companies. KONE Corporation continued to oversee the elevator, escalator, and building door services business, and Cargotec Corporation remained in control of the company's container and load handling operations. The transition was complete in June 2005 when both companies were listed as separate entities on the Helsinki Stock Exchange. KONE Corporation is led by President Matti Alahuhta; the founding Herlin family is represented by Chairman Antti Herlin.

Rising in Prewar Finland

KONE Corporation originated almost as an afterthought of the Finnish electric motor manufacturer, Strömberg. Although Strömberg's primary business was the manufacture and sale of new motors, it also had developed an active business of refurbishing its used motors. Rather than develop sales of the rebuilt units under its own name, however, Strömberg sought a new brand name for its refurbished motors. In 1910 Strömberg incorporated its electric motor refurbishing arm as a separate company, dubbing the company simply "KONE" (Finnish for "machine"). The KONE company began business as little more than a machine shop in a converted stable on the lot of Strömberg's Helsinki factory.

Another offshoot of Strömberg's electric motor business had been elevator sales and installation. The company did not produce the elevators itself, but instead acted as the Finnish licensee for Sweden's Graham Brothers, then the leading elevator manufacturer in Scandinavia. In 1912, Lorenz Petrell, head of Strömberg's elevator activities, was named managing director of its KONE subsidiary. Petrell did not abandon the elevator line, however; instead, he transferred all of Strömberg's elevator business, with its engineering, installation, and other personnel, to KONE. For the time, KONE continued to represent the Graham elevator line.

For more than a century Finland had been dominated by its Russian neighbor, which had made the tiny country a Grand Duchy at the start of the 19th century. In the years leading to World War I, Finnish manufacturers, including KONE, were called on to supply the Russian military effort. To meet production demands, KONE moved to larger Helsinki quarters. The Russian Revolution that followed on the heels of World War I gave Finland the long sought opportunity to declare its independence.

KONE, too, had decided that the time was ripe for independence. In 1918 the company ended its long-held licensing agreement with Graham Brothers, and began producing its own elevators, installing its first four elevators that same year. By then, the company had grown to 50 employees. The company's initial elevator experience was positive, prompting the company to turn its focus to elevators in the early 1920s. By then, the company, still a subsidiary of Strömberg, was producing more than 100 elevators per year. The company's sales focus was wholly on the Finnish market, which only had begun to develop multistory building structures necessitating elevator technology.

By 1924 KONE's parent company began to struggle financially; a member of its advisory board, Harold Herlin, recom-

Company Perspectives:

Over the years, KONE has proven its ability to adapt to a changing world as well as to create new opportunities for the company to grow. Stable ownership by four generations of the same family has created a strong and supportive environment for continuous development.

mended that Strömberg sell off its noncore businesses, including its KONE elevator division. Herlin, who held an engineering background, himself offered to buy KONE from Strömberg, an offer that was accepted. Herlin took the position as KONE's chairman, while assuming the chairman and president position of Strömberg as well. Lorenz Petrell, meanwhile, was named as KONE's president. The pair set to work building the newly independent KONE into the country's leading elevator manufacturer, hiring many of the failing Strömberg's engineering and commercial staff to boost KONE's development.

Helsinki was undergoing rapid expansion in the 1920s, and Herlin's variety of business interests, which extended into shipbuilding, utilities, and other construction, placed KONE in a strong position to furnish the growing market for elevators. In 1927 KONE moved into new, far larger production facilities, after buying a former margarine factory. By the end of 1928 the company had produced more than 1,000 elevators. In that same year the next generation of Herlins joined the company. With an engineering degree from Helsinki University of Technology, Heikki Herlin had spent four years working for Otis Elevator in the United States and for Brown Boveri in Germany, before joining what would become the Herlin family company. As KONE faced the Great Depression, Lorenz Petrell retired and was replaced by Heikki Herlin.

The younger Herlin proved to be an impassioned leader, whose engineering background enabled him to become involved in all aspects of the company. KONE, which had been struggling to compete against the higher technology of its foreign rivals, now began producing elevators again to meet international standards. The drop in elevator orders caused by the Depression economy paradoxically aided KONE in its technological advancement effort. Forced to look elsewhere for sales in the early 1930s, KONE saw an opportunity to move into the crane market, where it could easily adapt its elevator technology. At the same time KONE also began producing its own electric motors. This gave the company full control of its elevator manufacturing, enabling KONE to satisfy higher quality standards. During the 1930s the company's production continued to expand, into electric hoists, and then into conveyor belt systems.

Elevator production once again picked up at the end of the decade, enabling the company to top more than 3,000 elevators sold. World War II, and Finland's uncomfortable position, would interrupt KONE's elevator growth, as production was turned to supplying the country's effort against the Soviet army. Heikki Herlin took over the chairmanship of the company upon his father's death in 1941. Two years later KONE stepped up its production of industrial cranes, opening a new production plant in Hyvinkaa, outside of Helsinki. Supplying the war effort replaced much of KONE's production, however, while the company would maintain its prewar production levels to a large extent. On the losing side at the end of the war, Finland was forced to pay a heavy reparations bill. KONE's production was turned as well to this end, producing, at government cost, its elevators and other industrial equipment for the Soviet victors.

Postwar Diversity and Internationalization

KONE would find a positive note in its production for the Soviets. Despite receiving no profit from its production, which included 100 elevators and close to 200 cranes, paid for by the Finnish government, KONE found other benefits. For one, many of the elevators and cranes demanded by the Soviets were of a larger design, featuring more advanced technology than KONE had been using. As the company adapted to these requirements, it also was able to expand its production capacity, increasing not only the number of production units, but also their tonnage capacities. By the end of the 1940s, as reparations wound down, KONE had developed the technology to enter a new market, that of harbor cranes.

During the 1950s KONE continued to introduce new technology into its elevators, including automatic doors, hydraulic lifts, and advanced control features. The company also was growing into an important producer of cranes and hoists, as well as conveyor belts and other materials handling equipment technologies. A prime source of sales was Finland's dominant forestry and paper industries; in the 1960s KONE would increase its position in these industries with various lumber handling machinery. Yet elevators remained the company's core product; by the 1960s, KONE, which had become the leading elevator supplier for Finland, was finding little room for further domestic growth.

The arrival of the next generation of Herlins to the company's leadership would introduce a new era to KONE's history. When Heikki Herlin retired in 1964, he was replaced by son Pekka, who had joined the company in 1958. Unlike his engineering-oriented father and grandfather, Pekka Herlin held a degree in economics. The younger Herlin would chart a new course for the company: that of international growth. As such, KONE would become one of the first Finnish companies to eye international expansion, leaving the company with no predecessors upon which to model its expansion.

In 1966 the company opened a new, state-of-the-art elevator production facility in Hyvinkaa. Then the company began looking for new markets, in particular, across the borders of its Scandinavian neighbors. In 1968 KONE made its first acquisition, buying the elevator and escalator business of Sweden's ASEA. The purchase of the larger, yet money-losing ASEA-Graham unit (which, incidentally, gave the company control of its former supplier, Graham Brothers) catapulted KONE to the position of Scandinavian market leader. It would take six years for KONE to reverse its new subsidiary's losses. By then, however, the company had continued to fuel its overseas expansion, acquiring elevator subsidiaries throughout Europe. In 1974 the company bought out the entire European elevator and escalator production of Westinghouse, doubling KONE's revenues.

By the mid-1970s KONE was producing elevators, escalators, and the new ''autowalks'' under brand names such as

Key Dates:

1910: Strömberg incorporates its electric motor refurbishing arm as a separate company, dubbing the company simply "KONE" (Finnish for "machine").
1918: The company begins producing its own elevators.
1924: Harold Herlin buys KONE.
1966: The company opens a new, state-of-the-art elevator production facility in Hyvinkaa.
1968: KONE acquires the elevator and escalator business of Sweden's ASEA.
1974: KONE buys the entire European elevator and escalator production of Westinghouse.
1986: The conveyor and bulk handling businesses are sold.
1994: KONE's Wood division is sold to Austria's Andritz AG; the company buys Montgomery Elevator Company.
1996: Germany's O&K Rolltreppen is purchased.
1998: The company begins its partnership with Toshiba.
2005: KONE is separated into two separate publicly listed companies: KONE Corporation and Cargotec Corporation.

Graham, Hävemeier & Sander, Marryat & Scott, Armor, Sabiem, and Westinghouse, and the company featured production facilities in France, Germany, the United Kingdom, Austria, Sweden, Norway, Denmark, Spain, and elsewhere in Europe. Pekka Herlin also would continue the company's product diversification, adding electronic hospital and laboratory equipment, and expanding KONE's crane, harbor crane, and other materials handling businesses. Developing these activities led KONE into a new area, with the 1982 acquisition of Navire Cargo Gear and the 1983 acquisition of International MacGregor. These acquisitions did more than bring KONE into the cargo access market, including ship hatches and ramps and other materials for loading, unloading, and RoRo (rollin rollout) processing—adding Navire and MacGregor established KONE as the world leader in this category.

By the mid-1980s KONE had joined the ranks of the world's leading materials handling companies. Despite its diversification, KONE still relied on its elevator and escalator businesses for more than 63 percent of its sales, which continued to be heavily centered on Europe. The collapse of the worldwide building market, and the extensive economic recession that would grip Europe through much of the 1990s, would force KONE to rethink its global strategy.

Streamlining in the 1990s

By 1995 KONE had either sold off or spun off its non-elevator and non-escalator operations. First to go was the company's conveyor and bulk handling businesses, which were sold off in 1986. KONE would jettison its wood handling arm in 1994, selling its KONE Wood division to Austria's Andritz AG in 1994. Next, the company's cargo access wing, MacGregor-Navire, was sold to Incentive Group, based in Sweden, in 1993. The company's crane production subsidiaries were incorpo-

rated as a separate company, sold to Sweden's Industri Kapital, and then introduced as a public company on the Helsinki Stock Exchange as KCI KONEcranes International. Finally, the division grouping the company's high-tech analyzers, monitors, and other hospital and laboratory equipment businesses was spun off through a management buyout and reformed as KONE Instruments in 1995. In turn, KONE moved to reinforce its escalator arm, acquiring Montgomery Elevator Company, then the United States' fourth largest elevator and escalator company, which also gave KONE a major boost into the North American market. With the addition of 100 percent control of Germany's O&K Rolltreppen in 1996, KONE emerged firmly as the world's leading escalator and autowalk supplier.

The newly streamlined KONE had not finished its restructuring. Throughout its 20-year acquisition and development drive, KONE had maintained a hands-off policy on its new subsidiaries. The result was a collection of independently operating subsidiaries, each with its own culture, products, brand names, and production methods. In the 1990s KONE at last took steps to create a single corporate culture, enforcing the KONE brand name on a new generation of modular products. The company's push to restructure and homogenize its operations would be capped by the 1996 introduction of its Monospace elevator design. Hailed as revolutionary by the industry, the Monospace eliminated the need for a dedicated wheelhouse for the elevator's machinery, cutting its cost and reducing its energy requirements.

While building its new corporate culture, KONE also had been developing a new market area designed to complement its elevator and escalator core operations, as well as bridge that business's inherently seasonal, cyclical nature. In a program started during the 1980s KONE built a new maintenance services group, which during the 1990s would grow to become the company's strongest revenues provider. More than simply offering maintenance and repair services, KONE proposed a modernization program, enabling customers to upgrade, rather than entirely replace, their elevator parks.

As the company developed its maintenance and modernization arm, reaching more than 400,000 elevators under contract by 1998, the company's newly introduced Monospace design would help boost KONE's sales after years of a withering economic climate. KONE's strong push into the North American market promised to give the company greater balance during such economic cycles. Similarly, in the late 1990s KONE stepped up its efforts to expand into the developing Asian markets. Despite the faltering economy of much of the region, beginning in 1997 KONE continued to invest in production capacity, opening a new state-of-the-art production facility in Kunshan, China in October 1998.

The company also entered into a partnership with Toshiba Elevators and Building System Corp. in 1998. KONE and Toshiba expected to capture nearly 14 percent of the world market as a result of the deal. This strategic alliance was strengthened in 2001 when Toshiba gained the rights to manufacture and market elevators using KONE's state-of-the-art MonoSpace technology in Japan. During 2002, KONE invested EUR 158 million in Toshiba Elevators, securing a 19.9 percent stake in the company.

KONE also remained active on the acquisition front. It purchased Gustav Ad. Koch Maschinenfabrik KG and L. Hopmann Maschinenfabrik, two German elevator companies; London-based Cable Lift Installations; the United Kingdom's Chiltern Industrial Doors; and Neuwerth & Cie, an elevator concern based in Switzerland.

Changes in the New Millennium

As demand in the elevator industry leveled off in the early years of the new millennium, KONE looked for ways to increase sales and profits. It began to focus on bolstering its automatic building door business as well as its materials handling operations. As part of this strategy, KONE bought Finnish engineering firm Partek. Partek's container handling, load handling, forest machinery, and tractor operations were added to KONE's Materials Handling division. KONE opted to focus on its container and load handling business in 2003, selling off the tractor and forest machinery businesses that year. The Materials Handling division was renamed KONE Cargotec in January 2004. The division operated two main business segments: Kalmar and Hiab. Later that year KONE Cargotec spent EUR 186 million to acquire MacGregor, a cargo handling specialist it previously owned.

Pekka Herlin died in 2003 and Antti Herlin assumed the chairmanship. Matti Alahuhta was slated to become KONE's president in January 2005. Under this management team's leadership, KONE launched a strategic initiative that would significantly change the company's operating structure. In 2004, plans were set in motion to split KONE into two separately listed companies. KONE Corporation would continue to oversee the elevator, escalator, and building door services business while Cargotec Corporation remained in control of container and load handling operations. An April 2005 *Hugin Press Release* explained the strategy, claiming, "The objective of these developments is to increase customer focus, to become faster and better in responding to the differing needs of various market areas and to improve the productivity derived from common global functions and processes." The split was complete in June 2005 when Cargotec began trading on the Helsinki Stock Exchange.

During this transition, KONE was left to focus solely on its elevator-related operations. As such, the firm acquired Bharat Bijlee Ltd. of India and Thai Lift of Thailand. It also forged partnerships with Soolim Elevator Co. of Korea and China's Zhejiang Giant Elevator. On the product development front, the company launched a new systems platform, the KONE Maxispace, which eliminated the need for counterweights. In 2001, KONE teamed up with Nokia to develop wireless voice and data systems to be used to make its elevators and escalators safer and more reliable.

With 9 percent of the global market, KONE operated as the fourth largest elevator company in the world during 2005. The global elevator and escalator market—worth nearly EUR 30 billion a year—included the sale and installation of new equipment, maintenance, and the repair and modernization of old systems. The automatic door maintenance market was estimated to be worth EUR 5 billion. KONE continued to develop strategies to capture additional market share and appeared to be on track for success in the future.

Principal Competitors

Otis Elevator Company, Inc.; Schindler Holding Ltd.; ThyssenKrupp AG.

Further Reading

Burt, Tim, "Kone, Toshiba Expect Significant Lift from Alliance," *Financial Post,* May 28, 1998.

Frank, Jerry, "The Marriage of Kone Corp and MacGregor," *Lloyd's List,* December 3, 2004.

"KONE Announces Organizational Changes," *Hugin Press Release,* June 1, 2005.

"KONE Corporation Completes Demerger into Two Separate Companies," *Nordic Business Report,* June 1, 2005.

"Matti Alahuhta Named President of KONE," *Hugin Press Release,* November 22, 2004.

"Nokia and KONE Team to Extend Wireless Technology to Elevators and Escalators," *Telecomworldwire,* May 16, 2001, p. 1.

O'Mahony, Hugh, "Kone Buy-Out of MacGregor Aims to Raise the Stakes in the Elevator Market," *Lloyd's List,* May 10, 2005.

Simon, John B. (ed.), "Special History Issue," *New and Views Inhouse Magazine,* Helsinki: KONE Corporation, 1998.

—M.L. Cohen
—update: Christina M. Stansell

Kulicke and Soffa Industries, Inc.

2101 Blair Mill Road
Willow Grove, Pennsylvania 19090
U.S.A.
Telephone: (215) 784-6000
Fax: (215) 659-7588
Web site: http://www.kns.com

Public Company
Incorporated: 1956
Employees: 3,333
Sales: $717.8 million (2004)
Stock Exchanges: NASDAQ
Ticker Symbol: KLIC
NAIC: 333295 Semiconductor Machinery Manufacturing

Kulicke & Soffa Industries, Inc. (K&S) is the world's largest manufacturer and supplier of semiconductor assembly equipment. The company offers comprehensive assembly solutions to its many customers worldwide, including wire bonding equipment, packaging materials, and test interconnect products. According to the company, its wire bonders are used to connect very fine wires—made of gold, aluminum, or copper—between the bond pads of a semiconductor die and the leads on the integrated circuit package to which the die has been attached. K&S has an extensive network of 33 worldwide facilities which offer a wide range of sales, service and applications development. Although the company is headquartered in the sleepy town of Willow Grove, Pennsylvania, it has facilities in such highly diverse and far away locations as Israel, Taiwan, China, and Switzerland. In fact, approximately 80 percent of the company's total sales volume is generated overseas.

Company Origins in 1951

Like many other firms, the history of Kulicke & Soffa Industries begins with the biography of its founders, Fred Kulicke and Albert Soffa. Kulicke and Soffa were both educated as engineers and started working as employees for Proctor Electric upon their graduation from college. Based in Philadelphia, Pennsylvania, Proctor Electric was a well-known company specializing in con-

sumer electronics products. Ever since the end of World War II, with the growing prosperity of the American economy, the general public had been clamoring for more sophisticated consumer electronics products in order to make their lives more convenient. In order to meet this burgeoning demand, engineers like Kulicke and Soffa were hired to design consumer products. Shortly after the two men became employees of Proctor Electric, they found themselves designing such products as cake mixers and electric irons. In fact, it was a project to design electric irons that brought Kulicke and Soffa together for the first time.

Kulicke and Soffa were extremely ambitious and entrepreneurial young men, not satisfied with designing electric irons for a large company not their own. As the two men became more acquainted with one another, and started discussing their dreams and ambitions for the future, not surprisingly they discovered they had much in common. A close friendship developed as the two men worked on various projects at Proctor Electric and, after a short time, Kulicke and Soffa decided to strike out on their own and establish a custom engineering business. In the steamy month of July 1951, Fred Kulicke and Albert Soffa put their ambitions on paper and formed a partnership that was destined to last until one of them died. Thus Kulicke and Soffa Industries was born.

There was only one problem, and not a small one at that. The two men didn't have much money to start their business with. So they did what they could to raise the necessary funding, including raising loans from friends and acquaintances and pooling their own meager resources to begin operations. They established themselves in a small one-room office and began designing solutions to manufacturing problems by automating processes, while at the same time repairing broken machinery in order to pay the monthly rent and phone bills.

With their combined energy and technical ingenuity, Kulicke and Soffa aggressively contracted numerous small businesses and manufacturing firms throughout the greater metropolitan area of Philadelphia. When a packing firm approached them to stuff their sausages, the two entrepreneurs devised a machine to standardize and stuff sausage into casings in mass quantities. When a retail manufacturer asked them to design a machine to stretch kidskin for ladies' gloves, Kulicke and Soffa were only too happy to

Company Perspectives:

The K&S Strategy is to provide 'best in class' packaging assembly products supporting our customers' technology and cost roadmaps.

oblige with an innovative machine resulting in a significant increase in productivity and thus higher sales. Additional designs during their first years of business including innovative machines for cleaning beer cases as well as machines made to standardize the size of hamburger patties. In just of few short years, K&S became known as one of the most innovative and reliable custom engineering firms on the East Coast.

By 1956, K&S had been in business for five years. What transpired that year was to change the direction of the company's endeavors forever. The Nobel Prize in Physics was given to three engineers working at Bell Labs for the development of a semiconductor chip. Before the Nobel winners even returned home from the award ceremony in Stockholm, Sweden, the manufacturing division of Bell Labs, Western Electric, had decided to contract Kulicke and Soffa Industries to develop the equipment necessary to efficiently manufacture these early versions of semiconductor chips. The two partners, thrilled with the contract, agreed to it almost without hesitation. Then reality started to sink in, and Kulicke and Soffa realized what they had agreed to, namely, accepting the challenge of connecting microscopic wires from the transistor die in the semiconductor chip to the leads on its package. Within a few months, to the surprise of the electronics industry, Kulicke and Soffa had met the challenge, designing and beginning to manufacture the world's first wire bonder. Thus the company became one of the world's first designers and manufacturers of semiconductor assembly equipment.

From the moment the company introduced its wire bonder, it took a leading role in the semiconductor assembly equipment industry. In 1961, the owners decided that it was time to take the company public, so K&S made an initial stock offering of 100,000 shares on the NASDAQ. The company's shares were bought immediately and subsequent additional offerings were held throughout the decade. Fortunately, the partners had been at the right place at the right time and, as the semiconductor industry expanded by leaps and bounds throughout the 1960s, demand from around the world for K&S equipment skyrocketed. In addition to its legendary series of wire bonders, the company began to diversify its product line to include such items as manual and semi-automatic equipment for wafer preparation, wafer fabrication, die bonding, and micro-tools.

Growth and Expansion: 1960s–80s

One of the most important strategic decisions that the two men made early on in the organization and administration of their firm was to forge a commitment to research and development. Both owners were willing to invest more capital in research and development than was available from annual net profits. Nothing could have been smarter, since from the early 1960s, K&S became synonymous with technological leadership in the semiconductor industry. By this time, company operations had significantly outgrown the first machine shop where

the two entrepreneurs spent many hours building their business, so K&S moved to larger facilities in Willow Grove, Pennsylvania, while opening sales and services offices at the same time throughout the United States. Expansion was not limited to the United States. Due to the increasing demand for its products from around the world, the company established facilities in such strategic locations as Hong Kong, Switzerland, and Israel.

The mid-1970s brought with it a severe economic recession, and the semiconductor industry was hard hit. K&S suffered as a result, and the company was forced to either sell off or shutter all of its product line, except those focusing on semiconductor assembly operations. Still maintaining the priority of research and development in that core area, however, the company's engineers were able to introduce the first digitally-controlled, fully automatic wire bonders in the industry. This product, designed to operate at extremely high speeds with more accuracy and greater yield than any previous wire bonders, provided the firm's clients with the advantage of meeting the growing demand for PCS. Due to the introduction of this innovative product in 1976, Kulicke and Soffa Industries was able to recover from the losses suffered earlier and re-establish itself as the pre-eminent leader in the semiconductor assembly equipment industry.

The 1980s started well enough for K&S, and the company celebrated its 30th anniversary with much fanfare and celebration. During the early 1980s, management at the firm changed hands, but stayed in firm control of the Kulicke family. Even with this transition of leadership from one generation to the next, the company's long-term strategic goals remained the same, namely, a clear priority to research and development and a firm commitment to expanding its overseas markets. To this end in 1981, management decided to develop a major presence in the Japanese semiconductor market, which was growing by leaps and bounds at the time. Kulicke and Soffa (Japan) Ltd. opened for business in Tokyo and was soon competing with other major semiconductor assembly firms on their own turf. By 1984, company sales had reached their highest level ever.

The mid-1980s were not as kind to the fortunes of the company. The ever-volatile semiconductor industry took another severe downturn, and the new leadership was confronted with its first major financial crisis. Astute and prudent decision-making by management, however, enabled K&S to weather the gyrations of the market and continue its leadership in the industry by introducing a host of new and cutting-edge products for die bonding, wire bonding, and dicing. Such focus paid off handsomely as time went on. By the end of the 1980s, K&S had recovered financially and had introduced numerous innovative products that assured its technological leadership for years to come in the semiconductor assembly industry.

Growth in the 1990s

During the 1990s, the semiconductor industry grew in importance, with an accompanying worldwide dependence on K&S products. K&S profited immensely from the volume, complexity, and variety of semiconductor assembly equipment required by its ever-growing list of clients. With this explosion in the industry, the company expanded dramatically: technology centers were established in Willow Grove, Pennsylvania; Japan; Israel; and Singapore; customer resources centers were opened in Taiwan and The Philippines; Micro-Swiss facilities were constructed in

Hong Kong, Singapore, and Israel; fine wire operations were built in Alabama, Singapore, and Switzerland; a new Semitic manufacturing plant was opened in California, while a state-of-the-art Flip Chip Technologies wafer bumping manufacturing center was established in Arizona; an X-LAM Technologies research and development laboratory was dedicated in California, and an Advanced Polymer Solutions manufacturing facility was built at the company's headquarters in Willow Grove, Pennsylvania. The company also completed a massive 214,000-square-foot administrative, design and manufacturing facility to serve as a new headquarters to direct worldwide operations.

By 1999, K&S employed more than 2,200 people and controlled more than 50 percent of the global wire bonding equipment market. The largest supplier of semiconductor assembly equipment in the world, K&S was well-positioned to continue its dominance of the market. More than twice the size of its nearest competitor, the company was searching for ways to expand its presence in Asia and Europe, while maintaining its position of strength in the United States. As long as management continued to focus on research and development and introduced innovative products, there was no end in sight for the company's continued growth and expansion.

K&S in the New Millennium

K&S hit the ground running in the first year of the new millennium. Sales reached record levels—$899.3 million—in 2000. The company moved its ball bonder manufacturing to Singapore that year, anticipating significant cost reductions from the transfer of operations. It also introduced a series of new wire bonders that were considered to have the finest pitch and be the fastest in the world. K&S bolstered its holdings with the $65 million acquisition of Probe Technology Corporation and the $225 million purchase of Cerprobe Corporation The two companies were merged into K&S's new Test Interconnect operations.

The semiconductor industry proved its cyclical nature once again in 2001, leaving K&S and many of its competitors scrambling to make strategic business decisions that would cut costs and stabilize profits. The company's revenue fell sharply from the previous year, dropping to $555 million. As a result of the industry

downturn, K&S laid off nearly 500 employees and shuttered its manufacturing facility in Milpitas, California. It made Flip Chip Technologies a wholly owned subsidiary that year.

The slowdown continued in 2002 as revenues dropped further. The company posted a $274.1 million loss that year and was forced to rethink its expansion efforts. K&S took measures to control costs and streamline its operations—including the layoff of an additional 200 workers—and decided to focus on its wire bonders and test interface products business. The company divested its saw and hubless saw blade products line, nixed plans to develop its substrate business, and sold its Flip Chip unit in 2004.

K&S opened a manufacturing facility in China in 2003. Management eyed this region as a key growth area and expanded the plant's production capabilities in 2005. In addition, a wafer test manufacturing plant began operations in Taiwan in 2004.

K&S returned to profitability in 2004, a sure sign its strategy was paying off and that, perhaps, the semiconductor industry was slowly rebounding from its slump. The company launched its next generation wire bonding and stud bumping machines in 2005, which offered significant speed improvements. During this time period, the company continued to consolidate manufacturing operations while developing new state-of-the-art products. While the industry it served remained volatile, K&S had proved that it could weather difficult conditions. With a solid business plan in place, K&S management was confident the company would remain a leader in its field for years to come.

Principal Competitors

ASM International N.V.; SHINKAWA Ltd.; Sumitomo Metal Mining Co. Ltd.

Further Reading

Dorsch, Jeff, "Kulicke and Soffa Acquires Assembly Technologies," *Electronic News*, July 18, 1994, p. 2.
"K&S Expands Chinese Manufacturing Ops," *Electronic News*, September 19, 2005.
"K&S Opens China Manufacturing Operation," *Assembly*, November 1, 2003.
"Kulicke & Soffa Closing Plant, to Take $17 Mln Charge," *Reuters News*, August 27, 2002.
"Kulicke and Soffa Industries, Inc.," *Wall Street Journal*, August 22, 1996, p. B6(E).
"Kulicke and Soffa Revenues Dip In Quarter," *Electronic News*, April 27, 1998, p. 46.
"Kulicke Buys Probe Technology," *Wall Street Journal*, December 13, 2000.
Levine, Bernard, "Flip Chip Moves Accelerate," *Electronic News*, July 8, 1996, p. 8.
Levine, Bernard, "Kulicke and Soffa Wins Orders," *Electronic News*, August 16, 1999, p. 30.
Socolovsky, Alberto, "K&S Struggles To Make Money," *Electronic Business*, November 1992, p. 73.
"Tool Manufacturer Gets Key Benefits From Israeli Plant," *Industrial Engineering*, July 1992, p. 22.

—Thomas Derdak
—update: Christina M. Stansell

LaCie Group S.A.

17 rue Ampere
Massy
France
Telephone: +33 01 69 32 84 00
Fax: +33 01 69 32 83 66
Web site: http://www.lacie.com

Public Company
Incorporated: 1989 as Electronique D2
Employees: 341
Sales: EUR 289 million ($310 million) (2005)
Stock Exchanges: Euronext Paris
Ticker Symbol: 5431
NAIC: 334119 Other Computer Peripheral Equipment
  Manufacturing

LaCie S.A. is a leading developer and manufacturer of computer peripheral equipment, focusing especially on external data storage solutions, as well as display technologies. LaCie produces network drives, hard drives, and other storage drives, including tape-based storage devices, DVD and CD drives and writers, and high-end LCD monitors. The company incorporates high-speed transfer technologies into its devices, supporting USB 2.0, Firewire, SCSI, as well as cutting-edge technologies, such as SATA, introduced in 2005. The development of such high-speed protocols has proved a boon for the company, enabling external peripherals—the company's core niche—to achieve transfer speeds rivaling those of internal computer components. From its beginnings in a Paris apartment in 1989, LaCie has targeted the international market. As part of that strategy, the company has developed a local presence in Germany, Belgium, The Netherlands, Spain, Italy, the United Kingdom, Switzerland, Sweden, Japan, Hong Kong and China, Singapore, and the United States. Europe remains the group's largest market, at 53 percent of the group's revenues of EUR 289 million ($310 million) in 2005. The Americas account for 44 percent of the company's sales, and its Asian operations contribute just 3 percent. LaCie's growth in the 2000s has accelerated in large part because the company has expanded its product offering from a focus on the professional and corporate markets to target the retail consumer market. LaCie is listed on the Euronext Paris Stock Exchange. Company cofounder and Chairman Philippe Spruch is also its largest shareholder, with nearly 61.5 percent of shares.

External Ideas in the 1980s

Pierre Fournier and Philippe Spruch spotted a niche opportunity in the computer market in the late 1980s. Personal computers had become essential tools in a number of industries, such as the graphic design and nascent multimedia industries. Increases in computer technology, particularly the development of faster processors and more powerful graphics cards, introduced a new range of possibilities for professionals. Yet the advances in technology also created ever-larger file sizes. The relatively modest internal hard drives on most computers proved inadequate for many data storage needs. At the same time, the reliance on personal computers also highlighted the need to safeguard data through the creation of backup copies.

Unlike IBM-based personal computers at the time, Apple computers featured a built-in high-speed interface, called SCSI, to connect peripherals to the computer. Fournier and Spruch recognized the potential of adapting storage devices such as hard drives and tape drives to connect externally via the computer's SCSI port. The SCSI interface offered a second advantage in addition to transfer speed, in that several devices could be chained together to a single computer port. In 1989, the pair founded their own company, Electronique D2, in their apartment in Paris's 14th arrondissement. D2 became one of the first in Europe to exploit this new area of personal computing.

D2 at first focused on designing the cases to house existing drives, meeting with immediate success. By 1990, the company had outgrown its original location, and in that year, the company moved to a 900-square-meter site, still in the city of Paris. The move also accompanied a shift in the group's strategy. Fournier and Spruch understood that, in order to compete in an increasingly global market characterized by rapid technological progress, D2 would have to develop its own technological capacity.

D2 began hiring a team of engineers and building its own research and development team. By 1991, the company had launched its first in-house designed product, an internal SCSI card, bringing the transfer technology to the IBM PC market. Nonetheless, the Apple computer market remained the company's core focus into the mid-1990s.

In the meantime, D2 launched the second prong of its strategy, that of rapid international growth. In this way, the company sought to capitalize on the lack of a strong European player in the external data storage market. By 1991, D2 had opened its first subsidiary, in London. The following year, the company added subsidiaries in Belgium and Denmark.

Another important factor in the company's early success was its commitment to developing not only technologically advanced products, but also to providing its product with strong design features. As part of this effort, the company turned to a number of noted industrial designers, such as Philippe Starck, who helped design a whole line of D2 products in 1992. Neil Poulton became another prominent design partner for the company. The emphasis on design played an important role in the group's success: As external peripherals, the company's products were by nature exposed to view. At the same time, the company's core market of graphic designers and multimedia developers naturally responded to the stylish designs of the group's product range.

Acquiring a New Corporate Identity in the 1990s

D2 attacked a major limitation of IBM and Windows-based personal computers, which often lacked the physical capacity and software resources to house both the traditionally parallel port (used primarily for printers) and a SCSI port. In 1993, D2 released a new interface that housed both parallel and SCSI ports. The company also began work on a new cable to provide similar capability, launching the Shark cable in 1994. The Shark became one of the company's best-selling products into the middle of the decade.

With its European sales growing strongly, D2 moved to still larger premises in the town of Massy, a Parisian suburb, in 1993. The company also continued to expand its international network,

adding a subsidiary in Dusseldorf, Germany in 1993, and subsidiaries in The Netherlands and Switzerland in 1994. That year marked the group's transition to an international company, with 50 percent of its sales coming from outside of France.

The company continued its expansion, adding a subsidiary in Milan, Italy, and Madrid, Spain, in 1995. In order to fuel further growth, D2 brought in external investors, selling a 10 percent stake to venture capital group 3i (Investors in Industry) that year. The investment provided D2 with the capital it needed to enter the North American marketplace. By the end of 1995, the company had made its first major acquisition, that of Portland, Oregon-based LaCie, a subsidiary of hard drive manufacturer Quantum. Founded in 1987 and acquired by Quantum in 1992, LaCie had developed a range of products complementary to D2's own line, coupled with a strong brand name and proprietary software technologies. Yet LaCie offered other advantages to D2. The company's relationship with Quantum, a major supplier of drives used in D2's line, enabled D2 to renegotiate its purchasing agreement with Quantum. At the same time, LaCie enjoyed the exclusive rights to develop Apple-branded external hard drives.

The combined company now laid claim to being the largest aftermarket data storage supplier for the Apple computer market. D2 prepared for a new phase of growth, moving to larger headquarters in Massy in 1996. The company then went public, with a listing on the Paris Stock Exchange's "Nouveau Marché" that year.

The public offering helped the company in its next series of investments. In 1997, for example, the company made a brief foray into the after-sales repair and maintenance sector, buying up NATI. That effort proved less successful for the company, and D2 sold off NATI in 1999. In the meantime, D2 added new markets, including Sweden and Canada in 1996, and the launch of an Australian subsidiary in 1999.

By then, the company had decided to regroup its operations under a single brand name, LaCie. The company itself adopted the LaCie brand name in 1998, then opened a communications office in London as part of a worldwide public relations effort. Also in that year, the company acquired another U.S. company, APS.

Data Storage Peripherals Leader in the 2000s

An important factor in LaCie's continuing success was its ability to adapt to the changing computer market. Of importance, the company worked to reduce its reliance on the Apple computer market into the late 1990s, in part to distance itself from Apple's own struggles at the time, but also to take advantage of the surge in the worldwide PC market. The rise of multimedia-equipped computers in the mid-1990s created a new demand for larger and faster data storage solutions. LaCie responded with a number of innovative and highly successful products, such as its external 2.5-inch PocketDrive, launched in 2000. The company also expanded its presence in the high-end professional graphics and corporate markets with the launch of its own high-end flat-panel displays, such as an 18-inch display launched in 2001. LaCie expanded beyond its core European and American markets as well, adding a Japanese subsidiary that year.

Key Dates:

1989: Pierre Fournier and Philippe Spruch found Electronique D2 in Paris in order to develop external data storage systems.
1990: The company launches a research and development team.
1991: The company forms its first foreign subsidiary in London.
1992: Subsidiaries are opened in Belgium and Denmark.
1993: A subsidiary opens in Germany; the company moves to Massy, outside of Paris.
1995: The company acquires LaCie, in Oregon.
1996: A public offering is made on the Paris Stock Exchange's Nouveau Marché.
1998: The company changes its name to LaCie S.A.
1999: A subsidiary in Australia is added.
2000: A Japanese subsidiary is added.
2002: The company begins targeting the consumer retail market for the first time.
2003: The company launches a 500-gigabyte external hard drive.
2004: The company launches a one-terrabyte hard drive.
2005: The company launches a Silverscreen hard drive capable of displaying images directly on a television screen.

The development of a consumer market for high-capacity, high-speed storage devices encouraged LaCie to launch itself into the retail channel for the first time in 2002. Until then, the company's products had been sold through catalogs, or by value-added resellers, and remained geared toward the professional and corporate markets. Yet the consumer market, driven by music and video applications, became one of the data storage market's primary growth drivers. The arrival of new-generation high-capacity drives, as well as the CD writers, followed by DVD writers, opened a new range of possibilities for consumers.

LaCie launched its Big Disk in 2002, an external hard drive featuring 500 gigabytes of capacity. The company also responded to the development of a new generation of high-speed transfer protocols with the launch of its first Triple Interface hard drives, which featured USB 2.0 and Firewire transfer capacity, in addition to standard ATA transfer technology. The company also teamed up with the FA Porsche design team, developing a new line of sleek and sophisticated products.

LaCie continued developing high-capacity storage devices. In 2004, for example, the company launched its Bigger Disk, featuring one terrabyte of storage capacity. Also that year, LaCie teamed up with software developer Roxio to launch a new double-layer DVD burner for the Macintosh market.

More innovative products emerged from LaCie's research and development department in 2005. Among these was the Silverscreen, a mobile hard drive featuring 40 gigabytes of data space and the ability to connect and display video, music, and images directly to a television, without passing through a computer. In October of that year, the company launched another innovation, the Carte Orange USB drive, which, at the size of a credit card, plugged into a computer's USB port, with data storage ranging up to eight gigabytes. The company closed out the year with a new product for the corporate set, a hard drive with fingerprint recognition technology. LaCie stored the secrets of success in the global PC peripherals market.

Principal Subsidiaries

APS Tech (U.S.A.); LaCie Allemagne; LaCie Australia; LaCie Belgique (99.68%); LaCie China; LaCie Hollande; LaCie Italie (99.00%); LaCie Japan; LaCie Ltd. (U.S.A.); LaCie Peripherals (Canada); LaCie Royaume-Uni (99.90%); LaCie S.A.S. (France; 99.99%); LaCie Spain (99.95%); LaCie Suède; LaCie Suisse.

Principal Competitors

Teradata Corporation; ASUSTeK Computer Inc.; BenQ Corporation; Micron Technology Inc.; Sharp Electronics Corporation; Storage Technology Corporation; Lite-On IT Corporation; Hyperdata; Opengate S.p.A.

Further Reading

Cain, Chris, "LaCie Silverscreen: Portable Hard Disk Which Hooks Up to a TV," *Personal Computer World,* July 1, 2005, p. 65.
"Electronique D2, stimulant et branché," *L'Expansion,* July 10, 1997.
"High-Capacity USB Key," *Computer Active,* October 27, 2005, p. 7.
Joseph, Cliff, "LaCie Safe Mobile Hard Drive: Keep Your Data Safe from Prying Eyes," *Personal Computer World,* December 1, 2005, p. 52.
"LaCie and Roxio Team Up to Deliver First Mac DVD DL Solution," *DVD News,* June 2, 2004.
"LaCie Group Appoints New CEO," *M2 Presswire,* June 15, 1999.
"SUV Space in a Sports Car Body," *Computer Gaming World,* September 1, 2005.

—M.L. Cohen

LDI, Ltd.

LDI Ltd., LLC

54 Monument Circle, Suite 800
Indianapolis, Indiana 46204
U.S.A.
Telephone: (317) 237-5400
Fax: (317) 237-2280
Web site: http://www.ldiltd.com

Private Company
Incorporated: 1912 as U.S. Corrugated-Fibre Box
    Company.
Employees: 2,000
Sales: $855 million (2003 est.)
NAIC: 423120 Motor Vehicle Supplies and New Parts
    Merchant Wholesalers; 321918 Other Millwork;
    512120 Motion Picture and Video Distribution;
    551112 Offices of Other Holding Companies

LDI Ltd., LLC, is a privately owned management holding company that specializes in whole distribution of clothing, motorcycle parts, bicycle frames, and auto products. The company owns Tucker Rocky Distributing, a wholesale distributor of apparel and aftermarket equipment for the watercraft, motorcycle, and snowmobile markets. LDI also holds a majority stake in FinishMaster, Inc., a public company that is a leading independent distributor of automotive paints, coatings, and related accessories to the $2.5 billion U.S. automotive refinishing market.

Beginnings

The company began in 1912 when Howard J. Lacy co-founded the U.S. Corrugated-Fibre Box Company in Indianapolis, Indiana. His son, Howard J. Lacy II, took over the reins of the company in 1952. Upon his unexpected death from a heart attack in 1959, his wife Edna Lacy at the age of 53 immediately took over leadership responsibilities as president, chairman of the board, and treasurer of the company that her father-in-law had started. By this time, the company had six plants in Indiana, New York, Pennsylvania, Ohio, Connecticut, and West Virginia. Edna Lacy fended off offers to purchase the company with the intention to carry on the family run business.

Mrs. Lacy was born Edna Balz and raised in Indianapolis. After graduating from the University of Michigan in 1928 with a degree in education, she taught in the Indianapolis public schools. She married Howard Lacy in 1934 and settled into the role of conventional wife and mother. After she assumed the leadership of the company, Edna Lacy grew and diversified the business as a national leader in corrugated box production. In 1973, she acquired Jessup Door Company, a producer of solid wood panel doors, and, in 1972, the company changed its name to Lacy Diversified Industries to better reflect its diversification strategy. Edna Lacy retired from the day-to-day operations in 1983, handing over the reins to her son, Andre. She remained as chairman of the board, however.

The 1980s: New Leadership, New Direction

As LDI's new president and chief executive officer, Andre B. Lacy already had a long association with the family business. He began his career with the company as a child, distributing mail during summer breaks from school. After graduating from Denison University in 1961 with a bachelor of arts in economics, he worked in various positions of increasing responsibility, including as analyst, sales representative, plant manager, regional manager, and eventually, executive vice-president and chief operating officer. As LDI's president and CEO, Lacy soon grew unhappy with the company's direction and began a drastic restructuring. By closing down unprofitable facilities and upgrading others, he and his managers established the company as the nation's second largest independent box manufacturer.

The company made a profitable venture of selling cardboard to contain every conceivable product, but Lacy grew tired of the business. As a result, he decided to sell it. In recounting the reasons behind the divestment, Lacy told the *Indianapolis Business Journal* in 2004 that the industry "had a lower appetite for making money than we did." In the same year, he told the *Indiana Business Magazine* that in "1980 I wasn't comfortable where the company was headed. I thought we were coming up against a ceiling for what our company could be so we decided to make our move, make improvements and do an orderly divestment." Lacy's decision to sell the business initially ran into trouble with what he found to be an over-controlling and indecisive board, but the Lacy family and its outside board of trustees nevertheless soon began exploring other industries, especially those in which they could add value to the product or service. The corrugated box business was based primarily on a surrogate distribution model with the company buying a product, adding value, and selling it.

After divesting the corrugated box business in 1984, Lacy Diversified Industries became LDI Ltd., LLC, and Lacy began leading the company in the direction of acquiring and reinventing small niche distributors. It first acquired Major Video Concepts, a recorded-videotape distributor, followed in subsequent years by the purchase of eleven other distributors. LDI sought to invest in low-profile, small-niche distributors in industries with a total market of $3 billion to $5 billion and in which it could be a leading player. Such small distributors often escaped the notice or otherwise attracted little interest of large corporate giants. In 1989, LDI purchased Tucker Rocky Distributing, a Dallas wholesale distributor of after-market parts for power-sports industry, including motorcycles, snowmobiles, all-terrain vehicles, and watercraft. With this purchase, LDI also acquired Answer Products, Inc., a bicycle products distributor based in California, which was owned by Tucker Rocky. Two years later in 1991, the Tucker Rocky subsidiary acquired MS Racing, a leading off-road motorcycling distributor and apparel brand based in Riverside, California, for $1.7 million though bankruptcy court. The purchase gave the subsidiary exclusive rights to High-Point, MS Racing, and Malcolm Smith product brands. Tucker Rocky also acquired Biker's Choice (formerly NEMPCO), a leading cruiser aftermarket wholesaler.

The 1990s: New Acquisitions

In 1996, the private holding company LDI bought a 67 percent stake in publicly traded FinishMaster of Kentwood, Michigan, a distributor of automotive paints, coatings, and related materials to the automotive refinishing industry. Founded in 1968, FinishMaster grew to operate numerous outlets throughout the U.S. before being acquired by LDI. One year later in 1997, LDI promised to become a $1 billion company and the leader in the after-market auto finishes business with a $69 million offer to purchase of California-based Thompson PBE, Inc., FinishMater's main rival. The offer was made through LDI's controlling interest in FinishMaster for $8 a share of Thompson stock, and stood to give FinishMaster the number one market position in North America.

The two companies—which represented the largest players in the fragmented market of paint suppliers to auto-body shops and other metal-painting businesses—promised to create a company with sales of more than $300 million. Although both companies had proved profitable by doubling sales since going public in the early 1990s, their profits dropped off as they raced to consolidate the industry through acquisition. By comparison, in 1996, FinishMaster reported net income of $700,000 on revenue of $125 million, while Thompson posted $1.1 million on sales of $178 million. As Thompson's sales rose, its stock nose-dived, falling from $19.50 per share in June 1995 to $2.75 in April. FinishMaster's stock also had taken a hit, but the fundamental difference between the two firms was ownership. Unlike FinishMaster, Thompson was largely owned by institutional investors and a venture capital firm with expectations to show short-term results. As a subsidiary of a privately-owned firm, however, FinishMaster could afford to be patient in order to grow the business over the long term. With the precipitous decline of Thompson's stock price, Lacy saw opportunity in buying the firm to further his aims of consolidating and dominating the industry with an all-cash deal with bank loans. With the acquisition, FinishMaster hoped to battle the estimated 4,000 competitors in the $3.5 billion industry on a customer-by-customer basis. In subsequent years, FinishMaster winnowed down the numerous competitors through the acquisition of small distributors, merging them under the FinishMaster umbrella, and bolstering the sales force. At the time of LDI's offer for Thompson, the holding company also held a number of other firms, including Tucker-Rocky Distributing, a Dallas supplier of outdoor sports equipment; Answer Products, Inc., a California bicycle-products distributor; and Major Video Concepts, an Indianapolis firm that distributed videos to stores nationwide. In addition, LDI managed an investment portfolio valued at more than $100 million.

In 1998, LDI's power sports distributor Tucker Rocky announced an overhaul of its warehouse distribution network. At the time, Tucker Rocky reached more than 9,000 dealers, had 500 plus employees, and did business with most of the major vendors in the powersports market. The reorganization involved going from twelve branches/warehouses to eight, while at the same time tripling its total warehouse space. Tucker Rocky aimed to implement the changes to better serve manufacturers and retailers with a more up-to-date, state-of-the-art distribution network. The company believed that new technology would enable it to improve product forecasting, ordering, warehousing, and inventory management. The old warehouse system had evolved through a series of acquisitions rather than according to a master plan. The new locations for the implementation of purpose-built facilities were selected for their proximity to major shipping centers around the country. The reorganization also called for every warehouse to stock every part, which would allow the firm to efficiently serve its various dealers.

The 2000s: Continued Growth

In September, 2003 FinishMaster expanded into ten new markets with the acquisition of Germany-based BASF Corporation, which had operated under the name Automotive Refinish Technologies. The firm's sales outlets were in Atlanta and Augusta, Georgia; Austin, Texas; Buffalo, New York; Huntsville, Alabama; Las Vegas, Nevada; Memphis, Tennessee; Oklahoma City, Oklahoma; St. Louis, Missouri; and Spring-

Key Dates:

1912: Howard J. Lacy cofounds U.S. Corrugated-Fibre Box Company.
1952: Lacy's son, Howard J. Lacy II, takes over leadership of company.
1959: Edna Lacy, wife of Howard J. Lacy II, becomes company president, chairman of the board, and treasurer after her husband's death.
1972: Company changes name to Lacy Diversified Industries (LDI).
1983: Andre B. Lacy becomes company president and chief executive officer.
1989: LDI acquires Tucker Rocky Distributing Company.
1996: Company buys a 67 percent stake in FinishMaster.
2003: FinishMaster acquires German-based BASF Corporation.
2004: LDI sells Answer Products, Inc.

field, Illinois. The transaction called for FinishMaster to become BASF's national distributor for paint and materials sales earned through BASF's internet ordering site.

In March 2004, LDI sold Answer Products, Inc., which had become an industry leader in the making of handlebars and suspension systems for mountain bikes, to venture capitalist firm, Swander Pace Capital (SPC) for an undisclosed sum. The sale represented LDI's strategy of spinning off firms when it believed the industry had reached capacity. For example, it had sold its first venture, Major Video Concepts, in 2000 after riding the consumer market for home-videos from the beginning to almost the end. Answer's director of brand management and sales, Joel Smith, said the bicycle products firm was happy about the change and expected the sale would result in expanded business. Based in San Francisco, California, SPC operated as an investment firm with more than $660 million in capital. After being founded in 1996, the investment firm went on an aggressive buying spree, acquiring dozens of consumer product brands. The firm came to manage an eclectic assortment of companies, including glove and umbrella maker Totes-

Isotoner, Mrs. Fields cookies, Reef sandals, Skateboard World Industries, and others. Although LDI had nurtured Answer's growth since its acquisition in 1989, the bicycle firm's options were limited when the holding company began an exclusive focus on the distribution business. LDI had been looking to sell Answer for five years before concluding the deal with SPC. Nonetheless, LDI continued to see opportunities in Tucker Rocky and FinishMaster through developing a strong sales force and making sure the companies were client-friendly.

Principal Subsidiaries

FinishMaster, Inc.; Tucker Rocky Distributing.

Principal Competitors

Cannondale Corporation; Genuine Parts Company; Custom Chrome Inc.

Further Reading

Dooms, Tracy, "Coming on Board?," *Indianapolis Business Journal*, March 11, 1991.
——, "Panelists Want Proof of Citizens Gas Sale Benefits," *Indianapolis Business Journal*, September 23, 1991.
Eckert, Toby, "Mayor Starts Selling Biz on Pacers," *Indianapolis Business Journal*, March 17, 1997.
"Eight is Enough: Tucker Rocky/Nempco Distributing's Strategic Plan," *Dealernews*, June 1998.
"50 Most Influential People of the Century," *Indianapolis Business Journal*, December 1999.
"Indiana's Entrepreneurs of the Year," *Indiana Business Magazine*, September 1994.
"Investment Firm Swander Pace Picks Up Answer," *Retailer & Industry News*, March 15, 2004.
"LDI Subsidiary Acquires Motorcycle-Equipment Company," *Indiana Business Journal*, February 4, 1991.
Meyers Sharp, Jo Ellen, "Major Firms Expanding Operations in Region 7," *Indianapolis Business Journal*, May 24, 2004.
Pletz, John, "Buyout May Make LDI a $1 Billion Company," *Indianapolis Business Journal*, October 20, 1997.
"Seeds of Change were Planted in the '60s," *Indianapolis Business Journal*, December 27, 1999.

—Bruce P. Montgomery

Learning Care Group, Inc.

21333 Haggerty Road, Suite 300
Novi, Michigan 48375
U.S.A.
Telephone: (248) 697-9000
Toll Free: (866) 244-5384
Fax: (248) 697-9001
Web site: http://www.child-time.com

Public Company
Incorporated: 1995
Employees: 7,500
Sales: $212.2 million (2005)
Stock Exchanges: NASDAQ
Ticker Symbol: LCGI
NAIC: 624410 Child Day Care Services

Learning Care Group, Inc., formerly known as Childtime Learning Centers, Inc., offers child-care, preschool, and school-age educational services through its network of more than 459 centers in 23 states and the District of Columbia. Learning Care Group also has franchised locations in Hong Kong, the Philippines, and Indonesia. The company serves more than 30,000 families and provides care for children aged 6 weeks to 12 years through its learning centers and employer-sponsored, at-work facilities. Learning Care Group nearly doubled in size with its acquisition of Tutor Time Learning Centers Inc. in 2002.

Building Business in the Early Years: 1967–90

What eventually evolved into Childtime Learning Centers was founded in Illinois in 1967. The child-care firm was acquired by Michigan-based baby food manufacturer Gerber Products Company in 1973, and the name was changed to Gerber Children's Centers, Inc. The company grew swiftly and expanded into New York, Illinois, California, Florida, Oklahoma, Ohio, Michigan, Maryland, Virginia, Georgia, Texas, and Arizona by the late 1980s.

Gerber was a pioneer in the development of employer-sponsored child-care services, opening its first corporate child-care center in 1981 at the Hurley Medical Center in Flint, Michigan. The center provided daycare and child-care services to employees of the hospital as well as members of the community. Gerber followed up the success of the Hurley center with centers at the Fresno Hospital in Fresno, California, in 1983, on the campus of Prince Georges Community College in 1984, at Mercy Hospital in Oklahoma City, Oklahoma, in 1986, and at Henry Ford Hospital in Detroit, Michigan, in 1987. In early 1990 Gerber opened a center at Edward W. Sparrow Hospital in Lansing, Michigan, and one at William Beaumont Hospital, located in Royal Oak, Michigan. The Beaumont facility turned a profit after only six months in operation.

Gerber Children's Centers built a reputation for focusing on education, but its rapid expansion and what some in the industry viewed as poor management led to financial struggles in the late 1980s. The business suffered losses of about $3 million, and enrollment sagged—the centers, which numbered 115 in 1990, operated at about 60 percent of capacity at best, and 19 of the total were only half full. Attention from parent company Gerber Products was lacking as well; Gerber Products had diversified to the detriment of its primary business of baby food, and in the late 1980s the company began to shed its unprofitable, noncore operations, which included a trucking firm and businesses that manufactured toys, infant car seats, sleepwear, and children's furniture, in order to return its attention to baby food. The Gerber Children's Centers business was considered extraneous as well, and in 1990 Gerber Products announced the sale of its child-care subsidiary to KD Acquisition Corporation, a private investment firm based in New York. The sale was completed in July, and new ownership began the task of turning around the ailing business.

New Ownership and Restructuring in the Early 1990s

The U.S. child-care industry was highly fragmented, filled with many independent and local providers. In the early 1990s the largest child-care companies controlled only about 4 percent of the entire $15 billion market, leaving ample room for growth. The child-care industry was forecast to grow considerably as the number of working mothers increased, and the new owners of Gerber Children's Centers hoped to tap into this growth. As

Company Perspectives:

Our mission is to develop innovative learning care solutions which enable us to grow the number of children and families served, and to be recognized as the premier child and family education corporation in the world. Through our leadership and passion, we will: provide a secure, caring and enriched environment that promotes learning and the development of the whole child; develop lifelong relationships, create family solutions, and enhance the quality of life for our families; provide a fun, challenging work environment that fosters teamwork, inspires professional excellence, and encourages contribution by all team members; leverage technology to develop innovative learning products and solutions; provide superior levels of support and service to our franchisees; and achieve the best financial performance in the industry, allowing us to fulfill our mission.

Deborah Ludwig, executive vice-president and general manager of Gerber Children's Centers, explained in a company press release, "Nearly 75 percent of all preschool children will have employed mothers by 1995. . . . And more women with infants are choosing to stay employed than ever before in the history of this country. This, along with an overall rise in births—4.5 percent from July 1989 to July 1990—all point to growth opportunities for reputable providers of child care."

The new owners of Gerber Children's Centers wasted no time getting to work on reviving the company. Expansion, primarily in the growing field of employer-sponsored facilities, was a goal, and in December 1990 the company acquired Supertots, a provider of at-work child-care services, from Ogden Services Corporation. The purchase of the ten Supertots locations cemented the position of Gerber Children's Centers as one of the five largest child-care providers in the nation. Among the centers acquired by Gerber Children's Centers were those at Prudential Insurance Company of America in Iselin, New Jersey, and at Schering-Plough Corporation in Union, New Jersey.

Another major change for the company came in 1991. Under terms of the sale, KD Acquisition agreed to give up the Gerber name. To select a new company name, Gerber Children's Centers staged a contest that resulted in more than 3,000 entries. Two people came up with the winning name, Childtime Children's Centers, and for their efforts they were each given a $25,000 college scholarship bond.

The company moved its headquarters from Fremont, Michigan, to Brighton to be nearer to a major airport and assembled a new management team. Harold Lewis was recruited from Thomas Cook Travel Inc. to serve as president and CEO. Lewis, who had no previous work experience in the child-care industry, implemented a new management strategy that focused more heavily on the business aspect of running a child-care center. Lewis told *Crain's Detroit Business,* "We make it clear to our center directors that there's no inconsistency at all in being profitable and in caring for and teaching young children. . . . Without profitability, we can't invest back into the business in terms of new equipment for the children." Incentive programs that rewarded center directors for increasing enrollment and running more efficient operations were launched, and the company began offering management courses for directors that included classes on planning budgets, recruiting and firing staff members, marketing, and finance. Childtime also implemented a marketing program that targeted dual-income families with young children. The program used direct mail to entice prospective customers and marketed its services to businesses located close to Childtime facilities to attract working parents.

The emphasis on business and management did not mean Childtime ignored the care of children. The company installed computer systems in the majority of Childtime centers and hired an educational consultant to develop a curriculum for each age group served by the facilities. Childtime educational programs emphasized the process of learning and discovery, and children were placed into groups depending on their social, intellectual, emotional, and physical maturity. To retain business, Childtime made it a policy to keep parents informed regarding the activities and progress of their children, and thus the centers distributed the curriculum and periodic report cards to parents.

Childtime moved its headquarters again in 1992, to Farmington Hills, Michigan, and by the end of that year business was on the upswing—of the 19 centers that had been running at half capacity at the beginning of the decade, 16 had recovered and become profitable. By 1993 Childtime posted revenues of $44 million and a profit of $1 million. In 1993 the company opened two new at-work facilities, one at St. Francis Hospital in Evanston, Illinois, and one at the Northern Illinois Medical Center in McHenry. The following year Childtime began operating a facility for Blue Cross and Blue Shield of Mississippi and opened the Child Development Center at the Tulsa State Office Building in Oklahoma. To realize its goal of adding about 20 new centers a year, Childtime continued to expand through strategic acquisitions as well, and in 1994 the company bought Little Learners, a child-care provider in Syracuse, New York. The acquisition boosted Childtime's numbers to 135 centers covering 14 states and Washington, D.C.

By the mid-1990s Childtime's recovery seemed complete. For the fiscal year ended March 31, 1995, Childtime enjoyed record growth. The company reported revenues of $55 million, an increase of $7 million from the previous year, and net income of about $2.7 million. Harold Lewis commented on the company's accomplishments in a prepared statement and said, "Our growth over the past three years, in a very competitive market, is primarily the result of target marketing and focused management." Lewis also noted that the company's achievements were all the more remarkable when considering the slim profit margins in the child-care industry.

Steady Growth and Increasing Revenues in the Late 1990s

Childtime welcomed new challenges as it entered the second half of the decade. The company reincorporated as Childtime Learning Centers, Inc. in November 1995 and completed its initial public offering in February 1996. Childtime shares were offered on the NASDAQ at $10 a share. In addition, although the child-care industry was growing rapidly, Childtime planned to expand steadily but conservatively, aiming to open about 25 to 30 new facilities a year until the end of the decade. Lewis told the *Detroit News,* "The problem with expanding any faster is coming up with the capital and human resources. We don't want any handicaps. Our goal is to maintain steady growth with high-quality facilities." Each newly built center cost about $1 million to build. The spacious centers ranged from 6,400 to 8,000 square feet. To ensure the success of the centers it opened, Childtime sought locations in residential areas with a high density of dual-income families and in regions with numerous office buildings. The company also looked for opportunities managing employer-sponsored, at-work facilities.

Differing state regulations, high employee turnover, and low profit margins all posed problems to those in the child-care industry, but the potential for growth in the U.S. market outweighed the cons. Thomas Johnson of Kindercare Learning Centers, Inc., one of the largest child-care providers in the United States, explained in *Crain's Detroit Business* in 1996, "There are 51 million children under the age of 12. . . . Even if you total 50 of the largest for-profit child-care centers in the country, they'd be able to take care of only 1 percent of the nation's children." By the late 1990s the industry had grown to a $30 billion market, and consolidation had begun, indicating acknowledgment by investors of the growth potential of the business. In 1997 Kindercare was purchased by Kohlberg Kravis Roberts Co., and La Petite Academy was acquired by Chase Manhattan. In 1998 Children's Discovery Center was bought by Knowledge Universe, an investment company led by infamous junk bond dealer Michael Milken, Milken's brother Lowell, and Oracle Systems Corporation Chairman Lawrence Ellison.

Childtime's growth strategy proved successful, and the company's revenues grew steadily. Childtime's revenues for fiscal 1997 reflected a 20 percent increase over 1996 revenues and reached $78.63 million. The company opened 37 centers that year, including the takeover of Bureautots, an at-work facility serving employees of the U.S. Census Bureau in Suitland, Maryland. Childtime also won contracts to operate centers on the campus of the New Jersey Institute of Technology and the Veterans Affairs Medical Center in Pennsylvania. In 1997 the company made its entry into the state of Washington when it

acquired nine centers from Abundant Life Childcare Centers in Seattle. Childtime also secured a contract to assume operation of an at-work center sponsored by the General Services Administration in downtown Seattle.

By the end of fiscal 1999, which ended April 2, the number of Childtime facilities had grown to 270, spanning 19 states and Washington, D.C. Childtime's revenues reached $112.96 million, up from $97.83 million in 1998. Net income also increased, from $4.35 million in 1998 to $5.1 million. Enrollment in the centers had grown from 26,000 to 30,000 children, and the company added 30 new facilities. Childtime gained seven centers in Nevada through an acquisition, and two contracts involved the management of child-care facilities located at mass transit stops. The centers, in Baltimore, Maryland, and Des Moines, Iowa, were designed to promote mass transit commuting by working parents.

In August 1999 Childtime announced that its first quarter results would fall below estimates. The company blamed high electricity bills, caused by an unseasonably warm summer, and expenses from unsuccessful acquisition negotiations for the fall in earnings. Childtime also stated plans to close seven of its centers, which resulted in a severe one-day drop in the company's share price of 13.2 percent. The company indicated that it could possibly close six to ten additional underperforming centers during the year, but that plans to open 35 to 40 new facilities were in place.

Childtime may have hit a few snags as it neared the 21st century, but the company was not discouraged. The company was included on "The 200 Best Small Companies in America," an annual list compiled by *Forbes,* in 1999. Childtime continued to grow and expand, adding 11 new centers in North Carolina, Georgia, and Texas at the end of 1999 and winning a management contract for the Lovelace Child Development Center, which provided services for the employees and members of Lovelace Health Systems, a health maintenance organization. In September Childtime partnered with ParentWatch, an Internet company that provided parents with live video access via the World Wide Web to their children at participating child-care facilities. To enhance its educational programs, Childtime formed a joint venture with Oxford Learning Centres of Canada. Known as Oxford Learning Centers of America, the venture was designed to offer after-school tutoring and enrichment programs to children from kindergarten through the eighth grade.

In the course of one decade, Childtime not only had defied its demise but it also had grown from 115 centers to more than 280 facilities in 22 states and the District of Columbia. For the first nine months of fiscal 2000, Childtime reported revenues of $96.37 million, up from $84.88 million for the comparable period of 1999. Net income fell from $3.5 million to $3.2 million, but Childtime remained confident in its future. The company planned to continue growing and expanding to meet the demands of working families in the 21st century.

Changes in the New Millennium

Indeed, growth remained a cornerstone in Childtime's strategy during the early years of the new millennium. In 2002, the company announced plans to acquire Tutor Time Learning Centers Inc., a private Florida-based firm with 235 centers in 25 states. The deal would nearly double the size of Childtime and secure its position as the third largest for-profit child-care provider in the United States. While both companies eyed the purchase as a lucrative opportunity, a former Childtime vice-president and shareholder opposed the $22.5 million union, claiming that both companies were losing money and the deal, therefore, would fail to bolster shareholder value. Childtime Chairman James Morgan responded to the opposition in an August 2002 *Crain's Detroit Business* article stating, "Both companies have come through troubled periods. Both companies' troubles stem from, at minimum, questionable growth strategies, if not flawed growth strategies, and we have a lot of work ahead of us."

Sure enough, with Childtime and Tutor Time losing money, it was clear that the company's management team faced a difficult road ahead. During fiscal 2002, Childtime posted a net loss of approximately $4 million. That number climbed to $18 million in 2003. Revenue was rising, however, and by fiscal 2004, Childtime began to shore up its finances and posted a net loss of slightly less than $1 million. As part of its strategy, the company looked to strengthen operations at its franchise units and by fiscal 2005, the average U.S. Tutor Time franchise location was generating revenue of more than $1 million. That year the company returned to profitability, securing net income of $3.2 million.

As the company worked to integrate Childtime and Tutor Time, it adopted a new vision and mission statement to reflect its focus on child development and quality of life for families. The company also pledged to provide a fun and challenging work environment for its employees and provide top-notch levels of support to its franchisees. In August 2004, Childtime changed its name to Learning Care Group, Inc. According to the company, the new corporate moniker signaled its desire to remain neutral among its two flagship brands—Childtime and Tutor Time.

Learning Care planned to increase the number of both its franchise and corporate locations over the next decade. As one of the largest for-profit child-care operators in the United States, Learning Care appeared to be on track for success. Management was confident that its financial problems were a thing of the past and that families would continue to depend on Childtime and Tutor Time centers for years to come.

Principal Subsidiaries

Childtime Childcare, Inc.; Tutor Time Learning Centers LLC; Tutor Time Learning Centers International, Inc.; Tutor Time Franchise LLC.

Principal Competitors

Bright Horizons Family Solutions Inc.; KinderCare Learning Centers, Inc.; LPA Holding Corporation.

Further Reading

Adelson, Andrea, "Child-Care Industry Is Showing Signs of a Growth Spurt," *Austin American-Statesman,* August 1, 1998, p. 4.

Burge, Katrina, " 'What Did You Do in School Today, Darling?' Harold Lewis Is in the Business of Taking Care of Other People's Kids, But He's Smart Enough to Realize That His Real Customers Are the Parents," *Forbes,* December 1, 1997, p. 106.

Child, Charles, "Day-Care HQ in Brighton," *Crain's Detroit Business,* February 18, 1991, p. 1.

Fredrickson, Tom, "Childtime's Acquisition Takes Bite Out of Big Apple," *Crain's Detroit Business,* October 21, 2002.

Grugal, Robin M., "The New America—Childtime Learning Centers Inc.," *Investor's Business Daily,* October 31, 1996, p. A4.

Hoffman, Gary, "Childtime Learning Readies $18-Million Initial Stock Offering," *Detroit News,* January 10, 1996, p. E1.

Kosseff, Jeffrey, "Childtime Skins Knees: But Some Analysts See Upside to Closings," *Crain's Detroit Business,* August 23, 1999, p. 2.

"Learning Care Group Franchise Convention Celebrates Success, Growth Opportunities," *Market Wire,* April 22, 2005.

Raphael, Steve, "Minding Business: Chain Mixes Caring, Profits," *Crain's Detroit Business,* August 8, 1994, p. 3.

Seymour, Liz, "This Isn't Child's Play: Childtime Seeing Shamrock Green—Possibly $65M of It," *Crain's Detroit Business,* March 18, 1996, p. 3.

Smith, Joel J., "Day-Care Centers Running Out of Room," *Detroit News,* June 18, 1996, p. B1.

Snavely, Brent, "Childtime Plans to Buy Tutor Time," *Crain's Detroit Business,* February 11, 2002.

——, "Childtime Sprouts Up: But Child Care Company's Stock Hasn't Followed," *Automotive News,* December 20, 1999, p. 2.

——, "Former Childtime Exec Publicly Challenges Tutor Time Purchase," *Crain's Detroit Business,* August 19, 2002.

Waldsmith, Lynn, "Child Care Provider Gains in Earnings, Not on Market: Childtime Centers Sales Climb 20% Since Going Public in '96," *Detroit News,* September 9, 1997, p. B1.

—Mariko Fujinaka
—update: Christina M. Stansell

LENSCRAFTERS

LensCrafters Inc.

4000 Luxottica Place
Mason, Ohio 45040
U.S.A.
Telephone: (513) 765-6000
Fax: (513) 765-6249
Web site: http://www.lenscrafters.com

Wholly Owned Subsidiary of Luxottica SpA
Incorporated: 1983
Employees: NA
Sales: $1.33 billion (2003)
NAIC: 446130 Optical Goods Stores

A subsidiary of Italy's Luxottica SpA's Retail group, U.S.-based LensCrafters Inc. is North America's leading retailer of eyewear. The company was a pioneer of the "superoptical" segment during the 1980s and has grown to more than 880 stores in the United States, Canada, and Puerto Rico. Most of the company's stores are found in shopping malls and offer one-hour service, eye exams, contact lenses, and sunglasses. The company experienced significant growth under United States Shoe Corporation during the 1980s and early 1990s. Luxottica bought the company in 1995 and since that time has been building an optical empire by purchasing Sunglass Hut International Inc., OPSM Group, and Cole National Corporation.

Company's Founding in 1983

LensCrafters was founded in 1983 by Dean Butler, a 38-year-old who had previously worked at Procter & Gamble (P&G). A knowledgeable marketer, Butler had managed the Ivory liquid, Cheer laundry detergent, and Folger's instant coffee brands for the venerable Cincinnati consumer goods company.

At that time, the eyewear industry was on the cusp of radical change, a shift spurred by two vital legal decisions passed down in the late 1970s. The Federal Trade Commission freed patient choice by compelling vision professionals to give patients their prescriptions. A separate legal decision allowing advertising in this segment set the stage for the "superoptical" movement.

Butler was not the first to perceive this opportunity. New Jersey-based Eyelab gets credit for pioneering the concept, which featured mall-based stores, extended hours, onsite lens-grinding labs, thousands of frames, and rapid turnaround. Butler left P&G and launched his first 7,500-square-foot Precision LensCrafters (later simply LensCrafters) store just across the Ohio River from Cincinnati in Florence, Kentucky, in 1983. He was soon joined by another P&G colleague, Daniel Hogues.

Butler's version of the superoptical concept promised "glasses in about an hour." Since his stores were located in malls, customers could while away that hour shopping with other retailers. Guarantees helped instill confidence in customers who were accustomed to dealing with doctors. The "no risk sales guarantee" gave clients a full refund on glasses returned within 30 days of purchase. LensCrafters also offered to match competitors' prices as well as free lifetime maintenance. In a 1986 interview with *Forbes* magazine, Butler noted, "Marketing eyewear isn't much different from selling coffee. Retailing is what you do when customers walk into the store. But with a new idea, marketing comes first. Marketing is how you inspire customers to come to your door."

Notwithstanding naysayers who were convinced that the concept would fail, LensCrafters' first-year sales totaled $2 million. With support from a cadre of investors, the partners expanded to three outlets by early 1984, when their success drew the attention of a powerful backer: United States Shoe Corporation.

Acquired by U.S. Shoe in 1984

Also based in Cincinnati, U.S. Shoe was a billion-dollar company. Over the course of its more than 100 years in business, U.S. Shoe had diversified from its core footwear into retail apparel. Chains included Casual Corner and Petite Sophisticate. U.S. Shoe used its strong cash flow to fund a rapid expansion of LensCrafters.

With this backing, LensCrafters came not only to dominate its own industry, but also to take precedence over its own parent company's footwear and apparel businesses. From 1984 to 1987, LensCrafters' sales multiplied from $13.6 million or 1

Company Perspectives:

The L Guidance—We will help you navigate through the vast styles and sizes; Honesty—We will listen to what you want, tell you what works and even what doesn't; Knowledge—We know eyewear and can help you find what works best with your face, coloring and personality; Respect for your busy schedule. We know you're busy so we will help you find the glasses you love, quickly and without rushing you.

percent of U.S. Shoe's annual revenues to 241 units and $305 million in sales. In 1986 alone, the company opened new stores at the rate of almost two per week. In 1987 Bannus B. Hudson, an 18-year alumnus of Procter & Gamble who had come to work for LensCrafters in 1985, took the helm. (Founder Dean Butler had by this time resigned from the business. Following the expiration of a noncompete contract, he opened a rival chain dubbed Lens Lab.) By the end of 1989 Hudson had increased the number of stores to more than 350 and boosted sales to $532 million or more than one-fifth of U.S. Shoe's total revenues. Perhaps more important, LensCrafters' $30 million net income constituted nearly 40 percent of its parent's operating earnings by that time. That year U.S. Shoe tried to divest its lagging footwear business, but could not find any takers.

LensCrafters and other eyewear retailers were not content merely to wait for market growth in the form of aging baby boomers with deteriorating eyesight. Instead, they promoted the concept of eyeglasses as fashionable accessories in the same category as shoes or jewelry. This concept not only encouraged sales of designer eyeglasses, but also ownership of multiple pairs of glasses. As Butler told *Forbes* in 1986, "Right now, most people buy a single pair of glasses every two or three years. But what if we can sell eyewear as fashion, a tortoiseshell pair for work and some wire rims for play? We could double per capita sales of glasses."

LensCrafters also focused strongly on maintaining a positive corporate culture. This ideal was embodied in a list of nine Core Values enumerated in 1986. They included: nurturing individuals; building on people's strengths; accepting and learning from mistakes; focusing on winning, not individual scoring; pushing breakthrough ideas; thinking and acting like a long-term owner; demanding highest possible quality; constantly, measurably improving; and acting with uncompromising integrity. A tenth value, having fun, was added in 1990.

New Decade, New Leadership, New Strategies

By 1990, LensCrafters had grown to become U.S. Shoe's "crown jewel." That spring, Bannus Hudson succeeded Philip Barach as CEO of the parent company, and 30-year-old David M. Browne advanced to president and chief executive officer of LensCrafters. Browne, a five-year veteran of Procter & Gamble, joined LensCrafters in 1986 as the vice-president of the recently acquired Optica chain of upscale eyewear shops. He inherited a company that, while still successful, was faced with a number of challenges. The new CEO had hoped to launch 100 new stores in 1990, but was forced to scale back that aggressive growth strat-

egy when LensCrafters suffered its first-ever sales decline. The combination of the Gulf War and recession eroded consumer confidence while heavy competition squeezed prices and profits. Instead of pursuing growth, Browne was forced to restructure. He held job cuts to less than 100 of the company's 10,000 positions by relocating hundreds of employees. In spite of its difficulties, LensCrafters surpassed Pearle Vision Centers to become America's largest chain of eyeglass retailers in 1992, with an estimated $660 million or 4.5 percent of marketwide sales volume.

The company's new strategy targeted the bargain-minded customer via a joint venture with Kmart Corporation. In 1993, LensCrafters launched Sight & Save leased departments within existing Kmart stores. This new retail venture allowed LensCrafters to enter the discount segment without devaluing its namesake stores' focus on value and convenience.

LensCrafters' charitable activities started in 1988 as an extension of its optical services. In cooperation with Lions Clubs International, the company recycled used eyeglasses through its "Give the Gift of Sight" programs. Among other activities, this charity fashioned more than three million pairs of eyeglasses for disadvantaged people—especially children—in the United States and abroad from 1988 through 1996. In 1993, the company launched its Hometown Day project, wherein employees of each of the company's stores donated their time and expertise to needy recipients in their own communities. That same year CEO Browne committed the company to providing free eyecare to one million people by LensCrafters' 20th anniversary in 2003. It was almost halfway there by the end of 1997. The company's charitable activities earned it a Volunteer Action Award from President Bill Clinton in 1994.

International expansion proved a mixed bag for LensCrafters. The company became the first U.S. Shoe affiliate to establish an overseas presence in 1988 with the launch of nine Canadian superstores. In 1993, it became Canada's largest optical retailer with the acquisition of the 22-store Eye Masters Ltd. chain. The company fared well on its home continent. By the end of 1994, it had nearly five dozen Canadian locations. A foray across the Atlantic Ocean did not go as well. In 1990, LensCrafters opened stores in the United Kingdom. But by the fall of 1993, the company was ready to close all its U.K. stores, including locations under the LensCrafters and Sight & Save names.

LensCrafters also grew through domestic acquisitions during this period. It purchased Hourglass Inc. in 1990 and acquired Tuckerman Optical, a midwestern chain, in 1994. LensCrafters spent an estimated $45 million to $50 million on 12-year-old Opti-World Inc., a 59-store Atlanta-based chain, in March 1995.

Acquired by Luxottica in 1995

Italian eyewear manufacturer Luxottica SpA brought a $1.4 billion hostile takeover bid for U.S. Shoe in 1995. Owned by the Del Vecchio clan, Luxottica was not interested in U.S. Shoe's footwear or apparel, it was looking to round out its vertically integrated eyewear company to include retailing. Prior to its own acquisition, U.S. Shoe sold its footwear interests to Nine West Group Inc. for $600 million. Unable to find a buyer for U.S. Shoe's 1,300 money-losing apparel retailers, Luxottica transferred this division to a separate Del Vecchio interest.

The LensCrafters acquisition was a high-stakes gamble for Luxottica. The Italian company risked wholesale defection of its core customers—independent opticians and competing eyewear chains. Although many in these two groups did drop the Italian firm from their roster of suppliers, Luxottica was able to increase its sell-through at LensCrafters stores from 5 percent of frame revenues in 1995 to 43 percent by the end of 1996. In fact, the addition of LensCrafters more than doubled Luxottica's annual revenues from ITL 812.7 billion in 1994 to ITL 1.8 trillion in 1995.

In its first year under Luxottica, LensCrafters added 70 stores and 1,000 employees. In its zeal to focus on designer and high-end eyewear, however, Luxottica pushed LensCrafters to shutter its Sight & Save chain in 1996 and invest the proceeds in store refurbishings. LensCrafters also was testing new retail concepts, including Specttica in-store areas and SunCrafters sunglass kiosks. These outlets specialized in prescription and nonprescription sunglasses in airports and other high-traffic venues.

Despite the spinoff of both the U.K. and the Sight & Save operations in 1995 and 1996, LensCrafters' sales continued to grow rapidly under Luxottica. Revenues advanced slightly more than 5 percent from 1995 to 1996 to total $903.5 million, and the subsidiary was expected to contribute $1 billion to its parent company's top line in 1997.

On the occasion of LensCrafters' tenth anniversary in 1993, CEO Dave Browne said, "Looking to the future, I'm sure of only one thing—the inevitability of constant change and our readiness to face it. It will be harder to stay on top than it was to get there. We will have to recreate ourselves continuously in order to maintain our leadership position in an ever-changing category." That statement continued to hold true as the company faced the turn of the 21st century.

Lenscrafters in the Late 1990s and Beyond

Indeed, to remain competitive in the late 1990s and early years of the new millennium, Lenscrafters worked to create new strategies that would keep it one step ahead of its peers in the industry. In 1997, the company launched a Lenscrafters kiosk at the Cincinnati/Northern Kentucky International Airport. Management was optimistic that airport kiosks would become profitable and planned to add additional kiosks in airports throughout the United States. During that year, approximately 100 new stores opened their doors and sales surpassed $1 billion for the first time.

Along with new retailing formats, Lenscrafters also continued to offer cutting-edge products. In 1998, the company began outfitting its stores with equipment to make its Invisibles line of lenses available to customers in one hour. According to Lenscrafters, the Invisibles line reduced light reflections and glare off lenses by up to 90 percent when compared with traditional lenses. The company secured $1.3 billion in sales during 1999, which accounted for 63 percent of Luxottica's total revenue in 1999.

Lenscrafters entered the new millennium on solid ground with more than 858 locations in the United States, Canada, and Puerto Rico. The company launched a new marketing campaign in 2000 designed to promote Lenscrafters as the best choice for vision care, eyeglasses, and contact lenses. With the tagline, "My Personal Vision Place," the campaign proved successful as profits rose significantly during the campaign. At this time, more than 70 percent of the frames sold at a Lenscrafters outlet were manufactured by Luxottica.

As a Luxottica subsidiary, Lenscrafters held an enviable position in the eyewear industry. Often referred to as the 800-pound gorilla by independent eyewear retailers, Luxottica topped off its optical empire when it acquired Cole National Corporation in 2004. Cole National operated as the second largest optical retailer in North America and operated stores under the Pearle Vision, Sears Optical, Target Optical, and BJ's Optical monikers. Luxottica also had acquired Sunglass Hut and OPSM Group in 2001 and 2003, respectively, and had become the leading distributor of optical and sun products in North America and Asia Pacific as a result of its strategic purchases.

Meanwhile, Lenscrafters launched a new store design in 2003. The prototype opened in Tippecanoe Mall in Lafayette, Indiana and featured soft lighting and modern new fixtures, resembling an upscale apparel shop. A company spokesman commented on the new look in an April 2003 *Chain Store Age* article claiming, "We want people to feel good about buying eyewear and to think of the product not just as a medical requirement, but as something that can enhance their look."

With a strong focus on fashion and high-end brands, Lenscrafters aggressively moved into the Manhattan market during 2004 and 2005. The company planned to expand further, while offering the latest in eyewear. As a member of Luxottica's burgeoning Retail group, Lenscrafters had experienced marked success over the past ten years. With a solid strategy in place, the company appeared to be on track for continued growth in the years to come.

Principal Competitors

Eye Care Centers of America Inc.; National Vision Inc.; U.S. Vision Inc.

Further Reading

Bolton, Douglas, "LensCrafters Founder to Compete," *Cincinnati Post,* February 21, 1990, pp. 6B, 8B.
Butler, Elisabeth, "Local Eyewear Retailers Look Out for LensCrafters," *Crain's New York Business,* May 9, 2005, p. 4.

Comiteau, Jennifer, and Jim Kirk, "Looking for 20/20 Vision," *ADWEEK Eastern Edition,* March 13, 1995, pp. 1–2.

Davenport, Carol, "Bannus B. Hudson, 43," *Fortune,* June 19, 1989, p. 162.

De Lombaerde, Geert, "LensCrafters Turns Focus from Growth to Profits," *Business Courier,* January 15, 1999, p. 28.

Deutsch, Claudia H., "The Big Battle Over Eyewear," *New York Times,* November 26, 1989, p. F4.

Diamond, Michael, "A Decade Later, LensCrafters Sales Give Skeptics an Eyeful," *Cincinnati Business Courier,* May 3, 1993, p. 6.

Fasig, Lisa Biank, "LensCrafters' Vision," *Cincinnati Enquirer,* August 13, 1997, pp. I1, I16.

Feldman, Diane, "Companies Aim to Please," *Management Review,* May 1989, pp. 8–9.

Head, Lauren Lawley, "Lenscrafters 'Powerful Outlet' for Luxottica Frames," *Business Courier,* December 15, 2000, p. 32.

Kranz, Cindy, "Corporate Caring," *Cincinnati Enquirer,* April 25, 1997, pp. D1, D9.

McKenna, Joseph F., "Dave Browne's Style: Analysis, But Not Paralysis," *Industry Week,* September 3, 1990, pp. 19–20.

Merwin, John, "New, Improved Eyewear," *Forbes,* October 6, 1986, pp. 152–53.

Olson, Thomas, "Overseas Lures LensCrafters," *Cincinnati Business Courier,* September 3, 1990, pp. 1–2.

Reese, Shelly, "LensCrafters Leader in Eyeglass Retail Race," *Cincinnati Enquirer,* March 21, 1993, pp. F1, F10.

Schwartz, Judith D., "LensCrafters Takes the High Road," *Adweek's Marketing Week,* April 30, 1990, pp. 26–27.

Seckler, Valerie, "Luxottica Talks with U.S. Shoe Have Hit Snag," *WWD,* March 31, 1995, p. 11.

Sullivan, Ruth, "Luxottica Focuses on Dominating U.S. Market," *The European,* April 21, 1995, p. 16.

Teitelbaum, Richard S., "David M. Browne, 31," *Fortune,* July 2, 1990, p. 102.

Wessling, Jack, "Hudson Given U.S. Shoe Tiller," *Footwear News,* February 5, 1990, pp. 4–5.

Wilson, Marianne, "LensCrafters Makes a Fashion Statement," *Chain Store Age,* April 2003, p. 98.

——, "LensCrafters Polishes Image with Style," *Chain Store Age Executive with Shopping Center Age,* October 1996, pp. 144–45.

Zemke, Ron, and Dick Schaaf, "The Service Edge: 101 Companies That Profit from Customer Care," New York: New American Library, 1989.

—April D. Gasbarre
—update: Christina M. Stansell

Life Care Centers of America Inc.

3570 Keith Street N.W.
Cleveland, Tennessee 37312-4309
U.S.A.
Telephone: (423) 472-9585
Toll Free: (800) 554-9585
Fax: (423) 339-8341
Web site: http://www.lcca.com

Private Company
Incorporated: 1976
Employees: 30,000
Sales: $1.59 billion (2004)
NAIC: 623110 Nursing Care Facilities; 623311
    Continuing Care Retirement Communities; 623312
    Homes for the Elderly; 623990 Other Residential Care
    Facilities; 624110 Child and Youth Services; 624120
    Services for the Elderly and Persons with Disabilities;
    624190 Other Individual and Family Services

Life Care Centers of America Inc. (LCCA), a privately owned operator of retirement and health care services, manages more than 260 facilities in 28 states. The company offers a variety of retirement and health care services under eight divisions: Alzheimer's care, nursing care, assisted living, rehabilitation services, campus care, retirement center, home care, and specialty services. The Alzheimer's care division provides services for people suffering from Alzheimer's disease. The nursing care division offers skilled nursing care, and physical, speech, and occupational therapies at a patient's place of residence. LCCA's assisted living division offers assistance with scheduling medical appointments and medication management, and assistance with such daily living activities as bathing, dressing, grooming, and walking, as well as monthly blood pressure, weight, and nutritional checkups. The rehabilitation division provides physical therapy, occupational therapy, and speech-language pathology. Under the campus care division, the company operates multiple facilities, including retirement, assisted living, nursing care, respite care, Alzheimer's care, rehabilitation services, and wellness programs (blood pressure and health care screenings). LCCA

retirement center division operates almost 40 independent and assisted living communities in 20 states, providing hospital living conditions, dining services, security and emergency call system, and maintenance of facilities. The home care division addresses the needs of people who are recovering from an illness or surgery, or for individuals who are chronically ill. These services include skilled care services (injections, dressing changes, or administration of medication), physical therapy, occupational therapy, speech therapy, sitters and private services, live-in-services for patients unable to take care of themselves, and social services that address the social and emotional needs of the patient. The specialty services division provides respite care, sub acute care, wound care, hospice, and adult day care.

Origins

LCCA was founded in 1970 by Forrest L. Preston, who built his first facility, known as Garden Terrace Convalescent Center, in Cleveland, Tennessee. From 1970 to 1976, Preston built six more centers, five in Tennessee and one in Florida. He incorporated the company as Life Care Centers of America in 1976. In 1989, he established Garden Terrace as a division of Life Care as a specialty care center devoted to the care and treatment of patients with Alzheimer's disease and other dementias. He opened his first such facility in the fall of 1989 in Aurora, Colorado with the aim of building a chain of these specialized care facilities across the country.

1990s: Growth and Expansion

As part of its growth strategy, in 1994 LCCA teamed up with drugstore chain Jack Eckerd Corp., a manager of 710 drugstores in 13 states, to establish home health care centers within selected Eckerd drugstores. Eckerd saw the collaboration as a promising opportunity to broaden its health care services to customers. Under the deal, Life Care would own and operate the centers, which would provide a complete line of home health care products, including canes, crutches, safety side rails, sports braces, hospital beds, ostomy and incontinence supplies, wound care products, diabetes supplies, as well as respiratory therapy equipment. The centers, ranging in size between 700 to 1,000 square feet, would be staffed by trained nurses who would

Company Perspectives:

Life Care Centers of America is committed to being the premier provider of long-term care in America. It is our desire to be the facility of choice in any community in which we operate. Our programs, services and facilities must be designed and operated with superior quality in order to satisfy the needs of our residents.

conduct laboratory tests and orthotic fittings. The centers would also offer the services of physical therapists and medical social workers upon request.

In April 1994, Del Crane Medical Corporation, a maker of medical software and supplies, sued Life Care for allegedly violating its copyright of a software program and for not paying for its use. In the suit filed in federal court, Del Crane claimed that Life Centers interfered with contracts that Del Crane signed with the 140 nursing homes. Del Crane altered the 140 individual licensing agreements in early 1993 to one master agreement. In April 1993, however, the nursing homes notified Del Crane that they were changing to different software. The suit claimed that while some Life Care nursing homes continued to use Del Crane's software, others switched to almost identical software produced by former Del Crane employees. The suit claimed that the nursing homes that continued to use the software ceased making payments to Del Crane. In a separate suit filed at the same time, Del Crane charged Life Care with misusing a joint venture formed between the two firms. In 1990, the two companies created Del Care, a partnership to provide supplies and billing services to Medicare patients. According to the suit, Life Care was using Del Care's name and tax identification number for activities outside the joint venture.

In March 1995, Life Care broke ground on a new Garden Terrace Alzheimer's Center in Houston. The new center represented the first of its kind and one of only a few in the nation devoted exclusively to people with Alzheimer's disease. The 64,000-sqaure-foot, 120 bed center was anticipated to cost $6 million to build. Once built, the Garden Terrace facility offered 24-hour supervision and nursing care, in addition to respite care and day care. The center also provided residents with physical, occupational and speech therapies by licensed staff. The center was designed to offer residents in each stage of the disease a different environment and care plans. The center also included special types of lighting, color and interior décor to sooth people with Alzheimer's disease. Other amenities included private dining rooms, visitor lounges, outdoor patios, an ice cream parlor, a gift store, and a beauty and barber shop. The new facility joined the company's other specialized Alzheimer's care centers in Aurora, Colorado and Salt Lake City, Utah. The company began to build these specialized centers with an eye on the demographics. The Alzheimer's Association had estimated, for example, that 4 million Americans had the disease with more than 100,000 dying from it each year, making it the fourth leading cause of death among all adults. At the time when Life Care began building the Houston facility, more than 265,000 Texans were suffering from the degenerative disease with an estimated 25,000 of these people in the Houston area alone. Although members of the Texas

Council on Alzheimer's Disease and Related Disorders supported centers that care for Alzheimer's patients, it nevertheless was pushing for legislation that would require such care facilities as Garden Terrace to file disclosure statements with the state in order to receive certification. In subsequent years, Life Care opened other specialized Alzheimer's facilities in Fort Worth, Texas; Charleston, South Carolina; Overland, Kanas; Estero, Flordia; and Federal Way, Washington.

In June 1999, the institutional pharmacy services business, Omincare Inc., acquired Life Care's pharmacy services company. Omnicare purchased Life Care Pharmacy Services Inc., from Forrest Preston, the founder, chairman, and only shareholder of Life Care Centers of America. At the time of the acquisition, the Life Care's was providing pharmacy services to over 17,300 elderly residents in 12 states. With the acquisition, Omnicare's services covered approximately 617,000 residents in 8,600 long-term care facilities in 43 states.

Complaints, Lawsuits, and Looking to the Future

In February 2001, the magazine *Consumer Reports* named a Life Care Center in Oregon on its published nursing home watch list. The list, based on state survey reports between 1995 and 1998, was compiled by inspectors making surprise visits to home care facilities to observe care, examine sanitary conditions, and investigate complaints. Nevertheless, Jerry Weldon, an administrator who had been hired to improve operations at the facility said that there had been major improvements to clinical and staffing problems at the nursing home. In 1997, as Life Care proceeded to open a new facility in Lakeville, Massachusetts, the company paid a $650,000 settlement over a claim of negligence at its Raynham location. Another 79-year-old woman died in Life Care's West Bridgwater facility shortly after she moved in after a nurse accidentally gave a lethal overdose of morphine. The company fired the nurse and an investigation by the Plymouth County District, Department of Health, medical examiner concluded the death resulted from human error, rather than from company-wide substandard care. Like other companies in the industry, Life Care faced complaints of poor care, but overall the large for profit, private company was found to be on par with others in the retirement and health care services business.

In October 2000, Life Care's Plainwell, Michigan facility lost a National Labor Relations Board (NLRB) dispute with Local No. 79 of the Services Employees' International Union for refusing to bargain following the union's certification. Following an election on October 22, 1999, the union won certification on January 7, 2000, as the exclusive collective-bargaining agent of the employees of the nursing care facility. The company refused to both recognize and bargain with the union as the exclusive representative under Section 9(a) of the National Labor Relations Act. As a result, the NLRB found the company to have engaged in unfair labor practices and to be in violation of the Act.

The company moved to a web-based document and delivery storage management system in 2001 to streamline the printing and distribution of financial and other reports for its 230 eldercare facilities and seven regional offices in 28 states. The web-based system, called ReportSafe, was estimated to save Life Care $55,917 yearly by eliminating the piles of paper. The

---

Key Dates:

1970: Forrest L. Preston founds company as Garden Terrace Convalescent Center.
1976: Company is incorporated as Life Care Centers of America Inc.
1989: Company establishes Garden Terrace as division devoted to care and treatment of Alzheimer's disease.
1999: Omnicare Inc. acquires Life Care Pharmacy Services Inc.
2004: Hillhaven and Life Care Centers of America form joint venture called Medlife Pharmacy Network

---

company spent $20,250 on the cost of training and software implementation, and anywhere from $32,000 to $80,000 on the ReportSafe software. There was a downside to the software, however, requiring a long six-month implementation period as numerous rules needed to be written for the application to work with 500 users in almost 300 locations.

In 2003, a lawsuit was filed against Life Care's Las Fuentes Care Center in Phoenix, Arizona filed for alleging taking money out of employee paychecks for heath insurance but not paying the premiums. The Arizona Court of Appeals ruled that the company could not be sued in state court, stating that any claims employees had fell under the federal pension laws and must be filed in federal court. Court records evinced that Life Care, which operated the Las Fuentes Care Center, signed a 1998 agreement with Premier Healthcare of Arizona for health insurance for the Las Fuentes employees. Under the agreement, Las Fuentes would pay the monthly premiums financed by both employee payroll deductions and its own contributions. Three years later some of the employees filed a class action lawsuit in Maricopa County Superior Court, claiming the company had ceased remitting the payroll deductions.

In 2004, elder care provider Hillhaven and Life Care formed a joint venture under the name Medlife Pharmacy Network to provide pharmaceutical and medication delivery systems, infu-sion and enteral therapy services, and pharmacy consulting services to long term care and sub acute care facilities. With this venture, the company continued to look to expand in new ways in the $1.7 trillion U.S. health care services market, the world's largest.

Principal Divisions

Alzheimer's Care; Nursing Care; Assisted Living; Rehabilitation Services; Campus Care; Retirement Centers; Home Care; Specialty Services.

Principal Competitors

Beverly Enterprises Inc.; Sava Senior Care LLC; Sun Healthcare Group Inc.

Further Reading

Fischer, Howard, "Lawsuit Bounced to Federal Courts: Workers Sued Company Over Insurance," *Arizona Business Gazette*, January 23, 2003.

Gannon, Kathi, "Eckerd Opening Life Care Home Centers in Some Stores," *Drug Topics*, April 11, 1994.

Harding, Elizabeth U., "Distribution Tool Cuts Printing Costs at Life Care Centers," *Software Magazine*, Spring 2002.

Lewis, David, "Online Reporting's Return—Elder Care Facilities Use Web to Reduce Costs of Distributing Financial Reports," *Internet-Week*, September 24, 2001.

Miller, Nick, "Omnicare Buys Nursing Home Pharmacy Group," *Cincinnati Post*, June 4, 1999.

"Omnicare Acquires Life Care Pharmacy," June 3, 1999.

Peale, Cliff, "Software Firm Sues Nursing Homes for Copyright Cheating," *Cincinnati Business Courier*, May 2, 1994.

Rhoads, Gail J., "Fixing our Laundry Woes," *Nursing Homes*, February 1998.

Rising, David, "Firm's Impressive Record Marred by a Death, Court Case," Southwest Coast Today, September 11, 1997.

Schlegel, Darrin, "Tennessee Firm to Build New Alzheimer's Center," *Houston Business Journal*, March 1995.

—Bruce P. Montgomery

Lotte Confectionery Company Ltd.

23 Yangpyong-dong 4-ka, Youngdeungpo-ku
Seoul
South Korea
Telephone: +82 02 670 6114
Fax: +82 02 675 6600
Web site: http://www.lotteconf.co.kr

Public Company
Incorporated: 1948
Employees: 5,475
Sales: KRW 30 trillion ($1.09 billion) (2004)
Stock Exchanges: Seoul
NAIC: 311330 Confectionery Manufacturing from
    Purchased Chocolate

With a dual base in Korea and Japan, Lotte—known as Lotte Co. in Japan and as Lotte Confectionery Company Ltd. in Korea—is one of Asia's leading producers of confectionery and related products. The company's flagship is its line of chewing gums, and Lotte's brand family of chewing gums dominates its markets, with a market share of more than 60 percent in Japan, and similar levels in Korea. In addition to chewing gum, Lotte produces a wide range of candies, as well as cookies and other baked goods, and ice cream. Other operations under the company's direct control include the Lotteria chain of fast-food restaurants in Japan. The company has manufacturing and sales subsidiaries in Indonesia, China, Vietnam, the Philippines, and Thailand, as well as a production subsidiary in the United States. Together these operations combined to produce more than KRW 30 trillion ($1.09 billion) in annual sales in 2004. Lotte is itself part of the larger Lotte Group, controlled by the founding Shin/Shigemitsu family and company founder Shin Kyuk-ho (known as Takeo Shigemitsu in Japan). With interests including Lotte Shopping, Korea's largest department store group; the Lotte Hotel group; ownership of baseball teams (in Korea and Japan); travel and tourism; and real estate, including ownership of Lotte World, the world's largest indoor amusement park, shopping, entertainment, and hotel complex, Lotte Group is one of the ten largest corporations in Korea and one of the largest in the entire Asian Pacific region.

Bubble Gum Beginnings in the 1940s

Although later considered one of South Korea's largest companies, Lotte's origins actually traced back to post-World War II Japan. During the war, Shin Kyuk-ho, a native of Korea, came to Tokyo to study at a technical college in 1941 at the age of 19. After graduating, Shin remained in Japan, adopting the Japanese name of Takeo Shigemitsu. By 1946, Shigemitsu decided to go into business for himself, launching the Hikara Special Chemical Research Institute. This company produced soaps and cosmetics from surplus chemicals stocks left over from the war.

That company, although small, provided the basis for Shigemitsu's first fortune, and within a year he had amassed enough capital to launch a new company, dedicated to production of chewing gum. Introduced by American soldiers following the war, chewing gum quickly became popular among Japanese consumers eager to embrace all things American. In 1948, Shigemitsu founded Lotte Co., with ten employees. Shigemitsu's choice of the company's name came from his admiration for Goethe's *Sorrows of Young Werther,* particularly the character of Charlotte.

Using natural chicle, Lotte launched a number of chewing gum brands, including Orange Gum, Lotte Gum, Cowboy Gum, Mable Gum, and the highly popular Baseball Gum. The company backed up its products with strong advertising support, becoming one of the first in Japan to sponsor television programs, as well as its own baseball team and other events, such as beauty pageants. In the mid-1950s, the company sponsored the country's Antarctic Research Expedition Team, developing a chewing gum for the effort's training program. The company then launched the gum, known as Cool Mint Gum, for the consumer market, in 1956. The gum featured a penguin on the package, which became one of the country's most prominent consumer logos into the next century. Another Lotte sponsoring effort was the *Lotte Music Album* show on television, a popular music-oriented program that ran through the late 1970s.

Shigemitsu expanded his production interest to include candies, cookies, and snack cakes, and by the early 1960s, the

Company Perspectives:

We will always continue to take on new challenges based on three core themes. User Oriented. We think from the customer's perspective. First, we think about what is important for our customers. We provide them with products and services that enhance richer lives and greater satisfaction. This is the spirit that infuses our corporate philosophy. Originality. We continue to seek unique ideas. We constantly challenge ourselves to define new and unique products and services. This stance requires a total effort to develop new areas of business and advance into global markets with our challenging spirit, which is an important intangible asset. Quality. We will strive to achieve the highest quality in every aspect of our business. We have been making progress based on our philosophy, which places the highest value on quality as expressed in our slogan of 'sincerely producing the highest quality products made using the highest quality ingredients.' We will continue to insist on the highest quality, which enables our customers to enjoy the good taste and comfort of our family of quality products.

company had established itself as a rival to Japan's two largest confectionery groups, Meiji and Morinaga. The company's true breakthrough came during the 1960s, with its entry into the chocolate market. In 1964, the company launched its first milk chocolate, called Ghana, adapting Swiss-styled chocolates for the Japanese palate. The company supported this launch with a massive television advertisement campaign, firmly positioning the brand in the minds of consumers. The launch paved the way for Lotte's emergence as the number one chocolate manufacturer in Japan by the end of the century.

Although Lotte had successfully established itself as a truly Japanese company—in a country where ethnicity had always been a prominent part of the national identity—Shigemitsu had not abandoned his Korean roots. Lotte had established a presence in Korea as early as 1958, opening a factory producing chewing gum and other confectionery, as well as instant noodles, for the Korean market. The normalization of diplomatic relations between Japan and Korea in 1965, however, presented a new opportunity for the company. Lotte decided to move into Korea on a full scale, and in 1967, the company established a dedicated operation for South Korea, called Lotte Confectionery Co.

Adding Korean Operations in the 1960s

It was not long, however, before Shigemitsu—or, rather, Shin—found himself in trouble with the Korean government, then still under military dictatorship. The South Korean government was then in the process of building up its military strength as part of its cold war with North Korea. Seeking to establish its own industrial defense capacity, the government approached Shin with a request for him to contribute to this effort, encouraging him to enter military production as well.

Yet Shin, perhaps mindful of the negative publicity that a move into arms production would bring to the company's confectionery sales, refused. The refusal brought a series of difficulties

for Lotte Confectionery, which finally were resolved by the direct intervention of then president Park Chung-Lee. Rather than agree to invest in the country's defense effort, Shin agreed to transfer the center of Lotte's operations to South Korea. Lotte Confectionery now became the core of Shin's growing empire; nonetheless, the original Lotte Co. and the Japanese market remained the company's largest confectionery operation.

The move to Korea, however, opened a whole new series of business opportunities for Shin and for Lotte. Korea at the time had just begun its own effort to establish itself as one of the Asian region's industrial and technological giants, and Shin proved a shrewd investor, expanding the company's business interests to include department store ownership (the group's Lotte Shopping became the country's leading retailer); hotel ownership, through Lotte Hotels, created in 1973, and including Hotel Lotte Seoul, the largest in that capital city, in 1979; travel and tourism; and restaurant and convenience store operations. The company branched out into the outright ownership of baseball teams, buying up the Tokyo Orions (which became the Lotte Orions) in 1969, and also acquiring Korea's Giants and the Marines of Chiba, Japan, in 1971. Meanwhile, real estate development also became a prominent part of the company's growing empire, and later included Lotte World, the world's largest indoor amusement, entertainment, shopping, and hotel complex, opened in 1989.

These investments helped Lotte grow into one of Korea's top ten conglomerates by the end of the 20th century. Yet Lotte's diversification drive, unlike those of rivals such as Samsung, Hyundai, LG, and Daewoo, avoided an entry into heavy industrial operations, and instead focused on the light industry and services sectors. In Japan, for example, the company launched its own chain of fast-food restaurants, Lotteria, which shrewdly traded on its well-known and highly popular brand name. The first Lotteria opened in 1972, and by the end of that year the store had opened stores in Nihonbashi, Ueno, and Yokohama, before rolling the chain out on a national scale.

Another company extension was the creation of Lotte Denshi, which began developing novelty products such as lighters, pocket warmers, and cooler pouches, but also health foods and other goods. Closer to the group's core was the launch of its Lotte Trading subsidiary, founded in 1958, into the frozen desserts market in 1972.

Lotte launched its own bakery and baked goods operations in the early 1980s, including the establishment of subsidiary Mutter Rosa Co. in 1982. That company opened a string of bakeries, featuring freshly baked breads and related products. Through the 1980s, Lotte built up its backbone as well, adding subsidiaries involved in data processing, logistics and transportation, and machinery development, maintenance, and repair.

The company also continued to innovate with new confectionery products. These included the launch of the highly successful ice cream, Yukimi Daifuku, in 1981, and of the "half-unbaked cake" Choco Pie in 1983. The company created a new candy category, the "throat candy" with the launch of Nodo Ame in 1985. Lotte also enjoyed success with a number of new chewing gum brands, such as the sugarless Blueberry and the Giant chewing gum, both launched in 1993.

Key Dates:

1948: Korean native Shin Kyuk-Ho (also known as Takeo Shigemitsu) launches the Lotte chewing gum company in Japan, named after Charlotte, a character in Goethe's *Sorrows of Young Werther.*

1967: Lotte launches Lotte Confectionery in Korea, which becomes the focus of the Lotte Group's diversified development.

1978: The company launches U.S. production and a sales subsidiary.

1989: The company enters the Thai confectionery market; Lotte World, the world's largest indoor amusement part complex, opens.

1993: The company opens a production subsidiary in Jakarta, Indonesia.

1994: Lotte enters the Chinese market through a production joint venture in Beijing.

1995: Sales to Indonesia begin.

1996: The company launches a production and distribution subsidiary in Vietnam.

2002: The company forms the Lotte Snow Co. frozen dessert joint venture with Snow Brand Milk Products in Japan.

2005: Lotte acquires control of a confectionery production company in Qingdao, China.

International Success in the New Century

In the 1990s and 2000s, Lotte turned to the international market for further growth. The company had made its first international extension, other than in Korea, in the late 1970s. In 1978, Lotte set up a subsidiary in the United States, opening production facilities in Battle Creek, Michigan. The group's U.S. presence later expanded to include a sales office in Chicago, supporting sales of the group's chewing gums and cookies.

In the 1990s, Lotte turned to markets closer to home. The company established a subsidiary in Thailand in 1989, where it began producing and distributing candy and confectionery. In 1993, Lotte entered Indonesia, launching a subsidiary in Jakarta. This was followed by the creation of a joint venture for the mainland Chinese market, which established production facilities in Beijing in 1994. The company acquired full control of its Chinese operations in 2005. The Philippines became part of the Lotte empire in 1995, with the launch of a sales and distribution subsidiary in Manila. One year later, the company added production and sales operations in Ho Chi Minh, Vietnam, as well.

Continuing product development brought the company new successes as well. In 1996, the company launched its Chocolate Zero, claiming to be the world's first sugarless chocolate. The following year, Lotte became the first in Japan to launch a xylitol-based chewing gum. Because xylitol, unlike other sweeteners, did not produce acid when chewed, the company was able to promote its chewing gum as a cavity-fighting product. The company's interest in developing xylitol-based products continued into the 2000s, including the launch of the Xylitol Family Bottle, a beverage containing xylitol as a sweetener. In 2005, the company launched its Lotte Notime tooth-polishing chewing gum.

Lotte expanded its frozen dessert operations in 2002, forming a joint venture with troubled Snow Brand Milk Products, then involved in a beef-labeling scandal. The joint venture, Lotte Snow Co., was owned at 80 percent by Lotte, and launched production of Snow-branded ice cream products. In 2005, the company expanded its operations in China, buying up control of Qingdao-based Jinhu Shipin. That move was seen as part of the group's strategy to become a major confectionery group on a global scale. Lotte remained controlled by Shin Kyuk-ho, joined by his children and other family members. In less than 60 years, Shin had built Lotte from a small chewing gum producer into one of the world's top confectionery groups.

Principal Subsidiaries

Lotte China Foods Co., Ltd.; LOTTE Co., Ltd. (Japan); Lotte Confectionery Co. Ltd. (Korea); LOTTE Frozen Dessert Co., Ltd. (Japan); Lotte Hotel (Japan); Lotte Philippines Co., Inc.; Lotte Shopping Co. Ltd. (Korea); LOTTE Snow Co., Ltd. (Japan); LOTTE Trading Co., Ltd. (Japan); Lotte U.S.A., Inc.; Lotte Vietnam Co., Ltd.; LOTTERIA Co., Ltd. (Japan); Nihon Food Distribution Co., Ltd. (Japan); PT. Lotte Indonesia; Thai Lotte Co., Ltd. (Thailand).

Principal Competitors

Taiwan Sugar Corporation; Central Group of Cos.; Meiji Seika Kaisha Ltd.; Katokichi Company Ltd.; Ezaki Glico Company Ltd.; Lamson Sugar Co.; Morinaga and Company Ltd.; August Storck KG; Ferrero S.p.A.; Fujiya Company Ltd.

Further Reading

Lankov, Andrej, ''The Whole Lotte,'' *Korea Times,* July 24, 2005.

''New Chewing Gum from Lotte,'' *Japan Food Products & Service Journal,* February 25, 2005.

Nho, Joon-hun, ''Generational Transfer Taking Place at Lotte,'' *Korea Times,* May 12, 2003.

''Snow Brand Creates Lotte Joint Venture,'' *Dairy Markets,* July 4, 2002, p. 9.

—M.L. Cohen

Manning Selvage & Lee (MS&L)

1675 Broadway, 9th Floor
New York, New York 10019
U.S.A.
Telephone: (212) 468-4200
Fax: (212) 468-4175
Web site: http://www.mslpr.com

Wholly Owned Subsidiary of Publicis Groupe S,A.
Founded: 1938 as Selvage & Lee
Employees: 1,000 (est.)
Sales: $298 million (2004)
NAIC: 541820 Public Relations Services

A subsidiary of Paris-based Publicis Groupe S.A., one of the world's largest advertising and media services conglomerates, Manning Selvage & Lee (MS&L) is a public relations firm that concentrates on major corporate clients in four specialties: consumer marketing, corporate, health care, and technology. Services offered include branding, audience insights, message development, and the evaluation of the effectiveness of a public relations campaign. Major MS&L clients include Eli Lilly & Company, General Motors, Hasbro, JP Morgan, Nestle, Pfizer, Philips, Procter & Gamble, Western Union, and the U.S. Army. In addition to its headquarters in New York City, MS&L maintains approximately 40 other offices: 11 in North America, including Washington, D.C., Los Angeles, Chicago, Atlanta, and Toronto; two in Latin America; 16 in Europe, including London, Berlin, Paris, and Rome; seven in the Asia Pacific region, including Beijing, Hong Kong, and Tokyo; and a Middle East/Africa office in Dubai, United Arab Emirates. In addition, MS&L has 62 affiliates located around the world.

Public Relations Emerges in Early 1900s

The public relations (PR) profession grew out of the work of the press agents and publicists who in the main came from the newspaper field, promoting theatrical performances, circuses, boxing and wrestling matches, and other public spectacles. With the rise of the mass-circulation newspapers and magazines, progressive reformers around 1900 sought to harness the power of the media to shape public opinion. The government followed suit when in the mid-1910s it endeavored to mobilize support of America's entry in World War I. The Committee on Public Information that was created for this purpose would serve as a training ground for many of the PR specialists who plied the trade after the war in the service of corporations. During the war many of the techniques of contemporary mass manipulation were developed, including the news release, emotional appeals through advertising, the use of motion pictures (albeit silent), the enlistment of local "opinion leaders," and even the manufacture of "grassroots" campaigns. Among these early practitioners of public relations was Ivy Lee, credited with the development of the modern press release, but also castigated for his work in rehabilitating clients despised by the public, such as John D. Rockefeller, whose reputation went from robber baron to grandfatherly philanthropist. A nephew of Sigmund Freud, Edward Bernays, provide the profession with it first theorist. Borrowing from his uncle's ideas about human behavior, Bernays developed concepts on how the opinions of the masses could be shaped. In his 1928 book, *Propaganda,* he wrote: "Those who manipulate this unseen mechanism of society constitute an invisible government which is the true ruling power of our country." In his work for the tobacco industry in the 1920s, Bernays was able to persuade a large number of women to take up smoking by cleverly equating it with a demand for women's rights.

Following the stock market crash of 1929 that ushered in the Great Depression of the 1930s, American business was not held in high esteem by the public, offering public relations practitioners a wealth of business opportunities. In 1933 James P. Selvage (later of Manning Selvage & Lee) became a press agent and later public relations director for the National Association of Manufacturers (NAM), which strongly objected to President Roosevelt's progressive "New Deal" legislation. Part of Selvage's mandate was to create a public relations campaign "for the dissemination of sound American doctrines to the public." To achieve this end, Selvage created cartoons similar to the "Ripley's Believe it or Not" concept to present amazing facts about private enterprise and the American way of life; commissioned college professors to write newspaper columns criticizing the economic underpinnings of the New Deal; published the

You and Industry series of booklets for schools and the weekly school publication *And Young America*, which offered articles that put capitalism in the most favorable light. NAM also produced material for the movie theaters, such as the ten-minute episodes of *America Marches On* narrated by Lowell Thomas, portraying America as history's greatest industrial system. Selvage also utilized radio, creating a 15-minute program called *The American Family Robinson*, which centered on the lives of the Robinsons of the manufacturing city of Centerville, caught up in the problems of the Depression. With businessmen portrayed as heroes and labor organizers as villains, the clear message was that the free enterprise system would set things right. The more overt purpose of the show, according to Selvage, was to serve as ''industry's effective answer to the Utopian promises of theorists and demagogues at present reaching such vast audiences via the radio.'' In all likelihood he counted the president himself among that number, since Roosevelt had proven adept at using radio, especially in his famous ''fireside chats.'' Selvage would more directly oppose Roosevelt from 1943 to 1944, serving as the press agent for the Republican National Committee.

Late 1990s Launch of Selvage & Lee

In 1938 Selvage struck out on his own to start his own PR firm. He was soon joined by Morris M. Lee, Jr., information director for NAM and a former public relations executive at International Telephone & Telegraph, and the firm took the name Selvage & Lee. In the mid-1960s a third partner was added, James Stuart Howard, who had worked in his family's Cleveland PR firm, Edward Howard & Sons for nearly 20 years before moving to New York City to join Selvage and Lee. The firm now took the name Selvage, Lee & Howard, its focus on corporate and investor relations.

MS&L was formed in 1972 when Selvage & Lee merged with Farley Manning Associates and Howard's name was dropped. Farley Manning Associates was formed in 1954 by Farley Alden Manning, who started as a reporter in 1931, but became involved in public relations after joining the U.S. Army Air Corps in 1942, working under General James Doolittle for the Eighth Air Force. Following the war he became a senior account executive for New York's Dudley, Anderson, Yutzy, Public Relations, a position he held until forming his own PR firm.

The merger with Farley Manning Associates added consumer product and science/health practices to the firm. Following the merger, Manning served as MS&L's president and chairman and began expanding the operation. In 1975 an office in Washington, D.C., was added through the acquisition of Rainey, McEnroe & Manning; MS&L/Chicago was established through the purchase of Herb Kraus company; and a Pacific division was created through the acquisition of Paul Spindler & Company. The third of what contemporary MS&L considers its three predecessor companies, Bell & Stanton, was brought into the fold through a 1976 merger, adding an Atlanta office to the firm and further capabilities in consumer products. It had been established by Alan Bell and Edward Stanton in 1956.

While MS&L was expanding its expertise and offices in the 1970s, advertising agencies began to see the value of having public relations capabilities and began buying the top PR firms. The seventh largest in the industry, MS&L employed some 130 people at offices in New York; Los Angeles; San Francisco; Washington, D.C.; Chicago; Atlanta; and San Antonio. In addition, it partially owned a Toronto office and was involved in a joint venture in London. MS&L also had a sterling reputation as a Blue Chip PR firm, having served 60 of the Fortune 500 companies, making it a desirable acquisition. In 1980 MS&L was bought by one of the world's largest advertising agencies, Benton & Bowles, Inc. Fanning subsequently retired, and was succeeded by Robert Schwartz, named president and chief executive officer.

Global Expansion Begins in 1980s

With the deep pockets of a corporate parent, MS&L began to expand globally in the 1980s. The globalization trend began in the 1970s as American PR firms began serving the needs of multinational clients. MS&L inherited the Benton & Bowles public relations operations in West Germany in 1980, giving the firm a presence in Europe, but MS&L's worldwide expansion did not really accelerate until after Benton & Bowles merged with D'Arcy MacManus Masius Worldwide in November 1985, creating D'Arcy Masius Benton and Bowles Inc. (DMB&B) In the meantime, MS&L had beefed up its Washington, D.C. operation with the 1984 acquisition of Bill Rolle and Associates. Before the end of 1985, MS&L added a toehold in Australia by purchasing a 35 percent stake in Royce Australia. Three years the firm acquired a 51 percent controlling interest in the business. In 1987 MS&L opened a London office and a year later announced that it planned to strengthened its presence in Europe and looked to take equity positions in affiliated shops in the market. The strategy, in part, was to have public relations handled by nationals of a country, and by taking an equity position in an affiliate rather than buying complete control MS&L conferred upon a shop the kind of autonomy that would allow it to better compete in its local market. Kay Berger, director of European operations, told the press, ''There is a strong desire on our part to be a global agency. We have also been requested by clients to provide a global service.'' Working through a network of affiliates was a major part of the plan to develop this global reach.

In the early 1990s, MS&L was especially aggressive in pursuing its worldwide aspirations. In 1990 it became involved in Tokyo, entering into a joint venture with Tokyu Agences Intl. & Kyodo P.R. to form Tokyu/MS&L. In that same year, MS&L bought a 25 percent interest in a Dutch affiliate, Adviesbureaur en Van Der Mey in The Hague. In 1991, MS&L's parent company bought RSL/France to create RSL/MS&L. The firm was also active domestically during the early 1990s. In 1992 it acquired a Los Angeles-based Hispanic PR firm, Moya Villenueva, which was folded into MS&L's Los Angeles office. Then, the firm beefed up its Washington, D.C., operation, which was in sore need of an upgrade in order to attract the very

---

Key Dates:

1938: Selvage & Lee is founded.
1972: Selvage & Lee merges with Farley Manning Associates, creating Manning Selvage & Lee (MS&L).
1976: Bell & Stanton is acquired.
1980: Benton & Bowles acquires the firm.
1987: London office opens.
1991: Paris office opens.
1996: MS&L becomes part of the McManus Group.
1999: McManus merges with Leo Burnett, creating Bcom3 Group Inc.
2002: MS&L becomes a part of Publicis Groupe when the latter acquires Bcom3; Bcom3 is dissolved but MS&L remains a subsidiary of Publicis.

---

important business that was available in the nation's capital. Capitoline International Group Ltd., formed in 1991 by defections from Hill & Knowlton, was acquired by MS&L in January 1994, creating Capitoline-MS&L.

MS&L experienced some of its own attrition in the Atlanta office in July 1995 when several executives quit to form their own PR firm, Jackson Spalding Ledlie. MS&L tried to stop the move, claiming the former employees stole company secrets as well as top clients, but it failed to convince a federal judge to issue a restraining order. Jackson Spalding Ledlie countersued, alleging slander. After 20 months of legal wrangling, on the eve of a trial the two parties reached an out-of-court settlement, both agreeing to drop all claims and counterclaims. In the meantime, the MS&L Atlanta office had regained some its lost business by acquiring another local PR agency, which brought with it several health care clients and $850,000 in billings.

MS&L's corporate parent changed its name to The McManus Group, Inc., in 1996, and took steps to bring order to its far-flung collection of ad agencies and PR assets. Three years later MacManus merged with the Leo Group, parent of Chicago's Leon Burnett Company, Inc., creating an even larger entity in the rapidly consolidating advertising industry. The new company took the name Bcom3. Also in 1999, MS&L completed an acquisition of its own, buying Agnew, Carter, McCarthy, a 20-year-old Boston-based PR firm.

The 2000s saw even more consolidation among communication companies. In September 2002, Bcom3 was bought by France's Publicis Groupe, resulting in the world's fourth largest communications company, with operations in more than 100 countries spread across five continents.

Regardless of who owned the firm, MS&L continued to expand during the 2000s. In 2001 it moved into the investor relations field by acquiring Los Angeles-based Pondel/Wilkinson Group, which also maintained a key office in Washington, D.C. A year later MS&L filled in other gaps by adding six affiliates to its network, including Imre Communications of Baltimore; Morningstar Communications in Kansas, City, Kansas; Richard French & Associates in Raleigh, North Carolina; Strother Communications Group in Minneapolis; the Workman Company in St. Louis, and Schroder & Schombs Public Relations GmbH, in Berlin. One area that MS&L had shied away from had been high-tech. That discretion paid off following the burst of the dot com bubble. Having avoided taking on the debt that saddled rivals, MS&L in the early years of the 2000s was well positioned to continue its global expansion.

Principal Operating Units

Consumer Marketing; Corporate; Health Care; Technology.

Principal Competitors

Burson-Marsteller; Edelman; Hill & Knowlton, Inc.

Further Reading

Fones-Wolf, Elizabeth, "Creating a Favorable Business Climate: Corporations and Radio Broadcasting, 1934 to 1954," *Business History Review,* Summer 1999, p. 221.
"From the Bronx to the Board—Lou Capozzi, Chairman/CEO, Manning Selvage & Lee," *PR Week,* March 5, 2004, p. 19.
Lohr, Greg A., "MS&L Deal Brings Public, Investor Relations Closer," *Washington Business Journal,* February 9, 2001, p. 5.
"Manning Selvage and Lee Plans to Buy One or More Consultancies," *PR Week,* October 24, 19991, p. 1.
Rabin, Phil, and Carolyn Myles, "Four Agencies Become Two as Double Weddings Rings in New Year," *Washington Times,* January 5, 1994, p. B9.
Roush, Chris, "Two Atlanta PR Firms Reach Settlement, Drop Claims," *Atlanta Journal and Constitution,* March 25, 1997.
Stanton, Edward M., "PR's Future is Here: Worldwide, Integrated Communications," *Public Relations Quarterly,* Spring 1991, p. 36.
Warner, Judy, "MS&L Acquires Agnew, Carter," *Adweek,* August 23, 1999, p. 5.

—Ed Dinger

MARSH.

Marsh Supermarkets, Inc.

9800 Crosspoint Boulevard
Indianapolis, Indiana 46256-3350
U.S.A.
Telephone: (317) 594-2100
Fax: (317) 594-2704
Web site: http://www.marsh.net

Public Company
Incorporated: 1933 as Marsh Food Stores, Inc.
Employees: 14,300
Sales: $1.74 billion (2005)
Stock Exchanges: NASDAQ
Ticker Symbol: MARSA
NAIC: 445110 Supermarkets and Other Grocery (Except
    Convenience) Stores; 445120 Convenience Stores

Marsh Supermarkets, Inc., is one of the largest regional supermarket chains in the United States, despite limiting its operations almost entirely to Indiana and western Ohio. The company has 117 supermarkets that operate under the Marsh, LoBill Foods, O'Malia's Food Markets, Arthur's Fresh Market, and Savin*$ Mercado banners. Marsh also operates 161 Village Pantry convenience stores and several McNamara florists. Its Crystal Food Services subsidiary provides upscale catering, cafeteria management, and related services. Supermarket operations accounted for more than 78 percent of company revenues in fiscal 2005.

A Depression-Era Success

The first attempt by a member of the Marsh family to enter the grocery business came in 1922, when Wilmer Marsh left farming to buy a small grocery and general goods store in North Salem, Indiana, population 75. All seven of Marsh's children helped in running the store, but it was Ermal Marsh, the second youngest at 12 years old, who took the most interest in the store's operations, taking charge of the books and ordering merchandise. The store did well enough; but in 1925, during a holdup by a member of the Al Capone gang, Wilmer Marsh was shot in the head. Although he suffered only a flesh wound, Wilmer Marsh sold the store and returned to farming.

Two years later, however, Wilmer Marsh bought a new store in New Pittsburg, Indiana, population 50. That store was successful enough for Marsh to open a second store in Ridgeville, Indiana, in 1929. Ermal Marsh, then completing his first year of college at Ball State, left school to manage the new store. Grocery stores of the era were small, about 2,400 square feet, and sold a variety of dry goods in addition to foods, which the grocer would gather from the shelves for the customers. For the new store, Ermal Marsh joined the Independent Grocers Association (IGA), which advocated new selling techniques, such as advertising and allowing the customer to choose their purchases for themselves. Three weeks after the Ridgeville store opened, the stock markets crashed, and the Depression era began. Despite the bleak economy, the new store proved successful and was operated by brother Estel, when Ermal Marsh returned to college.

In order to finance his education, Ermal Marsh opened his own store in Muncie, Indiana, in 1930, borrowing $2,900 from an older brother. The first day's sales totaled $7. Yet the store, an IGA affiliate, proved successful enough for the newly graduated Ermal Marsh to open a second store two years later. The following year, Marsh closed that store and moved its stock to a new store located in Muncie's commercial district. He also incorporated his business as Marsh Food Stores, Inc., listing himself as secretary and treasurer, and his older brother as president.

Marsh sought financing to expand his company, but banks were reluctant to lend in the early Depression years, especially to the low-margin grocery business. By 1935, however, Marsh had arranged sufficient financing to open a third Muncie grocery. The next year, Marsh closed his second store and reopened it in a new, larger location. The new stores, both IGA affiliates, featured meat counters, fresh produce, and a sound system providing background music and in-store announcements. By the end of the decade, Marsh sought to expand again. He sold one store and opened another, larger store. Then, together with several other store owners, Marsh formed the Carload Buyers Association to purchase dry goods at wholesale for distribution to its member stores. The association next teamed up with another wholesaler, changing its name to Mundy Sales, Inc.

The U.S. entry into World War II barely slowed Marsh's growth. By 1943, Ermal Marsh had added three more stores to

Company Perspectives:

Marsh Supermarkets, Inc., strives to attain and maintain a position of leadership and market dominance in Indiana and other outlying territories through a commitment to aggressive marketing of new products, service innovation, and support by a first class sales organization, support staff, and community involvement.

his operations. The following year, he opened his first store outside of Muncie, in the Jay County town seat of Portland. Two more stores were added that same year, in Dunkirk and Marion, and in 1946, Marsh opened a new store in Muncie, closing his original store. Marsh's biggest advancement, however, would occur the following year.

Postwar Growth

Marsh opened two new groceries in 1947 and planned to open a third, somewhat larger store that year, complete with a parking lot. Unable to get permission to break the curbstones for entrances, Marsh decided to use the parking space to expand the size of the store. The new store, at 6,430 square feet, became Marsh's—and Muncie's—first supermarket. Called Marsh Foodliner, the store proved profitable in its first week. Encouraged by the store's success, Marsh determined to convert his operation entirely to supermarkets. The company began to expand its corporate staff; by then Marsh operated its own fleet of trucks to service its stores. Over the next three years the company opened four more stores—including a second Foodliner in Muncie, helping to prove the viability of the supermarket concept. Store size was reaching 9,000 square feet. The company started its own bakery in 1949, and then added a new sideline business, making ice cream in the basement of one of the stores. Sold in gallon containers, Marsh Ice Cream proved immediately popular with customers—selling five million gallons by 1957 and eventually making Marsh the country's largest distributor of gallon ice cream—beginning a long line of Marsh private-label products.

By 1951, Marsh was outgrowing its facilities. In that year, the company purchased an abandoned milk condensery in Yorktown, Indiana, and began construction there on the Marsh Food Center, housing production, distribution and warehouse facilities, and corporate headquarters. To finance the construction, Marsh went public, issuing 40,000 shares of nonvoting stock. The following year, Marsh restructured the company's various operations as a single entity under the name Marsh Foodliners, Inc. The supermarket chain had grown to 16 stores, all in Indiana. That changed in 1956, when Marsh opened its first two stores in western Ohio. Until this time, Marsh supermarkets were found only in mid-sized towns and cities. In 1957, the company opened its first store in a large urban market, Indianapolis. Sales for that year reached $34 million.

Marsh stepped up its expansion in the final years of the 1950s when it acquired the eight-store Food-Lane Stores, Inc., chain based in South Carolina and Georgia. Marsh followed that acquisition with the purchase of Bellman Markets, a five-store supermarket chain with an average store size of 13,000 square

feet, based in Toledo, Ohio. Ermal Marsh's five-year plan called for even faster growth, but he did not get to see completion of his plan. Ermal Marsh died in 1959 when the plane he was piloting crashed.

Settling In: 1960s–70s

Marsh's brother Estel, then serving as executive vice-president, took over as head of the company, now renamed Marsh Supermarkets, Inc., and continued the pattern of growth set by Ermal Marsh. By 1960, the chain had expanded to 62 stores, reaching annual sales of $80 million. The company maintained its rapid expansion, adding 34 stores between 1960 and 1963. By 1966, Marsh had topped $100 million in sales. By then, the supermarket concept had captured the grocery market, ending the era of the small grocer. The demise of the small stores opened a new market for the increasingly mobile American public. Convenience stores had begun to appear in various parts of the country, but Indiana's restrictive laws regarding sales of beer and gasoline—the most profitable aspects of the convenience store business—left that state mostly free of competitors.

Marsh opened its first Village Pantry convenience store in Muncie in 1966. That division, led by then executive vice-president Don Marsh, oldest son of Ermal Marsh, grew quickly, adding nine more Village Pantries in two years. The company also experimented with another type of store concept, called Family Market, which offered a no-frills concept. When Estel Marsh was appointed chairman in 1968, Don Marsh was named president of the company. Following the lead of other supermarket chains, Marsh moved into the drugstore business, opening its first Marsh Drug Store in 1969. Under Don Marsh's leadership, the company exited the food production business, contracting with outside companies to supply its private-label products, in order to concentrate on its growing retail empire. Marsh closed out the 1960s with revenues of $122 million.

Marsh continued to expand its operations at the start of the 1970s, but a slowdown in the economy, rising building costs, and increasing price competition with other supermarket chains cut deeply into the company's profits. With a 49 percent drop in net income in 1971, the company closed its Family Market operation, and then sold its truck fleet in a sale-leaseback arrangement. The company stepped up the growth of its Village Pantry chain, bringing the total to 30 stores by 1973. In that year, the company acquired 15 convenience stores from Nite Owl Food Marts, Inc., and, with the addition of more Village Pantries, the convenience store division reached 62 stores by 1974. By then, however, the Arab oil embargo and the resulting surge in inflation began to restrict Marsh's growth.

Nevertheless, Marsh made international news in 1974 when its Troy, Ohio, supermarket became the first in the world to offer Universal Product Code (UPC) scanning. The new system would greatly enhance the company's ability to track its customers' purchases; linked to inventory, scanning also helped streamline its ordering and delivery processes. Before long, UPC scanning became ubiquitous in the supermarket industry and soon spread to nearly every retail industry.

Through the second half of the 1970s, Marsh, by then topping $200 million in annual sales, continued adding to its chains, although its growth was slowed somewhat by the eco-

Key Dates:

1927: Wilmer Marsh buys a grocery store in New Pittsburgh, Indiana.
1930: Ermal Marsh opens his own store in Muncie, Indiana.
1933: Ermal Marsh incorporates the company as Marsh Food Stores, Inc.
1947: Marsh Foodliner, a 6,430-square-foot supermarket, opens its doors in Muncie.
1956: Two stores open in Ohio.
1959: Ermal Marsh dies in a plane crash.
1966: Marsh opens its first Village Pantry convenience store in Muncie.
1969: The first Marsh Drug Store opens.
1974: The company's Troy, Ohio, supermarket becomes the first in the world to offer Universal Product Code scanning.
2001: CSDC is sold to McLane Company Inc.
2004: The Arthur's Fresh Market concept debuts.
2005: The company opens its first store in Naperville, Illinois.

nomic problems of the day. To aid in its expansion, the company adopted a "last-in, first-out" accounting method. During this time, Marsh also began moving away from leasing its Village Pantry locations to owning them outright. The advantages of owning also led the company into acting as its own building contractor for the construction of new Village Pantries. Meanwhile, Marsh unveiled a new supermarket concept in the mid-1970s when it opened its first integrated supermarket-drugstore site. The new prototype stores, called "Combos," were former Marsh supermarkets that had been expanded to an average 25,000 square feet. Two years later their success led the company to developing an all-new store concept, this time built from the ground up, with selling area and warehouse space growing to more than 35,000 square feet.

Estel Marsh retired in 1978 and was replaced by Don Marsh as CEO and chairman. By the end of the 1970s, the company had grown to include, in addition to its supermarket chain (which had launched a new, expanded prototype called Marsh Xtras) 109 Village Pantries; 15 Marsh Drug Stores; and three new ventures—the first of a chain of restaurants called Foxfires; a seven-store chain of Tote 'N' Save markets, a return to the no-frills shopping concept; and the first store of another division, called Farmer's Market, specializing in produce sales. None of these new ventures would survive the coming decade, however.

Price Wars in the 1980s and 1990s

Marsh had successively competed in its Indiana market with other, national supermarket chains, but a new type of grocer soon threatened the company. The 1983 entry of Cub Foods and its warehouse concept stores into Indiana sparked a vicious price war that would last more than two years, driving down the profits of the larger chains and forcing at least 35 independent grocers to close. Yet Marsh, which saw its net income drop to $1.6 million on sales nearing $600 million in 1984, managed to come out of the

fray intact. Better, the company actually saw an increase in its market share, capturing many of the customers of the failed supermarkets. Marsh responded to the store wars by increasing its operating efficiency and cutting out luxury expenditures, such as the company's fleet of jets. Marsh also began heightening its customer service, adding bulk food items, increasing its range of fresh foods, such as cheese, and including other services such as in-store banking and video rental. By 1985, despite a meager 4 percent revenue growth, to $628 million, over the previous year, Marsh was able to post a net profit of $4.7 million.

Not all of the Marsh empire came out unscathed. The company sold off its drugstore division to the Peoples drugstore chain. Marsh also unloaded its restaurant division, and shut down both its Tote 'N' Save and Farmer's Market divisions. The company instead returned its focus to its supermarkets and Village Pantries, raising the number of Marsh supermarkets to 76 and the number of Village Pantries to nearly 170 by the end of the decade. The company also picked up CSDC to serve its Village Pantry stores and other convenience stores in the Midwest. By 1990, sales had topped $1 billion.

The 1990s brought a new growth spurt to the company, which moved its headquarters to Indianapolis in 1991. The launching of a new superstore concept—with stores of 60,000 to 80,000 square feet—sparked several years of intensive capital investment. The company also rolled out its Lo Bill store concept, offering lower prices and more limited selection—and offering the company the ability to convert its older, smaller Marsh supermarkets to the new concept. The company added another new division, Crystal Food Services, bringing the company into the catering and foodservice area.

In the mid-1990s, the company faced the emergence of a new competitor in its core Indiana market. Michigan-based Meijer, a chain of "hypermarkets" with warehouse-style stores averaging 200,000 square feet, entered Indiana in 1993—with a reputation for allowing new stores to take losses until they had beaten competitors. Marsh responded by adding warehouse-style departments to its superstores, launching more superstores, and expanding the fresh foods departments of existing stores, while appealing to six decades of Marsh family service to its Indiana and Ohio customers. The strategy appeared to be working. Despite the entry of 14 direct competitors, Marsh's revenues rose to $1.4 billion, and net income increased to $9 million.

Competition Leading to New Concepts in the Late 1990s and Beyond

The company spent the remaining years of the 1990s successfully fending off intense competition. Marsh spent heavily on information technology, opened new stores, and rolled out fresh and updated store formats for its existing locations. It also purchased three Cox Supermarkets in late 1999. As a result, Marsh entered the new millennium on solid footing with sales and profits on the rise.

During this time period, the company made several moves to increase its share of the regional market. Marsh bolstered its holdings in 2000 with the acquisition of five Ross Supermarkets. One year later it added O'Malia Food Markets to its arsenal. In order to focus on core retailing operations, the company sold its Convenience Store Distributing Company (CSDC) to McLane Company Inc. in 2001.

Marsh also launched several new concepts in order to remain competitive in the consolidating grocery industry. The first Savin*$ Mercado, a store developed in a large Hispanic neighborhood, opened its doors in 2002. During 2004, the company's Trios Di Tuscanos debuted in Noblesville and marked one of the first times a supermarket chain opened a stand-alone restaurant. The Tuscan-style eatery featured a wide variety of food, including gourmet pizzas and rotisserie chicken. Further expansion in the Midwest was dependent on the success of the concept in the mid-2000s. Marsh also launched Arthur's Fresh Market that year. The 22,000-square-foot store offered fresh food, prepared meals, baked items, salads, sushi, and wine in upscale neighborhoods.

Another new concept in Marsh's strategy was the Lifestyle supermarket. The first Lifestyle location opened in early 2004 and featured 66,000 square feet of shopping space catering to customers looking for gourmet, natural, and organic foods. The store included a coffee bar with sofas, plasma televisions, magazines, and books; a kid's club that gave away free gifts each week; and a floral department that included a gas fireplace. A January 2004 *Supermarket News* article described the unique look of the new store, reporting that it was designed in ''a double-racetrack format, with an expansive produce department and coffee bar occupying most of the center area of the store and various departments in separate 'rooms' around the perimeter.'' Marsh entered the Illinois market for the first time in 2005 when it opened a store with the Lifestyle format in Naperville.

While developing its new concepts, Marsh's revenues and net income had fluctuated over the past several years. The company's financial instability demonstrated just how volatile the grocery market had become with large competitors including Wal-Mart, Kroger, and Meijer eating away at market share. During fiscal year 2005, the company's revenue and net income rose slightly while management remained focused on securing stronger financial results by cutting costs. By opening new stores with the Lifestyle design and by introducing new store formats, Marsh was optimistic that it would differentiate itself from the competition and remain a leading regional chain for years to come.

Principal Subsidiaries

Marsh Drugs, Inc.; Marsh Village Pantries, Inc.; Mundy Realty, Inc.; Mar Properties, Inc.; Marlease, Inc.; Marsh Drugs, Inc.; Marsh Village Pantries, Inc.; Marsh International, Inc.; Marsh Supermarkets of Illinois, Inc.; North Marion Development Corporation; Contract Transport, Inc.; Crystal Food Services LLC; LoBill Foods LLC; Marsh Supermarkets LLC; Crystal Cafe Management Group LLC; Crystal Food Management Services LLC; Butterfield Foods LLC; Floral Fashions LLC; O'Malia Food Markets LLC; McNamara LLC.

Principal Divisions

Supermarket; LoBill Foods; O'Malia Food Markets; Pharmacy; Village Pantry; Food Service; McNamara; Floral Fashions.

Principal Competitors

The Kroger Company; Meijer Inc.; Wal-Mart Stores Inc.

Further Reading

Albert, Barb, ''Indianapolis-Based Supermarket Chain Plans Acquisitions,'' *Indianapolis Star,* August 4, 1999.

''Distributor Shake Up,'' *Convenience Store News,* October 21, 2001.

Hamstra, Mark, ''Marsh's New Lifestyle,'' *Supermarket News,* January 26, 2004.

Higgins, Will, ''Marsh Benefits from Price War Industry Fallout,'' *Indianapolis Business Journal,* June 24, 1985, p. 9.

Johnson, J. Douglas, ''CEO of the Year: Don Marsh,'' *Indiana Business,* December 1993, p. 8.

Kukolla, Steve, ''Marsh Takes on Meijer, Disputes Meager Predictions by Analysts,'' *Indianapolis Business Journal,* June 27, 1994, p. 3.

Lasting Values: The First Half-Century of Marsh Supermarkets, Inc., Yorktown: Marsh Supermarkets, Inc., 1984.

''Lifestyle 101,'' *Progressive Grocer,* November 1, 2005.

Marsh, Don E., *Marsh Supermarkets, Inc.: Sixty-Four Years of Continuous Smiles,* New York: The Newcomen Society of the United States, 1996.

''Marsh Knows Supermarketing,'' *Progressive Grocer,* December 1992, p. M6.

''Marsh Supermarkets Opens Standalone Eatery in Noblesville, Ind.,'' *Indianapolis Star,* April 14, 2004.

''Marsh Supermarkets Readies for Illinois Debut,'' *Progressive Grocer,* August 8, 2005.

Sherman, John, ''Don Marsh Talks Shop,'' *Indiana Business,* March 1986, p. 46.

Zwiebach, Elliot, ''Marsh Rolls Out 'Refresh' Program,'' *Supermarket News,* August 9, 2004.

—M.L. Cohen
—update: Christina M. Stansell

Mazzio's Corporation

4441 South 72nd East Avenue
Tulsa, Oklahoma 74145-4692
U.S.A.
Telephone: (918) 663-8880
Fax: (918) 641-1236
Web site: http://www.mazzios.com

Private Company
Incorporated: 1987
Employees: 4,000
Sales: $207 million (2004 est.)
NAIC: 722110 Full-Service Restaurants

Mazzio's Corporation is a privately-owned Tulsa, Oklahoma-based holding company that operates two regional Italian casual restaurant chains, Zio's Italian Kitchens and Mazzio's Pizza, as well as a pizza delivery service. The 17-unit Zio's is the more upscale of the two concepts, offering brick-oven pizzas and traditional Italian cuisine. Mazzio's Pizza numbers nearly 200 units, about half of which are franchised operations. Mazzio's restaurants are located in Oklahoma, Texas, Arkansas, Mississippi, Georgia, Tennessee, Missouri, Illinois, Kansas, and Iowa. The company is headed by its founder, Ken Selby.

Selby Meets Pizza in Mid-1950s

Ken Selby was born and raised in southern Oklahoma, then earned a teaching degree from Northeastern State University in 1958. Two years earlier, while on a trip to Chicago, he visited a pizza parlor for the first time in his life. "I had never even heard the word 'pizza' before," he told the *Tulsa World* in a 2000 profile, adding, "I thought it was the best food I'd ever eaten." It was an experience that would eventually change his plans to make teaching a career.

Selby's introduction was not that unusual for the time. Although pizza had been available for decades, it was mostly limited to major cities, primarily the East Coast and its large population of Italian Americans. However, a pizza craze swept the country after World War II, resulting in a large number of mom-and-pop pizza parlors. Pizza soon attracted entrepreneurs in America's Heartland with bigger plans. In 1958 Frank and Dan Carney opened the first Pizza Hut in Wichita, Kansas, and a year later opened their first franchise unit in Topeka, Kansas. While Pizza Hut was devoted to a table and chairs environment for pizza, Detroit native Tom Monaghan founded Domino's Pizza in 1960 and pioneered the delivery concept. A short time later Michael Ilitch, also from Detroit, founded Little Caesars, which focused on the carry out of inexpensive pizza. While each man would take his concept to a national stage, the demand for pizza was so strong that there remained a place for small pizza shops and regional chains. In 1960, for example, Pizza Inn was launched in Dallas to compete in the pizza restaurant category, and a short time later Ken Selby planted the seeds for his own regional chain in Tulsa, Oklahoma.

After graduating from Northeastern, Selby taught high school chemistry in Missouri before moving to Tulsa to take a position in a local junior high school. To supplement his income he worked part-time as a cook at a small pizza shop. In 1961, at the age of 24, he launched his own pizza business, renting a tiny vacuum sweeper shop in Tulsa for $150 a month, and cobbling together the rest of the operation. He found a used stove, moved in some old tables and chairs, and had a sign that read "Used Cars" repainted to read, "The Pizza Parlor." Using his own recipe for sauce and mixing the dough in a No. 2 washtub, Selby opened for business on Saturday, November 11, 1961. With a ten-inch pepperoni pizza selling for $1.50, he rang up $35.25 in sales that first day.

The Pizza Parlor was a hand-to-mouth business for several months, as the till was raided each day to pay for ingredients. Selby continued to teach chemistry from 8 a.m. to 4 p.m., then baked pizzas until midnight. He hired his first employee, an art student at the University of Tulsa named Bill Williams. For the first three months Selby was unable to pay him, although he did help the young man with his rent and car payments until the Pizza Parlor was generating enough cash flow to allow for a regular pay check. Not only did Williams help make pizzas, he used his art talent to paint a mural of an Italian village on the restaurant wall and even designed the placemats and a pizza man logo that Selby used for several years.

The Road to Expansion in Mid-1960s

For four straight years, Selby taught school during the day
and ran his business at night. Finally in 1965 he was able to quit
teaching, launch a second pizza parlor in Tulsa, and devote
himself to his restaurants full time. He also changed the name of
his stores to something slightly less generic than The Pizza
Parlor, adopting the name Ken's Pizza Parlor. He also became
interested in franchising Ken's, an idea that was gaining currency in the fast food industry with the success of McDonald's
and others. In 1966 he sold his first franchise, which relied on
his special sauce and thin crust pizza dough. The chain enjoyed
steady, although not meteoric, growth over the next decade. By
1975 the Ken's Pizza chain totaled 100 company-owned and
franchised units and had spread beyond the Oklahoma borders.

Along the way, Selby began to have regrets about using
"Ken's," feeling it was a name more appropriate to an auto
repair shop than an Italian eatery. He recalled reading *From Here
to Eternity* during college and an Italian-American character
named Maggio. "If I had just thought," Selby told Oklahoma
City's *World Reporter,* "I wouldn't have named those places
Ken's. I would have named them Maggio's." In the late 1970s he
decided to create a second, larger, more upscale restaurant format
that would include the increasingly popular thick-crust pizza and
a greater variety of Italian fare and a large salad bar. Selby
planned to call it Maggio's, but his attorney soon discovered that
a Philadelphia food processor had already appropriated the name.
One of Selby's employees suggested he replace the two G's in
Maggio's with the two Z's from pizza and call the restaurants
Mazzio's. Thus in 1979, Mazzio's Pizza premiered and proved to
be an immediate hit with customers. He set a goal of opening 145
company and franchised Mazzio Units in five years, a number he
easily surpassed. A major factor in the company's success was
advertising. Until the late 1970s, before Mazzio's, Ken's spent no
money on advertising beyond direct mail. Selby hired his first
employee with marketing experience and began to try running
television spots. He told *Restaurant Hospitality* in a 1988 article:
"It was very effective for us. We became real believers because it
really moved the needle for us. From that point, we evolved,
moving away from direct mail/newspaper advertising to television when we had the option."

In 1982 Selby changed the name of his company to Ken's
Restaurant Systems. Two years later he launched a pizza delivery operation called Scooter's Pizza Delivery, electing to use
the Scooter's name until the bugs were worked out. In 1987 it
became Mazzio's Pizza Delivery. By now, Mazzio's was the
company's key brand. The old Ken's Pizza units were now
converted to the Mazzio's concept, with only a handful of stores
in Tulsa retaining the Ken's name because of long-term market
loyalty. Because of this conversion to a single name, Mazzio's

increased its buying power in such areas as logo goods (pizza
boxes and napkins) as well as advertising. Ken Restaurant System also changed its name to Mazzio's Corporation in 1987. At
this stage the company operated 133 company-owned restaurants to go along with 148 franchised units, spread across 17
Sun Belt states. It also began to diversify its menu, adding a
number of pasta entrees.

Mazzio's again changed directions in the early 1990s, as it
became clear that it was losing dinnertime business to a new
breed of casual restaurants, including the likes of Bennigans,
Chili's, and TGI Fridays, which offered an extensive menu and
a full bar. Selby and his management team decide in 1992 to
develop their own Italian cuisine entry in this category, the goal
to offer quality food in ample portions at affordable prices,
serviced in a comfortable atmosphere. The result of 14 months
of effort was the 1994 opening of the first Zio's Italian Kitchen
in Tulsa, a 5,000-square-foot-freestanding structure modeled
after an Italian villa, capable of seating 250 guests. The concept
proved immediately popular and led to larger units opening in
Oklahoma City, Kansas City, and Springfield, Missouri. In
March 1998 a Zio's opened in Houston and appeared to be well
on its way to enjoying success but on the third night of operation, with the restaurant packed, smoke was detected. It quickly
became apparent the attic was on fire. Everyone was quickly
evacuated and within a matter of minutes the structure burned to
the ground. Not only did Mazzio's rebuild on the same location,
before the end of the year it opened a second Houston location.

At the time Zio's opened, the Mazzio's chain totaled more
than 230 units generating $130 million in sales. However, as
Mazzio's was upgrading its menu and Zio's was going more
upscale, the company felt that it was forgetting about it's long-
term customer base, the value-oriented family market. To appeal to this segment, Mazzio's launched the Pizzetti's $2.99 all-
you-can eat concept. It was supposed to attract large families,
the members of which would eat varying amounts. Over time
the restaurants simply attracted big eaters, and a high volume,
low-margin business to begin with became even less profitable.
The parent company preferred to invest its money on its other
concepts. Pizzetti's units outside of Tulsa were sold, and the
handful located in Tulsa were converted to Mazzio's.

During the 1990s Mazzio's made regular changes to its
menu. In 1992 it began offering specialty pizzas that instead of a
traditional red sauce used an Alfredo sauce. The chain then
moved to products with much the same appeal as pizza. In 1994
Mazzio's introduce a calzone ring, essentially a stuffed pizza
brushed with garlic butter seasoning and served with a marinara
dipping sauce. This item was followed a year later by stromboli.
In 1997 Mazzio's began to offer wraps, and in 1998 it unveiled
the quesapizza, an ultra-thin-crust pizza that came with a salsa
dipping sauce.

While the focus of Mazzio's had shifted toward the casual
dining arena and greater variety in the menu, it did not neglect
pizza and the pizza delivery business. It established call centers
in Tulsa and Moore, Oklahoma, to field calls from a single
advertised number of delivery and takeout. The orders were
then routed to the closest restaurant. In the late 1990s Mazzio's
leveraged the power of the Internet and created a virtual private
network to link units outside of Oklahoma to the two call

Key Dates:

1961: Ken Selby opens The Pizza Parlor in Tulsa, Oklahoma.
1965: Selby opens a second unit, called Ken's Pizza.
1966: The first franchise unit opens.
1979: Mazzio's Pizza is launched.
1987: Ken's Restaurant Systems becomes Mazzio's Corporation.
1994: First Zio's Italian Kitchen unit opens.
2000: The upgraded Mazzio's format begins replacing Mazzio's Pizza unit.

Zio's beyond the Texas-Oklahoma corridor in which they had been operating, opening eight restaurants. The hope was to have 24 units opened by the end of 2001, but the company failed to reach that number. The company had to contend with pizza price wars that hurt margins. If 2003 was a challenge, 2004 proved even more so, impacted by rising dairy and gas prices, and a faltering economy. Rather than the pizza category growing, companies were simply swapping customers. Mazzio's did better than most of the competition by continuing to update its stores and upgrade its menu. The chain dipped below 200 units in size, but in the long run it was better positioned than if its had stayed the course and remained Mazzio's Pizza. Although not as widespread as management had hoped by this point, Zio's was also succeeding in its markets. Ken Selby was well into his 60s but indicated that he had no plans to step away from the business he founded on a shoestring budget in 1961.

centers. In this way, instead of $800 a month to connect to the Oklahoma call centers, an amount that was cost prohibitive, a remote restaurant could now link up at a cost of about $100 per month, making it worth while to join the system.

Late 1990s Upgrade of Mazzio's

By 1998 the Mazzio's Pizza chain numbered 250 units, of which about 110 were company-owned. The decision was now made to elevate the concept and establish it in the casual dining category, albeit a much smaller operation than a Zio's. The company devoted more than two years developing the new concept, which would simply be called Mazzio's, dropping Pizza from the name since pizza would now be just a small part of what the full-service restaurants had to offer, including wine and beer, appetizers, salads, entrees, pastas, and desserts. Because the Mazzio's name was so connected to pizza rather the casual dining, the company had to prove to franchisees as well as to itself that the new concept would work. Hence, it closed a successful Mazzio's unit and converted it into a prototype. Converting a less profitable unit, then producing an increase in sales would not have proven the viability of the new Mazzio's concept. The prototype was a success as it turned out, and the company began to switch the older Mazzio's Pizza shops to the new Mazzio's casual dining restaurant concept at a cost of about $150,000 per unit.

As a private company, Mazzio's Corporation did not have the financial resources to quickly transform the Mazzio's chain to the casual dining format or expand Zio's as rapidly as management would like. In 2000 the company began to expand

Principal Operating Units

Mazzio's; Zio's Italian Kitchen.

Principal Competitors

Pizza Inn, Inc.; Happy Joe's Pizza and Ice Cream Parlors, Inc.; Paul Revere's Pizza International, Ltd.

Further Reading

Berta, Dina, "Pizza Chains Hit by Rising Commodity Costs, Intensified Competition," *Nation's Restaurant News,* July 26, 2004, p. 108.
Colberg, Sonya, "Oklahoma Founder of Pizzerias Tops Classic Ideas with new Concepts," *Oklahoman,* October 22, 2000.
——, "Pasta and Profits Selby Translates Energy, Italian Cuisine Into Empire," *Tulsa World,* June 18, 2000, p. 1.
Dees, Synthia, "Mazzio's Pizza Helps Parent Get Bigger Slice of Pie," *Tulsa Business Chronicle,* November 30, 1987, p. 7.
Festa, Gail, "Mazzio's Magic," *Restaurant Hospitality,* June 1988, p. 91.
Lester, Terrell, "Pizza King Selby Rolling in Dough," *Tulsa World,* November 10, 1991, p. G1.
Littman, Margaret, "As Italian as Apple Pie," *Chainleader,* September 2000.
Tiernan, Becky, "A Saucy Business Flair Marketing Skills Perpetuate Selby's Restaurant Success," *Tulsa World,* April 5, 1997, p. 1.
Zuber, Amy, "Mazzio's Changes the Dough, Continues to Rise," *Nation's Restaurant News,* May 11, 1998, p. 8.

—Ed Dinger

MeadWestvaco

MeadWestvaco Corporation

1 High Ridge Park
Stamford, Connecticut 06905
U.S.A.
Telephone: (203) 461-7400
Fax: (203) 461-7468
Web site: http://www.meadwestvaco.com

Public Company
Incorporated: 1930 as The Mead Corporation, 1888 as
    Piedmont Pulp and Paper Company
Employees: 29,400
Sales: $8.2 billion (2004)
Stock Exchanges: New York
Ticker Symbol: MWV
NAIC: 322121 Paper (Except Newsprint) Mills

MeadWestvaco Corporation, formed in early 2002 by the merger of Mead Corporation and Westvaco Corporation, operates as a leading packaging company that serves the food and beverage, media and entertainment, personal care, cosmetic, and healthcare industries. The company also has interests in consumer and office products and specialty chemicals. MeadWestvaco has facilities in more than 29 countries and owns approximately 1.2 million acres of forestlands. In 2005, the company sold its Paper division and half of its forestlands in a $2.3 billion deal.

The History of Mead

The Mead Corporation began as Ellis, Chafflin & Company. Founded in 1846 by Colonel Daniel Mead and his partners, the company produced book and other printing papers at a mill in Dayton, Ohio. In 1856 Mead bought out his original partners with a friend from Philadelphia, Pennsylvania, forming Weston and Mead. This company became Mead and Weston in 1860, then Mead and Nixon in 1866. In 1873 Daniel Mead spearheaded a reorganization of the firm as the Mead & Nixon Paper Company, and in 1881 Mead bought out Nixon, establishing the Mead Paper Company in 1882. He immediately upgraded the Dayton mill and in 1890 purchased a facility in nearby Chil-

licothe, Ohio. During the first decade of its existence, Mead Paper Company averaged annual profits of $22,000, peaking at nearly $50,000 in 1891, the year of Mead's death.

In the years after Mead's death, the management of the company passed to his sons, Charles and Harry, who became president and vice-president, respectively. Despite the fact that Mead had left a thriving business, Mead Paper soon fell on hard times, owing in large part to personal overdrafts by family members amounting to more than $200,000, as well as to the substantial salaries drawn by Harry and Charles Mead and Charles's travel expense and cash accounts, which in 1900 amounted to $13,800. Combined losses for 1901 and 1902 added up to more than $36,000, and banks began calling in the company's loans. By 1904 the Teutonia National Bank instituted a suit that resulted in trusteeship of the company by bankers in Dayton, Chillicothe, and Cincinnati, Ohio.

As Mead Paper Company teetered on the brink of total collapse in 1905, the banker-trustees turned to George Mead, Harry Mead's independent and business-minded son, requesting that he take over the helm at Mead. George, then about to leave his post at the General Artificial Silk Company in Philadelphia, accepted the opportunity to rejuvenate the family company. He reorganized it as the Mead Pulp and Paper Company and was appointed vice-president and general manager. George Mead's business philosophy would influence the company substantially during his 43-year tenure.

Mead Pulp and Paper made its first public stock offering in 1906. A year later operations were consolidated at the Chillicothe mill, costing the company more than $32,000. The economic recession of 1907 and the tremendous cost of moving almost destroyed Mead once again, but the sale of the Dayton property saved the company. Finally, in 1908, the company made profits of almost $25,000, and it continued to operate in the black until the Great Depression.

Growth via Acquisitions: 1910s–40s

During the 1910s, Mead expanded through acquisition and began to maximize machine output by restricting its product lines. In 1916 Mead purchased a share in the Kingsport Pulp

Company Perspectives:

MeadWestvaco's innovation, customer relationships and strength throughout the packaging value chain drives our leadership. From excellence in engineering unique paperboards to innovative uses of multiple materials to world-class expertise in package design, converting and systems, we deliver integrated packaging solutions throughout the world—creating value for customers, consumers and shareholders. We are a leader in consumer and office products, specialty chemicals and specialty papers, where innovation is essential to market leadership. Our businesses are dedicated to addressing customers' most pressing challenges.

Corporation of Kingsport, Tennessee, and in 1917 it acquired full control of the Peerless Paper Company of Dayton. George Mead had been reducing the number of different types of paper made at Mead since his entry in 1905, when the company produced 15 different grades of paper. Seeing that profits would be maximized if each machine could concentrate on producing one type of paper rather than continually changing production methods for different papers, Mead specialized his mills as far as possible.

Toward this end, in 1917 Mead secured a five-year contract to produce magazine paper for Crowell Publishing Company. The magazine paper called for 75 percent of the Chillicothe mill's production. Consequently, Crowell remained Mead's principal customer throughout the decade. In 1918 the Management Engineering and Development Company was established in Dayton as a separate firm to supervise engineering of new Mead plants and to market Mead's engineering services to other paper companies. In 1921 the Mead Sales Company was established as a separate corporation to sell white paper produced by Mead mills and other U.S. and Canadian mills.

In 1920 Mead bought out the other owners of Kingsport Pulp. The plant began white paper production in 1923 and became a central Mead factory. Mead began to diversify its product lines in the 1920s as it started to manufacture paperboard. By 1925 Mead research led to the discovery of the semichemical pulping process by which wood chips from which tannin had been extracted could be converted into paperboard. Mead expanded the paperboard business in the late 1920s with the purchase of mills throughout Appalachia that produced corrugating medium from wood waste. In 1927 The Mead Paperboard Corporation was founded as a holding company for the paperboard operations, including the Sylvia Paperboard Company, The Harriman Company, The Southern Extract Company, and the Chillicothe Company.

The Mead Corporation was incorporated on February 17, 1930, and George Mead was appointed president. The company subsumed the operations of the Mead Pulp and Paper Company, The Mead Paperboard Corporation, and the Management Engineering and Development Company, although the separate legal existence of these organizations continued for some years. At that time, the company had 1,000 employees and plants in four states. In 1935 Mead's common and preferred stock were listed on the New York Stock Exchange.

During the 1930s Mead made substantial acquisitions that diversified its lines. Although concentration on a few types of paper was necessary when the company was small, Mead had grown large enough to produce a number of grades of papers profitably. Mead's own major mills had attempted to sell business, envelope, and writing papers, but they had no luck. Two major purchases were Dill & Collins in 1932 and Geo. W. Wheelwright Company in 1934. Each of these companies had established names and well-developed distribution systems. This allowed Mead to market effectively large quantities of specialty papers produced at Chillicothe as well as smaller quantities produced in the acquired mills.

In 1938 Mead entered two joint ventures in an effort to reduce its dependence on imported pulp and to enter the kraft linerboard business. With Scott Paper Company, it formed the Brunswick Pulp & Paper Company at Brunswick, Georgia to supply both parent companies. In addition, with the holding company of the Alfred du Pont estate, Almours Security Company, it built a huge pulping plant in Port St. Joe, Florida. By 1937 the Brunswick mill was producing 150 tons of pulp per day. Soon the Port St. Joe facility was yielding 300 tons of pulp and 300 tons of linerboard daily. It was widely regarded as the leading linerboard mill in the country and by 1940 was making $1 million a year before taxes. Relations with the Almours Security Company deteriorated, however, and Mead sold its share of the operation. Mead intended to launch another linerboard mill immediately, but World War II halted this plan.

In 1942 George Mead became chairman of the board and Sydney Fergusen, who had been with the company since the 1910s, became the corporation's president. In the same year, Mead purchased a small white-paper mill from the Escanaba Paper Company in Michigan's upper peninsula. Eventually the Escanaba mill would become one of Mead's largest operations. Two other acquisitions were made, in 1943, that of the Manistique Pulp and Paper Company, of Manistique, Michigan and, in 1946, that of the Columbia Paper Company in Bristol, Virginia. The Manistique plant was sold in the early 1950s, and the Virginia company was consolidated with the Wheelwright plant in 1946. Other plants bought to meet postwar demand were subsequently sold.

Although Mead had continued production at a breakneck pace to meet domestic and overseas container and paper requirements, wartime price and profit controls, as well as raw material shortages, stunted the company's growth. In 1945 Mead's assets had risen only $2.1 million from a prewar figure of $37 million.

Immediately following the war, however, Mead was back on course. Its well-defined postwar plan allotted $23 million for plant expansion. In the brown paper division, plans were readily revived to build a kraft linerboard plant to replace the Port St. Joe operation. Mead firmly entrenched itself in paperboard-making through its joint projects with Inland Container Corporation. The companies first collaborated in 1946 to found the Macon Kraft Company to build and operate a paperboard mill in Macon, Georgia. This was followed by successive joint mills built in Rome, Georgia, in 1951 and Phenix City, Alabama, in 1966.

Key Dates:

1882: Colonel Mead establishes the Mead Paper Company.
1889: William Luke establishes the Piedmont Pulp and Paper Company.
1897: West Virginia Paper merges with West Virginia Pulp Company to become West Virginia Pulp and Paper Company (WVPP).
1927: The Mead Paperboard Corporation is founded as a holding company for the company's paperboard operations.
1930: The Mead Corporation incorporates.
1955: Mead enters the container business with the acquisition of Jackson Box Company of Cincinnati, Ohio.
1969: WVPP changes its name to Westvaco Corporation.
1977: Franklin Container Corporation of Philadelphia and Tim-Bar Corporation file a $1.2 billion antitrust suit against Mead and eight other box makers.
1994: Mead Data Central is sold.
1995: Westvaco sells its corrugated container operations.
2002: Mead and Westvaco merge to form MeadWestvaco.
2005: The company sells its writing and printing papers business and 900,000 acres of forestland.

Diversification Beyond Paper Products in the 1950s

Mead saw a rapid succession of presidents after Fergusen, who in 1948 became chairman of the board and handed the presidency on to Charles R. Van de Carr, Jr. In 1952 Howard E. Whittaker became president, and five years later he was replaced by Donald R. Morris. The year 1955 marked the beginning of a new period of growth for Mead, as the company diversified beyond its traditional paper products. A 1957 acquisition, the Atlanta Paper Company, led Mead into the packaging business and was the forerunner of Mead's packaging division, which invented the familiar paper six-pack carrier for bottled beverages and became the largest supplier of paperboard beverage packaging in the world. The specialty paper division, which produced papers for filters and insulation, was started with the purchase of Hurlburt Paper Company of South Lee, Massachusetts in 1957.

Mead entered the container business in 1955 and 1956 with the acquisition of Jackson Box Company of Cincinnati, Ohio. This firm became the nucleus of Mead's containerboard division. In 1960 Mead's rapid expansion in paperboard manufacture prompted the Federal Trade Commission (FTC) to file a complaint against Mead, alleging that Mead's growth since 1956 was anticompetitive. Mead and the FTC settled in 1965 when Mead signed a consent decree, agreeing to sell seven of its plants over five years and place a ten-year moratorium on paperboard acquisitions.

Mead began its wholesale distribution network with the acquisition of Cleveland Paper Company in 1957. Mead's aggressive expansion of its wholesale force provoked a 1968 suit by the Justice Department. The suit claimed that Mead's acquisition between 1957 and 1964 of six paper wholesalers with 38 outlets caused an unlawful concentration in the paper industry.

Mead agreed in 1970 to sell within two years 22 of the outlets operated by Chatfield & Woods Company, acquired in 1961, and Cleveland Paper Company.

Acquiring Businesses Unrelated to Papermaking in the 1960s

With the retirement of Chairman Howard E. Whitaker and President George H. Pringle in 1968, the new president, James W. McSwiney, began to acquire businesses that were unrelated to papermaking. During the 1950s, and with the 1968 allocation of $50 million for the expansion of the Escanaba mill, Mead had spent in excess of $400 million on maintaining and improving its papermaking facilities. Then its business emphasis in paper products shifted from production to marketing. The paper markets, however, were fairly mature, and growth had to be sought elsewhere. Mead's management anticipated a boom in family spending and homebuilding and bought companies that would benefit from such a boom. Mead's acquisition of an educational products supplier in 1966 was followed in 1968 by the purchase of Woodward Corporation, a maker of pipe and pipe fittings, castings, and chemicals and of Data Corporation, which produced computer software. In 1969 Mead bought a furniture maker.

1970s Recession Leading to Divestments

These purchases did not shield Mead from an economic recession in the early 1970s. In 1971 the Escanaba mill was operating at a loss despite a $15 million investment in upgrading the plant. Another $45 million investment went into the plant the following year, but profitability continued to elude the operation. As a result of its flagging profits, Mead began to sell off some of the acquisitions it had made only a few years earlier.

Mead managers sold more than $80 million of interests in low-growth markets between 1973 and 1976. For example, lower-grade tablet paper and low-volume colored envelope interests were eliminated. Mead sold off facilities such as the corrugated-shipping-container plant it had built at a cost of $3.5 million in Edison, New Jersey, in 1967, but which had never made a profit. Mead's corrugated-paper business was concentrated in Stevenson, Alabama in 1975. Mead also directed its attention to potential growth in paper; for example, the company responded to an anticipated hike in mail rates by investing $60 million in a computer-controlled paper machine to make lightweight paper.

Mead retained substantially diverse operations, including furniture factories, foundries, and Alabama coal mines. Despite these far-flung interests, in 1974, about 24 percent of Mead's pretax earnings came from paper, 35 percent from paperboard, and 5 percent from wholesaling. Metal products contributed 11 percent and furniture 5 percent, while about 20 percent was derived from sundry jointly owned forest products operations. Mead lost an estimated $85 million in sales owing to strikes at several pulp and paper mills. By 1975, however, sales and profits were on the upturn.

In 1977 the consolidation of the box-making business became problematic as two small Pennsylvania paper-box makers, Franklin Container Corporation, of Philadelphia, and Tim-Bar Corporation, filed a $1.2 billion antitrust suit against Mead and eight other box makers. The suit charged the defendants with price fixing and with attempting to push smaller makers out of the market by buying independent box makers and opening operations where they would compete with smaller businesses. The suit was one of the largest price fixing lawsuits in U.S. legal history. Mead was found not guilty in a 1979 criminal trial, but a jury found the company guilty in a civil class-action suit of 1980. The other defendants had settled out of court prior to the civil suit, and Mead was left with a potential liability of $750 million. Finally, Mead also settled out of court in 1982 for $45 million, considerably less than it might have had to pay in court, but still five times more than any of the other defendants paid.

1980s Highlighted by the Increasing Success of Mead Data Central

In 1979 Mead ranked fourth among forest products companies and hit its all-time earnings peak of $5.19 a share while fending off an unwanted takeover by Occidental Petroleum Corporation. By the early 1980s, earnings began to fall from their 1979 peak of $141 million to a loss of $86 million in 1982—Mead's first loss since 1938. Among the factors responsible were a drastic decrease in demand for lumber products and the costly settlement of the box suit. In addition, Mead's $1.5 billion five-year expansion plan begun in 1978 may have equipped it to benefit from the next paper market boom, but it also left the company in 1983 with a debt amounting to more than half of its total capitalization. Mead whittled away at the sum by selling several noncore businesses. By 1984 debt was down to 42 percent of capital, still a dangerously high level but better than in the previous year.

Business improved in 1984, as Mead's electronic information-retrieval services became profitable. Mead Data Central Inc. (MDC), the subsidiary whose primary product was LEXIS, a service that made case law and statutes available through online computer searches, had been growing at a rate of 43 percent a year. Unveiled in 1973, LEXIS took in about 75 percent of the computerized legal research market by the late 1980s. The system's success was enough to spark its own court battle with West Publishing Company, which claimed that MDC intended to infringe on its copyrights by distributing its information with West's pagination. Mead in turn filed its own antitrust suit against West. The case was settled in 1988 with a licensing agreement permitting MDC to offer West-copyrighted material via the LEXIS service.

By 1988 MDC boasted 200,000 subscribers, who bought $300 million worth of information. In 1988 LEXIS was responsible for MDC's 33 percent growth. LEXIS accounted for an estimated $215 million of MDC's $307.6 million revenues. MDC's other products included NEXIS, which distributed newspaper and magazine reprints. MDC also carried other services, such as LEXPAT, which distributed patent information, and LEXIS Financial Information Service, which provided stock information. Micromedex, a subsidiary acquired in 1988, provided information about poison and emergency medicine on compact disc.

In 1988, to enhance the scope of its service to attorneys, paralegals, and the court, MDC purchased The Michie Company, a legal publisher based in Charlottesville, Virginia, publishing statutes from 24 states in printed form. MDC made these statutes searchable electronically through the LEXIS service and developed compact disc products combining case law and statutes.

In addition to the promising enterprises at MDC, in 1988 Mead unveiled Cycolor, a new paper for color photocopying. The specially coated paper contained a chemical that, like an instant film, performs the reproduction internally, eliminating the complex machinery formerly needed to create color photocopies. Mead contracted several Japanese companies to manufacture copiers compatible with the paper. By 1990, two Japanese companies were marketing copiers using Cycolor. Development of this product was costly, and it diminished Mead's earnings from 1986 to 1990. After losing almost $200 million developing the special paper, Mead closed its Cycolor division in December 1990.

While developing these nonpaper interests, Mead also undertook some rationalization of its traditional sectors. Most important was the restructuring of its paperboard operations to focus on the production of coated board. Mead dissolved its partnerships with Temple-Inland in the Georgia Kraft Company, sold six of its container plants, and doubled its coated board capacity. The Macon mill was sold in 1987 to Pratt Holding, Ltd., an Australian firm; Temple-Inland took control of the Rome, Georgia plant; and in 1988 Mead took full control of the Phenix City coated board mill. In 1991, Mead completed a $580 million expansion of this mill, which added 370,000 tons of coated board annually. Mead also sold its share of the Brunswick pulp and paper mill in August of 1988 and sold its recycled products business to Rock-Tenn Company in 1988.

Steven Mason Leading 1990s Turnaround

These rationalization moves were important, but Mead's revenues were flat from 1988 through 1992 and net earnings fell from a record $352.7 million in 1988 to $38.5 million in 1990, $6.9 million in 1991, and $71.6 million in 1992. After ten years as chairman and CEO, Burnell Roberts retired in 1992 and was replaced by Steven Mason, who had been president and vice-chairman. A third-generation Mead employee with 35 years at the company, Mason moved quickly and boldly to turn Mead around.

In mid-1992 Mason announced the start of a three-year performance-improvement plan that aimed to increase both productivity and customer satisfaction. As part of the plan, Mead laid off about 1,000 employees, setting up a $95 million special reserve for expenses such as severance pay, retraining, relocation, counseling, and outplacement. Another component of the plan called for overall productivity increases of 3 percent per year, which would lead to annual savings of about $60 million. By year-end 1996 Mead had successfully hit this target, as it had achieved an overall productivity gain of 12 percent since 1992. During this same period Mead's customer satisfaction rankings markedly improved; in 1992 less than half of the company's business units were ranked first in customer satisfaction compared with Mead competition, but by 1996 three-quarters were ranked first.

Equal in significance to the performance-improvement plan was Mason's decision to refocus Mead on core value-added forest products. In addition to selling its imaging and reinsurance businesses, Mead reduced its uncoated paper operations through the 1995 sale of the loss-making Kingsport, Tennessee uncoated paper mill. The largest divestment, however, came in December 1994 when the company sold Mead Data Central to Anglo-Dutch publishing giant Reed Elsevier for $1.5 billion, taking Mead out of the electronic publishing business. Following these moves, Mead had three core areas of operation: paper (primarily coated paper, a sector with more growth potential than uncoated paper), packaging and paperboard, and distribution and school/office supplies.

Much of the $1 billion after-tax proceeds from the MDC sale was used to pay down debt and make stock repurchases. Overall, from 1992 to 1996 Mead was able to reduce its debt-to-capital ratio from 47 percent to 36 percent. Meanwhile, company shareholders were kept happy through repurchases of 8.7 million shares valued at $459 million.

To shore up its core areas, Mead spent heavily to upgrade and add machinery to its mills and also made one strategic acquisition. The Escanaba and Chillicothe coated paper mills were the recipients of large capital investment programs, with $200 million spent in 1994 and 1995. In November 1996 Mead increased its coated paper capacity by 600,000 tons a year with the $640 million purchase of a coated paper mill located in Rumford, Maine from Boise Cascade. The mill also brought with it 667,000 acres of woodlands, which increased Mead's timber holdings to 2.1 million acres in eight states, a 65 percent increase over 1992 holdings.

Mead's paperboard capacity also was increased through the 1996 completion of a 225,000-ton-per-year, $176 million corrugating medium machine at the Stevenson mill. That same year the company announced a second phase to the capital upgrades at this mill, whereby the new machine's output would increase to 390,000 tons annually when virgin pulp-making capability, a wood fuel boiler, and additional dryers were added by 1999. The second phase was expected to cost an additional $224 million.

Following record-breaking revenues of $5.18 billion and robust net earnings of $350 million in 1995—a year with market conditions favorable to paper companies—Mead celebrated its 150th anniversary in 1996 with solid revenues ($4.71 billion) and earnings ($195.3 million). Mason's various initiatives as chairman and CEO clearly had borne fruit. The company's future also seemed bright, as the April 1996 appointment of Jerome F. Tatar, a 23-year Mead veteran and former president (over an eight-year period) of Mead's Fine Paper Division, as president and chief operating officer (and expected Mason successor) pointed to the likelihood that Mead would continue on a steady course into the early 21st century.

The History of Westvaco

Born into a Scottish papermaking family, Westvaco founder William Luke came to the United States in 1852. Ten years later he began running a plant for Jessup & Moore Paper Company in Harper's Ferry, West Virginia. Although employed by Jessup & Moore until 1898, he set up a small plant of his own with his two sons in 1889. Originally established in Piedmont, West Virginia, a shift in the Potomac River and a 1922 municipal name change eventually put the same facility in Luke, Maryland, where Westvaco still operated a mill in the late 1990s.

The mill was one of many mills that, during the late 1800s, imported and developed automated wood-pulping technologies. Called the Piedmont Pulp and Paper Company, it became the first commercially successful sulfite pulp mill in the United States. Eventually U.S. makers used the sulfite process to make 83 percent of their paper. The Piedmont plant employed 60, and by 1891 it began production of printing paper under the name West Virginia Paper.

U.S. timber supply and automated processes lowered the price of paper and accelerated its consumption. In 1897 West Virginia Paper merged with West Virginia Pulp Company of Davis, West Virginia and became West Virginia Pulp and Paper Company (WVPP). It expanded along with the United States' growing demand, and it established a business headquarters in New York City. In addition to its white printing paper, it marketed pulp and chemical byproducts. In 1904 William Luke relinquished the presidency of the company to his son John Luke, who held the position until 1921. William Luke died in 1912, at which time the company had four mills operating in West Virginia, Pennsylvania, Virginia, and New York.

Post-World War I Diversification

During the post-World War I recession, prices plummeted and strikes hit two-thirds of the industry, including WVPP. Sales and earnings reached a record level, however, in 1920, which would be unequaled for 20 years.

While white paper production volume remained relatively constant, diversification accounted for virtually all growth after World War I. The company produced its first kraft paper in 1921, the first year of David Luke's tenure as president. David Luke was another son of the founder. Used in U.S. packaging since 1907, kraft paper replaced many wood and textile shipping containers. As trees in the southern states were more suitable for kraft, between the world wars kraft production in the region skyrocketed. West Virginia's kraft output grew steadily for 15 years but then leveled off.

In 1929 WVPP introduced containerboard, a heavier, corrugated paper used for boxes. Federally approved for shipping in 1914, use of this material grew tremendously during the world wars.

During the 1920s WVPP began purchasing woodlands to supply its own wood pulp, but self-sufficiency in fiber supply remained a long-term prospect. By the 1930s very little virgin timber remained in the southern states. WVPP continued to buy land close to its mills and eventually owned extensive woodlands. The immaturity of the trees in its holdings, however, forced it to rely on outside suppliers for its pulp supply and prevented diversification into finished wood products.

Another son of William Luke, Thomas Luke, became president in 1934, inheriting a company with young diversification attempts and old mills. Three years later the company built a new mill to produce kraft and containerboard. By 1939 all five mills operated 24 hours per day.

The company's mills continued to operate at capacity throughout World War II. Wartime allocations made scarce the materials for expansion and repair, however. Although its facilities produced 20 percent more volume by war's end, WVPP's facilities emerged from the war badly in need of modernization.

David L. Luke Initiating a Series of Expansion Programs: 1945–63

Ascending to president in 1945, David L. Luke, a grandson of the founder, established the company's modern growth pattern. He immediately began the first of many expansion programs, spending the $17.5 million the company had accumulated during the war. The company also used some of its cash surplus to acquire more land, selling the trees too mature for papermaking to provide additional financing.

Wartime research greatly expanded paper's uses, particularly in containers. Postwar demand continued to grow so explosively that only production volume and market share concerned papermakers. The industry enjoyed favorable prices, consolidating competition, and growing demand in all areas of paper products.

The industry set high prices, required more prompt payment, and used the cash influx to build new mills during the late 1940s. Capacity caught up with demand by the late 1940s, and surpassed it by the mid-1950s, creating the need for more development leading to automation, product consistency, and new uses for paperboard. Although still reliant on white paper, WVPP put much of its postwar development efforts into these areas.

Profit margins in the commodity-based paper industry remained slim during the 1950s, and a company's technological efficiency determined its success. The cyclicality of the industry meant that for the next 30 years papermakers invested in capacity additions. When they did so, they lowered prices precipitously. David L. Luke's expansion programs, however, coincided with the industry downturns. While occasionally requiring more debt than that to which the company was accustomed, automation allowed it to cut its work force for each of the next ten years.

The first major work stoppage since World War I occurred in 1952, when 4,000 employees struck. Labor relations flared up more frequently in the postwar era, decreasing earnings on occasion, well into the 1970s.

The company got more short-term use of its land in 1952 when it discovered a use for its hardwoods. Traditionally, only younger and softwood trees had been used for paper. Hardwoods on WVPP's land holdings used for paper allowed the company to reduce production costs.

Encouraged by the premature utility of its land, over two years the company aggressively increased its holdings 75 percent to 749,000 acres. Most of the money spent on expansion in the 1950s, however, went to equipment modifications required by the technology.

WVPP sold its output mainly to companies that converted it to finished products. Priced as a commodity, paper prices often changed dramatically, making earnings erratic. Demand, however, constantly increased, providing a greater cash flow.

Use of paperboard, a noncorrugated material for consumer product containers, grew explosively during David L. Luke's presidency. Just as kraft paper and containerboard accounted for the company's prewar growth, paperboard made up most postwar growth.

The 1953 acquisition of Hinde & Dauch Paper Company, a box maker, allowed WVPP to bypass distributors and represented the first major move toward integration. Hinde & Dauch (H&D) used WVPP's paperboard to produce its parent company's first finished paper products. Bleached paperboard was found to take colors as well as printing papers, making it highly adaptable to packaging uses. In 1955 WVPP purchased color presses to produce paperboard finished to client specifications.

West Virginia Pulp & Paper Company slowed expansion and improvement during the mid-1950s in its traditional sectors of printing papers, kraft, and containerboard, in favor of its new division. The company closed H&D's paper mills but built more than 20 new assembly plants for it during the next ten years, to make the most of H&D's knowledge of package design and experience with marketing finished products. These new plants allowed for the first increase in WVPP's workforce since World War II. By constantly automating to reduce labor costs, its number of employees began to level off again by the early 1960s.

WVPP purchased a Brazilian paper box maker in 1953. By the end of the 1950s, the Brazilian subsidiary financed its own production expansion with fewer employees.

Demand for white printing papers began its first large increase in decades in 1954 as a population boom and renewed prosperity increased consumption of printed materials. Demand for all paper products grew so explosively in the 1950s that by 1956 the industry could not meet demand. WVPP's earnings increased out of proportion to sales, peaking at $16.3 million in 1956 after five successive years of gains.

The industry responded by rapidly expanding its capacity. WVPP typically upgraded one machine at a time, rather than building or buying new mills. This method slowly consolidated production into larger and fewer facilities. By 1959 WVPP completed its largest spending program, doubling capacity at the Luke mill; but when domestic growth slowed, prices collapsed. Despite annual sales records, for the next five years WVPP's earnings fluctuated wildly—at one point dropping to as low as $8 million. Other factors that depleted earnings included new technology that produced more pulp from harvested trees as well as price wars following the entry of forestry and container companies into paper. WVPP, which also sought to enter new markets, lowered prices as well.

Many companies waited for demand to catch up, but West Virginia Pulp & Paper continued its ten-year expansion plan. It focused on relatively inexpensive converting plants rather than mills, but its debt grew more sizable. The timing of the expansion speeded WVPP's recovery; by 1962 demand began to catch up to the capacity added in recent years. The spending program was completed and the company issued only $60 million in bonds.

The length of the industry's recession and the growth of H&D encouraged a renewed push toward finished products. In 1957 West Virginia purchased Virginia Folding Box Company, an assembler of cigarette packaging. It eagerly expanded the acquisition and reorganized itself into six divisions, four of which were in the business of converting: bleached boards, building boards, fine papers, H&D, kraft, and merchant paper. The company decentralized each division and provided each with its own sales force.

As new materials, particularly plastic, threatened to replace older forms of paper packaging, technical research intensified during the mid-1950s and the early 1960s. Higher than the industry average, WVPP's research expenditures enhanced its reputation for product development. Research and development spending quadrupled during the ten-year period, ending 1961 at $4 million annually.

WVPP pioneered several processes, including the use of electronic controls in production, the marketing of waste by-products in the chemicals division, the use of hardwoods, and the development of Clupak, a more elastic kraft paper. The company typically licensed or sold new technologies to pay for additional research.

By 1959 packaging grades of paper made up two-thirds of West Virginia's production volume. By 1960 the demand for office and printing papers (at one time WVPP's primary product) provided growth to the long-stagnant industry. Then oriented toward finished products and marketing, WVPP set up a separate sales force to sell directly to printers and paper converters.

When paper prices improved in the early 1960s, WVPP made the most of its recently completed investment program. The renewed efficiency and a change in its accounting method finally pushed 1965 earnings past the 1956 level. The downturn, however, had raised the competitive level of the industry. Like its competitors, WVPP came out of the late 1950s and early 1960s more diversified, integrated, and less production oriented.

WVPP exported negligibly until 1960, when 3 percent of sales went overseas. Although it did not pursue international markets actively for another 20 years, in 1962 it set up an international division to explore manufacturing possibilities abroad and established foreign subsidiaries in Europe and Australia.

David L. Luke retired in 1963. During his tenure the company had changed dramatically. At the end of World War II, West Virginia Pulp & Paper Company had produced commodity grades of paper for a few hundred customers, but by 1959 it had its own sales force selling a variety of finished paper products to a customer base of 11,000. The company had developed the marketing techniques and made the necessary acquisitions to get it started in finished conversion while keeping debt to a minimum.

Diversification and International Expansion: 1963–88

Hesitant to join his family's company at first, David L. Luke's son David L. Luke III became CEO in 1963, after working 11 years for WVPP. He maintained the product development momentum initiated by his father and continued to upgrade efficiency with frequent spending programs. Like the rest of the industry, however, he reevaluated the use of debt in the coming decade. In 1962 the Luke family controlled 30 percent of the company's stock; by 1984 it controlled only 2 percent.

Still pursuing self-sufficiency in fiber supply, the company's land holdings were constantly becoming more productive. WVPP acquired its millionth acre in 1964. Research into forestry techniques produced hybrids that were not only more disease resistant but capable of growing three times the wood fiber per acre than the strains of 15 years earlier.

Shrinking timber reserves nationwide escalated land value further. Beginning in the late 1960s, WVPP developed land of commercial value and purchased additional timberland closer to its mills. Operating in 22 states, this latter strategy proved important when transportation costs inflated during the 1970s. Lower land values in the early 1970s allowed additional land purchases. Even though these lands provided only 10 percent of its raw material requirements, in the long term they stood to raise the degree of self-sufficiency.

During the mid-1960s, the growth rate in earnings once again outpaced sales. Operating near capacity once again, the company was able to reduce the debt it had assumed to complete its expansion program. Most of this investment went to make its three main mills more efficient. Nearly half of sales in 1967 came from products introduced in the previous ten years. This success and resulting heavier cash flow tempted the company to offer consumer products, a segment profiting several of its competitors. WVPP purchased C.A. Reed Company in 1968, maker of disposable paper products. Although the disposables market soared in the 1960s and 1970s, WVPP sold it after only seven years.

White printing papers used by business systems also boosted sales. Although the industry began to see overruns again, WVPP began another expansion program in 1967. It included the building of a new white paper mill in Kentucky. At $90 million, it was the largest project ever attempted by the company. In 1969 the company changed its name to Westvaco Corporation. Growing dependence worldwide on North American pulp and timber helped make Westvaco less dependent on the health of the domestic economy, exporting 10 percent of sales by the early 1970s.

Commodity-type production continued to plague the industry. In the early 1970s the industry suffered once again from too much capacity, higher production costs, and low prices. Tougher environmental standards and a weaker economy hastened closure of plants industrywide. Westvaco closed plants, but its frequent incremental upgrades kept shut-down costs low. Leaner by default, turnaround came quickly.

During the early 1970s the government kept paper prices and labor costs stable but put a freeze on earnings as well. U.S. paper production reached record levels. By 1972 the government loosened its restrictions on paper somewhat, but fierce price competition negated a 4 percent price increase approval in 1971.

Wage and price controls were lifted altogether in 1974, allowing the industry to pass on production costs. Like the industry's recession in the early 1960s, these price controls contributed to integration, as producers sought to increase earnings in areas outside federal control, particularly finished paper products.

The paper industry was now increasingly accountable to federal regulations. The Federal Energy Administration forced

Westvaco and 12 other paper companies to convert certain plants to coal burning from oil. The Department of Justice blocked an attempt by Westvaco to acquire the remainder of U.S. Envelope, the largest domestic producer of envelopes, of which Westvaco owned 58 percent. The paper industry had been investigated repeatedly for antitrust compliance and been named in private suits. Although Westvaco settled suits out of court it had never been indicted.

In the ten years ending 1975, Westvaco almost doubled sales, while simultaneously reducing its workforce. During the mid-1970s demand in all sectors began to catch up with capacity, but growing production costs dampened earnings.

Energy shortages of the early 1970s prompted Westvaco to turn to its land holdings once again by mining coal for its own consumption. By 1974 it achieved 40 percent fuel self-sufficiency by burning its own waste from the production process. Such conservation efforts would help earnings substantially in the late 1970s.

The 1980s were turnaround years for papermakers. The industry started to spend on capacity once again. Although Westvaco now converted more than one-third of its paper production in its own plants, growth in the use of the personal computer and in the publishing industry gave way to rapid increases in demand for Westvaco's traditional printing papers.

By the mid-1980s, Westvaco emerged from one of the worst five-year periods for the industry with six straight earnings records. In addition, it had completed its spending program. These programs drained earnings, but at their conclusion the company earnings jumped dramatically, and the company produced more paper with larger, more efficient units and less labor. David Luke III began four such programs in his 24 years as CEO.

By employing its own sales force, Westvaco diversified not by acquisition, but by tailoring products for customers. Research and sales forces emphasized new uses for bleached board in microwave food packaging and liquids packaging.

During the mid-1980s, the company took a series of anti-takeover steps. Although at record levels, debt was lower than in most companies in the forest products and packaging industries. David Luke III's final spending program of $1.6 billion was financed 80 percent internally. Unlike those before it, the program intensified product development instead of production efficiency.

Westvaco set up trade offices in Tokyo and Hong Kong in the mid-1980s to tap the skyrocketing Asian and Pacific markets. Finished products paved the way for increased activity overseas, and by the late 1980s exports reached 15 percent of sales. The consistently profitable Brazil operations began to export, after holding 20 percent of Brazil's corrugated box market for decades.

Significant growth in the printing industry in the late 1980s led to capacity expansion. Westvaco emphasized heavier-weight printing papers, despite the industry's cyclicality, which forced buyers to cut costs occasionally.

Emphasis on "Differentiation" in the Late 1980s and Early 1990s

During David Luke III's 24 years as CEO, Westvaco did more than most papermakers to free itself from the cyclicality of commodity production. His program that accomplished this, "differentiation," continued under his successors—his brother John A. Luke, who became CEO in 1988, and John A. Luke, Jr., whose attainment of the CEO position in 1992 represented the fifth generation of Lukes at the company helm. For Westvaco, differentiation meant manufacturing specialized products that met specific market segment needs. By lessening its reliance on commodity grade products, Westvaco would thus protect itself from the inevitable downturns of the cyclical paper industry; and, in practice, differentiation had proved to be a successful strategy for Westvaco through the mid-1990s.

Westvaco's specialty chemicals were a prime example of differentiated products. This business segment was bolstered in 1992 with the acquisition of North American Carbon. By 1995 Westvaco held a virtual monopoly of the U.S. market in carbons for automotive emission control devices, a sector that generated $15 to $20 million each year. The company sought to strengthen its position further when it announced late in 1995 a plan to spend $80 million to build a new activated carbon plant near its Wickliffe, Kentucky, fine papers mill, with operations scheduled to begin in mid-1997.

In the early 1990s differentiated products accounted for two-thirds of company sales, compared with only one-third a decade earlier. John A. Luke, Jr., aimed to increase this further, to about three-quarters of overall sales. A major step toward this goal came in 1995 when Westvaco sold its corrugated container operations to Weyerhaeuser for an estimated $85 million, the rare occurrence in company history of an asset sale. Westvaco's exit from the corrugated container business promised to free up capacity at its Charleston, South Carolina, mill for production of additional differentiated products, such as decorative laminates for kitchen countertops, which were made from saturating kraft paper.

Westvaco also continued to expand overseas as another basis for future growth. Subsidiaries were established in South Korea and Singapore in 1992 and in China, the Czech Republic, and India in 1995. Brazil, however, continued to be Westvaco's largest foreign beachhead, and the company's operations there were increased in 1996 with the opening of a new container plant in Pacujus and the purchase of a consumer packaging plant in Valinhos. Almost one-quarter of Westvaco's 1996 revenues were generated outside the United States, and John A. Luke, Jr., set a goal to increase that figure to one-third within ten years.

Westvaco enjoyed an exceptionally strong year in 1995, fueled in part by a market upturn, with record revenue of $3.27 billion and record net income of $280.8 million. The company's stock split three for two that August. Meanwhile, environmental issues came to the fore when the Council on Economic Priorities placed Westvaco on its 1995 list of the country's eight worst corporate polluters, citing 1992 toxic emissions more than three times the industry average. For its part, Westvaco announced plans in early 1995 to spend $140 million to upgrade its bleached pulpmaking plants so as to eliminate the use of elemental chlorine. Environmental groups had been lobbying paper companies to eliminate this use of chlorine because of the creation of the highly toxic chemical dioxin as a byproduct.

In early 1996, David L. Luke III retired from the Westvaco chairmanship, and John A. Luke, Jr., added the post of chairman to his roles as president and CEO. In September of that same year Westvaco formed a joint venture with SCANA Corporation to build and operate a $160 million power cogeneration facility at Westvaco's North Charleston, South Carolina, kraft paper mill. The new facility would enable Westvaco to make future expansions in its manufacturing operations at North Charleston. The company also announced plans to build a $20 million technical center in North Charleston with laboratories and offices for its specialty chemicals division.

From the late 1980s through the mid-1990s, Westvaco had been one of the steadiest-performing companies in the paper industry. Westvaco's emphasis on differentiated products and its reinvestment programs may have cut earnings over short-term periods, but it provided a sounder basis for long-term growth. The company was also well positioned to take advantage of an increasingly open world market, all of which added up to a promising future.

A Merger in the New Millennium

By the start of the new millennium, the paper and forest products industry was undergoing significant change by way of consolidation. An influx of companies offering similar products forced prices to fall and left paper concerns scrambling to shore up profits and control costs. Large companies, including International Paper Company and Georgia-Pacific Corporation, were buying up smaller companies and Mead and Westvaco alone were considered to be takeover targets. The two companies, however, decided to join forces in a $3.1 billion deal that would position it as the second largest producer of coated papers.

Before its merger with Mead, Westvaco had bolstered its holdings with strategic acquisitions including a bleached paperboard mill in Evadale, Texas, and two packaging suppliers—Mebane Packaging Group and IMPAC Group Inc. By 2001, both Mead and Westvaco were pursuing options that would allow them to remain competitive in the ever-changing industry. Mead and Westvaco struck a deal in August 2001 and announced their intent to merge.

The union that created MeadWestvaco was viewed as a merger of equals and because the deal was structured as such, the new company would assume very little debt. Meanwhile, its competitors were straddled with significant debt due to recent acquisitions. As a stock-for-stock exchange, Mead shareholders received one share of the new company for each share of Mead stock held as well as a cash payment of $1.20 per share. Westvaco shareholders received 0.97 shares of MeadWestvaco for every share of Westvaco stock held. Westvaco's offices in Connecticut became MeadWestvaco's company headquarters.

The deal was completed in January 2002 and MeadWestvaco was born. In one fell swoop, the company had become a major player on par with the likes of International Paper and Georgia Pacific, with operations in coated and specialty paper, packaging, consumer and office products, and specialty chemi-

cals. The company expected to save at least $325 million as a result of the merger, and as part of the integration process, it shuttered three paper machines and facilities in Chillicothe, Ohio, as well as a plant in Front Royal, Virginia.

With John Luke, Jr., at the helm of MeadWestvaco, the new company made several keys moves over the next few years. As part of its acquisition strategy, it purchased pharmaceutical packaging manufacturer Kartoncraft Ltd. of Ireland and stationery products concern AMCAL Inc. Tilibra S.A. Productos de Papelaria, an office products manufacturer based in Brazil, was acquired in 2004.

MeadWestvaco also began divesting certain assets, including parcels of forestland. In 2003, the company announced plans to cut 1,000 jobs and close several plants in order to increase earnings. As part of that plan, it consolidated its consumer and office products operations.

The company made its most significant move in January 2005 when it announced plans to sell its papers business to NewPage Corp., a private buyout company controlled by Cerberus Capital Management LP. The $2.3 billion deal included paper mills in Ohio, Michigan, Maryland, Maine, and Kentucky, and 900,000 acres of forestland in Illinois, Kentucky, Michigan, Missouri, Ohio, and Tennessee.

The sale of these assets was a major initiative in MeadWestvaco's strategy to focus on its packaging products business. The sale also would allow the company to pay down nearly $900 million in debt. NewPage completed its purchase in May 2005, leaving MeadWestvaco with three core segments: Packaging, Consumer and Office Products, and Specialty Chemicals. MeadWestvaco had indeed experienced significant change in the early years of the new millennium, but as 2005 came to a close, the company's management team was confident that its activities over the past several years left it well positioned for success in the future.

Principal Subsidiaries

MeadWestvaco Coated Board, Inc.; MeadWestvaco Consumer Packaging Group, L.L.C.; MeadWestvaco Forestry, L.L.C.; MeadWestvaco Maryland, Inc.; MeadWestvaco Texas, L.P.; MeadWestvaco Virginia Corporation; Rigesa, Celulose, Papel E. Embalagens Ltda. (Brazil).

Principal Divisions

Packaging; Consumer and Office Products; Specialty Chemicals.

Principal Competitors

Crown Holdings Inc.; International Paper Company; Weyerhaeuser Company.

Further Reading

Baker, Don, "$13M Parachute Will Ease Mead CEO's Exit," *Business Courier,* November 30, 2001, p. 34.
Carr, William H.A., *Up Another Notch: Institution Building at Mead,* New York: McGraw-Hill, 1989.

David, Gregory E., ''A Machine Called Chief: How Modest Steve Mason Saved Mead from Mediocrity,'' *Financial World,* March 14, 1995, pp. 42–43.

Ducey, Michael J., ''Mead, Westvaco: Merger of Equals,'' *Graphic Arts Monthly,* October 2001, p. 58.

Ferguson, Kelly, ''Westvaco Corp.: 'Differentiation' Means Key to Success,'' *Pulp & Paper,* April 1995, pp. 36–37.

Fischl, Jennifer, ''Mead and Boise: The Long and the Short,'' *Financial World,* November 18, 1996, p. 24.

Hodgson, Richard S., ed., *In Quiet Ways: George H. Mead, The Man and the Company,* Dayton, Ohio: The Mead Corporation, 1970.

Jaffe, Thomas, ''Paper Values,'' *Forbes,* August 20, 1990, p. 124.

Kim, Queena Sook, ''Paper Merger Attains Size Without Adding Huge Debt,'' *Wall Street Journal,* August 30, 2001, p. B4.

Livingston, Sandra, ''Mead Corp.: Attention to Detail Boosts Productivity,'' *(Cleveland) Plain Dealer,* June 26, 1996.

''MeadWestvaco to Sell Paper Business for $2.3 Billion,'' *New York Times,* January 19, 2005.

''MeadWestvaco Will Eliminate 600 Jobs to Cut Costs,'' *New York Times,* August 6, 2004.

Narisetti, Raju, ''Mead Corp. Decides To Go Back to Its Roots, Literally: Company Bets Future on Forest Products, Not Electronic Data Services,'' *Wall Street Journal,* May 27, 1994, p. B4.

——, ''Mead to Buy Coated-Paper Mill, Woods from Boise Cascade for $650 Million,'' *Wall Street Journal,* October 1, 1996, p. A4.

Parker, Marcia, ''Quietly, Paper Giant Girds for Downturn,'' *Crain's New York Business,* March 18, 1991, pp. 3, 25.

Plishner, Emily S., ''The Old Guard: Why Straitlaced Westvaco Should Interest Value-Minded Contrarians,'' *Financial World,* January 30, 1996, pp. 52, 54.

Sender, Henny, ''MeadWestvaco to Sell Paper Business,'' *Wall Street Journal,* January 19, 2005, B2.

Westvaco 1888–1988: Centennial Recognition—The Early Years, New York: Westvaco Corporation, 1988.

Young, Jim, ''Mead: Performance Improvement Program on Track,'' *Pulp and Paper,* June 1994, pp. 30–31.

—Elaine Belsito, Ray Walsh
—updates: David E. Salamie, Christina M. Stansell

Métropole Télévision S.A.

89 avenue Charles de Gaulle
92200 Neuilly-sur-Seine, Paris
France
Telephone: (+33) 1 41 92 66 66
Fax: (+33) 1 41 92 66 10
Web site: http://www.m6.fr

Public Company
Incorporated: 1986
Employees: 1,362
Sales: $1.7 billion (2004)
Stock Exchanges: Paris
Ticker Symbol: MMT
NAIC: 513120 Television Broadcasting Networks;
   512110 Television Show Production

Métropole Télévision S.A. is one of France's leading television broadcasters and programming producers. Métropole Télévision's flagship station is the M6 television channel, which ranks second behind Société Télévision Française 1's TF1 station. Métropole Télévision taps into the under 50 viewing market with over 14 themed channels and also has interests in home shopping services, music, publishing, rights acquisitions, and film distribution. The company also owns 34 percent of digital television provider Télévision Par Satellite (TPS). Métropole Télévision secured EUR 598.8 million in advertising revenue during 2004, which accounted for just over half of its total sales. RTL Group owns a 48.8 percent stake in the company.

'Little Station That Could' in the 1980s

Until the early 1980s, France's television broadcasting networks remained under the tight control of the French government, which restricted the number of available stations to just three: TF1, which was privatized in 1987, and the government-owned Antenne 2 and Antenne 3. The appearance of privately owned television stations marked something of a revolution for the French television viewer. The first of the new breed of channels was Canal Plus, a subscription-based service requiring a set-top decoder, which began broadcasting in 1984. Canal Plus was soon followed by La Cinq, broadcasting on France's channel five. Plans for a sixth channel, TV6, to be operated by radio programmer NRJ and advertising agency Publicis, foundered by mid-decade.

In 1987, however, a new station joined France's airwaves. Called M6, the station quickly became known as the French version of the "Little Engine That Could." Starting on a budget of just FRF 500 million per year—which represented only one-fourth of the budget for La Cinq—M6 definitely faced an uphill battle. As CEO and founder Jean Drucker told *Le Point*, "We didn't start from zero. We started from less than zero." One of the station's largest hurdles was that its broadcast network remained severely limited, with reception assured in less than one-third of France, in part because of government reluctance to allow the station to expand its network of transmitters nationwide. Industry analysts were also skeptical that the French market could support a sixth television channel. Métropole Télévision's first year's balance sheet seemed to bear out the skeptics, as the company posted losses mounting to FRF 380 million.

Yet Drucker, who had previously served as president of Antenne 2 (later renamed France 2), not only had extensive experience in television, but also the deep pockets of financial backers Lyonnaise des Eaux and CLT (Compagnie Luxembourgeoise de Télédiffusion, later CLT-UFA), which each held 25 percent of Métropole Télévision. Drucker put his broadcasting experience to good use, focusing on establishing a strong identity for the new station. The company developed the M6 logo, and a "look" for the station that set it apart from its competitors. Standing apart was also extended to M6's broadcast schedule as well. In a country where the eight o'clock news broadcast was known as the "high mass," M6 dared to be different, offering an array of counter-programming initiatives that increasingly brought it to the attention of France's television viewers, in particular the younger viewing markets.

M6's counter-programming took on various forms, including broadcasting television series—chiefly American-made—during the traditional news time, as well as a CNN-inspired six-minute newscast presented in the time slot just before 8 p.m., when all of the other stations were still broadcasting commer-

Key Dates:

1987: M6 television station begins broadcasting.
1988: Potential viewing audience reaches 18 million households.
1994: Company is listed on Paris Stock Exchange.
1995: Company purchases interest in Télévision Par Satellite (TPS).
1998: Home Shopping Service and Fun TV stations are launched.
2000: Share of national audience tops 13.5 percent.
2002: Company acquires additional shares of TPS.
2004: Suez S.A. sells its interest in the company; RTL Group remains a majority shareholder.

cials. M6's choice of programming often placed the company in difficulties with the CSA (the French television authority) and requirements that stations devote certain percentages of their broadcast time to French- and European-produced programming. American shows such as *Cagney and Lacey* and *The Cosby Show* gave M6 an increasing share of the French viewing public. M6 also developed its appeal with the youth market, devoting much of its broadcasting time to music videos.

Despite a strong showing in its urban markets, where the channel pulled in as much as 15 percent of the viewing audience, M6 remained the smallest kid on the block. With just 2 percent of the national audience—in a system that largely lacked local advertising—M6 remained far from its break-even point of 10 percent. This situation began to change early in 1988, when the extension of the company's transmitter network allowed it to triple the number of television households it could reach. By then, with remote controls in hand, more and more television viewers were tuning into M6.

Diversifying in the 1990s

By 1991, M6 had captured a 9 percent share of France's viewing public. Although the station continued to rely heavily on music videos and U.S.-imported shows, Métropole Télévision had begun to show its own programming muscle. M6-produced programs included *Capital,* a highly respected news magazine with an emphasis on corporate and financial matters, and *Culture Pub,* a program devoted to advertising around the world, both of which began to make a mark on the French television scene. Nevertheless, the company continued to face industry criticism for its lack of French- and European-made television programming, especially from France's producer's guild, but also from many political leaders who did little to hide their interest in seeing M6 disappear altogether.

Similar pressures, and viewer disinterest, led to the demise of La Cinq by 1992, suggesting that the country indeed was not ready for six television stations. However, M6's fortunes continued to rise, gaining points not only from the closing of La Cinq (which was later replaced by station Arte, a French-German broadcaster oriented toward cultural programming), but also from France's Big Three: TF1, France 2, and France 3. As the company neared the 10 percent break-even point, it was

also moving from net losses toward net profits. By 1991, with revenues of FRF 800 million, the company had cut its losses back to just FRF 140 million. Nevertheless, with the end of La Cinq, many in the industry began sounding the death knells for M6, with its total of FRF 1.4 billion in losses during its first five years of business. Métropole Télévision turned to its two largest shareholders for continued financing; in turn, Lyonnaise des Eaux and CLT both increased their shares to 34 percent.

The year 1992 proved to be M6's turning point. With its share of the television viewing audience topping 10 percent for the first time, M6 became profitable, posting net profits of FRF 100 million for the year. The company's fortunes continued to rise. By 1993, as its national share of 12 percent gave it a growing percentage of the nation's total advertising expenditures—reaching 14.9 percent that year—net profits topped FRF 230 million on revenues of FRF 1.8 billion. In 1994, Métropole Télévision was ready to go public, posting just 9 percent of its shares on the Paris Stock Exchange. Priced at FRF 260 per share, the listing was oversubscribed some 38 times, making it one of the year's most successful initial public offerings.

Métropole Télévision invested its new capital in diverse activities. The rollout of satellite television, under preparation in the mid-1990s, and the extension of cable television offered the company new programming perspectives. New channels proposed by the company included Téva, a channel featuring programming for the women's market; M6 Music, taking over the company's music video programming as M6 itself turned more and more toward programming fiction and news and entertainment magazines; and Série Club, devoted to broadcasting French and U.S.-made series. Métropole Télévision also bought into the TPS satellite network; the company's participation, together with the strong share positions of CLT and Lyonnaise, gave Métropole Télévision a leading role in TPS's operations.

By 1995, Métropole Télévision had succeeded in shedding its debts. The company continued to post steady gains in profits, despite its share of the loss-making TPS network, only slowly beginning to gain momentum. In 1996, M6 faced once again the ire of the CSA. Where M6 had enjoyed the regulatory body's lenience toward the station's disregard of its programming quotas, the company's success now forced it to toe the line, especially during the 5 p.m. to 11 p.m. time slot. The tightening of its requirements led the company to increase its own production investments. By 1998, Metropole's own productions were helping to drive the company's success, forming the majority of its top audience-generating programs.

The company's satellite television investments began to pay off in the late 1990s as well. Growing public interest in satellite broadcasting, spurred by sharp drops in the prices for satellite dish receivers and decoders, placed TPS as one of the leaders, alongside CanalSatellite, for the French market. After increasing its own participation in TPS to 25 percent, Métropole Télévision quickly made plans to create more new channels, including Fun TV, oriented toward the youth market, and the Home Shopping Service.

Métropole Télévision was also making advances on other entertainment fronts. The company's M6 Interactions subsidiary made strong inroads with its magazines, video and compact disc, and software products. Métropole Télévision also joined the big screen, providing production and financing for a number of cinema projects, including *Quasimodo* and *Peut-être*, among others. The company also began preparations for two new television channels, to be launched after the turn of the century, M6 Famille, devoted to family programming, and TV.com, featuring multimedia and computer-oriented programming. On the multimedia front, Métropole Télévision created a new subsidiary, M6 Web, grouped under its M6 Interactions subsidiary, to govern its Internet and multimedia activities. The growing importance of its multimedia activities was highlighted by M6 Interactions' growing share of the company's annual revenues: some 30 percent of 1998's FRF 3.5 billion.

In 1999 Métropole Télévision extended itself into a new arena—that of the sports arena. In May of that year, the company joined shareholder CLT-UFA in the purchase of the Girondins soccer club of Bordeaux. The purchase not only gave the company an entry into the sports market, it also gave it the possibility to include live sports broadcasting on its stations for the first time.

Métropole Télévision in the New Millennium

Métropole Télévision entered the new century with the announcement that it had gained the second place position among France's general-programming stations, with a 13.6 percent share nationwide. The ''little station that could'' had certainly proved that it could assert itself as a leader in the French television market. Indeed, the company's actions over the next several years would solidify its position in the French television industry. One such move came along in 2002, when Métropole Télévision increased its ownership in TPS to 34 percent.

Founder Jean Drucker died in 2003 leaving Nicholas de Tavernost at the helm of M6. Under his leadership, the firm continued to diversifying its holdings in order to shield itself from drops in advertising revenue. The strategy worked. By 2003 revenues from its other businesses had reached EUR 601.7 million while advertising-related revenues were EUR 575.2 million.

With both sales and profits on the rise, Métropole Télévision was known throughout the industry for its branding ability, which allowed it enter and be successful in established markets including music, retail, and publishing. De Tavernost commented on the company's branding initiatives in a June 2003 *Financial Times* article claiming, ''If the umbrella brand is not good, the diversification would be bad too. We built our brand name very, very carefully. It's a brand that's specifically for young people, for the under-35s.'' He went on to comment, ''We have an affinity with our audience. When we sell our products with our trademark, people recognize it immediately.''

Suez S.A., a French water and energy conglomerate that held a 37 percent stake in Métropole Télévision sold off its interest in 2004. RTL Group S.A., owned by Bertelsmann AG, retained a controlling 48.8 percent interest. At this time, government regulations did not allow a foreign company to own more than 49 percent of a terrestrial broadcaster. Previous agreements made with M6, Suez, and RTL kept the latter's voting rights to 34 percent in an effort to preserve M6's editorial independence.

In 2004, Métropole Télévision looked for ways to expand its soccer coverage. It attempted to purchase the rights to France's top-flight soccer matches but lost out to competitor Canal Satellite. It also relaunched its shopping channel as M6 Boutique La Chaine and acquired the television channel Paris Premiere.

During this time period, the advertising market remained in a state of flux. The French government began lifting certain bans allowing newspapers and magazines to advertise on mainstream terrestrial television channels for the first time in 2005. Large retailers were expected to enter the television advertising scene in 2007. As such, Métropole Télévision set plans in motion to increase its programming spending in an attempt to profit from these changes in the future.

While the television industry remained highly competitive, Métropole Télévision had carved out a defined space as one of top stations in France. M6 was the only national channel to increase its viewing share in 2004, a sure sign that the company was on track for success in the years to come.

Principal Subsidiaries

TPS SNC (34%).

Principal Operating Units

M6 Boutique; M6 Music; M6 Music Black; M6 Music Rock; Paris Premiere; Serie Club; Teva; TF6; Fun TV.

Principal Competitors

Canal + Group; Société Télévision Française 1.

Further Reading

Aubert, Philippe, ''Une télé pas comme les autres,'' *Le Point*, January 4, 1988, pp. 74–75.

Equirou, Marine, ''Jean Drucker: M6 réalisera en 98 un bénéfice au moins égal à celui de 97,'' *Les Echos,* September 10, 1998, p. 24.

''EU Clears Bertelsmann Metropole,'' *Daily Deal*, March 16, 2004.

''French TV Channel M6 *Les Echos,* Seeks to Build Up Soccer Coverage,'' *Dow Jones International News*, April 28, 2004.

''Jean Drucker, M6 Founder, Dies,'' *Music & Media*, May 3, 2003.

''M6 to Be Bound by Broadcast Quotas,'' *Tech Europe*, January 9, 1996.

''M6 Ups Program Spending Ahead of Rule Change,'' *Dow Jones International News*, March 8, 2005.

''Metropole Television,'' *Financial Times*, June 17, 2003, p. 24.

Short, David, ''Small Networks Reap Big Rewards,'' *European*, October 7, 1994, p. 25.

''TF1, M6 Acquire Another 25% of French Broadcaster TPS,'' *Wall Street Journal Europe*, July 19, 2002, p. N4.

Tieman, Ross, ''Suez Favors Public Offering for M6,'' *Daily Deal*, November 25, 2003.

—M.L. Cohen
—update: Christina M. Stansell

MOCON®

Mocon, Inc.

7500 Boone Avenue North
Minneapolis, Minnesota 55428
U.S.A.
Telephone: (763) 493-6370
Fax: (763) 493-6358
Web site: http://www.Mocon.com

Public Company
Incorporated: 1966 as Modern Controls, Inc.
Employees: 116
Sales: $25.1 million (2004)
Stock Exchanges: NASDAQ
Ticker Symbol: MOCO
NAIC: 334519 Other Measuring and Controlling Device
Manufacturing

Mocon, Inc., is a Minneapolis-based company that provides gas detection, analysis, and control products and services for a wide variety of industries, including chemical, electronics, food and beverage, life sciences, oil and gas, paints and coatings, pharmaceuticals, plastics, and vision care. Mocon's instruments measure the rate at which oxygen, carbon dioxide, water vapor, and other molecules leak through packaging, thereby helping determine the shelf life of a product. Moreover, Mocon is able to help clients calculate the cost-effective thickness of packaging material needed to achieve a certain shelf life. Other products include instruments to sort, weigh, and move pharmaceutical tablets and capsules. In addition to its Minnesota headquarters, the company maintains facilities in Lyons, Colorado, and Round Rock, Texas. About 50 international distributors sell the products, which can be found in more than 60 countries. Mocon is a public company listed on the NASDAQ.

1950s Origins

The man behind the founding of Mocon was Howard (Les) Demorest. Born in Tacoma, Washington, in 1921, Demorest served in the Navy during World War II and later moved to Minnesota to study physics at the University of Minnesota.

After graduating, he stayed in the area to become involved in heart valve research at the Minneapolis Veterans Medical Center. He then went to work for General Mills, Inc., in Minneapolis, taking a position in the applied sciences division. In 1957 he began working on the infrared H2O technology that would be at the heart of his first permeation instrument. After five years of effort he had developed a viable device, which he called the Infra-Red Diffusometer.

The Infra-Red Diffusometer was the world's first dynamic instrument for measuring trace amounts of moisture permeating through barrier films, an important aspect in the development of packaging materials. The instrument worked by using a heated saturated salt solution to establish a condition of 90 percent relative humidity at 100 degrees Farenheit on one side of a film and a condition of 0 percent relative humidity at 100 degrees Farenheit on the other side using a stream of warm dry air. When the source of dry air was cut off, vapor from the moist side of the film was drawn to the dry side. The rate at which this occurred was sensed by an infrared detector and provided the water vapor transmission rate (WVTR), which became a baseline value that allowed films to be compared in terms of their ability to serve as a moisture barrier.

As Demorest's research was about to bear fruit in the early 1960s, General Mills sold its applied sciences division, prompting many of the unit scientists to strike out on their own and start companies. Demorest was one of them. Frugal by nature, he was able to start Demorest Instruments in the basement of his home in 1963. He spent another two years developing the Infra-Red Diffusometer before putting the device on the market in 1966. He also incorporated his business as Modern Controls, Inc., and made the first use of the name Mocon.

Demorest took Modern Controls public in 1968, making an initial offering of stock over the counter in Minneapolis. Soon the young company began developing a second product, the Ox-Tran 100, to measure the permeation of oxygen through flexible materials, an important consideration in the food packaging industry. Ox-Tran made use of a Hersch cell, an oxygen analyzer invented by Paul Hersch in the late 1950s. It employed a pair of electrodes immersed in an electrolytic fluid, such as potassium hydroxide. It was the hydroxide ions that was measured moving from one side of a barrier film to the other, where a lead anode was located. The lead then reacted to form lead oxide producing an electric current that was proportional to the oxygen concentration of the sample gas. In this way the oxygen transfer rate of a barrier film could be determined. Ox-Tran became available for sale in 1971.

NASDAQ Listing in the Late 1970s

In 1975 Modern Controls introduced the first multi-cell permeation instruments: the Permatran-W, which measured WVTR, and the Ox-Tran 10/50, which measured oxygen transfer. Two years later the company introduced the first Pac Guard CO2 leak detector. Used in production line quality assurance, the device could quickly detect weak heat seals, large leaks, or even small pin holes in finished products. In 1979 Modern Controls began to offer its first high speed check weigher for the pharmaceutical industry, the Vericap 1200. In that year it also began to import a head space analyzer (the Mocon/Toray LC-700F), used to measure the amount of air space surrounding a product in a package. Also of note in the 1970s, the company moved its headquarters from Minneapolis to Elk River, Minnesota, in 1978 and a year later its stock gained a listing on the NASDAQ.

Modern Controls introduced the Ox-Tran Twin and Vericap 1800 products in 1981 and also opened a standard testing laboratory to offer permeation testing services. The company unveiled a carbon dioxide transmission measuring system, the Permatran C-IV, in 1982, which found a ready market with soft drink bottlers, who were replacing glass containers with plastic to eliminate the expense of recycling, cleaning, and sterilization. The one drawback with plastic, however, was how quickly carbon dioxide passed through its walls, leaving the soda "flat." Permatran C-IV helped bottlers to create plastic containers that could better contain carbonated beverages.

Modern Controls made a misstep in the early 1980s when it attempted to diversify its business mix by becoming involved in the manufacture of flat-panel computer displays. The bid failed and the company soon returned its focus to its profitable niche in package testing. In 1983 Modern Controls introduced the world's first computerized permeation instrument, the Ox-Tran 1000. A year later it brought out the AB-1 (AB standing for Automatic Balance). Originally developed for the pharmaceutical industry to weigh and sort tablets and capsules, the instrument found other application weighing individual pieces or parts. In 1985 an improved version, the AB-2, was introduced, as was Vericap 2110, an upgrade of the Vericap 1800. In that same year, Modern Controls began offering a new permeation instrument called Multi-Tran, which tested permeability of such gases as nitrogen, argon, helium, and hydrogen.

Modern Controls continued to fill out its product lines during the second half of the 1980s. After the 1986 acquisition of the Winzen Research film thickness division, it introduced

the Profiler product line of film thickness gauges. In 1987 the first Ox-Tran models capable of determining precise relative humidity were put on the market. A year later the first precise WVTR test system, the Permatran-W, was also offered. Modern Control closed out the decade by adding improved Ox-Tran and Profiler models, as well as introducing a leak and burst tester, SKYE, and the PG-1 carbon dioxide head space analyzer. Also of note during the decade was the 1988 retirement of Les Demorest, who was replaced by Bill Mayer. The elder Demorest continued to serve on the board of directors until 1996. He died of emphysema in 1999 at the age of 78. He and Mayer had known each other from their days at General Mills.

As Modern Controls entered the 1990s, permeation products accounted for about 70 percent of revenues, while gauging products accounted for another 15 percent. Revenues in 1989 approached $10 million and net income topped $2.1 million. The company's pattern of increasing sales and income continued until 1992, when Modern Controls encountered a serious drop in international business, which by this point accounted for about 40 percent of revenues. Sales to Germany and Japan were cut in half, resulting in two straight years of declining revenues and income before Modern Controls was able to regain its momentum. Nevertheless, the company was able to continue to pay shareholders a dividend.

Modern Controls also continued to bring out new models of proven products in the early 1990s. In 1991 it introduced the Ox-Tran 2/20, the first modular unit in the line, and the SKYE 2000, an improved leak and burst tester. Further offerings in 1991 included Veritab, a high-speed device to check and weigh tablets for the pharmaceutical industry, and Aromatram, an instrument that determined the transmission rates of organic vapors and gases, including menthol, d-limonene, and propane. In 1992 Modern Controls introduced its first modular WVTR test system, the Permatran-W model 3/30. Also in 1992, the company brought out the HS-751, used to determine the amount of oxygen in the head space of a package.

After dipping as low as $10.4 million in 1993, sales began to creep up in 1994 and 1995, then began to accelerate in 1996 as exports began to rebound despite continued softness in orders from Japan and Germany. The company was well-positioned to enjoy strong growth during the second half of the 1990s. It had plenty of cash on hand to pay for acquisitions and was also excited about the potential of a new process the company was developing, Transorption, which allowed it to conduct permeation tests on substances other than film, such as layers of paint or circuit boards. Moreover, Modern Controls was able to use this new technology to take advantage of a corporate trend to outsource testing, providing it with customers in industries it had never served before. The Transorption technology was a major part of the company's new Consulting & Developmental Services unit.

Sales in 1996 increased to a record $14.8 million while net income topped $3 million for the first time in company history. Business continued to grow in 1997, as revenues improved 15 percent to more than $17 million and net income 21 percent to $3.7 million. To keep pace with demand, Modern Controls in 1997 expanded its sales force and made changes in its geographic distribution to better serve the markets for its products.

Key Dates:

1963: Les Demorest founds Demorest Instruments.
1966: Business is incorporated as Modern Controls, Inc.
1968: Company stock is floated over the counter.
1971: The Ox-Tran oxygen-permeation measuring device is introduced.
1979: Modern Controls stock is listed on NASDAQ.
1982: Permatran introduced.
1986: Profiler product line is introduced.
1988: Les Demorest retires.
1999: Company changes its name to Mocon, Inc.
2000: Founder's son, Robert L. Demorest, becomes president, CEO, and chairman.

Sales did not improve as expected in 1998, however. Revenues slipped to $15.1 million, although Modern Controls was able to produce net income of $2.3 million, a healthy 15 percent return. Long in the market for acquisitions the company was finally able put some of its cash to use by completing a pair of acquisitions. Modern Controls bought Austin, Texas-based Microanalytics Instrumentation Corporation in early 1998. At the close of the year it picked up Boston-area Lab Connections, Inc. The addition of these analytical instrument companies provided Modern Controls with technology in chromatography and mass spectrometry, and opened up new marketplaces for the company, such as chemical analysis, drug discovery, aroma/odor studies, and life sciences.

For years the company had been informally known as Mocon, and in May 1999 Modern Controls formally changed its name to Mocon Inc. Business also rebounded, as the company recorded sales of $17 million and net income of $2.9 million. Mocon's performance was also recognized by *Forbes* magazine, which ranked the company 177 on its annual list of 200 Best Small Companies in America.

Son of Founder Takes Charge in 2000s

In April 2000 Mayer retired and was replaced as CEO and chairman by the son of Les Demorest, Robert L. Demorest, who for the prior several years had served as Mocon's president. He took charge of a company that was in solid shape. In 2000 it recorded its 20th consecutive year of profitability, with sales improving to $17.3 million and net income to $3.3 million. It was also well-positioned for continued growth, as the consulting business continued to gain credibility in the marketplace, and the technology acquired through acquisition was being used to improve older products and spur renewed sales in them. In addition, Mocon improved the software interface on some of its instruments to increase speed and accuracy.

Mocon completed another acquisition in 2001, paying $3.6 million for Questar Baseline Industries Inc. of Lyons, Colorado, from Questar Corporation. Baseline offered gas analysis and monitoring instruments for use in the oil and gas exploration, industrial hygiene and safety, and other applications. The addition of Baseline technology bolstered the gas detection and chromatography business it had added in previous acquisitions. Despite difficult economic conditions in 2001, Mocon continued to prosper, increasing revenues to $19.3 million and net income to $3.4 million.

Mocon also made additions to its product lines in the early 2000s. It began selling the first Permatran-W WVTR instrument in 2002 and offered the Ox-Tran 702 in 2003. Mocon also acquired the Vaculok product line of vacuum-insulated panels in December 2003 but soon thought better of venturing too far afield from its core gas detection and measurement businesses and sold the Vaculok assets in July 2005. Another acquisition, the purchase of Lippke GmbH in Germany in January 2004, was more in keeping with Mocon's successful business model. For more than three decades Lippke had been Mocon's main European distributor. Its addition greatly enhanced Mocon's sales and service capabilities in Europe and could also be used to import new products to the U.S. market.

After hovering in the $19 million sales range for three years, Mocon enjoyed a surge in 2004 and for the first time topped the $25 million mark in sales, along with $2.4 million in net income. Moreover, its operations in Texas, Colorado, and Minnesota were all reorganized to operate more efficiently. Mocon continued to spend money on research and development to spur growth organically. New products included hand-held analyzers that found a receptive market in the food and beverage industry. In addition, Mocon still had sufficient money on hand to make strategic acquisitions. The company, a dominant player it its niche market, was clearly well placed to enjoy ongoing growth.

Principal Subsidiaries

Microanalytics Instrumentation Corporation; Lab Connections, Inc.; Baseline-Mocon, Inc.; Mocon FSC, Inc.; Paul Lippke Handels-GmbH Prozess-und Laborsysteme (Germany).

Principal Competitors

Agilent Technologies, Inc.; O.I. Corporation; PerkinElmer, Inc.

Further Reading

Brammer, Rhonda, "Bad Break," *Barron's,* July 15, 1996, p. 18.
Fiedler, Terry, "Seduced by Technology," *Minnesota Business Journal,* June 1985, p. 44.
Her, Lucy Y., "Howard (Les) Demorest, 68 Dies of Emphysema," *Star Tribune* (Minneapolis), December 19, 1999, p. 7B.
"Mocon Acquires Colorado-Based Baseline Industries," *Finance and Commerce Daily Newspaper, MN,* October 26, 2001.
"Modern Controls Inc," *Minneapolis-St. Paul City Business,* May 6, 1991, p. 23.
"Small Companies That Are Great Values," *Kiplinger's Personal Finance Magazine,* July 1997, p. 18.

—Ed Dinger

The National Bank of South Carolina

1241 Main Street
Columbia, South Carolina 29201
U.S.A.
Telephone: (803) 929-2062
Web site: http://www.nationalbanksc.com

*Wholly-Owned Subsidiary of Synovus Financial
Corporation*
Incorporated: 1905 as Farmers Bank and Trust
Employees: 600 (est.)
Total Assets: $3.5 billion (2005)
NAIC: 522110 Commercial Banking

The National Bank of South Carolina, a subsidiary of Synovus Financial Corporation, is a leading bank in South Carolina. Formed in the farming town of Sumter in 1905, the bank focused on the Pee Dee region of the state, in the northeastern corner, for its first several decades. At the time of its 100th anniversary, NBSC was still building its presence in the state, buying a number of smaller banks and building new branches. The company operated fairly autonomously from its Columbus, Georgia-based corporate parent.

Origins

The National Bank of South Carolina (NBSC) dates back to 1905. In that year, Farmers Bank and Trust was founded in the farm town of Sumter, South Carolina by C.G. Rowland. Rowland, a station agent for the Atlantic Coastline Railroad, had been assigned to the area 18 years earlier.

Originally operated from a grocery store, the bank moved into the former county courthouse in 1907. It was the only one of seven Sumter banks to survive the Great Depression. A branch was opened in the state capital of Columbia in 1965. In the early 1970s, assets were up to $80 million and the company had nine branches centered on the Pee Dee area.

Takeover Target in the 1980s

The holding company NBSC Corporation was set up in 1983. The bank, the seventh largest in South Carolina with deposits of $170 million, was already viewed as a takeover target as regulations were relaxed regarding banking acquisitions. NBSC had repulsed an offer from Greenville, South Carolina-based Southern Bancorp Inc. in 1982, saying the offer was too low. It was also discussing merger prospects with at least one other bank, Southern National Corp. of Lumberton, North Carolina, according to a later story in the *News & Observer.*

NBSC renewed its interest in selling after asking prices for banks began to fall later in the decade. Discussions with Southern National Corporation simmered until 1990, when the $3 billion bank, based in Lumberton, North Carolina, made a serious bid to acquire NBSC, which had assets of $540 million. Southern National proposed an all-stock deal worth $53 million. NBSC's retail emphasis was considered complementary to Southern National's mainly corporate-centered business. "This is a good fit for us," said NBSC chairman Marvin D. Trapp. Southern National had the deal approved by the NAACP—which had questioned the bank's record of reinvesting in poor or minority communities—but called off the merger after a couple of months, citing "unexpected obstacles."

NBSC had pursued a few acquisitions of its own in the last half of the 1980s, buying the $5 million Bank of Summerton and the larger Lake City State Bank, assets $51 million, which dated back to 1940. It was also opening brand new offices in greater Columbia and Myrtle Beach.

NBSC followed other banks in the region by relaxing its loan requirements and withdrawal penalties in the wake of Hurricane Hugo. The October 1989 storm affected all of the bank's branches, noted *American Banker,* including the main office in Sumter, 100 miles from shore.

NBSC ended the 1980s as South Carolina's third largest bank. It had 28 offices in the state, total assets of $563 million, and about 450 employees.

Waking Up in the 1990s

Marvin D. Trapp, NBSC's CEO since 1973 and chairman since 1985, stepped down in 1991. He had first joined the company in 1963 as assistant vice-president for business development and advertising. Trapp's successor was Robert V.

Key Dates:

1905: Farmers Bank and Trust launched in Sumter, South Carolina.
1965: Branch established in Columbia.
1983: NBSC Corporation holding company is formed.
1985: The Bank of Summerton acquired.
1986: Assets are $350 million; company files public stock offering.
1988: New offices built in Irmo, Myrtle Beach; Lake City State Bank acquired.
1992: Branches opened in Camden, Florence, and Mount Pleasant; First Trident S&L acquired.
1993: Offices open in Upstate, Hilton Head Island.
1995: Synovus Financial Corporation acquires NBSC in deal worth $153 million.
2000: Carolina Southern merged with NBSC.
2005: At time of 100th anniversary, NBSC has assets of $3.5 billion.

Royall, Jr., formerly head of Citizens and Southern National Bank of South Carolina (C&S of SC) and C&S Corporation's vice-chairman. Royall was also chairman of the South Carolina Ports Authority. He had left C&S after it merged with Sovran Financial Corporation.

Royall immediately made sweeping changes at the "very, very sleepy bank." He hired a handful of executives from C&S and restated 1990 earnings, shifting $1 million of net profit to loan-loss reserves.

NBSC was venturing into the Upstate in 1993, opening offices in Spartanburg, Greenville, and Greer. The area was growing rapidly, spurred by BMW's new North American plant. NBSC had also opened a branch at the other end of the state, Hilton Head Island, and had bought out couple of thrifts. By this time, it had branches in two dozen communities and assets of $974 million. NBSC Corporation also owned Sunsbank Life Insurance Company.

Another wave of consolidation was rolling over banks in the Carolinas, and though it was "the largest independent bank headquartered in South Carolina," this time NBSC would not escape this time without itself being taken over by a larger competitor. It was able, though, to put off the inevitable for a couple of years.

According to *American Banker,* NBSC was stealing customers from the large North Carolina banks (such as First Union Corporation, NationsBank Corporation, and Wachovia Corporation) as they consolidated their Palmetto State acquisitions. "We set out from the very beginning to be the local bank," said one of Royall's early hires. "Our goal became one of stealing customers and selling our name. . . . If we only sold rate, we'd lose every time."

Acquired by Synovus in 1995

Synovus Financial Corporation, based in Columbus, Georgia, acquired NBSC in February 1995 for stock worth $153 million, or twice NBSC's book value. Synovus, which had assets of nearly $6 billion before the merger with NBSC, had gobbled up more than 30 banks in the previous ten years. It allowed them to remain relatively autonomous, however, and this would be the case with NBSC, which was allowed to keep its name and continued to refer to itself as a "community bank." The NBSC merger was Synovus' largest to date and marked its entry into the South Carolina market.

An analyst told the *Atlanta Journal-Constitution* that NBSC had below average return on assets and very high overhead.

NBSC was operating 43 branches at the time of the merger. Total assets topped $1 billion.

William L. Pherigo, NBSC's president since 1991, was promoted to CEO in 1995. Robert Royall remained chairman. Pherigo was one of the many who followed Robert Royall to NBSC. Another, Fred L. Green, III, became NBSC's CEO in 1997.

A good word from one of NBSC's influential friends raised questions in 1999, at least among Democrats. Republican House Speaker David Wilkins appeared in a newspaper ad for the bank that listed his credentials as both speaker of the House and member of NBSC's board of directors. According to state Democratic chairman Dick Harpootlian, this went against a state law barring public officials from using their positions to promote business interests. "He has disgraced his office and should resign," said Harpootlian, adding that Wilkins had supported legislation favorable to the banking industry.

Synovus boosted its holdings in the Upstate by acquiring Spartanburg-based Carolina Southern Bank in 2000. Carolina Southern had been founded in 1989 and had four branches. Synovus lumped the new bank into NBSC, increasing NBSC's assets to more than $2 billion.

The National Bank of South Carolina celebrated its 100th anniversary in 2005. Assets had grown to $3.5 billion. It had a new president and CEO: Chuck Garnett, who was a C&S alumnus like his predecessors.

Principal Competitors

BB&T Financial Corporation; First Union Corporation; NationsBank Corporation; Wachovia Corporation.

Further Reading

Atkinson, Bill, "National Bank of S. Carolina Trying to Bulk Up for Battle with Invaders," *American Banker,* December 14, 1993, pp. 6+.
Bandy, Lee, "South Carolina Democrats Call on Republican House Speaker to Resign," *State* (Columbia), October 8, 1999.

"CEO Interview: NBSC Corp.," *Wall Street Transcript,* May 16, 1994.

Cline, Kenneth, "NBSC of South Carolina Said Considering Offers," *American Banker,* September 28, 1994, p. 22.

——, "Synovus to Pay $153M in Stock for NBSC, Or Twice Book Value," *American Banker,* October 7, 1994, p. 5.

Cooper, Jeanne Dugan, "National Bank of South Carolina Joins Lenders Easing Rules After Hurricane," *American Banker,* October 4, 1989, p. 23.

Dietrich, R. Kevin, "Synovus-Owned National Bank of South Carolina to Merge with Carolina Southern," *Carolina,* September 20, 2000.

Ivey, Page, "Planning, Strategy Are Royall's Business Trademarks," *State* (Columbia), October 21, 1991.

Jackson, C. Grant, "Columbus, Ga.-Based Bank Holding Company Names Vice President," *State* (Columbia), December 3, 2003.

Jean, Sheryl, "South Carolina Bank Executive to Retire," *Knight Ridder Tribune Business News,* October 22, 1997.

Kenneson, Kim R., "Southern National Will Buy S.C. Bank," *News & Observer* (Raleigh), September 21, 1990, p. C7.

"NAACP Drops Protest of Southern National, NBSC Merger," *PR Newswire,* November 28, 1990.

"The National Bank of South Carolina Acquires Standard Federal Savings and Loan Association," *PR Newswire,* September 27, 1993.

"National Bank of S. Carolina to Open 2 Offices," *American Banker,* January 3, 1993, p. 2.

"NBSC and First Trident Announce Merger Plans," *PR Newswire,* April 21, 1992.

"NBSC and Lake City State Bank Announce Plans to Merge," *PR Newswire,* March 17, 1988.

"NBSC Announces Plans to Open Two Offices in Spartanburg," *PR Newswire,* December 21, 1993.

"NBSC Cleared to Buy Bank in Sumter, S.C.," *Wall Street Journal,* July 7, 1983.

"NBSC Corp. Files Registration with SEC for Public Offering of 215,000 Shares of Common Stock," *PR Newswire,* July 10, 1986.

"NBSC Corporation's Marvin Trapp Announces Retirement at Year-End," *PR Newswire,* January 29, 1991.

"NBSC's Parent Company Sees Growth in Loans, Bank Fees," *The Post and Courier* (Charleston), July 19, 2001.

Seward, Christopher and Rodney Ho, "Synovus to Merge with Bank in S.C.," *Atlanta Journal-Constitution,* October 6, 1994, p. E1.

"Southern National, NBSC Agree to Merger," *PR Newswire,* September 20, 1990.

"Southern National Terminates Merger Negotiations with NBSC," *PR Newswire,* December 3, 1990.

"Synovus Financial Announces Completion of Historic NBSC Merger," *PR Newswire,* February 28, 1995.

Ward, Timothy, "NBSC: Looking Forward to the Next 100 Years," *Greater Columbia Business Monthly,* May 2005, pp. 52, 54, 56.

Werner, Ben, "Bank Survived Depression, Takeover Era," *State* (Columbia), February 17, 2005.

Winston, Chris, "Spartanburg, S.C., Bank Bought Out by National Conglomerate," *Herald-Journal* (Spartanburg), September 22, 2000.

—Frederick C. Ingram

Nobel Learning Communities, Inc.

1615 West Chester Pike
West Chester, Pennsylvania 19382
U.S.A.
Telephone: (484) 947-2000
Toll Free: (888) 886-6235
Fax: (484) 947-2004
Web site: http://www.nobellearning.com

Public Company
Incorporated: 1984 as Rocking Horse Child Care Centers
    of America Inc.
Employees: 3,800
Sales: $164.2 million (2005)
Stock Exchanges: NASDAQ
Ticker Symbol: NLCI
NAIC: 611110 Elementary and Secondary Schools;
    62441 Child Day Care Services

Nobel Learning Communities, Inc., operates private schools that serve students from preschool through high school. The company runs approximately 150 schools in 14 states, including its largest school operation, the California-based Merryhill School system, which consists of 30 preschools, elementary schools, and middle schools. The company builds and acquires its educational facilities in clusters, thereby creating a network within a community that can accommodate a child throughout his or her primary and secondary education. Nobel schools are generally open between 6:30 a.m. and 6:00 p.m., providing child supervision for the company's target customers, single-parent and double-income families. Nobel schools operate under various names, including Merryhill School, Chesterbrook Academy, Northwest Schools, and Houston Learning Academy. The company also operates corporate child-care centers and summer camps. Educational conglomerate Knowledge Universe owns 25 percent of Nobel Learning.

Origins

It took roughly a decade before Nobel arrived at the strategy, the corporate structure, and the leader capable of achieving

consistent success. The years in between were difficult, a period when Nobel operated under a different name and pursued a different corporate mission. Nobel began operating in 1984 as Rocking Horse Child Care Centers of America Inc., a Cherry Hill, New Jersey-based operator of private child-care centers.

Rocking Horse began modestly, with a single child-care center that recorded $48,000 in revenue during its first year of operation. Rocking Horse did not expand until April 1986, but once it began developing into a chain of day-care centers, the company did so with fervor. By the end of 1986, the company's revenue total had increased mightily, swelling to nearly $3 million as it began an aggressive acquisition campaign. Between April 1986 and October 1987, Rocking Horse acquired 31 child-care centers and constructed two new facilities, extending its operating territory to an eight-state area. The company's energetic growth, however, did not translate into profitability. Rocking Horse posted a net loss of $3.2 million in 1986, $300,000 more than it collected in revenue.

Despite the loss, the company continued to expand into the late 1980s. Rocking Horse raised $5 million in a public offering of stock in October 1987, the capital from which was used, as its president, John W. Quaintance, told the *Philadelphia Business Journal* in the October 12, 1987, issue, "to continue our acquisition strategy." By the end of 1988, the company operated 41 of what it called "preschool learning centers." There were ten each in Georgia and Florida, eight in South Carolina, four each in Illinois and Pennsylvania, three in New Jersey, and one each in Maine and Massachusetts. Rocking Horse held licenses to accommodate 5,538 children, allowing an average of 135 children per center. The company charged between $43 to $140 per week for its child-care services, the nature of which represented the hidden and unexploited strength of the chain. To distinguish itself from the scores of other child-care companies in existence, Rocking Horse used professionally developed educational and recreational programs administered by trained supervisors and teachers. By tailoring itself as more than a traditional day-care provider, the company's management hoped to attract parents and their children away from the competition, but the strategy never worked, at least not financially. By the end of the decade, Rocking Horse was a company suffering from profound financial problems.

As Rocking Horse entered the 1990s, the signs of financial distress were alarmingly abundant. Saddled with an extremely large bank loan it could not pay, Rocking Horse had difficulty convincing its bank to approve a lease on a company vehicle. The company had a negative net worth of $3.8 million and was reeling from the effects of successive annual losses. After Rocking Horse defaulted on its loans, the accounting firm of Coopers Lybrand issued a statement based on the child-care provider's 1991 results, stating that it was unsure if Rocking Horse had the capacity to survive.

Clegg Leading Revival in 1992

The task of rescuing Rocking Horse fell to a new management team headed by A.J. "Jack" Clegg, whose arrival marked the beginning of a new and decidedly more successful era. Clegg's professional background included the 1979 founding of Empery Corporation, an operator of cable television and printing business. At Empery, Clegg served as chairman, president, and chief executive officer from 1979 to 1992, but his duties at Empery represented only a fraction of his business background in the decade preceding his arrival at Rocking Horse. Between 1983 and 1993, Clegg served as chairman and chief executive officer of TVC, Inc., a distributor of cable television components. During the same period he also held identical titles at Design Mark Industries, a manufacturer of electronic senswitches. Clegg served as chairman and chief executive officer of Globe Ticket and Label Company from 1984 to 1991 and was on the board of directors of Ferguson International Holdings PLC. In the academic world, he was a member of the Advisory Board of Drexel University, an honor bestowed on the then-50-year-old Clegg in 1989.

When Clegg joined Rocking Horse in May 1992, he inherited a company that had lost $10.2 million during the previous two years. The losses were out of control, delivering staggering blows to a company that only generated roughly $30 million in annual sales. Clegg worked quickly to trim the company's liability, reducing Rocking Horse's debt by nearly $7 million within a year. He raised money for much-needed restructuring

through private placements, initially raising $2 million by selling stock and private holdings and raising another $2.5 million in 1993. Thanks to Clegg's restorative efforts, Rocking Horse reversed it losses, going from losing $3.8 million in 1991 to posting a profit of $1.8 million in 1992. Revenues slipped during the first stages of the turnaround, dropping from $34.7 million in 1991 to $33.5 million in 1992—a consequence of having to divest several child-care centers—but the company was on the mend. After the restructuring and divestitures, the company operated 44 child-care centers in 11 states, with the most significant addition in northern California where Rocking Horse operated 29 schools called the Merryhill County Schools. As Clegg looked beyond the immediate need to arrest the company's money-losing ways, the Merryhill system would serve as his blueprint for the future.

Aside from Clegg's focus on financial matters, the survival of Rocking Horse depended on another contribution from its new chairman, president, and chief executive officer. In the course of inspecting Rocking Horse's properties, Clegg visited one of the company's Merryhill schools, then operating as a division of Rocking Horse. During his visit, Clegg noted the focus on offering curriculum-based programs to the children. Rather than merely offering custodial care, Rocking Horse, Clegg realized, was offering something beyond the services of a babysitter. "The company never really took advantage of the fact that it had something relatively unique," Clegg told the *Philadelphia Business Journal* in a May 23, 1997, interview. Educational programs represented Rocking Horse's distinguishing mark, a specialty that Clegg intended to use as the emphasis underpinning Rocking Horse's expansion.

With a clear vision of what the company should become, Clegg began making wholesale changes. He began converting the company's child-care centers into curriculum-based preschools, a shift in strategy that called for a new corporate title. In 1993, Rocking Horse Child Care Centers of America was dropped in favor of Nobel Education Dynamics, Inc. Once the company's financial health was restored, Clegg also began acquiring and expanding preschools, elementary, and middle schools, a mode of expansion that touched off in 1994. An integral aspect of the company's expansion strategy involved grouping its properties around each other. Clegg did not try to establish a presence in a wide geographic area; instead, he only moved into new territory if he was able to acquire additional nearby properties, a strategy he likened to playing the board game Monopoly. "If we go into a brand-new area," Clegg explained in his May 23, 1997 interview with the *Philadelphia Business Journal,* "we will buy [an existing] school and use that school base to build clusters." According to the plan, the acquisition or construction of a preschool was followed by the addition of other preschools within the same vicinity. After establishing a network of preschools in a given area, the company next built centrally located elementary and middle schools, thereby creating a system that could accommodate the same pupil through his or her preschool, elementary, and middle school years.

Adhering to its blueprint for expansion, Nobel began acquiring facilities within roughly the same geographic area that Rocking Horse had penetrated. By the end of 1995, the company had 101 facilities in operation within an 11-state region.

Key Dates:

1984: Rocking Horse Child Care Centers of America is founded.

1988: Following the company's first acquisition campaign, there are 41 Rocking Horse child-care centers in operation.

1992: A.J. Clegg is hired as chairman and chief executive officer.

1993: Rocking Horse changes its name to Nobel Education Dynamics, Inc.

1998: The company is renamed Nobel Learning Communities, Inc.

2003: Knowledge Universe increases its stake to 25 percent; Jack Klegg resigns.

The process of acquiring and converting preschools into accredited private elementary schools was in full swing, as Clegg targeted the children of single-parent families and two-income families to fill his growing number of educational facilities. Nobel schools provided child supervision from 6:30 a.m. to 6:00 p.m., a schedule that conformed to the work schedule of most parents. Public schools, by contrast, typically provided child supervision from 8:30 a.m. to 3:00 p.m., which generally required single parents or double-income parents to pay for after-school child-care services. The savings partially offset Nobel's average tuition of $5,500, a fee that was 17 percent below the average $6,630 tuition at private nonparochial schools. Educationally, Nobel schools also compared favorably to other private schools, with Nobel students scoring one to two grades above their grade level, according to the Stanford Achievement Test, a standardized reading and math test.

Nobel's operating hours, its curriculum, and its tuition fees distinguished the company from many of its competitors. The company presented itself as an intriguing alternative to a specific sector of the market, leading one industry analyst to remark, "Nobel is the first private educator to provide solutions at a price the middle class can afford," as quoted in the January 1996 issue of *Money* magazine. Of importance, Clegg's approach to education operated on a sound financial footing as well. The company's primary schools earned 22 percent profit margins, a figure that was achieved in large part because Nobel operated with minimal overhead and without burdensome bureaucracy. Nobel's facilities were modest structures without the manicured lawns and architecturally elegant buildings found at the most expensive private schools. Nobel schools typically employed fewer support personnel than their private and public counterparts, and teachers' salaries averaged 41 percent less than the $37,000 average salary of public school teachers. Despite the lower pay, teachers welcomed the opportunity to work at Nobel, where average class sizes were smaller than at public schools—17 students per class versus 24 students per class—and where the pupils were generally more committed to learning, in large part because the schools had the ability to turn away children with disciplinary problems.

With a proven business model, Clegg entered the latter half of the 1990s ready to expand his concept by creating clusters of

Nobel communities. By the beginning of 1996, 13 of the company's properties in California had been converted to elementary schools catering to students from kindergarten through the eighth grade. Clegg intended to nearly triple the number of converted schools during the next two years, as well as to convert approximately 70 percent of Nobel's 51 preschools to kindergarten through second-grade schools. Clegg also announced aggressive acquisition plans, endeavoring to dramatically increase the $44 million in sales the company recorded at the end of 1995.

Late 1990s Diversification

As Clegg pursued his ambitious expansion plans, another change in the company's corporate title was needed to more accurately reflect the strategy driving it forward. In 1998, the company adopted the name Nobel Learning Communities, Inc., indicative of Clegg's desire to serve the educational needs of all children within a given community. Toward this end, the company's acquisition campaign enabled Clegg to create a more entrenched position within Noble communities—between 1994 and 1999, 68 schools were acquired—but the last years of the decade also saw Nobel target other segments of a community's student base. In 1998, the company formed a joint venture with Developmental Resource Center, Inc. (DRC), owned by Dr. Deborah Levy, a developer of special education programs. Under the terms of the agreement, Paladin Academy LLC was formed, a joint venture project 80 percent owned by Nobel and 20 percent owned by DRC. The joint venture gave Nobel control of three schools in Florida that specialized in full-day programs, summer camps, testing services, and clinics for kindergarten through 12th grade students challenged by learning disabilities such as dyslexia and attention deficit disorder. In 1999, Nobel added three more Paladin Academy locations, offering the specialized educational programs in the classrooms of existing Noble schools. Based on the performance of the new Paladin Academy schools, the company planned to open additional schools in areas where Nobel schools were clustered.

Nobel also moved in several other new directions in 1999, as Clegg shaped the company into a comprehensive education facility for the next century. Late in 1999, Nobel began offering tutorial and diagnostic programs under the name Nobel Learning Advantage. The programs, which the company planned to market to Nobel students and non-Nobel students both, were offered at two of Nobel's schools in 1999, with a companywide rollout scheduled to begin in January 2000. Nobel entered the charter school market in 1999 as well, facilitating a nonprofit entity's application for a charter from the School District of Philadelphia. Under the terms of a five-year management contract, Nobel agreed to provide administrative and construction management services to the charter school, which funded its own operations through payments from the School District of Philadelphia. The last year of the decade also saw Nobel acquire the Houston Learning Academy, an operator of five specialty high schools in Houston, Texas. The schools offered half-day curriculum programs focused on individualized attention.

As Nobel prepared for further expansion in the 21st century, the achievements of the 1990s suggested that energetic growth lay ahead. The company eclipsed the $100 million-in-sales mark in 1999, recording $109 million in sales, more than twice the total collected five years earlier. With the additions to the company's operating scope made in 1999, the opportunities for growth increased commensurately, positioning Nobel to attract students of all ages and abilities within a given community. After righting a floundering enterprise, Clegg demonstrated the ability and willingness to expand aggressively and strategically, a behavior he promised to display in the years ahead.

Changes in the 2000s

Nobel had long been compared with another very visible for-profit, publicly-traded education company, Edison Schools. Edison had well-known figures at its head, its media mogul founder Chris Wittle and Chairman Benno Schmidt, who had been president of Yale. Edison enjoyed a rising stock price in the early 2000s, yet the company lost money and was not expected to reach profitability for several more years. In contrast, Nobel was profitable from the mid-1990s through the dawn of the 21st century. It was still a relatively small company, and its stock traded much lower than Edison's, yet it seemed to have something going for it that its more visible competitor did not. Clegg explained his company's success in a profile in *Inc.* (December 2000) by saying education was "not a money problem. It's a money-management problem." Nobel kept its overhead low, and instead of requiring its separate schools to conform to a complex financial pattern, it asked its executives to be accountable for three key cost-control measures. The company kept an eye on general and administrative expenses as a percentage of tuition, strived for a high occupancy rate for each school, and kept down school employee costs as a percentage of tuition. Clegg's formula seemed to work even as the U.S. economy stumbled into recession with the end of the long bull market of the 1990s. Part of this may have been because, although economic conditions were generally poor in the United States in the early 2000s, the education market continued to grow. The total K-12 market was estimated at $2.5 billion in 2001, and it was growing at around 20 percent annually. The for-profit education industry seemed to be a protected niche, and Nobel seemed to be insulated from the economic stress that damaged other industries at the time.

Yet the rosy forecasts of the first few years of the new millennium did not seem to come true for Nobel Learning. The company began to lose money, a proposed merger fell through, and senior management left the company. The first clue that the situation was changing at Nobel came when the company announced in mid-2002 that it was being bought out and taken private by an entity formed by two investment companies and certain Nobel senior executives. The buyout was offered for $7.75 per share, which came down to some $110 million, including the assumption of debt. Chairman and CEO Clegg welcomed the offer when it was first made. The deal did not go through, however, with the buyout group claiming that it did not think the merger was financeable at the price it had offered. A few weeks after the termination of the merger in early 2003, Nobel announced that Knowledge Universe, the education holding company that already owned approximately 16 percent of the company, would invest an additional $5 million and take what amounted to 25 percent ownership. Two Knowledge Universe executives gained seats on Nobel's board of directors. When the two new directors joined Nobel Learning, the company announced that it would split the chairman and chief executive position. Both jobs had been held by Jack Clegg, and the company began searching for a new CEO. A few months later, in July 2003, Nobel announced that it had gotten another big investment, this time $6 million from a Baltimore-based private equity firm called Camden Partners. Camden's founder, David Warnock, served on the boards of several education companies, and he joined Nobel's board as well. One month later, Nobel announced that Chairman and CEO Jack Clegg had resigned.

By the end of fiscal 2003, it was clear that Nobel had lost more than $11.5 million on revenue of almost $150 million. Aside from Jack Clegg, many others in senior management left the company, including the chief operating officer and the chief financial officer. Nobel began to close some of its schools, and sought to refinance its debt. The company's new management team, led by the new president and CEO George Bernstein, worked to increase enrollment at its schools, to evaluate the company's real estate portfolio, and to bring in independent directors with education experience to its board. A year later, the company had reduced its debt, brought in money through sales of assets, and raised its school operating profit, but Nobel still finished 2004 with a net loss of close to $6.6 million.

Nobel closed more schools, bringing its total number from 179 in early 2003 to 150 at the end of 2005. Revenue grew to $164 million, and the company finished 2005 in the black, with a profit of some $2.5 million. Nobel further reduced its debt, and its school enrollment began to grow for the first time since 2002. The new management team was at work on a variety of fronts, improving marketing, investing in new curricula, training its staff, and putting money into its buildings and real estate. The company seemed to have reversed its poor performance of the last two years.

Principal Subsidiaries

Merryhill Schools, Inc.; Merryhill Schools Nevada, Inc.; Chesterbrook Academy; Northwest Schools; Houston Learning Academy.

Principal Competitors

Bright Horizons Family Solutions, Inc.; Edison Schools Inc.; Imagine Schools, Inc.

Further Reading

Abelson, Reed, "Rocking Horse Offering Aimed at Expansion," *Philadelphia Business Journal,* October 12, 1987, p. 10.

Davis, Jessica, "Venture Firm Invests in For-Profit School Company," *Philadelphia Business Journal,* September 2, 1994, p. 3.

Edwards, Brian, and Mary Ann Sabo, "Investing in Education Is Not Just a Platitude," *Chicago Tribune,* May 22, 2001, p. 3.

Ellis, Junius, "A Potential 48% Gain Puts These Education Stocks at the Head of the Class," *Money,* January 1996, p. 25.

Geiger, Mia, "Nobel's ABCs of Private Schooling," *Philadelphia Business Journal,* May 23, 1997, p. B1.

——, "Rocking Horse Changes Image After Quick Financial Turnaround," *Philadelphia Business Journal,* June 28, 1993, p. 6B.

Gubernick, Lisa, "Midmarket Schools," *Forbes,* July 31, 1995, p. 46.

"Inc. Case Study," *Inc.,* December 2000, p. 88.

Mylchreest, Ian, "Business Profile: Merryhill Schools, Company Shows That Education Can Be Profitable in a Variety of Ways," *Las Vegas Business Press,* May 10, 2004, p. 14.

"Rocking Horse Child Care Centers of America Inc.," *Philadelphia Business Journal,* December 12, 1988, p. 26.

Spencer, Theodore, "A Tale of Two Education Stocks," *Fortune,* January 22, 2001, p. 144.

"The Vision Thing," *Inc.,* December 2000, p. 88.

Woodall, Martha, "Media, Pa.-Based Education Firm Plans Philadelphia Charter School," *Knight-Ridder/Tribune Business News,* November 11, 1998.

—Jeffrey L. Covell
—update: A. Woodard

Nu Skin Enterprises, Inc.

75 West Center Street
Provo, Utah 84601
U.S.A.
Telephone: (801) 345-6100
Fax: (801) 345-2799
Web site: http://www.nuskinenterprises.com

Public Company
Incorporated: 1984 as Nu Skin International Inc.
Employees: 10,000
Sales: $1.14 billion (2004)
Stock Exchanges: New York
Ticker Symbol: NUS
NAIC: 325411 Medicinal and Botanical Manufacturing

Nu Skin Enterprises, Inc., is one of the world's largest direct selling or multilevel marketing (MLM) firms. In 41 nations, more than 820,000 independent distributors buy Nu Skin products for their own use, sell them at retail prices, and recruit others to become distributors as well. The company offers more than 200 skin, hair, cosmetic, oral care, general nutritional, sports nutritional, weight management, and botanical products. It also offers Internet services and various communication products through its Big Planet division. Nu Skin opened retail locations in China in 2003.

Origins and Early Expansion

The year was 1984, Ronald Reagan was in the White House, and Blake Roney graduated from Brigham Young University (BYU) with a business finance degree and great hopes for the future. He and his sister Nedra Roney and their friend Sandie Tillotson decided to start their own business. Blake Roney invested $5,000 of his own money in a business idea—to make personal care products that contained "All of the Good, None of the Bad," the core principle when Nu Skin International (NSI) was founded in June 1984. On October 15, 1984, the company was incorporated.

Since the new firm had limited funds for advertising, it decided to rely on the growing method of network or multilevel marketing (MLM), whereby independent self-employed Nu Skin distributors would sell products one-on-one and recruit others to do the same.

Initially the company met in the apartment of Nedra Roney. After several rejections, it finally found an Arizona company to make its first skin and hair products, which were sent to Nedra's place. Then the founders spooned their products from ten-gallon containers into jars or whatever receptacles their customers brought. By word of mouth the new business spread to family and friends and was off and running out of its home in Provo, Utah.

By 1989 sales were exploding at double-digit rates every month. That year Nu Skin hired Brent Ririe as director of management information systems, the firm's first technical employee. He helped the company choose new computer systems so that commission checks could be mailed on time and other company functions could operate efficiently. Other serious problems, however, waited around the corner.

Legal Challenges Beginning in 1991

In March 1991 the Michigan attorney general told Nu Skin to prove it was not an illegal pyramid scheme or face a lawsuit. At least four other states (Ohio, Pennsylvania, Illinois, and Florida) also investigated the rapidly growing firm that by 1991 claimed more than 100,000 distributors in the United States, Hong Kong, Canada, and Taiwan.

Nu Skin in late December 1991 issued a press release indicating that it had negotiated an agreement with Michigan in which it would strengthen its buy-back policy by offering its distributors a 90 percent refund on any unused products and sales aids, without any limit since the time of purchase. The Direct Selling Association, which Nu Skin joined, recommended a 90 percent buy-back policy to prevent building up too much inventory. Georgia, Maryland, Louisiana, Wyoming, and Massachusetts required that 90 percent refund policy.

Without admitting any illegal activity in its Michigan settlement, Nu Skin also agreed to reemphasize its retail sales and pay Michigan $25,000 for its investigative expenses. Nu Skin spokesman Jason Chaffetz said in the December 28, 1991, *Provo Daily*

Herald that his company was encouraged by the settlement after what he said was "the longest, hardest look at us."

Meanwhile, the Food and Drug Administration (FDA) investigated Nu Skin to make sure its products were safe and clearly labeled without making any illegal healing claims. It should be noted that no federal laws had been passed covering multilevel marketing. Rules and regulations of the FDA and Federal Trade Commission (FTC) applied, but most government oversight came from state laws. The FTC's senior attorney said in the November 1991 issue of *Kiplinger's* that most states considered MLM as an illegal pyramid "when the money is coming in from the recruitment of people, not the sale of products."

Such governmental checks, national media exposure, and its expanding operations brought Nu Skin more attention in 1991. In May 1991, for example, it opened its new $8 million warehouse/distribution center in Provo's East Bay. Without going into debt, Nu Skin built a 200,000-square-foot center to consolidate its nine previous Utah County warehouses. The company also built a recreation facility, basketball and volleyball courts, and picnic areas for its Provo employees.

In 1992 Nu Skin completed its new corporate headquarters. After using four other Provo offices, the firm finally had its permanent home in the ten-story Nu Skin Tower, Provo's tallest downtown building. It included fiber optics and computers to administer a growing international network of distributors and a visitors' center and theater.

In the early 1990s Nu Skin faced allegations of sex discrimination from 28 former and current female employees. In one lawsuit filed December 29, 1992, in U.S. District Court in Salt Lake City, six former employees charged that Nu Skin denied them advancement opportunities and equal benefits and paid men more for comparable work. Judge David Winder on August 6, 1993, denied the women's effort to make this a class action and dismissed the case with prejudice, so that it could not be refiled. This lawsuit was settled out of court under undisclosed terms, but both sides said they were pleased with the results. Since about half of Nu Skin's work force was women, this was a very significant case.

The FTC in January 1994 confirmed that it had reached a settlement with Nu Skin, which agreed to pay $1.2 million without admitting any wrongdoing. The FTC had alleged that the Provo firm had made false statements about three of its products and also had exaggerated earnings claims without telling prospective distributors that very few actually made large incomes.

Meanwhile, Nu Skin in 1992 introduced a new line of products called Interior Design Nutritionals, or IDN. Eventually the firm offered more than 50 IDN products of four types: general nutrition, sports nutrition, botanicals, and weight management.

Success and Frustrations in Asia in the Early to Middle 1990s

Nu Skin commenced its Asian operations in Hong Kong in September 1991. Operating from this base through the subsidiary Nu Skin Hong Kong, several leading distributors through their downlines eventually entered other Asian markets. In February 1995 Nu Skin Hong Kong began operating in Macau.

January 1992 marked Nu Skin Taiwan's opening date. About two million individuals or 10 percent of the total population of Taiwan were estimated to be involved in some form of direct marketing, mostly of nutritional products. Because of so much participation, the government strictly regulated this new form of business. Nu Skin Taiwan believed that in 1997 it was the largest direct marketing firm in that nation. Revenue growth there increased an average of 41 percent annually through 1997.

Nu Skin Japan commenced operations in April 1993 and quickly became the major success story for Nu Skin in Asia. In 1992 some $30 billion worth of goods and services were sold by direct sales in Japan, making it the world's largest direct sales market, with about twice the amount sold in the United States.

Not surprisingly, in the early 1990s several other MLM firms also entered the Japanese market. For example, more than one million Amway distributors in Japan recorded $1 billion sales in 1992, and the local company Pola Cosmetics sold twice that amount in 1992. Avon and Mary Kay Cosmetics also operated in Japan.

Because of the success of other MLM companies in Japan, *Business Week* on May 31, 1993, wisely included an article on Nu Skin's entry into that market. "Japan will be Nu Skin's biggest market," predicted retired baseball player Leron Lee, a major Nu Skin distributor in Tokyo. Statistics from the Nu Skin 1997 annual report (i.e., 297,000 active distributors generating revenue of nearly $600 million) proved Lee right.

What accounted for the success of MLM in Japan? Part of the answer involved close social networks already in place. "Organizations from college clubs to tea ceremony schools provide ready-made distribution frameworks," said the author of the *Business Week* article. Another likely reason was that many Japanese consumers preferred high-priced, high-quality products, unlike many Americans who always seemed to be shopping for a bargain.

Products in the Late 1990s

Nu Skin in 1998 offered a wide diversity of products for consumer use. Its facial care items included cleansing bars and various lotions, muds, moisturizers, face lift formulas, and IdealEyes creme to reduce dark circles and wrinkles around the eyes. For body care, Nu Skin sold bar and liquid soaps, deodorants, moisturizers and lotions, and Sunright sunscreens, lip balm, and sunless skin tanning lotion. The HairFitness line covered shampoos, styling gel, mousse, and hair conditioners. The company's AP-24 oral care products featured floss, breath

Key Dates:

1984: Nu Skin International is established.
1991: Several states launch an investigation into the company; Asian operations begin.
1992: Construction is completed on the ten-story Nu Skin Tower in Provo, Utah.
1993: Nu Skin Japan is launched.
1996: Nu Skin Asia Pacific, Inc. (NSAP) is incorporated under Delaware laws and launches an initial public offering.
1998: NSAP is renamed Nu Skin Enterprises Inc.; Generation Health Holdings, Inc. is acquired.
1999: Big Planet Inc. is purchased.
2003: The company expands into China.

spray, mouthwash, a toothbrush, and two kinds of toothpaste. Nu Skin also sold Nutriol products, described in a product brochure as "Advanced Care from Europe," including nail liquid, mascara, eyelash formula, shampoo, and hair conditioner. The firm's Nu Colour Cosmetics included mascaras, blushes, lipsticks, eye liners, and finishing powder. For the exercise crowd, Nu Skin offered five trademarked ProSync products: hair and body shampoo, antibacterial deodorant bar, antiperspirant and antideodorant, muscle rub, and a face and body lotion. Nu Skin also sold the Believe line of fragrances inspired by model Christie Brinkley, the company's spokesperson. For children, it distributed specially designed gentle skin and hair products, sunscreen, toothpaste, and floss under the Jungamals brand name.

Nu Skin developed its trademarked Epoch line with plant ingredients acquired from native cultures. From the Polynesians, Nu Skin gained an extract of the ava puhi plant used for its Epoch shampoo/hair conditioner. Generations of Polynesians also used two other indigenous plants (Cordyline terminalis and Orbignya phalenata) for moisturizing and soothing skin; Nu Skin incorporated them in its Firewalker Moisturizing Foot Cream. Other Epoch products featured botanical ingredients originally from several American Indian and Mayan cultures.

From native Haitian plant experts, Nu Skin acquired knowledge of the botanical Citrus aurantium that it included as a key ingredient in its Epoch deodorant. As part of its Force for Good Campaign, Nu Skin donated 25 cents from the purchase of every Epoch product to help indigenous peoples protect their habitats and traditional cultures.

Further Developments in the Late 1990s

Nu Skin Asia Pacific, Inc. (NSAP) was incorporated under Delaware laws on September 4, 1996, as the exclusive distribution unit for Nu Skin International products sold in Asia. On November 20, 1996 a corporate reorganization resulted in Nu Skin Japan, Nu Skin Taiwan, Nu Skin Hong Kong, Nu Skin Korea, and Nu Skin Personal Care (Thailand) becoming wholly owned subsidiaries of Nu Skin Asia Pacific. NSAP's initial public offering (IPO) of 4.75 million shares of Class A common stock was completed on November 27, 1996, resulting in net

proceeds of $98.8 million. Nu Skin Asia Pacific, renamed Nu Skin Enterprises, Inc., on March 27, 1998, completed its acquisition of Nu Skin International and its affiliated companies in Europe, South America, New Zealand, and Australia. Nu Skin USA was acquired in 1999.

In the late 1990s, Nu Skin began operations in the Philippines and started a new compensation plan and the new Scion product line, both designed for use in low per capita income nations. In 1998 the firm also started in Poland and Brazil.

In October 1998 Nu Skin Enterprises completed its acquisition of Generation Health Holdings, Inc., the private parent company of Pharmanex, Inc. Founded in 1994, Pharmanex researched and produced a line of 38 natural health supplements, including five proprietary formulas. From its base in Simi Valley, California, Pharmanex ran several research and production facilities, primarily in the People's Republic of China but also in Chile. The company employed about 40 scientists and collaborated with UCLA, Scripps Institute, Columbia University, and Beijing University on various projects.

Just one month after the Nu Skin acquisition, Pharmanex announced on November 18, 1998, that it was removing all its products from some 30,000 mass retail stores so that it could rely completely on Nu Skin's network marketing methods. "Pharmanex's move is calculated to take advantage of the growth in direct sales in the United States," said Pharmanex President Bill McGlashan in a press release. "We have confidence in Nu Skin's distributor force. . . . As successful as we have been in securing coveted retail shelf space, direct selling represents a more attractive way to differentiate the benefits and unique attributes of Pharmanex products—an education that cannot be communicated adequately in the mass retail setting." Pharmanex products continued to be available from the firm's catalog, a toll-free telephone line, its Internet store, health food stores, and independent pharmacies across the nation.

Nu Skin in 1999 continued under the leadership of Blake Roney and at least two others who helped start the company in 1984. Roney was president and CEO of Nu Skin International (NSI) until May 1998 and board chairman of Nu Skin Asia Pacific from November 1996 to May 1998, when he became Nu Skin Enterprises' board chairman.

Steven J. Lund, a graduate of BYU Law School, practiced law before helping Roney found Nu Skin. He served as NSI vice-president from 1984 to 1996, when he became president/CEO of Nu Skin Asia Pacific. In May 1998 he was chosen as the president/CEO of Nu Skin Enterprises.

Sandie N. Tillotson, a third founder, also graduated from BYU, as did almost all Nu Skin officers and directors. She helped develop the original products and create the multilevel marketing system. In 1993 *Working Woman* magazine named Tillotson one of the nation's top ten female business owners. She served as NSI vice-president from 1984 to May 1998, when she became a senior vice-president of Nu Skin Enterprises.

Nu Skin's finances continued to improve in the late 1990s. Its revenues grew from $358.6 million in 1995 to $678.6 million in 1996 and $890.5 million in 1997. Net income also rose steadily, from $40.2 million in 1995 to $81.7 million in 1996 and $93.6 million in 1997.

Nu Skin's expansion illustrated the growing popularity of direct sales among more and more consumers. In 1997 direct sales, which were mostly one-on-one transactions, totaled $22 billion in the United States and more than $80 billion worldwide, a doubling of sales in a decade.

It was also part of a major trend of more individuals working from their home. A 1997 Telecommute America survey estimated that about 11 million Americans used their computers and telecommunications devices to telecommute to work, instead of driving to work. In addition, the 1990 U.S. Census found that 54 percent of home workers were self-employed, compared with just 5.5 percent of workers outside the home who were self-employed. Network marketers like those in Nu Skin thus played a significant part in this dramatic economic shift from the factory and office to the home.

Nu Skin also demonstrated the important role that the state of Utah played in the expanding network marketing field and the natural products industry. Several other herbal or natural products companies that used MLM started in or moved to Utah, including Nature's Sunshine Products, Inc., USANA Inc., and the Sunrider Corporation. Many of these firms supported the Utah Natural Products Alliance, a Salt Lake City-based trade industry association.

Nu Skin's future looked bright in 1999. With an increasing number of high-quality products and good leadership, it continued to attract more distributors, many with high levels of education and successful careers in other fields. It faced plenty of tough competitors, however, including Amway and several other corporations involved in multilevel marketing of personal care and nutritional products.

In order to remain a step ahead of the competition, Nu Skin expanded its holdings in August 1999 with the $37 million purchase of Big Planet Inc., an Internet services company. The Republican National Committee selected Big Planet as its Internet Service Provider for its GOPNET.com web site in 1999.

Nu Skin in the New Millennium

Nu Skin remained focused on growth as it entered the new millennium. While its international business was booming, its U.S. operations were stagnating. The company attempted to bolster this region's sales by developing new nutrition products and by launching new distributor compensation initiatives. Nu Skin purchased First Harvest International and its Nourish the World network marketing program in 2002. The deal gave the company rights to sell the dehydrated food product Vitameals and also afforded Nu Skin the opportunity to distribute the product to malnourished children across the globe.

The company made significant expansion efforts in China during 2003 by opening more than 100 retail outlets in January alone. Chinese laws prevented Nu Skin from implementing its direct selling model but management eyed the retail stores as lucrative inroads to the Chinese market, which was expected to be one of the top direct selling markets in the world within the next five years. In order to reach its goal of $500 million in Chinese

revenues by 2008, Nu Skin planned to develop its distributor leadership even further, introduce its Pharmanex products to the market, and continue expansion throughout China.

Nu Skin celebrated its 20th anniversary in 2004. The company had come a long way from its humble beginnings in Nedra Roney's apartment. In fact, sales surpassed $1 billion that year. Nu Skin attributed much of its success to its new product, the Pharmanex BioPhotonic Scanner. In a published press release the company described the scanner as, "the first to use innovative laser technology to non-invasively measure the concentration of carotenoid antioxidants in the body's tissue; antioxidants protect the body at the cellular level against the effects of aging and the environment." The scanner could provide a score that measured a person's diet and nutritional health. By June 2005, there were more than 4,000 scanners in operation across the globe and more than two million people had been scanned.

During 2004, the company focused on strengthening its operations in Latin America and Eastern Europe. The firm planned on future expansion into Russia and Indonesia. With sales and net income on the rise, Nu Skin Enterprises appeared to be well positioned for growth in the years to come. Indeed, management was confident that the next 20 years would bring even more success its way.

Principal Subsidiaries

Nu Skin International, Inc.; Nu Family Benefits Insurance Brokerage, Inc.; Nu Skin Asia Investment, Inc.; Nu Skin Enterprises Australia, Inc.; Nu Skin Belgium, N.V. (Belgium); Big Planet, Inc.; Nu Skin Brazil, Ltda. (Brazil); Nu Skin Canada, Inc.; Nu Skin Enterprises Singapore Pte. Ltd. (Singapore); Nu Skin Europe, Inc.; First Harvest International L.L.C.; Nu Skin France, S.A.R.L. (France); Nu Skin Germany, GmbH (Germany); Nu Skin Guatemala, S.A. (Guatemala); Nu Skin Enterprises Hong Kong, Inc.; Nu Skin International Management Group, Inc.; Nu Skin Italy, S.r.l. (Itlay); Nu Skin Japan Company Limited (Japan); Nu Skin Japan, Ltd. (Japan); NSE Korea, Ltd.; NSE Korea, Ltd. (Korea); Nu Skin Malaysia Holdings Sdn. Bhd. (Malaysia); Nu Skin Mexico, S.A. de C.V. (Mexico); Nu Skin Netherlands, B.V. (Netherlands); Nu Skin Enterprises New Zealand, Inc.; Niksun Acquisition Corporation; Pharmanex, L.L.C.; Nutriscan, Inc.; Pharmanex (Huzhou) Health Products, Co., Ltd. (China); Nu Skin Enterprises Philippines, Inc.; Nu Skin Enterprises Poland Sp. z.o.o. (Poland); Nu Skin Poland Sp. z.o.o. (Poland); Nu Skin Scandinavia A.S. (Denmark); Nu Skin (China) Daily-Use and Health Products Co., Ltd. (China); Nu Skin Spain, S.L. (Spain); Nu Skin Taiwan, Inc.; Nu Skin Enterprises (Thailand), Ltd.; Nu Skin Personal Care (Thailand), Ltd. (Thailand); Nu Skin U.K., Ltd. (United Kingdom); Nu Skin Enterprises United States, Inc.; Zhejiang Cinogen Pharmaceutical Co., Ltd. (China); Nu Skin Israel, Inc.; Nu Skin Pharmanex (B) Sdn. Bhd. (Brunei); Pharmanex Electronic-Optical Technology (Shanghai) Co., Ltd. (China); Nu Skin Enterprises, RS, Ltd. (Russia); PT Nu Skin Distribution Indonesia (Indonesia).

Principal Divisions

Nu Skin; Pharmanex; Big Planet.

Principal Competitors

AMS Health Sciences Inc.; Amway Corporation; Herbalife International Inc.

Further Reading

Anderson, Duncan, ''The New Elite,'' *Success,* December 1995.

Bullinger, Cara M., ''Nu Skin Tells Its Story,'' *Utah Business,* October 1991, pp. 49–50.

Cilwick, Ted, ''Women at Nu Skin Pile Up Claims of Sex Discrimination,'' *Salt Lake Tribune,* September 19, 1993, pp. F1, F3.

Conover, Christi, ''Nu Skin, Michigan May Soon Have Agreement,'' *Provo Daily Herald,* December 28, 1991, p. A1.

Free, Valerie, ''Magic Marketing,'' *Success,* March 1992.

Godfrey-June, Jean, ''Can a Skin Cream Save the Rain Forest?,'' *Elle,* July 1996.

Gross, Neil, ''They've Got Their Feet in the Door,'' *Business Week,* May 31, 1993.

Klepacki, Laura, ''Nu Skin Celebrates 20 Years,'' *Women's Wear Daily,* February 20, 2004.

May, Dennis, ''Nu Skin Addresses FDA Concerns,'' *Utah County Journal,* October 22, 1991, p. A3.

''Nu Skin Closes Big Planet Acquisition for $37 Million,'' *Dow Jones Business News,* July 20, 1999.

Omelia, Johanna, ''Direct Sellers Expand in Asia/Pacific Rim,'' *Drug & Cosmetic Industry,* September 1996.

Roha, Ronaleen R., ''The Ups and Downs of 'Downlines,' '' *Kiplinger's Personal Finance Magazine,* November 1991, pp. 63–64, 66, 68–70.

Romboy, Dennis, ''High-Level Expansion Has Nu Skin Shedding Low-Key Image,'' *Deseret News,* June 12, 1991, p. B4.

Von Daehne, Niklas, ''Techno-Boom,'' *Success,* December 1994.

Warner, Laura, ''Nu Skin Has Evolved into a Giant,'' *Deseret Morning News,* March 8, 2004.

——, ''Nu Skin Marks 20th Anniversary,'' *Deseret Morning News,* June 4, 2004.

—David M. Walden
—update: Christina M. Stansell

Obrascon Huarte Lain S.A.

C/Gobelas No. 35-37, El Plantio
Madrid
Spain
Telephone: +34 91 348 41 00
Fax: +34 91 348 44 63
Web site: http://www.ohl.es

Public Company
Incorporated: 1911 as Sociedad General de Obras y
    Construcciones Obrascón S.A.
Employees: 11,033
Sales: EUR 2.23 billion ($2.82 billion)(2004)
Stock Exchanges: Madrid
Ticker Symbol: OHL
NAIC: 236220 Commercial and Institutional Building
    Construction; 221320 Sewage Treatment Facilities;
    236210 Industrial Building Construction; 237310
    Highway, Street, and Bridge Construction

Obrascon Huarte Lain S.A. (The OHL Group) is one of Spain's largest and most diversified construction groups. The company's primary area of operations remains in the large-scale construction, public works and infrastructure sectors, including road building and highway management and maintenance, harbor and port construction and maintenance, and the like. Since the early 2000s, however, OHL has been investing heavily in its diversification effort, boosting its operations in waste management and water treatment, urban and infrastructure services, and "social" construction, primarily of hotels and other tourism-market related structures, as well as shopping centers and retirement homes. OHL has coupled its diversification effort with an a geographic expansion effort. Although the company has long participated in foreign construction projects—the group's first contract, in fact, was for the construction of a port in Portugal in 1912—the company has been stepping up its international operations into the mid-2000s. Latin America has been a primary focus of the group's efforts in this regard, especially in Brazil, Argentina, Chile and Mexico. The company also has operations in North Africa. The company has also targeted the Eastern European market, acquiring Czech Republic construction leader ZS Brno as the springboard for further expansion in the region. OHL itself is the result of the merger of three midsized Spanish construction groups, between Obrascon and Huarte in 1998, and with Lain in 2001. The company's revenues of EUR 2.23 billion (US$ 2.82 billion) in 2004 place it among the top five Spanish construction groups. OHL is listed on the Madrid Stock Exchange. Chairman of the board Juan-Miguel Villar Mir is also the group's major shareholder.

Iberian Infrastructure Specialist in the 1910s

Sociedad General de Obras y Construcciones Obrascón, S.A., was founded in Bilbao, Spain in 1911. Obrascon's original shareholders were the Banco de Bilbao and the Banco de Vizcaya, which had begun to take an interest in financing infrastructure projects in the Iberian peninsula, and elsewhere. The company first project came from Portugal, when Obrascon won the contract to build two docks in the port of Lisbon. The construction of seaport infrastructures became a company specialty over the following decades.

Obrascon also retained a strong international focus. By 1918, the company had completed its first projects in North Africa. And in the years following World War II, Obrascon entered the American markets, and especially the Latin American region. The company's international expansion also encouraged the group to expand its focus, and in the 1960s Obrascon developed into a general construction group, with an emphasis on large-scale public works and infrastructure projects.

The company meanwhile had changed owners. In 1953, the Banco de Bilbao acquired full control of the company, a holding it maintained until 1973. Obrascon's ownership was then transferred to Altos Hornos de Vizcaya. But the company's growth effort quickly ran out of steam. By the mid-1980s, the company had begun to struggle amid falling profits. By 1987, Obrascon's losses had topped one billion pesetas—compared to the group's total capitalization value of just 900,000 pesetas.

Obrascon was rescued that year by Juan-Miguel Villar Mir. Born in Madrid in 1931, Villar Mir had started his career as a civil servant in the late 1950s, rising to a number of high-level

Company Perspectives:

The ultimate mission of the OHL Group is to create value in conditions of economic, social and environmental sustainability, catering to the specific interests of its clients, of the human team comprising the Group, of the investors and of all of the individuals and entities having a stake in the proper functioning of the company.

administrative positions in the 1960s. Villar Mir left the government to enter the private sector at the end of the decade, in order to take over a failing company. The rescue of failed companies became something of a specialty for Villar Mir.

Villar Mir briefly returned to politics after the death of Franco—Villar Mir's political career included a stint as Spanish vice-president between 1975 and 1976. Disagreement with the new Spanish government led Villar Mir to abandon politics for the private sectors. Villar Mir at first invest in real estate, until he spotted a new opportunity with the collapse of Obrascon.

Paying a symbolic price of just one peseta, Villar Mir took over Obrascon and set it on a new course. Among other features of the new Obrascon strategy was a commitment to strong profit margins. As such, Obrascon began to shed its low-profit operations. Instead, the company focused its efforts on its building its infrastructure business. Into the 1990s, the company adopted a conservative approach to growth, based on its insistence on maintaining strong profit margins for its operations. By 1991, the company was strong enough financially to be listed on the Madrid Stock Exchange. The company then made an attempt to enter a number of other, related high-margin areas, such as building its own real estate portfolio. In 1991, the company joined with the United Kingdom's Northumbrian Water to develop a water distribution business for the Spanish market. Into the mid-1990s, the company remained a medium-sized business, posting annual revenues of the equivalent of just EUR 135 million.

Consolidating to Survive in the 1990s

Spain's entry into the European Union and the requirements of the Maastricht Treaty introduced a new era in the Spanish construction sector. Among other requirements, the Spanish government was required to reduce its level of public works spending significantly. As a result, the Spanish government inaugurated a new policy of transferring an increasing number of public works and infrastructure projects to the private sector. This decision, while opening the market for new projects to a variety of players, including banks and larger corporations, as well the construction groups themselves, nevertheless presented a significant hurdle to potential players. Companies were now expected to finance the construction of new projects from their own treasuries. At the same time, regional governments, which took over the awarding of civil contracts, began demanding that potential candidates establish a permanent presence in the region.

The new industry situation meant that companies hoping to establish themselves as a major players in the national construction market had no choice but to expand. Not only were companies required to expand geographically, in order to provide

national coverage, they were also forced to build up the scale of their operations in order to develop the financing necessary to compete for and carry out new projects. The consolidation of the Spanish construction sector began in earnest in the mid-1990s. By the end of the decade, the sector, which previously counted nearly 30 larger groups, had been reduced to just 11 major players.

Obrascon emerged as one of the leaders of the consolidation effort. Abandoning its commitment to the high-margin, short-term profit-driven strategy that had enabled the group to rebound into the 1990s, the company launched a series of acquisitions, starting with the purchase of Elsan in 1996. That business posted revenues roughly equivalent to Obrascon's, although at lower profit levels. The addition of Elsan, however, added its specialty in asphalt-based construction, including roads, airports, parking lots and the like. Elsan also brought its subsidiary, Fernandez Constructor, which offered its specialty in bridge and special structures.

After spending some ESP 1.5 billion acquiring Elsan, the company closed out 1996 with the ESP 1 billion purchase of SATO. That company specialized in ports and other maritime and coastal civil works projects. Also that year, Obrascon announced its intention to sell off its real estate division and to exit the water distribution market. Instead, the company turned to the waste treatment sector, more closely related to its construction operations, acquiring 60 percent of Cida Hidroquimica. Also in 1996, Obrascon acquired a 40 percent stake in Ondagua, a company specialized in urban services infrastructure and water treatment. The company bought full control of Ondagua in 1998.

International Player in the 2000s

Villar Mir, who had in the meantime had orchestrated the rescue of a number of the failing companies, brought that specialty to Obrascon's benefit in 1997, acquiring, at first on a personal basis, a major stake in struggling construction rival Huarte. Established in 1927 by two Pamplona based families, Huarte had grown into one of the Spanish construction sectors major players. Into the mid-1990s, however, Huarte stumbled, and by 1995 the company had been forced to seek bankruptcy protection. The following year, Huarte and Obrascon began developing a working relationship, leading to Villar Mir's acquisition of a major stake in Huarte. As part of that purchase, Huarte's capitalization was reduced to zero, absorbing the group's debts.

The merger between Obrascon and the larger Huarte was carried out in 1998. The move reduced Villar Mir's stake in the newly renamed Obrascon Huarte to below 50 percent. Yet the company now emerged as one of the top ten Spanish construction groups. Obrascon also continued to build out its regional coverage, acquiring Malvar in 1999, and adding that group's focus on the Galicia region.

Obrascon continued to seek scale amid the general Spanish consolidation effort. The company found the next piece in its puzzle in 1999, when it agreed to merge with rival group Construcciones Lain, in a deal worth some $900 million. Lain had been founded in 1963 as the Spanish arm of British construction group John Laing Construction. Laing exited Spain in 1988, selling the Spanish subsidiary to a management buyout,

Key Dates:

1911: Sociedad General de Obras y Construcciones Obrascón S.A in Bilbao, Spain.
1912: First contract to build two ports in Lisbon, Portugal.
1918: First North African construction projects.
1960s: Transitions from ports specialist to general construction.
1987: Juan Miguel Villar Mir acquires Obrascon for one peseta.
1991: Obrascon listed on Madrid stock exchange.
1996: Launches drive to build scale and acquires Elsan, a road building specialist.
1998: Merger with Huarte, founded in 1927.
1999: Merger with Construcciones Lain, founded in 1963.
2003: Acquires controlling stake in ZS Brno, a leading construction group in Czech Republic, as part of effort to expand into Eastern European market.
2005: Announces plans to list Brazilian subsidiary on Sao Paulo stock exchange.

which renamed the company as Construcciones Lain, then took it public in 1991. Lain too had launched an effort to acquire scale in the mid-1990s, buying up railway construction specialist Guinovart in 1995, the moving into the Basque region with the purchase of Sobrino in 1996. In 1998, Lain merged with Pacsa, a diversified group engaged in general construction, road building and renovation.

The merged Obrascon Huarte Lain (OHL) became Spain's fifth-largest construction group. OHL also established a clear strategy to become a diversified construction group for the new century, and especially targeting high-margin, high-growth areas such as urban services, and ''social'' construction— including hotel and tourism infrastructure projects, as well as shopping centers and retirement facilities and the like.

As it turned toward the new century, OHL also adopted a renewed strategy of international growth. As part of this effort, the company especially targeted the Latin American and North African markets. OHL at first focused on building up its road-building and toll road management and maintenance business, acquiring Chile's Infrasestructura 2000 from Endesa Chile, and its operations of the highway between Santiago and San Antonio, and the construction of the highway linking Santiago-Colina and Los Andes. The company also bought majority control of the AEC consortium building the Ezeiza-Canuelas freeway. In that year, also, the company briefly entered talks to acquire troubled Mexican construction group Tribasa. Those talks fell through, however.

By 2001, OHL had also begun to roll out an ambitious diversification strategy, announcing that it had developed plans for some US $1 billion in investments in Mexico alone for that year. The company also acquired parking lots operations in Santiago, and in 2002, the company also announced its intention to expand its presence in that sector.

OHL took a break from its South American expansion in 2003 to turn its sights on the promising Eastern European

market. As a first step toward a proposed regional expansion effort, the company acquired a 61.1 percent stake in ZPSV Uhersky Ostroh, which owned ZS Brno, one of the leading construction groups in the Czech Republic.

In 2004, OHL stepped up its fast-developing hotel construction operations, announcing a new US$ 1 billion investment program to build up to four luxury hotels. That effort came as part of a strategic alliance with Fairmont Hotels & Resorts, and the Rosewood and Starwood hotel groups. Among the alliance's project was the construction of a two May Koba-branded hotels along the Mayan Riviera.

By 2005, OHL's Latin American operations included three highways, for a total of 909 kilometers, in Brazil as well. In that year, the company announced its plans to list its Brazilian subsidiary on the Sao Paulo exchange, as part of an effort to boost its operations in that country. OHL had successfully transformed itself from a mid-sized company in the Spanish market to a fast-growing, diversified player on the international construction market.

Principal Subsidiaries

Ambient Serviços Ambientais De Riberao Preto S.A. (Ambient); Autopista Del Sol S.A.; Autopista De Los Libertadores S.A.; Autopista Los Andes S.A. (Chile); Autopista Eje Aeropuerto CESA; Autopista Ezeiza Cañuelas S.A. (Aecsa) (Argentina); Autovias S.A (Brazil); Avalora, Tecnologías De La Información S.A.; Centrovias Sistemas Rodoviarios S.A. (Brazil); Concesionaria Mexiquense SA de CV (Mexico); Construcciones Adolfo Sobrino S.A.; Construcciones Enrique de Luis S.A. (Celsa); Desalant. S.A. (Chile); Desalinizadora Arica Ltda. (Desalari) (Chile); Electrificaciones Y Montajes Guinovart S.A.; Elsan-Pacsa S.A.; Ingenieria De Los Recursos Naturales S.A. (Irena); Inima Servicios Europeos De Medio Ambiente S.A.; Inima Usa Corporation; Jose Malvar Construcciones S.A.; Morkaitz S.A.; Muelles Y Espacios Portuarios S.A.; Ohl Central Europe, A.S. (Czech Republic); Ohl Concesiones, S.L.; Pabellon Cuauhtemoc SA de CV (Mexico); S.A. Trabajos Y Obras; Terminales Marítimas Del Sureste S.A.; Žsbrno, A.S. (Czech Republic); Žspv Uherský Ostroh A.S. (Czech Republic).

Principal Competitors

ENCOL S.A.; Roggio E Hijos Benito S.A.; Fomento de Construcciones y Contratas S.A.; Construtora Lider Ltda.; CMB S.A.; El Corte Ingles S.A.; ACS Actividades de Construccion y Servicios S.A.; Sacyr Vallehermoso S.A; Acciona S.A.; Sociedad General de Aguas de Barcelona S.A.; Abengoa S.A.;

Further Reading

Becker, Robert, ''Spanish OHL to Build Hotels in Mayan Riviera,'' *El Economista*, February 9, 2004.
Davis, Paul, ''OHL May Sell Off Water Environ Subsidiary,'' *Business News Americas*, July 1, 2003.
Johnstone, Chris, ''Spain's Obrascon Huarte Lain Buys Majority Stake in Brno Building Group,'' *Prague Business Journal*, April 21, 2003.
''Juan Miguel Villar Mir: Visión para hacer fácil lo difícil,'' *El Mundo*, October 3, 1999.

''OHL Invests US$1.0 billion in Tourism Sector,'' *Internet Securities*, February 7, 2004.

''OHL Looks to Raise US$222mn in IPO – Brazil,'' *America's Intelligence Wire,* June 29, 2005.

''Spain's OHL Talks Up Mexico Plans,'' *Internet Securities*, November 26, 2001.

''Spain's OHL to Control ZS Brno Through Purchase of ZPSV Group,'' *Europe Intelligence Wire*, April 14, 2003.

Tizón, Alvaro, ''El Empresario que surgió de la crisis,'' *El Mundo*, February 7, 1999.

—M.L. Cohen

expect the world from us

The Oppenheimer Group

11 Burbidge Street, Suite 101
Coquitlab, British Columbia V3K 7B2
Canada
Telephone: (604) 461-6779
Toll Free: (888) 321-6779
Fax: (604) 468-4780
Web site: http://www.oppyproduce.com

Private Company
Founded: 1858 as Oppenheimer Bros. and Company
Employees: 215
Sales: $415 million (2004)
NAIC: 422480 Fresh Fruit and Vegetable Wholesalers

Based near Vancouver, British Columbia, Canada, and privately owned, The Oppenheimer Group is composed of three companies. David Oppenheimer & Associates (Canada) and David Oppenheimer & Co. LLC (United States) combine to make one of North America's largest distributors of produce, offering more than 100 varieties of fresh fruits and vegetables from some 25 countries, including an increasing number of its own branded items. Offices are located in Vancouver and Calgary in Canada, as well as U.S. cities Seattle, Washington; Los Angeles and Visalia, California; Nogales, Arizona; Houston, Texas; Chicago, Illinois; Wilmington, Delaware; and Miami and Tampa, Florida. Oppenheimer also maintains a procurement office in Santiago, Chile. The third Oppenheimer company is David Oppenheimer Transport, a ground transportation company that operates out of the Vancouver, Los Angeles, and Wilmington offices. Oppenheimer is well known in its field, responsible over the years for the introduction of a number of fruits and vegetables to North America, including Granny Smith apples and kiwifruit.

Founders Immigrating to North America in the Mid-1800s

The origins of The Oppenheimer Group date to 1848 when five brothers—David, Charles, Godfrey, and Isaac Oppenheimer, as well as their brother Meyer, who was often neglected by historians—left Bavaria as young men to escape the persecution visited upon German Jews during that era. They originally settled in New Orleans, Louisiana before relocating to Sacramento, California at the height of the gold rush. The sons of a wine dealer, they elected to pursue careers as merchants catering to the miners rather than prospecting for gold themselves. Meyer launched a successful business in Sacramento, while David and his wife ran a hotel in the nearby town of Columbia. After the California gold fields were played out, many of the miners headed north to take part in the Fraser River Gold Rush in British Columbia, and in 1858 the Oppenheimers followed to supply their needs. Charles arrived first and established a trading business known as Charles Oppenheimer and Co. The family partnership expanded when David and Isaac Oppenheimer opened a general store in Yale, British Columbia, to outfit prospectors, and soon expanded to other mining camps, such as Fort Hope and Lytton. In 1858 the brothers formed Oppenheimer Bros. and Company, a full-service grocery company to supply their stores. As the gold rush moved north, the brothers opened a store in Barkerville in 1862.

Charles withdrew from the family business to take on a contract to build a road through the region, leading to the company changing its name to Oppenheimer & Co. Charles would later move back to San Francisco, where he died in 1890. Godfrey died in 1880, leaving David and Isaac Oppenheimer as partners. As the northern gold rush waned in the mid-1880s, the brothers elected to stay in British Columbia, as did a large number of miners. David and Isaac settled in Vancouver in 1885, where they established the first wholesale provisionary warehouse in the city's first brick building, and also became civic leaders and played a key role in the incorporation of Vancouver in 1886. They had already become large landowners in the city through their Vancouver Improvement Company and had been actively promoting Vancouver as the ideal location for the Pacific terminus of the Canadian Pacific Railway (CPR), Canada's first transcontinental railroad. Not only would they become wealthy from their real estate holdings when Vancouver indeed became the CPR's West Coast anchor, they prospered by supplying provisions to the road builders. David Oppenheimer was elected as Vancouver's mayor from 1888 to 1891 and was responsible for so many improvements in the city

---

Company Perspectives:

We've built our company on determination, innovation and trust. For nearly a century and a half, we've been pioneering new fresh produce varieties, nurturing direct relationships between the world's leading growers and North American retailers, cultivating sophisticated delivery networks and setting standards for food safety and quality. This depth of experience now provides us—and our customers—with a world of advantages.

---

that he would be regarded by many as a founding father of Vancouver. He would die in 1897 at the age of 63. Isaac left Vancouver four years later, eventually settled in Spokane, Washington, and died in 1922 at the age of 88.

The Oppenheimer brothers left a thriving grocery wholesale business to their descendants and also established a tradition of introducing new fruits and vegetables. In 1884 the family firm forged an alliance with the Japan Fruit Growers Cooperative and began importing mandarin oranges, each piece of fruit wrapped in tissue and packed in a wooden box. The oranges were originally sent to Canada as gifts for relatives who came to work on the CPR, but they would become part of the Christmas tradition in western Canada, as children looked forward to the Christmas orange in their stocking, and the boxes they came in would be transformed into treasure chests, doll houses, and sleds.

Produce Gaining in Importance: 1920s and 1930s

Produce eventually became such a major part of Oppenheimer's grocery distribution business, enjoying strong growth in the 1920s and 1930s, that a separate department was created and served as a sales agent for growers. With the advent of World War II, the longstanding ties with Japanese exporters had to be severed and mandarin oranges went missing from Christmas for a few seasons. When trade resumed after the war, Oppenheimer quickly reestablished its relationship with the Japanese growers. In the days before refrigerated trains, Oppenheimer commissioned special trains, the cars painted orange, to take the oranges straight from the ships to the eastern Canadian cities, where the residents knew the holiday oranges had arrived by the sight of the brightly colored railcars.

The 1950s was a decade of strong growth for Oppenheimer's produce business. In addition to sourcing produce, the company became increasingly involved in produce merchandising and promotional campaigns, which included in-store materials. A major reason for this expanded operation was the arrival during the 1950s of southern hemisphere Chilean and New Zealand produce, much of which was new to North American consumers, who would have to be educated and urged to give the new items a try. Chile began exporting a variety of products to North America during this period, including onions, honeydew, melons, and garlic. Chile is uniquely positioned to supply North America because of its unusual north-south geography. The country is composed of six distinct climatic regions, stretching some 1,200 kilometers. As a result, the harvest of fruits and vegetables is staggered, allowing Chile to supply produce to

markets over an extended period of time. Moreover, because Chile is located in the southern hemisphere it became an ideal source of produce during the winter months for North America. Each year, Chile increased its volume of produce as well as its variety. The availability of refrigerated shipping space was also a key factor, as the amount of Chilean produce shipped to North America increased dramatically in the early 1960s.

Oppenheimer also established ties to New Zealand in the 1950s and, by chance more than design, was responsible for the introduction of the Granny Smith apple to North America. A shipment of 5,000 cases of the tart, green apples bound for Hawaii was diverted to Vancouver because of a longshoreman strike in Hawaii. Oppenheimer's salesmen pitched the new variety to retailers with the slogan, "not every green apple will give you a bellyache." In just one week they sold the errant shipment, and then in the following season the company sold the apple throughout Canada as well as the West Coast of the United States. Soon the Granny Smith apple was introduced to the rest of North America. Oppenheimer's success also forged a bond with New Zealand growers that led to the introduction of more than a dozen other apples to North America, including Royal Gala, Braeburn, Fuji, Pacific Rose, and Jazz. Taylor's Gold pears from New Zealand also would be marketed by Oppenheimer.

By the early 1960s the produce industry was undergoing a sea change, moving from a regional business to a global one. Not only was there jet transportation capable of supplying North America with produce from around the world, but the grocery industry was undergoing consolidation, and retail chains were interested in differentiating themselves by offering greater variety as well as extending the seasonality of produce. In 1962 the Oppenheimer produce operation had grown large enough that the family company was reorganized, divided into two separate companies: the grocery brokerage business of David Oppenheimer Bros. & Company, Ltd., and David Oppenheimer and Associates to concentrate on produce. The latter would be led by David Oppenheimer III, a grandson of one of the original Oppenheimer brothers. The newly independent company soon had it first marketing success, again courtesy of New Zealand growers, when in 1963 it introduced western Canadians to kiwifruit and also sold it to markets in the northwestern United States and California. At the time it was known as "Chinese gooseberry," a name not easily marketed. As a result, the fruit would be named after New Zealand's national bird, the kiwi, thus becoming kiwifruit, which gradually gained in popularity.

The next major step in the expansion of Oppenheimer came in 1985 when the company formed a U.S. subsidiary, David Oppenheimer & Co. L.L.C., and opened its first office in Seattle, Washington. Over the next seven years six more U.S. offices were opened in strategic locations as Oppenheimer expanded to serve new markets.

With that expansion came the need for a consolidated approach to ground transportation to manage the movement of produce across the continent. In 1993 David Oppenheimer Transport was formed and established operations in Oppenheimer's Wilmington, Delaware, office. At this point, the David Oppenheimer Group was formed to serve as a holding company

Key Dates:

1848: The Oppenheimer brothers immigrate to North America.
1858: Oppenheimer Bros. and Company is founded in British Columbia.
1885: Business operations move to Vancouver.
1962: The produce business is split off as David Oppenheimer and Associates.
1985: The first U.S. subsidiary opens in Seattle.
1993: The David Oppenheimer Group is formed as a holding company for three related subsidiaries.
2002: The name is shortened to The Oppenheimer Group.

for David Oppenheimer & Associates, David Oppenheimer & Co. LLC, and David Oppenheimer Transport. Initially limited to serving the East Coast of the United States, David Oppenheimer Transport would establish operations in Los Angeles, California in 2002, to serve the markets of the U.S. West Coast. Two years later, another branch was established in Vancouver to service the western part of Canada.

New CEO in the Early 1990s

In 1993, Oppenheimer's current president, chief executive officer, and chairman, John Anderson, was named CEO. He literally worked his way up through the organization. When he was a teenager and helping his father set up equipment for a figure skating and concert event, his hard work caught the eyes of an Oppenheimer executive who offered him a job. Anderson was uninterested, intent on following his dream of becoming an airline pilot. He was only looking for part-time employment as he devoted as much time as possible to flight training. A strike at the Safeway supermarket chain prompted the young man's contact at Oppenheimer to call him up to offer him work unloading a railcar, which turned out to be packed with broccoli, cauliflower, and ice. In just two hours Anderson managed to shovel out the car. His hard work once again prompted a job offer that he once more refused.

At the age of 18 Anderson began his own one-aircraft airline, but when that did not succeed he went to work for Oppenheimer with the understanding that he would eventually leave to be an airline pilot. While he pursued his lifelong dream, Anderson worked his way up from the loading docks at Oppenheimer to a sales job and then management. Then, just when he was on the verge of taking a job with an airline, Oppenheimer made him a counteroffer, eager to keep Anderson and promising him that there was no limit to how high he could rise in the organization. It was Anderson who opened and managed the Seattle office in 1985. He became chief operating officer in 1988 and by 1992 opened and managed another six U.S. offices. In 1980, Anderson realized his original dream and founded a successful charter airline service in Vancouver, Anderson Air. The company would service Oppenheimer employees along with many other companies in British Columbia and beyond.

When Anderson became CEO in 1993, he took over a company that was rich in history as well as baggage. According to

BC Business, "Anderson concluded that almost a century-and-a-half's worth of corporate culture was going to have to be overhauled in order to drag the company into the 21st century." He explained, "I could see it was getting to be a global business and we had to become a full-service international marketer so that we would be able to control our own destiny, as opposed to somebody else controlling it for us. That meant getting into transportation, quality control, marketing, promotions, warehousing, all the things we weren't in before." To sell his vision to the rank and file, Anderson visited each of the offices and met with every manager. According to *BC Business,* he allowed "them to voice their concerns, but [demanded] hard work and loyalty once the course had been set."

To reach the next level, Oppenheimer upgraded its technology infrastructure. In 1996, the company launched a custom-designed management information system that was the envy of the produce industry. Oppenheimer's advanced technology provided a competitive edge in an increasingly global market, allowing it to realize economies of scale by integrating its worldwide supply base and bring all of its marketing resources to bear to provide value-added services to its retail and foodservice customers. The system became so advanced that the company could take a box of its fruit from a store and trace it back to the section of the farm on which it was grown.

Later in the 1990s Anderson changed the way the company approached its business, adopting the concept of category management. Deal managers now became category managers, responsible for a single product category. In this way the unique needs of a particular product could be addressed, including quality control, the proper way to transport it, and market it. By 2000 Oppenheimer had established several main product categories with year-round availability, including pipfruit (apples and pears), stone fruit, citrus, grapes, kiwifruit, mangoes, pineapple, and greenhouse-grown vegetables. Products with more limited availability continued to be coordinated by deal.

In 2002 the David Oppenheimer Group shortened its name to The Oppenheimer Group and introduced a new corporate logo, the first change in the logo in about 20 years. A year later the logo would begin to enjoy greater visibility as the company introduced the first Oppenheimer-branded packaging. Further branding work took place in 2004 with the unveiling of a brand promise, "expect the world from us," which replaced the phrase, "International Marketers of Fresh Produce," at the foot of the new logo. With a refined image and solid long-term relationships with both growers around the world and North American foodservice customers and retailers, supported by a robust infrastructure, Oppenheimer appeared poised to enjoy even greater prosperity in the future.

Principal Subsidiaries

David Oppenheimer & Associates (Canada); David Oppenheimer & Co. LLC (United States); David Oppenheimer Transport.

Principal Competitors

Dominion Citrus Ltd.; Fresh Del Monte Produce Inc.; Services Group of America.

298   **The Oppenheimer Group**

Further Reading

Christmas, Jane, ''David Oppenheimer Group,'' *Financial Post,* December 12, 2001, p. SR4.

MacNeill, Ian, ''The Sky's the Limit,'' *BC Business,* October 2002, p. 60.

''The Oppenheimer Group,'' *Food Institute Report,* January 31, 2005, p. 6.

''The Oppenheimer Group Unveils New Look,'' *Produce News,* January 29, 2002.

—Ed Dinger

Orrick, Herrington and Sutcliffe LLP

405 Howard Street
San Francisco, California 94105-2625
U.S.A.
Telephone: (415) 773-5700
Fax: (415) 773.5759
Web site: http://www.orrick.com

Private Company
Founded: 1885 as Jarboe, Harrison & Goodfellow
Employees: 800
Sales: $448 million (2003)
NAIC: 541110 Offices of Lawyers

A long-time San Francisco law firm known for its work in municipal bonds, Orrick, Herrington and Sutcliffe LLP has grown aggressively since the early 1990s, adding a variety of practices and opening offices around the world. The firm employs some 750 lawyers in 13 practice areas. Transactional practices include Bankruptcy and Debt Restructuring, Compensation and Benefits, Corporate Global Finance, Mergers and Acquisitions, Public Finance, Structured Finance, Real Estate, and Tax. Litigation practices include Litigation, Intellectual Property, Employment Law, and Securities Litigation. Clients include the likes of Salomon Smith Barney, Charles Schwab, and IBM. In addition to its San Francisco headquarters, Orrick maintains domestic offices in New York (largest in size), Los Angeles, Orange County, Sacramento, Silicon Valley, the Pacific Northwest, and Washington, D.C. International offices are located in London, Paris, Milan, Rome, Moscow Hong Kong, Taipei, and Tokyo. The driving force behind the firm's expansion is chief executive officer Ralph H. Baxter, Jr., who took the helm in 1990.

Firm Origins Date to 1860s

Orrick traces its lineage to attorney John R. Jarboe, Jr. He was born in 1836 in Maryland of French descent (his family had accompanied Lord Baltimore when he founded the city that bore his name) and spoke French as his native tongue. Injured as a child, he was confined to bed for three years and became quite studious. Although the youngest member of his class at Yale University, he graduated near the top in 1855. A year later he moved to California and taught briefly before deciding to study law in the San Francisco office of Jesse B. Hart, at a time when there were no law schools and attorneys "read" with those already established in the profession. In 1858 he became a clerk at Shattuck, Spencer & Reichert and in that same year was admitted to the bar and soon became a practicing attorney. According to company lore his examiners were so impressed by his knowledge of the law they dropped the subject and asked if the young man knew how to make a brandy punch. He replied that he did not, but confided that he had discovered an excellent one was served at a saloon across the street, adding, "And I would be pleased if the learned committee would join me in testing one." The attorneys quickly agreed upon a change of venue.

Upon Reichert's death, the firm became Spencer & Jarboe, and following Spencer's death Jarboe practiced on his own for about eight months, his specialty real estate, before taking on partners. He became partners with Ralph C. Harrison in 1867, and they worked together until Harrison was elected to the Supreme Bench of the State. W.S. Goodfellow would join them, and in 1885 they founded Jarboe, Harrison & Goodfellow, the firm that Orrick considered its forefather. In 1891 Harrison was elected a justice to the California Supreme Court, and the partnership was dissolved. Two years later, Jarboe, always of poor health, died at the age of 57.

William Orrick Joins Firm in Early 1900s

Goodfellow carried on the firm's tradition, and in 1901 formed a new partnership with Charles Eells, who would play an important role following the 1906 earthquake that leveled San Francisco. Eells helped to save Fireman's Fund Insurance Company by implementing a reorganization plan that allowed the insurer to pay off some of its claims with company stock. The behind the Orrick name, William H. Orrick, joined the firm in 1910, the beginning of a 50-year tenure that would last until he was well into his 80s. Another attorney, Stanley Moore, joined the firm in 1914, and in that year the partnership changed its name to Goodfellow, Eells, Moore & Orrick.

The Herrington in Orrick, Herrington and Sutcliffe LLP was George Herrington who became a partner in 1927 and joined the

---

Company Perspectives:

The firm exists to help our clients achieve their goals and solve their problems by performing effective, challenging and innovative legal work on their behalf, with financial results that will permit the firm to advance and flourish.

---

firm under unusual circumstance. Orrick was well known for his insistence on thoroughly researching his subjects, notorious for the prodigious assignments he gave to associates, but he also demanded as much effort from himself. While Herrington studied law at the University of California, Berkeley's School of Law—Boalt Hall, he worked part-time at the library, charged with opening it on Sunday mornings. One more than one occasion he found Orrick sitting on the steps waiting to get in. Years later Orrick would quip that he only hired Herrington to make sure he showed up to work on time.

Five years after Herrington, Eric Sutcliffe joined the firm in 1932. During this period the firm became involved in one of the most high profile bond issues in its history: the building of the Golden Gate Bridge. While Sutcliffe contributed to the effort by providing research, Herrington played a key part in making sure the bridge was built. The Golden Gate Ferry Company, backed by the deep pockets of its corporate parent, the Southern Pacific Railroad, fought against the bridge project which threatened to undercut its business and challenged the bond issue. When it ultimately passed, Herrington's reputation was established and the firm became a major West Coast law firm.

Sutcliffe would play a more prominent role in the future, however. In 1947 he became the firm's managing partner, the start of a 30-year tenure at the top. The modern era of the firm, which after a regular shuffle of partners settled on its present name in 1980, began after Sutcliffe's retirement. At the time, Orrick was a quiet, conservative law firm, content to stick to its knitting in San Francisco.

Orrick did not open its second office until 1983 when it set up shop in Sacramento. A new chairman, William McKee, appointed a year later had more ambitious goals. He had been with the firm since 1950 and was responsible for launching Orrick's tax practice. During his term as chairman from 1984 to 1986, McKee oversaw the upgrading of the firm's time-keeping methods and merit-based compensation, and modernized the business practices. He also opened the firm's first non-California office, establishing an important beachhead in New York City. Taking advantage of its reputation in California municipal bonds, Orrick was able to recruit half-a-dozen lawyers from a major New York law firm, Brown & Wood. While Orrick looked to make inroads with New York financial companies, other major San Francisco law firms were building up their Silicon Valley offices to attract more business from the high-technology sector. Orrick opted to stay out of Silicon Valley, a questionable move at the time, and instead opened an office in Los Angeles in 1985.

Orrick's prospects in the New York market appeared dim after the passage of the 1986 Tax Reform Act, which curtailed the number of tax-exempt bonds and set limits on legal fees on bonds issued for private development projects. Business in this area was also adversely impacted by uncertain interest rates that scared off many insurance companies. Small firms exited the bond business, larger firms cut back, and Orrick was close to shuttering its New York office. Instead, it decided to expand, diversify the practice and also beef up its public finance practice. A key move came in July 1987 when Orrick lured away nine bond specialists from Hawkins Delafield, bringing with them some major clients, including New York City's Municipal Assistance Corp. and the Port Authority of New York and New Jersey. As a result, business surged and in 1988 Orrick was involved in more bond business than any law firm in the country, according to trade newspaper *The Bond Buyer,* after ranking fourth the year before. The momentum stalled for the New York office by the end of the decade, and the firm was at a crossroads. It experienced some lackluster years, the average per partner profits dropped well below other leading San Francisco law firms, and some key lawyers defected.

New Chairman Leads Firm Into the 1990s

In 1990 the Orrick partners elected Ralph H. Baxter, Jr., a labor litigator, as their new chairman. He quickly took steps to improve the firm's balance sheet and grow partner profits to a much high level. He cut staff and eased out partners who were not producing enough work, and he also embraced a strategy of geographic expansion and placed less emphasis on the San Francisco market. At the time Los Angeles had 30 lawyers, New York 50, and San Francisco 175. Baxter's goal was to build the Los Angeles and New York offices to the same size as San Francisco. Because the California economy soon slowed, Baxter had to adjust his plans, cutting back on his Los Angeles aspiration. In 1983 Orrick opened a Washington, D.C., office, but New York remained the key to the firm's future. According to Krysten Crawford, wiring for *The American Lawyer* in a 1998 profile on Baxter, "As the financial center of the world, New York is where the deals get done—the mergers, the project financings, the securitizations. New York is also the link to other markets such as London, Hong Kong, and Latin American. In Baxter's mind, a firm that seeks to be a global player—a truly exceptional law firm—must first make a stand in New York."

Orrick used its ties to investment banks to build up existing practices and add others in New York. The first target was securitization (turning loans, mortgages, and the like into tradable securities), followed by project finance. The firm's success in New York in these areas then served to reinforce Orrick's position on the West Coast in securitization work. The size of the New York office grew steadily in the 1990s, reaching 165 lawyers by 1998 to become larger than the San Francisco office, which now employed 155 lawyers.

The 1990s also saw Orrick make a belated entry into the Silicon Valley. By this point its rivals had long since carved up the best corporate work, so in 1995 Orrick's new Palo Alto office focused on intellectual property litigation. To jumpstart the practice, the firm lured a high-profile litigation lawyer, Terrence McMahon, from a chief rival. McMahon, nicknamed "Mad Dog," was an impressive calling card for the office. "We don't intend to be a quiet, insignificant member of Silicon Valley," Baxter told *San Francisco Business Times.* "And Terry is far from quiet and insignificant."

Key Dates:

1885: Law firm Jarboe, Harrison & Goodfellow established in San Francisco.
1910: William H. Orrick joins firm.
1927: George Herrington named partner.
1932: Eric Sutcliffe joins firm.
1947: Sutcliffe begins 30-year tenure as firm's managing partner.
1980: Firms settles on name: Orrick, Herrington and Sutcliffe LLP.
1984: New York office opens.
1990: Ralph H. Baxter, Jr., named chairman.
1995: Silicon Valley office opens.
1998: London office opens.
2002: Paris office opens.
2005: Offices in Moscow and Hong Kong open.

One area sorely lacking in the late 1990s was Orrick's litigation capability. To address that need, Orrick entered into talks in 1987 to merge with an old-line New York law firm Donovan, Leisure, Newton & Irvine, which had been struggling since a decline in antitrust work in the 1980s and was now considered too small by many potential clients. It appeared to be a good fit for both firms, and Donovan, Leisure's partner voted to approve the merger, but talks faltered in early 1998, due in large part, according to press accounts, to a legal conflict: Donovan, Leisure was being sued by a mutual client. In the end, about 40 of Donovan, Leisure's 60 lawyers were hired by Orrick, which essentially took the ones it wanted, and Donovan, Leisure was dissolved. As a result, Baxter told the press, "We will now have one of the most complete law practices in New York City." While Orrick was acquiring a litigation practice, it was also taking steps to become an international law firm. A Tokyo office was opened in 1997, followed by a London office in 1998.

Orrick continued its aggressive expansion with the start of the 2000s, looking to grow both domestically and overseas. The firm opened an office in Seattle in 2000 to mainly seek work from clients involved in the Internet and telecommunications industries. To beef up its Pacific Northwest presence, Orrick looked to add to its roster of lawyers. It soon identified a group of lawyers employed in Portland, Oregon-based Ater Wynne LLP, who were hired away in March 2003. Most of the lawyers worked in Ater Wynne's finance group, but what made them especially attractive was their involvement in the fast growing practice of Indian tribal deals, an area Orrick had begun to

purse. In one stroke, the firm became a leader in the practice area. Also in the United States during this period, Orrick opened an office in Orange County, California, by acquiring intellectual property lawyers from the firm Lyon & Lyon.

Orrick was even more aggressive on the international front in the early 2000s. In 2002 it established an office in Paris by acquiring the 42-lawyer operation of Watson, Farley & Williams. It would focus on cross border and domestic transactions involving structured finance, leasing, and asset financing. A year later, Orrick hired 23 lawyers from Ernst & Young legal affiliate Studio Legale Tributario and opened an office in Milan, Italy, to help the firm in its cross-border business in Europe and Asia. In 2004 a Rome office was added through the hiring of the 16-lawyer firm Studio Legale e Tributario, which focused on banking and finance and administrative law. In that same year, the Tokyo office expanded, hiring a number of lawyers, including its first partner to deal with South Korea. Orrick opened an office in Moscow in 2005, and supplemented it with the launch of a Russian practice in London and Washington, D.C. By acquiring a 25 lawyer group from Coudert Brothers in 2005, Orrick also opened an office in Hong Kong, which gave it entry to the potentially lucrative market of the People's Republic of China.

Principal Operating Units

Transactional Practices; Litigation Practices.

Principal Competitors

Clifford Chance LLP; Pillsbury Winthrop Shaw Pittman LLP; Skadden, Arps, Slate, Meagher & Flom LLP.

Further Reading

Crawford, Krysten, "The House That Ralph Built," *The American Lawyer,* March 1998, p. 50.
Dockser, Amy, "Orrick Herrington Led U.S. Law Firms In Volume of Municipal Bond Work in '88," *Wall Street Journal,* January 9, 1989, p. 1.
Hogarth, Marie-Anne, "William McKee, 78, Orrick Partner and Firm Chairman," *The Recorder,* October 29, 2004.
Kellher, Kevin, "Orrick, Herrington Joins Silicon Valley's legal Fray," *San Francisco Business,* March 24, 1995, p. 1.
Pearlman, Laura, "Alas, Poor Orrick," *American Lawyer,* May 2001, p. 21.
Petersen, Melody, "Donovan, Leisure, Old-Line Law Firm, to Shut Its Doors," *New York Times,* April 20, 1998, p. D2.
Rauber, Chris, "Orrick Eschews Overseas Offices for U.S. Growth," *San Francisco Business,* September 6, 1991, p. 17.

—Ed Dinger

Pappas Restaurants, Inc.

642 Yale Street
Houston, Texas 77007-2534
U.S.A.
Telephone: (713) 869-0151
Fax: (713) 869-4932
Web site: http://www.pappas.com

Private Company
Founded: 1976
Employees: 10,000
Sales: $320 million (2003)
NAIC: 722110 Full-Service Restaurants; 722212 Cafeterias

The family-owned Pappas Restaurants, Inc., chain operates in more than 60 locations in Houston, Dallas, Austin, San Antonio, Beaumont, Atlanta, Chicago, Denver, and Phoenix. The restaurants encompass a variety of concepts, including Pappas Bros. Steakhouse, C&H Steakhouse, Pappadeaux Seafood Kitchen, Pappas Seafood House, Pappasito's Cantina, Pappas Bar-B-Q, Pappas Burger, Pappas Pizza, Yia Yia Marys. The company is run by brothers Christopher and Harris Pappas, who also serve as the executive team at Luby's, Inc., a cafeteria chain in several states.

Origins

The origins of the family-operated Pappas Restaurants date back several generations, beginning with H.D. Pappas, who emigrated from Greece in 1897 and opened restaurants in Arkansas, Tennessee, and Texas. In 1945, H.D. Pappas's sons, Pete and Jim, moved to Houston where they obtained a franchise to sell beer coolers in South Texas. The brothers eventually built the venture into a successful restaurant supply business, selling chairs, booths, refrigerators, and other kitchen equipment. The business was cyclical, however, and the brothers soon decided to try the restaurant field in 1967 with the opening of a Dot Coffee Shop in downtown Houston. In 1970, Jim Pappas's son, Harris, joined the family business, soon followed by his other sons, Christopher and Greg. Although the 1970s proved to be a heyday for the restaurant business, the Pappas family largely sat out the prosperous times, preferring a more conservative approach of buying and owning property rather than leasing it. The company also pursued a strategy of expanding during economic downturns when land prices were relatively cheap and startup costs were affordable.

Beginnings of Company Growth

The company had modest success in opening and operating several casual dining spots, including two Dot Coffee Shops, a Brisket House barbecue, and the Strawberry Patch American bistro. The Pappas family also continued to operate the restaurant supply business, becoming its sole client. With the attitude that they could do things better themselves, the Pappas family built and supplied their own equipment, including wood-burning grills, chairs, sinks, and stoves. A business owned and operated by a sister, Victoria Giannukos, supplied the uniforms and awning designs. With the 1980 opening of the first Pappas Seafood House, the company realized that it had entered a lucrative market. However, the business also had its failures. In 1979, the family opened the Circus Restaurant with a Barnum & Bailey theme but terminated the venture in 1985. The company's taqueria concept called Pappatacos also proved a failure.

New Markets in the 1980s

After Jim Pappas's death in 1982, his sons aggressively expanded the business, opening up more seafood restaurants, in addition to profitable Mexican and cajun restaurants. The Pappas family eventually turned their business into a 50-unit chain worth hundreds of millions of dollars. The Pappas brothers grew the business on a tireless attention to detail, value, and service. The brothers also made their mark by offering large portions at moderate prices at restaurants with highly visible locations. What the restaurants tended to lose in higher food costs, they made up for with volume and considerable customer turnover. The company had a competitive edge on publicly owned restaurant chains, which were under pressure to build new units in a hurry and to improve their bottom lines from one quarter to the next. Unlike these competitors, the Pappas business could take its time in building a high quality restaurant, devoting as much labor to the project as was required.

In 1989, after concentrating their business in Houston where they had more than 25 Pappas dining spots, the family began expanding into Dallas and Austin. The company had several firmly established and profitable concepts, including Pappas Seafood House, Café Pappadeaux, Little Pappas Seafood Kitchen, Pappamia Cucina Italiana, Pappasito's Cantina, and Pappas Brisket House barbecue place. In 1992, the business broke into the San Antonio market with one of its Pappasito's Cantina Mexican food eateries. The company planned to open another Pappasito's and the Pappas' Cajun seafood concept, Pappadeux Seafood Kitchen, in San Antonio by the fall of 1993. Each of these restaurants included 10,000 to 12,000 square feet of space, was designed by the Pappas' architectural staff, and was built by the company's in-house construction crew.

Legal Challenges and Expansion

Amidst the company's growing success, it ran into legal woes. In 1995, the company settled a class-action complaint by the U.S. Equal Employment Opportunity Commission, claiming that four Pappas restaurants in Houston had discriminated against Hispanics, African Americans, and workers older than 40 in better-paying dining-room jobs in favor of younger, white workers. The lawsuit also alleged that the company hired mostly Hispanic workers for such jobs as dishwashers and busboys. The company settled the suit without admitting any wrongdoing. The agreement provided that Pappas Restaurant, Inc., offer dining room jobs to as many as 1,073 African Americans and 1,177 Hispanics who applied for those positions between January 1, 1988, and February 28, 1993. The agreement also stipulated that older and minority applicants who were denied jobs during that period might be eligible for monetary damages.

The company was also shaken when Greg Pappas died in a car accident on a Houston highway. With his death in February 1995, the company lost an important member of its executive team as well as its main architect.

In 1996, the company's gamble on a new concept—an upscale steakhouse with a cigar room, impressive wine cellar, and playful art—raised the business to new heights. The company opened its first Pappas Bros. Steakhouse on the spot of the Strawberry Patch American bistro, an eatery they opened in

1975 and closed in 1993 after the venture had run its course. The steakhouse represented a departure from its other causal dining restaurants and poised the company for future growth. Another Pappas Steakhouse was opened in 1998, located in the restaurant row that had developed along Northwest Highway in Dallas. The company took more than a year to build the restaurant, spending $6 million on the wine inventory alone. With a wine list of 1,600 selections, a cigar room, and other amenities, the restaurant proved a success in catering to business executives and others with a taste for fine food. At the same time, the company continued to expand its family empire with the opening of new restaurants in Chicago and Atlanta.

The company ran into more legal trouble in 1997 after a three-year federal investigation found the 54-unit restaurant chain to be in violation of federal immigration laws. In a plea bargain signed August 13, 1997, the company agreed to pay a $1.7 million fine, the largest ever in an Immigration and Naturalization Service enforcement case. Federal raids at six Pappas-owned restaurants in the Dallas area had found more than 100 undocumented workers, primarily from Mexico and Central America. In the plea bargain, the company admitted that it had hidden illegal aliens during raids and altered personnel records by changing the names of undocumented workers as they were moved from one restaurant to another.

Luby's Acquisition in the 2000s

In December 2000, the Pappas brothers acknowledged the purchase of more than a million shares of Luby's Inc., a financially troubled San Antonio-based business with a chain of cafeteria-style restaurants in ten states. Brothers Christopher and Harris Pappas bought 1.3 million shares, nearly 6 percent of Luby's stock, in increments between October 16 and December 22. At the same time, the Pappas brothers began negotiating for possible board seats, an active role in its management, and possible further investment in the company. The deal marked the Pappas brother's first ownership in a publicly traded company. Luby's stock value had plunged by more than 75 percent in three years. It had further suffered from high management turnover, declining sales, a controversial president who resigned in September 2000, and a proxy fight with a small group of shareholders who had tried to oust some of company's board members at its January annual meeting.

In March 2001, with Luby's in dire financial straights, the company named Christopher J. Pappas as company president and CEO and Harris J. Pappas as chief operating officer. The Pappas brothers also joined Luby's board of directors and agreed to invest an additional $10 million in the company. As the brothers stepped into their respective management roles, Luby's posted a second-quarter loss of $9.4 million and was in default with its syndicate of lenders. Luby's financial fortunes continued to plunge with its stock price bottoming at 95 cents a share on May 7, 2003. By August 2005, however, the Pappas brothers had begun to turn the troubled company around by investing in better kitchen facilities, introducing new food selections, and launching a new marketing campaign. When the brothers took over the company in 2001, the chain had 190 cafeteria restaurants and was assuming debt that eventually totaled $108.6 million. They decided to close 50 of the chain's worst performers and worked to cut debt to $29.8 million. In

---

Key Dates:

1897: H.D. Pappas emigrates to the United States from Greece and opens up restaurants in Arkansas, Tennessee, and Texas.
1945: H.D. Pappas's sons, Jim and Pete, enter refrigeration business in South Texas.
1976: Brothers Jim and Pete Pappas open the Dot Coffee Shop.
1989: Company expands business into Dallas and Austin.
1992: Company breaks into San Antonio market.
1995: Company settles class-action discrimination complaint by the federal government.
1996: Pappas brothers open their first upscale restaurant, Pappas Bros. Steakhouse.
1997: Company is found in violation of federal anti-immigration laws.
2001: Christopher and Harris Pappas are named executive managers of Luby's Inc.

June 2005, Luby's third-quarter sales had increased 6.5 percent to $77 million, fueled primarily by the introduction of new combo plates such as lemon basil salmon, Cajun etoufee, and sweet sesame pork. Christopher and Harris Pappas also moved Luby's headquarters from San Antonio to Houston, where the Pappas chain of restaurants was based. Although growth for the cafeteria chain remained in the distance, the Pappas brothers sought to improve profitability through increasing same store sales, improving brand through advertising, and introducing new entrees. Along with the success of their Pappas restaurant chain, the Pappas brothers appeared to be making headway in improving Luby's prospects as well.

Principal Competitors

Brinker International Inc.; Consolidated Restaurant Operations, Inc.; Landry's Restaurants, Inc.

Further Reading

Allen, Elizabeth, "Famous Houston Restaurateurs Buy Stake in San Antonio-Based Chain," *San Antonio Express-News*, December 28, 2000.

Bajaj, Vikas, "Houston Restaurateurs Buy Stock in San Antonio-Based Cafeteria Chain," *Knight Ridder/Tribune Business News*, December 27, 2000.

"Changing the Recipe," *San Antonio Express-News*, August 7, 2005.

Elder, Laura Elizabeth, "Hefty Helpings, High Volume," *Houston Business Journal*, October 25, 1996.

"Head of Luby's Hints at Menu Changes to Boost Cafeteria Chain," *Knight Ridder/Tribune Business News*, March 29, 2001.

Moore, Paula, "Pappas Poised to Shake Up City's Tex-Mex Industry," *San Antonio Business Journal*, March 27, 1992.

"Pappas Bros. Make Investment in Luby's," *PR Newswire*, December 27, 2000.

Ruggless, Ron, "Chris Pappas," *Nation's Restaurant News*, January 1997.

——, "Pappas Agrees to Pay $1.75 M for Employing Illegal Aliens," *Nation's Restaurant News*, August 25, 1997.

Tanner, Lisa, "Dining for Dollars," *Dallas Business Journal*, September 29, 2000.

"Texas Business Briefs Column," *Amarillo-Globe News*, January 2, 2001.

"Under New Management, Luby's Faces Financial Squeeze," *Austin Business Journal*, March 23, 2001.

—Bruce P. Montgomery

Picard Surgeles

37b rue Royale
Fontainebleau
France
Telephone: +33 01 64 45 14 00
Fax: +33 01 64 69 80 65
Web site: http://www.picard.fr

Private Company
Incorporated: 1920 as Les Glacières de Fointainebleau-
   Etablissements Picard
Employees: 3,000
Sales: EUR 785 million ($920 million)
NAIC: 445110 Supermarkets and Other Grocery (Except
   Convenience) Stores; 445210 Meat Markets; 445299
   All Other Specialty Food Stores; 311412 Frozen
   Specialty Food Manufacturing; 311411 Frozen Fruit,
   Juice, and Vegetable Processing; 311712 Fresh and
   Frozen Seafood Processing

Picard Surgeles is France's leading frozen foods specialist. The Fontainebleau-based company operates as both a manufacturer and a distributor, with a network of more than 500 retail stores throughout most of France. The company also operates an e-commerce capable web site and offers home delivery services. Picard's revenues of more than EUR 785 million ($890 million) gives it a market share of more than 12 percent of the total French frozen food market, as well as approximately one-third share among the country's frozen food specialists retailers. Picard has distinguished itself through a commitment to high quality and innovation. Some 95 percent of the more than 1,000 products on offer at the company's stores are either produced by Picard or produced exclusively for the company, and sold under the company's own brands, especially the Picard name. Other brands include a line of prepared exotic meals under the Cuisine Evasion brand; ice cream, sorbets, and other frozen desserts under the François Théron name; Formule Express, for microwaveable meals; and Le Soleil, for Mediterranean dishes. Originally focused on the Parisian region, Picard has been steadily completing its national coverage, backed by a strong logistics support system. The company also has begun a foray into the international market, operating 45 stores in Italy, and offering delivery services to Belgium. Picard is led by Chairman and CEO Xavier Decelle. In 2005, the company was acquired by investment group BC Partners.

Retail Frozen Foods Pioneer in the 1970s

Picard's growth into France's leading frozen foods specialist began only in the 1970s, when the company was acquired by Armand Decelle. Nonetheless the Picard name had already been associated with the frozen products market since as early as 1906, when Raymond Picard began producing ice blocks and delivering them to local restaurants, cafes, and homeowners in Fontainebleau. By 1920, Picard's business had become known as Les Glacières de Fontainebleau—Etablissements Picard. Other sources, however, date the establishment of the Picard family business to the 1940s.

That year marked a revolution in the international grocery industry. Clarence Birdseye had recognized the potential for flash-freezing foods while on a trip to the Arctic. Returning to the United States, Birdseye developed a method for flash-freezing foods on an industrial scale, and the frozen foods industry was born. The frozen food revolution—which allowed the nutrients and flavors in foods to be preserved far longer than was the case with fresh foods—was slow in reaching France, however, where freezers, and even refrigerators, remained rarities through the first half of the century.

This situation changed in the years following the post-World War II period. France entered a period of extended economic boom. At the same time, as disposable income levels grew, the country embraced home appliances on a large scale. The growth of a leisure industry also encouraged the growth of a convenience foods industry, enabling consumers to spend less time in the kitchen. Refrigerators grew in size and added freezer compartments. Meanwhile, restaurants and cafes installed dedicated refrigeration and freezer capacity.

By the early 1960s, the Picard family had recognized that its traditional business of providing ice was doomed; instead the company converted itself to a wholesale supplier of freezers and

---

Company Perspectives:

Picard is unique on the French frozen food market because it is both a distribution label and a brand name. The strength of this innovative concept enables us to offer our customers the double guarantee of a well-known brand and our own distribution network that now comprises more than 600 points of sale and 23 home delivery bases. For 30 years Picard has selected and created the best products and perfected the best recipes in order to enable our customers to enjoy the pleasure of eating well every day.

---

frozen foods to the commercial sector. In 1962, the company changed its name to Etablissements Picard. The company's earliest products included chopped meat, breaded fish, spinach, and other vegetables. Over the next decade, the company continued to add to its catalog, and by the beginning of the 1970s, the company handled more than 300 frozen food items.

By then, a new consumer market for frozen food products had begun to develop in France. At first confined in large part to the rural and agricultural sector, where large-sized freezers were more practical, the market began to expand to include urban markets as well. The relatively young supermarket industry responded to demand by broadening their frozen food offerings. At the same time, the country saw a boom in catalog-based home delivery services. Picard itself decided to enter this category, launching its catalog in 1971, backed by a small fleet of trucks. The family-owned company's operations remained decidedly local. With just 10 employees, the company posted sales of only $750,000 into the early years of the 1970s.

The Picard name's fortune changed dramatically in 1973, when Armand Decelle bought the company from the Picard family. Decelle had already had a successful career as CEO of Compagnie Générale de Conserve, a canned good business later known as Secab-Daussy. Decelle had recognized the huge potential of the frozen foods business—in large part because of the superior quality, and convenience, of frozen foods over fresh and canned goods.

Decelle broke with Picard's past, however, steering the company's focus to the consumer retail market. The company maintained its small home delivery business (which later grew into a significant part of the group's business), but now turned its attention to the retail store channel. In 1974, Decelle opened a first Picard frozen foods supermarket, on the Rue de Rome, in Paris. The operation of the store not only served as an outlet, it also placed the company in greater proximity to its customers and allowed it to tailor its product offering to client needs.

Picard quickly built up a range of some 400 frozen food items. The success of the first store encouraged Decelle to open a second store, in Pavillions-sur-Bois, followed by several others through the decade. Supporting the company's growing retail network was a new logistic facility in Saint-Ouen L'Aumone in 1976. The opening of this site permitted the company to take control of its supply and transport requirements and backed Picard's first growth phase. By the end of the decade, the company operated more than 20 Picard stores.

Establishing a Frozen Foods Brand in the 1980s

In 1980, the company adopted a new store name, Picard Les Surgeles, as well as a new logo featuring a blue snowflake. By then, however, Picard was facing with growing competition from the supermarket sector, which not only had begun capturing the major share of the Paris region's fresh foods market, but also was coming to dominate frozen foods. Picard's suppliers soon favored the larger supermarket groups; faced with difficulties of supply, lower quality standards, and higher pricing than its competitors, Picard made the strategic move of launching its own branded line of foods, starting with vegetables.

The company soon took over much of the processing and packaging of much of the Picard line, which was launched with some 400 items, and later doubled. In support of this effort, the company moved to a new headquarters in Nemours. The site housed a new state-of-the-art warehouse facility, as well as a packaging plant and a small quality laboratory. The company established strict quality standards, firmly positioning itself on the high end of the consumer foods market. Although the company's prices were higher than those of the supermarkets (and even higher than the prices at the small grocery shops), Decelle, joined by twin sons Xavier and Olivier, put into place the company's promotional pricing policy.

Each month, the company's stores and catalog placed a number of items on promotion, with discounts ranging up to 40 percent off. Unlike promotional items at other retailers, however, which tended toward unsold and de-stocked items, Picard's promotions featured only ongoing items normally available at its shops. In fact, Decelle's original motivation for the discount pricing policy was to encourage its customers to try new food items. Yet the company quickly recognized the added benefit of the discounted pricing, in that the lower prices on those items allowed a customer to balance his spending at the Picard store, bringing their total purchases more in line with the prices at the supermarkets. Sales of the group's monthly promotions regularly accounted for 25 percent of total sales and more, and remained a mainstay throughout the company's expansion.

Picard invested little in promotional activities, preferring to generate new customers through word of mouth. In 1986, however, the company began publishing a monthly newsletter, *Lettre Picard,* which was distributed at the group's stores as well as in the Parisian editions of two television program guides.

Picard's commitment to quality and innovation resulted in the establishment of a full-scale laboratory in Nemours in 1986. The company also set into place a team of food engineers, assigned the task of developing new products and recipes for the group's ever-expanding line. Consumer testing of new products, however, remained in the field. Rather than invest in costly consumer research polling and studies, the company instead preferred to place products directly in its stores. Products were then given a four-month period to prove themselves.

The company took a similarly organic approach to the expansion of its sales network. After establishing some 100 stores throughout the Paris region, the company decided to expand to the south of France, including the regions of Lyons and Nice, as well as the Antibes. The group's choice of new target markets was dictated by the reasoning that these were popular vacation

Key Dates:

1906: Raymond Picard begins producing and delivering ice blocks in Fontainebleau.

1920: The company becomes Les Glacières de Fontainebleau—Etablissements Picard.

1940s: Picard begins the first wholesale sales of frozen foods and freezers.

1962: The company changes its name to Etablissements Picard and focuses on the distribution of wholesale foods and freezers.

1971: The company launches the first frozen foods catalog and home delivery sales.

1973: Armand Decelle acquires Picard company.

1974: The first Picard retail store opens.

1979: Headquarters are moved to Nemours.

1980: The Picard frozen foods brand is launched.

1987: The company opens its 100th store; the first store outside of the Paris region opens.

1991: Carrefours buys a 10 percent stake in Picard.

1994: Carrefour boosts its stake to 79 percent and backs an accelerated store expansion program.

1999: Picard acquires 50 Gel Market stores in Italy from Gel 2000.

2001: Carrefour sells Picard to a management buyout backed by an investment consortium led by Candover.

2004: Candover sells the Picard stake to investment group BC Partners.

destinations for its Parisian consumer base, providing a ready-made consumer base for the brand. The first stores outside of Paris opened in 1987, supported by a new logistics center at Vitry-sur-Seine. The following year, Armand Decelle turned over leadership of the company to sons Olivier and Xavier, who became co-CEOs.

Changing Owners in the New Century

As it continued its expansion, the Decelles decided to open up the company's capital to outside investors. In 1991, the company sold a 10 percent stake to French hypermarket giant Carrefour. The company now launched a new expansion drive, opening as much as 15 new stores each year. By 1994, the company's network had expanded to 300 stores, and the group had opened a new logistics center in Avignon to support its rising sales. In order to achieve still faster growth, the Decelles agreed to sell a majority stake in the company to Carrefour that year. Carrefour now took control of 79 percent of Picard, paying the Decelles, who retained 21 percent of the company, nearly EUR 140 million.

Despite the change in ownership, the Decelle brothers remained at the head of the company and continued to lead Picard as an independent operation. Yet the backing of Carrefour enabled the company to shift its expansion into overdrive;

through the rest of the decade, the company began opening as many as 40 and even 50 new stores each year. By the end of the decade, Picard had established itself as a national chain, with more than 500 stores. The company also had launched an effort to replicate its successful retail formula on an international level, buying up the 45-store Gel Market from struggling French rival Gel 2000.

Picard also launched its own e-commerce capable web site. The group's Internet sales, while limited to the larger metropolitan markets, built on the strong home delivery unit, which boasted more than 20 delivery bases throughout France into the 2000s.

Carrefour's takeover of Promodes, creating not only France's leading distribution group, but also one of the world's largest retail companies, led to a change of strategy. In 2001, Carrefour sold Picard to a management buyout, led by the Decelle family, and backed by an investment consortium headed by British buyout specialist Candover. The buyout marked Olivier Decelle's exit from the company's direction; Xavier Decelle continued as sole chairman and CEO.

With Candover's financial backing, Picard continued on its growth course, boosting its store network to 600 stores by the end of 2004. The company began eyeing the possibility of going public. Instead, in December 2004, the company announced that it was being sold to a new investment group, BC Partners, in a secondary buyout that enabled Candover to nearly triple its initial investment. Despite the change in ownership, Xavier Decelle remained as head of the group, which in just 30 years had established itself as the French frozen foods leader. Picard hoped to build on this position, establishing its brand on an international scale into the new century.

Principal Competitors

Carrefour S.A.; Etablissements E. LeClerc S.A.; ITM Entreprises S.A.; Groupe Auchan; Rallye S.A.; Toupargel-Agrigel S.A.; Thiriet S.A.; Maximo.

Further Reading

"Carrefour Sells Frozen Food Division to Consortium," *Grocer,* February 24, 2001, p. 14.

O'Donnell, John, "Backers to Cash in Picard Chips," *Sunday Times,* May 5, 2002, p. 2.

Mitteaux, Valérie, "Nous voulons gagner la bataille du quotidien," *e-marketing.fr,* March 1, 2002.

"Picard, le bon élève de la galaxie Carrefour," *e-marketing.fr,* April 1, 2000.

"Picard manie les P et refroidit ses rivaux," *Challenges,* September 5, 2002.

"The Secondary Buyout of French Frozen Food Retailer Picard Surgeles by BC Partners Has Been Backed by 913m [euro] of Debt," *Acquisitions Monthly,* March 2005, p. 62.

"Sur toute la chaîne, Picard reste de glace," *Challenges,* September 1, 2000.

—M.L. Cohen

Pittsburgh Brewing Company

3340 Liberty Avenue
Pittsburgh, Pennsylvania 15201-1394
U.S.A.
Telephone: (412) 682-7400
Web site: http://www.pittsburghbrewingco.com

Private Company
Incorporated: 1899
Employees: 200
Sales: $22.3 (2004 est.)
NAIC: 312120 Breweries

Pittsburgh Brewing Company is one of the oldest beer makers in the United States, and one of the 15 largest. The firm's signature brands are Iron City and I.C. Light, and it also makes Augustiner, American, Brigade, and Old German. They are distributed in the eastern United States and to a few countries overseas. Pittsburgh Brewing has been owned since 1995 by an investment group led by vice-chairman Joseph Piccirilli. Faced with mounting debt, in December of 2005 the company filed for Chapter 11 bankruptcy protection.

Origins

The roots of Pittsburgh Brewing date to 1861, when German immigrant Edward Frauenheim and several partners founded a small brewery in the rapidly-growing city of Pittsburgh, Pennsylvania. The firm (officially known as Frauenheim, Miller & Company) began with a golden-hued lager beer, reputedly the first of its type in the United States, which it named Iron City in honor of Pittsburgh's leading industry.

After several years the beer began to catch on, and in 1866 the company moved into a new $250,000, four-story brewery. With growth continuing unabated, in 1869 an additional three-story structure was added. In the 1880s the firm became known as Frauenheim and Vilsack when Leopold Vilsack bought the stakes of Frauenheim's original partners. The brewery now had annual capacity of 50,000 barrels, making it one of the largest outside of the East Coast.

In 1899 the company merged with 20 other regional breweries to form the Pittsburgh Brewing Company, after which some operations were consolidated and others were shut down. Total capacity was now more than one million barrels per year. By 1918 the publicly-traded company's annual revenues reached $7.7 million, and it recorded a profit of $800,000. Total production for the year was 855,795 31-gallon barrels.

Prohibition Ends Beer Production in 1920

In 1920 production of alcoholic beverages was outlawed in the United States, and the firm was forced to reconfigure its business model to survive. During the 13 years of Prohibition Pittsburgh Brewing produced nonalcoholic "near beer," soft drinks, and ice cream, and ran a cold storage business. A new unit, Tech Food Products Company was formed to oversee some of these operations. In 1921 sales fell to $1.8 million and a loss of $667,000 was recorded, and the company continued to operate in the red until 1930.

When beer production resumed in 1933 after Prohibition was repealed, the firm elected a new president, John W. Hubbard, and formed a new subsidiary, Iron City Brewing Company Its products included Iron City Pilsner, Iron City Lager, Tech Beer, Dutch Club Beer, and Blue Label Beer. In 1947 a new $1 million expansion and upgrade was begun, and despite labor strife involving the Teamsters, by the mid-1950s Iron City had become the best-selling beer in the Pittsburgh area, where it was especially popular with steelworkers.

An annual tradition begun during this period was the production of a beer called Olde Frothingslosh. Invented as an on-air joke by a Pittsburgh disc jockey whose pseudo-commercials used the tagline "the pale stale ale with the foam on the bottom," the firm sent out 500 cases of Tech beer with Olde Frothingslosh labels to shareholders in 1955 as a Christmas gift. The idea was a hit, and the mythical brew was manufactured each winter thereafter for public consumption. By 1960 its popularity had increased to the point that $200,000 was budgeted to promote it, comprising the company's largest ad campaign to date.

In 1962 Pittsburgh Brewing made beer industry history with the introduction of the easy-opening "snap-top" can, devel-

Company Perspectives:

An innovator in the industry, PBC has continued through the years to introduce new products yet maintain the same emphasis on excellence that its ancestors did. Pittsburgh Brewing has remained for 142 years dedicated to all of its products and to the public it serves—a public that returns that favor by continuously showing interest in and enthusiasm for the hometown brew.

oped by locally-based Alcoa aluminum. It was soon adopted as an industry standard, as was a later company innovation of this era, the twist-off bottle cap. The firm was also one of the first to use a new cold filtration process that made canned beer taste more like draft. By 1964 annual sales had risen to $17 million.

In 1965 an attempt to buy major Pennsylvania rival Duquesne Brewing was blocked by the U.S. Justice Department, but in 1967 a smaller area company, DuBois Brewing Company, was acquired. That firm had long brewed a beer called Budweiser, and a decades-old legal dispute over the name with Anheuser-Busch was settled several years later with a reported $1 million payment to Pittsburgh Brewing. In 1969 the company also signed an agreement with Dr. Robert Cade, inventor of Gatorade, to brew a lemon/lime malt beverage he had developed called Hop 'N Gator.

An 11-month boycott of Iron City beer by Pittsburgh's African American community in 1971 resulted in the firm agreeing to hire more blacks, but that settlement was followed by an even larger boycott by racist whites. Sales declined by an estimated 15 percent and the firm's union workers went on strike for two months. Despite these problems, Iron City continued to be the number one brand in the Pennsylvania-West Virginia-Ohio market.

The year 1972 also saw the firm purchase the rights to a number of other brand names including Gamminus, Robin Hood Cream Ale, Augustiner, and Mark V. The latter was a low-calorie beer that was considered the forerunner to the light beers that became popular later in the decade. In 1973, the company closed the former DuBois brewery.

In the late 1960s and 1970s the high-powered marketing campaigns of national firms like Anheuser-Busch and Miller took their toll on regional brewers, and the company's beers gradually came to be seen as budget-price brands outside of their local stronghold. For much of the 1970s Pittsburgh Brewing operated in the red, despite efforts to broaden distribution to states like Florida and Illinois.

New Products in the 1970s

In 1978 the struggling firm enticed retired executive Harry Glenn Wolfe back to serve as chairman, and he brought in an old friend, Miller Brewing veteran William F. Smith, for the job of president. Under their leadership the company introduced a new low-calorie beer called I.C. Light, which was marketed aggressively to younger drinkers and soon captured more than two-thirds of light beer sales in the area. The campaign also

helped restore the luster of the Iron City brand, and in 1980 the company reported a net profit of $1.3 million on revenues of $38.4 million, up from $25 million just a year before. Total production now topped one million barrels.

In 1981, after settling a brief strike by the company's employees, Smith left to head troubled industry giant Pabst (which later unsuccessfully sought to buy Pittsburgh Brewing). His place was taken by Robert Seymour, who moved to the post of chairman a few months later when former Gimbel's head Harvey Sanford was named to the posts of president and CEO.

In 1982 the company started a five-year, $12 million modernization program that would add warehouse space and boost bottling capacity by 50 percent. The year 1984 saw introduction of a new premium beer, I.C. Golden Lager, which quickly grew to take a 5 percent share of all beer sales in southwestern Pennsylvania, one-eighth of the firm's total share of 40 percent. The company was again working to upgrade its image by dropping some brands and reducing its distribution area to focus primarily on Pennsylvania, where 80 percent of sales were made. For 1984, revenues topped $44.7 million.

In 1985 a management-led group offered $26.5 million to take the company private, but they were topped by Australian financier Alan Bond's Bond Corporation Holdings Ltd., which was seeking entrée into the American beer market. After the $28.5 million deal was completed Swan Export Lager was introduced to American drinkers, and Pittsburgh Brewing's distribution area was expanded.

The firm was now using its excess brewing capacity to produce beers for other companies under contract, including Pennsylvania Pilsner, Olde Heurich, Thirteenth Colony Amber, and Samuel Adams Boston Lager. The latter, brewed for the Boston Beer Co., would eventually come to account for more than a third of total production.

American Beer Falls Flat in the Late 1980s

In 1987 Pittsburgh Brewing took the bold step of launching a new brand called American Beer that was intended to compete nationally against the likes of Budweiser, Miller, and Coors. Industry analysts gave it little chance of success and the effort was scuttled the following spring, though the beer would later be reincarnated as a low-priced brew that was exported to such countries as Poland and Russia.

In January 1988 the company was reorganized as a unit of new $1.2 billion Bond acquisition G. Heileman of Wisconsin, at which time CEO Harvey Sanford resigned. During this period the firm introduced a number of new drinks, including flavored malt beverage I.C. Cooler, I.C. Ice, I.C. Dry, Classic Draft, Classic Draft Light, and a non-alcoholic brew called Keene's.

Alan Bond's acquisitions had left him with an unwieldy $4 billion debt load, and in 1990 he was forced to sell his Australian breweries and resign from the firm that bore his name. In 1991 G. Heileman filed for bankruptcy and a group of Pittsburgh Brewing employees led by retired CEO Harvey Sanford once again made an attempt to buy the company. This time they lost out to the $28.5 million offer of Michael Carlow, a 40-year old businessman who (in partnership with his father Frank) had

Key Dates:

1861: Edward Frauenheim begins brewing Iron City beer in Pittsburgh, Pennsylvania.
1899: Firm unites with 20 other area brewers to form Pittsburgh Brewing Company.
1920: Prohibition begins; company provides cold storage; makes near beer, soft drinks.
1933: Beer production resumes.
1950s: Iron City becomes Pittsburgh area's top-selling brand.
1962: Firm introduces industry's first "snap-top" beer can.
1978: I.C. Light is introduced and becomes company's best selling product.
1986: Australian Alan Bond acquires firm as part of efforts to bring his beers to United States.
1992: Michael Carlow buys Pittsburgh Brewing from Bond for $28.5 million.
1995: Carlow is charged with fraud and steps down; Joseph Piccirilli-led group buys firm.
2004: New aluminum bottle introduced to strong sales.
2005: Debt-ridden company files for Chapter 11 bankruptcy protection.

recently taken control of the troubled Pittsburgh-based candy maker D.L. Clark Company.

The summer of 1992 saw beer sales boosted with a new ad campaign that spotlighted local beer drinkers' fantasies and the tagline "It's a 'Burgh Thing." In 1993 the firm responded to the growing interest in "craft beers" like Sam Adams by introducing J.J. Wainwright Select, which was named after one of the 21 companies that had originally banded together in 1899 to form Pittsburgh Brewing. The firm was also having success with exports of American Beer to Russia, which accounted for 7 percent of revenues.

In February 1994, after the Carlow-owned City Pride Bakery unexpectedly closed, a Pittsburgh *Post-Gazette* investigation of the man once touted as a savior of local jobs uncovered a checkered past which included bad debts and much ill will. In early 1995 Carlow's lender, PNC Bank N.A., accused him of a "check-kiting" scheme in which he had allegedly stolen $31.3 million. In February, the brewery's owner was forced to declare bankruptcy.

New Ownership in the 1990s

In the summer of 1995 Keystone Brewers, headed by 32-year old former trash hauling company owner Joseph Piccirilli and financier James M. Gehrig, agreed to pay $12.4 million and assume $17 million in debt to buy the firm, narrowly beating out yet another offer from a Harvey Sanford-led group. After the acquisition Piccirilli and Gehrig began putting in long hours to repair the damage caused by Carlow, and by year's end sales had begun to improve and the firm was looking at the possibility of expanding beyond its 14-state territory.

In May 1996 Michael Carlow pleaded guilty to bank fraud, conspiracy, embezzlement, wire fraud, and filing false income

tax returns, and he was later sentenced to eight years in prison and ordered to pay $2.3 million in restitution and back taxes. His predecessor as brewery owner, Alan Bond, was now also behind bars, serving time for art fraud.

Meanwhile, Piccirilli, who had no formal management training, was cutting costs by dismissing the firm's veteran sales team and instituting frequent week-long shutdowns of the brewery, as well as dropping three long-time local distributors in favor of a fourth that had offered to pay a fee for the privilege. In March 1997 more than 100 members of one of the company's unions walked off the job to protest a work scheduling decision, and Piccirilli immediately fired many of them. He later rehired most but sued the union for the work stoppage, after which an arbitrator ruled that the firm had to rehire all of the fired workers and give them back pay.

In 1998 Pittsburgh Brewing acquired the rights to more than 20 older brands from bankrupt Evansville Brewing Company, including Wiedemann, Falls City, Drewry's, and Sterling, but efforts to merge with two other breweries failed and the contract to brew Sam Adams ended and was not renewed. In 1999 another merger deal with distributor Capital Beverage fell apart, while James Gehrig and several other top executives left the firm to work for a new Cleveland-based brewery. Pittsburgh Brewing subsequently sued the latter over the alleged similarity of its label design to the recently-revived 1950s red circle Iron City logo. In 2000 a new "superpremium beer," Augustiner Lager, was introduced, and the following year some of the firm's brews were packaged in plastic bottles for sale at sporting events.

Debt Mounts in Early 2000s

Production was now steadily declining, and with money tight needed upkeep and improvements to the company's aging brewery were being ignored. Pittsburgh Brewing was also having trouble making payments on a $1.4 million loan from the Pennsylvania Industrial Development Authority, a $358,000 energy bill, nearly $200,000 owed the state treasury department, and some $3.7 million due the Pittsburgh Water & Sewer Authority, which in 2002 threatened to shut off the firm's water supply if it was not paid. Though a payment plan was soon worked out, the company disputed its sewer bill, arguing that a substantial portion of the water became beer so that the standard ratio of water to sewage used to calculate service charges did not apply.

In August 2004 the company's sagging fortunes were boosted by the successful introduction of a new aluminum bottle for Iron City beer, which was said to make the beverage stay cold longer. Though already available in Japan, Pittsburgh Brewing was the first large U.S. firm to use the container. Sales were brisk, and the can was named one of the ten best new products of the year by Business Week magazine. A few months later I.C. Light was also made available in the bottle. During 2004, according to *Modern Brewery Age* magazine, the firm brewed 372,000 barrels of beer, down from 927,000 a decade earlier, making it the eleventh-largest brewer in the United States.

In 2005 Pittsburgh Brewing asked the U.S. government's Pension Benefit Guaranty Corporation to take over its pension plan, which had a $5.6 million deficit, claiming it would go bankrupt if the request was not granted. Over the summer the federal government also filed a $750,000 lien against the firm because of unpaid excise taxes, while the still-unresolved dispute with the water and sewer authority continued to simmer. When the company was unable to meet an early December deadline to pay $2.5 million owed in the latter case, it filed for Chapter 11 bankruptcy protection. Industry analysts held out hope that the firm could recover, citing the iconic status of the Iron City brand in Pittsburgh and the success of other brewers in returning from bankruptcy.

After nearly 150 years of operation, the Pittsburgh Brewing Company was facing one of the biggest challenges in its history. As its owners and employees fought to keep the company alive, the firm entered bankruptcy with hopes for an eventual return to profitability.

Principal Subsidiaries

Wainwright Brewing Company; Commonwealth Brewing Company.

Principal Competitors

Anheuser-Busch Companies, Inc.; Miller Brewing Company: Coors Brewing Company; Pabst Brewing Company; D.G. Yuengling & Son, Inc.; City Brewing Company; InBev USA.; High Falls Brewing Company.

Further Reading

Alden, Robert, ''Advertising: Frothingslosh Makes a Splash,'' *New York Times*, December 6, 1960, p. 71.

Boselovic, Len, ''Aluminum Beer Bottle Puts Charge in Iron City,'' *Pittsburgh Post-Gazette*, January 23, 2005, p. A1.

——, ''Beermaker in Bankruptcy,'' *Pittsburgh Post-Gazette*, December 8, 2005, p. A1.

——, ''Piccirilli Gets Brewery in Bidding War,'' *Pittsburgh Post-Gazette*, September 13, 1995, p. C7.

——, ''Strategy For Renewal,'' *Pittsburgh Post-Gazette*, July 14, 2000, p. D1.

——, ''The Carlow Way: His Gutsy Style Revived 3 Companies in Pittsburgh, But Has Left a Long Trail of Bad Debts Elsewhere,'' *Pittsburgh Post-Gazette*, February 20, 1994, p. A1.

Boselovic, Len, and Cristina Rouvalis, ''Iron City's House Rocker - Joe Piccirilli's Enthusiasm, Inexperience Fermenting Change at Pittsburgh Brewing,'' *Pittsburgh Post-Gazette*, September 15, 1996, p. C1.

Boselovic, Len, and Steve Massey, ''PNC's Allegation Unseats Carlow,'' *Pittsburgh Post-Gazette*, February 7, 1995, p. A1.

DeParma, Ron, ''Pittsburgh Brewing Improves Market Share,'' *Tribune Review*, January 30, 1996, p. D3.

Earl, Greg, ''Setback for Bond in US Beer Market,'' *Australian Financial Review*, May 27, 1988, p. 19.

Fahey, Alison, ''Iron City Beer: It's a 'Burgh Thing,'' *Brandweek*, January 25, 1993, p. 14.

''From Beer to Ice Cream,'' *Wall Street Journal*, November 28, 1921, p. 12.

Gannon, Joyce, ''Clark Bar Maker Buys an 'Iron,' '' *Pittsburgh Post-Gazette*, November 5, 1991, p. 1.

Halvonik, Steve, ''The Final Deal: Carlow Sentenced to 8 Years for His White-Collar Crime,'' *Pittsburgh Post-Gazette*, August 16, 1996, p. B10.

Harris, Roy J., Jr., ''Some Blue Collar Workers Shun Their Favorite Beer After the Brewery Signs a Pact to Hire More Blacks,'' *Wall Street Journal*, June 8, 1972, p. 30.

McIlwraith, John, ''Bond Moves into US Beer,'' *Australian Financial Review*, January 29, 1986, p. 1.

McKay, Jim, ''Brewery Workers Ordered Reinstated,'' *Pittsburgh Post-Gazette*, September 5, 1997, p. E1.

''Pittsburgh Brewing: Big-Time Tactics With a Hometown Touch,'' *Business Week*, September 29, 1980, p. 124.

''Pittsburgh Brewing Co. Plans to Enter Markets Outside Pennsylvania,'' *Wall Street Journal*, August 13, 1984.

Richard, Christine, ''Brewer Seeks to End Obligations for Pensions Without Bankruptcy,'' *Wall Street Journal*, October 19, 2005, p. B4.

—Frank Uhle

Princes Ltd.

6th Floor Royal Liver Building
Pier Head
Liverpool
United Kingdom
Telephone: +44 0151 236 9282
Fax: +44 0151 255 1440
Web site: http://www.princes.co.uk

Wholly Owned Subsidiary of Mitsubishi Corporation
Incorporated: 1880 as Simpson, Roberts
Employees: 3,525
Sales: £750 million ($1.2 billion) (2004)
NAIC: 424410 General Line Grocery Merchant
    Wholesalers

Princes Ltd. is the United Kingdom's leading importer of canned foods products, and one of its major processed foods and soft drinks producers. The company has been associated with the United Kingdom's canned fish market for more than 125 years, and remains one of the country's top two canned tuna brands. Princes also has expanded its brand name to include a range of food and cooking oils, as well as processed foods including canned meats and other ready-to-eat meals, ready-made sandwiches, and sauces. Princes has been extending its brand portfolio in the 2000s, adding brands such as Napolina Italia Foods, Shippams, Mazola, Cookeen, and Crisp N' Dry. In 2005, the company entered the ambient ready-to-eat meal segment with the launch of the Quick Eat brand. Since the 1990s, Princes also has been present in the soft drinks market, with a full range of juices, carbonated beverages, and mineral water marketed under the Princes, Jucee, Twist n' Squeeze, and, since 2005, Aqua Pura brands. In addition to its U.K. manufacturing operations, Princes operates production facilities in The Netherlands and on the island of Mauritius. The company has set itself a target of doubling its sales, from 2004's £750 million, through the second half of the 2000s. As part of that strategy, the company expects to expand its operations further onto the European continent. In addition to its subsidiary in The Netherlands, the company controls the Vier Diamanten canned tuna brand, the largest in the Austrian market. Princes has been wholly owned by Japan's Mitsubishi Corporation since the late 1980s.

Canned Fish Importer in the 1880s

Princes' origins stretched back to the late 19th century and the formation of Simpson, Roberts. The company, formed as a partnership in 1880, specialized in importing canned fish to the United Kingdom, especially salmon and other fish from Canada. Operating from headquarters in Liverpool, the company eventually launched its own line of canned fish under the Princes brand. By 1900, the partnership had formed a dedicated subsidiary for its canned food products, Princes Pure Foods Ltd.

Simpson, Roberts remained focused on its import business into the mid-20th century. By 1946, however, the company had begun its first move into manufacturing, setting up a processing and production facility in Southport. The company also established a production facility in The Netherlands, in 1960. Nonetheless, the great majority of the company's operations remained focused on its fish imports, and the company was essentially recognized as a commodities business. By the late 1950s, the company also had gone public, although the Dickinson family, who had been among the original partners, remained as the company's leadership; indeed, the group's chairman, W.T. Dickinson, served with the company for 80 years until his death in 1962.

The transition toward a branded food products group began in the early 1960s. In 1962, the company changed its name, adopting its popular Princes brand name as its corporate identity. Through the 1960s, the company successfully positioned its line of Princes-branded canned fish as one of the United Kingdom's leading brands.

The company's effort came in the midst of a dramatic change in the U.K. grocery sector. Once dominated by small, locally owned grocer's shops, supplied by a myriad of small production companies, the grocery market had begun to shift toward the rapidly developing supermarket model. The supermarket format quickly established itself as a dominant force in the grocery sector. By the late 1960s, a small number of large,

Company Perspectives:

Our Responsibilities: Princes recognises that, as a major international manufacturer and supplier, the company has a responsibility towards the environment, its employees and the communities in which it operates. Princes constantly strives to ensure that its business activities provide sustained environmental, social and economic benefits in the countries in which it operates. The company complies fully with the labour, health and safety and employment laws of the respective countries in which it operates. The same compliance is expected from all Princes' suppliers, which are regularly audited by the company.

regionally and nationally operated supermarket chains had begun to transform the U.K. food industry in general. Many smaller grocers disappeared, while others were forced to consolidate.

The arrival of supermarkets placed food producers and importers under a new and unprecedented pressure. The consolidation of the sector and the concentration of consumer spending was coupled with the tendency of supermarket groups to focus on a narrower range of branded products. Producers were forced to compete for limited store shelf space.

This new fact of the grocery industry sparked a wave of consolidation among British food companies in an effort to gain the national scale to supply the largest supermarket groups. Princes, with its popular brand name, became a fixture on supermarket shelves. Nonetheless, by the late 1960s, the company became caught up in the industry consolidation. In 1968, Bibby & Co., which produced paper products as well as foods, including its Trex line of fats and vegetable oils, launched a takeover offer for Princes. The company initially rejected the offer as too low. Yet Princes' management held just 10 percent of the group's shares. When Bibby raised its offer, the company had no choice but to accept, and Princes ceased to be an independent company.

Bibby's expansion effort floundered, however, into the early 1970s. The company's problems were especially attributed to the Princes acquisition, which, still chiefly a commodities business, had not generated the hoped-for synergies with Bibby's other operations. In 1973, Bibby decided to restructure, and sold off its foods division, including Princes Foods and its Trex fats and oils business, to Italy's Buitoni. That family-owned company, based in Italy, had been making its own drive to expand internationally, and the Princes acquisition provided Buitoni with a solid entrance into the United Kingdom.

Princes grew strongly as part of Princes Buitoni. The company expanded its canned goods business, adding new products such as imported canned vegetables and canned corned beef and other meats. By the end of the decade, the company held the U.K. market leadership in some 11 different canned goods categories. From sales of £33 million in 1980, the Princes division grew to turnover of £200 million at the end of the decade. The Princes brand alone represented some 93 percent of these sales.

Building a Brand Family in the 2000s

Nestle acquired Princes Buitoni in 1988, then sold off the Princes Food division to Mitsubishi the following year. Backed by one of the world's largest corporations, Princes now began to diversify its operations, expanding its range of brands, as well as its production capacity. On the one hand, Princes enjoyed continued independence of operation under Mitsubishi. On the other, the company was able to take advantage not only of Mitsubishi's financial clout, but also of its extensive, worldwide presence.

Princes' first product extension came in 1991, with the purchase of G. Barraclough Limited. That company added soft drinks production and distribution to Princes' operations, including the Gee-Bee brand of carbonated beverages and "squashes." The company continued to develop its soft drinks wing, buying Cima Foods Limited in 1993. That purchase extended the company's operations to the fruit juice and fruit drinks category.

Beverages remained the company's primary acquisition target through the end of the decade. In 1997, Princes bought Barber Springdale and its line of juices, squashes, and carbonated beverages. The company then bought the Juices Division from Waterford in 1998.

As the new decade approached, however, Princes' acquisition interest turned toward developing its food categories. In 1999, the company bought up rival Oxbridge Foods Ltd., a producer of canned foods, including vegetables, fruits, and fish. That year the company also made an unsuccessful attempt to buy up Shippams Ltd., which produced fish pastes, canned chicken, and pate, and which had been in operation since the late 18th century. However, in 2001 Princes made a successful bid to acquire Beta Foods, finally gaining control of the Shippams operation.

By then, Princes had expanded its canned fish production capacity, buying up a cannery on the island of Mauritius in 1999. The company took a break from its foods expansion to add to its beverage division again in 2000, buying Wells Soft Drinks. In that year, as well, the company completed its acquisition of oils group Leon Frenkel, after acquiring 50 percent of that business in 1998. In 2001, after the Shippams acquisition, the company bought up Italian foods group Napolina Italia Limited.

In the early 2000s, Princes began developing goals for expansion onto the European mainland. The company began producing for the private-label market, expanding in The Netherlands, Sweden, and Spain. The company also formed a partnership with Italian canned tomato producer AR Industrie Alimentarie, forming the Russo joint venture in 2000. In 2002, in keeping with its growth goals, the company restructured its operations. As part of this process, the company created three new divisions: Princes Foods Trading and Manufacturing, which focused on its U.K.-based businesses; Princes Foods International, which included its Netherlands, Mauritius, and Italian holdings, focused on developing the group's European operations; and Princes Soft Drinks, which included the group's beverage business in the United Kingdom and Europe. The company hoped the restructuring would achieve its goal of doubling in size into the second half of the 2000s.

Key Dates:

1880: The Simpson, Roberts partnership is established in Liverpool to begin importing canned fish.
1900: After developing the Princes brand, the company establishes the Princes Pure Foods subsidiary.
1962: The company adopts the new name of Princes Foods Ltd.
1968: The company is acquired by Bibby & Co.
1973: Bibby sells the foods division, including Princes and the oils operations, to Buitoni of Italy.
1988: Nestle acquires Princes Buitoni.
1989: Mitsubishi acquires the Princes foods division from Nestle.
1991: Princes makes its first acquisition, entering the beverage market through the purchase of G. Barraclough.
1993: The fruit juice group Cima Foods Ltd. is acquired.
1997: Carbonated beverage company Barber Springdale is acquired.
1999: Rival Oxbridge Foods Ltd. is acquired.
2000: A joint venture is formed with Italy's AR Industrie Alimentari; Wells Soft Drinks is acquired; the Leon Frenkel Ltd. oils group is acquired.
2001: Beta Foods and its Shippams subsidiary are acquired.
2002: The company restructures operations ahead of a European expansion drive.
2003: Dairy Crest's chilled juice division is acquired.
2004: The company enters the bottled mineral water market with the purchase of Well Well Well Ltd. and its Aqua Pura brand.
2005: The company acquires the licenses to the Mazola, Flora, Cookeen, Spry Crisp 'n' Dry, and Olivio oil brands.

A new extension to the group's brand family came in 2002, when Princes gained the franchise for Virgin Drinks, including the popular Virgin Cola, launched in the early 1990s. Under Princes, Virgin redeveloped its recipe in order to differentiate itself from competitors. In 2003, the company further extended its beverage line with the acquisition of Dairy Crest's chilled fruit juice operations. A year later, the company entered the bottled mineral water market, a rapidly expanding beverage segment in the United Kingdom, with the purchase of Well Well Well Ltd. and its Aqua Pura brand.

In addition to its acquisition drive, Princes launched an in-house effort to extend its operations into new product categories. In 2000, for example, the company launched its own branded line of ambient dips. The company also began to target the ready-to-eat market, introducing its own prepared canned meals. Included in this effort was a partnership with Slimming World, and the launch of 12 tuna-based, Slimming World-branded ready-to-eat products. In 2005, the company launched a new line of ready-to-eat ambient meals. Originally developed for Marks & Spencer, the popularity of the line led the company to launch the line under its own Quick Eat label.

With sales of £750 million—and a target to reach £1.5 billion during the decade—Princes continued seeking expansion opportunities. In 2005, the company made a new acquisition, buying up the licenses to a range of oil brands, including Flora, Mazola, Cookeen, and the olive oil brand Olivio. After 125 years, Princes remained a leading name in the U.K. foods industry.

Principal Subsidiaries

Stretton Hills Mineral Water Company; Eden Valley Mineral Water Company; Princes Foods B.V. (Netherlands); Napolina Italia Ltd.; Princes Tuna (Mauritius) Ltd.

Principal Divisions

International Trading and Manufacturing; Soft Drinks; Foods Manufacturing.

Principal Competitors

John West Foods Ltd.; Thai Union Frozen Products plc; Bumble Bee Seafoods LLC; StarKist Foods, Inc.

Further Reading

"Acquisition Takes Princes into Bottled Water," *Grocer,* June 12, 2004, p. 6.
"Battle to Be the Biggest Fish Brand," *Grocer,* September 10, 2005, p. 52.
Beddall, Clive, "A Place in the Sun," *Grocer,* February 24, 2001, p. 40.
Chomka, Stefan, "Princes' Quick Way to Fill Gap," *Grocer,* October 15, 2005, p. 74.
Jorro, Richard, "Princes' Progress," *Super Marketing,* July 5, 1991, p. 36.
"Princes Finally Seizes Beta Foods," *Grocer,* March 3, 2001, p. 14.
"Princes Restructures to Spread Further Across EU," *Grocer,* March 17, 2001, p. 13.
"Princes to Dip Another Toe in the Market," *Super Marketing,* September 8, 2000, p. 16.
"Tasty Way to Boost Sales," *Grocer,* July 23, 2005, p. S20.
"You Know You Always Can with Princes," *Grocer,* February 1, 2003, p. 44.

—M.L. Cohen

Rexnord Corporation

4701 Greenfield Avenue
Milwaukee, Wisconsin 53214
U.S.A.
Telephone: (414) 643-3000
Fax: (414) 643-3078
Web site: http://www.rexnord.com

Private Company
Incorporated: 1892 as the Chain Belt Company
Employees: 4,800
Sales: $811 million (2004)
NAIC: 333131 Mining Machinery and Equipment Manufacturing; 333319 Other Commercial and Service Industry Machinery Manufacturing; 333613 Mechanical Power Transmission Equipment Manufacturing; 333922 Conveyor and Conveying Equipment Manufacturing; 334513 Instruments and Related Products Manufacturing for Measuring, Displaying, and Controlling Industrial Process Variables; 336340 Motor Vehicle Brake System Manufacturing; 336350 Motor Vehicle Transmission and Power Train Parts; 336413 Other Aircraft Parts and Auxiliary Equipment Manufacturing

Rexnord Corporation is a major supplier of power transmission and conveying components to a variety of industries around the globe. Headquartered in Milwaukee, Wisconsin, the company operates from more than 35 manufacturing locations worldwide. Products include power transmission components; bearings; brakes, clutches, and electronic components; conveying equipment, including bucket elevators, industrial elevators, and apron conveyors; couplings; drive products; engineered chain and roller chain; and more. Rexnord was acquired by The Carlyle Group in 2002 and was reorganized under the parent company RBS Global Inc. In 2005 Rexnord acquired its own Milwaukee neighbor, gear and coupling manufacturer The Falk Corporation.

Origins in 1892

The company was first incorporated in Wisconsin on February 20, 1892, as the Chain Belt Company, to manufacture a chain belt that would replace the leather belting then used to drive agricultural equipment. The company was established in Milwaukee by inventor C.W. LeValley and two foundry operators, F.W. Sivyer and W.A. Draves. After proving that chain belts worked well on farm machinery, the concept was applied to conveying equipment and construction machinery. During the 1890s the company manufactured chain-driven material handling conveyors and bucket elevators for Milwaukee breweries. The company also worked with customers to develop chain drives for new applications.

By 1894 the company had started developing international markets, with the export of chain to Europe and the opening of a sales office in England. The company paid its first dividend that year and would never miss a dividend payment as long as it was a publicly owned company.

The company reached its first significant milestone in 1913, when annual sales reached $1 million. At that time the company's products were organized into three major divisions: chain products for power transmission; a line of chain-driven construction machinery; and chain-powered bulk conveying equipment. In 1914 it introduced the Rex brand-name, which was first used on a chain-driven concrete mixer. It soon became a widely recognized trademark.

Sales continued their upward trend throughout the 1920s and 1930s. In 1941, sales passed the $10 million mark for the first time. Research and development was credited with the growth in sales, as the company focused on developing new products, new methods, and new markets. It was the beginning of Rexnord's tradition of manufacturing technologically advanced products of the highest quality.

Growth and a Name Change in the 1960s

At the beginning of 1964 the company changed its name to Rex Chainbelt, Inc. Sales for the year reached the $100 million mark for the first time. A highly developed marketing and distribution system was in place. A growing commitment to international development had resulted in increased sourcing capabilities around the world. The company's product development efforts focused on several promising growth areas.

Under the company's new management sales went from $100 million to $1 billion in a 25-year period. William C.

Company Perspectives:

The company's mission is to be a leading marketer and world class manufacturer of power transmission, aerospace, and specialty components, products & systems and provide superior growth and command sustainable competitive advantage.

Messinger joined the company in 1963 as president and in 1967 became chairman of the board, with Robert V. Krikorian as president. Under their leadership, Rexnord would grow from a small capital goods manufacturer into a highly diversified corporation serving worldwide markets with sales surpassing $1 billion by 1980.

It was in the late 1960s that management set the company on a new course, to minimize the business cycles that capital goods companies were subject to. Prior to this time, sales followed a cyclical pattern, with two or three good years followed by a down year. The company's new strategy called for a broader line of products, especially those that were consumed in use or required proprietary replacement parts. Management felt that demand for these products would continue, even when capital spending had to be curtailed. The goal, therefore, was to build a portfolio of businesses with offsetting economic cycles as well as to achieve geographical diversity by operating on an international basis.

When Messinger later retired in 1980 at the age of 65, more than half of Rexnord's sales came from components and replacement parts. Two countercyclical business segments, process machinery and environmental control equipment, accounted for approximately one-third of total sales, and international sales accounted for 28 percent of the company's total revenues.

Acquisitions in the 1970s

In 1970 the company made the significant acquisition of the Nordberg Manufacturing Company. The acquisition of Nordberg broadened the company's markets and put it strongly into minerals mining and aggregate (crushed stone) equipment. Affected by changing price levels for minerals and by worldwide demand for crushed stone, these markets were considered countercyclical to the domestic economy, as were sales of environmental control equipment.

At the beginning of 1973 the company adopted a new name, Rexnord, Inc., and undertook a new corporate identification program. A brochure, ''Serving the Needs of the People,'' was issued as the second part of the company's two-part annual report in 1974. At this time the company had five major business segments: power transmission components, mineral and rock crushing and processing machinery, environmental control equipment, material handling equipment, and construction machinery. Its international operations consisted of subsidiaries in West Germany, Belgium, and Australia, that produced construction machinery, power transmission components, and pollution control equipment. Operations also included Racine Hidraulica S.A. in Brazil, which manufactured hydraulic components and systems. Altogether, Rexnord operated 29 plants in 14 countries during 1973.

Sales continued to grow at a 10 to 20 percent annual rate throughout the 1970s, reaching $1.01 billion in 1979. Profitability also continued to rise. During this time, the company pursued a carefully planned strategy of product and market diversification to offset weakness in one by strength in another. International growth was planned and timed to avoid becoming overly dependent on the economy of any one nation. Rexnord also concentrated on products that were either consumed in use or required Rexnord replacement parts. Such a product mix provided a continuity of earnings, even when industry conditions might restrain capital expenditures. The company audited all of its product lines on a regular basis. During the 1972 to 1977 period, for example, it sold or discontinued product lines with annual sales of $51 million, but that had losses of $2.7 million.

New Management and Challenges in the 1980s

During 1979 management changes were put into effect in anticipation of Messinger turning 65 in January 1980 and retiring. Krikorian, president since 1967, was elected vice-chairman and CEO, then he succeeded Messinger as chairman of the board in 1980. Donald Taylor was elected president. He had joined Rexnord in the Nordberg merger of 1970. The next year Rexnord honored Messinger by naming its Milwaukee research center after him.

By 1980 Rexnord's five business segments were grouped into two major product groups, components and machinery. The components product group, consisting of power transmission components and specialty fasteners, accounted for 59 percent of Rexnord's sales and more than 72 percent of operating income in 1980. They were the company's most profitable businesses and had received the bulk of capital expenditures in recent years. The machinery product group included process machinery, which emphasized products having a strong replacement parts business, environmental control equipment, and construction machinery.

Rexnord began the 1980s with more than 17,000 employees in 51 U.S. and Canadian plants and in 22 overseas facilities. Like many other businesses, it experienced difficulties in the post-inflationary recessionary early 1980s. In spite of high interest rates and a generally weak economy, Rexnord achieved its 20th consecutive year of sales growth in 1981 when sales reached $1.13 billion, up from $1.084 billion in 1980. However, real unit volume declined 2 percent. The company's strengths were its replacement parts business, which provide more than half of its 1981 volume, and international markets, which accounted for nearly one-third of sales.

During 1981 the company divested several product lines, including its European construction machinery operations and its subsidiary Rockford Aerospace Products, located in California. In 1982 it sold two significant businesses for approximately $70 million: the Construction Machinery Division and the Fluid Power Division. It also closed its process machinery foundry in Milwaukee. With a worldwide recession and high long-term interest rates, 1982 was a difficult year for operations, with the company emphasizing cost reduction programs, significant restructuring, and continued investment in research and development. Capital goods spending had been in decline for the past year and a half, and Rexnord reported reduced earnings and its

Key Dates:

1892: Chain Belt Company is formed to make chain belts for agricultural equipment.
1913: Sales reach $1 million.
1914: Rex brand introduced.
1941: Sales exceed $10 million.
1964: Company is renamed Rex Chainbelt, Inc.; sales reach $100 million.
1970: Acquisition of Nordberg Manufacturing Company expands company into mining equipment.
1973: Company is renamed Rexnord.
1980: Sales exceed $1 billion.
1981: Rexnord begins divesting major businesses in early 1980s recession.
1984: Acquisitions strengthen component products, industrial process control lines.
1987: Cleveland's Banner Industries acquires Rexnord.
1992: Rexnord goes public on the New York Stock Exchange.
1994: Rexnord is acquired by Britain's BTR plc (later renamed Invensys plc).
2002: The Carlyle Group investment firm buys Rexnord from Invensys.
2005: Rexnord acquires The Falk Corporation.

first sales decline in 20 years, down 17 percent. It now had three major business segments: power transmission components, specialty fasteners, and process equipment (which included the company's water, wastewater, and related sludge conditioning and treatment equipment and systems). During the year it acquired Contech, Inc., for $16 million in cash. With sales of more than $29 million, the 16-year-old company manufactured and marketed a wide line of adhesives, sealants, caulkings, and specialty chemicals used in building construction, maintenance, and renovation.

Sales again declined in 1983 to $804.5 million, compared to $936.6 million in 1982, while net income dropped to $3.93 million, compared to $7.15 million in 1982. Orders for industrial machinery products remained at low levels and overall sales were 14 percent below 1982 levels.

With four acquisitions in 1984, sales increased to $921 million. Acquired for $68.8 million, Clausing Corporation was the largest acquisition of the year. Clausing manufactured component products in plastics engineering, which added to Rexnord's portfolio of component products for use in a broad cross-section of industrial markets. Clausing's products served the automotive and electronics markets and could be used to develop new markets. Its industrial process control products supported Rexnord's strategy of strengthening and expanding its electronics-related businesses. Clausing also brought to Rexnord a profitable Industrial Distribution Group, which handled several lines of high-quality metal-working machine tools and accessories imported from European countries.

During the year Rexnord created a Process Controls Division and was building a major instrumentation and controls

business in the process control and industrial automation markets. Two of its 1984 acquisitions, Tano Corporation and Insta-Read Corporation, further expanded Rexnord's instrumentation and control capabilities in the industrial automation area. Tano was an industry leader in the design and manufacture of computer-based electronic systems for marine, oil and gas and energy management applications. Tano manufactured moving beam laser bar code scanners, with applications on the shop floor and in warehouse inventory control. These scanners complemented Rexnord's own omnidirectional bar code scanner, called Lasertrak.

The year 1985 was one of moderate growth in sales, earnings, and dividends for Rexnord. The company further expanded its instrumentation and control capabilities in the industrial automation area when it purchased Electronic Modules Corporation (EMC) for $46 million in cash and 42 million shares of Rexnord common stock in April 1985. With 1984 sales of $68 million, EMC designed and manufactured industrial and factory process controls. With EMC as its flagship, Rexnord created a new subsidiary, Rexnord Automation, that included its former Process Controls Division.

Since June 1981, Rexnord had divested 15 businesses with annual sales of $220 million, for $145 million. The company announced in 1985 that its major divestitures had been completed, although it said that there may be more in the future. In 1985 Robert Krikorian retired as chairman. Donald Taylor, formerly vice-chairman and CEO, became chairman and CEO. John P. Calhoun became president and chief operating officer.

Acquisition by Banner Industries in 1987

With the company in the process of repositioning itself, 14 percent of Rexnord's stock was acquired by Banner Industries of Cleveland, Ohio, in 1986. When Rexnord announced in December 1986 that it was planning a massive restructuring, including selling most of its capital goods businesses and moving toward higher technology products, Jeffrey J. Steiner, chairman of Banner Industries and Rexnord's largest stockholder, opposed it.

In March 1987 Banner completed its acquisition of Rexnord. In connection with the acquisition, Banner entered into a $550 million credit agreement with a group of financial institutions. Proceeds from the sale of certain Rexnord assets were to be used to reduce $420 million in term loans that were part of the $550 million credit agreement. As of June 30, 1987, approximately $105.8 million of Rexnord's net assets were held for sale.

By the end of 1987 Banner had sold one subsidiary of Rexnord, Mathews Conveyor of Kentucky, while employees of the Louisiana-based Rexnord Instrument Products purchased the division from Rexnord. Texas-based Rexnord Automation was also put up for sale, after the company decided it did not have the resources to compete in the automation sector. Additional assets were sold by February 1988 to finance the acquisition.

After offering $500 million earlier in 1988, Banner Industries acquired PT Components, Inc., of Indianapolis, Indiana, an auto brake systems manufacturer, for an undisclosed amount in August 1988. Interestingly, PT Components had a history longer than and somewhat parallel to that of Rexnord. It was originally founded in the 1870s as Ewart Manufacturing Company in Indianapolis, Indiana, by W.D. Ewart, a co-worker of Rexnord's founder, C.W. LeValley. Ewart had beaten inventor LeValley in the race to patent detachable link belts, but LeValley discovered a way to develop a link belt product that did not infringe on Ewart's patent and established his own company. The two companies were competitors in this field. Ewart Manufacturing later became the Link Belt Company and eventually PT Components.

Banner then organized Rex-PT Inc. as a combination of the Mechanical Power Division of Rexnord, Inc., and PT Components, Inc. Rex-PT would be a $500 million supplier of industrial couplings, conveying chain, and other industrial chains, bearings, reducers, clutches, brakes, and drives.

In September 1988 Banner Industries sold its 60 percent majority ownership in Rex-PT Holdings, Inc., to a group of investors, and kept a 40 percent interest. Rex-PT Holdings was the parent of Rex-PT, Inc., which was renamed Rexnord Corporation by the end of 1989. The sale of its majority interest resulted in an after-tax gain in excess of $45 million for Banner. Net proceeds were $360 million, including an increase of $260 million in cash and debt reduction of $100 million.

In June 1989 Banner Industries acquired the outstanding common stock of Fairchild Industries, Inc., for $18 per share. The transaction was valued at approximately $400 million and included the assumption of certain liabilities. Effective November 15, 1990, Banner Industries changed its name to The Fairchild Corporation.

At this time, Rexnord became one of Fairchild's operating subsidiaries. In 1991 Rexnord's fastener operations were merged with the fastener operations of Fairchild Industries. While Rexnord had mainly served the industrial and military markets, Fairchild primarily served the commercial aviation industry.

By 1991 Rexnord was focused as a leading manufacturer of mechanical power transmission components. Its products were sold to such major industries as food and beverage processing, aerospace, construction, energy, and agriculture. Major product lines included chains, conveying equipment, bearings and seals, couplings, clutches, brakes, and drives. Some 55 percent of sales were for replacement parts. The international market continued to be a significant component of Rexnord's overall business, with 28 percent of sales coming from overseas customers in fiscal 1991. Outlook was good for growth in Europe, the Far East, and South America. Rexnord's 1991 sales were $552 million, compared to $567 million in 1990. During 1991, the Fairchild Corporation owned a 42 percent interest in Rexnord Corporation. In 1992, it was a 45 percent stake.

Public in 1992

In 1992 Fairchild's recapitalization program transformed Rexnord into a publicly traded company listed on the New York Stock Exchange. Prior to the recapitalization, Rexnord Corporation was merged into its immediate parent, Rex-PT Holdings, Inc, in June 1992. The Fairchild Corporation continued to own a controlling interest, through subsidiaries, of about 45 percent of the outstanding common stock. In July 1992 Rexnord made an initial public offering (IPO) of more than nine million shares of

common stock at $17 per share to raise money to redeem notes and preferred stock and to pay the costs of recapitalization. It also issued $172.5 million worth of unsecured ten-year corporate bonds (senior notes at 10.75 percent interest) for similar purposes. Immediately prior to the IPO, Rexnord was merged into Rex-PT Holdings, Inc., which was the surviving corporation. Rex-PT Holdings subsequently changed its name to Rexnord Corporation.

As a result of the IPO, the company was much less leveraged and had improved financial flexibility with more liquidity. The company was committed to a continuing program of cost reduction as well as plant consolidation. At the time of its IPO Rexnord's business consisted mainly of manufacturing and supplying mechanical power transmission components and related products. Principal products included engineered, conveying, flat top, and roller chains; various types of anti-friction bearings, speed reducers, shaft couplings and seals; and idlers, sprockets, and electric motor brakes and clutches. Major markets included food and beverage processing, pharmaceutical, commercial aerospace, chemical, petrochemical, coal oil field, transportation, sanitation, construction, machinery, cement, forest products, farm machinery, and industrial equipment industries.

In 1993 Rexnord achieved an operating profit of $82.7 million, up 21 percent from 1992 levels. Sales increased by 3.4 percent over the previous year. Recessionary conditions in Europe and in the commercial aerospace markets served by Rexnord were offset by aggressive cost reductions to preserve profit margins until full economic recovery. Rexnord's market value increased to approximately $140 million, some $80 million higher than the value carried on Fairchild's books. The investment was seen as a valuable, though undervalued, asset that would help Fairchild's ongoing recapitalization and debt reduction plans.

Sale to BTR in 1994

In December 1993 the pending acquisition of Rexnord by BTR plc, an international holding company based in London, England, was announced. BTR offered to purchase all of Rexnord's outstanding shares at $22.50 a share, with the total purchase price estimated to be approximately $420 million. Rexnord's stock value rose, and the company expected a bond upgrade from Moody's Investors and Standard & Poor's credit rating services. By the end of December Fairchild had sold its stock interest in Rexnord Corporation at a premium price, resulting in a pre-tax gain of $129.1 million. Fairchild received $181.9 million in cash. On December 23, 1993, the sale of Fairchild's 43.9 percent interest in Rexnord to BTR Dunlop Holdings, Inc., an American subsidiary of BTR plc, was completed. Approximately eight million shares were sold at $22.50 per share. In January 1994 the proposed merger with BTR Dunlop Holdings, Inc., a subsidiary of BTR, was approved at a special shareholders meeting. By this time, BTR Dunlop had acquired 52.8 percent of Rexnord's outstanding common stock. The merger took place between a wholly owned subsidiary of BTR Dunlop and Rexnord, with Rexnord being the surviving corporation. With BTR PLC as its ultimate parent company, Rexnord Corporation continued as a premier supplier of power transmission and conveying components to many different industries worldwide.

Rexnord made fewer major acquisitions in the second half of the decade. It did buy Addax Inc. in 1998. Addax, based in Lincoln, Nebraska, made mechanical power transmission components using advanced composite materials.

During this time, the Rexnord companies were part of the BTR's PowerDrives Group. In 1999, BTR merged with Siebe plc to form Invensys plc; Rexnord's ownership would soon change. By 2000, Rexnord employed 5,000 people at more than 30 plants around the world, and sales were about $700 million a year. Rexnord was investing considerable resources into replacing its sometimes antiquated equipment with state-of-the-art technology. This included optical inspection systems and new CNC grinding machines for producing roller bearings.

New Ownership in the Early 2000s

By 2002, parent company Invensys was struggling with debt and looking to focus on energy and production management. A buyer for Rexnord was found in The Carlyle Group, the famously well-connected investment group in Washington, D.C., which paid $880 million for Rexnord. The deal also included an infusion of $33 million in working capital. When the deal was completed in November of that year, RBS Global, Inc., became the holding company for Rexnord Corporation. It was a private company but filed annual reports with the SEC to accommodate the terms of some of its debt.

Company officials tied Rexnord's prospects to the health of the manufacturing sector at large, and the economy as a whole was not faring very well in 2003. Rexnord management made plans to shift about 50 jobs from Milwaukee to a plant in Morganton, North Carolina, but canceled the move after the unionized Wisconsin employees agreed to wage cuts of $3 an hour, or 13 percent, on average. Rexnord then decided to shut down the Morganton factory, which employed 160 people, even though it was not unionized. "Clearly the competitive pressures facing the business dictated that extraordinary efforts would be required," explained a company spokesperson.

Rexnord made a major acquisition in 2005, buying industrial power transmission product manufacturer The Falk Corporation from the Hamilton Sundstrand unit of United Technologies Corporation, which had owned Falk since 1968. The deal was worth $295 million and made Rexnord a $1 billion company again. Falk, also based in Milwaukee, had entered the gear business in 1899. In the early 2000s, Falk had plants in six countries, about 1,100 employees and annual sales of about $200 million. While Falk and Rexnord had competed in gear drives and couplings, Falk also had strengths in the mining industry. Falk continued to operate independently though plans were to integrate it into Rexnord over time.

Company representatives told the *Milwaukee Journal Sentinel* that Rexnord was able to combine operations and cut costs

following the merger; a recovery in the aviation industry was also playing to its benefit. Before the merger, Rexnord had posted net income of $21.6 million, up 51 percent, on revenues of $811.0 million, up 13.8 percent for its 2005 fiscal year.

Principal Subsidiaries

Rexnord S.A. (France); Rexnord Correntes Ltda. (Brazil); Rexnord FlatTop Europe BV (Netherlands); Rexnord Kette GmbH (Germany); Rexnord Marbett Srl (Italy).

Principal Competitors

Emerson Electric Company; Renold plc; Rockwell Automation, Inc.; Tsubakimoto Chain Company.

Further Reading

Barrett, Rick, "Rexnord Shows Signs of Merger's Benefit," *Milwaukee Journal Sentinel,* August 12, 2005, p. D3.

——, "Rexnord to Buy Competitor Falk; Longtime Local Firms Make Gears, Other Industrial Equipment," *Milwaukee Journal Sentinel,* April 6, 2005, p. 1.

"BTR to Buy Rexnord at $22.50 a Share," *Reuters Business Report,* December 2, 1993.

Content, Thomas, "Rexnord Corp. Again Up for Sale," *Milwaukee Journal Sentinel,* February 23, 2002, p. 1D.

Fauber, John, "Rexnord Sold to British Firm," *Milwaukee Journal,* December 2, 1993.

Fromstein, Ruth, *Milwaukee, The Best of All Worlds: A Contemporary Portrait,* Chatsworth, Calif.: Windsor Publications, 1990.

Holman, Kelly, "Rexnord Buys UT Unit for $295M," *TheDeal.com,* April 6, 2005.

Kirchen, Rich, "Rexnord Likes Long-Term Outlook," *Business Journal* (Milwaukee), December 4, 1993.

Knoche, Eldon, "Rexnord President and Art Benefactor Krikorian Emphasized Business Ethics," *Milwaukee Journal Sentinel,* April 10, 1999, p. 1.

McBride, Janet, "Invensys Sells Unit to Carlyle for $880 Mln," *Reuters News,* September 28, 2002.

MacFadyen, Ken, "Carlyle Group to Buy Rexnord from Invensys PLC," *Buyouts,* October 21, 2002.

Mecia, Tony, "Milwaukee-Based Equipment Maker Changes Deal, Will Shut Morganton, N.C., Plant," *Charlotte Observer,* March 11, 2003.

Radkowski, Leo, "Getting a Bonus: When This Company Traded Its Vintage ID Grinders for CNC Machines, It Got More Grinding Capacity/Capability Than It Expected," *Modern Machine Shop,* December 2001, pp. 82+.

Sandler, Larry, "Rexnord Buyout Boosts Stock Price," *Business Journal* (Milwaukee), December 3, 1993.

"Steelworkers Agree to Concessions at Rexnord West Milwaukee Plant," *Associated Press Newswires,* March 6, 2003.

—David Bianco
—update: Frederick C. Ingram

RWD Technologies, Inc.

5521 Research Park Drive
Baltimore, Maryland 21228
U.S.A.
Telephone: (410) 869-1000
Toll Free: (888) 793-8324
Fax: (410) 869-3002
Web site: http://www.rwd.com

Private Company
Incorporated: 1988
Employees: 700 (est.)
Sales: $104 million (2004 est.)
NAIC: 541490 Other Specialized Design Services

RWD Technologies, Inc., is a Baltimore, Maryland-based professional services company that helps companies maximize technology through training, information technology consulting, and organizational performance improvement solutions. Privately held, RWD divides its business into three categories: Performance Solutions, which helps automakers to launch new vehicles, railroads to improve reliability, and the petroleum and chemical industries to increase worker productivity; Enterprise Learning Solutions, providing training and other services to companies that use Oracle, PeopleSoft, and SAP software; and Applied Technology Solutions, helping pharmaceutical and other regulated industries integrate software systems, as well as develop custom applications. Although a relatively small company, with annual sales less then $150 million, RWD boasts a client list that includes a large number of Fortune 500 companies. It serves 20 industries, including automotive, chemical, consumer products, finance, manufacturing, medical, petrochemical, pharmaceutical, rail, and telecommunications. RWD maintains 19 offices in the United States, Australia, Belgium, Canada, France, Germany, Japan, and the United Kingdom.

Founder Jumpstarts Education During World War II

The letters RWD stand for the company's founder Robert William Deutsch. He was born in Far Rockaway, New York, in 1924, the son of a grocer, and grew up interested in math and science. In 1941 he entered Queens College to study engineering, choosing the school simply because it was affordable. Within a matter of weeks, the United States military base at Pearl Harbor, Hawaii was attacked by Japanese forces, Germany subsequently declared war on the United States, and the country found itself at war. Deutsch remained in school for two years before enlisting in the Army, which then sought to take advantage of his training. Deutsch was sent to study electrical engineering at the Massachusetts Institute of Technology, and afterwards dispatched to Europe, where he helped in the communications between U.S. and French forces.

Following the war, Deutsch returned to MIT in 1946, earned a Bachelor of Science degree in physics. He then went on to graduate school at the University of California at Berkeley, and in 1953 earned a Doctorate in high-energy physics. Deutsch next took a position at the General Electric Knolls Atomic Laboratory in Schenectady, New York, involved in the development of nuclear reactors that could be used by submarines. In 1957 he went to work for Florida-based General Engineering Company, and after that company was sold four years later Deutsch became a physics consultant on aerospace projects for Martin Marietta, a move that brought him to Baltimore. He then became a professor of Nuclear Engineering at Catholic University in Washington, D.C., in 1962, while continuing to serve as consultant for companies involved in nuclear power plants.

To bring in more consulting work, Deutsch tried his hand as an entrepreneur in 1965 with the launch of General Physics Corporation, which trained nuclear plant operators. The nuclear power industry was on the rise and General Physics prospered under his leadership as chief executive officer. Most of the work was on government contract, mostly for the Navy and nuclear power plants. Deutsch took the company public in 1982, retaining a quarter interest, but in 1986 National Patent Development Corporation acquired a controlling interest in General Physics, which by this point was generating about $115 million in annual revenues. In late 1987 National Patent wanted Deutsch to step down as CEO and offered him what *Forbes* in a 1998 profile called a "face-saving retirement package." He rejected it and, according to *Forbes*, "he told the world he'd been fired and sold his family's 24% stake in National Patent for $18 million. Less than three weeks later, in January 1988, Deutsch used some of the cash to get back in the training business.''

The 63-year-old Deutsch recruited his chief operating officer at General Physics, John H. Beakes, formed RWD Technologies and set up shop in Columbia, Maryland, the goal to provide high-tech services to commercial companies. It was a welcome change of direction for Deutsch, who had already concluded that both defense contracting and the nuclear power industry offered a meager opportunity for growth. He saw an opening to train workers on how to make the best use of the advanced technology that was being introduced in all industries. ''Deutsch got the idea for his second act,'' according to *Forbes,* ''after watching the frustration corporate management often experiences when it invests in new technology. Too often the employees don't really know how to use the new equipment properly, so the buyers don't reap maximum productivity gains.'' Deutsch explained the genesis of the problem to the *Washington Post* in a 1995 interview: ''The big companies tend to work from the top down. Someone sells top management on the idea of a new technology, but doesn't give them a system that's user-friendly. Top management forgets about the people who have to use the system.'' The primary goal of RWD was to customized those systems, then train the workers who would actually have to use them, but the greater mission was to help American manufacturers regain a competitive edge in the world.

RWD's early work was done with Chrysler Corporation, involved in the development of training programs that helped workers in the launch of new vehicles. Unlike most consulting firms that preferred to work with management, RWD liked to go directly to the shop floor to deal with problems from the bottom up. Deutsch told *Forbes,* ''Big consulting companies, when they do go into factories, talk down to the workers. It's just not in their culture to work with people who use their hands and with the nondegreed.'' In order to gather the kind of personnel comfortable with this approach, Deutsch eschewed MBAs, preferring instead to hire engineers and computer science graduates, while also avoiding graduates of premiere schools like MIT and Stanford or applicants with a perfect 4.0 grade point average. ''It means the person did nothing but study and did not have any social or athletic life,'' Deutech explained to *Forbes.* ''That person would have a hard time working in a place like this with our team environment.''

Success with Chrysler led to work with Ford Motor Company to help implement lean manufacturing methodologies in an engine plant. This would lead to RWD working with Ford to implement the Ford Production System in its factories around the world. RWD also learned lessons from its automotive work that could be applied to other industries. For example, the work it did with Ford on a new production line for automobile transmissions was useful in solving a problem for Frito-Lay Inc.,

which was trying to install a new potato chip production line that kept burning the chips. By changing the flow of oil, a lesson learned at Ford, the RWD troubleshooters solved the problem.

After three years RWD was profitable and established enough to not need a marketing department, a decision that also reflected the company's philosophy. ''Salesmen tend to promise solutions engineers can't deliver,'' Deutsch commented in the 1998 *Forbes* article, which added, ''RWD often approached an account by first asking if it can talk with workers: Before pitching to a food manufacturer, recently, an RWD project manager spent the day riding around with one of its deliverymen.''

Early 1990s SAP Work

In the early 1990s RWD expanded into computer systems. It helped Dow Chemical make changes to its training program to help implement the SAP enterprise resource planning (ESR) software it purchased. This project led to other SAP implementations, and RWD expanded its expertise to include other ERP packages, including Oracle and PeopleSoft. As a result, the client list swelled to include a wider variety of industries. RWD also beefed up its information technology capabilities in order to offer custom IT systems for corporate customers. For example, it helped office furniture manufacturer Steelcase to create a user friendly laptop ordering system for its salesmen and helped Holiday Inn develop an easy-to-use worldwide reservation system.

Revenues grew at a rapid clip in the 1990s, totaling $18.4 million in 1993 and topping the $65 million mark in 1996, when net income approached $5.2 million. In June 1997 the company was taken public, after twice postponing the initial stock offering because of poor market conditions. Not only did RWD raise $38 million, it was able to create a stock option plan for employees after they had been with the company for 12 months. Moreover, being public added credibility to RWD as it attempted to attract more Fortune 500 customers. On the downside, the company now had to spend hundreds of thousands of dollars each year on Securities and Exchange Commission filing fees, extra attorney and accountants' fees, investor mailings, and insurance to cover directors and officers. As long as the business continued to grow, the cost of being a public company was acceptable, but that situation would change within a few years. In the meantime, RWD continued to enjoy an upward trend in business. Sales totaled $85.7 million and net income topped $9 million in 1997. RWD was serving seven of the top ten of the Fortune 100 and 25 overall. The company was also becoming more of a global player, as 10 percent of revenues came from international sales, compared to just 2 percent in 1996, prompting RWD to open an office in Europe. Most of that growth was connected to RWD helping Ford implement its lean manufacturing production system at plants in the United Kingdom and Europe.

RWD enjoyed another strong year in 1998, when sales improved by 34 percent to $114.7 million and net income totaled $13.1 million. The company was listed among *Forbes* 200 Best Small Companies and *ComputerWorld* named it one of the Best IT Places to Work. By now the ERP practice was the fastest growing part of the business, but RWD also enjoyed significant successes in the IT area. For example, in 1998 the company developed an intranet-based diagnostic system for

5,300 Chrysler dealer repair shops, providing mechanics with up-to-date vehicle information. A similar system was then set up for John Deere equipment dealerships for their technicians to use in the field.

Business began to tail off in 1999, due in large measure to clients diverting money away to address the Y2K problem. Although RWD's revenues increased to $124.4 million in 1999, it was less than expected, and net income decreased 60 percent to $5 million. In addition, the price of RWD stock tumbled. After starting 1999 as a company with a market capitalization of $300 million, it ended the year worth half as much.

In June 1999 RWD acquired Merrimac Interactive Media Corp., an Internet-based technical training and testing solutions provider, and then in 2000 RWD established a new subsidiary called Lattitude360 to provide just-in-time training programs. RWD appeared to be on the rebound in 2000, as business increased during each of the first three quarters of the year before sagging in the fourth quarter. In the end sales improved to $133.7 million while net income slipped to $4.2 million. However, the slowdown at the end of the year was a harbinger of more difficult conditions to follow in 2001.

Poor Economy In Early 2000s Hinders Growth

Despite a retooling of its business models in 2000, RWD simply could not overcome a downturn in the economy that led clients to cut back on investments. Sales dropped to $118 million and the company reported a loss of $9 million in 2001. The reduction in corporate spending on IT services continued in 2002, when revenues decreased further to $117.5 million and RWD lost another $22.4 million. To make matters worse, the accounting scandals at such companies as Enron and Worldcom, resulted in new and costly regulations. To remain a public company would now cost RWD about $1 million a year. Given the company's size and struggle to regain profitability, Deutsch decided in 2003 to take the company private once again and eliminate these costs as RWD waited until economic conditions improved. Deutsch used a company he owned with his family, Research Park Acquisition Inc., to acquire the outstanding shares of RWD stock. The transaction was completed in September 2003.

Sales continued to slide in 2004, falling to $107 million. The company sought new business opportunities to turn things around, as Deutsch once again looked to military and other government work. In October 2004 the company created a new business group dedicated to the training of federal employees, anticipating that a large number of baby boomers were on the verge of retirement, creating a need for their replacements to be trained. The initial focus was on ERP software training. RWD also developed software that in November 2005 received certification for the Navy Marine Corps Intranet, capable of distributing documents and training materials and providing online help. In addition, in 2005 RWD hired a pair of executives to expand the Applied Technology Solutions division in hopes of drumming up more business from the pharmaceutical and other regulated industries.

Principal Divisions

Performance Solutions; Enterprise Learning Solutions; Applied Technology Solutions.

Principal Competitors

BrightStar Information Technology Group Inc.; International Business Machines Corporation; Sapient Corporation.

Further Reading

Ey, Craig S., "A Senior Entrepreneur," *Baltimore Business Journal,* January 28, 2000, p. 21.
Hirsh, Stacey, "Columbia, Md.-Based Technology Consulting Firm to Save Money by Going Private," *Baltimore Sun,* May 2, 2003.
Hughlett, Roger, "RWD Launches dot-com unit," *Washington Business Journal,* April 7, 2000, p. 93.
Novack, Janet, "A Well-Rounded Life," *Forbes,* March 9, 1998, p. 186.
Southerland, David, "RWD Technologies Finds a Lot of Room to Grow," *Washington Post,* October 16, 1995, p. F14.
——, "RWD Technologies Grows by Helping Corporate Giants," *Washington Post,* October 18, 1993, p. F08.
Stipe, Suzanne E., "In the Public Eye," *Baltimore Business Journal,* March 27, 1998, p. 27.

—Ed Dinger

THE

SCRIPPS

RESEARCH

INSTITUTE

The Scripps Research Institute

10550 North Torrey Pines Road
La Jolla, California 92037
U.S.A.
Telephone: (858) 784-1000
Fax: (858) 784-8118
Web site: http://www.scripps.edu

Not-for-Profit Company
Incorporated: 1924 as Scripps Metabolic Clinic
Employees: 2,600 (est.)
Operating Revenues: $265.22 million (2004)
NAIC: 541710 Research and Development in the
    Physical, Engineering, and Life Sciences

The Scripps Research Institute is one of the largest nonprofit research organizations in the United States. Based in La Jolla, California, the Institute is composed of eight departments: cell biology, chemistry, immunology, experimental medicine, infectology, molecular biology, neurobiology, and neuropharmacology. The Scripps staff includes 270 professors, with three Nobel Prize winners among its ranks, 800 postdoctoral fellows, 1,500 laboratory technicians, and 126 Ph.D. students. Most of the Institute's funding comes from grants from the National Institutes of Health (NIH) and alliances with pharmaceutical companies. In the 2000s Scripps began building a second research center in southern Florida, geared toward biomedical research, advanced technologies, and drug discovery.

Founder: 19th-Century Champion of Women's Rights

The Scripps Research Institute bears the name of its founder, Ellen Browning Scripps, a member of the family that also founded the Scripps chain of 21 daily newspapers, today part of the media holdings of The E.W. Scripps Company. Her father, a native of Great Britain and acclaimed bookbinder, relocated the family to Rushville, Illinois, when she was just seven years of age. An avid reader, she became one of the first women in the United States to attend college, graduating from Knox College in Illinois in 1858. She taught school for several years and then

in 1873, following the death of her father, she joined her brother, James E. Scripps, in launching the *Detroit Evening News,* investing all of her savings in the venture. Given that the country had just tumbled into one of its deepest economic depressions, it was a bold decision, but one that paid off handsomely. Not content to serve just as a proofreader, she began writing a daily front page column called ''Matters and Things,'' which became a highly popular vehicle for her opinions on topics such as prohibition and women's suffrage. Her column, which she authored for the next 60 years, became syndicated by some 1,000 newspapers. In the meantime, she also proved to be an adept businessperson. In 1878 she invested in an effort of her brother, Edward W. Scripps, to launch a Cleveland daily newspaper, the *Penny Press,* aimed at urban workers. It was the start of a chain of newspapers, many of which Ellen Scripps would invest in, and became the foundation of today's E.W. Scripps empire. Never married, she moved to San Diego, California, with Edward and his family in 1891, and then moved to La Jolla in 1896. She made even more money speculating in La Jolla real estate, and then in 1900 inherited a fortune from her brother, George H. Scripps. She treated the inheritance as a bequest and over the last third of her life devoted much of her time to philanthropic endeavors in southern California.

In 1924 Ellen Scripps broke her hip and was confined to a La Jolla sanitarium that was far from ideal. She decided to replace it with a first class hospital, and in that year she and her brother funded the 44-bed Scripps Memorial Hospital along with the Scripps Metabolic Clinic. The early focus was on caring for patients with diabetes, a disease that afflicted the Scripps family, and on researching treatment for diabetes. Ellen Scripps passed away in 1932, but the institutions she helped found lived on, including the Metabolic Clinic.

Modern Era Dating to the 1950s

The Clinic reached a turning point in 1955, a year that marked the birth of the Institute known today. It was renamed the Scripps Clinic and Research Foundation (SCRF) and most of its reserves were now committed to the construction of a new first-class research facility and the recruitment of leading biomedical scientists. A major coup for the Institute occurred in 1961 when renowned immunologist Frank Dixon and four of his colleagues left the University of Pittsburgh School of Medicine to establish the Department of Experimental Pathology at SCRF. The group of scientists focused its research on autoimmune diseases, with the funding mostly coming from NIH grants. SCRF began to gain in prominence, as reflected by a member of the faculty, Gerald M. Edelman, winning a 1972 Nobel Prize for his discoveries related to the chemical structure of antibodies. SCRF also expanded its scope during this period. In 1974 The General Clinical Research Center was established to test discoveries made in the Scripps laboratories in a clinical setting. By this time a number of research programs had developed, and in 1977 they were formally brought together under SCRF, which was reorganized as the Research Institute of Scripps Clinic.

Another turning point for the Institute occurred in the early 1980s, when immunology was becoming increasingly dependent on new molecular biology technologies. According to Yvonne Baskin, writing for *Science* in 1991, Dixon "considered it critical to propel the institute into molecular biology. But by then NIH funding was plateauing, and the institute's labs were full. 'We had no hard money, no endowment, and the medical end of this operation has always been a financial drag,' Dixon [said]." The solution on which the Institute settled was a commercial partnership with a pharmaceutical company. In 1982 Scripps signed a long-term licensing agreement with Johnson & Johnson. In exchange for funding, which would amount to about $10 million a year, Scripps gave Johnson & Johnson first rights to the fruits of its research through 1996. The pharmaceutical company also funded the construction of a new molecular biology building, and in 1983 Scripps founded its Molecular Biology Department. In 1985 Scripps forged another commercial alliance, this time with PPG Industries, and doubled the size of the building. PPG gained first rights in areas not covered by the Johnson & Johnson agreement, such as polymer chemistry and plant molecular biology. The company also had second rights on Scripps's discoveries passed up by Johnson & Johnson. NIH funds did not dry up, however. "In 1986," according to Baskin, "when the total of its grants from the National Institutes of Health (NIH) passed the $39 million mark, the Scripps Research Institute began billing itself as the nation's largest 'independent, nonprofit biomedical research center.' The unspoken rival Scripps had surpassed was the Mayo Clinic."

Scripps grew on other fronts as well as the 1980s came to a close. Dixon stepped down as director in 1987, replaced by protégé Richard Lerner. Two years later Lerner recruited K.C. Nicolaou from the University of Pennsylvania to establish a new chemistry department. In keeping with a Scripps tradition

of working across disciplines, Nicolaou soon launched a program in biorganic synthesis that quickly became a leader in the field. Lerner also established Scripps's first graduate program in 1989 in Macromolecular and Cellular Structure and Chemistry. A program in chemistry, with an emphasis on bioorganic synthesis, would follow two years later.

Reorganization in the 1990s

More organizational changes occurred in 1991. SCRF and Scripps Memorial Hospitals were reaffiliated, both placed under a parent organization, Scripps Institutions of Medicine and Science. SCRF now became a separate corporation, taking on the name The Scripps Research Institute.

Scripps established its Department of Neurobiology in 1992. At the close of that year, four full years before the agreement with Johnson & Johnson was set to expire, the Institute arranged a new drug development alliance with Swiss pharmaceutical Sandoz AG, a ten-year deal worth $300 million set to begin in January 1997. It was a good fit for the parties, given that both concentrated on immunology, central nervous system disorders, and cardiovascular diseases. Although Johnson & Johnson would no longer provide general research funding, it continued to work with Scripps on development projects for specific drugs. The agreement with Sandoz, however, sparked some unexpected controversy, as some critics questioned the propriety of Sandoz gaining the rights to research partially funded by the federal government. A January 1993 editorial in the *San Diego Union Tribune* questioning the arrangement caught the attention of a U.S. Congressman, Democrat Rob Wyden of Oregon, who was investigating the price of new drugs and began examining arrangements between government-funded research institutions and drugmakers. He then wrote a letter to the NIH asking the agency to look into the matter. Subsequent pressure from Congress and the NIH, which threatened to restrict future grants to the Institute, forced Scripps and Sandoz to rework their agreement in June 1993. In the end, the fundamentals of the deal remained $300 million over ten years, but Sandoz would not receive first rights to all Scripps's research, just the research it directly funded.

In the second half of the 1990s, Scripps continued to expand its interests. It established the Skaggs Institute for Chemical Biology in 1996, the result of a $100 million commitment from Aline and Sam Skaggs through their charitable entities. The mission of the new unit was to conduct research where chemistry and biology converged in order to develop cures for diseases. In 1999 contributions from the Harold L. Dorris Foundation led to the creation of The Harold L. Dorris Neurological Research Center to conduct research into neurological disorders, such as epilepsy, Alzheimer's disease, and Parkinson's disease.

The early 2000s saw more centers opening within the Scripps Research Institute. In 2001 the Institute for Childhood and Neglected Diseases was established to focus on diseases such as epilepsy, mental retardation, malaria, cystic fibrosis, chronic pain, and depression. The following year the Helen L. Dorris Institute for the Study of Neurological and Psychiatric Disorders of Children and Adolescents was founded. The mission of this center was to investigate the pathological basis of

Key Dates:

1924: The Scripps Metabolic Clinic opens.
1955: The clinic changes its name to Scripps Clinic and Research Foundation.
1977: Research programs are brought under the Research Institute of Scripps Clinic.
1982: An alliance is forged with Johnson & Johnson.
1991: The Scripps Research Institute name is adopted.
1997: Johnson & Johnson is replaced by Sandoz AG.
2004: Scripps Florida opens.

mental disorders in order to develop therapies. In 2003 Scripps established the Pearson Center for Research on Alcoholism and Addiction, funded by an anonymous gift. The goal of this center was to develop new clinical treatments to help people free themselves from alcohol and drug addictions. During this period of time Scripps also added two more Nobel Prizes. K. Barry Sharpless won the 2001 Nobel Prize in Chemistry for his work on chirally catalyzed oxidation reactions. A year later his colleague, Kurt Wuthrich, was awarded the Nobel Prize in Chemistry for the development of nuclear resonance spectroscopy, used to determine the three-dimensional structure of biological macromolecules in solution.

In June 2003 Scripps's facilities were visited by Florida Governor Jeb Bush, who began talks with the Institute's officials in an effort to convince them to launch a second research facility in Florida's Palm Beach County. The two sides came to an agreement, which was signed in January 2004, calling for the creation of Scripps Florida, a division of The Scripps Research Institute. In the hope of adding more than 40,000 jobs that would develop around the new research facility and transform South Florida into a center for the life sciences, Scripps received a one-time $310 million appropriation of federal economic development funds from Florida. In addition, Palm Beach County provided 100 acres of undeveloped land and $137 million for the construction of a temporary and permanent facility. Palm Beach County was chosen as the site for Scripps Florida because of its reputation as the state's philanthropic center, an important consideration because the new research institute would depend on private donations. Nevertheless, the state and local governments expected to be paid back handsomely on their investment. They estimated that over the course of the next 15 years Scripps Florida would bring in about $1.6 billion in income to the area and increase Florida's gross domestic product by $3.2 billion. Moreover, beginning after the

seventh year, Scripps promised to repay up to $155 million to Florida's Biomedical Research Trust Fund.

Scripps Florida opened in a small temporary facility on the campus of Boca Raton's Florida Atlantic University in the spring of 2004. It was quick to launch a doctoral program at the school. A year later the unit moved into a new 40,000-square-foot laboratory building located on the university's Jupiter, Florida, campus. In that year, ground was broken on the main facility, a 350,000-square-foot state-of-the-art campus on the 100 acres provided by Palm Beach County, slated to open in 2007.

While a great deal of attention was received by Scripps Florida, the parent Institute continued to thrive in southern California, where it had already proven to be an important catalyst in the $6.3 million biotech industry that had developed in the La Jolla area. In 2002 it forged another important commercial alliance, this time with Xerox Corporation's Palo Alto Research Center (PARC). The partnership was dubbed the Scripps-PARC Institute for Advanced Biomedical Studies and began work on the development of new cancer detecting tools. Two years later, PARC and Scripps established a separate institute to carry on the work.

Principal Operating Units

The Skaggs Institute for Chemical Biology; Institute for Childhood and Neglected Diseases; The Helen L. Dorris Institute for the Study of Neurological and Psychiatric Disorders of Children and Adolescents; The Harold L. Dorris Neurological Research Center; The General Clinical Research Center; The Center for Integrative Molecular Biosciences; The Pearson Center for Research on Alcoholism and Addiction.

Further Reading

Anderson, Christopher, "Scripps Backs Down on Controversial Sandoz Deal," *Science,* June 25, 1992, p. 1872.
——, "Scripps-Sandoz Deal Comes Under Fire," *Science,* February 12, 1992, p. 889.
Baskin, Yvonne, "Manifest Destiny at the Scripps Research Institute," *Science,* July 12, 1991, p. 140.
Cole, Jonathan E., et al., "Scripps Is Catalyst for Florida's Life Sciences Industry," *Venture Capital Journal,* March 1, 2005, p. 1.
Hilts, Philip J., "Research Group's Tie to Drugmaker Is Questioned," *New York Times,* June 18, 1993.
Lauer, Nancy Cook, "Florida Lawmakers Get Acquainted with Scripps Research Institute," *Tallahassee Democrat,* October 22, 2003.
Seemuth, Mike, "Science Friction: The Launch of Scripps Florida," *South Florida CEO,* June 2005, p. 106.

—Ed Dinger

Sirti S.p.A.

Via Stamira d'Ancona 9
Milano
Italy
Telephone: +39 02 95881
Fax: +39 02 95883333
Web site: http://www.sirti.it

Public Company
Incorporated: 1921 as Società Italiana Reti Telefoniche
    Interurbane
Employees: 4,725
Sales: EUR 456.4 million ($550 million) (2004)
Stock Exchanges: Milan
Ticker Symbol: SIT
NAIC: 334210 Telephone Apparatus Manufacturing;
    334220 Radio and Television Broadcasting and Wireless
    Communications Equipment Manufacturing; 334290
    Other Communication Equipment Manufacturing

Sirti S.p.A. specializes in developing telecommunications networks and systems. The company's operations span the full range of services, from design and engineering, to the physical deployment of cable-based and wireless networks, to their maintenance. Sirti's expertise includes fiber optic networks, satellite link base stations, digital television transmission networks, and wireless communications systems. The company also builds traffic control networks for highways and railways, and electrical power transmission and distribution networks. The company, formerly part of Telecom Italia, remains Italy's leading provider of telecommunications networks, and is also a world-leading specialist in this sector. In the mid-2000s, Sirti's maintenance operations oversaw more than 35,000 miles of fiber optic cable, and more than 2.5 million access lines. Sirti also develops software and provides software support services for its network operations. Since the 1990s, the company has worked to reduce its reliance on Italy and Telecom Italia. The company has operations in Spain, through subsidiary Seirt, and also operates a subsidiary in Argentina, through which Sirti has established a base for expansion into the rest of the South American market. The company also has subsidi-

aries in France and Switzerland, and holds stakes in Sirti-branded joint ventures in the United Kingdom and Germany. Telecom Italia sold Sirti in 2000 to the Wiretel investment consortium including Techint S.p.A. and Stella International S.p.A., as well as the Benetton family's 21 Investment, among others; in 2005, Wiretel sold 69.5 percent of Sirti to a buyout partnership involving fellow Sirti shareholders Clessidra SGR and Investindustrial. Clessidra and Investindustrial have indicated their interest in acquiring full control of Sirti.

Cabling Italy in the 20th Century

Sirti had its origins in the years following World War I, when Piero Pirelli, of the Pirelli industrial empire, and Vitorrio Teschino founded a company in order to lay cable and provide long-distance connections among Italy's cities. Founded in 1919, the company was formally incorporated as a limited liability company in 1921 under the name Società Italiana Reti Telefoniche Interurbane.

Sirti's primary customer was the telecommunications bodies set up under the auspices of the Ministry of Post and Telecommunications, and the Italian PTT later became not only Sirti's only customer, but also its parent company. Sirti's first project was the construction of a telephone network linking the cities of Milan, Turin, and Genoa. Through the 1920s and 1930s, the company remained a privileged partner of the PTT, responsible for connecting many more of the country's cities into a unified national telephone market. A major project for Sirti came in 1932, when the company deployed a 270-kilometer undersea cable connecting the island of Sardinia with the Italian mainland. Sirti also followed the Italian PTT in its operations overseas, becoming a telecommunications infrastructure specialist.

The post-World War II economic boom and the rise in demand for telephones in Italy placed Sirti at the forefront of the growing national telecommunications market. Placed under the national telecommunications entity, STET, Sirti played a primary role in the modernization of the country's telephone system, and in turn in the country's modernization in general. During the 1950s, Sirti began developing a new telephone network combining coaxial cable technology with radio-based wireless technol-

Company Perspectives:

Sirti: tradition and innovation in telecommunications. Sirti is the Italian leading company in engineering and realization of telecommunication networks and systems. The wide experience achieved and the in-depth technical expertness allow Sirti to provide customers with solutions of a high technological level in the different segments of telecommunications and ICT. All those who need a strategic asset, such as a network infrastructure aimed to business development, for instance telecommunication operators both incumbent or newcomers, big public or private users, such as Public Administration, Railways, Public services providers, great Corporations, find Sirti as the perfect partner able to analyze all problems and propose solutions tailored both on the technological and economic point of view. To achieve these targets, Sirti has set up an operating organization spread on the national territory, ready to timely and effectively react, and that is able to manage the project in the strictest respect of the time scheduled.

ogy. Work on the network continued through the 1960s. STET's position in overseas markets, including its longstanding operations serving the Latin American markets, also gave Sirti continued access to those markets over the next decades.

Nearly all of the company's revenues came from Italy, however, and was based on its work for just two customers, SIP and ASST, both parts of STET. The company nevertheless enjoyed steady turnover growth—by as much as 20 percent and more per year into the 1990s—and even posted double-digit net profit growth. The decision to upgrade Italy's national telephone network, replacing the coaxial network with fiber optic cables, played a large role in Sirti's growth. Launched in the 1980s and continued into the 1990s, the "Eighties Project," as it was called, involved not only the replacement of the country's phone cables, including across the mountainous regions as well as the submarine lines connecting Sicily and Sardinia to the mainland, but also a networkwide upgrade of the country's terminals and related switching and transmission infrastructure for future digital compatibility.

Into the mid-1990s, however, as the Italian government began making progress toward the privatization of the country's telecommunications sector, Sirti began a quest for diversifying its operations, both geographically and in seeking other areas of operations. As part of the group's effort to expand, Sirti entered a number of new markets during the 1990s, including France, Spain, and Germany, as well as the East European market, and, through a subsidiary in Argentina, the South American market. The company supported this effort with the acquisition of a number of smaller companies as well as through the creation of joint ventures. The company entered Portugal, for example, after Spanish subsidiary Seirt acquired a small company there, broadening Sirti's reach to the whole of the Iberian peninsula.

As a result of Sirti's internationalization effort, the company reduced its Italian revenues to just 83 percent of its total by 1993, and to approximately 70 percent by 1997. Yet Italy

remained the group's sole source of income for much of this time, as its foreign operations, such as Sirti's U.K. operations, set up as a joint venture, struggled to gain a foothold in the new markets.

Europe became a natural target for Sirti's expansion. Yet Sirti's ability to acquire scale on the continent was hampered by the fact that during the period, Sirti was the only specialist company of its kind. As a result, the company found no acquisition opportunities of a significant size. Instead, the company continued its expansion by organic growth, as well as completing smaller acquisitions and through establishing partnerships. Already in the 1980s, the company had formed a partnership with Olivetti, called Eurolan, which specialized in the development and deployment of local area networks. Sirti also developed an expertise in developing network management systems and the customized software needed to guide them.

Independent in the New Century

Through the 1990s Sirti's range of operations expanded to include Poland, where, in 1995, the company won a contract worth ITL 22 billion to install a 1,400-kilometer fiber optic network in Poland. The company also had entered the Middle East, leading a consortium to win a $100 million contract to construct a fiber optic telephone network in Beirut from Siemens AG. Meanwhile, Latin America, supported by the group's base in Argentina, remained a primary foreign market for the company. By the mid-2000s, Sirti had become active in Brazil, Chile, and Bolivia. Elsewhere, the company completed contracts in Saudi Arabia, Gabon, Libya, and Egypt.

The Italian government, in the meantime, had been preparing the much-anticipated privatization of the country's telephone monopoly, regrouped and renamed as Telecom Italia in the mid-1990s. As part of Telecom Italia's own effort to become a leading global telecommunications player, the company began a program of selling off its noncore operations, including Sirti.

By 1995, the Italian government had reduced its stake to just 49 percent. A first effort to complete the privatization was made in 1997, when Telecom Italia began negotiations with the Pirelli group, a deal that would have brought Sirti full circle, as it were. By the end of the decade, however, the two sides were unable to agree and the deal fell through. Instead, Telecom Italia sold its remaining share of Sirti to a consortium, called Wiretel, led by Techint S.p.A., the Italian steelmaker, which also had extensive operations in Latin America. Other members of the consortium included Stella, the Italian timber group, and the Benetton family's investment vehicle, 21 Investimenti.

Under its new owners, Sirti focused its efforts on expanding its operations in Italy and Spain, especially. The company recognized the emergence of new technologies—such as high-speed and wireless Internet transmission, and the emergence of digital television broadcasting—and new markets. One of these was the railway market, which offered a built-in potential for network development. Sirti also expanded into the satellite broadcasting and transmission networks, as well as military network applications.

By 2005, Sirti had successfully shed its former reliance on Telecom Italia and had emerged as a truly independent—and

Key Dates:

1919: Piero Pirelliand Vitorrio Teschino found a company in order to lay cable and provide long-distance connections among Italy's cities.

1921: The company is incorporated as Società Italiana Reti Telefoniche Interurbane.

1932: A submarine cable is laid, linking Sardinia to the Italian mainland.

1950s: The company develops a new coaxial cable- and radio-based telecommunications network in Italy.

1980s: The ''Eighties Project'' begins, replacing Italy's telephone network with fiber optic cables and a digital-ready infrastructure.

1995: The Italian government, through STET (later Telecom Italia), sells 51 percent of Sirti.

2000: Telecom Italia sells the remaining share to a Wiretel investment consortium.

2005: An investment partnership between Clessidra SGR and Investindustrial LP acquires Wiretel's 69.5 percent stake and announces its intention to buy out the minority shareholders.

international—company. With its sales rising to EUR 456 million ($550 million), up from approximately $100 million at the beginning of the decade, Sirti had become a major international specialist in telecoms engineering and services. Sirti also had found new owners as it turned toward the mid-century. In 2004, an investment partnership between Clessidra SGR and Investindustrial agreed to buy Wiretel's 69.5 percent of Sirti. The new majority owners of the company then announced their intention to buy out Sirti's minority shareholders as well. With more than 70 years of experience, Sirti prepared to extend its network expertise into the 21st century.

Principal Subsidiaries

EPlanet S.p.A. (22.85%); Seirt SAU (Spain); Setelco Lugano Fr. (Switzerland); Sirti Argentina S.A.; Sirti GmbH (Germany; 19%); Sirti Ltd. (U.K.; 20%); Sirti Progetto Reti S.p.A.; Sirti S.A. (France); Sirti Sistemi S.p.A.

Principal Competitors

Bechtel Group, Inc.; Autostrade - Concessioni e Costruzioni Autostrade S.p.A.; Eiffage S.A.; Autoroutes du Sud de la France; Telindus Group N.V.; Dycom Industries, Inc.

Further Reading

Gelfi, Francesco, ''Sirti Linking the Past and Future,'' *Business Week,* November 20, 1989.

Lane, David, ''Italian PM Aims for Stet Sales This Year,'' *Privatisation International,* June 1996, p. 8.

O'Brian, Heather, ''Majority of Sirti Bought Out,'' *Daily Deal,* September 15, 2004.

''Siemens AG to Construct a Fiber Optic Telephone Network,'' *Fiber Optics News,* October 10, 1994, p. 9.

''Sirti Installing Telecommunications for the Europe of Tomorrow,'' *Business Week,* December 24, 1990, p. IS 29.

''Sirti Shareholders Approve Merger,'' *IPR Strategic Business Information Database,* June 22, 1999.

''Sirti Signs Fiber Deal with Polish Telecom,'' *Newsbytes,* July 3, 1995.

''Telecom Italia to Sell Sirti Cable Laying Business,'' *Financial Times,* August 4, 2001, p. 21.

—M.L. Cohen

SPARTECH Corporation

Spartech Corporation

120 South Central Avenue
Suite 1700
Clayton, Missouri 63105-1705
U.S.A.
Telephone: (314) 721-4242
Fax: (314) 721-1447
Web site: http://www.spartech.com

Public Company
Incorporated: 1960 as Permaneer Corporation
Employees: 3,750
Sales: $1.12 billion (2004)
Stock Exchanges: New York
Ticker Symbol: SEH
NAIC: 326130 Laminated Plastics Plate, Sheet, and
Shape Manufacturing; 326113 Unsupported Plastics
Film and Sheet (Except Packaging) Manufacturing

Spartech Corporation operates as a leading manufacturer of engineered thermoplastic materials, polymeric compounds, and molded and profile products. Its products are used in a wide variety of items, ranging from subzero refrigerators to kayaks and food jars. Spartech serves the packaging, transportation, building and construction, and the recreation and leisure markets. The company has 43 manufacturing facilities in the United States, Canada, Mexico, and Europe. Together, these facilities have an annual production capacity of more than 1.4 billion pounds.

A Bumpy Road to Success Since the 1960s

Spartech originated as Permaneer Corporation in St. Louis, Missouri in 1960. Founded by Allen Portnoy, Permaneer manufactured doors, paneling, furniture, and other wood products. The company was successful through the decade, and it went public in 1968. Portnoy took Permaneer on an expansion spree in the early 1970s, borrowing heavily. By the mid-1970s, the company was collapsing under its debt load, and in 1975 Permaneer's creditors forced Portnoy's resignation. One year later, Permaneer declared bankruptcy.

Portnoy was not ready to give up, however. In 1977, Portnoy joined with Lawrence Powers, a Wall Street securities lawyer with a background in public offerings and acquisitions, to form Spartan Manufacturing Corporation. Spartan won bankruptcy court approval to take over Portnoy's former company. Portnoy took the titles of president and chief executive officer, Powers was named chairman, and, together with general counsel Martin Green, they controlled some 80 percent of Spartan's stock. The partners, determined to avoid Permaneer's fate, attempted to protect Spartan by taking it on the then-popular diversification route. Over the next several years, Spartan built itself into a conglomerate of nine separate businesses, ranging from plastics to computer equipment to oil well pipe couplings, and including store fixtures, precision machines, copper tubing, and a computer lease brokerage business. These acquisitions took the form of leveraged buyouts or were arranged through secured financing. In its initial years, Spartan enjoyed the tax breaks brought by Permaneer's financial problems, helping reduce the income tax on Spartan's earnings. An early, yet troubled, centerpiece of the company was a plastic extrusion plant in Union, Missouri, a business that predated Spartan's formation. In 1980, the company acquired Alchem Plastics, with a plant in Los Angeles producing extruded custom sheet plastic, and a second plastics company, Koenig Plastics Co., a plastic scrap reprocessor, and bundled its plastics businesses under the Alchem name.

Spartan grew quickly. Starting with about $2 million in sales in 1977, Powers and Portnoy built annual revenues to $20 million in 1978, $56 million in 1979, and $79 million in 1980. In those early years, Spartan's earnings appeared to keep pace, rising from $467,000 in 1978 to $1.5 million in 1979 and $1 million in 1980. Many of Spartan's businesses were already bleeding, however, when the company ran head on into the recession of the early 1980s. By 1982, Spartan was losing money—posting a loss of $4 million for the year despite sales topping $100 million—and Portnoy and Powers were besieged once again by creditors. Spartan began divesting its businesses as the company's fortunes continued to slide. Powers and Portnoy reorganized the company, renaming it Spartech, around its plastics and computer business. In 1983, the company posted a loss of $10 million. Relations between Portnoy and Powers also cooled. As Powers told the *St. Louis Post-Dispatch,* "I lost

---

Company Perspectives:

Our mission is a simple one. All of us at Spartech endeavor: to meet the needs of our customers with the highest standards of value, quality, service, and integrity; to provide our employees with a safe and healthy work place where each has an equal opportunity to succeed; to operate our facilities in such a manner as to protect the environment; and to aim for a consistent and superior return on equity for all shareholders.

---

confidence in [Portnoy's] management of Spartech and he lost confidence in my willingness to follow his lead as we lurched from one dispute with creditors to another in 1982–83.''

Portnoy and Powers agreed to split in 1983. Spartech, led by Powers, would keep its plastics business, while Portnoy would take control of the company's computer equipment business, spun off as Digitech. That company worked on technology that would allow computer speech recognition. Digitech, however, proved to be a money pit. Portnoy poured his personal savings and stock into the company to keep it afloat, but it finally went bankrupt in 1990.

Deja Vu in the 1980s

Powers, meanwhile, had been training as a manager, attending Harvard Business School's executive management program from 1982 to 1983. It was there that Powers hit upon the idea of restructuring Spartech around its plastics business to restore the company to profitability. Joined by Buechler, who took charge of the Alchem Plastics division, Spartech completed its divestiture of unrelated businesses and concentrated on rebuilding itself as a plastics manufacturer. The company started with negative assets of some $2 million, with sales of $24.5 million and a net loss of nearly $11 million. By 1985, however, the company had turned itself around, raising revenues to nearly $33 million and posting a profit of nearly $1.3 million.

Buechler oversaw the day-to-day management of the company at its Missouri headquarters while Powers, working out of his New York office, led Spartech on a new buying spree (and into renewed losses by the end of the decade). During the mid-1980s, however, Spartech grew strongly, retaining its focus on the plastics industry. In May 1985 the company made its first new acquisition, of Southwest Converting for $2.5 million in cash and notes, adding that company's $7.5 million revenues. But Spartech was already preparing two more acquisitions that would double the company's size. The first acquisition, of Adams Industries, with revenues of $25 million, extended Spartech into a new area of plastics, polyethylene film manufacturing. The second acquisition followed in January 1986, adding the $30 million Franklin Plastics, a specialty plastics compounder, as a third Spartech division. At the same time, the company began paying attention to its internal growth, stepping up its capital expenditures. By 1986, the company's revenues had climbed to $70.6 million, providing a net income of $1.5 million. Spartech's stock, which had traded as low as 50 cents per share, was beginning to rise. Yet Spartech was only starting on its newest acquisition drive.

By 1988, Spartech had added seven more acquisitions, including rigid sheet producers Atlas Plastics and Eagle Plastics; specialty alloy and compounder The Resin Exchange; polyethylene film maker Favorite Plastics, for $18 million; the Burlington South compounding plant from Occidental Chemical Corp., for $6.2 million; and Koro Corp., a Boston-based rigid plastic sheet producer. The acquisitions helped boost Spartech's revenues to $138.4 million by 1987 and to $221.8 million in 1988 and gave Spartech the lead in the rigid sheet plastic market. The company was also profitable, generating $9.4 million in 1987. Financing for this activity came in part with a $12 million dollar investment by Trust Co. of the West subsidiary TCW Capital in 1986, which also helped to head off a hostile takeover attempt, followed by $40 million raised through a $25 million debenture offering and a $15 million subordinated financing agreement, the latter arranged through TCW Capital.

By 1988, however, Spartech's profits were beginning to slip beneath the weight of its debt load, which, at $100 million, had reached an 11-to-1 debt-to-equity ratio. Profits fell to $3.3 million for the year. The Koro unit was failing (the company sold it less than a year after its acquisition), as was its Favorite Plastics acquisition, leading Spartech to charge that company with inflating its revenues prior to its acquisition by Spartech. The company looked to sell its profitable Atlas-Alchem division to help maintain its profits. Instead, however, the company agreed to sell 28 percent of Spartech's stock to British Vita plc, the largest rigid sheet plastic producer in Europe, which had seven plants to complement Spartech's six U.S. rigid sheet plants.

By 1989, Spartech was again seeing red, in the amount of $12.7 million on $185 million. The loss included the closing of Spartech's failing polyethylene film division, the disposition of which was completed only in 1991. Spartech's losses continued, reaching $17.7 million for 1991, which included a charge for $12 million against the closing of its polyethylene film plants. Under pressure from Spartech's major shareholders, British Vita and TCW, Powers resigned from the company in October 1991. He was replaced as chief executive by Buechler.

Third Time's the Charm in the 1990s

Under Buechler's leadership, Spartech again regrouped, now around its rigid sheet and rollstock division and its compound group. With the polyethylene unit's losses gone, and the company's overhead reduced (Spartech closed Powers's New York office and consolidated its headquarters in Clayton, after paying Powers a parachute of some $2.5 million) Spartech again returned to profitability, posting $4.2 million on 1982's $168.8 million in revenues. Buechler next turned to reducing the company's $75 million in debt. In April 1993, he reached agreement with the company's creditors to convert $30 million of subordinated debt into new shares of common and preferred stock, reducing the company's debt-to-equity ratio to 1.2-to-1.

Meanwhile, Spartech returned to expansion through acquisition. In January 1993, the company purchased plastic custom extrusion equipment and related business from Penda Corp., adding $15 million to company sales. That purchase was followed in March of the next year by the $8 million acquisition of Product Components, Inc., adding two new manufacturing plants and extending Spartech's plastic sheet line. In September

Key Dates:

1960: Permaneer Corporation is created.
1968: The company goes public.
1976: Permaneer declares bankruptcy.
1977: Allen Portnoy and Lawrence Powers form Spartan Manufacturing Corporation.
1980: Alchem Plastics and Koenig Plastics Co. are acquired.
1982: The company is reorganized as Spartech Corporation.
1983: Portnoy and Powers split; Powers remains head of Spartech.
1985: Adams Industries is acquired.
1986: Spartech purchases Franklin Plastics.
1989: British Vita plc buys a 28 percent stake in the company.
1996: Portage Industries Corporation and Hamelin Group Inc. are acquired.
1998: Three purchases are made, including Anjac-Doron Plastics Inc., Polycom Huntsman, and Prismaplast Canada Ltd.
2002: British Vita begins selling off its stake in Spartech.
2005: Buechler retires; George Abd is named his successor.

1994, Spartech, which had been looking to expand its Midwest operations, bought the extrusion and color concentrates units of Wichita, Kansas-based Pawnee Industries, Inc. These acquisitions helped Spartech boost its share of the rigid sheet market to 28 percent, while expanding its compounding capacity as well. The company's revenues rose to $256.6 million in 1994, for net earnings of nearly $11 million.

To prepare for further acquisitions as well as a second public offering, Spartech raised $50 million in a private share placement and arranged an unsecured credit line of $40 million. By January 1996, Spartech moved to grow again, purchasing Wisconsin-based Portage Industries Corp. for $16 million and adding that company's $35 million in sales and two sheet extrusion and light-gauge thermoforming plants. The Portage acquisition boosted Spartech's total production capacity to 450 million pounds per year.

Having entered the thin-wall thermoforming business with the Portage acquisition, Spartech moved to consolidate that capability, and also to enter a new market, injection molding. In June 1996, Spartech acquired Montreal-based Hamelin Group, Inc., and its sheet extrusion, color concentrate, and injection molding units. The purchase, for $55 million, brought Spartech into Canada for the first time and added some $80 million to Spartech's revenues, while boosting the company's production to 550 million pounds. The acquisition of Hamelin's injection molding business also was seen as a strategic move for the company, bringing it into the consumer market, which offered less volatility during economic downturns.

Spartech's sales continued to gain strongly due to its acquisition, rising from $352 million in 1995 to $391 million in 1996. The Hamelin addition was expected to swell Spartech's revenues to more than $475 million in its 1997 fiscal year. The company also reported continued strength in its earnings, with income of $14.5 million in 1995 and $18.3 million in 1996. In September 1996, Spartech posted a second public offering of six million shares. With its stock, which had slipped below $1 per share in the early 1990s, trading at $9.50 per share, Spartech finally appeared to have found its course.

Spartech in the Late 1990s and Beyond

By 1997, Spartech controlled nearly one-third of the rigid plastic sheet and rollstock extruder market. The company made several acquisitions during the late 1990s that left it well positioned for additional growth. In 1998, the company bought Anjac-Doron Plastics Inc., Polycom Huntsman, and Prismaplast Canada Ltd. Five acquisitions were made in 1999, including Lustro Plastics Company and Alltrista Plastic Packaging. Overall, Spartech's buying strategy left it with an expanded product line and a stronger foothold in many of its markets.

As such, the company entered the new millennium on solid ground. It continued its growth-through-acquisition policy by adding Uniroyal Technology Corporation's plastics division to its arsenal in 2000. The deal placed Spartech in the mass transit and aerospace markets for the first time. During the following year, the company announced its ''Creating Positive Change'' management plan, which included several initiatives that would result in the consolidation and divestiture of 12 plants in order to cut costs and reduce debt. British Vita plc, a U.K.-based company that had accrued a 46 percent interest in Spartech, began selling off its stake in the company in 2002. It sold all remaining shares in 2004.

The manufacturing economy during this time period was weak, forcing Spartech to focus on product marketing, strengthening its cost structure, and new product development in order to remain competitive. The company continued to view strategic acquisitions as a crucial component in its growth strategy. Indeed, Spartech completed three acquisitions in 2002 that led to its expansion into Mexico. Polymer Extruded Products was bought the following year. In 2004, the company bolstered its holdings with three acquisitions, expanded its facility in Donchery, France, and opened a Product Development Center in Warsaw, Indiana. Sales surpassed $1 billion in 2004.

George A. Abd was named president and CEO of Spartech in 2005 after Bradley Buechler announced his retirement. With new blood at the helm of the company for the first time in 14 years, Spartech launched several restructuring initiatives that included shutting down several facilities and selling off unprofitable businesses. Spartech moved to strengthen its financial position late that year as high resin prices and skyrocketing production costs began eating away at the company's bottom line. While the company's acquisition strategy was temporarily put on hold as a result, management set forth a goal to increase Spartech's global market penetration over the next five years. It also remained focused on investing in people, products, technology, and globalization. With this strategy in place, Spartech appeared to be on track for future growth.

Principal Divisions

Custom Sheet and Rollstock; Color and Specialty Compounds; Molded and Profile Products.

Principal Competitors

CYRO Industries; PolyOne Corporation; Primex Plastics Corporation.

Further Reading

Allen, Leslie J., "Spartech Cuts Debt, Sees Growth Ahead," *St. Louis Post-Dispatch,* May 20, 1990, p. 1E.

Esposito, Frank, "Spartech Acquires Prismaplast," *Plastics News,* May 4, 1998.

Evans, Tavia, "Higher Resin Costs Stunt Spartech Strategy," *St. Louis Post-Dispatch,* October 20, 2005, p. E2.

Ezer, Andrew, "After False Starts, Spartech Achieving Steady Profit Climb," *St. Louis Business Journal,* March 23, 1987, p. 12A.

Hanford, Desiree J., "Spartech Sticks with Its Successful Growth Plan," *Dow Jones News Service,* March 22, 2000.

Lauzon, Michael, "Spartech Buying Hamelin," *Plastics News,* June 17, 1996, p. 1.

Manor, Robert, "Founder Gets $2.5 Million to Leave," *St. Louis Post-Dispatch,* October 13, 1991, p. 1E.

——, "Portnoy Had Faith in Firm," *St. Louis Post-Dispatch,* February 24, 1991, p. 1E.

Melnick, Robert, "Spartech Plans To Double Its Size with Two Acquisitions," *St. Louis Business Journal,* May 13, 1985, p. 10A.

Pryweller, Joseph, "Abd Outlines Big Changes for Spartech," *Plastics News,* June 13, 2005.

Renstrom, Roger, "Spartech Adding Sheet Lines," *Plastics News,* September 13, 1999.

"Spartech Corporation's Growing Role in the Plastics Business," *St. Louis Commerce,* November 1995, p. 28.

"Spartech Stake to Go," *Urethanes Technology,* October 1, 2001.

—M.L. Cohen
—update: Christina M. Stansell

SSOE Inc.

1001 Madison Avenue
Toledo, Ohio 43624-1535
U.S.A.
Telephone: (419) 255-3830
Fax: (419) 255-6101
Web site: http://www.ssoe.com

Private Company
Incorporated: 1948 as A.H. Samborn & Associates
Employees: 600
Sales: $81 million (2004)
NAIC: 54310 Architectural Services; 5431330
   Engineering Services

SSOE Inc. is a leading architectural and engineering firm with 11 offices in California, Michigan, Ohio, Tennessee, Washington, Puerto Rico, and Shanghai, China. The company employs approximately 600 professionals, providing various services in a wide range of markets, including automotive and part suppliers, chemical, commercial, education and athletic, energy, food, healthcare, manufacturing, personal care, pharmaceutical, and retail. The company operates one wholly owned subsidiary, SSOE Systems, Inc., a provider of integrated solutions with single point responsibility from design and startup, to procurement and troubleshooting.

1940s Origins

SSOE Inc. began in 1948 when founder A.H. Samborn, a structural engineer, signed his first contract with Spurgeon Conveyor Company to design a material handling system for converting a boiler plant from oil to coal. Samborn called his company A.H. Samborn & Associates, but renamed it Samborn, Steketee and Associates after fellow structural engineer Jack N. Steketee joined the firm in 1949 to help with the increasing number of projects. The fledgling company initially worked only on small material handling design and structural steel detailing projects. In 1950, the company completed its first industrial architectural project by building a diesel repair shop for Toledo Terminal Railroad, and provided all the structural steel detailing for the Allen County War Memorial Coliseum, then the largest all-welded rigid frame structure in existence. Over the next few years, the company took on new challenges, including projects for such clients as The Andersons, Ford Motor Company, and Surface Combustion, the firm's first repeat client.

By 1953, the firm had 32 employees, and the following year the company diversified into highway design services with its first project in designing highway improvements for U.S. Rte. 24 between Defiance and Napoleon, Ohio. In 1955, upon the recommendation of the Ford Motor Company, the firm won a major commission from National Carbon Company (later renamed UCAR Carbon) to design a warehouse and manufacturing facility in Tennessee. With its growing business and services, the firm added architects Erwin J. (Burrie) Otis, Jr., and John H. Evans in 1956, setting the stage for a major expansion in business. In that same year, the company established a Cleveland, Ohio, office to provide structural detailing services to the surrounding area. From 1957 to 1961, the company set up an affiliate partnership under the name Hatch, Samborn, Steketee to pursue highway design projects. In 1958, the company changed its name to Samborn, Steketee, Otis and Evans, Engineers and Architects, later known as SSOE. By the end of the decade, the company had diversified its operations into plumbing, fire protection, power distribution, lighting and communications. It had won its first international project in 1959 from UCAR Carbon, a $10 million contract for a graphitizing plant in Monterrey, Mexico.

The 1960s: Company Expands and Diversifies

In 1960, with a staff of 58 including six partners and two office locations in Ohio, the company began to diversify the types of projects it undertook and its client base in the Toledo area. The company's design label appeared on a range of business projects, from Blue Cross of Northwest Ohio, to Lutheran Welfare Services in West Toledo, to the Anderson Office Building in Maumee. The company's 1961 project involving Crestview Club Apartments, a full care retirement community, was the first of many health care projects to come. In 1962, the company won several contracts from Libbey-Owens-Ford at its facilities in Ohio, Iowa, Illinois, West Virginia, California, and Canada. The highlight came with a $20 million design contract for a flat-glass production facility in Italy.

The company continued to expand and diversify its business throughout the remainder of the 1960s with its entrance into new fields of engineering and architectural design. By the late 1960s, the company had added new services, including environmental control, industry process design, and fast track construction techniques. These services enabled the firm to undertake new projects in the chemical and refining industries. To keep pace with technological advances, the firm established a computer division to assist in the design process. The company now designed anything from manufacturing plants, to post offices, to office buildings.

The 1970s: Slower Times

Although the 1960s was a profitable time for the company, the 1970s proved less prosperous amidst a declining domestic economy. Nonetheless, the firm's early diversification enabled it to weather the slower times. SSOE completed design projects for such major clients as Champion Spark Plug, Owens-Illinois, and longtime client Union Carbide. It also branched out into the international arena, completing projects in Puerto Rico, Venezuela, Singapore, Japan, Spain, Italy, England, South Africa, Brazil, Mexico, India, and France. In 1977, the firm underwent its first organizational change when Samborn stepped down as president and was replaced by Steketee, his long time partner. Samborn remained on as chairman of the board of directors. By 1978, the firm had offices in Toledo, Ohio, and Flint, Michigan, and had acquired the firm, Dunbar Associates of Monroe, Michigan.

The 1980s: Boom Times and New Directions

The 1980s returned the firm to more prosperous times. This renewed prosperity stemmed in part from the addition of computer graphics to its core business, helping to boost the firm's reputation for innovative design and technical expertise. In 1980, the firm established SSOE Systems as a wholly owned subsidiary to provide turnkey integrated components for process and building systems. The firm also contributed to Honda Motor Company's building of its first U.S. plant at Marysville,

Ohio. In that same year, after merging its Flint office with the firm of Lantz-Griggs, the company developed the enterprises into a self sustaining, full-service design firm with approximately 150 employees. This development enabled the Flint office to obtain in 1982 its largest project award, a $90 million contract to modernize the Rock Island Arsenal in Illinois. Partners Otis and Steketee died in 1982 and 1984, respectively. Before his death, however, Steketee had passed the mantel of leadership in 1981 to Byron West. In 1984, the firm Samborn, Steketee, Otis and Evans officially renamed itself SSOE Inc. Thereafter, in 1986 Samborn retired from the company. With most of the original partners gone, SSOE's new leadership took the firm in new directions by intensifying marketing, increasing computerization, expanding into new cities, and entering into new fields of specialization. The acquisition of Nashville, Tennessee-based Pickney & Associates in 1987 both increased the size of the firm and enabled SSOE to pursue more challenging projects with a regional presence. The acquisition also brought with it such established clients as Ford Nashville Glass, General Motors, and Bridgestone Tire. By 1988, SSOE had risen to national prominence, leading the magazine *Building Design & Construction* to rank it the nation's 12th largest in size among engineering and architectural firms.

The 1990s: Continued Growth

In 1990, SSOE expanded to the state of Washington to serve the growing business on the West coast. The company's primary focus was industrial with Boeing as a major client. Among the firm's projects in the early 1990s were the Glass Bowl Stadium, a $5 million expansion of Honda's engine plant in Aurora, Ohio, and a new high school in Archbold, Ohio. SSOE also designed the master plan for the 2,000-acre Maumee Bay State Park, one of the public parks, forests, and wildlife refuges that line the shores of Lake Erie in northwestern Ohio. The total cost of developing the park and its 120-room lodge was $50 million. In 1991, SSOE also established a presence in Detroit with the opening of a Troy, Michigan, office. Two years later in 1993, Frank McAuliffe retired as CEO and was replaced by 28-year company veteran, Gary McCreery. The company set up a new leadership training and development program in 1995 to mentor in-house leadership and professional skills. In 1996, the firm established SSOE Studios as a strategic business unit in the Toledo office to focus on architectural and engineering design in the commercial, educational, and healthcare markets. At the same time, SSOE's Nashville operation was working on projects for a variety of businesses, including Nissan and Toyota.

SSOE's Tennessee office also was selected to design the corporate headquarters building for U.S. Xpress in Chattanooga. The firm designed the structure with a metal skin, consisting of Alucobond Material, to accommodate U.S. Xpress's desire for a building that would symbolize high technology and forward thinking. The design team drew up plans for a three-story, cantilevered triangular building, featuring 105,000 square-feet. The building was designed with neither a designated front nor rear with the axis through the structures culminating at the boardroom balcony. In addition, in 1998, SSOE served as the lead architectural and engineering design firm for the construction of DaimlerChrysler's new $1.2 billion assembly plant of the 21st century.

Key Dates:

1948: A.H. Samborn & Associates opens for business and lands first contract with Spurgeon Conveyor Co. to convert boiler plant from oil to coal.
1949: Jack N. Steketee joins firm, which is renamed Samborn, Steketee and Associates.
1956: Architects Erwin J. Otis, Jr., and John H. Evans join firm.
1958: Company changes name to Samborn, Steketee, Otis and Evans, Engineers and Architects.
1959: UCAR Carbon grants firm its first international project in Mexico.
1969: Company establishes Flint, Michigan, office.
1977: Founder A.H. Samborn steps down as president.
1984: Company changes its name to SSOE Inc.
1987: SSOE acquires Pickney & Associates and establishes a Nashville, Tennessee, office.
1990: Company opens Washington state office to serve growing business on West Coast.
2004: SSOE opens Puerto Rico office.
2005: SSOE opens office in Shanghai, China.

Continued Growth and Globalization in the New Century

The firm won a contract in May 2001 as the lead architectural and engineering firm for a $930 million Nissan assembly plant near Canton, Mississippi. In 2003, SSOE's expanded its presence to Portage, Michigan; Irvine, California; and Cincinnati and Lima, Ohio. In the same year, SSOE and San Antonio-based Marmon Monk won a joint contract to design Toyota's planned pickup plant. SSOE was well suited for the project as about 30 percent of its business came from automotive industry work. The partners, which were the recipients of the first contract toward the plant's construction, called for drafting plans for the facility's grading, foundation, structural steel, utilities, heating and air conditioning, shops, cafeteria, and administration building.

In 2005, SSOE opened an operation in Shanghai, China, to manage a variety of projects in and around the country. The firm hired Enzo Colonna, an experienced international manager of diversified industrial business sectors, to man the one-office shop. Colonna, who spoke four languages, brought with him 32 years of consulting, architectural, engineering, and construction experience from such companies as Lockwood Greene International and Philip Holzmann International. The move followed China's relaxation of market barriers after its three year membership in the World Trade Organization that made it more profitable for U.S. companies to do business in the country. SSOE had numerous clients setting up operations in China, prompting the firm to follow with an eye on the Chinese auto industry. The Shanghai office came after SSOE's opening in 2004 of a Puerto Rico operation to serve the island's growing pharmaceutical industry.

Principal Subsidiaries

SSOE Systems, Inc.

Principal Competitors

The Day & Zimmerman Group Inc.; Jacobs Engineering Group Inc.; Foster Wheeler Corporation; Kellogg Brown & Root Inc.

Further Reading

"Design in Motion," *Buildings*, November 1999.
Jefferson, Greg, "Toyota Picks San Antonio Firm as One of Two Designers for Area Plant," *San Antonio Express-News*, October 1, 2003.
"Metal Recovery, SSOE in Dezincing Agreement," *American Metal Market*, April 22, 1997.
Pakulski, Gary T., "Glass Firm Joins Spate of Companies Opening Offices in China," *Knight Ridder/Tribune Business News*, February 16, 2005.
"Projects Awarded," *Building Design & Construction*, May 2001.
Radulski, John P., "Restaurant-Hotel Design International," *Nature Study*, October 1991.

—Bruce Montgomery

Sun-Rype Products Ltd.

1165 Ethel Street
Keiowna, British Columbia V1Y2W4
Canada
Telephone: (250) 470-6405
Toll Free: (888) 786-7973
Fax: (250) 762-3611
Web site: http://www.sunrype.com

Public Company
Incorporated: 1946 as B.C. Fruit Processors Ltd.
Employees: 428
Sales: CAD 115.2 million ($95.6 million) (2004)
Stock Exchanges: Toronto
Ticker Symbol: SRF
NAIC: 31999 All other Miscellaneous Food Manufacturing

Sun-Rype Products Ltd. is a Canadian company that sells fruit juices and fruit snacks. It is located in British Columbia's Okanagan Valley near Washington state, which because of its climate and soil is ideally suited for the growing of fruit, including apples, apricots, cherries, peaches, pears, plums, and strawberries. Sun-Rype is best known for its 100 percent apple juice, which is also used to produce other fruit juice blends, such as Apple Orange Passionfruit, Apple Orange Peach, and Apple Pineapple Banana. Sun-Rype also sell other 100 percent fruit juices, including grape, raspberry, tropical, mango tangerine, wildberry, fruit medley, and strawberry kiwi. In addition, Sun-Rype offers orange juice and citrus blends as well as varieties of Fruit & Veggie Juice. Sun-Rype natural fruit snacks include apple sauce and Fruit to Go fruit "leather," Canada's top selling fruit snack, and FruitSource bars. Sun-Rype is a public company listed on the Toronto Stock Exchange.

Okanagan Valley Begins Raising Fruit in 1800s

Western Canada's Okanagan Valley initially attracted gold prospectors in the 1860s to 1880s to the surrounding mountains, but the valley itself was soon recognized as a good place to raise livestock and plant fruit orchards. In 1889 the B.C. Fruit Grow- ers Association was formed to serve the interests of the many small fruit farmers in the valley. With the introduction of new species of disease-resistant trees in the 1920s the valley began to truly prosper, then in 1939 British Columbia passed new legislation that led to the establishment of a new growers' agency, B.C. Tree Fruits, which took charge of selling the valley's abundance of apples, apricots, cherries, peaches, pears, and plums. It also became the dominant entity, as B.C. Fruit Growers essentially served as the fruit growers political arm.

The apple growers of the Okanagan Valley had a problem, however. There was no market for their sub-grade fruit, cull apples. As a result they had to pay to have the packing plant haul away rejects to be dumped. Thus, in 1946 B.C. Tree Fruits instructed B.C. Fruit Growers to form a company called B.C. Fruit Processors Ltd., which the association would own on behalf of its 3,300 grower members as a cooperative, to turn cull apples into 100 percent apple juice and apple sauce. The new company bought a pair of struggling juice plants and for a brand name chose "Sun-Rype." In addition to apple juice and apple sauce, the company in the early years also manufactured pie filling and dehydrated apples.

In 1959 B.C. Fruit Processors took the name Sun-Rype Products Ltd. and launched Blue Label Apple Juice, which became the company's flagship product and over time became the dominant brand of apple juice in Western Canada. A major factor in the product's success was the forging of a joint venture in 1963 with the Fraser Valley Milk Producers Association, which distributed juice on established milk routes.

Because it was a cooperative, Sun-Rype distributed profits each year to members of the B.C. Fruit Growers. Then, in 1979 the arrangement was changed. Sun-Rype began to retain the profits to build the business. It upgraded its production lines and in 1979 became the first juice processor in Canada to offer tetra-packaging for 250 milliliter and one-liter packs. Richard Skelly wrote in a 1996 story for *BC Report,* "Earnings eventually stalled at about CAD 5.9 million, says grower and Sun-Rype chairman Merv Geen. Expenses kept rising, and, by 1992, 'we had a balance sheet that was out of whack with our debt covenants to the bank,' he said. 'The growers were not willing to put in more money. Under co-operative rules, you come in with nothing and you leave with nothing. So, as a grower, you'd get no recognition for contributing any capital.' " Moreover, Sun-Rype was overly dependent on apple juice, with Blue Label apple juice accounting for about 60 percent of sales. As a result, the company was put in a difficult position whenever there was a shortage of cheap cull apples. Moreover, it was operating in a limited marketplace in Western Canada.

Early 1990s Restructuring

In order to begin addressing its myriad of problems, Sun-Rype in 1993 underwent a financial reengineering. According to Skelly, Sun-Rype was "recapitalized by issuing 10.2 million shares. Enter investor Allied Strategies, which purchased 3.46 million shares. The Vancouver holding company paid CAD 8.7 million in return for a 30 percent stakes of the available Class B shares. A further 5.9 million B shares, one for every dollar of historic retained earnings, were divided on a pro-rata basis among grower." Some of the remaining shares were sold to growers and employees or award to management instead of salary. Another 430,500 shares were use to acquire a dried fruit and granola bar manufacturer, Okanagan Dried Fruits.

The addition of Okanagan Dried Fruits provided much needed diversity for Sun-Rype, which still had to contend with the uncertainty of its apple supply. The company expected a shortage in 1993 and tried to hedge its position by guaranteeing prices for apples that turned out to be much higher than necessary. Then, in 1995, Sun-Rype failed to hedge, a shortage developed, and the company was forced to pay a steep price for process-grade apples. It was able to remain profitable because of Okanagan Dried Fruits as well as the sale of blended beverages, which were cheaper to make and becoming increasingly popular with consumers.

During this period in the early 1990s, Sun-Rype's management developed ambitious goals, as laid out in a document called Vision 2000. In it, the company's stated mission was to become a leading international food and beverage company by the year 2000. There was talk in the press about growing revenues to CAD 500 million by then, which would represent a dramatic jump given that sales in 1993 totaled CAD 63.2 million. The company began taking steps to realize that dream. Research and development spending, which had totaled about 0.1 percent of sales was increased ten-fold to bring to market new products. Sun-Rype also began to spread its marketing reach eastward with the goal of serving all of Canada, and it looked to international markets as well. The company exported its products to the United States, the Philippines, Singapore, and Thailand, and was especially excited about the prospects for doing business in China. Management paid a number of trips to China in the early 1990s in hopes of arranging a joint venture to produce fruit juice from concentrates.

By the end of 1995, according to Skelly, "Sun-Rype executives faced new hurdles. Allied strategies wanted out of its Sun-Rype investment. Allied president William Sleeman tried and failed to persuade the growers' association to allow his firm to take control of Sun-Rype. Rebuffed, Allied bought Okanagan Springs Brewery instead. And when Mr. Sleeman purchased a similar craft brewery in Ontario, his eastern partners insisted he exit other beverage endeavors.''

In search of a buyer, Sleeman looked to an Allied board member, Douglas Mason, who had made a splash with the launch of Clearly Canadian Beverage Corporation, a new age beverage company that began selling sparkling, fruit-flavored water in the late 1980s and enjoyed a meteoric rise in the price of its stock. Sales began to tail off in 1993, so Mason jumped at a chance to buy into Sun-Rype and recharge the fortunes of Clearly Canadian. He offered Allied CAD 6.5 million for its stake, then approached the Sun-Rype board with an offer in March 1996 to buy more stock and take control. The Sun-Rype board dismissed the overture and exercised its right to match any outside bid for Allied's shares, paying CAD 6.3 million but on terms that were faster than the CAD 6.5 million Mason had proposed. He then engineered a CAD 40 million hostile take-over bid of Sun-Rype, going over the heads of the board and appealing directly to the grower-members. Mason's team set up shop in a nearby hotel and began to woo growers in what became a nasty scrap with Sun-Rype management, who Mason accused of having its own agenda and using fear-mongering with shareholders to defeat his proposal. In the end Mason failed to persuade enough of the shareholders to trust his vision for growing Sun-Rype. In addition, for those shareholders who wanted to cash in their stake in Sun-Rype they only had to wait until the end of 1996 when Sun-Rype stock went public on the Toronto Stock Exchange.

Late 1990s: New Management Team

In the mid- to late-1990s, Sun-Rype made little inroad in achieving the goal of generating CAD 500 million in sales by 2000. Revenue totaled CAD 80.3 million in 1994, dipped to CAD 77.4 million in 1995, rebounded to CAD 80.2 million in 1996, and topped CAD 88.3 million in 1997 before tailing off in 1998 to CAD 83.8 million. More so, in 1997 Sun-Rype posted a CAD 5.8 million lost due to its failure to launch a business in China after four years of trying. A new management team was installed in 1998, as long-time Sun-Rype executive Lawrence Bates was named the company's chief executive officer just as he was on the verge of retirement. "When I assumed my position, the first job was fixing the basement," Bates told *National Post* in 2000. "We got back to basics." One move was to withdraw from the highly competitive granola bar business. Instead, Sun-Rype concentrated on the fruit snack business where there were no major players and was more in keeping with the company's core business. Fruit leathers and fruit bars had been essentially relegated to home kitchens due to the 24-hour drying time of the pureed fruit. It wasn't until Sun-Rype researchers discovered new technology in California that cut the drying time to three to four hours, that the company was able to mass produce the fruit snacks. The Fruit to Go fruit leathers were introduced in March 1997, then early in 1999 Energy to Go fruit bars, later renamed FruitSource, went on

Key Dates:

1946: Company formed as a co-operative, B.C. Fruit Processors Ltd.
1959: Name changed to Sun-Rype Products, Ltd.
1979: Profits now retained to invest in business.
1994: Company recapitalized; 30 percent acquired by Allied Strategies Inc.
1996: Company taken public on Toronto Stock Exchange.
1999: Fruit bars are introduced.
2002: Sun-Rype surpasses CAD 100 annual sales mark.

sale. Bates used both brands as a spearhead to introduce Sun-Rype to central and eastern Canada markets where the company's juice brands had not penetrated due to shipping costs. Also in 1999 Sun-Rype took another major step in its transformation from an agricultural co-operative to a modern, growth-oriented company when the company's nine Class A shares, held in trust on behalf of the fruit growers' association, were redeemed. Each of the shares, accord to *BC Report,* controlled "a whopping 50 million voting rights on each share. Even assuming they all agree on an issue, Class B shareholders would always lose by almost 440 million votes if the grower's association disagreed." With the association relinquishing its voting control, Sun-Rype gained greater flexibility and become more of an attractive investment. In 2000 Canadian entrepreneur and billionaire Jim Pattison bought nearly 15 percent of Sun-Rype's stock. Over the next few years Pattison would increase his stake to 25 percent.

Sales reached a record CAD 96.4 million in 1994, and Sun-Rype appeared well positioned to top the CAD 100 million, a far cry from the CAD 500 million dream of a few years earlier, but still an impressive performance. The company was spreading eastward and the fruit snack business was just beginning to spin off new products. A decline in process grade apples in the 1999 harvest, however, temporarily halted Sun-Rype's sales momentum, as revenues dipped to CAD 88.2 million in 2000. But net income improved from CAD 3.7 million in 1999 to more than CAD 4.9 million in 2000. More importantly, Energy to Go was available in 90 percent of Canada and Fruit to Go had a 96 percent national distribution. The products, supported by a national advertising campaign, both enjoyed sizable sales increases over the previous year.

Sun-Rype upgraded its beverage processing and packaging facilities in 2001 as part of an effort to revitalize its beverage portfolio. The company also added to its snack offerings by launching Sun-Rype Fruit & Veggie bars in September 2001. Sales rebounded to CAD 92.6 million in 2001, while net income totaled CAD 4.4 million. Sales in central and eastern Canada were also growing at a healthy 27 percent clip.

New product development continued in 2002 with the introduction of Sun-Rype's first entry in the "functional" beverage market, Calcium Enriched Orange Juice. The company was also successful in landing food contract manufacturing business, co-packing, an area of growth for Sun-Rype. Over the next two years its secured business from customers in both the United States and Europe. As a result of growth on all fronts, Sun-Rype cracked the CAD 100 million revenues mark in 2002. Sales improved to CAD 108 million in 2004 and CAD 115.2 million in 2004. Net income during this period increased from CAD 4.9 million in 2002 to nearly CAD 5.9 million in 2004. Through the first three quarters of 2005, revenues and earnings were also on record pace. There was every reason to believe that Sun-Rype was just beginning a period of sustained growth.

Principal Competitors

Del Monte Foods Company; Dole Food Company, Inc.

Further Reading

Attard, Yvonne, "Fifty Golden Years," *Food in Canada,* September 1996, p. 50.
Damsell, Keith, "Doug Mason Can See Clearly Now," *Financial Post,* July 27, 1996, p. 12.
Holloway, Andy, "Ripe for the Picking," *Canadian Business,* December 10, 2001, p. 30.
McCullough, Michael, "Just Add Hype," *Canadian Business,* December 1996, p. 130.
Schreiner, John, "Is Sun-Rype Ripe For a Takeover by Jim Pattison?," *National Post,* October 28, 2000, p. D7.
——, "Sun-Rype Sets $500M Goal Heading into Global Market," *Financial Post,* April 28, 1994, p. 51.
Skelly, Richard, "Ripe for the Picking?," *BC Report,* August 19, 1996, p. 28.

—Ed Dinger

Tata Tea Ltd.

1 Bishop Lefroy Road
Kolkata 700 020
West Bengal
India
Telephone: +91 33 2281 3891
Fax: +91 33 2281 1199
Web site: http://www.tatatea.com

Public Company
Incorporated: 1964 as Tata Finlay Ltd.
Employees: 56,099
Sales: INR 30.76 billion ($707 million) (2005)
Stock Exchanges: Bombay
Ticker Symbol: 500800
NAIC: 311920 Coffee and Tea Manufacturing

Tata Tea Ltd. is one of India's leading tea companies and is the second largest supplier of branded tea in the world. Vertically integrated, Tata Tea produces 40 million kilograms on 18,000 hectares on about three dozen plantations in India and Sri Lanka. Branded tea accounts for 86 percent of sales, with the remainder coming from bulk tea, coffee, and investments. The subsidiary Tata Coffee has 8,000 hectares under production, producing more than 9,000 metric tons a year. Tata accommodates every budget with its brands sold in India, which include Tetley, Kanan Devan, Chakra Gold, Gemini, and Tata Tea (one of the country's top sellers). The company has the largest instant tea processing facility outside the United States, which produces exclusively for export from India. Two-thirds of sales came from the United Kingdom's Tetley Group, which Tata Tea acquired in 2000 in the largest takeover of a foreign company by an Indian one to date. Tetley then became the company's main brand for world markets with Tata doing business in 40 countries. Tata also has an instant tea plant in Florida, where its U.S. subsidiary is based. Since the mid-1980s, Tata Tea has been progressively shifting away from the risk-laden plantation business into the marketing of tea (and coffee) to the consumer. In 2005, the company began selling its tea estates to their workers.

Origins

Tata Tea's origins can be traced back to the James Finlay Group. In 1893 James Finlay of Glasgow, Scotland, acquired the concession for tea cultivation in Travancore, Kerala, on South India's Malabar Coast, which faces the Arabian Sea. In the early days, according to Sir Percival Griffiths' *History of the Indian Tea Industry,* in South India, tea was secondary to coffee and other crops. However, in the second half of the 20th century tea was the exclusive crop in Kerala. Most tea in the south was grown on hillsides, notes Griffiths, in contrast to the plains in the north.

Local planters began to turn to growing *cinchona* (quinine) and later tea, as coffee leaf disease spread to the area in the 1870s. James Finlay & Company's Sir John Muir acquired concessions for the North and South Sylhet Tea Companies in 1893. The Consolidated Tea and Lands Company was established to take over these interests. Finlay's 2,500 acres and other estates were acquired in 1897 by the Kanan Devan Hills Produce Company, which was named after the prominent geographical feature in North Travancore.

India's Tata Group conglomerate formed the Tata Finlay joint venture with in 1964 to develop value-added tea, beginning with instant tea. The company took over James Finlay's operations in 1976 and in 1983 it bought out the Finlay Group, forming Tata Tea Ltd. At the time, the industry was slogging through a global depression. A U.S. unit, Tata Tea Inc., was formed in 1987.

Focus on the Consumer in the 1980s

In the early 1980s the tea industry in India was experiencing rising input and labor costs and dwindling margins as well as ''capricious'' taxes, according to Britain's *Financial Times.* India was facing competition on the world market not just from China, but other countries entering the business. However, by 1983, the industry was well in the black, with record profits being reported by most companies, including Tata Tea, which had sales up 42 percent to INR 1.1 billion ($95 million) and a pre-tax profit of INR 236 million, up five-fold. The amount of black tea sold was only slightly larger, 384 million kilograms.

Key Dates:

1837: Tetley established in Yorkshire, England.
1893: James Finlay & Company acquires tea concessions in Travancore, India.
1897: Kanan Devan Hills Produce Company takes over venture.
1953: Tetley introduces tea bag concept to United Kingdom.
1964: Tata Finlay formed as joint venture between James Finlay and Tata Group.
1983: James Finlay interests bought out; company renamed Tata Tea Ltd.
1987: U.S. subsidiary established.
1992: Tata Tetley joint venture formed.
1995: Tata Tea attempts to buy Tetley Tea.
2000: Tata acquires Tetley for £271 million.
2005: Tata announces plan to sell Munnar tea estates to workers.

The company had been spending millions of rupees to upgrade its facilities.

Tata Tea decided to move from the commodities business to consumer branding in 1983. Its first brand was Tata Tea. This was followed by Kanan Devan, Agni, Gemini, and Chakra Gold. However, the concept of branded teas would be slow to catch on in the domestic market, which was the world's largest.

Global in the 1990s

Tata Tea took its brands to the global market in the 1990s. It formed an export joint venture with Britain's Tetley Tea in 1992. Other new enterprises included a majority interest in Consolidated Coffee Ltd. (Tata Coffee Ltd.) and a joint venture to manage agricultural estates in Sri Lanka.

Tata's brands ended the decade with a market share of 25 percent in India, making it second to Hindustan Level Ltd., which dominated the market. The company had 74 tea gardens and was producing 62 million kilograms of tea a year, two-thirds of it packaged and branded. According to the *Economic Times,* while no one sold more tea than Unilever, Tata Tea was the largest integrated producer.

The tea business was complicated by a drought in much of India in 1999. In addition, Russia, once the largest buyer of Indian tea, temporarily withdrew from the market. Also, Tata's attempt to launch ice tea did not curry favor with the Indian market.

The Tetley Acquisition in 2000

A bid to buy The Tetley Group Ltd. from Allied Domecq in 1995 failed due to a lack of financing. However in 2000 Tata was able to acquire the company from Schroders Private Equity Fund in a £271 million ($432 million) leveraged buyout. Tata Tea reportedly outbid the American conglomerate Sara Lee in what was described as the largest takeover of a foreign company by an Indian one to date.

Tetley, based in the United Kingdom, was the world's second largest tea company after Unilever's Brooke Bond-Lipton and had annual turnover of £300 million. It was the market leader in Great Britain and Canada and a popular brand in the United States, Australia, and the Middle East.

Tetley had been founded in 1837 by brothers Joseph and Edward Tetley, who had traveled the Yorkshire moors selling salt and other wares. By the end of the 19th century was well known in the United States as well as England. Tetley had a history of innovative packaging, including bringing the tea bag to Britain from America in 1953, and developing the first round tea bags in 1989. Its factory in Eaglescliffe in northeast England, established in 1969, was considered the world's largest tea bag plant.

Part of the rationale for the Tetley buy was the impending liberalization of the Indian tea market, which was the world's largest, consuming about 650 million kilograms a year, less than half of it in packets. While Tata Tea was broadening its marketing reach via the Tetley takeover, rival Unilever was buying several plantations to boost its production capacity. The international tea business was as much as ever a contest dominated by two global brands, Unilever's Lipton and Tetley, which Tata was bringing to India for the first time in 2002. However, a plethora of regional brands claimed more than one-third of the domestic market and remained a threat, along with loose tea.

Tata had a variety of other initiatives in play. It was an investor in a domestic coffee bar chain called Barista. Tata Tea, a market leader in India, was reportedly considering entering another huge tea market: China. Once a major supplier of pepper, it decided to exit the business in 2004, closing the Cochin Spices Centre it had built in 1990.

With the antioxidants in tea making headlines for cancer-fighting properties, the tea manufacturers were doing a brisk business. However, Tata's exports fell by about one-sixth in the 2003–04 fiscal year, largely due to reduced trade with Iraq.

In 2005, Tata announced a plan to sell its 17 tea plantations in Munnar to the 12,500 employees there. Tata Tea would retain less than 20 percent of the equity. This was part of the company's shift in emphasis to brand marketing rather than production. In October 2005, Tata's Tetley plc acquired a small California maker of specialty teas called Fmali Herb Inc. and Good Earth Corporation.

Principal Subsidiaries

Tata Coffee Ltd.; Tata Tea Inc. (United States); Tata Tea (GB) Ltd. (United Kingdom; 98.58%); Watawala Plantations Ltd. (Sri Lanka; 50%).

Principal Divisions

Plantations; Packet Tea; Instant Tea; Global Business Division.

Principal Competitors

Hindustan Lever Ltd.

Further Reading

Bhushan, Ratna, "Coffee's Rather Romantic; Tea's More a Habit," *Business Line,* August 8, 2000.

"Fulfilling a Global Vision—The Saga of Tata Tea," *Hindu,* April 5, 2000.

Goodwin, Jason, *A Time for Tea: Travels Through China and India in Search of Tea,* New York: Alfred A. Knopf, 1991.

Griffiths, Percival, *The History of the Indian Tea Industry,* London: Weidenfeld and Nicolson, 1967.

"It's Official: Tata Tea Seals Tetley Deal," *Economic Times* (India), February 28, 2000.

Mahanti, P.C., "A Year of Mixed Fortunes," *Financial Times* (London), Survey: Indian Industry XI; Tea Production, January 26, 1983, p. XI.

Mandal, Kohinoor, "Tata Tea Mulling Options to Enter Chinese Market," *Business Line,* February 14, 2004.

Menon, Shyam G., "Quality Upgrade Has Helped Tata Tea," *Business Line,* February 20, 2002.

Puliyenthuruthel, Josey, "Indian Tea Rivals Buy Brands," *Daily Deal,* October 14, 2005.

Sriram, R., and Rakhi Mazumdar, "Can Tata Tea Blend Its Global Brew with Tetley?," *Business Today* (India), July 7, 1999, p. 46.

Subbu, Ramnath, "After Cement, It's Consolidation in Tea," *Hindu,* March 6, 2000.

"Taste, Touch and Feel. . . . That's What the (Tea) Market Needs," *Financial Express,* May 19, 2002.

"Tata Tea to Close Its Cochin Spice Centre," *Financial Express,* September 12, 2004.

"Tata Tea to Sell Munnar Estates to Employees," *Hindu,* February 12, 2005.

—Frederick C. Ingram

Telekom Malaysia Bhd

Level 51, North Wing
Menara Telekom
Off Jalan Pantai Baharu
Kuala Lumpur 50672
Malaysia
Telephone: +60 3 2240 9494
Fax: +60 03 22832415
Web site: http://www.telekom.com.my

Public Company
Incorporated: 1984
Employees: 27,000
Sales: MYR 13.25 billion ($3.2 billion) (2004)
Stock Exchanges: Kuala Lumpur
Ticker Symbol: TLMM.K
NAIC: 517110 Wired Telecommunications Carriers;
    423430 Computer and Computer Peripheral
    Equipment and Software Merchant Wholesalers;
    511140 Database and Directory Publishers; 517212
    Cellular and Other Wireless Telecommunications;
    517910 Other Telecommunications

Telekom Malaysia Bhd (TM), the former telecommunications monopoly in that country, since privatization remains Malaysia's top telecom group and a fast-growing international player in the Asian region. The company continues to hold the *de facto* monopoly on the country's fixed-line telecom market, with more than 4.6 million access lines. However, the relatively low penetration rate of just 17.2 lines per 100 population (compared with nearly 65 per 100 in the United States) provides room for TM's future growth, as well as a potential entry point for competitors. In addition to its fixed line business, TM is one of Malaysia's leading cellular telephone provider, a position solidified following the company's 2003 acquisition of Technology Resources Industry (TRI) and its Celcom mobile telephone unit. Celcom is a long-time leader in the Malaysian cellular market, with a market share approaching 30 percent. TM also operates the country's leading Internet provider, TMNet, which is also the sole broadband provider in the country. In addition to its operations in Malaysia, TM has developed

a network of subsidiaries and investments internationally, with a focus on the Asian region. The company is present in Sri Lanka (where it holds more than 90 percent of Dialog Telekom), Cambodia, Indonesia, Bangladesh, Guinea and Malawi. As part of its future international expansion plans, the company formally adopted a new brand identity, TM, in 2005. The company is listed on the Kuala Lumpur Stock Exchange. In 2004, TM posted revenues of MYR 13.25 billion ($3.2 billion).

A State Telecoms Agency in the 1950s

Malaysia's first telephone line was installed in 1874, linking the British colonial government's Resident's Office in Perak with one of its administrative offices. The colonies, then known as Malaya, remained unconnected. Over the next decade underwater cable was laid linking Perak with the island of Panang. However, the country's first telephone exchange was not installed until 1891 in Kuala Lumpur.

In 1964, Malaysia became a country independent of British rule. The years immediately following were turbulent as Indonesia sought control of the area and Singapore seceded from the new country. Once the government was stable, however, it took control of the country's telephone network, already organized as Jabatan Telekom Malaysia (JTM). Telephone penetration had remained extremely low in the country, and by 1960 had not yet reached 50,000 lines, for a total market penetration of less than 1 per 100.

As a government agency, JTM took a first step toward developing a corporate culture when it received authorization in 1971 to begin operating as an independent, profit-driven enterprise. In 1982, the Malaysian government announced its intention to privatize JTM during the decade, and to deregulate the Malaysian telecommunications market. JTM braced itself for the change, restructuring its operations.

In the meantime, JTM had continued to build up the country's network, topping one million access lines and raising the penetration rate to nearly 7 per 100 by the mid-1980s. The company had also installed a national network of pay telephones, counting more than 60,000 by the end of the decade. In the meantime, JTM launched Malaysia's first cellular telephone service in 1985. That service, called ATUR 450, was based on the NMT analog standard technology. By the end of the decade, the company had developed a new generation of cellular telephone service, based on the ART 900 standard. An important step forward for the country's national telephone backbone came with the installation of a 1,500-kilometer underwater fiber optic cable linking the Malaysian peninsula with the Sabah and Sarawak regions.

The deregulation process of the Malaysian telecommunications market was formally launched in 1987, when JTM was split into two entities. The first, and smaller, retained JTM's industry regulation arm, and remained a government-run department. The second, which took over JTM's fixed-line and mobile telecommunications operations, became Telekom Malaysia (TM).

TM's privatization was slated for 1990. As part of the preparation for that process, the company sold off its ART 900 cellular business in order to create a competitor for the soon-to-be-privatized telephone monopoly. As part of the government's efforts to promote the commercial interests of the ethnic Malay community, which, while politically powerful had long played a secondary role to the economic clout of the country's ethnic Chinese community, the cellular company was sold to Tajudin Ramli for just MYR 250,000 (less than $110,000). Included in the sale was a guarantee of a five-year monopoly for cellular services in Malaysia. Ramli launched the cellular services as a company called Celcom in 1989. As a result, TM was locked out of the cellular market and became one of the few incumbent telecommunications monopolies not to control the fast-growing mobile market in the late 1990s.

International Interests in the 1990s

The Malaysian government moved forward with TM's privatization in 1990, placing 25 percent of the company on the Kuala Lumpur Stock Exchange. As such, TM became one of the first in the region to emerge from under government protection. The government continued to reduce its stake through the decade, selling another 5 percent of the company to private shareholders, and placing a further 5 percent among TM's employees by mid-decade.

The public offering enabled TM to launch a massive investment program in the early 1990s. The company's expansion effort came as part of the Malaysian government's ambitious

"Vision 2020," a long-term plan meant to raise the country to developed nation status by 2020. The role of the telecommunications sector in general placed TM at the center of the government's plans, and as such the company received the backing for its own MYR 17 billion ($5.6 billion) investment program, launched in 1994.

By the end of the 1990s, TM had boosted its total number of access lines to four million and its penetration rate to 19 per 100 population. The company had also expanded its exchange capacity, launching a fully digital network with a capacity of nearly six million lines.

The end of Celcom's five-year monopoly allowed TM to enter the cellular market in the mid-1990s, when the company received one of the country's eight new mobile telephone licenses. TM launched its own network, called TM Touch. At the same time, the government issued new licenses allowing entry into the country's fixed-line and international telephone markets. Yet the high cost of entry, especially into the fixed-line local market, meant that TM maintained a de facto monopoly on this market into the mid-2000s.

While building its network at home, TM also turned its attention to the regional telecommunications player. The company's first international effort came in Sri Lanka, where it backed the launch of that country's MTN (later Dialog) Telekom in 1993. By mid-decade, TM had also added a joint venture in India, where it began operating GSM-based cellular phone services in the Calcutta market, as well as paging services in six other cities. The company also expanded into Malawi, formed a 60–40 joint venture with Malawi Telecommunications Ltd. to launch the TNM GSM-based cellular service in 1995. In that year, also, the company acquired 60 percent of Sotelgui SA, the former government-controlled fixed-line and mobile service provider in Guinea. Bangladesh became another target market for the company, and in 1995 TM formed a joint venture with AK Khan & Co. to launch the Aktel GSM cellular service.

In Malaysia, TM responded to the growing interest in internet access with the launch of its own Internet service provider, TMNet. That operation became the country's second, and soon largest ISP. TM's control of the nation's fixed lines also enabled it to capture the broadband market into the 2000s. The company then entered Cambodia acquiring a 19.4 percent stake in Samart in 1997, then acquiring a 51 percent stake (to Samart's 49 percent) in mobile telephone provider Casacom in 1998.

Mobile Leader in the New Century

TM expanded its Malaysian cellular business in 1998, taking control of Mobikom, founded in 1993. Mobikom had built a network based on the AMPS protocol, covering all of the Malaysian peninsula, as well as Sabah and Sarawak. In order to overcome incompatibilities between the two companies' networks (TM's TM Touch network operated on the GSM 1800 standard) TM announced its intention to roll out a dual-band handset. Nonetheless, TM's cellular phone operation remained a small, money-losing operations, lagging far behind leaders Celcom, Maxis, and GiGi.

Incompatibility was only one of the problems dogging the Malaysian mobile telephone market. The presence of eight

Key Dates:

1874: The first telephone line in Malaysia is installed.
1891: The first telephone exchange is installed in Kuala Lumpur.
1946: A state-run telecommunications agency, Jabatan Telekom Malaysia (JTM), is established.
1971: JTM begins operating as a for-profit corporation.
1985: JTM launches a cellular phone service.
1987: Privatization and deregulation begins as JTM is split into two bodies, and Telekom Malaysia (TM) is created as telecommunications provider.
1989: Cellular service is sold to Tajudin Ramli, who establishes Celcom.
1990: Government sells a 25 percent stake in TM to the public.
1994: TM acquires control of cellular service in Sri Lanka (later Dialog Telekom) and launches its own cellular service, TM Touch.
1995: TM enters a joint venture to provide cellular service and pager services in India
1996: An Internet access service, TMNet, is launched.
2002: The company acquires an initial stake in Celcom and gains control the following year.
2004: Launches 3G high-speed cellular service.

cellular providers had proved to be too many for the Malaysian market. Into the early 2000s, therefore, the Malaysian government began encouraging a consolidation of the market. TM played its part in that effort, acquiring a stake in Celcom's parent company, Technology Resources Industry (TRI), in 2002. By 2003, the company had acquired full control of TRI, and of the country's leading cellular service provider. TM then received one of only two licenses for the new "3G" high-speed cellular phone services. By 2004, the company had launched its first 3G service. Because of low initial demand for the service, however, the company's 3G offered remained on a limited scale serving only a few hundred subscribers in the country's so-called "Multimedia Super Corridor."

Elsewhere, TM's regional ambitions hit a setback when it failed to win its 2001 bid for a stake in Indonesian Satellite, thwarting TM's attempt to enter the Indonesian cell phone market. The company had also run into trouble with an attempt to enter Ghana's telecommunications market, where its investment reached some US$ 150 million.

TM bounced back toward mid-decade. In July 2005, the company brought its Sri Lankan operations to the Colombo Stock Exchange, selling a 9.6 percent stake in what became that country's largest-ever initial public offering (IPO). Soon after

the company joined with Malaysian state investment agency Khazanah Nasional to acquire a 17.7 percent stake in Singapore's MobileOne, becoming the cellular service provider's largest shareholder. Meanwhile, TM had found its entry into the Indonesian market, buying a 27.3 percent stake in Excelcomindo, owner of that country's third-largest mobile phone provider. In order to consolidate its growing international profile, Telekom Malaysia announced in 2005 that it was adopting TM as its new brand identity. Telekom Malaysia expected to become a major player in the international telecommunications market in the new century

Principal Subsidiaries

Cambodia Samart Communications Co. Ltd.; Celcom (Malaysia) Bhd; Fiberail Sdn Bhd (60%); GITN Sdn Bhd; Intelsec Sdn Bhd; Mediatel (Malaysia) Sdn Bhd; Meganet Communications Sdn Bhd; Menara Kuala Lumpur Sdn Bhd; Mobikom Sdn Bhd; MTN Networks Ltd (Sri Lanka); Parkside Properties Sdn Bhd; Rebung Utama Sdn Bhd; Societe des Telecommunications de Guinee (Papua New Guinea; 60%); Tekad Mercu Bhd; Tekekom Enterprise Sdn Bhd; Telekom Applied Business Sdn Bhd; TM Global Inc. (United States); TM International (Bangladesh) Ltd.; TM International Sdn Bhd; TMI International Lanka Ltd. (Sri Lanka); TMI Mauritius Ltd.

Principal Competitors

V KDDI Corporation; Nippon Telegraph and Telephone Corporation; China Railway Communication Corporation; Hutchison Whampoa Ltd.; PT Elnusa Tbk; China Telecom Corporation Ltd; China Mobile Communications Corporation; China Telecoms Corporation Ltd; Myanma Posts and Telecommunications; PT Astra International Tbk.

Further Reading

Arnold, Wayne, "Telekom Malaysia Pushes for the Fast Lane," *New York Times*, February 21, 2003, p. W1.

Colquhoun, Lachlan, "Testing the Waters in KL," W*ireless Asia*, January–February 2004, p. 9.

Llyod-Smith, Jake, "Khazanah, Telekom Malaysia in M1deal," *Financial Times*, August 18, 2005, p. 27.

Montagu-Pollock, Matthew, "A Conservative Approach to Telecoms," *Asiamoney*, December 2000, p. S25.

Tanner, John C., "3G Results Play the Wild Card in Malaysia's Cellco Shuffle," *Wireless Asia*, August 2002, p. 7.

"Telekom Malaysia: A Leader in Telecommunications," *Institutional Investor International Edition*, June 2004.

"Telekom Malaysia: Committed to Providing World-Class Service," *Institutional Investor*, December 1995, p. A16.

"Telekom Malaysia is Seeking a Controlling Share in Excelcomindo," *Wireless Asia*, January–February 2005, p. 12.

—M.L. Cohen

Tessenderlo Group

rue du Trone 130
Brussels
Belgium
Telephone: +32 02 639 18 11
Fax: +32 02 639 19 99
Web site: http://www.tessenderlogroup.com

Public Company
Incorporated: 1919 as Produits Chimiques de
  Tessenderlo
Employees: 8,181
Sales: EUR 2.08 billion ($2.63 billion) (2004)
Stock Exchanges: Brussels
Ticker Symbol: TESBr
NAIC: 325188 All Other Inorganic Chemical
  Manufacturing; 325131 Inorganic Dye and Pigment
  Manufacturing; 325181 Alkalies and Chlorine
  Manufacturing; 325211 Plastics Material and Resin
  Manufacturing; 325312 Phosphatic Fertilizer
  Manufacturing

Tessenderlo Group is a Belgium-based, globally active specialty chemicals company. One of Belgium's largest chemicals firms, Tessenderlo has established a position for itself on an international level by focus on a narrow range of core niche chemicals. The company is the world's top producer of hydrochloric acid, fertilizers based on liquid sulfur, sodium hydrosulfide, benzyl alcohol, acetate, and chloride, among others. Tessenderlo holds number two positions in the production of animal feed-grade phosphates and potassium sulphate and the number three position worldwide in the production of gelatin. While targeting a global market, backed by a network of 66 factories and 40 sales offices, Tessenderlo is a highly European group. In Europe, the company is the largest producer of glycine, and number two in caustic potash; the company also holds leading positions in the production of plastic compounds and polyvinyl chloride (PVC). Europe accounts for 84 percent of the company's total sales, including 39 percent from Belgium and 23 percent from France. The United States adds 10 percent of the group's sales, while the rest of the world, including operations in China, Chile, and Brazil, among others, adds 6 percent to sales. The company posted revenues of EUR 2.08 billion ($2.6 billion) in 2004. Since 2005, Tessenderlo has been structured in three primary divisions: Chemicals; Specialties, including fine chemicals, gelatin, and natural derivatives; and Plastics Converting, including the production of PVC-based profiles, pipes and fittings, and compounds. Tessenderlo is listed on the Euronext Brussels Stock Exchange and is led by Chairman and CEO Gérard Marchand.

19th-Century Origins

The first association of the town of Tessenderlo, in Belgium, with the country's developing industry occurred in the late 19th century with the founding of Exploitation des Procédés Raynaud in 1892. That company began manufacturing chloric acid and sodium sulfate, used in various industries and products such as detergents. Following World War I, the site was acquired by L'Union Française des Produits Chimiques & Matières Colorantes, which despite its name was owned by Belgian interests. The formation of this company marked the start of the later Tessenderlo Group. The site was redeveloped and in 1920 launched the production of the sulfate-based fertilizer potash and hydrochloric acid, a byproduct of the sulfate production process. In that year, the company was renamed Produits Chimiques de Tessenderlo.

In the 1920s, Tessenderlo's production featured a number of company mainstays, including feed phosphates, fertilizers, and sulfates. These products remained central to the company's operations throughout the century and into the beginning of the 21st century. The decade also marked the beginning of Tessenderlo's relationship with France, which became the company's second largest market after Belgium. In 1923, Tessenderlo formed a sales agreement with France's Société Commerciale des Potasses d'Alsace. That agreement led to the creation of a joint venture between the two companies, called Produits Chimiques de Limbourg, formed in 1929. The creation of the joint venture, which involved the merger of the Tessenderlo and Alsace companies' operations, also marked the entry of French investment into the Belgian company. The

---

Limbourg-based joint venture built a new plant in the town of Ham and began producing potassium sulphate and dicalcium phosphate. Exports formed a major part of the joint venture's operations, and by 1930 exports accounted for some 80 percent of the company's total production.

Yet the deepening of the economic crisis in the 1930s forced Produits Chimiques de Tessenderlo to withdraw from the joint venture with Potasses d'Alsace in 1936. Instead, Tessenderlo set up its own independent operation, focused on the main Tessenderlo site, for the production of new salt and potash derivatives, including sulfuric acid, dicalcium phosphate, chlorine, and caustic soda. The company went public the following year, listing on the Brussels Stock Exchange.

The years of World War II and the Nazi occupation of Belgium culminated in an explosion at the main site, which killed nearly 200 and left 800 wounded in 1942. Following the war, the company rebuilt its operations. In 1954, however, the Tessenderlo company's development once again coincided with that of Potasses d'Alsace, now known as Mines de Potasses d'Alsace. This time, the French company acquired its Belgian counterpart outright. Under its new owners, later to be known as Entreprise Minière & Chimique, the Tessenderlo site remained focused on its sulfate-based production, and its core Limbourg region, into the 1960s.

Diversifying from the 1960s

Tessenderlo launched its first effort at diversification, accompanied by its first expansion beyond the Limbourg region, in 1964 when it acquired a company in Vilvoorde-based Pont Brûlé. That company, which like Tessenderlo produced sodium sulphate and dicalcium phosphate, added the production of gelatin to Tessenderlo's sphere of operations as well. Gelatin, derived from slaughterhouse byproducts, was produced by hydrolyzing the bones and skins of pigs and cattle, a process that made use of hydrochloric acid. As Tessenderlo had already emerged as a major producer of hydrochloric acid, the extension proved a natural fit. Gelatin and, later, other specialty products such as natural derivatives were used in flavorings.

Tessenderlo's production of chlorine provided the launch pad for its next extension at the end of the 1960s. In 1969, the company teamed up with DSM to begin production of vinyl chloride monomer and, later, polyvinyl chloride (PVC). For this effort, the companies created a joint venture, Limburgse Vinyl Maatschappij, and built a new production facility, which came onstream in 1972. The company also changed its name that year, becoming Tessenderlo Chemie.

Tessenderlo's growing gelatin operation formed the basis for the creation of another subsidiary, PB Gelatins. Formed in 1972, PB Gelatins began to expand through acquisitions, starting with the purchase of Colles et Gelatines, based in Zaventem, in 1973. In 1975, the gelatin production subsidiary added a site in Germany, acquiring Nienburger Gelatine.

Tessenderlo extended its operations again with the launch of a fine chemicals division, which began producing benzyl chloride, another chlorine derivative, as part of a joint venture, in 1976. That business was expanded in 1980 with the purchase of 100 percent control of Benzyl Chemie. The company also boosted its vinyl chloride operations as well, buying up France's Société Artésienne de Vinyl in 1976. Meanwhile, the company had added another company, Limburgse Rubber Producten, in 1975, and then launched construction of a new electrolysis facility.

By the early 1980s, Tessenderlo had completed, in large part, its diversification efforts. In 1983, the company restructured its operations, bringing all of its subsidiaries under a single holding company, named Tessenderlo Chemie N.V. The newly reorganized company now boasted four main areas of operations: Inorganic and Chlor-alkali Chemicals; Fine Chemicals; Gelatin; and Natural Derivatives. By focusing on niche products, the company successfully avoided direct competition with the world's chemical industry giants. Over the next 20 years, Tessenderlo established itself as a European and/or global leader in many of its product groups.

Tessenderlo's vinyl chloride monomer and PVC production led it to an interest in developing downstream activities as well. In 1984, the company launched a strategy to add a new business division, that of Plastic Conversion. As part of this effort, the group launched a new series of acquisitions, starting with French plastic pipe manufacturer Sotra in 1984. The following year, the company began producing window profiles through the purchase of Plastival, located in Clerval, France. By the end of the decade, the company had added Dyka, a pipes and fittings maker active in The Netherlands and Belgium, acquired in 1987. Into the 1990s, the group boosted its plastic products operations with the purchase of Deltaplast, in The Netherlands, in 1993, and Seperef, a pipes producer in Quincieux, France, in 1996.

Niche Leader in the New Century

Tessenderlo continued building up its other core business areas through the 1990s as well. The group's Gelatin operation grew with the acquisition of a production facility in Treforest, marking the company's entrance into the United Kingdom, in 1985. In a related move, the company acquired Caillaud, based in France, which specialized in collecting and processing slaughterhouse byproducts, and provided a stable supply of raw materials for the group's gelatin production. A decade later, the company's gelatin subsidiary made a major step toward becoming the world's leading gelatin producer through its acquisition of Baert-Verlee, based in Belgium, which also produced animal meal and fats.

Tessenderlo expanded its basic production operations with the acquisition of a chlorine, alkali, and mineral chloride production facility from Produits Chimiques de Loos in 1988. The following year, the company acquired full control of the Lim-

<table>
<tr><td colspan="2" align="center">**Key Dates:**</td></tr>
<tr><td>**1919:**</td><td>L'Union Française des Produits Chimiques & Matières Colorantes is established on a chemicals site in Tessenderlo dating from 1892.</td></tr>
<tr><td>**1920:**</td><td>The company becomes Produits Chimiques de Tessenderlo (PCT).</td></tr>
<tr><td>**1929:**</td><td>PCT merges into a joint venture, Produits Chimiques de Limbourg (PCL), with Potasses d'Alsace.</td></tr>
<tr><td>**1936:**</td><td>PCT exits the PCL joint venture.</td></tr>
<tr><td>**1937:**</td><td>PCT goes public on the Brussels Stock Exchange.</td></tr>
<tr><td>**1954:**</td><td>Mines de Potasse d'Alsace acquires control of PCT.</td></tr>
<tr><td>**1964:**</td><td>The company acquires Pont Brûlé and begins production of gelatin.</td></tr>
<tr><td>**1972:**</td><td>The company name is changed to Tessenderlo Chemie; PVC production is launched.</td></tr>
<tr><td>**1976:**</td><td>The company begins fine chemicals production.</td></tr>
<tr><td>**1983:**</td><td>All operations are merged under the Tessenderlo Chemie N.V. holding company.</td></tr>
<tr><td>**1984:**</td><td>The company begins an extension into production of PVC-based products, including pipes and fittings, window profiles and compounds.</td></tr>
<tr><td>**1986:**</td><td>The company acquires Caillaud of France and enters the natural derivatives market.</td></tr>
<tr><td>**1995:**</td><td>The company acquires the Wymar group, producer of window profiles, and enters the U.S. and Chinese markets.</td></tr>
<tr><td>**1999:**</td><td>The company enters Eastern Europe with the acquisition of a PVC compound plant in Poland.</td></tr>
<tr><td>**2001:**</td><td>The company acquires Accordis Fine Chemicals and John Davidson Pipes in the United Kingdom.</td></tr>
<tr><td>**2005:**</td><td>The company restructures operations along three primary business divisions: Chemicals; Specialties; and Plastics Converting.</td></tr>
</table>

burgse Vinyl Maatschappij joint venture. Tessenderlo also extended its downstream operations, buying up Tiffauges, France-based Thermoplastiques Cousin Tessier in 1991. The purchased marked Tessenderlo's entry into the production of PVC compounds and thermoplastic elastomers. In 1995, the company bought the Wymar group of companies, active in France and Belgium, but also in Canada, marking the group's expansion into the North American market. Wymar was a major producer of PVC-based window profiles.

Until then, Tessenderlo's operations had focused on its European base. In the late 1990s, however, the group began its expansion into the Americas. A major part of this effort was accomplished with the purchase of Hickson Kerley, the U.S. arm of Hickson International. Completed in 1996, the acquisition gave Tessenderlo control of a major producer of specialty chemicals, including sulfur-based agricultural and industrial products in the U.S. market. The Kerley acquisition also gave the company its first foothold in the Latin American markets.

The move into the United States came as part of Tessenderlo's effort to develop itself as an internationally operating company. Tessenderlo continued to add operations in the United States, such as Chelsea Building Products in Pennsylva-

nia, acquired in 1996. In Italy, the company purchased a chemicals plant in Pieve Vergonte in 1997. The company entered Eastern Europe in 1999, buying a PVC compound production facility in Warzaw, Poland. The group also had entered China, creating the joint venture Lianyungang Chemical Factory in 1995, in order to produce benzyl chloride and other chemicals.

Tessenderlo's expansion continued into the 2000s, notably with the purchase of Accordis Fine Chemicals, based in Leeds, England, and a chloroluene operation from Atofina in Widnes, also in the United Kingdom, both in 2001. In 2003, the company expanded its gelatin business, adding a site in Davenport, Iowa, and in Santa Fe, Argentina, marking the first international expansion of that division. Both operations were purchased from Australia's Goodman-Fielder. In 2004, the company added to its extensive French presence, where 25 of the group's 65 production facilities were located, with the purchase of Acome, a PVC profiles producer.

The growth of all of its core operational divisions led Tessenderlo to undertake a new restructuring in 2005. As part of that process, the company created three core business groups: Chemicals, including inorganics, chlor-alkalis, and PVC; Specialties, including gelatin, natural derivatives, and fine chemicals; and Plastics Converting, including profiles, pipes and fittings, and compounds. Already a world leader in most of its product categories, Tessenderlo was prepared to continue its expansion on a global scale into the late 2000s.

Principal Subsidiaries

Aliphos S.A.S. (France); Baert-Verlee & Zoon BVBA; Ets. Caillaud S.A.S. (France); Calaire Chimie S.A.S. (France); Ets. Charvet Père et Fils S.A.S. (France); Chelsea Building Products Inc. (United States); Chemilyl S.A.S. (France); Cofipar S.A. (Netherlands); Dyka B.V. (Netherlands); Dyka GmbH (Germany); Dyka Plastics S.A. (Belgium); Fairbrook PLC (United Kingdom); Farchemia S.R.L. (Italy); John Davidson Holding Ltd. (United Kingdom); Kerley Trading Inc. (United States); Lianyungang Taile Chemical Industry, Co. Ltd. (China); Limburgse Vinyl Maatschappij S.A. (Belgium); PB Gelatins France S.A.S.; Produits Chimiques de Loos S.A.S. (France); Tessenderlo Chemie S.A. (Belgium); Tessenderlo Chemie Hungaria Kft; Tessenderlo Chemie International S.A.; Tessenderlo Fine Chemicals Ltd. (United Kingdom); Tessenderlo Italia S.R.L.; Tessenderlo Kerley Inc. (United States); Tessenderlo Kerley Latino Americana S.A. (Chile); Tessenderlo Kerley Mexico S.A. de C.V. (Mexico); Tessenderlo Polska Sp. z.o.o.; Tessenderlo Schweiz AG; Tessenderlo U.S.A. Inc.; Tessenderlo UK Ltd.

Principal Competitors

Repsol YPF S.A.; BASF AG; Sungai Budi Group; Dow Chemical Company; OMK United Metallurgical Company; Lanzhou Chemical Industry Company; Zigong Honghe Chemical Company Ltd.; Votorantim Participacoes S.A.; E.I. du Pont de Nemours and Co.

Further Reading

Higgs, Richard, ''Tessenderlo Invests in Brazil Profile Firm,'' *Plastics News,* December 21, 1998, p. 4.

"Tessenderlo Expands in Gelatine," *International Food Ingredients*, April–May 2003, p. 14.

"Tessenderlo Group's Double Investment," *Fertilizer International*, January–February 2005, p. 42.

"Tessenderlo Opens a New Chapter," *Fertilizer International*, September–October 1996, p. 53.

Walsh, Kerri, "Tessenderlo Buys Accordis Unit," *Chemical Week*, August 29, 2001, p. 23.

Warmington, Andrew, "Soap Stars: What Are the Competitive Issues in Fragrance Ingredients for Household and Personal Care Applications?," *Specialty Chemicals*, February 2004, p. 10.

—M.L. Cohen

Ticketmaster

8800 Sunset Boulevard
Los Angeles, California 90069
U.S.A.
Telephone: (213) 639-6100
Fax: (213) 386-1244
Web site: http://www.ticketmaster.com

Wholly Owned Subsidiary of IAC/Interactive Corporation
Incorporated: 1982
Employees: NA
Sales: $743 million (2003)
NAIC: 561599 All Other Travel Arrangement and
   Reservation Services

Ticketmaster is the world's largest ticket distribution company in the United States, completely dominating its market niche. The company distributes tickets for more than 10,000 clients whose events range from professional wrestling matches and rock concerts to Broadway shows and operas. Tickets are sold at roughly 3,300 outlets worldwide, as well as through 19 telephone call centers and through the ticketmaster.com web site. The company's ReserveAmerica subsidiary manages campsite reservations across North America. Ticketmaster also owns several regional ticketing service companies and TicketWeb, a provider of ticketing software and services. Ticketmaster is itself a subsidiary of IAC/InterActive Corporation, the media vehicle of entrepreneur Barry Diller.

Early Years

Ticketmaster was started by two Arizona State University students who were looking for a solution to a problem they encountered when buying concert tickets. At the time, the buyer of a ticket was forced to select from the seats that had been allotted to the particular vendor from whom he or she was purchasing the ticket. If the vendor was nearly sold out, the buyer might be forced to buy bad seats even though better seats were available through other ticket sellers. Melees occasionally erupted when ticket buyers, after standing in line for hours at one place, found that the vendor was sold out or that better seats

were available elsewhere. The system also was inefficient for promoters and owners of venues, who often had difficulty selling all of their tickets, despite unmet demand.

In 1978, the two budding entrepreneurs developed a solution to the problem. They created an innovative computer program that networked several computers in such a way that a person buying an event ticket at a box office could quickly select from the total reserve of seats available. Thus efficient computerized ticket vending was born, and Ticketmaster—the company that sprouted from student innovation—became one of several small vendors in the late 1970s and early 1980s that pioneered the industry. When it was starting out, in fact, Ticketmaster was just one of many small ticket-vending companies competing for a small share of the industry; the business had come to be dominated by ticket distribution giant Ticketron. Nevertheless, Ticketmaster, with its unique computer-based vending system, managed to increase its ticket sales to about $1 million annually by 1981. That amount was still less than 1 percent of the business controlled by Ticketron, however.

Ticketmaster's fate was changed in 1982, when Chicago investor Jay Pritzker purchased it. Pritzker, the wealthy owner of the Hyatt Hotel chain, paid $4 million for the entire company. He immediately brought in Fred Rosen as chief executive to manage the operation. Rosen, an attorney and former stand-up comic, brought energy and vision to the enterprise. He believed that the future of the ticket industry was in concert sales, rather than sporting events, in part because sporting event-goers often were able to circumvent service fees charged by ticket sellers by purchasing season tickets. But his feeling also arose from his observations about the dynamics of the concert industry. Indeed, if concert fans wanted to see a show badly enough, they would buy on impulse and would be willing to pay higher prices for tickets. Furthermore, the long lines that formed at box offices for rock concerts indicated a great need for Ticketmaster's computerized service.

Aside from new computer and information technologies, other forces were at work in the ticket industry in the early 1980s that boded well for an innovator like Ticketmaster. In fact, the rock concert industry, among other entertainment businesses, was becoming much more complicated. Prior to the

Company Perspectives:

Our mission: for clients—to provide the best systems, services, and tools for the optimal sale of tickets to the widest possible audience; for consumers—to provide convenient, secure, and fair access to the best possible ticket offered by our clients.

1970s, bands were paid a lump sum—usually in cash just a few minutes before they went on stage—by the promoter of the concert. The promoter would agree beforehand to pay the band, say, $20,000, and any money left over would be used to pay the promoter's expenses and profit.

In the 1970s, however, bands started demanding more. They started charging minimum appearance fees, for example, and wanted a cut of the money generated from concessions and parking. The demands, in part, were the result of a feeling by top bands that promoters were taking advantage of them. But the increased cost of traveling and putting on a show also contributed to the bands' desire for better compensation; fans came to expect much more in the way of expensive sound systems and special effects, for example.

One result of the new demands was that, after a concert, the band's manager and the promoter typically negotiated, or argued, about exactly how much the promoter and other involved parties would be paid. The new system increased the bargaining power of the bands, eventually boosting their take to 75 percent or more of the gross receipts. Meanwhile, the promotion industry was pinched. Many promoters saw their profit margins deteriorate to as little as 1 percent, despite the fact that they were still bearing much of the risk of a failed concert. To get the big name bands, however, promoters had to be willing to accept that risk and honor many of the group's requirements.

A New Strategy in the Late 1970s and 1980s

That was the environment still evolving when Rosen took the helm at the fledgling Ticketmaster. Realizing the folly of trying to compete with the mammoth Ticketron using conventional industry tactics, he devised a strategy that exploited the frustrations of the promoters. He effectively offered to limit inside charges—the money taken from promoters and facility owners—thus reducing the promoter's risk. He would accomplish this by raising service charges on individual ticket sales and giving promoters a percentage of the proceeds. In return, the promoters agreed to give Ticketmaster the exclusive rights to ticketing for their shows. To boost service fees, Rosen implemented new sales techniques, particularly telephone sales service, which gave customers an alternative to standing in line. For the convenience, Ticketmaster was able to charge as much as a 30 percent premium, or higher in some instances.

Many promoters gave exclusive rights to Ticketmaster. Indeed, aside from guaranteed fees, the promoters benefited from Ticketmaster's state-of-the-art ticketing system. The company's computers could sell 25,000 tickets in just a few minutes, if necessary, which substantially reduced the promoter's advertising and related costs and improved customer satisfac-

tion with the overall event. The arrangement worked so well that Ticketmaster eventually was able to secure long-term contracts with several major promoters for handling ticketing for all of their events. Promoters also viewed Ticketmaster as a preferable alternative to the giant Ticketron, which many promoters believed had become arrogant and sloppy.

Despite steady gains, Ticketmaster lost money in the late 1970s and early 1980s as it scrambled to implement its expensive strategy. By the mid-1980s, though, the company was posting profits. To boost sales and market share, Ticketmaster began buying out smaller competitors in an effort to broaden its reach into major cities. It acquired Datatix/Select-A-Seat in Denver, for example, and SEATS in Atlanta. As it bought up more companies and drove others out of business, the number of competitors in the industry declined. At the same time, Ticketron's supremacy was rapidly waning. Aside from complacency, part of Ticketron's problem was that it lacked the investment capital afforded by Ticketmaster's deep-pocketed owner. Its ticketing systems soon became obsolete in comparison with those in use at Ticketmaster.

By the late 1980s, Ticketmaster had become a top player in the ticketing business and Ticketron was scurrying to duplicate Rosen's successful revenue-sharing strategy. But it was too late; Ticketmaster had mastered the recipe and was rapidly increasing the number and size of its contracts. In fact, Ticketmaster's relationship with, and control over, its promoters had evolved to the point where Ticketmaster was deeply entwined in the promotion business. That involvement was evidenced by a relationship in Seattle that finally ended in a lawsuit. In 1989, Ticketmaster made a loan and credit line guarantee valued at $500,000 to two of the area's top promoters. The promoters used the money to start a new operation promoting concerts in The George, a facility in central Washington. In that same year, one of the promoters launched another venture, PowerStation, to sell tickets in competition with Ticketmaster. Enraged Ticketmaster executives responded by withholding cash from the promoter's ticket sales through Ticketmaster. The promoter sued and finally settled with Ticketmaster out of court, but the PowerStation was shuttered and both promoters left the concert business.

Market Dominance in the Early 1990s

By the end of the 1980s, Ticketmaster was selling more than $500,000 worth of tickets annually. Ticketron was still considered an industry power, but its status was diminished and its long-term prospects were dismal. The only other competition consisted of a smattering of local and regional companies struggling to combat Ticketmaster. Ticketmaster finally delivered the crowning blow to Ticketron in 1991, when it purchased some of the company's assets and effectively rendered the company no more than a lesson in corporate history. Questions were raised about whether or not the buyout would give Ticketmaster a monopoly on the industry, but the U.S. Department of Justice approved the deal. With Ticketron out of its way, Ticketmaster was virtually dominant and its sales began rising rapidly toward the $1 billion mark.

Because it had so much control in the ticket industry, Ticketmaster came under fire from numerous critics following the demise of Ticketron. Some fans complained that Ticketmaster

Key Dates:

1978: Ticketmaster is founded by two Arizona State University students.
1982: Jay Pritzker purchases the company, beginning a period of growth.
1991: Main rival Ticketron is acquired, giving the company market dominance.
1996: Ticketmaster goes public, launches online, travel, and magazine ventures.
1997: Online service is merged with CitySearch; Barry Diller acquires 47 percent of the company.
1998: Diller's USA Networks acquires the remainder of Ticketmaster; the online operations are spun off.
1999: The U.S. Supreme Court refuses to review an antitrust lawsuit appeal in a victory for the company.
2000: The company acquires Admission Network and ETM Entertainment Network.
2001: The company buys back a controlling stake in Ticketmaster Online-Citysearch, and the merged companies begin to operate as Ticketmaster Corporation.
2003: Diller's USA Networks changes its name to IAC/Interactive Corporation.
2005: The company forms a new unit called TicketmasterArts, dedicated specifically to ticketing and fundraising for arts organizations.

was raising its fees, reflecting a monopoly on the industry. Similarly, some promoters argued that Ticketmaster wielded too much power and that it was willing to abuse that power to get its way. Finally, some rock bands complained that Ticketmaster was gouging their profits with excessive fees, knowing that the bands had nowhere else to turn. Ticketmaster countered, citing rising operating costs and relatively modest overall company profits. Still, criticism continued.

Band discontent with Ticketmaster's tactics culminated in one of the most visible disputes with Ticketmaster on record: a complaint filed with the Justice Department by the popular rock band Pearl Jam alleged that Ticketmaster engaged in monopolistic practices. Pearl Jam wanted Ticketmaster to drop its service fees to $1.80 per ticket, but the company refused to drop below $2.50. Pearl Jam rejected the offer and threatened to work without Ticketmaster. The band planned to find venues, such as fairgrounds and racetracks, that were not subject to Ticketmaster's exclusive contracts. Their efforts eventually failed and their concert tour fell apart. It was then that the band filed the complaint, and the Justice Department launched an investigation.

Ticketmaster argued that from about $1 billion worth of tickets sold in 1993, it generated revenues of $191 million in 1993, only $7 million of which was earned as net profit. That amounted to less than ten cents in profit per ticket. Critics complained that Ticketmaster was simply concealing the profitability of the business, but Rosen and his fellow executives were adamant that the industry was still competitive. "Fifteen years ago, there was another company everybody said had a monopoly—Ticketron," said Larry Solters, Ticketmaster spokesperson, in the July 31, 1994, *News & Observer*. He added, "Ticketmaster

did ticketing better. And I wouldn't be surprised if somebody else comes up with a better system someday. There are a million ideas out there. . . . It's not that tough."

After posting record sales and profits in 1993, Ticketmaster's fate was changed again when Paul Allen beat out several big media players in a bid to purchase controlling interest in the company. The 40-year-old Allen, who had gained fame as the cofounder of Microsoft, paid an estimated $300 million for his stake. Following his departure from the software giant, he had assembled an interesting portfolio of investments, many of which were related to the emerging information highway. He also owned the Portland Trailblazers basketball team and a charitable foundation, among other interests. Allen retained Rosen as CEO, but he had new plans for the company. In fact, he wanted to increase its sales threefold to fivefold within five years and expand into different distribution avenues.

Ticketmaster sold a whopping 52 million tickets to entertainment and sporting events in 1994 and captured about $200 million in revenues. Having nearly cornered the ticket market, it was setting its sights on several other media-related ventures. The company already was distributing a regional monthly events guide to about 600,000 customers, and it planned to use that as a base for creation of a new entertainment magazine. Ticketmaster also was working on a new online service, hoping to position itself as a one-stop shopping center for entertainment and event needs.

The company launched its new magazine, *Live!,* in February 1996. Critics saw the publication as a thinly veiled attempt to brighten Ticketmaster's tarnished image. The magazine field was definitely a difficult one to break into, and *Live!* lost money from the start, costing its owners $11 million in the first two years. Other ventures introduced during 1996 included a hotel and airline reservation service, Ticketmaster Travel and Ticketmaster Online. The latter was an instant success, topping $3 million a month in revenues within a short time.

1996 Public Offering

The biggest story for Ticketmaster in 1996 was its decision to go public. Paul Allen kept his stake, retaining control of 54 percent of the company after the initial public offering (IPO). The initial offering price had been considered high by many analysts, and it soon fell off. Within a year it recovered, however, rising to nearly double the original figure.

On April 28, 1997, Ticketmaster filed suit against Microsoft over that company's practice of deep linking from its web site to an inner page of Ticketmaster's site, bypassing the company's home page and its logo and advertising content. To some users, it could appear that the Ticketmaster page was generated by Microsoft, rather than Ticketmaster. The suit was later settled out of court, with Microsoft agreeing to link only to Ticketmaster's home page. The year also saw the company's online ticket service merge with CitySearch's entertainment guide web site, and new investments in Australian and French ticketing companies. A joint venture with Jack Nicklaus's Golden Bear Golf to market golfing reservations was launched as well.

In May 1997 Barry Diller's HSN, Inc. (later to be known as USA Networks, Inc.) announced plans to buy out Allen's stake in

Ticketmaster. The following year the company became a subsidiary of USA Networks when the remainder of its stock was acquired. After the acquisition, Fred Rosen stepped down as CEO, allegedly due to clashes with Diller. He was replaced by Terry Barnes. At about this time Diller acquired City Search, Inc., merged it with Ticketmaster's online operation to form Ticketmaster Online-CitySearch, Inc., and spun it off as a public company, retaining 60 percent ownership. This resulted in two Ticketmasters, the one representing the traditional part of the business and the awkwardly named Ticketmaster Online-CitySearch as its own Internet-only company. This was at a time when Internet stocks were the high fliers on Wall Street, and many companies split off their online divisions as separate companies. For example, bookseller Barnes and Noble made a freestanding unit out of its online seller barnesandnoble.com. So this seemed a sensible business strategy with many imitators in the late 1990s.

In December 1997 a contract was signed with event promotion giant SFX Entertainment that guaranteed Ticketmaster exclusive ticketing rights for seven years. Diller and SFX Chairman Robert F.X. Sillerman had earlier engaged in a very public battle of words, but were able to bury the hatchet when it came time to do business.

A lawsuit over Ticketmaster's alleged monopoly on ticket distribution reached the Supreme Court in 1999. The court let a prior ruling, which was in Ticketmaster's favor, stand. Also during the year, an attempt to merge Ticketmaster Online-CitySearch with Lycos and USA Networks failed when Lycos shareholders rebelled.

In late 1999 and early 2000, Ticketmaster acquired several more of its competitors. These included Alabama-based TicketLink, multilingual ticketer Admission Network, Inc. of Canada, and ETM Entertainment Network, Inc., which had contracts with the Los Angeles Dodgers and New York Mets, among others. The company also sued Tickets.com, in conjunction with Ticketmaster Online-CitySearch, over alleged deceptive practices involving its web site. The appeal of buying tickets online was growing steadily, with 40 percent of some events' seats selling over the Internet. As a result, Ticketmaster's telephone operators were taking fewer orders, and the company shut down several of its call centers. Tickets purchased online were still mailed to customers, but new technology was being tested that would allow them to be printed at home, further streamlining the process.

Reunited Company in the 2000s

When Barry Diller took over Ticketmaster in 1997, he had moved quickly to capitalize on what looked like the most vital part of the company by spinning off the online ticketing business as Ticketmaster Online-Citysearch. The new Internet company's stock had initially gone way up, and shortly after the IPO, Ticketmaster Online-Citysearch was worth as much as $3.4 billion. The soaring stock price allowed Diller to make several acquisitions, trading the stock for small ticket companies such as 2b Technologies, a museum ticketing firm, and a Microsoft subsidiary called Sidewalk that made city guides. These acquisitions may have cost the company too dearly. And there were other problems as well. Although Ticketmaster was ostensibly a separate operation from Ticketmaster Online-

Citysearch, the companies still overlapped in many ways. For example, Ticketmaster's telephone call centers were staffed with Ticketmaster employees, but these employees were at times asked to do things that specifically benefited Ticketmaster Online-Citysearch. Communication between the two companies was apparently rocky. John Pleasants, who was CEO of the online company, claimed in an interview with *Fortune* magazine (March 5, 2001) that "There was an issue every day," meaning conflict between the two firms was ongoing.

By the end of 2000, when the high-tech market had crashed, Ticketmaster Online-Citysearch's stock had gone from a high of more than $80 to less than $12 a share. The company had lost some $337 million over two years. In November 2000, Barry Diller agreed to buy back a controlling stake in Ticketmaster Online-Citysearch. A few months later, he announced that the two companies would once again operate as one. Diller became cochairman of the new combined Ticketmaster Corporation, with Ticketmaster CEO Terry Barnes sharing the post. The new company was to have more than 12 million customers and sell some 80 million tickets a year.

Barry Diller remained extremely active in the Internet world, buying the Internet travel firm Expedia for $4.6 billion in 2003 and Hotels.com later that year. In June 2003, Diller's USA Networks changed its name to IAC/Interactive Corporation. Ticketmaster was part of a media empire that also contained the home shopping channel HSN and the web-based mortgage lending company LendingTree. Ticketmaster was not a fast-growing company, but it did remain profitable after its merger with its online sister, and it made some acquisitions and changes in its way of doing business. In 2003, the company experimented with auctioning off event tickets. Many concert tickets were already auctioned off electronically in the secondary market, selling on eBay sometimes for much much more than the original price. Ticketmaster, which sold close to 100 million tickets overall in 2002, was looking at so-called "dynamic pricing" as a way to ease problems caused by unscrupulous "scalpers" (secondary market sellers) and to sell difficult seats such as ones in the back of an auditorium, that often went empty. Ticketmaster also moved into new international markets in the early 2000s, expanding into Sweden, Norway, Denmark, and Finland. Ticketmaster also operated in Scotland, Wales, Ireland, England, and The Netherlands. The company also formed a new unit in 2005 called TicketmasterArts, dedicated specifically to ticketing and fundraising for arts organizations. The new division worked with venues like the Kennedy Theater and the North Carolina BTI Center for the Performing Arts.

In 2005, Ticketmaster's parent corporation, IAC/Interactive, went through another upheaval, splitting off its travel division Expedia and some other Internet travel companies into a new entity. Ticketmaster remained part of the main company IAC/Interactive, along with HSN, LendingTree, and the Internet search engine Ask Jeeves. While the parent company did not break out financial results for the subsidiaries, Ticketmaster was considered a stable and profitable company in IAC's mix. The parent company had projected 2005 sales of $5.7 billion.

Principal Competitors

Tickets.com; TicketCity.com

Further Reading

Andrew, Paul, "Paul Allen's Ticket to Future," *Seattle Times,* November 23, 1993, p. E1.

Balzer, Stephanie, "That's the Ticket," *Business Journal—Serving Phoenix & The Valley of the Sun,* August 25, 2000, p. 1.

Corr, O. Casey, "Big-Ticket Troubles: Concert Industry Rolls in Money, But Where Is It All Going," *Seattle Times,* August 21, 1994, p. A1.

Francis, Mike, "Paul Allen Slowly, Surely Steps into Public Light," *Oregonian,* August 14, 1994, p. F1.

Gaulin, Jacqueline, "Consumer Groups Go After Ticketmaster," *Washington Times,* March 22, 1995, p. B7.

Helm, Leslie, "Ticketmaster IPO Set at $14.50 a Share," *Los Angeles Times,* November 19, 1996, p. D2.

Menconi, David, "Ticketmaster's Money Tree—A Giant with It Made in the Shade," *News & Observer* (Raleigh, N.C.), July 31, 1994, p. G1.

Philips, Chuck, "Ticketmaster Cleared; Justice Department Drops Antitrust Probe," *Washington Post,* July 6, 1995, p. C2.

Reilly, Patrick M., "Ticketmaster Gears Up to Launch a New Entertainment Magazine," *Wall Street Journal,* October 25, 1995, p. B5.

"Rosen Reflects on Ticketmaster," *Amusement Business,* May 25, 1998, p. 1.

Saylor, Mark, "Ticketmaster's Tough CEO Ready for the Next Act," *Los Angeles Times,* November 30, 1997, p. D1.

Shapiro, Eben, and Bruce Orwall, "Roadshow Spurs Battle of SFX, Ticketmaster," *Asian Wall Street Journal,* August 4, 1998, p. 13.

Sloan, Allan, "Scalped at Ticketmaster? Paul Allen Leaves Investors in the Lurch," *Newsweek,* June 16, 1997, p. 76.

Spring, Greg, "Ticketmaster Sets Sights on New Ventures," *Los Angeles Business Journal,* February 13, 1995, p. 6.

Stooksbury Guier, Cindy, "Ticketmaster Changed the Face of Live Entertainment," *Amusement Business,* July 27, 1998, p. A10.

—Dave Mote
—updates: Frank Uhle, A. Woodward

Toupargel-Agrigel S.A.

13 Chemin des Pres Secs, Zone Industrielle
Civrieux d'Azergues
France
Telephone: +33 04 72 54 10 00
Fax: +33 04 72 54 10 3033
Web site: http://www.toupargel.fr

Public Company
Incorporated: 1947 as Toupargel S.A.
Employees: 3,502
Sales: EUR 360 million ($490.10 million) (2004)
Stock Exchanges: Euronext Paris
Ticker Symbol: TPGEL.PA
NAIC: 454113 Mail-Order Houses; 311412 Frozen
  Specialty Food Manufacturing; 311411 Frozen Fruit,
  Juice, and Vegetable Processing; 311712 Fresh and
  Frozen Seafood Processing

Toupargel-Agrigel S.A. is the leading provider of home delivery grocery services in France. Originally specializing in the delivery of frozen foods, which continues to account for more than 90 percent of group sales, Toupargel-Agrigel has expanded to include the delivery of fresh food and groceries as well. The company's frozen food operations are carried out under the Toupargel and Agrigel brand names. The company expects to integrate its two brands (Agrigel was acquired in 2003) under a single brand by 2007. Together, the two brands control 34 percent of France's frozen foods home delivery market, and more than 6 percent of the total frozen foods market. Toupargel-Agrigel's fresh foods and groceries operations brand, Place du Marché, was created in 2000. Led by Roland Tchenio, Toupargel-Agrigel has developed a proactive sales system. The company places calls to each of its more than 1.4 million customers up to 14 times per year in order to take their order; the company also operates an e-commerce web site. Orders are then delivered to customers within 48 hours. Customer support is handled through 35 call centers around France, as well as its own freezing and cold storage facilities, logistics platforms, and fleet of refrigerated vehicles. Toupargel-Agrigel

is listed on the Euronext Paris Stock Exchange's Secondary Market. Roland Tchenio, the driving force behind the group's growth since 1982, is also its majority shareholder, with 56 percent of company shares.

New Home Delivery Model in the 1980s

Roland Tchenio completed his studies at France's elite HEC business school before earning an MBA at Harvard. Returning to France at the beginning of the 1970s, Tchenio worked first for French conglomerate Schlumberger before joining rival group Chargeurs in 1977. Tchenio developed a specialty in turning around struggling companies, with an emphasis on the retail sector. As Tchenio told *Tremplins:* "I've always worked in the distribution sector. My strength? A developer's profile. I'm able to take a concept, an idea, and understand how a company will be able to evolve."

Yet, as part of these rapidly growing conglomerates, Tchenio barely had the opportunity to enjoy the fruits of his success before moving on to the next acquisition. In 1982, therefore, Tchenio decided to set out in business on his own. Instead of founding his own company, Tchenio decided to put his career expertise to work, and favor the developer's role over that of entrepreneur.

Tchenio's target fell on Toupargel, a small company based in Civrieux d'Azergues. Founded in 1947, Toupargel originally specialized in the production of frozen vegetables and other foods. In 1969, Toupargel decided to enter the retail market, and began selling its products directly to consumers. The company's model mirrored that of the home grocery delivery market in France, using a small fleet of trucks outfitted as small grocery stores. These trucks served primarily a rural population; indeed, into the 1970s, the presence of freezers in French households remained limited in large part to the country's agricultural population. The appearance of large-scale supermarkets, and later hypermarkets, launched a shift in consumer grocery shopping habits in much of France. Nonetheless, the country's growing retail giants focused especially on larger urban markets. France's rural region, while accounting for a significant proportion of the country's population, remained underserved by the retail sector.

Company Perspectives:

Toupargel Agrigel is a specialist in the home delivery of quality food products to individuals, with two main businesses: Frozen Foods, which account for 96% of its sales, and Fresh Foods and Groceries. Our company business model distinguishes us from traditional distribution· telesales followed by delivery within 48 to 72 hours, after semi-automated preparation of sales orders at dedicated logistical platforms. This sales approach was created and perfected by the Group's Frozen Foods business, and now has been duplicated at the Group's Fresh Foods and Groceries business.

When Tchenio purchased Toupargel in 1982, it was a small but profitable business, with 70 employees and six truck stores and annual sales of less than $10 million per year. Tchenio immediately set out to develop the business, using his experience in the integration of acquisitions to expand the company. As he told *Tremplins:* "When I bought this company more than 20 years ago, I recognized immediately how I was going to develop it, notably by focusing on external expansion with regional companies."

Tchenio launched Toupargel on a long series of acquisitions, buying up many of the company's smaller rivals in the surrounding region, before beginning to expand on a national scale. By the early 1990s, Toupargel had completed some 30 acquisitions. The company's external growth effort continued through the 1990s, adding another ten companies into the next century.

From the start, however, Tchenio recognized the inefficiency of Toupargel's original model. The company's truck stores were too small to carry the range of goods offered by the larger supermarkets, which had begun to dominate the French market in the 1980s. While the company's existing clientele remained relatively loyal, developing new clients became more and more difficult. At the same time, sending out the company's fleet of trucks with no firm orders had become an inefficient use of the group's resources, especially following the oil crises of the 1970s.

Tchenio sought a new way of doing business, telling *Creascope:* "We saw that the truck store market was in decline. We tried out a system where the salesmen made house calls in order to take customers' orders, which were delivered afterward. We recognized that that wasn't working."

The solution came through the company's acquisition drive, which, in addition to increasing the group's client base and fleet, also gave the company the opportunity to explore different ways of approaching the home delivery market. As Tchenio explained: "In 1983, I acquired a company in Annecy who only did business by mail order. In 1985, I acquired a company in Poitiers that had used traveling salesmen but had decided to switch to telephone sales."

Tchenio decided to combine a catalog-based mail-order approach with use of telephone-driven sales. In 1986, the company began investing in its new model, converting its truck fleet and installing a computer-based ordering system. "Once we

had found this solution, we needed to develop specific tools," Tchenio told *Creascope.* Toupargel quickly took the telephone sales model to a new level. Rather than send out its catalog and wait for customers to call, the company adopted a proactive approach. In support of this, Toupargel established its own network of call centers, responsible for contacting customers at regular, scheduled intervals—typically some 14 times per year in order to take their orders. Customers were able to prepare their orders at their leisure, and know in advance when the Toupargel sales personnel were to call.

The conversion to this new sales model had the added benefit, for both Toupargel and its customers, of allowing the company to expand its range of products. "In the truck stores, we couldn't offer more than 200 items. Today, with the telephone, we have about 1,000," Tchenio told *Creascope.* Meanwhile, the company's delivery schedule was adapted to the new model, allowing the company to make more efficient use of its fleet.

Home Delivery Leader in the 2000s

Toupargel grew rapidly through the end of the 1980s and into the 1990s. By 1992, the company's sales had topped the equivalent of $50 million. By 1997, Toupargel's revenues had climbed past $85 million. In that year, the company went public, listing its stock on the Paris Stock Exchange's Secondary Market.

The public offering came in support of a change in the group's strategic direction. By the late 1990s, the French frozen foods home delivery market had more or less reached maturity, and future expansion of the market appeared less likely. A factor contributing to this was the consolidation of the supermarket sector in general. Limits imposed on the expansion of the hypermarket format—with new store openings becoming severely restricted in the 1990s—forced the larger distribution groups to seek other means to continue their own expansion by developing new store formats, including smaller shops targeting smaller and local population areas. A number of frozen food retail specialists had grown as well, including the nationally operating Picard and Thriet chains, providing more direct competition for Toupargel. Meanwhile, the promise of Internet shopping, although slow to develop, presented another threat to Toupargel's growth.

In response, Toupargel sought to expand its own base of operations away from its focus on frozen foods and to adapt its successful telephone-based sales system for the fresh foods and groceries market. Once again, Toupargel turned toward external growth to accomplish its strategy. In 1998, the company made two key acquisitions, buying Néodis and Selecta. Both companies operated home delivery services in the northeast of France. After their acquisition, the two companies were merged into a single operation in 1999. Renamed as Place du Marché ("Market Square"), the new operation was then converted to a telephone-based sales system. For this, Toupargel invested some EUR 16 million in the creation of a new, dedicated logistics center. Place du Marché also put into place its own call centers, based on the Toupargel model.

Place du Marché quickly added to its product offering, jumping from 500 items to more than 2,200 by the end of 2002.

Key Dates:

1947: Toupargel is founded as a frozen foods producer.
1969: Toupargel begins home deliveries of frozen foods.
1982: Roland Tchenio buys Toupargel and begins an expansion program, acquiring 40 companies over the next 20 years.
1986: Toupargel adopts a telephone-based sales system.
1997: Toupargel goes public on the Paris Stock Exchange's Secondary Market.
1998: Toupargel acquires Néodis and Selecta, specialized in fresh foods and groceries home delivery.
2000: After merging together, Néodis and Selecta adopt the Place du Marché brand name and begin a telephone sales system.
2003: Toupargel acquires Agrigel, French leader in the frozen foods home delivery market, from Unilever for EUR 81 million.
2005: Agrigel is converted to a telephone sales system and achieves 95 percent of its sales over the telephone.

Yet converting the operation's existing client base proceeded less smoothly than expected. As a result, Toupargel was forced to backtrack a bit, returning to a truck-based store system for its existing clientele, while retaining the telephone-based system in order to convert these customers in the future, and attract a new generation of customers. By the beginning of 2003, Toupargel's sales had topped EUR 110 million.

While it continued to build up its fresh foods division, Toupargel soon found a new—and faster—approach to its expansion. In 2003, the company agreed to buy up Frigedoc, a subsidiary of Cigesal-Miko, a part of Unilever. Toupargel paid EUR 81 million for the acquisition, which gave it control of Frigedoc's Agrigel brand, the French frozen foods home delivery leader. The addition of Agrigel forced Toupargel into debt for the first time, yet the acquisition also tripled Toupargel in size, establishing it as the clear leader in its market.

The integration of Agrigel into Toupargel, which renamed itself as Agrigel-Toupargel, went smoothly. The company dedicated most of 2004 to converting Agrigel, previously a truck store-based operation, to Toupargel's telephone sales system. The convergence of the two operations, especially the generation of operational synergies, continued through 2005. By the end of that year fully 95 percent of Agrigel's sales were generated through the telephone.

The integration process was expected to continue through 2006, at which point Toupargel-Agrigel expected to convert its operations to a single brand name. With annual sales of nearly EUR 360 million ($400 million), Toupargel-Agrigel had built up a solid position in the French home delivery market. Under Roland Tchenio, named one of Ernst & Young's French Entrepreneurs of the Year for 2004, Toupargel-Agrigel appeared certain to maintain a prominent spot in the French retail market.

Principal Subsidiaries

Agrigel S.A.; Place du Marché S.A.

Principal Competitors

Carrefour S.A.; Casino S.A.; Etablissements E. LeClerc S.A.; Picard S.A.; Thriet S.A.

Further Reading

"Croître par rachats successifs," *Tremplins,* January–March 2005.
Henin, Nicolas, "Du surgelé par téléphone à l'épicerie sur Internet," *Creascope,* October 12, 2000.
Jaouën, Muriel, "Toupargel fondu de la vente," *Centre d'appels,* November 1, 2000.
Lejoux, Christine, "Toupargel Shares Dragged Down by Results," *La Tribune,* November 22, 2004.
Pourprix, Claire, "Toupargel avale plus gros que lui," *BREF Online,* April 2003.
"Roland Tchenio: l'homme qui venait du froid," *BREF Online,* September 2000.
Todd, Stuart, "Galeries Lafayette Eyes Sale of Telemarket," *just-food.com,* June 23, 2005.

—M.L. Cohen

Tree Top, Inc.

220 East 2nd Avenue
Selah, Washington 98942
U.S.A.
Telephone: (509) 697-7251
Fax: (509) 697-0421
Web site: http://www.treetop.com

Cooperative
Incorporated: 1960
Employees: 900
Sales: $295.7 million (2004)
NAIC: 311423 Dried and Dehydrated Food
    Manufacturing; 311421 Fruit and Vegetable Canning

One of the largest apple cooperatives in the United States, Tree Top, Inc., processes more than 500,000 tons of fruit every year to make apple juice and cider, as well as apple sauce and other fruit-based products and concentrates. Owned by 1,460 growers in Washington, Oregon, and Idaho, its customers include distributors and retailers throughout the nation, as well as manufacturers in the food industry worldwide. Tree Top's corporate headquarters are located in Selah, Washington. Five of its processing facilities are in the state of Washington, with another one located in Oregon. The company also has a bottling facility in Rialto, California. While apple juice and cider remain the backbone of Tree Top's retail sales, it also markets other consumer packaged goods, such as blended fruit juices and fruit bars, and produces and sells a wide variety of dried and frozen fruit products used as ingredients in the food industry. Tree Top's juice-testing laboratories are considered world class and it has the only ''trained taste profile panel'' in the apple juice industry.

1940s Roots

Tree Top's roots can be traced back to the late 1940s, when entrepreneur Bill Charbonneau and his family moved from southern California to central Washington's Yakima Valley. Charbonneau bought a small apple processing plant on ''Produce Row'' in Selah, Washington. Charbonneau's mission was to develop a high-quality brand of apple juice. His original product line would include apple juice and apple cider, each available to consumers in three sizes.

The name Tree Top came about from the winning entry in a brand-naming contest Charbonneau held among his employees. The name was not only catchy but meaningful in that at the time the popular belief was that the best fruit grew at the top of the trees.

Charbonneau kept his office in the plant facility so that he could closely oversee production. He personally tried a sample of freshly produced juice each time a batch of apples was pressed. If he did not approve of what he tasted, Charbonneau ordered the plant's entire 5,000-gallon holding tank of apple juice to be poured down the drain.

During this time, apples were overly abundant in the state of Washington; so much so that in 1950, *Life* magazine featured a double-page spread of 5,000 railway cars of fruit being dumped into the Columbia River because there was a lack of processors to handle it all.

By 1960 orchard owners in the state of Washington were selling their fruit for $5 a ton, and those were the lucky ones. The rest were paying to have their fruit dumped or buried in canyons and rivers. Not knowing what to do with their inferior apples and tired of wasting their fruit—not to mention paying to have it hauled away—a few Washington growers banded together to save money by forming a cooperative that would handle and process the excess apples. This group of growers approached and purchased Tree Top from Charbonneau.

New Structure and Pioneering Processes in the 1960s

After the cooperative's inception in May 1960, the number of orchardists to join it increased until it reached its 1980s peak of more than 3,700 grower-owners, who were based not only in Washington, but Oregon and Idaho as well.

Recognizing that freezing juice was an economically prudent way to ship, Tree Top pioneered frozen apple juice concentrate in 1963. The next challenge was to convince consumers on the idea of frozen apple juice; they managed to accomplish their mission. Then, eight years after the becoming a cooperative,

Tree Top decided not to limit itself to juicing the apples and began to slice them as well.

By the late 1960s, Tree Top had two plants specializing in dried apple products, and they would eventually become the largest supplier of dried apple products in the world. In 1970, with the consumer demand for organic foods on the rise, Tree Top introduced an unfiltered apple juice. It also began marketing frozen concentrated cider that same year.

In 1975, Tree Top succeeded in marketing juice blends. It introduced a pear-apple and other pear-based fruit blends to provide its members with an outlet for processing pears.

The first 20 years was a high time for growth and development for Tree Top. During this time, the cooperative returned more than $85 million to its membership—on what was once a waste product dumped by the ton into rivers and canyons.

The 1980s

By 1985 the rationale for apple growers to band together had changed. To compete with much larger companies that dominated the food market (such conglomerates as Procter & Gamble, Unilever, Cadbury Schweppes, and Nestle) Tree Top decided to move away from being a traditional co-op and adopt the business practices of a corporation. Recognizing that it had become less of an apple handler/processor and more of an apple marketer, Tree Top executives changed its equity structure. The company paid its now 3,500 members based on the current market price, rather than the old method of basing payments on the number of tons processed. The change gave the company more capital for marketing new products such as dried apples and apple fiber, and it guaranteed that growers would get the fair market value for their fruit every year. Tree Top began to purchase additional presses and plant facilities. In 1988 Tree Top was the largest apple juice producer for the retail market in the world. It had become a global company, selling to Japan and buying from Europe and South America.

In February 1989, the Natural Resources Defense Council (NRDC), an environmentalist and consumer watchdog group, issued a report that said children who eat a lot of apples run a higher risk of cancer due to the use of Alar, a chemical sprayed on apples to make them redder and crisper. Yet because Tree Top didn't sell fresh apples and thus didn't care about the chemically-enhanced appearance of fresh fruit, it had always rejected apples from growers who used Alar and had urged the U.S. Environmental Protection Agency to the prohibit use of the chemical.

Their anti-Alar stance didn't help Tree Top in the end. The NRDC report led to a led to a nationwide fear of apple consumption. Despite the fact that the U.S. Food and Drug Administration (FDA) challenged that the Alar present in apples was far below safe levels for humans, the NRDC mounted a strategic media campaign against Alar use, which included celebrity backing and a television feature on CBS's *60 Minutes* television program.

Tree Top expanded its ban, refusing apples from growers who used Alar on any apple trees. The company also fought back with its own $1 million advertising blitz and media campaign. By May, however, the matter led Tree Top president Dennis Colleran to resign due to a related dispute with the board.

The 1989 Alar controversy and Mother Nature's drop in apple crop yield resulted in a record decline from 1988's return of $30.4 million. To reduce costs, Tree Top chopped is management staff by 10 percent, abandoned its plans to open a facility in the southeastern part of the country, and sold its recently acquired Sunnyside division to the National Grape Cooperative Association, which did business as Welch's.

New Challenges in the 1990s

By the early 1990s, things were getting back on track. In 1990 the Schweppes U.S.A. division of Cadbury Beverage of North America struck a 15-year deal with Tree Top for the exclusive franchise rights to its juice line in 11 western states, as well as Alaska and Hawaii. Mott's was already dominating the eastern states for Cadbury Schweppes.

By now Tree Top was now making more money than it ever had, despite the fact that it was processing fewer apples. The company was capitalizing on its name as a quality apple juice producer, still the nation's largest seller of juice with 8 percent of the market and selling to 21 countries. The company's industrial operations, which provided dehydrated apple products to the food industry for use in hot and cold cereals and fruit-filled cookies, for example, were now making up 25 percent of its industrial sales. Its Wenatchee plant was slicing, dicing, drying, and freezing apples to transform into 400 different types of dehydrated and frozen products that were sold to major food companies, such as Campbell's Soup, Kellogg, Nabisco, Pillsbury, Sara Lee, and Ralston Purina. The company could even take low-moisture apples and turn them into other fruits, like blueberries, raspberries and strawberries by using flavors and colors.

Creating more juice blends and targeting products to adults as well as kids would be marketing milestones of the 1990s. The company also met market demands by switching from glass to plastic bottles and selling products in vending machines.

Yet Tree Top recognized the fact that it would continue to face challenges, including fluctuating crop volumes, too much competition, the relative easiness of entering the juice business, and shipping a heavy product. Economic reasons such as these kept Tree Top from expanding to the eastern part of the country.

Tree Top restructured in 1996 as a response to the growth of its ingredient business. It separated into two divisions: one for consumer packaged goods and one for ingredients. The restructure did not lead to layoffs, though the number of employees continued to shrink as the company invested in equipment.

fresh market, leaving less for processing—the exact opposite of what led growers to form the co-op in 1960.

In the 21st century, Tree Top executives were fully aware that diversification would be key to survival. Despite continued challenges, Tree Top remained optimistic. Diversification would not be the only tactic to keep the former apple co-op on top. Its use of state-of-the-art technology at its processing plants, an experienced work force, and strong brand-recognition would also play major roles to the company's success, because Tree Top insisted that apple juice would remain the core of its business.

Principal Divisions

Ingredients; Consumer Packaged Goods.

Principal Competitors

Dole Food Company, Inc.; Mott's Inc.; Tropicana Products, Inc.

Further Reading

Broberg, Brad, "Market Forces are Testing Tree Top's Fruit Growers," *Puget Sound Business Journal,* June 25, 2004.

Dickson, Barbara, "A Leaner Tree Top Regroups After the 1989 Panic Over Alar," Puget Sound Business Journal, July 2, 1990.

Freeman, Paul, "Tree Top Juices Up for the Future," *Puget Sound Business Journal,* June 26, 1998. p. 44.

Hieger, Jennifer, "Juice Industry Targets Grown-Ups," *Yakima Herald-Republic*, May 25, 1997. p. F1.

"How Do You Like Them Apples?," *Food Research & Development,* January 1995, p. 14.

Jalonen, Wendy. "Tree Top Alters Equity Plan to Keep Its Juice on Top." *Puget Sound Business Journal.* September 9, 1985.

"Market Forces are Testing Tree Top's Fruit Growers." *Puget Sound Business Journal.* June 25, 2004.

Meyer, Ann, "Watching Out for the Watchdogs - Consumer Groups and the Food Industry," *Prepared Foods,* August 1989.

Sudermann, Hannelore, "U.S. Imposes Apple-Dumping Penalty," *Spokesman Review,* April 8, 2000. p. A8.

"Tree Top Rolling Out Flat Fruit as Juice Profits Sag," *Puget Sound Business Journal,* November 7, 2003.

Virgin, Bill, "Fruit Cooperative Posts Profitable Year," *Seattle Post-Intelligencer,* October 21, 2001, p. D6.

——, "Tree Top Presses Ahead with Expansion Plans Despite Overabundance of Apples, Competitors Bearing Fruit," *Seattle Post-Intelligencer,* October 2, 1995, p. B3.

Wilhelm, Steve, Tree Top Inc. "Finding that Less Can Really Be More," *Puget Sound Business Journal,* June 18, 1993.

—Kimberly Burton

Key Dates:

1940s: Bill Charbonneau founds Tree Top Inc.
1960: Group of Washington orchardists buy Tree Top to form a co-op.
1963: Tree Top pioneers frozen juice concentrate.
1975: Company markets juice blends.
1988: Tree Top is the world's largest apple producer for the retail market.
1989: Industry-wide ban on chemical Alar affects the company's profits.
1996: Company restructures into two divisions: ingredients and consumer packaged goods.

At the same time, China, with its vast orchards, became a bigger threat to the industry. Between 1995 and 1998 Chinese apple juice imports grew by more than 1,200 percent, while the average price for apple juice fell by 53 percent. In 1999 Tree Top and five other U.S. juice concentrate businesses petitioned the U.S. Department of Commerce to investigate several Chinese companies they claimed were selling concentrate into the United States market for less than cost of production. The following year, in a response to aid U.S. juice makers, the Department of Commerce began to charge a duty of nearly 52 percent on apple juice imports.

A New Century

Yet in 2001 a worldwide apple surplus drove down prices paid to growers, with juice market values falling from $112 a ton in 2000 to almost $43. This latest slump felled Tree Top's membership, although the overall acreage represented remained steady.

Stagnant prices and strong competition out of China further compelled Tree Top to experiment with non-juice products. In 2003 it test marketed a new line of snack products called Flat Fruit. The company was also forced to lay off employees and reduce production down to one processing plant.

In addition to fierce global competition in not only the juice industry, but the entire beverage industry, Tree Top also occasionally experienced a shortage of apples to process, being second in line for the crops produced by growers, who grew primarily for the more lucrative fresh fruit market and not the processing market. If the quality of a given year's crop was particularly high, the majority of the crop would be sold to the

United Natural Foods, Inc.

United Natural Foods, Inc., is the leading distributor of natural foods and related products in the United States. Originally known as Cornucopia Natural Foods, Inc., the company has expanded through strong internal growth, acquisitions, and mergers. United Natural has more than 20,000 customers—including independent retailers, natural superchains, conventional supermarkets, and restaurants—across the country. The company is the primary supplier to a majority of its customers, offering them a mix of more than 40,000 high-quality national, regional, and private-label natural products. These products include groceries and general merchandise, nutritional supplements, bulk and foodservice products, perishables and frozen foods, and personal care items. For more than ten years, United Natural has been the primary distributor to the two largest natural superchains: Whole Foods Markets, Inc. and Wild Oats Markets, Inc. To complement its distributorship, the company also owns and operates the National Retail Group (NRG), which consists of 12 retail stores selling natural products in the eastern United States. The company has organized its ten distribution operations into four principal units: United Natural Foods in the Eastern Region (previously Cornucopia Natural Foods, Inc. and Stow Mills, Inc.); United Natural Foods, Western Region; Albert's Organics; and Selection Nutrition. For the fiscal year ending July 31, 2004, United Natural generated net sales and operating income of $1.7 billion and $31.9 million, respectively.

The 1970s: Going Back to Nature for Business

The 1970s could be seen as a time of search for relevance between "the world that had been" and "the world that was becoming." Entrepreneurs made and sold tofu; they raised and marketed herbs as well as organic and natural foods. Yoga gained popularity as a calming form of exercise. According to Elaine Lipson's comment in the February 1999 issue of *Natural Foods Merchandiser,* in 1979 the editorial staff of that periodical used typewriters to chronicle the growth of the natural products world. There were no fax machines, web sites, or compact/digital-video discs and players. The period of transition between the rebellions of the 1960s and the excesses of the 1980s, Lipson wrote, was a "perfect breeding ground for natural products visionaries ready to blend alternative lifestyles with business potential."

One of these visionaries was Norman A. Cloutier, who founded Cornucopia Natural Foods, Inc. (Cornucopia) in Coventry, Rhode Island. From 1977 to 1978 he operated Cornucopia as a retail store for natural foods. In 1979, however, Cloutier changed his focus from retailing to the distribution of natural foods and related products. Although most natural products were food products (which included organic foods), the natural products industry encompassed a number of other categories, such as nutritional and herbal supplements, toiletries and personal care items, naturally based cosmetics, natural/homeopathic medicines, and naturally based cleaning agents.

As a matter of fact, by changing from retailing to distribution, Cloutier zeroed in on an emerging need in the rapidly expanding natural products industry. Suppliers of natural products found it difficult to meet the demands of an increasing number of retail outlets; they relied on distributors to reach a fragmented customer base and to provide information on consumer preferences at the retail level. Retailers wanted more frequent deliveries, greater product selection, higher fill rates, more information on product movement, and specialized programs—such as financing information, merchandising assistance, marketing support, and assistance in consumer education. Cloutier envisioned the possibility

360

of meeting these needs through a national natural products distribution business that would provide the sourcing, purchasing, warehousing, marketing, and transportation of natural products from suppliers to retailers.

Launching a National Presence: 1980–95

At first, Cornucopia grew by acquiring other distributors of a variety of natural foods and related products. For example, in 1985 the company purchased two distributors to strengthen its position in the New England market and to establish distribution in the mid-Atlantic states: Harvest Provisions, Inc. of Boston, and Earthly Organics, Inc. of Philadelphia. Cornucopia also acquired two specialty suppliers of natural products. In 1987 the company bought Natural Food Systems, Inc., a distributor of seafood and owner of the ''Natural Sea'' brand; in 1990, Cornucopia acquired certain assets of BGS Distributing, Inc., a regional distributor and manufacturer of vitamins and the holder of distribution rights to several additional product lines. Furthermore, in 1991 the company made its way into the southeastern United States by opening a distribution center in Georgia.

Then, in 1993, Cornucopia added retailing to its distributor operations by forming the Natural Retail Group with the intention of acquiring retailers of natural products. The NRG strategy consisted of buying independent stores but keeping the former owners to run the stores. By April 1995 Cornucopia owned and operated eight natural food stores located in Connecticut, Florida, Maryland, Massachusetts, and New York. The company believed that these stores received a number of advantages: Cornucopia provided its financial strength and marketing expertise, economies of scale resulting from group purchases, and access to a wider selection of products. The NRG retail stores offered products in each of Cornucopia's six main distributor categories as well as produce, meat, poultry, fresh seafoods, baked goods, and other prepared foods. In addition, NRG provided consumer education through informational brochures, promotional flyers, seminars, workshops, cooking classes, and product samplings.

On the other hand, benefits also accrued to the parent company, which was both the owner of, and distributor to, its retail stores. Cornucopia controlled the purchases made by these stores; increased the distribution and marketing of its private-label products; and stayed in touch with the retail marketplace. Furthermore, in these NRG stores, the company could test and evaluate consumer reaction to select products before offering them to a broader, national customer base.

Having established itself in the eastern United States, in May 1995 Cornucopia reached across the country to purchase Seattle, Washington-based Nutrasource, Inc., a distributor of natural products in the Pacific Northwest region. Then in July the company acquired Denver-based Rainbow Natural Foods, Inc. (Rainbow), the largest distributor of natural products in the Rocky Mountains and the Plains areas.

1996–99: Stabilizing a National Presence

Cornucopia buttressed its entry into the West in 1996 when it completed a merger with Auburn, California-based Mountain People's Warehouse, Incorporated, the largest distributor of natural products in the western portion of the United States, to form a new company: United Natural Foods, Inc. Cloutier had succeeded in crossing the country with his company. On the other hand, Michael S. Funk, founder and president of Mountain People's, thought the merger broadened ''Mountain People's buying power and enabled the company to offer more services and a wider selection of natural foods and products,'' according to the April 20, 1996 issue of the *Sacramento Bee.* United now had five distribution centers strategically located in the states of California, Colorado, Connecticut, Georgia, and Washington, as well as two satellite staging facilities in Florida and Pennsylvania. The company was well positioned to offer nationwide distribution services: namely, next-day delivery service to a majority of its active customers and multiple deliveries each week to its largest customers. Cornucopia could better coordinate its inventory management with regional purchasing patterns and realize significant operating efficiencies. The company also was able to eliminate geographic overlaps in distribution; integrate administrative, finance, and accounting functions; expand marketing and customer-service programs; and upgrade information systems.

United Natural, however, did not centralize the making of decisions for the majority of its purchasing, pricing, sales, and marketing. These managerial activities remained at the regional level in order to expedite response to the preferences of regional and local customers. Each of the three 1996 regional operators (Cornucopia, Rainbow, and Mountain People's) were better suited to make these decisions because they had extensive knowledge of the local and regional taste preferences in their particular marketplace and could provide products to accommodate local trends. By the end of fiscal 1995, the company's net sales had risen to $283.32 million, compared with $124.37 million at the end of fiscal 1992. United Natural filed an initial public offering on September 4, 1996 and began to trade its stock on the NASDAQ under the ticker symbol UNFI on November 1, 1996.

The company's private-label products addressed the preferences of customers wanting products not offered by other suppliers. For instance, in 1997 United Natural launched an organic infant food product called Organic Baby. In the February 1997 issue of *Natural Foods Merchandiser,* Emily Esterson commented that sales in baby food were declining because ''baby boomers' children were past baby-food age.'' In most natural products stores, the only available organic baby food was that of Earth's Best, owned by Pittsburgh-based H.J. Heinz. United Natural was interested in expanding to serve innovative, highly specialized niche markets. Other private-label products included Clear Spring Waters, Farmer's Pride eggs, Guardian vitamins and supplements, Natural Sea fish products, and Gourmet Artisan pasta and oils. Each year United Natural studied both existing and anticipated consumer preferences in order to evaluate more than 10,000 new products in the natural, organic, ethnic, gourmet, and specialty areas. The company purchased products from approximately 1,800 suppliers and also sourced products from suppliers throughout Europe, Asia, South America, Africa, and Australia.

United Natural reached its goal of being the nation's largest distributor of natural foods and related products in November 1997 when it completed a merger with Chesterfield, New Hampshire-based Stow Mills, Inc., a distributor of natural foods and related products in New England, New York, the Mid-Atlantic states, and the Midwest. According to Emily Esterson's article, "United Adds Stow, Strengthens Midwest Region," in the August 1997 issue of *National Foods Merchandiser,* Stow had sales of $208 million for fiscal 1996 and distributed 12,000 products to stores in the Northeast, the Midwest, and the Mid-Atlantic regions. The merger "filled gaps in United Natural's services by adding warehouses in New Hampshire and Pennsylvania, plus a Chicago facility that Stow Mills acquired when it bought Rainbow Distributing in 1996," Esterson wrote.

Cloutier also pointed out that Stow brought additional natural products expertise to the company because "Stow is a well-established, sophisticated operation with experienced and talented staff. There is no shortage of good ideas in the industry, but what

separates the successful from the unsuccessful is organizations with the expertise to execute plans," said Cloutier. Furthermore, he noted that "despite the growth of the company and concerted efforts to reach conventional grocers, United remained loyal to independent retailers, which made up approximately 60 percent of the company's sales." According to the June 30, 1997 issue of *Sacramento Business Journal,* United Natural President and Vice-Chairman Funk commented that by 1997 the natural foods industry was increasing by 15 percent a year and that conventional supermarkets were selling more and more natural foods products. "More people are aware of diet and how it affects our health and are into self-healing," Funk said, and added that an aging population would fuel continued growth of the industry.

In February 1998 United Natural acquired Hershey Import Co., Inc., a business specializing in the international trading, roasting, and packaging of nuts, seeds, dried fruits, and snack items. In September of the same year United Natural bought Albert's Organics, Inc., a company specializing in the purchase, sale, and distribution of produce and other perishable items. Albert's was the country's largest organic produce wholesaler, according to the March 17, 1997 issue of *Business News New Jersey.* Since 1985 United Natural had successfully completed 20 acquisitions and/or mergers of distributors, suppliers, and retail stores. The company's net sales increased to $728.9 million for fiscal 1998, compared with $634.8 million for fiscal 1997.

1999–2000: Reorganizing for a New Millennium

United Natural became a primary source of supply to a diverse base of customers having significantly varied needs. To meet these needs the company distributed more than 26,000 products consisting of national brands, regional brands, and private-label brands. The company held distribution rights to more than 1,000 nationally known products. More than 800 regional brand products were distributed to consumers in specific geographic regions. United Natural's decentralized purchasing practices enabled regional buyers familiar with consumer demands in their respective regions to offer products of special appeal to these regional consumers.

During fiscal 1999, after an operations and logistics study, United Natural found that $3.4 million could be saved in the northeast region if the company operated two warehouses instead of three in that area. Consequently, the business of the Chesterfield, New Hampshire-based warehouse of Stow Mills was integrated into the Dayville, Connecticut, facility and into the expanded New Oxford, Pennsylvania, warehouse. Continuing problems and expenses related to the consolidation resulted in lower sales, lower gross margins, and higher operating expenses in the East for the first quarter of fiscal 2000. Furthermore, Chairman and CEO Norman Cloutier resigned for personal reasons, and top management had to be restructured. Michael S. Funk, United's vice-chairman and president, was elected to succeed Cloutier as CEO. Thomas B. Simone was elected chairman of the board, where he had served since 1996; he was president and CEO of Simone & Associates, a consulting company for healthcare and natural products investment.

The change of management came at a time when sales of natural foods were still spiraling upward. According to industry analyst David Wanetick, who chaired the 1999 Natural Foods Industry Conference, sales of natural products continued to grow because of increased accessibility. "While there were fewer than 90 natural products stores in 1990 with more than 5,000 square feet," Wanetick told *Natural Food Merchandiser,* he expected "the number of these stores to reach 1,000 by the year 2000." Wanetick commented that another factor propelling sales of natural foods was Americans' increased health consciousness: "Millions of American adults are now watching their fat intake and monitoring their dietary cholesterol," he explained. Among other trends beneficial to the natural foods industry, Wanetick noted, were the fact that rising costs of healthcare led more people to take better care of their health and that gourmet cooks advocated the use of natural products to ensure better taste. Yet, "despite all these growth drivers, natural foods have barely penetrated their markets. Since natural foods account for only 2.5 percent of the total food market, natural goods still have a great deal of potential," Wanetick emphasized.

Indeed, as the 20th century drew to a close, mainstream customers "were moving in unprecedented numbers into the natural products channel," according to trends in the natural marketplace reported in the December 1999 issue of *Natural Foods Merchandiser.* Uppermost in the minds of these consumers was "the concept of 'whole health'—an aggregation of many different lifestyle and shopping choices into a self-directed program of healthful living." From its earliest days of operation under predecessor Cornucopia Natural Foods, United Natural had seen the business potential of a focus on natural foods and related products. Because of the company's remarkable past performance and of growing consumer awareness of "whole health," it was possible to assume that the difficulties United Natural experienced during the first quarter of fiscal 2000 were a temporary setback and that the company would continue to prosper.

Success in 2000 and Beyond

Sure enough, United Natural experienced success due to industry conditions as well as its growth strategy. Acquisitions, coupled with the expansion of its distribution centers, allowed the company to enter new geographic markets, increase its customer base and market share, and broaden its burgeoning product line. During 2001, United Natural strengthened its foothold in the southwestern United States by leasing a new distribution center in the Los Angeles, California area. In addition, it bought Palm Harbor Natural Foods, a Florida-based company.

The firm faced a major setback in 2002 when Wild Oats Markets, one of its largest customers, chose competitor Tree of Life Inc. as its supplier. Wild Oats began to experience problems with its new primary supplier, however, and quickly returned to United Natural. In January 2003, a new five-year contract was signed and in April of that year, United Natural resumed its position as Wild Oats' main distributor. The company also signed a deal with Sodexho USA to supply its 6,000 foodservice outlets with natural and organic foods. During 2004, United Natural renewed its contract with Whole Foods.

In 2002, United Natural acquired Blooming Prairie Cooperative, the Midwest's largest volume distributor of natural foods, in a $31 million deal. It also completed its merger with Northeast Cooperatives, a distributor serving more than 2,800 customers in the Northeast and Midwest.

In January 2003, Steven H. Townsend was named president and CEO. Late that year he assumed the chairman position as well. Industry conditions bode well for United Natural as demand for natural and organic products continued its upward trend. The company became the first and largest certified organic distributor in North America in 2003. United Natural received its certification from Quality Assurance International, an independent, third-party organization responsible for verifying organic integrity and quality.

United Natural had added more than 1,400,000 square feet of capacity since 2000, increasing its distribution capacity by 93 percent by 2005. A total of 97 percent of its deliveries were completed on time, putting the company in an enviable position among its competitors. Its profits had more than doubled since 2001, and the company's financial future looked promising. United Natural completed another acquisition in 2005, adding Roots & Fruits Cooperative to its arsenal. Townsend announced his retirement in October 2005 and Michael Funk once again assumed the role as president and CEO. Townsend was expected to leave the chairman post in December of that year.

Principal Subsidiaries

Albert's Organics, Inc.; Natural Retail Group, Inc.; Nutrasource, Inc.; Rainbow Natural Foods, Inc.; Select Nutrition Distributors, Inc.; Stow Mills, Inc.; United Natural Foods Pennsylvania, Inc.; United Natural Foods West, Inc.; United Natural Trading, Inc. Co.; United Natural Transportation Co.; United Northeast LLC.

Principal Competitors

Kehe Food Distributors, Inc.; Tree of Life Distribution, Inc.; Nature's Best, Inc.

Further Reading

"Creating Healthy Business," *Sacramento Bee* (California), April 20, 1996.

Esterson, Emily, "United Adds Stow, Strengthens Midwest Region," *Natural Foods Merchandiser,* August 1997.

Granato, Heather, "The Changing Distribution of Natural Foods," *Organic and Natural News,* November 1999.

"Healthy Deals," *Business News New Jersey,* September 28, 1998, p. 3.

Johnson, Kelly, "Merger Propels Food Firm to Top," *Sacramento Business Journal,* June 30, 1997, pp. 1–2.

Lambert, Emily, "Natural Selection," *Forbes,* January 10, 2005, p. 144.

Lipson, Elaine, "Humble Beginnings Become Big Business," *Natural Foods Merchandiser,* February 1999.

Marilyn, Much, "Distributor Keeps on Truckin' Thanks to Demand," *Investor's Business Daily,* March 18, 2004.

Plank, Dave, "Healthy Food Viewed As Key Lifestyle Choice," *Natural Foods Merchandiser,* December 1999.

"United Natural Foods Acquires Roots & Fruits," *Progressive Grocer,* July 14, 2005.

"United Natural Foods Chooses New Chief," *Progressive Grocer,* January 1, 2003.

"United Natural Foods Has Completed Its $31 Million Acquisition of Blooming Prairie Cooperative," *Frozen Food Age,* November 1, 2002.

Wells, Danny, "20 Years . . . and Still Going," *Natural Foods Merchandiser,* February 1999.

—Gloria A. Lemieux
—update: Christina M. Stansell

Valassis Communications, Inc.

19975 Victor Parkway
Livonia, Michigan 48152
U.S.A.
Telephone: (734) 591-3000
Toll Free: (800) 437-0479
Fax: (734) 591-4994
Web site: http://www.valassis.com

Public Company
Incorporated: 1970 as George F. Valassis & Co.
Employees: 4,100
Sales: $1 billion (2004)
Stock Exchanges: New York
Ticker Symbol: VCI
NAIC: 323110 Commercial Lithographic Printing

Valassis Communications, Inc., created the industry of free-standing inserts, the four-color coupon booklets distributed in newspapers. The company's coupons are added mechanically to papers throughout the week, but are carried most prominently in Sunday newspapers, where as many as a dozen separate inserts are common. These appear in single or multiple folded sheets, printed in full color. Valassis was the leading company in this market for most of its history. In the 2000s, the company met a formidable competitor in News America Marketing, a subsidiary of media giant News Corporation. Valassis fell to the number-two slot in the market in the 2000s, and holds about 46 percent of the market share, with the News Corp. subsidiary taking the remaining 54 percent. Valassis coupons are distributed to more than 60 million American households in more than 550 different newspapers. About half of its income comes from this area. The company also produces specialized promotional materials and has stakes in firms that provide Web-based coupon distribution, data warehousing, and direct-mail advertising services. Valassis has a growing international presence, carrying out coupon and marketing services in Italy, Spain, Germany, and England, as well as across the United States, Canada, and Mexico.

Beginnings

The company had its origin in 1970, when George Valassis opened a small sales agency in his home in suburban Detroit. He handled contract printing for numerous products, including computerized form letters. After purchasing his own printing press in 1971, however, he found it difficult to keep the machine in operation due to a lack of business.

In 1972, Valassis decided to solicit coupon advertising from a variety of retail product companies. After locating merchandisers who wished to promote their products with cents-off coupons, he then printed the coupons and purchased distribution arrangements with local newspaper publishers that would insert the coupon sheets in their papers. The business proved to be highly successful, as product manufacturers discovered the advantages of cooperative coupon advertising. The inserts were effective at enticing consumers to try virtually any product and, unlike advertising, their influence on buying patterns was highly measurable.

The inserts developed by Valassis were freestanding sheets containing bold four-color promotions. Because each sheet could be divided into 8, 10, 16, and even 24 or more different coupons, each a small advertisement, Valassis could piggyback several different companies' promotions on the same printing. This created a need to assign coupon spots carefully, since competing colas or brands of raisin bran, for example, could not be satisfactorily run on the same page. Valassis's solution was to encourage large manufacturers to purchase several coupon spots at once. These companies would place coupons for several nonrelated products, from breakfast cereal to cleanser, thereby creating demand for additional sheets from competitors.

Valassis immediately won business from companies such as General Foods, Procter & Gamble, General Mills, Nabisco, and Kellogg, but, still unable to purchase newspaper distribution rights on an efficient scale, the company lost money for several years as it pioneered a path in the new industry. Undeterred, George Valassis purchased additional printing machinery and increased his sales and production staff to 46 employees. By 1974, circulation of his freestanding inserts had grown to 25 million households on sales of $5.7 million.

Finally, in 1976, with virtually the same circulation, sales rose to $11.8 million, nearly double the 1974 figure. This confirmed for Valassis that manufacturers placed a high value on coupon advertising and encouraged him to continue efforts to expand the business.

Upgrading and Expanding in the Late 1970s and Early 1980s

Valassis began replacing his older equipment with newer, state-of-the-art machinery that featured added functionality. This included large, eight-page inserts and an oversized "super page." To house the operation, Valassis purchased a new production facility at Livonia, in west suburban Detroit. With sales growth at nearly 40 percent per year, Valassis marked sales of $23.5 million on a circulation of 27.8 million in 1978, and $33.7 million in sales on a circulation of 30 million a year later.

The company's employee roll grew to 193 people in 1979, and additions to staff included a young marketing manager from Procter & Gamble named Dave Brandon. Brandon, who played football at the University of Michigan, found employment at Procter & Gamble after graduation through a recommendation from coach Bo Schembechler. Brandon remained in touch with a former teammate, Larry Johnson, who joined Valassis after marrying George Valassis's daughter. Brandon brought to Valassis a powerful personal style. Although he began in the company performing some low-priority jobs, his potential was quickly appreciated. As he ascended to higher levels of management, he developed an open, folksy style within the company, giving personal attention to the human, as well as the business, aspects of Valassis. This atmosphere later won Valassis inclusion in a publication that identifies the best 100 companies for which to work. One component of that atmosphere is an across-the-board employee profit-sharing plan that can augment annual salaries by as much as 15 percent.

By 1982, circulation had grown to 38 million (50 percent more than in 1977) and sales had increased to more than $90 million, representing a fivefold increase over the period. This expansion led Valassis to build a second plant at Durham, North Carolina, in 1983, which would enable the company to more easily distribute its materials in southeastern markets. In 1985, a third plant was established in Wichita, Kansas.

With the expansion of printing capacity, Valassis's sales more than doubled in 1984, to $200 million. Now in a position to consolidate its market, Valassis bought out its largest competitor, Newspaper Co-op Couponing (NCC) in 1986. In an effort to streamline operations, Valassis dissolved NCC's freestanding insert operation and added two new printed promotional products to the operation. Nearing saturation of the freestanding insert business, in large part as a result of good expansion and a rise of upstart competitors, Valassis began run-of-press advertising, in which coupon space is reserved on pages of the newspaper itself. The primary market for run-of-press coupons was the typical weekly food section of daily newspapers, again featuring cents-off coupons for a variety of products.

A second extension was specialty printing, including production of brochures, catalogs, posters, and magazine inserts that concentrated on foodservice and fast-food promotions. More sophisticated specialty printing included scratch-and-sniff and lottery-style rub-off contests. Primary customers included Pizza Hut, Arby's, McDonald's, and LensCrafters.

Run-of-press and specialty printing were aggressively promoted as complements to the standard freestanding insert promotion. The success of the formula also propelled Valassis into a new function, that of promotional consultant. Now advertisers could retain Valassis much as they did ad agencies or public relations firms and receive advice on specific campaigns.

Acquisition by Consolidated Press Holdings in 1986

The consolidation of NCC also made Valassis an attractive takeover target. With an extremely strong record of sales growth and a favorable position in a market that included competition only from much smaller companies that lacked the finances of a larger operation, Valassis was discovered by Kerry Packer, chair of Consolidated Press Holdings, an Australian publishing conglomerate. The Australian publishing industry, dominated by a handful of media barons, had been exhausted of virtually all of its independents. With few investment opportunities in Australia, Packer and other barons such as Rupert Murdoch and Robert Holmes Court began shopping for deals in the American and British markets. The acquisition of Valassis in 1986 represented an unusual departure for Packer, who had confined his takeovers mostly to magazines and other periodicals. Rupert Murdoch's company, News Corporation, was evidently on the same track as Packer. Valassis's principal competitor in the freestanding insert market beginning in the early 1990s was News America, a subsidiary of News Corp.

After the takeover by Consolidated Press Holdings, George Valassis left the company for retirement. His company, however, benefited from numerous press arrangements made possible by its association with Packer. Sales increased by nearly $100 million by 1987, to $381 million. Packer placed David Brandon in charge of Valassis. The arrangement, in which Packer maintained a hands-off approach from 12,000 miles away, suited Brandon well. He maintained his folksy style, insisting on personally meeting each new hire. But with the

Key Dates:

1970: George Valassis founds a small printing sales agency in a suburb of Detroit.
1972: Valassis introduces the first ''freestanding inserts'' of newspaper ads.
1970s: The company grows with the success of the inserts, and moves its operations to Livonia, Michigan.
1983: A Durham, North Carolina, plant is opened.
1985: A Wichita, Kansas, facility is added.
1986: Newspaper Co-Op Couponing is acquired; Kerry Packer buys Valassis.
1989: Valassis Impact Productions is formed to produce specialized promotional items.
1992: Valassis goes public on the New York Stock Exchange.
1995: Canadian marketing company McIntyre & Dodd is purchased.
1997: Packer sells his stake in Valassis; the new corporate headquarters is completed.
1999: Valassis begins investing in companies that distribute coupons on the Internet.
2003: The company purchases NCH Marketing.
2004: Revenue passes $1 billion.

added responsibility came larger compensation. When Brandon's million-dollar-plus salary became known, his relationship with employees suffered somewhat.

Brandon kept Valassis on track and ensured that all sales and growth targets were met. For the most part, this kept Packer content and in Australia, but by 1992, Packer decided the time was ripe to reap the benefit of his investment in Valassis. In March of that year, he engineered the sale of 51 percent of the company's shares to the public. More than 22 million shares were issued through the New York Stock Exchange, yielding Packer's Consolidated Press Holdings a profit of about $900 million. The company continued to trade publicly, but was dominated by Consolidated's 49 percent interest.

Meanwhile, Valassis's business continued to expand. Because more than three-quarters of American households used coupons, they were proven sales aids. In Brandon's words, Valassis's coupon business was analogous to printing money. ''We bring it to your home and lay it on your doorstep and say 'use whatever you will.' '' But manufacturers' customers are always retailers, rather than consumers. Retail grocery stores stock, on average, 18,000 items, all of which compete for shelf space. As the coupons drive up consumer demand for a product, retailers are ''pushed'' into distributing—and giving favorable shelf display—to that product.

In 1995 Valassis acquired McIntyre & Dodd, a Canadian company that produced freestanding inserts and sold mail-order gifts. It was subsequently renamed Valassis of Canada. Two years later, Valassis's new corporate headquarters in Livonia was completed. The building featured a gym, salon, cafeteria, and in-house physician, keeping intact the company's commitment to its employees' well-being. Also that year Kerry Packer

sold his shares of the company, and Valassis's Mexican operations and a French joint venture were shuttered.

CEO David Brandon stepped down in 1998 to make way for Alan F. Schultz, who had been serving as executive vice-president and chief operating officer. Under his leadership, Valassis began to invest in a variety of new ventures. In 1999 the company purchased a majority stake in Independent Delivery Services, Inc., a provider of home-shopping software products for supermarkets. Valassis also bought 30 percent of Relationship Marketing Group, Inc., a company that utilized retailers' frequent shopper card data to send direct mail offers to consumers. Late in the year the company restructured its Canadian operations, eliminating mail-order subsidiary Carole Martin Gifts due to poor performance.

Valassis also entered the world of cyberspace in 1999. An investment in Merge LLC, subsequently renamed Save.com, gave the company a 52 percent stake in an online coupon distributor. In October, Net's Best LLC, an Internet marketing company, was acquired. This was followed in 2000 by the purchase of a minority stake in Coupons.com, which offered coupons online. Save.com also purchased MyCoupons.com and Direct Coupons.com, further expanding the company's presence on the Internet. CEO Schultz described Valassis's intentions as follows: ''Valassis will be the leader in online promotions.''

Competition in the 2000s

In August 2000 the company's Valassis Data Management subsidiary acquired 80 percent of PreVision Marketing for $30 million plus 145,000 shares of stock. PreVision was a Massachusetts-based customer relationship management firm. Prevision had revenues of about $14 million, and handled so-called relationship marketing for large retail clients such Toys R Us and The Gap, whereas Valassis worked only with grocery chains in this service area. Relationship marketing was defined as efforts to enhance customer loyalty, and included management strategies, information science such as database mining, and direct-mail marketing. It was a relatively new business area that had become hot in the high-tech run-up in the late 1990s.

As the long bull market of the 1990s drew to a close and high-flying technology stocks dropped precipitously, overall economic conditions in the United States became more difficult. The recession of the early 2000s was not expected to hurt Valassis, however, because typically coupons became more popular as consumers tightened their spending. The coupon market had risen by more than 10 percent in the recession of the early 1990s, for example. Yet the early 2000s did not see a comparable surge in coupon use, and Valassis did suffer somewhat. Whereas its revenue stood at more than $849 million in 2001, with net income of almost $118 million, for 2002 the company brought in only slightly more than a year earlier, $853 million, and net income shrank to slightly more than $95 million. Valassis posted a loss for the fourth quarter of fiscal 2002. Although its coupon business still seemed strong, Valassis's investments in web-based coupon companies and in relationship marketing had not done as well. Changes in accounting law also required Valassis to take some charges related to its recent acquisitions.

Valassis hoped to bolster its revenue with a new acquisition in 2003, an Illinois company called NCH Marketing Services, Inc. Valassis spent $60 million to buy NCH's expertise in managing promotion information and managing coupon marketing. NCH had large clients such as the department store chain Target Corp., the drugstore chain Walgreens, Kraft Foods, consumer products manufacturer Procter & Gamble, and the world's largest retailer, Wal-Mart Stores Inc. It worked for these companies to recover coupon money from manufacturers, and it also had data management capabilities. NCH provided a way for Valassis to expand internationally, as the newly acquired company already had substantial business in Europe.

Valassis expected to raise its sales because of the NCH acquisition, and it knew it needed to, as a formidable competitor was eating into its market share. The News Corp. subsidiary News America had appeared on the horizon around the time Packer bought Valassis. By the early 2000s, News America was about the same size as Valassis, and Valassis steadily lost customers to the Australian-owned company. The competition forced Valassis to lower prices, and its net income declined. A shareholder filed suit against Valassis in 2004, alleging that the company had not revealed that it was losing market share because of the competition with News America. In 2005, the Federal Trade Commission (FTC) began investigating Valassis on suspicion of price fixing relating to its competition with News America. The battle between the two companies led prices for freestanding inserts to fall by almost 20 percent over the first half of the 2000s. By the mid-2000s, News America had passed Valassis in market share, holding an estimated 54 percent of the market to Valassis's 46 percent—this in an industry that Valassis had invented and for years dominated as the sole big player.

Despite the troubling loss of ground to News America, Valassis still seemed to have its strengths. Its revenue surpassed $1 billion in 2004, with earnings of slightly more than $100 million. The company renewed its commitment to the city of Livonia, buying a $30 million building from Northwest Airlines in 2005 in order to consolidate its employees from three buildings to one. The company had close to 1,000 employees in its headquarters city, with another 3,000 at various plants and offices across the United States and abroad. The company's European marketing, which it had pushed with the purchase of NCH in 2003, seemed to be doing well, and the company planned to expand certain coupon and free sample business projects in Spain, Italy, France, and England over the next few years.

Principal Subsidiaries

Valassis Canada; Prevision Marketing LLC; Promotion Watch; Valassis Relationship Marketing Systems LLC; NCH Marketing Services, Inc.

Principal Competitors

News America Marketing; Vertis, Inc.; ADVO, Inc.

Further Reading

Adams, Cheryl, "King of Coupons," *Printing Impressions,* April 1, 2000, p. 26.

Flass, Rebecca, "Valassis Acquires Prevision, Expands Retail Niche," *Adweek New England Edition,* August 21, 2000, p. 5.

Gallagher, Kathleen, "Multiyear Contracts Provide Marketer with Growth Potential, Analyst Says," *Milwaukee Journal-Sentinel,* June 6, 1999, p. 3.

Gargaro, Paul, "After a Great Quarter, Valassis Wants Growth," *Crain's Detroit Business,* August 24, 1998, p. 3.

Hunter, George, "Valassis Ready to Roll: Pennies Add Up for Livonia Coupon Company," *Detroit News,* May 29, 1997, p. D1.

Keeton, Ann, "Valassis Sees $1 Billion Internet Opportunity," *Dow Jones News Service,* May 12, 1999.

Markiewicz, David A., "Clip Job," *Detroit News,* March 14, 1993.

Moses, Lucia, "Valassis' Bid for New Biz Worries Newspapers," *Editor & Publisher,* August 11, 2003, p. 4.

Neff, Jack, and Jennette Smith, "Valassis Not Counting on Boom in Coupons As Economy Slows," *Crain's Detroit Business,* November 12, 2001, p. 4.

Pachuta, Michael J., "Valassis Looks for New Ways to Stuff Bargains into Papers," *Investor's Business Daily,* May 27, 1997, p. B12.

Palm, Kristin, "Perks (and Pooches) Can Help Keep Your Employees in Place," *Crain's Detroit Business,* May 24, 1999, p. E-19.

"Quicken, Valassis to Bring 700 Workers to Livonia," *Detroit Free Press,* February 14, 2005.

Roush, Matt, "Don't Discount Valassis," *Crain's Detroit Business,* February 19, 1996, p. 2.

——, "Valassis Takes a Clipping: But Analysts Expect '97 to Be a Cut Above," *Crain's Detroit Business,* February 3, 1997, p. 2.

Smith, Jennette, "Relationship-Marketing Ventures Take Toll on Valassis Earnings," *Crain's Detroit Business,* March 3, 2003, p. 4.

——, "Valassis Buys N'West Center," *Crain's Detroit Business,* January 31, 2005, p. 3.

——, "Valassis' Price War with Rival Draws Attention from FTC," *Crain's Detroit Business,* November 15, 2004, p. 4.

Stoffer, Jason, "Valassis Communications, Inc.," *Crain's Detroit Business,* September 6, 1999, p. 18.

"Valassis Answers Probe," *Detroit Free Press,* March 16, 2005.

—John Simley
—updates: Frank Uhle, A. Woodward

VeriFone Holdings, Inc.

2099 Gateway Place, Suite 600
San Jose, California 95110
U.S.A.
Telephone: (408) 232-7800
Fax: (408) 232-7811
Web site: http://www.verifone.com

Public Company
Incorporated: 1981
Employees: 1,016
Sales: $390.1 million (2004)
Stock Exchanges: New York
Ticker Symbol: PAY
NAIC: 334119 Other Computer Peripheral Equipment
   Manufacturing

VeriFone Holdings, Inc., is a leading provider of technology that enables electronic payment transactions. Along with point of sale (POS) software and terminals, the company provides systems that process a variety of payment types including signature and PIN-based debit cards, credit cards, contactless, smart cards, prepaid gift and store-value cards, electronic bill payment, check authorization and conversion, signature capture, and electronic benefits transfer. VeriFone's customers include global financial institutions, payment processors, petroleum companies, large retailers, government organizations, healthcare companies, quick service restaurants, and independent sales organizations that resell VeriFone's products and services. The company changed ownership several times during the late 1990s and early years of the new millennium. Hewlett-Packard Co. acquired the company in 1997 and then sold it to Gores Technology Group in 2001. Private equity firm GTCR Golder Rauner bought a controlling interest in VeriFone the following year. The company launched a second initial public offering in April 2005.

Pioneering Transaction Automation in the 1980s

William Melton already had more than a decade of experience in payment processing before founding VeriFone in 1981.

Ten years earlier, Melton had founded Real-Share, Inc., in Hawaii, a pioneer in the use of computers and other database and telecommunications systems for check authorization and guarantees. In 1980, Melton sold Real-Share to TeleCheck Services, later part of First Financial Management Corporation for some $3 million and used this money to start up VeriFone in Honolulu the following year. Initially, the company provided retailers with access to information on people known to have written bad checks. The company started at the local level, but soon spread throughout the islands. Part of Melton's operating philosophy was to place his sales and support staff close to the company's customers. To maintain contact among his widely dispersed employees, Melton turned to the nascent networking and portable computer industries, outfitting the company with early e-mail messaging and online database capabilities.

A development in the still-young credit card industry, however, caused Melton to change the focus of the company. The use of credit cards first became widespread during the 1970s. By the beginning of the 1980s, the major credit card companies began seeking methods to reduce processing costs and losses due to fraud. In 1981, Visa and MasterCard began offering merchants discounts on their transactions if they agreed to use newly developed automated transaction technology for all credit card purchases greater than $50. This move opened the way for the creation of an industry devoted to producing POS authorization systems. Early systems typically had starting prices of $900.

VeriFone introduced its first POS product in 1982. By slashing operating costs and lowering manufacturing costs by outsourcing production, VeriFone brought its first system to the market at $500. In financing this effort, Melton received help from Lexis-Nexis founder William Gorog, who had sold that company and founded Arbor International to produce credit card authorizations systems under contract for Tymnet. When Tymnet management decided not to pursue the POS market, Gorog agreed to finance VeriFone with letters of credit. He next brought VeriFone in contact with a venture capital firm for additional financing. In return, Arbor received the right to sell VeriFone products east of the Mississippi.

Working with Visa, VeriFone quickly captured a strong share of the POS market. In 1984, however, the company took a major step toward achieving industry dominance with the introduction of its ZON credit card authorization system, which, taking advantage of improvements in processor speeds and the lowering cost of both processors and memory, cost as little as $125, making it easier to convince retail merchants to install the system in their stores. The following year, the company's revenues grew to $15.3 million, earning a net profit of $864,000. In that year, VeriFone moved its headquarters to Redwood, outside of San Francisco, to be closer to that area's software and hardware engineering talent pool, as well as to its customers and investors.

The company doubled revenues, to about $30 million, in 1986. But VeriFone's products were beset by quality problems, the company was barely producing profits, while in constant need of new financing, and investors were critical of the company's management. As one early investor told *The New York Times*, VeriFone was led by ''management by reactive panic mode.'' The venture capitalists behind VeriFone urged Melton to bring in a new president and CEO.

Melton chose Hatim A. Tyabji. Born in Bombay, India, Tyabji had moved to the United States at the age of 22 to attend graduate school, eventually earning two graduate degrees. Tyabji joined Sperry Corporation as a junior project manager, but in 13 years rose to become president of information systems products and technologies. When Sperry was bought up by Burroughs Corporation, forming Unisys Corporation, Tyabji decided to leave. Named president and CEO of VeriFone, Tyabji worked to turn the company around. Quality problems were quickly addressed; by 1988, Tyabji moved to create manufacturing as a core competency, opening VeriFone's first manufacturing plant in Taiwan. The company also acquired Arbor International, for an exchange of stock, giving it full control of marketing and sales of its products. Tyabji sought to transform the company into Melton's original vision of a virtual operation. Laying down a corporate philosophy, Tyabji encouraged the growth of the company's computer network, outlawing paper-based communications and mandating that employees make constant use of the network's e-mailing and database functions. Employees and operations were placed close to the company's customers, enabling Tyabji to institute what the company calls its ''culture of urgency,'' allowing for 24-hour-per-day product development and sales and marketing efforts.

By January 1988, VeriFone controlled more than 53 percent of the POS systems market. Revenues had reached $73.4 million, with net earnings of more than $6 million. The following year, the company increased its dominance in the industry with the purchase of the transaction automation business of Icot

Corporation, then second in the market with a 20.5 percent share. The acquisition boosted VeriFone's revenues to $125 million. By then, VeriFone had entered the international market, starting with Australia in 1988 and placing its millionth ZON system in Finland in 1989. Tyabji added chairman to his titles after Melton retired from the company in 1989, taking a seat on the company's board.

New Directions for the 1990s

VeriFone went public in March 1990, raising more than $54 million. As the credit card industry matured, VeriFone pushed to install its systems into new markets, such as restaurants, movie theaters, taxis, and fast food restaurants, while developing software capacity to bring its systems into the health care and health insurance markets and to government functions, such as state welfare systems. International sales also began to build, as use of credit cards became increasingly accepted in foreign markets. VeriFone was also building its global operation, opening facilities in Bangalore, Singapore, England, Dallas, and Ft. Lauderdale, in addition to its Hawaii and California facilities. Rolling out its Gemstone line of transaction systems, which added inventory control, pricing, and other capabilities, VeriFone was aided by announcements from Visa and MasterCard that the companies would no longer provide printed warning bulletins, while requiring merchants to seek authorization for all credit card transactions by 1994.

These moves further stimulated demand for VeriFone's products. Revenues jumped from $155 million in 1990 to $226 million in 1992. By then, VeriFone had placed its two millionth system (in Fouquet's restaurant, near Paris, in 1991); by 1993, VeriFone systems were in place in more than 70 countries, including its three millionth system, in Brazil, representing the company's expansion in the Latin American market. International sales, which had contributed less than 10 percent of revenues before 1990, now accounted for more than 30 percent of the company's nearly $259 million in annual revenues.

New opportunities arose as banks began rolling out debit cards in the mid-1990s. VeriFone was quick to launch itself into this new market, producing terminals designed with key pads for customers to punch in their PIN numbers. But as the domestic credit and debit card markets neared saturation, VeriFone made ready to launch itself in new directions. While continuing its international expansion, topping four million installed systems in 1994, and maintaining its manufacturing capacity, doubling production capacity with a new plant near Shanghai in China in 1994, VeriFone had already evolved its primary focus to producing software applications, offering vertically integrated systems solutions, including applications for standard computer operating systems.

VeriFone moved to take the lead in the coming smart card revolution, teaming up with GemPlus, a France-based maker of the cards, and MasterCard to form the joint venture SmartCash. Smart cards replaced the magnetic stripe of typical credit cards with tiny processors. The chips, which could contain as much as one megabyte of RAM, could be encoded with a variety of information, such as the amount of money available to the cardholder. Purchases made using a smart card were automatically deducted from the holder's account. Transactions were

```
┌─────────────────────────────────────────────┐
│                  Key Dates:                   │
│                                               │
│ 1981: William Melton establishes VeriFone.    │
│ 1982: VeriFone introduces its first point of  │
│       sale (POS) product.                     │
│ 1984: The ZON credit card authorization       │
│       system is launched.                     │
│ 1990: The company goes public.                │
│ 1995: VeriFone launches its smart card.       │
│ 1997: Hewlett-Packard Co. acquires VeriFone.  │
│ 2001: VeriFone is sold to Gores Technology    │
│       Group.                                  │
│ 2002: GTCR Golder Rauner LLC gains a majority │
│       interest in the company.                │
│ 2005: VeriFone, reorganized as a holding      │
│       company, launches an initial public     │
│       offering.                               │
└─────────────────────────────────────────────┘
```

immediate, require no authorization, and thus enabled the card to be used in low denomination purchases that would be too expensive or time-consuming with the typical credit or debit card. In addition, smart cards could be encoded with much more information, including a person's health insurance information, as well as that person's various credit card accounts.

To place the company close to technological developments in France and the rest of Europe, VeriFone opened its Paris research and development center in 1994. The company launched its smart card in May 1995. The company introduced its Personal ATM, a palm-sized smart card reader capable of reading a variety of smart card formats, in September 1996, with the product expected to ship in 1997. Among the first customers already signed to support the P-ATM were American Express, MasterCard International, GTE, Mondex International, Visa International, Wells Fargo Bank, and Sweden's Sparbanken Bank. Contracts for each called for the purchase of a minimum of 100,000 units; the total market potential for the device was estimated at more than 100 million households. In addition, VeriFone began developing smart card readers to supplement and eventually replace its five million credit and debit card authorization systems.

In 1995, VeriFone began the first of its aggressive steps to enter an entirely new area, that of Internet-based transactions. In May 1995, the company partnered with BroadVision Inc., a developer of Internet, interactive television, computer network, and other software, to couple VeriFone's Virtual Terminal software—a computer-based version of its standard transaction terminal—with BroadVision's offerings, thereby extending VeriFone's products beyond the retail counter for the first time. In August 1995, however, VeriFone took an even bigger step into the Internet transaction arena, with its $28 million acquisition of Enterprise Integration Technologies, developer of the S-HTTP industry standard for safeguarding transactions over the World Wide Web. VeriFone followed that acquisition with a $4 million investment in William Melton's latest venture, Cyber-Cash Inc., also working to develop Internet transaction systems.

By 1996, VeriFone was ready with its Payment Transaction Application Layer (PTAL) lineup of products, including the Virtual Terminal interface for merchants conducting sales with consumers; Internet Gateway or vGATE, to conduct transactions between merchants and financial institutions; and the Pay Window interface for consumers making purchases on the Internet. After securing agreements from Netscape, Oracle, and Microsoft to include VeriFone software in their Internet browsers, VeriFone and Microsoft announced in August 1996 that VeriFone's virtual point of sale (vPOS) would be included in the Microsoft Merchant System to be released by the end of the year. VeriFone's announcement of the P-ATM, able to be attached as a computer peripheral, wedded the company's smart card and Internet transaction efforts.

The success of these ventures depended on the long-term acceptance of the new technologies, and VeriFone faced powerful competition as the industry struggled to achieve international standards and specifications. However, with Hatim Tyabji leading the company in its culture of urgency, VeriFone hoped to become as ubiquitous on the screen as it had become on the store counter. During the late 1990s, "transaction automation," as the company called its industry, would become increasingly less reliant on physical products and instead turn to a virtual realm where cash would perhaps become obsolete. VeriFone was at the forefront of this transition, shifting its own emphasis from manufacturing hardware to designing complete software solutions.

Changes in the Late 1990s and Beyond

While technology was changing at breakneck speed during the late 1990s, VeriFone worked to stay ahead of the game. Its position in the burgeoning industry and strong revenue growth made it an attractive takeover target for Hewlett-Packard Company (HP). At the time, HP was looking to tap into Internet commerce and believed VeriFone could be its next cash cow. Thus HP made a $1.3 billion play for VeriFone and completed the deal in 1997. Tyabji retired shortly thereafter, leaving Robin Abrams—the first woman to head VeriFone—at the helm.

As a division of HP, VeriFone continued to develop new products and services. The company launched its Omni 3200 payment terminal in 1999 and it quickly became its best selling terminal to date. The group also developed an integrated payment solution and a new global payment platform.

While VeriFone's future looked bright, the company began to face challenges in the new millennium. Profits began to suffer as intense competition and ever-changing technology demands ate away at its bottom line. With VeriFone's market share falling, many analysts began to speculate that its union with HP had been a mistake. Sure enough, HP announced a major restructuring effort in 2001. As part of its reorganization, it sold the VeriFone division to buyout firm Gores Technology Group, which was led by Douglas G. Bergeron. Bergeron summed up his thoughts on HP's management of VeriFone in a September 2001 *Bank Network News* article claiming, "They gummed it up with H-P bureaucracy and sucked the entrepreneurial oxygen out of it."

Under Bergeron's leadership, VeriFone quickly returned to profitability by focusing on its POS products and services. During 2002, Bergeron and venture capital firm GTCR Golder Rauner LLC recapitalized VeriFone. When the dust settled on the deal, Bergeron was left as the company largest private investor while GTCR retained a controlling interest. VeriFone Holdings, Inc., was created to oversee the operations of VeriFone Inc.

With the changes in management behind it, VeriFone was left to focus on the future. VeriFone began to tap into the quick service restaurant and drive-thru industry in 2003 as fast food establishments began to allow customers to pay with credit and debit cards. The company also launched several new versions of its Omni payment terminal, worked to shift Food Stamp benefits from a paper-based system to an electronic benefits transfer program, and partnered with McAfee to develop virus protection for POS payment terminals.

Bouyed by strong sales and profits, VeriFone launched an initial public offering on the New York Stock Exchange in April 2005. The company also launched its MX870, a new secure payment product for multi-lane retailers with video and sound that allowed for branding, promotion, and advertising at the POS terminal. VeriFone had recovered from the problems it experienced as a division of HP. Keeping up with technological demands while fending off competitors remained at the forefront of VeriFone's strategy. With a strong hold on the U.S. market, VeriFone management hoped to increase its overseas market share in the years to come.

Principal Subsidiaries

VeriFone Inc.

Principal Competitors

Hypercom Corporation; Ingenico S.A.; NCR Corporation.

Further Reading

Alva, Marilyn, ''VeriFone Holdings San Jose, California; Supplier of Electronic Payment Gear Cashes in on Cashless Trend,'' *Investor's Business Daily*, November 7, 2005.
''An ATM in Every Home Is VeriFone's Platform,'' *Bank Network News*, October 11, 1996.
Beltran, Luisa, ''VeriFone IPO Sputters,'' *TheDeal.com*, May 2, 2005.
Daly, James J., ''Out of the Box,'' *Credit Card Management*, November 1995, pp. 102–108.
Daniels, Jeffrey, ''Payment Systems Firm VeriFone To Go Public in $56 Million Offering,'' *Investor's Daily*, March 2, 1990, p. 28.
Epper, Karen, ''Money Creators: Point of Sales Pioneers Setting Sail on the Internet,'' *American Banker*, February 10, 1995, p. 14.
Fitzgerald, Kate, ''VeriFone, HP Duo Focuses on Net,'' *Card Technology News*, July 12, 1998.
Freedman, David H., ''Culture of Urgency,'' *Forbes*, September 13, 1993, p. 25.
''Gores Relinquishes VeriFone Control,'' *Bank Network News*, June 20, 2002.
''H-P to VeriFone: Start Packing,'' *Credit Card Management*, June 1, 2001.
Kutler, Jeffrey, ''Terminal Maker Stakes Future on the Net,'' *American Banker*, December 5, 1995, p. 5A.
——, ''VeriFone's Unconventional Chief: 'Lucidly Crazy,' '' *American Banker*, April 20, 1995, p. 12.
Louis, Arthur M., ''No Place to Call Home: VeriFone Is a ''Virtual' Workplace,'' *San Francisco Chronicle*, October 22, 1996, p. C1.
Nee, Eric, ''Hatim Tyabji,'' Upside, September 1996, pp. 84–93.
Pollack, Andrew, ''Company's Rise Is Built on Credit,'' *New York Times*, August 3, 1990, p. D1.
''A Rejuvenated VeriFone Faces a Sluggish Market,'' *Bank Network News*, September 20, 2001
Taylor, William C., ''At VeriFone It's a Dog's Life (And They Love It!),'' *Fast Company*, June 6, 1996.

—M.L. Cohen
—update: Christina M. Stansell

Viel & Cie

253 Boulevard Pereire
Paris
France
Telephone: +33 01 56 43 70 20
Fax: +33 01 55 37 91 99
Web site: http://www.viel.com

Public Company
Incorporated: 1920
Employees: 1,910
Sales: EUR 557.2 million ($$704.7 million) (2004)
Stock Exchanges: Euronext Paris
Ticker Symbol: 50049
NAIC: 523120 Securities Brokerage

Paris-based Viel & Cie is one of the world's top three over-the-counter (OTC) financial brokers; that is, the company acts as an impartial intermediary brokering major financial deals. Viel has acted as a driving force in the rapid consolidation of this market, which is expected to narrow to just a handful of major players in the mid-2000s, and as few as three leader-specialists in each of the financial broker segments. Viel, however, has long taken a diversified approach to the financial market, and as such has built up a network of subsidiaries spanning the full range of brokering sectors, including the markets for exchange rates, equities, commodities, and interest rates, among others. In support of its diversified base, the company has established a globally oriented network of subsidiaries and offices in the major financial cities in 18 countries. Acquisitions have provided the motor for Viel & Cie, and include the purchase of a 35 percent stake in Singapore's Ong First Pte Ltd. in 2005, and of Chapdelaine & Co. in New York in 2004, among others. The latter purchase has boosted the share of the United States in Viel's overall revenues to nearly 50 percent. The company's other major revenue producers operate in London and Tokyo. Although financial brokering remains Viel & Cie's primary operation, the company also has launched its own online brokering subsidiary, Bourse Direct, which operates the Capitol.fr web site, one of France's top five online brokers with 9,000 customers. Viel & Cie is listed on the Euronext Paris Stock Exchange, and is led by Patrick Combes, chairman of the board and architect of Viel's expansion. In 2004, the company posted revenues of EUR 557.2 million ($$704.7 million). The acquisition of Chapdelaine is expected to boost total revenues past EUR 700 million ($900 million) in 2005.

Building a Broker in the 1980s

Viel & Cie was founded in Paris in 1920 and operated as a financial broker, with a specialty as a broker for the Parisian money market. The company went public in 1962. At the end of the 1970s, however, Viel & Cie remained a small-scale operation, with just three employees and annual revenues of less than FRF 600,000 (approximately $100,000) per year.

In 1979, however, Patrick Combes, a French native who had spent the early part of his career working in the financial sector in the United States, took over Viel & Cie. Then just 27 years old, Combes gave himself six months to see if he would be able to build the brokerage into a viable, competitive broker. Of note, Combes decided to break with the brokerage sector's tendency at the time to focus on niche markets. As Combes told *Entreprendre:* "The logic of a niche, especially in the financial professions, is very difficult. One might be able to juxtapose niches, but surviving on just one without having a critical size means taking the risk that at any moment one may become a target, or see oneself completely overtaken by the turn of events. In addition, there are criteria such as scale and minimum product coverage that one must take into account."

Combes established initial strategic goals of gaining market leadership in France and taking Viel & Cie public. To achieve these goals, the company quickly began putting into place Combes's strategy of diversifying its range of services. In 1982, for example, the company began brokering interest rate options, becoming the first in France to take on this niche. The following year, the company became the first in the market to establish a dedicated currency exchange operation, which formed the basis of a new international department. The company continued to boost its currency business, boosting its operations particularly in the French franc exchange market at the middle of the decade.

Company Perspectives:

The broker is a completely independent player in over-the-counter (OTC) financial markets. Its role primarily consists of providing a point of contact for institutional clients seeking to buy or sell financial products. Regulatory constraints require the broker to act as a pure intermediary, taking no positions or dealing risks in the financial markets. Working at the very heart of the markets, the broker is in continual contact with leading players in the major financial centres (banks, insurance companies, large private companies, etc.), enabling it to acquire a unique, comprehensive knowledge of financial markets. Its chief functions are therefore: To ensure market liquidity and respond rapidly to its clients' needs; To respect the confidential nature of its clients' transactions. The broker receives a commission on each client transaction. The professionalism of its clients demands sophisticated expertise on the part of the broker in order to meet integrally its clients' needs. This expertise entails: A perfect knowledge of financial markets; A good understanding of its clients' needs and objectives; Providing superior quality, high value added service. VIEL & Cie is an acknowledged leader in the rapidly moving world of financial brokerage, adhering to the fundamental principles of confidentiality, expertise, competence and sophisticated service.

Viel & Cie began putting into place a structure for its future public offering at the middle of the decade. In 1986, the company created a new holding company, Viel & Cie Finance. This vehicle, which retained control of a majority share of Viel & Cie, also permitted the company to expand its range of operations beyond Viel & Cie's core business, without implicating Viel & Cie itself. In the same year, for example, the company created a new subsidiary, STAFF, which stood for Société de Transaction et d'Arbitrages sur Future Financiers, and permitted Viel & Cie Finance to extend the group's range of operations into the French futures and arbitrage markets.

Viel & Cie continued expanding its own range of financial products as well. In 1987, the company expanded into the brokering of treasury bills, which required a doubling of the company's size. This necessity, and the need for further capital to expand its operations—notably, to an international level—brought Viel & Cie to the Paris Stock Exchange's Secondary Market in 1988. Viel & Cie Finance nonetheless retained majority control of the business, and continued to hold nearly 55 percent of the company into the mid-2000s.

Acquiring Scale in the 1990s

The public offering provided Viel & Cie with greater name recognition. Combes also welcomed the constraints imposed by opening the group's shareholding structure to outside investors, telling *Entreprendre:* ''It's a good thing to live with the worries of a listed company—whether in good times or bad times, it's necessary to develop solutions.'' Following its public offering, Viel & Cie expanded its range of operations again, into securities, in 1990, establishing a dedicated subsidiary, MIA, in that year.

With its new capital backing, Viel & Cie began acquiring scale in France in the first half of the 1990s. The company bought out part of the operations of interbanking specialist Degez in 1991, then acquired control of the banking intermediary specialist Julien Olivier & Cie. The following year, the company was merged into Viel & Cie's operations. At the same time, Viel & Cie Finance returned to Degez, buying up that company altogether. In 1995, the company redeveloped its government securities business into a separate, dedicated subsidiary, Viel Eurovaleurs.

By then, Viel & Cie had established itself as the number two player in the French financial broker market. Yet on a global level, with annual sales of the equivalent of just EUR 34 million, Viel & Cie remained a minor player. Indeed, the global financial broker market had long been dominated by British and, to a lesser degree, American brokers.

Combes, however, became determined to guide Viel & Cie to the top ranks of the global markets. Recognizing that establishing its own operations from scratch into the various financial capitals would require an extreme investment, in effort and financial capital, the company developed an expansion strategy based on acquisition of existing companies. Viel & Cie took its first step internationally in 1995, when it acquired fellow French firm Maison Debeausse, giving it control of its New York-based subsidiary, Debeausse Inc. The company also moved into the Luxembourg market that year, acquiring Arbitrage Change S.A. that year.

Viel's most significant acquisition came the following year, with the purchase of a 61 percent stake in Switzerland's Compagnie Financiere Tradition (CFT), then the world's sixth largest broker. CFT had been founded by André Levy in 1959 as Compagnie Financiere et de Credit, and had originally specialized in eurodollar deposits. The company quickly became international, opening a subsidiary in London in 1961. In 1968, the company changed its name to CFT, and in 1973 went public with a listing on the Geneva Stock Exchange. In that year, CFT opened an office in New York as well. The company continued to expand internationally in the following decades, adding an office in Hong Kong in 1978, in Singapore in 1979, and in Italy in 1980, as well as operations in Tokyo (through its share of the Meitan Tradition Co. joint venture) in 1985 and Luxembourg in 1987.

In 1988, CFT itself became part of Banque Pallas Stern (BPS), which acquired a 61 percent stake. Yet that company's bankruptcy in 1995 gave Viel & Cie its opportunity, and in 1996 Viel acquired BPS's 61 percent of CFT. The takeover immediately boosted Viel's international presence and CFT became a major subsidiary in the Viel & Cie group. Viel & Cie continued buying up shares of CFT, boosting its holding to 74.5 percent in 1997. The takeover of CFT also gave the company control of Tradition Financial Services (TFS), a market-leading provider of OTC brokerage services.

Global Top Three in the New Century

The takeover of CFT and TFS established Viel & Cie as the leading financial broker on the European continent, and gave the company a place among the world's top five. As the new century approached, Viel became determined to crack the top

Key Dates:

1920: Viel & Cie is created in Paris.
1962: Viel & Cie goes public on the Paris Stock Exchange.
1979: Patrick Combes takes over Viel & Cie, then a three-person firm, and leads its diversification and expansion.
1982: The firm launches interest rate options brokering.
1986: A new holding company, Viel & Cie Finance, is created.
1988: Viel & Cie goes public on the Paris Stock Exchange.
1996: The company acquires control of Compagnie Financiere Tradition of Switzerland and becomes the top continental European broker and one of the top five worldwide.
1999: The company establishes the subsidiary Bourse Direct and launches Capitol.fr online brokerage.
2004: The company acquires Chapdelaine & Co. in the United States.
2005: The company acquires 35 percent of Ong First Pte Ltd. in Singapore.

three. Part of the group's strategy for this effort was to position itself as a global technological leader. To this end, in 1999, the company acquired 47 percent of Infotec, boosting the company's technological capacity. Viel also recognized the Internet as an important brokerage tool for the future, and in 1999 created a new subsidiary, Bourse Direct, which launched an online brokerage, Capitol.fr. That site grew into one of the top five in the French online broker segment by the mid-2000s.

Viel also maintained the pace of its acquisitions. In 1999, the company bought up nearly 90 percent of Prominnofi, a specialist in European government debt transactions. In 2000, Viel added voice recognition capacity when it bought a stake in Vecsys, as part of its effort to position itself as a technology leader. Also in that year, the company boosted its New York presence through the acquisition of Asiel & Co. LLC. Created in 1878, Asiel had been a founding member of the New York Stock Exchange. Following its acquisition by Viel, the company was renamed Tradition Asiel, becoming part of CFT/TFS.

Viel's expansion continued into mid-decade. The company increased its technology capabilities with the creation of a joint venture with Volbrokers in 2001. In 2004, Viel acquired BCV Finance France from the Banque Cantonale Vaudoise. The company also purchased 10 percent of spread-betting specialist IFX Group plc, based in the United Kingdom. By the end of

2004, the company further enhanced its U.S. presence through the acquisition of Chapdelaine & Co., based in New York, with offices in Chicago, Palm Beach, and Long Island.

Viel established a presence in the South American market as well, opening a subsidiary in Santiago, Chile, at the beginning of 2005. Also in that year, the company boosted its presence in the Asian markets, buying 35 percent of Ong First Pte Ltd., a leading broker in Singapore. By the end of that year, Viel & Cie had grown into one of the global financial brokerage leaders, with a presence in 18 countries and annual sales expected to top EUR 750 million ($900 million).

Principal Subsidiaries

Arbitrage Change S.A. (Luxembourg; 99.93%); Arpège Finances; BCV Broking; Bourse Direct; Capitol; Compagnie Financiere Tradition (Switzerland; 70.42%); Elite Broker S.A. de C.V. (Mexico); Finacor & Associés S.A. (Belgium); Finacor Belgique S.A.; Finacor Deutschland GmbH; Financière Vermeer B.V. (Netherlands); Fincor SGPS (Portugal; 20%); Meitan Tradition Co. Ltd. Japan; 55.34%); Monecor (London) Ltd.; SCS Gestion Privée; SP Angel & Co. Ltd. (United Kingdom); TFS (Switzerland; 98.79%); The Recruitment Company Holdings Inc. (United States; 79%); Tradition (Asia) Ltd. (Hong Kong); Tradition (North America) Inc. (United States); Tradition (UK) Ltd.; Tradition Argentina S.A.; Tradition Asiel Securities Inc. (United States); Tradition Australia Pty. Ltd. (Australia); Tradition Bond Brokers Ltd. (United Kingdom); Tradition Chile Agentes de Valores Limitada; Tradition Financial Services GmbH (Germany); Tradition Financial Services Inc. (United States); Tradition Italia Sim S.p.A. (Italy); Tradition S.A. (Switzerland); Tradition Service Holding S.A. (Switzerland); Tradition Singapore (Pte) Ltd. (Singapore); Tradition Wertpapierhandel GmbH (Germany); VIEL Debeausse and Co. Inc. (United States; 91%); VIEL Tradition S.A.

Principal Competitors

ICAP (Garban Intercapital); Maxcor; Cantor Fitzgerald; Prebon; Tullett & Tokyo; GFI.

Further Reading

"Compagnie Financiere Tradition," *Euroweek,* May 21, 2004, p. 29.
"Patrick Combes, PDG de Viel & Cie: Le financier qui monte," *Entreprendre,* May 1, 2000.
Vlad, Mirela, "Viel Plans Further Acquisitions," *Wall Street Journal Europe,* August 18, 2000, p. 16.
Walker, Susanne, "French Brokerage Announces Intent to Acquire Chapdelaine & Cos.," *Bond Buyer,* December 21, 2004, p. 28.

—M.L. Cohen

Votorantim Participaçoes S.A.

255 Rue Amauri
Sao Paulo, Sao Paulo 01448-000
Brazil
Telephone: (55) (11) 3704-3300
Fax: (55) (11) 3167-1550
Web site: http://www.votorantim.com

Private Company
Incorporated: 1918 as S.A. Fábrica Votarantim
Employees: 4,500
Sales: BRL 18.4 billion ($6.28 billion) (2004 est.)
NAIC: 11310 Orange Groves; 113210 Forest Nurseries and Gathering of Forest Products; 221122 Electric Power Distribution; 311411 Frozen Fruit, Juice, and Vegetable Processing; 322110 Pulp Mills; 322121 Paper (Except Newsprint) Mills; 325181 Alkalies and Chlorine Manufacturing; 326112 Unsupported Plastics Packaging Film and Sheet Manufacturing; 327310 Cement Manufacturing; 327320 Ready-Mix Concrete Manufacturing; 331312 Primary Aluminum Production; 518210 Data Processing, Hosting, and Related Services; 522110 Commercial Banking; 523110 Investment Banking and Securities Dealing; 551112 Offices of Other Holding Companies

Votorantim Participaçoes S.A. is the operational holding company for the Votorantim group, the second-largest family-owned industrial group in Brazil, that of the de Moraes family. This group consists of holdings in cement, pulp and paper, metals, flexible film, chemicals, agribusiness, and energy, partly financed by the group's own bank. It is highly integrated, supplying itself with many or most of the raw materials it needs to turn out products and the electricity needed in its manufacturing processes. A few cement holdings are in North America. Votorantim also has subsidiaries in Belgium, Germany, and Singapore.

Creation and Growth of an Industrial Empire: 1918–73

Votorantim was founded by Antônio Pereira Ignácio, who was brought to Brazil in 1874 by his Portuguese parents. He started his career as the semiliterate proprietor of a small shoe shop but later became owner of a cottonseed-oil mill. By 1918 he was prosperous enough to buy at auction, with Nicolau Scarpa, a textile manufacturer that was in receivership because its owner, a bank, had failed. The mill, about 60 miles from Sao Paulo, was a few miles from Sorocaba, in the district of Votorantim, from which it got its name. It was already a substantial enterprise, with 1,300 looms and 25,000 spindles.

Perreira Ignácio gained a strong right arm in the person of José Ermírio de Moraes, who married his daughter in 1925. De Moraes, an engineering graduate of the Colorado School of Mines, had ambitious plans and based his operations in Sao Paulo in 1932. In order to exploit the rich lime deposits around Sorocaba, he and Perreira Ignácio founded Santa Helena, a cement works, in 1936. The following year they established, with Brazilian and U.S. partners, Companhia Nitro Química Brasileira to manufacture "synthetic cotton" (rayon). De Moraes traveled to the United States and acquired machinery there for the factory, which opened in 1940. In 1938 Votorantim established Usina Siderúrgica Barra Mansa, a company manufacturing steel bars, and in 1941, Companhia Brasileira de Alumínio (CBA). Although Brazil has plentiful deposits of bauxite (aluminum ore), CBA was the first Brazilian-owned company to produce aluminum there, but construction did not begin until after World War II. Because the only other producer—the Brazilian subsidiary of Canada's Alcan Inc.—refused to provide the electrical power needed for the plant, Votorantim built its own hydroelectric facilities, enabling aluminum production to begin in 1955.

As the Votorantim group—S.A. Indústrias Votorantim—expanded, it continued to concentrate on basic-process commodity products with common technology and a limited number of intermediate customers. It also organized vertically. Although the group never extended forward to the production and distribution of goods to the final user, it integrated backwards, buying huge tracts of land containing the raw materials it needed, such as bauxite and other ores, and generating its own electricity to avoid government-determined rates. Votarantim's so-called fortress mentality served it well during Brazil's frequent boom-and-bust economic cycles. The group financed itself out of its profits, avoided entangling ties with government, and kept its companies largely independent of one another, with necessary coordination generally confined to a few family members at the top. Votorantim never lost money.

The Second Generation Rules: 1973–2001

Perreira Ignácio died in 1951 and was succeeded by de Moraes as president of the Votarantim group. Among the new businesses created during his presidency was Companhia Minera de Metais, a zinc producer, in 1967. But by the time of his death in 1973, de Moraes, a senator and ambassador, had for many years been dedicating his time almost exclusively to politics, leaving administration of the group chiefly to the eldest two of his three sons: José Ermírio, Jr., who succeeded him as president, and Antônio Ermírio, who became superintendent. Both were alumni of the Colorado School of Mines and well-drilled in their father's work ethic. Antônio Ermírio, who *Forbes* placed on its 1987 list of the world's richest people, with a fortune estimated at $1.5 billion, was said by the magazine's Patrick Duggan to be the one who "called the shots." He also found time to run (unsuccessfully) for state governor of São Paulo and write books, plays, and newspaper columns. In a country plagued by kidnappings of the rich for ransom, he traveled without bodyguards and left instructions not to pay anything if he were taken captive.

At the time of the passing of the senior de Moraes, Votorantim consisted of 46 companies with 33,000 workers. In 1982 Votarantim was a group consisting of 92 companies in 17 states, with 60 factories, 54,500 employees, and combined annual revenue of 376.6 billion cruzeiros (about $1.88 billion). It was producing 35 percent of the cement in Brazil, 30 percent of the aluminum, 60 percent of the zinc, and 25 percent of the refractory materials. Companhia Níquel Tocantina, founded in 1981—as the result of 20 years of planning—added nickel to its products. The group's textile goods were being sold by its 30-unit Casa Jaraguá chain. Sugar and alcohol were being produced in the state of Pernambuco. Nitro Química was turning out rayon, soda, chlorine, and phosphates. One company had been making transparent paper since 1948; another was producing cardboard cartons. About 70 percent of the group's energy consumption came from its own facilities. In 1981 the group

established its own investment bank, Banco Votorantim. In 1985 Votorantim was the fourth-largest private (that is, nongovernment) enterprise in Brazil owned by Brazilians rather than foreigners. It was the largest industrial group and largest private-sector employer in Brazil.

The group's determination to control costs was illustrated by its headquarters in the former Hotel Esplanada in the center of Sao Paulo, where the senior de Moraes had married Perreira Ignácio's daughter. This vast and sumptuous hotel had been stripped of its furnishings and assumed the ambience of a hospital. José Ermírio, Jr.'s, bare-walled quarters were decorated only with plastic plants in a vase. Until recently employees who wanted a new pencil had needed to return the old one. No one was given an exclusive personal secretary. And even in the corridor of the president's office, the lights were turned off during the lunch hour.

The group's holdings, in 1987, consisted of almost 100 companies with combined net worth of nearly $2 billion and more than 60,000 employees. The debt came to only 8 percent of its capital. Despite investment of more than $120 million in 1986, only one subsidiary loaned money from a bank. There were, however, changes in direction during this decade. Votorantim sold its sugarcane, alcohol, refractory-materials, textile, cellophane, and rayon holdings. It expanded its interests in the pulp and paper industry in 1988, when it purchased Celpav Celulose e Papel Ltda., a company based in the state of Sao Paulo. In 1992 the group acquired Industrias de Papel Simao S.A., the fifth-largest Brazilian company in its field, for $230 million. Celpav became a subsidiary of Papel Simao, which became Brazil's third-largest pulp and paper producer and was renamed Votorantim Celulose e Papel S.A. (VCP) in 1995. The group entered the field of concentrated citrus-fruit juice by means of Citrovita Agro Industrial in 1989. This company claimed to own the world's largest orange grove, in which it planted 3.5 million trees.

In 1992 José Ermírio, Jr., announced that he, Antônio Ermírio, their younger brother, Ermírio Perreira de Moraes, and their brother-in-law, Clóvis Scripilliti, were resigning their positions. Although remaining on the group's board, they would turn over day-to-day operations to their 13 male heirs. But he ran into an insuperable obstacle in the form of the six-foot-three, 220-pound Antônio Ermírio, who worked more than 12 hours each weekday at headquarters and spent weekends visiting Votorantim factories when not at the Portuguese community hospital in Sao Paulo, where he served as unpaid chairman. The 63-year-old expressed his desire to die working.

Since the matter could not be resolved, the group was parceled out. Antonio Ermírio received control of the metallurgical and mineral enterprises; José Ermírio, the cement and pulp and paper ones; Ermírio Pereira, the chemical and citrus-juice ones; and Scripilliti, the businesses in north and northeastern Brazil.

The rift between José Ermirio and Antônio Ermírio was underlined by the scandal that brought down the president of Brazil, Fernando Collor de Mello. Reportedly on José's orders and over Antônio's objections, Votorantim contributed $300,000 to a slush fund that enriched Collor and his associates. Many other large Brazilian business enterprises also paid the president's operatives to secure contracts or other favors. The exposure of these payoffs eventually forced Collor to resign his office at the end of 1992.

Only small stakes in Votorantim's cement and paper holdings were in public hands, but in 1997 the group, for the first time, solicited the world capital markets by selling $400-million worth of bonds. Votorantim entered a consortium that sought to acquire Companhia Vale do Rio Doce (CVRD), Brazil's largest mining company, but was outbid by the giant privatized steel manufacturer Companhia Siderúrgica Nacional (CSN). However, it formed with two partners, VBC Energia, an electricity-generating joint venture, and purchased controlling shares in two electricity distributors based in the industrialized south of Brazil.

As of 1999, Votarantim enterprises ranked first in nickel, zinc, and cement production in Brazil. The group was third in aluminum and fourth in pulp and paper production (although first in paper sales). It was also third in orange-juice production. With its partners Banco Bradesco S.A. and the construction firm Construçoes e Comércio Camargo Corrêa S.A., it was the nation's second-largest distributor of electricity. Votorantim's $3.6 billion in revenue came from: cement, 36 percent; metallurgy, 29 percent; pulp and paper, 21 percent; agroindustry and miscellaneous, 5 percent each; and chemicals, 4 percent. Despite its size, the group was much leaner in personnel than in the past; its 22,000 employees were only about a third of its labor force at the 1980s peak.

New Century, New Administration

A new company, Votorantim Venture Capital (VVC), was organized in 1999. The purpose was to form alliances with entrepreneurs and other groups and inject new technologies in traditional businesses with the aim of increasing their value. Another purpose was to create electronic portals for the group. Other areas of interest included biotechnology, bioinformation, biodiversity, and data-center and call-center services. Alellyx engaged in genetic research intended to raise the yield of the group's oranges, sugarcane, and eucalyptus trees. Scyla worked on developing information-technology services and software. OptiGlobe provided data-center services for Latin American businesses seeking to outsource their information-technology needs. Some $300 million was earmarked for VVC over five years, and a biotechnology cluster took shape in Techno Park, a high-technology center about 60 miles from Sao Paulo. Renamed Votorantim Novos Negócios (VNN), this enterprise consisted in 2004 of eight companies with BRL 400 million (about $137 million) in annual sales, but was not yet profitable.

VVC was the group's first initiative given over exclusively to the third de Moraes generation, which was now reaching, or had already reached, middle age. José Ermírio, Jr., died in 2001, leaving Antônio Ermírio as the senior member of the older generation. A new model of governance for the group was announced that year, soon after Votorantim Participaçoes was founded as the group's operational holding company. Mindful of a study showing that family enterprises rarely lasted more than three generations—largely because of internal feuding— the 23 third-generation heirs announced that, while forming an eight-member executive council with the final authority over strategy and acquisitions, they would, over a five-year transi-

tional period, yield day-to-day administration to executives who were not family members. Located in a Sao Paulo commercial building, the offices of Votorantim Participaçoes presented a marked contrast to the old headquarters with ample light filtered by venetian blinds through the large windows, blond-wood paneling, and glass dividers.

The process of turning over administration to outside executives was not yet complete in 2005. Even before 2000, Votorantim had in recent years recruited executives from outside, often from competing multinational companies. Later, an Alcan Inc. executive was hired to run Votorantim Mineraçao e Metalurgica (VMM), a division created in 1997. The chief executive of a large Brazilian mining company became head of VCP, and a Citigroup Inc. banker was appointed chief financial officer of Votorantim Cimentos. However, analysts questioned whether there was enough managerial talent to meet the group's goal of expanding and operating successfully outside Brazil.

Despite its growing interest in new technology, the group's largest sector continued to be in a traditional business—cement. In 2002 Votorantim Cimentos Ltda. was a company consisting of several cement, mortar, and lime subsidiaries comprising 22 plants throughout Brazil, where they held a combined 42 percent share of the Brazilian market. In that year the company also entered the ready-mix concrete market by purchasing Engemix, which gave it 20 percent of the domestic market in that field. It began expanding outside Brazil in 2001, when it purchased Toronto-based St. Marys Cement Inc. for $680 million. St. Marys held a half-share of Florida's Suwannee American Cement and factories in the Great Lakes region of the United States, making it the world's eighth-largest cement company. In 2005 Votorantim Cimentos purchased more Great Lakes factories from the Mexican multinational giant CEMEX S.A. de C.V. for $389 million, raising its share of the U.S. cement market to about 6 percent.

VCP had become a company with, in 2004, $1 billion in net sales, almost half from exports. It owned about 195,000 hectares (about 480,000 acres) of land in the state of Sao Paulo, where fast-growing eucalyptus was planted in some 260 tracts. Production from two mills came to 1.4 million metric tons of wood pulp and 610,000 metric tons of paper per year. In 2004 VCP and another large pulp and paper producer, Companhia Suzano Celulose e Papel, joined forces to jointly acquire Ripasa S.A. Celulose e Papel for $720 million. (VCP began selling shares in the United States in 2000.)

CBA had revenue of BRL 2.2 billion ($751 million) in 2004 and ranked second to Alcoa's Brazilian subsidiary. But, because 60 percent of its electricity came from the Votorantim group's own generating plants, its profit came to BRL 716 million ($244 million), almost twice as large as Alcoa's. CBA was the only enterprise in Votorantim's portfolio being administered personally by Antônio Ermírio de Moraes.

The Brazilian business magazine *Exame* had given CBA its award as best enterprise of the year in 1983. In 2000 the award went to Votarantim Cimentos. Three years later, Votorantim as a whole was honored by *Exame* as the best enterprise of the last 30 years. Its consolidated net sales of 18.4 billion BRL in 2004 ($6.28 billion) was 17 percent higher than in 2003, according to

Financial Times Ltd.'s Business News America. (*Exame* gave a figure of $8.55 billion.) The consolidated net profit of 4.14 billion BRL ($1.66 billion) was 20 percent higher than in 2003. Among major private groups in 2003, Votorantim ranked tenth in sales, second in profits, and fourth in estimated net worth. It was still tenth in sales in 2004.

Vontarantim Participaçoes was the operational arm of Hejoassú, the controlling de Moraes family holding company. As of 2000, the four children of the senior José Ermírio de Moraes held equal shares of this company. Each of the four branches was entitled to appoint two members of the next generation to serve on the executive council of Votarantim Participaçoes. The presidency of the council was to rotate between the eight. Of the fourth generation of heirs, 60 or so in number, some 15 were undergoing apprenticeships presided over by Scripilitti, but with no guarantee that they would ever rise to an executive position in the group.

Principal Divisions

Votarantim Finance; Votarantim Industrial; Votarantim New Business.

Principal Subsidiaries

Banco Votarantim S.A.; Companhia Brasileira de Alumínio; Votorantim Agroindústria; Votorantim Celulose e Papel S.A.; Votorantim Cimentos Ltda.; Votorantim Energia Ltda.; Votorantim Filmes Flexiveis Ltda.; Votorantim International do Brasil Ltda.; Votorantim International Europe GMBH (Germany); Votorantim International Europe N.V. (Belgium); Votorantim International North America (United States); Votorantim Metals; Votorantim Novos Negócios; Votorantim N.V. (Singapore); Votorantim Química.

Principal Competitors

Aracruz Celulose S.A.; Banco Bradesco S.A.; Banco Itaú S.A.; Brasken S.A.; Cimento Rio Branco S.A.; Companhia Energética de Minas Gerais; Klabin S.A.; Suzano Papel e Celulose.

Further Reading

"Against the Odds," *World Cement,* October 2002, pp. 23–24.

Attuch, Leonardo, "Enfin sob o mesmo teto," *Exame,* February 15, 1995, p. 73.

Blecher, Nelson, "De olhos bem abertos," *Exame,* June 28, 2000, pp. 116–26.

——, "En busca da eternidade," *Exame,* June 11, 2003, pp. 40–41.

"Brazil Boosts Aluminum Production," *Business Week,* July 19, 1952, pp. 152, 154.

Caixeta, Nely, "Melhor de 30," *Exame,* June 9, 2003, pp. 50–54

"CBA/Votorantim A EMPRESA DO ANO," *Exame,* May 10, 1983, pp. 28–37.

Duggan, Patrick, "Straight Man," *Forbes,* October 5, 1987, pp. 156–57.

"Easy Now," *Economist,* June 20, 1998, pp. 76–77.

Ferraz, Eduardo, "Antes tarde do que nunca," *Exame,* June 27, 2001, pp. 62–65.

Kandell, Jonathan, "The CVRD Factor," *Institutional Investor,* October 1997, pp. 191–92.

Nelson, Reed E., "Is There Strategy in Brazil?," *Business Horizons,* July/August 1990, p. 22.

Samor, Geraldo, "Votorantim Mines for Growth," *Wall Street Journal,* January 18, 2005, p. B3.

Scantimburgo, Joao de. *José Ermírio de Moraes.* Sao Paulo: Companhia Editora Nacional, 1975.

Simonetti, Eliana, "O império loteado," *Veja,* December 16, 1992, pp. 90–93.

—Robert Halasz

Widmer Brothers Brewing Company

929 N. Russell
Portland, Oregon 97227
U.S.A.
Telephone: (503) 281-2437
Fax: (503) 281-1496
Web site: http://www.widmer.com

Private Company
Incorporated: 1984
Employees: 130
Sales: $33 million (2004 est.)
NAIC: 312120 Breweries

Widmer Brothers Brewing Company is a Portland, Oregon-based ''craft brewer'' that produces several distinctive varieties of beer. The firm's brews include top seller Hefeweizen, an unfiltered wheat beer; black raspberry-flavored Widberry; Drop Top Amber; Blonde Ale; seasonal varieties like Okto and Snowplow Milk Stout; and others that are brewed for sale on draft only. Hefeweizen is available in most American states, and the rest are found primarily on the West Coast. The firm is run by brothers Kurt and Rob Widmer, who sold a minority stake to Anheuser-Busch in 1997 to gain access to the industry leader's distribution network.

Beginnings

Widmer Brothers Brewing Company was founded in 1984 in Portland, Oregon by Kurt and Rob Widmer. Older brother Kurt had come to appreciate a wide variety of beer while living in Germany in the 1970s, and had begun making his own beer when he returned to the United States. He used a traditional strain of yeast obtained from the Brewing Research Institute in Weihenstephan, Bavaria, and later returned to Germany to fine-tune his craft at a brewery in Dusseldorf. By the early 1980s he had developed a recipe for beer that produced consistently good results.

In 1984 the Widmer brothers decided to found a brewery, and raised more than $50,000 from family members and an outside investor. With their father Raymond, they assembled a small brewery out of used dairy and restaurant equipment, and by fall had begun running test batches. The first Widmer offering, Altbier (German for ''old beer''), was offered for sale in early 1985, and the richly flavored brew was soon joined by a lighter variety, Weizen, which used wheat as an ingredient. Unlike German wheat beers, which had a slight flavor of bananas and cloves, the Widmers' recipe produced a less noticeable aftertaste.

Whereas the United States had once been home to thousands of regional breweries, 13 years of Prohibition had reduced the number to about 800, after which national competition, mergers, and bankruptcies had pared the total to just 50 by the 1980s. At this time home-brewers like Kurt Widmer were starting to make traditional varieties of beer that giants like Anheuser-Busch, Miller, and Coors had abandoned, while a relaxed legal environment began to lower the barriers to brewing beer for local consumption. Portland was an early locus of such activity, with the Cartwright Brewing Company founded there in 1980, followed four years later by the Bridgeport Brewing Company and Widmer Brothers.

Not everyone was ambitious enough to try the beers of these unfamiliar new companies, however, and the brothers faced an uphill battle to get taverns to offer them (Widmer Brothers sold its beer in kegs only, believing flavor was degraded by the bottling process). To boost interest they formed the ''Widmer Designated Drinker'' program, in which the brothers and their friends rented vans (driven by nondrinkers) and traveled to clients' bars where they ordered copious amounts of the company's beer. For the new firm's first year production totaled 400 31-gallon barrels.

The Creation of Hefeweizen in 1986

In 1986 a variation on Widmer's wheat beer was introduced that would prove a turning point in the firm's evolution. Faced with demand for a third variety of beer, but limited by their ownership of just two brewing vessels, the brothers reluctantly filled a keg with Weizen without filtering it to remove the wheat proteins and yeast particles that made it appear cloudy. Bar owner and early company supporter Carl Simpson liked the resultant

Company Perspectives:

Widmer Brothers Brewing Company currently produces an extensive line of European and American style beers year-round. These offerings include America's Original Hefeweizen, Drop Top Amber Ale, Widmer Blonde, and Widberry "O." Seasons and holidays inspired Widmer Brothers to be the first brewery to introduce seasonal beers to America—an idea that has spawned such favorites as Snow-plow and Okto, returning each year by popular demand. In keeping with the tradition of hand-crafted brewing, the Widmer Brothers continue to develop new and exciting beers.

hazy, golden appearance, and when he served it in 22-ounce glasses with lemon wedges his customers did, too. Dubbed Hefeweizen, it would soon go on to become the firm's top seller.

Annual production increased each year, and by 1989 the maximum capacity of the company's brewing equipment had been reached, forcing the Widmers to turn away business. That year the firm bought two adjoining historic buildings in Portland that were slated for demolition, which would be refurbished to house a new brewery. The 100-year-old Smithson and McKay Buildings featured Italianate and Romanesque Revival brickwork and a unique cast-iron storefront, and were listed on the National Register of Historic Places. They required extensive interior work, however, which made the renovation costs significantly higher than constructing a new facility from scratch.

In June 1990 the firm began moving into its newly completed brewhouse, whose state-of-the-art equipment had twice the 8,000-barrel annual capacity of the original location. The new site also had room for a pub, offices, basement storage, and possible banquet rooms and rental apartments.

Once it was fully operational the new brewery enabled the firm to increase production dramatically, but demand was growing even faster. In 1992 Widmer Brothers began laying plans to build an expansion adjacent to its new brewery that would once again double production. Output for the year reached 27,400 barrels, 20,550 of which was Hefeweizen. The Widmers continued to distribute their beer in kegs only, as they strove to offer the best-tasting beer possible.

In early 1994 the company sued a former employee who was planning to open a new brewery in Portland, claiming he was violating a noncompete agreement he had signed. The case was later settled out of court with a payment to Widmer. During the year the firm also added a new beer called Dunkel Weizen and leased a closed G. Heileman plant in Milwaukee to brew Hefeweizen, but the facility was reportedly not able to produce the beer to Widmer's satisfaction and the deal was terminated.

In March 1995 a pub and restaurant, the Widmer Gasthaus, was opened adjacent to the company's brewery, and a major expansion was begun across the street on property the firm had acquired. In September the Widmers sold a stake to Desai Capital Management for $10 million to fund the new construction. The company had also recently engaged CKS Partners to handle advertising, which was initially budgeted at $1 million

per year. Production for the year reached 69,200 barrels, of which 58,820 was Hefeweizen, and revenues hit an estimated $10 million.

Oregon now had 70 breweries or brewpubs (where beer was brewed for sale on-site), and the state's drinkers led the nation in consumption of craft beers, with nearly 9 percent of the total consumed in 1995 coming from local firms. Widmer sold a greater portion of this amount than any of its competitors, though its out-of-state presence was reduced because it did not bottle its beers.

Bottling Beginning in 1996

In the spring of 1996 the firm's new $20 million brewery opened, with its brewing vessels and utilities connected to the older one via under-the-street tunnels. It would focus exclusively on brewing Hefeweizen, and included a new bottling line that met the Widmers' strict standards for maintaining flavor. Several other varieties would be bottled there, including Amberbier, Blackbier, and Widberry.

On May 6 Hefeweizen reached store shelves in Oregon and Washington in 22-ounce bottles and six-packs of 12-ounce bottles. The public response was overwhelming, and in June the firm reported that demand of 15,000 barrels (206,700 cases) was more than double the anticipated production of 6,000 barrels (82,600 cases). Plans for a $1.5 million expansion to the new plant were soon announced that would boost annual capacity to 310,000 barrels.

Widmer was now producing 11 different beers, some of which were only offered on draft. They included Hefeweizen, Widberry Weizen, Blackbier, Amberbier, Altbier, and Weizen year-round; and Doppelbock, Oktoberfest, and Winternacht on a seasonal basis. The firm's distribution area extended to Oregon, Washington, California, Wyoming, Colorado, Montana, Nevada, Idaho, and Alaska and a handful of other markets around the United States.

The company's success was not lost on the brewing industry's leaders, who had been warily eying the upstarts around the country that were taking a small but growing portion of their business. Some, including Miller and Coors, had launched pseudo-microbrews like Red Dog and Killian's whose packaging obscured their corporate origins, while others began seeking to take over the most successful new firms. The number of small brewers also was reaching critical mass, and distributors had started to drop slower-moving brands, while Anheuser-Busch's wholesalers were strongly urged to commit a "100 percent share of mind" to its brews, with incentives offered if they jettisoned other lines. Meanwhile, imported beer sales were rebounding through the aggressive efforts of firms like Corona, and makers of distilled spirits were working to reclaim their own share of the alcoholic beverage market. As its growth began to level off, in January 1997 the company laid off 11 employees.

Selling a Stake to Anheuser-Busch in 1997

In September 1996 August A. Busch, the chairman of Anheuser-Busch (A-B), met with the Widmers at their brewpub in Oregon, initiating a dialogue between the two firms. A-B had

Key Dates:

1984: Kurt and Rob Widmer found Widmer Brothers Brewing Company.
1986: Hefeweizen unfiltered wheat beer debuts.
1990: The firm opens a new brewery/headquarters facility.
1996: A second brewery and bottling plant is added across the street.
1997: Anheuser-Busch buys a 27 percent stake in the firm for $18 million.
2003: The company begins brewing Hefeweizen at the New Hampshire Redhook plant.
2004: Widmer and Redhook form the Craft Brands Alliance to handle West Coast sales.

---

already purchased a stake in Seattle's Redhook Ale Brewery and then helped it reach a national market, and in April 1997 Widmer Brothers sold a 27 percent stake in the firm to the industry's leader for $18.25 million. The move helped strengthen the company financially at a time when many craft brewers were in trouble, though some critics grumbled that the sale was contrary to the principles with which brewers like the Widmers had entered the business. A-B made approximately 45 percent of the beer sold in the United States, and its distribution network would give Widmer Brothers the ability to reach a national market.

The year 1997 also saw the firm introduce several new brews, including Widmer Vienna and Czech Pilsner, as well as a hard cider beverage. The company was now making seven year-round brews and a changing lineup of three seasonals, which included Golden Bock, Sommerbrau Kolsch, and Hop Jack Pale Ale. During the year the firm ran into distribution trouble in Denver, Colorado, when its local distributor there went under, and it took more than a year before its products were restored to the area.

In early 2000 Widmer Brothers unveiled redesigned packaging, which emphasized the "W" initial in the firm's name and featured more colorful graphics. Distribution was continuing to roll out around the United States, and in 2003 the company began brewing Hefeweizen at a Redhook-owned brewery in Portsmouth, New Hampshire that was similar to the firm's Portland facility. Redhook also would distribute the beer for Widmer, while dropping production of its own Hefeweizen in the East. The new arrangement would halt the flow of other Widmer products to the area, however, as the firm would no longer truck them the long miles from Oregon. The year 2003 also saw introduction of Drop Top Amber Ale, which was touted for its smooth flavor and slightly fruity aroma. Widmer was now ranked as the fourth largest craft brewer in the United States, behind Sierra Nevada of California, New Belgium of Colorado, and Redhook, which had brewed 229,000 barrels in 2003 to Widmer's 170,000.

Forming the Craft Brands Alliance in 2004

In 2004 Widmer Brothers expanded its relationship with Redhook to create a joint sales and marketing organization called Craft Brands Alliance LLC that would handle both companies' products on the West Coast. The move was expected to help the firms cut costs by utilizing common staff for a number of tasks. The two companies would sell their beers to Craft Brands, which would then handle all advertising and marketing, distributing the product through A-B wholesalers.

The year also saw the introduction of a seasonal brew called Snowplow Milk Stout, which had been developed by the Oregon Brew Crew, a homebrewers club to which the brothers belonged and with which the firm had begun collaborating in 1997. Widmer Brothers had been honored a number of times over the years in beer tasting contests, and in 2004 the company was named Brewer of the Year at the Great American Beer Festival in Colorado, while its Hefeweizen won a gold medal at the 2004 World Beer Cup. Production increased yet again during the year to 199,000 barrels, an increase of more than 17 percent over 2003.

In April 2005 the firm turned 21, the legal drinking age in the United States, and the Widmer brothers celebrated with an Octoberfest party at the brewery in September. The company's beers were now available in 45 states across the United States.

After more than two decades in operation, Widmer Brothers Brewing Company had established itself as the largest brewer in Oregon, and one of the leading craft brewers in the United States. The firm's ties to Anheuser-Busch and joint marketing agreement with Redhook, along with numerous still-untapped markets, made future growth a certainty.

Principal Subsidiaries

Craft Brands Alliance LLC (50%).

Principal Competitors

Redhook Ale Brewery; Pyramid Breweries; Deschutes Brewing Company; Anchor Brewing Company; Full Sail Brewing Company; Portland Brewing Company; Boston Beer Company; Sierra Nevada Brewing Company; New Belgium Brewing Company.

Further Reading

Berne, Steve, "Manufacturing Excellence: Five That Strive," *Prepared Foods,* June 1, 1997, p. 72.
Bonino, Rick, "Brew News at Widmer," *Spokesman Review,* May 14, 1997, p. D1.
Bradford, Julie Johnson, "Widmer's Is on Tap," *News & Observer* (Raleigh, N.C.), April 18, 2003.
"Brewer May Save Threatened Buildings," *Seattle Times,* February 27, 1989, p. B4.
Brinckman, Jonathan, "Widmer, Redhook Plan Joint Sales, Marketing Unit," *Portland Oregonian,* February 4, 2004, p. D1.
Cristy, Nick, "Taking Off and Breaking Away, Widmer Brothers Attempts to Soar," *Beverage World,* January 31, 1998, p. 29.
Forder, Tony, "Betting the Time Is Ripe for Unfiltered Brew," *The Record,* June 11, 2003, p. F2.
Foyston, John, "Drinking Age at Last: Widmer Is 21," *Portland Oregonian,* September 17, 2005, p. C1.
Francis, Mike, "Anheuser-Busch Brewing's 1,000-Pound Gorilla," *Portland Oregonian,* October 4, 1997, p. E1.

——, ''Brew Baron Turns Heads at Brewpub,'' *Portland Oregonian,* September 22, 1996, p. G1.

——, ''For Brewers, These Are Heady Times,'' *Portland Oregonian,* April 28, 1991, p. K1.

——, ''Widmer Faces Slowdown, Lets 11 Go,'' *Portland Oregonian,* January 15, 1997, p. E2.

——, ''Widmer Joins King of Beers' Realm,'' *Portland Oregonian,* April 18, 1997, p. A1.

——, ''Widmer Plans a Leap,'' *Portland Oregonian,* October 25, 1994, p. B16.

Gonzales, Gloria, ''Making It with Hefeweizen,'' *Portland Oregonian,* April 28, 1996, p. F1.

Kreck, Dick, ''Oregon Microbrew Favorite Returning to Colorado,'' *Denver Post,* July 21, 1999, p. E3.

McBride, Sandra, ''Craft Quality,'' *Beverage World,* February 15, 1997, p. 70.

Sullivan, Ann, ''Landmarks Commission OKs Widmer Brewing Co's Expansion Plans,'' *Portland Oregonian,* September 28, 1992, p. B2.

Tripp, Julie, ''The 'Give Me a Bud' Refrain Wanes As Oregon Microbrewers Make Gains,'' *Portland Oregonian,* June 10, 1990, p. 1.

''Widmer Bros. Brewing Co. Begins Bottling Operations,'' *Modern Brewery Age,* May 6, 1996, p. 2.

—Frank Uhle

Younkers

331 West Wisconsin Avenue
Milwaukee, Wisconsin 53203
U.S.A.
Telephone: (414) 347-4141
Fax: (515) 247-7174
Web site: http://www.younkers.com

Wholly Owned Subsidiary of Saks Inc.
Incorporated: 1904
Sales: $500 million (2004 est.)
NAIC: 45211 Department Stores

Younkers is a Midwestern department store chain with 47 stores scattered throughout Illinois, Iowa, Michigan, Minnesota, Nebraska, South Dakota, and Wisconsin. Younkers' stores are generally located in midsized to smaller cities where competition is more limited than in major metropolitan areas. Younkers' stores sell apparel and accessories for men, women, and children, as well as home furnishings and furniture. Younkers and its peers in Saks Incorporated's Northern Department Store Group were put up for sale in 2005.

An Iowa Institution: 1856–1978

Younkers (originally Younker & Brothers) was founded in Keokuk, Iowa, in 1856 by three young Polish-born brothers: Lipman, Samuel, and Marcus Younker. The general store was a base from which they strapped packs of merchandise on their backs that they carried into the neighboring countryside to farmers and others too busy or isolated to shop in town. They founded Iowa's first synagogue and closed the store on Saturdays, the Jewish Sabbath. Another brother, Herman, joined them in 1874 and opened a 1,320-square-foot dry goods store in Des Moines on their behalf with a $6,000 grubstake. "We have come here to live and mean to do what is right," the store declared in a newspaper advertisement taken out on its opening.

With the closing of the Keokuk store in 1879, Des Moines became headquarters for Younker Brothers. In 1881 it became the first Des Moines store to hire female sales clerks, and in 1900 this store moved to its location at Seventh and Walnut Streets and remained opened until 2005. Younker Brothers was a place to meet as well as to shop. Women lunched at the elegant Tea Room upstairs and teenagers took their dates there for dinner and dancing. Just about every organization in town met at the Tea Room. The store even had a knitting classroom. It installed Iowa's first escalator in 1939 and was the first department store in the United States to air condition its entire building.

Younker Brothers grew by acquiring Grand Department Store in 1912, Wilkins Department Store in 1923, and J. Mandelbaum & Sons in 1928. Originally incorporated in 1904, it merged with Harris-Emery Co. in 1927, thereby becoming the largest department store chain in Iowa, and reincorporated under Delaware law. Its net sales (excluding leased departments) rose from $8.4 million in 1938 to $26.4 million in fiscal 1948 (the year ended January 31, 1948). Net profit rose in this period from a low of $308,000 in 1939 to a high of nearly $2 million in fiscal 1947. At the end of 1947 it acquired a Sioux City, Iowa store from Davidson Brothers Co. and had, since 1941, opened branch stores in Ames, Fort Dodge, Marshalltown, and Mason City. Younker Brothers went public in December 1948 to retire bank loans, offering a minority of its common stock at $26 a share. Much of its stock remained in the hands of three Des Moines merchandising families: the Frankels, Mandelbaums, and Rosenfelds.

As the largest store in Iowa, the Younkers of this period carried the old adage that the customer is always right beyond the call of duty. A *Business Week* article cited the case of a lady who brought back her fur coat, complaining it did not fit, after allowing her weight to balloon over the winter. The store remodeled it without argument. Morey Sostrin, president and general manager, said, "We figure that the advertising value of such cases in small towns in Iowa is worth far more than the adjustment cost." Younkers was known for liberal credit policies (including 60,000 charge accounts) and a mail-order service. It also was running three Des Moines restaurants.

During the 1950s Younker Brothers acquired another Sioux City store and opened branch stores in Iowa City, Oskaloosa, and Ottumwa, Iowa; Omaha, Nebraska; and Austin, Minnesota. The Omaha store, opened in 1955, was its first in a shopping center.

Company Perspectives:

Through the years, Younkers has defined, and will continue to offer, the style and quality that customers have come to expect and enjoy.

Net sales, after reaching $45.5 million in fiscal 1956, slumped to $37.1 million the next year and did not surpass the 1956 figure until 1962. Net income dropped from $2.4 million in 1956 to $1.4 million in 1957 and did not top the 1956 figure until 1965. In 1961 the company acquired Kilpatrick's Department Store of Omaha.

Although the biggest downtown department store in Des Moines, the Younkers flagship retained a reputation for "small town friendliness." This six-story, 400,000-square-foot, block-long building was responsible for 42 percent of corporation sales in fiscal 1965. At the end of the decade, in addition to the main Des Moines and Sioux City stores, there were 16 Younkers branch stores in Iowa, more than half in major shopping centers. Net sales (including leased departments) reached a record $83.5 million in fiscal 1970, and net profit was a record $3.8 million. Apparel was accounting for nearly 80 percent of sales, with home furnishings, furniture, and appliances next in importance. Dividends had been paid each year since 1935. The long-term debt was $10 million.

Equitable of Iowa Subsidiary: 1979–92

By 1978 Younkers had added branch stores in Des Moines and Davenport, Iowa; Moline, Illinois; and Sioux Falls, South Dakota, plus a main store in a Cedar Rapids shopping center and the Merle Hay Mall in Des Moines, which had a separate store for homes. This last store was destroyed by a fire that year in which ten employees were killed. Net sales came to $135.5 million in fiscal 1978, and net profit amounted to $5 million. In 1979 Equitable of Iowa purchased Younker Brothers for $72.2 million and made the retailer a subsidiary named Younkers. Des Moines breathed a sigh of relief, since Equitable was controlled by Iowa's first family, the Hubbells. "The loss of an independently-owned business always is sad," the *Des Moines Tribune* declared in an editorial. "But the acquisition of Younkers by another Des Moines-based firm avoids the drawbacks of absentee ownership and promises to be good for the community."

The Younkers chain of 29 stores (25 in Iowa) grew slowly during the next four years. Sales increased from $141.9 million in 1979 to $188.7 million in 1984. After net income slumped from $4.8 million in 1983 to only $723,000 in 1984, William Friedman, Jr., a descendant of the group of families that had controlled Younkers since the 1920s, was ousted as president and chief executive officer, allegedly for alienating customers by turning Younkers into an upscale boutique. The Ottumwa store was closed, and 200 jobs were eliminated.

Under W. Thomas Gould, who first assumed the presidency and later became chief executive officer as well, Younkers shifted its focus back to the middle class. It updated its "Satisfaction Always" motto, adopted in 1936, to stress customer service even more than previously. Although not paying a commission on sales, the company adjusted wage rates every

six months on a sales-per-hour basis. Salespeople were expected to acknowledge a customer within 30 seconds of arrival in a department at a distance of no more than 30 feet. Gould closed eight of the 37 Younkers stores that he felt were too small in markets that offered little growth opportunity, and he eliminated the chain's only furniture store.

Net income improved appreciably in 1986, and at the end of the year Younkers agreed to purchase a major competitor, Brandeis & Sons, which was operating 11 department stores in Iowa and Nebraska. This acquisition boosted Younkers' revenues by almost $100 million, and in 1988 the 37-store chain earned a record $8.3 million on revenues of $313.4 million. Gould and other Younkers managers chafed under Equitable's direction, however, because its profits were absorbed by the parent organization instead of being earmarked for expansion, which company managers felt was needed to generate the economies of scale needed to compete with Kmart and Wal-Mart on price. Between 1985 and 1992 Younkers paid Equitable about $63 million in dividends.

In June 1989 Equitable announced its intention to sell Younkers but rejected offers of about $90 million as inadequate. Sales grew slowly in subsequent years, but after the company earned a record $12.8 million on sales of $330 million in 1991, almost all of the common stock was put on the market at $12.50 a share. Some of the proceeds from the 6.17 million shares sold in 1992 were used to reduce Younkers' long-term debt from $104 million to $89 million.

Public Company Again: 1992–95

Gould, who as chairman remained at the helm of Younkers, continued to stress customer service. Interviewed by *Daily News Record* [DNR] in 1992, he said, "The '80s were merchandise and marketing driven. The '90s are customer driven. . . . We have to totally reverse the hierarchy of the '80s where the buyers and merchandisers were on top and the sales associates were on the bottom." His philosophy was to stress basics rather than trendy but unsuitable merchandise. "Former management thought the American consumer had gotten thin and rich overnight," Gould told a *Business Week* reporter. In fact, the average female customer was consuming so many calories that Younkers was making one-quarter of its women's apparel sales in sizes 14 and higher and, therefore, was featuring large women in its catalog and fashion shows.

During fiscal 1992 (ended January 30, 1993) Younkers had net earnings of $17.6 million on net sales of $473.4 million. In April of that year Younkers purchased the department store division of financially troubled H.C. Prange Co., a privately owned chain with 25 stores, 18 of them in Wisconsin, for $67 million in cash and assumption of $9 million in debt. Prange proved harder to digest than expected, however, and although Younkers' sales rose to $597.9 million in fiscal 1993, net earnings fell to $12.2 million and, on an earnings-per-share basis, only half the previous year's level. During fiscal 1994 sales and earnings barely rose. The value of a share of Younkers stock fell from a high of $32.50 in 1993 to $12.25 in June 1994, making the company vulnerable to a takeover by a bigger store chain.

A battle royal for control of Younkers broke out in 1994, when Milwaukee-based retailer Carson Pirie Scott & Co. made

Key Dates:

1856: Younker & Brothers is established by the Younker brothers.
1881: The company is the first Des Moines store to hire female sales clerks.
1927: Younker Brothers merges with Harris-Emery Co.
1948: The company goes public.
1979: Equitable of Iowa purchases Younker Brothers for $72.2 million and makes the retailer a subsidiary named Younkers.
1986: Younkers agrees to purchase Brandeis & Sons.
1992: Almost all of the company's common stock is put on the market at $12.50 a share; H.C. Prange Co. is acquired.
1996: Younkers becomes a subsidiary of Proffitt's, Inc.
1998: Proffitt's acquires Carson Pirie Scott & Co. and Saks Holdings Inc. and adopts the Saks Incorporated corporate moniker.
2005: The company's flagship store in Des Moines closes its doors; Saks puts Younkers up for sale.

an unsolicited $152 million ($17 a share) takeover bid for the company. Carson already held 12 percent of the stock. Younkers not only rejected the bid as inadequate but adopted a poison-pill defense intended to make the acquisition prohibitively expensive.

Undeterred, Carson raised its bid to $19 a share in 1995 and won a nonbinding resolution from Younkers shareholders to put the company up for sale to the higher bidder, but Younkers' board voted not to sell. Carson, which would have closed Younkers' headquarters and the downtown Des Moines store, then sued Younkers' directors for "gross breaches of fiduciary duty."

Sale to Proffitt's in 1996

By late 1995 Younkers' position was more attractive to alternative offers, because the former Prange stores had become an asset, accounting for more than 40 percent of the company's total sales. In February 1996 the company quickly accepted a $24-a-share, $216 million offer from Proffitt's, Inc., a department store chain based in Tennessee. Younkers, which became a Proffitt's subsidiary as well as a division, preserved its name and much of its independence, although about one-fifth of the jobs at Des Moines headquarters were eliminated. (The flagship Des Moines store, a money loser, remained open only because of a city financial aid package.) Even Carson voted its shares in favor of the merger.

Gould became vice-chairman of Proffitt's, yielding the CEO position at Younkers to Robert Mosco. Mosco resigned in October 1996 to become president of Proffitt's newly formed Merchandising Group. Three unproductive Younkers stores were closed in 1996, and two others were sold to a third party. New Younkers units were scheduled to open, however, in Iowa City, Iowa, and Grandville, Michigan, in 1998. During fiscal 1997 (ended February 3, 1997) women's apparel accounted for 32 percent of Younkers' sales, men's apparel for 16 percent,

home furnishings for 16 percent, and cosmetics for 11 percent. Children's apparel, accessories, leased departments, lingerie, and shoes accounted for the remainder of the division's sales, in that order.

Changes in the Late 1990s and Beyond

Despite fending off advances from Carson Pirie Scott & Co. in 1995, Younkers found itself inextricably linked to the company in 1998 after its parent acquired the chain in February 1998. Later that year, Proffitt's shelled out $2.1 billion to acquire Saks Holdings Inc. and adopted the Saks Incorporated corporate moniker.

As a Saks subsidiary, Younkers continued its slow and steady growth. In 1999, the company set plans in motion to open a store in Muskegon, Michigan. It also opened two new stores in Lansing and Okemos, Michigan. At the same time, unprofitable stores began to shut their doors. Its location in Bettendorf, Iowa, closed and the Younkers on College Avenue in Appleton, Wisconsin, shut down.

In the early years of the new millennium, competition was fierce for department store operators. An increase in sales at discounters like Wal-Mart and Kohl's as well as specialty retailers began to hurt Younkers' business. As such, Saks took several measures to shore up the company's profits. Younkers left its home in Des Moines as company headquarters were moved to Wisconsin during the latter half of 2002 and into 2003. Almost 300 jobs were cut as part of the reorganization. The company's merchandising, advertising, marketing, and other support functions were integrated into Carson Pirie Scott & Co.'s operations.

At the same time, several of Younkers' stores were shuttered. Its location at the Crossroads Mall in Omaha, Nebraska closed. The company also said goodbye to its flagship store in downtown Des Moines in August 2005. The location had proved to be unprofitable and its closure was part of Carson Pirie Scott & Co.'s strategy to focus on its most productive and profitable locations.

During this time period, profits at Saks were falling. To top it off, the U.S. Securities and Exchange Commission had launched an investigation into the company's accounting practices. Several Saks executives were fired as a result of the investigation, which found that the company had improperly collected allowances from several of its vendors. Saks was operating with two main business segments at this time: the Saks Department Store Group (SDSG) and Saks Fifth Avenue Enterprises (SFAE), which included the Saks Fifth Avenue stores, Saks OFF 5th stores, and saks.com.

During 2005, Saks decided to focus solely on its high-end SFAE business and began to look for buyers for the stores in its SDSG segment. As such, Saks began to entertain offers for its Northern Department Store Group, which included Younkers, along with Herberger's, Carson Pirie Scott, Bergner's, and Boston Store. Bon-Ton Stores Inc. swooped in with a $1.1 billion offer in October 2005. Bon-Ton, which had used acquisitions to fuel much of its growth throughout its history, would double in size as a result of the purchase. Saks and Bon-Ton were expected to close the deal in the coming months. With a new parent company on the horizon, only time would tell what was in store for Younkers in the years to come.

Principal Competitors

Federated Department Stores Inc.; Marshall Field's; Sears, Roebuck and Co.

Further Reading

Byrne, Harlan S., "Younkers," *Barron's,* September 13, 1995, pp. 35–36.

Chandler, Susan, "This Takeover Goes Way Past Hostile," *Business Week,* July 3, 1995, pp. 72–73.

"City Store Wins State Buyers," *Business Week,* May 28, 1949, pp. 56–58.

Couch, Mark P., "Peeking into Younkers' Executive Suite," *Business Record,* May 2, 1992, p. 1.

Day, Bill, "What's Next for Proffitt's?," *Des Moines Business Record,* July 27, 1998, p. 22.

Dewitte, Dave, "Downtown Des Moines Younkers Store to Close," *The Gazette,* June 4, 2005.

"The Dismantling of Saks," *Women's Wear Daily,* July 5, 2005.

"Equitable of Iowa Says Friedman Removed As Younkers Chief," *Wall Street Journal,* January 4, 1985, p. 24.

"Equitable Puts Younkers Chain on the Block," *WWD (Women's Wear Daily),* June 1, 1989, pp. 1, 11.

Ford, George C., "Younkers Owner Still Exploring Sale of Chain," *Knight Ridder Tribune Business News,* October 19, 2005.

Hajewski, Doris, "Headquarters Could Grow in Deal," *Milwaukee Journal Sentinel,* November 1, 2005.

Hartnett, Michael, "Younkers," *Stores,* March 1993, pp. 16, 18, 20.

"Insurance Firm Agrees to Buy Younker Bros.," *Daily News Record,* August 4, 1978, p. 3.

Kasler, Dale, "Surprise Bid Puts Younkers on the Market," *Des Moines Register,* October 29, 1994, 1A, 6A.

——, "Tom Gould, CEO," *Des Moines Register,* November 7, 1993, pp. 1G, 7G.

——, "Younkers," *Des Moines Register,* February 3, 1996, pp. 12S, 11S.

——, "Younkers Becomes a Part of Proffitt's," *Des Moines Register,* February 3, 1996, pp. 1A, 10A.

——, "Younkers Bid Caps Year of Troubles," *Des Moines Register,* October 30, 1994, pp. 1A, 7A.

——, "Younkers President Taking New Job," *Des Moines Register,* October 26, 1996, pp. 12S, 7S.

Oliver, Suzanne, "Milan Proposes, Des Moines Disposes," *Forbes,* July 19, 1993, pp. 88, 92.

Poxon, Jeffrey, "Younker Brothers, Inc.," *Wall Street Transcript,* January 10, 1972, p. 26,774.

Schuyler, David, "Saks to Move Younkers HQ to Milwaukee Office," *Business Journal of Milwaukee,* October 1, 2002.

Sharoff, Robert, "An Independent Voice in the Midwest," *DNR (Daily News Record),* February 3, 1992, p. 16.

Sloane, Leonard, "Iowa's Younkers: Friendly Store," *New York Times,* April 11, 1966, pp. 55, 59.

"Two Younkers Are Better Than One," *Birmingham Business Journal,* September 26, 2002.

—Robert Halasz
—update: Christina M. Stansell

INDEX TO COMPANIES

Index to Companies

Listings in this index are arranged in alphabetical order under the company name. Company names beginning with a letter or proper name such as Eli Lilly & Co. will be found under the first letter of the company name. Definite articles (The, Le, La) are ignored for alphabetical purposes as are forms of incorporation that precede the company name (AB, NV). Company names printed in bold type have full, historical essays on the page numbers appearing in bold. Updates to entries that appeared in earlier volumes are signified by the notation (upd.). Company names in light type are references within an essay to that company, not full historical essays. This index is cumulative with volume numbers printed in bold type.

TGEL&PCo. *See* Tucson Gas, Electric Light & Power Company.
TH:s Group, **10** 113; **50** 43
Tha Row Records, 69 350–52 (upd.)
Thai Airways International Public Company Limited, 6 122–24; **27** 463–66 (upd.)
Thai Lube Blending Co., **56** 290
Thai Nylon Co. Ltd., **53** 344
Thai Union Frozen Products PCL, 75 370–72
Thalassa International, **10** 14; **27** 11
Thales S.A., 42 373–76
Thames Trains, **28** 157
Thames Water plc, 11 509–11; **22** 89
Thameslink, **28** 157
THAW. *See* Recreational Equipment, Inc.
Theatrical Syndicate, **24** 437
Thelem SA, **54** 267
Therm-o-Disc, **II** 19
Therm-X Company, **8** 178
Thermacore International Inc., **56** 247
Thermador Corporation, **67** 82
Thermadyne Holding Corporation, 19 440–43
Thermal Dynamics, **19** 441
Thermal Energies, Inc., **21** 514
Thermal Power Company, **11** 270
Thermal Snowboards, Inc., **22** 462
Thermal Transfer Ltd., **13** 485
ThermaStor Technologies, Ltd., **44** 366
Thermo BioAnalysis Corp., 25 475–78
Thermo Electron Corporation, 7 520–22; **11** 512–13; **13** 421; **24** 477; **25** 475–76; **52** 389
Thermo Fibertek, Inc., 24 477–79
Thermo Instrument Systems Inc., 11 512–14; **25** 475–77
Thermo King Corporation, 13 505–07
Thermoform Plastics, Inc., **56** 378–79
Thermoforming USA, **16** 339
Thermogas Co., **35** 175
Thermolase Corporation, **22** 410
Thermos Company, 16 486–88
TheStreet.com, **34** 125
THHK Womenswear Limited, **53** 333
ThiemeMeulenhoff BV, **53** 273
Thies Companies, **13** 270
Thiess Dampier Mitsui, **IV** 47
Things Remembered. *See* Cole National Corporation.
Think Entertainment, **II** 161
Think Technologies, **10** 508
Thiokol Corporation, 8 472; **9** 358–59, 500–02 (upd.); **12** 68; **22** 504–07 (upd.)
Third Age Inc., **71** 137
Third Coast Capital, Inc., **51** 109
Third National Bank. *See* Fifth Third Bancorp.
Third National Bank of Dayton, **9** 475
Third Wave Publishing Corp. *See* Acer Inc.
ThirdAge.com, **49** 290
Thirteen/WNET. *See* Educational Broadcasting Corporation.
Thistle Group, **9** 365
Thistle Hotels PLC, 54 366–69
THM Biomedical Inc. *See* Kensey Nash Corporation.
Thom McAn. *See* Melville Corporation.
Thomas & Betts Corporation, 11 515–17; **14** 27; **54** 370–74 (upd.)
Thomas & Howard Co., **II** 682; **18** 8
Thomas and Judith Pyle, **13** 433
Thomas Bros. Maps, **28** 380

Thomas Cook Group Ltd., **17** 325; **57** 195
Thomas Cook Travel Inc., 9 503–05; **33** 394–96 (upd.); **42** 282
Thomas De La Rue and Company, Ltd., **44** 357–58
Thomas H. Lee Co., 24 480–83
Thomas Industries Inc., 29 466–69
Thomas J. Lipton Company, 14 495–97
Thomas Jefferson Life Insurance Co., **III** 397
Thomas Kinkade Galleries. *See* Media Arts Group, Inc.
Thomas Linnell & Co. Ltd., **II** 628
Thomas Nationwide Transport. *See* TNT.
Thomas Nationwide Transport Limited. *See* TNT Post Group N.V.
Thomas Nelson Inc., 8 526; **14** 498–99; **24** 548; **38** 454–57 (upd.)
Thomas Publishing Company, 26 482–85
Thomas Y. Crowell, **IV** 605
Thomaston Mills, Inc., 27 467–70
Thomasville Furniture Industries, Inc., 12 474–76; **74** 339–42 (upd.)
Thompson and Formby, **16** 44
Thompson Aircraft Tire Corp., **14** 42
Thompson-Hayward Chemical Co., **13** 397
Thompson Medical Company. *See* Slim-Fast Nutritional Foods International Inc.
Thompson Nutritional Products, **37** 286
Thompson PBE Inc., **24** 160–61
Thomsen Greenhouses and Garden Center, Incorporated, 65 338–40
Thomson BankWatch Inc., **19** 34
Thomson-Brandt, **II** 13, 116–17; **9** 9
The Thomson Corporation, 8 525–28; **10** 407; **12** 361, 562; **17** 255; **22** 441; **34** 435–40 (upd.); **44** 155
Thomson International, **37** 143
Thomson-Jenson Energy Limited, **13** 558
THOMSON multimedia S.A., 18 126; **36** 384; **42** 377–80 (upd.)
Thomson-Ramo-Woolridge. *See* TRW Inc.
Thomson, S.A., II 31, 116–17; **7** 9; **13** 402; **50** 300; **59** 81. *See also* THOMSON multimedia S.A.
Thomson Travel Group, **27** 27
Thonet Industries Inc., **14** 435–36
Thor Industries, Inc., 39 391–94
Thorn Apple Valley, Inc., 7 523–25; **12** 125; **22** 508–11 (upd.); **23** 203
Thorn EMI plc, I 52, 411, 531–32; **19** 390; **24** 87; **26** 151; **40** 105; **59** 228. *See also* EMI plc; Thorn plc.
Thorn plc, 24 484–87
Thorncraft Inc., **25** 379
Thorndike, Doran, Paine and Lewis, Inc., **14** 530
Thornhill Inc, **64** 217
Thornton Baker. *See* Grant Thornton International.
Thornton Stores, **14** 235
Thorntons plc, 46 424–26
Thoroughgood, **II** 658
Thorpe Park, **55** 378
Thorsen Realtors, **21** 96
Thos. & Wm. Molson & Company. *See* The Molson Companies Limited.
Thousand Trails, Inc., 13 494; **33** 397–99
Thousands Springs Power Company, **12** 265
THQ, Inc., 39 395–97; **52** 191
Threads for Life, **49** 244
Threadz, **25** 300

Three-Diamond Company. *See* Mitsubishi Shokai.
The 3DO Company, 10 286; **43** 426–30
3 Guys, **II** 678, **V** 35
3 Maj, **25** 469
Three Ring Asia Pacific Beer Co., Ltd., **49** 418
Three Rivers Pulp and Paper Company, **17** 281
Three Score, **23** 100
3 Suisses International, **12** 281
3Com Corporation, 11 518–21; **34** 441–45 (upd.). *See also* Palm, Inc.
3D Planet SpA, **41** 409
3dfx Interactive Inc., **54** 269–71
3Dlabs, **57** 78, 80
3i Group PLC, 73 338–40
3M Company, 61 365–70 (upd.)
360 Youth Inc., **55** 15
360networks inc., **46** 268
Threshold Entertainment, **25** 270
Thrift Drug, **V** 92
Thrift Mart, **16** 65
ThriftiCheck Service Corporation, **7** 145
Thriftimart Inc., **12** 153; **16** 452
Thriftway Food Drug, **21** 530
Thriftway Foods, **II** 624; **74** 365
Thrifty Corporation, **25** 413, 415–16; **55** 58
Thrifty PayLess, Inc., 12 477–79; **18** 286; **19** 357
Thrifty Rent-A-Car. *See* Dollar Thrifty Automotive Group, Inc.
Throwing Corporation of America, **12** 501
Thrustmaster S.A., **41** 190
Thummel Schutze & Partner, **28** 141
Thunder Bay Press, **34** 3–5
Thüringer Schokoladewerk GmbH, **53** 315
Thurmond Chemicals, Inc., **27** 291
Thurston Motor Lines Inc., **12** 310
Thyssen AG, IV 195, 221–23, 228; **8** 75–76; **14** 169
Thyssen Krupp AG, 28 104, 452–60 (upd.); **42** 417
Thyssen-Krupp Stahl AG, **26** 83
Thyssengas, **38** 406–07
TI. *See* Texas Instruments.
TI Corporation, **10** 44
TI Group plc, 17 480–83
TIAA-CREF. *See* Teachers Insurance and Annuity Association-College Retirement Equities Fund.
Tianjin Automobile Industry Group, **21** 164
Tianjin Bohai Brewing Company, **21** 230; **50** 202
Tianjin Paper Net, **62** 350
Tibbett & Britten Group plc, 32 449–52
Tiber Construction Company, **16** 286
Tichenor Media System Inc., **35** 220
Ticketmaster, 13 508–10; **37** 381–84 (upd.); **76** 349–53 (upd.)
Ticketron, **13** 508–09; **24** 438; **37** 381–82
TicketsWest.com, **59** 410, 412
Tichnor & Fields, **10** 356
Ticor Title Insurance Co., **10** 45
Tidel Systems, **II** 661; **32** 416
Tidewater Inc., 11 522–24; **37** 385–88 (upd.); **59** 402
Tidewater Utilities, Inc., **45** 275, 277
Tidi Wholesale, **13** 150
TIE. *See* Transport International Express.
Tien Wah Press (Pte.) Ltd., **IV** 600
Tierco Group, Inc., **27** 382
Tierney & Partners, **23** 480

INDEX TO INDUSTRIES

Index to Industries

BIOTECHNOLOGY

CHEMICALS

CONSTRUCTION

ENGINEERING & MANAGEMENT SERVICES

ENTERTAINMENT & LEISURE

FINANCIAL SERVICES: BANKS

MATERIALS

MINING & METALS

PUBLISHING & PRINTING

TOBACCO

GEOGRAPHIC INDEX

Geographic Index

United States

NOTES ON CONTRIBUTORS

Notes on Contributors

BRENNAN, Gerald E. Writer based in Germany.

BURTON, Kimberly. Writer and editor based in Michigan.

COHEN, M. L. Novelist and business writer living in Paris.

DINGER, Ed. Bronx-based writer and editor.

GREENLAND, Paul R. Illinois-based writer and researcher; author of two books and former senior editor of a national business magazine; contributor to *The Encyclopedia of Chicago History, The Encyclopedia of Religion,* and the *Encyclopedia of American Industries.*

HALASZ, Robert. Former editor in chief of *World Progress* and *Funk & Wagnalls New Encyclopedia Yearbook;* author, *The U.S. Marines* (Millbrook Press, 1993).

HAUSER, Evelyn. Researcher, writer and marketing specialist based in Germany.

INGRAM, Frederick C. Utah-based business writer who has contributed to *GSA Business, Appalachian Trailway News,* the *Encyclopedia of Business,* the *Encyclopedia of Global Industries,* the *Encyclopedia of Consumer Brands,* and other regional and trade publications.

MONTGOMERY, Bruce. Curator and director of historical collection, University of Colorado at Boulder.

STANSELL, Christina M. Writer and editor based in Louisville, Kentucky.

UHLE, Frank. Ann Arbor-based writer; movie projectionist, disc jockey, and staff member of *Psychotronic Video* magazine.